TEXTBOOK RENTAL SERVICE

a. For your protection,
sign your name below.

b. DO NOT ABUSE THIS TEXTBOOK.

c. Return this textbook before
each semester's deadline.

d. A penalty   per book
will be charged for late
returns.

NAME	ADDRESS & PHONE
V. Porazinski	Gabbard #22
Michelle	

Choices in Relationships

An Introduction to Marriage
and the Family

■

THIRD EDITION

Choices in Relationships

An Introduction to Marriage
and the Family

■

THIRD EDITION

David Knox

EAST CAROLINA UNIVERSITY

Caroline Schacht

EAST CAROLINA UNIVERSITY

WEST PUBLISHING COMPANY

Saint Paul   **New York**   **Los Angeles**   **San Francisco**

Copyediting: Cheryl Wilms
Composition: Carlisle Communications
Cover/Interior Design: Kristen Weber
Index: Schroeder Editorial Services
Cover Art: Pierre Auguste Renoir, In the Garden.
Scala-Art Resource, New York.

Printed in the United States of America

98 97 96 95 94 93 92 91   8 7 6 5 4 3 2 1 0

Library of Congress Cataloging-in-Publication Data

Knox, David, 1943-
   Choices in relationships : an introduction to marriage and the
family / David Knox, Caroline Schacht. -- 3rd ed.
      p. cm.
      Includes bibliographical references and index.
      ISBN 0-314-78709-7
      1. Family life education. 2. Marriage--United States.
I. Schacht, Caroline. II. Title.
HQ10.K57   1991
306.8'0973--dc20   90-20121
                                    CIP ∞

To Dave, Lisa, and Isabelle
who continue to make choices
in relationships for themselves.

T HIS THIRD edition of *Choices in Relationships: An Introduction to Marriage and the Family* continues the theme of the earlier editions—encouraging you to take control of your life by making deliberate choices in your personal relationships, especially marriage and the family. Rather than passively reacting to events in your life so that choices are made for you, the text encourages you to make active choices and select courses of action for your life. By doing so, you increase the control over your own happiness and the happiness in relationships with others.

The text features a new coauthor, Caroline Schacht, who brings to each chapter a more balanced perspective of choices in relationships than is possible when the views of only one gender are presented. Although her influence is evident throughout the text, the two specific areas that benefit most from a more balanced perspective are found in the chapters on Gender Roles and Sexuality in Relationships. The text also features a new table of contents and begins with a chapter containing an overview of the important choices that people make in relation to marriage and the family. Subsequent chapters follow a developmental framework, examining relationships from first meeting through marriage, having and rearing a family, divorce, and remarriage. Along the way, we look at singlehood, gender roles, love, sexuality, communication, violence, dual-income marriages, and stepfamilies.

Each page of the third edition has been reviewed, revised, and updated. Examples of new information in this edition include new legal definitions of the family, dating the second time around, theories of marital communication, effective communication, adjustment to divorce, sexual addictions, miscarriage, day care, parenting adolescents, death of a child, divorce mediation, becoming a successful stepfamily, and the effect of AIDS on sexual patterns.

Because of their success in the earlier editions, the unique features of the text have been continued. The goal of these features is to provide you with a basis for making the best possible interpersonal choices. These features are described here:

Choices

At the conclusion of each chapter, a special section emphasizes the choices that are relevant to the content of that chapter. Examples of the issues discussed include: ''Is Marriage for You?,'' ''Should You Live with Your Partner?,'' ''Should You Call Off the Wedding?,'' ''How Long Should You Live with Your Parents?,'' and "Is a Dual-Career Marriage for You?". Over 50 choices are examined in 17 chapters.

Impact of Social Influences on Choices

Although the theme of this book is to take active control of your life, it is important to be aware of the social forces that influence and limit your choices. For example, the choice of a marital partner may be influenced by the approval of parents/peers and by social norms. Interracial marriages today represent less than one percent of all marriages because approval from parents/peers may be lacking and present social norms are not supportive of marriages between individuals of different racial groups.

Age, Racial, and Ethnic Balance

Another feature of this third edition is a continued emphasis on choices in relationships made by individuals representing a variety of ages and racial and ethnic backgrounds. Although white students from 18 to 22 years of age comprise the largest percentage of those enrolled in college, one-fourth of college students are over age 30. Enrollments of individuals from different racial groups are also increasing. Black, Hispanic, Asian, Native American, and foreign students represent about 20 percent of all students in U.S. colleges and universities today. Although many marriage and family choices are similar regardless of racial background, some unique differences will be examined.

African Americans or blacks (31 million or 12 percent of the U.S. population), Mexican Americans or Hispanics (21 million or 7 percent of the U.S. population), Asian Americans (8 million or 3 percent of the U.S. population), and Native Americans (2 million or less than one percent of the U.S. population) comprise the largest racial and ethnic groups in our society (Schaefer, 1990; Henry, 1990). By 2010, as many as 38 percent of Americans under the age of 18 will belong to minority groups (Schwartz & Exter, 1989). Because of their increasing population and presence in American society, their marriage and family patterns will influence current patterns (Mindel et al., 1988).

Self-Assessment Inventories

To be consistent with the theme of making decisions, every chapter includes an inventory or scale to enhance decision making in various areas of marriage and the family. Examples include the Love Attitudes Scale, the Sexual Attitudes Scale, and the Relationship Involvement Scale. You might want to complete these self-assessment inventories to learn more about yourself.

Considerations

Sprinkled throughout the text are short paragraphs that also could be labeled "What this may mean for you" or "The point is . . . if you haven't thought of this." These considerations encourage you to relate what you have been reading to your life and your interpersonal relationships.

Data

Because the study of marriage and the family (also referred to as "family science") is a social science, we present data on who does what as reported in various professional journals. These data help us to gather as much information as possible with which to make decisions. For example, data showing that those who marry after having known each other for only a short time have a higher divorce rate than those who marry after having known each other for at least two years may be important in deciding when to marry a person you are very much in love with but have known for only a short time.

Exhibits

The exhibits offer practical illustrations (and sometimes suggestions) in reference to particular issues. Examples are "The Feminization of Poverty" and "Two Views of One Dual-Career Marriage."

Acknowledgments

The third edition of *Choices in Relationships: An Introduction to Marriage and the Family* is a result of the work of many people. Peter Marshall, again, provided cutting-edge information in regard to critical issues in marriage and the family and how faculty and students want these issues addressed. Maralene Bates and Jane Bacon provided quick turnaround on reviews and kept the project on track. Angela Deadwiler secured permissions and Jeff Carpenter served as production editor in St. Paul.

We would also like to thank Kim Tripp for her thorough library research and typing throughout the project, Mary Elesha-Adams for sharing her research on human sexuality, Suzanne Kellerman for her contributions to the sections on STDs and contraception, Jack Turner for his insights on communication and divorce adjustment, Delene Rhea for her continued insights about social influences on choices, and Christa Reiser for her resources on gender roles. A number of professors who teach the course for which this text is written read the manuscript and provided valuable insights and suggestions:

Cliff Barber
Colorado State University

Mary Beaubien
Youngstown State University

Carol Bennett
Illinois State University

Jan Copeland
Emporia State University

Peggy Draughn
Louisiana State University

Laura Kells
Wichita State University

John Engel
University of Hawaii

Jerry Gale
University of Georgia-Athens

Ann Goetting
Western Kentucky University

Ted Greenstein
University of Texas-Arlington

Janet Koenigsamen
College of St. Benedict

Larry Dangloif
California State University-Los Angeles

Owen Morgan
Arizona State University

Louise Paxton
Western Oklahoma State College

Dorothy Pomraning
James Madison University

Les Whitbeck
Iowa State University

Miles Whitney
North Adams State College

David Knox
Caroline Schacht

CONTENTS
IN BRIEF

:: PART V   TRANSITIONS   501

:: PART VI   SPECIAL TOPICS

CONTENTS

Chapter 2: Love Relationships   37

Chapter 3: Gender Roles   63

Chapter 4: Sexual Values and Behaviors   99

▪▪ PART II   DECISIONS   121

Chapter 5: Lifestyle Alternatives   123

Chapter 6: Living Together   149

Chapter 7: Dating and Mate Selection   167

Chapter 9: Two-Income Relationships   245

Chapter 10: Communication in Relationships   283

Chapter 11: Sexuality in Relationships   319

Chapter 12: Violence and Abuse in Relationships   357

▪▪ PART IV   FAMILIES   391

Chapter 13: Planning Children and Birth Control   393

Chapter 14: Having Children   437

Chapter 15: Rearing Children   467

:: PART V   TRANSITION   501

Chapter 16: Divorce and Widowhood   503

⣿ PART VI   SPECIAL TOPICS   567

Special Topic 1: Budgeting, Investing, Life Insurance and Using Credit   569

Special Topic 2: Sexual Anatomy and Physiology   581

Special Topic 3: AIDS and Other STDs   589

Special Topic 4: Resources and Organizations   603

Index   607

□

Perspectives

THERE IS AN old joke among professors who teach marriage and family courses that they can use the same tests year after year because even though the questions remain the same, the answers keep changing. The percentages of women and men who choose to remain single, who enter marriage as virgins, and who have a dual-career marriage change continually. Heraclitus said, ''Nothing endures but change.'' This is certainly true of marriage and the family.

Women no longer look to marriage and the family for total fulfillment. Although these relationships continue to be a major source of enjoyment, they are supplemented by success in the work world and by interactions with coworkers and friends. Likewise, although the job remains a primary source of satisfaction for most men, it is being supplemented by an increased interest in the family unit. In particular, some men are becoming more involved in their role as father.

C H A P T E R

1

Choices in Marriage and the Family: A First View

CONTENTS

IS IT TRUE?

1. By the year 2010, most people will probably choose to remain single rather than to get married.

2. Social class background is a more powerful predictor of choices in marital and family behavior than racial heritage.

3. Marriage and the family are basically the same concept.

4. Gay and lesbian couples cannot be considered a family.

5. Today, people are more likely to ask, ''Is it good for me?'' rather than ''Is this best for my family?''

1 = F; 2 = T; 3 = F; 4 = F; 5 = T

B UT I THINK the simple reality that we all have to face is that you can't do everything in life. There really are genuine forks in the road, where in order to do one thing, you give up the opportunity to do something else.

—Pete Dawkins

These words by a former winner of the Heisman Trophy in college football emphasize the importance of making choices. Making choices in your relationships—particularly in regard to marriage and the family—is the most important set of decisions you will make in your life, and will involve your greatest joys and sorrows. In no other area of life will choices be so crucial.

⠿ Basic Choices

Although you will make an array of interpersonal choices (see Exhibit 1.1) throughout your life, most people will face the most basic choices.

Singlehood or Marriage?

Although more than 90 percent of us eventually marry (*Statistical Abstract of the United States: 1990*), whether to remain single or to marry remains a choice. Some people who do not marry are homosexual persons. Some heterosexuals are not suited to marriage and should not marry just because they feel society expects them to. According to one person:

> I can't stand living with other people. I need my own place with no one else there. Sure, I enjoy other people and they come over to my place, but I don't want anyone

EXHIBIT 1.1

Sixty Choices in Relationships

Life style
Marriage?
Singlehood?
Live together?

Marriage
Premarital counseling?
Premarital agreement?
Traditional or egalitarian relationship?
Who manages the money?
Live with parents?
Partner's night out?
Separate or joint vacations?

Communication and Conflict
How much should you tell?
Talk about issues or avoid them?
Consult a therapist?
Marriage enrichment weekends?
Role responsibilities?

Sex
Intercourse before marriage?
Infidelity?
Open marriage?
Heterosexual, homosexual, bisexual?
Consult sex therapist if problems?

Employment
Job or career?
Part-time or full-time work?
One- or two-income marriage?
Move if one career requires?
Who does what chores at home?
Hire outside help?

Birth Control
Use of a contraceptive?
Which contraceptive?
Sterilization?
If become pregnant, keep child, abort, or give up for adoption?

Children
Have children?
When?
Adopt children?
Number of children?
Single parent by choice?
Artificial insemination by husband?
Artificial insemination by donor?
Ovum transfer?
Test-tube fertilization?
Amniocentesis?
Surrogate mother?
Home or hospital birth?
Day care for child?
Public or private school?

Divorce
Stay married or divorce?
Divorce mediation?
Custody to one parent?
Joint custody?
When and how to tell parents?
What to tell children?
Relationship with ex-spouse?
Amount of child support?
Remarry?
Remarry person with children?
Remarry person against your children's wishes?

Widowhood
Living will?
Life insurance?
Remarry?

living there but me. Marriage means that you are burdened with having to interact and to consider another person in everything you do. I'm simply not cut out for that kind of life.

Other people enjoy the intimacy of marriage. One spouse said, "If you've got a good marriage, you've got the best there is." The "best" this spouse is referring to not only includes the intimacy but the companionship and mutual support that marriage may provide.

Children—Yes or No?

Just as most people marry, 90 percent express a desire for and eventually have children. However, some people do not want children. Children take time and are a drain on financial and emotional resources. Individuals who are not eager to share their lives with an infant, child, and teenager may decide not to have children.

One- or Two-Income Marriage?

I'm learning that the twice we're earning doesn't mean it's twice the fun.
—A DUAL-CAREER SPOUSE

The fact that about 70 percent of all married couples have two incomes illustrates their involvement in employment and their need for money. One partner, more often the wife, has a job that permits easy entrance and exit from the labor force to accommodate the needs of the family. Couples who decide that both partners will pursue a career may enjoy personal and economic advantages but may also have less time for each other, particularly if they have children. For the childfree couple, two careers are easier to manage.

Fidelity

Two flavors confuse the palate.
—CHINESE PROVERB

Most of us expect emotional and sexual fidelity from our partner. Yet about 50 percent of all husbands and wives (Thompson, 1983) have sexual relationships with someone other than their spouse. In one British study, 73% of the respondents reported sexual intercourse outside the marriage (Lawson, 1988). Although most couples remain married after such involvements occur, each spouse may need to decide (more than once) whether to be monogamous. "Someone is always available if you want to have an affair," said one spouse. "It's really up to you whether you do or not."

Positive or Negative View?

A final—and perhaps the most important—basic choice is deciding how you wish to view something. Life has positive and negative aspects. Your choice of whether to focus on the positives or on the negatives is critically important to your personal and interpersonal happiness.

Most people are about as happy as they have made up their minds to be.
—UNKNOWN

When you look at your partner, you can focus on his or her loving eyes or on facial pimples. Similarly, you can focus on the times your partner did something you liked or on the times he or she did something that offended or hurt you. You can focus on your partner preparing a meal rather than forgetting to put the ketchup on the table. In dissolving a relationship, you can view it as the end of a life or as the beginning of a life.

In other words, how you choose to view a situation will often have more to do with your happiness than the situation itself. A positive perception affects not only your psychological health but also your physical health (Trotter, 1987).

:: Some Facts about Choices

When you make choices, it is important to keep several issues in mind.

Not to Decide Is to Decide

It is important to recognize that not making a decision *is* a decision. The act of not deciding for something is to decide against something. For example, if you are sexually active and do not use birth control, you have decided for pregnancy. As a childfree career woman, if you don't decide to have a baby, you may be deciding not to have one forever. Choosing—through action or through inaction—means taking responsibility for the consequences of your decisions. Such responsibility also implies making informed decisions. The maxim, "If you don't know your choices, you don't really have any choices" emphasizes the importance of looking carefully at alternative courses of action.

> What is not possible is not to choose, but I ought to know that if I do not choose, I am still choosing.
> —JEAN-PAUL SARTRE

Choices Are Only Probabilities

The outcome of any choice is at best a probability, because it is difficult, if not impossible, to know exactly what the best choice is for all time. We can only make decisions based on the information available to us at the time of the decision. Later we may become aware of new information which, had we known it initially, may have influenced us to have made a different decision. Even though choices are only probabilities, those based on knowledge are certainly better than choices based on default.

> Chance favors only the mind that is prepared.
> —LOUIS PASTEUR

Choices Are Continual

Making choices is a continual process. Life is not one or two BIG decisions. It is a series of some big decisions and a constant stream of smaller ones. For example, if you choose to be single, you can live alone, with another partner in a heterosexual or homosexual relationship, or with a roommate. You can live in a one-room apartment or on a communal farm with 300 others (as on the Farm in Tennessee). If you choose to marry, you can select from a variety of marital styles (traditional, open, dual-career, childfree). If you decide to separate and eventually to divorce (as most of us visualize "somebody else" doing), you will be making an additional choice to remain single or to remarry. Remarriage will involve still other choices, including whether to marry a person with children or to be childfree.

> Life is what happens while you are making other plans.
> —JOHN LENNON

You will continually be faced with choices; in fact, you may be faced with the same choice more than once. Choices to continue or end a relationship, to have children, or to be disclosing to your partner are often made more than once.

☐　　　　C O N S I D E R A T I O N　　　　☐

Whereas the single person makes a decision to get married, the married person makes a decision to stay married. "I think sometimes I would be better off if I were single . . . but then again I think marriage isn't so bad," said one spouse. We do not "decide"; we continue to decide.

Choices Involve Trade-offs

Any choice you make involves gains and losses. Barbra Streisand once considered having her nose altered by a plastic surgeon, but she was told that to do so might also alter the nasal sound and timbre of her voice. The trade-off was not worth the risk for her.

Interpersonal choices also involve trade-offs. For example, one spouse said:

> Everything is a trade-off. If you get married, you are less free; if you don't get married, you may be more lonely. If you have kids, they cost money, make noise, and tear up the house; if you don't have kids, you may miss them. If you have an affair, you feel guilty and may lose your marriage; if you don't have sex with others, you wonder what it would be like. So what's the answer?

Trade-offs occur in the choice of lifestyle and family life. Spouses with large homes, expensive cars, and a vacation cottage may (unless they are of the elite social class) need to spend time away from each other earning the money to pay for the lifestyle. "Generally, such success can be achieved only at some sacrifice of family life" (John, 1988, 355).

Some Choices Are Revocable; Some Are Not

Whether your choices involve a philosophy of life, a career, or selecting a mate, most of them are revocable. Although the emotional or financial price is higher for certain choices than for others (for example, backing out of the role of spouse is somewhat less difficult than backing out of the role of parent), you can change your mind. Most choices can be modified or changed. However, once you decide to get married, you can never return to your previous status (never married); if you dissolve the marriage, you will acquire a new status (divorced).

Choices Are Influenced by Social Context and Social Forces

You do not make choices in a vacuum. Your choices are influenced by the social context in which they occur. *Social context* refers to what significant others (people you care about) are saying and doing. Their behavior provides a model that guides your own behavior. If all of your friends are married and have children, you are much more likely to choose both marriage and parenthood. Significant others also reward and punish your choices. If you elect to marry a person twice your age, your peers may question your choice, which may influence your eventual decision to marry that person.

Social variables that influence your choices also operate at the larger societal level (see Exhibit 1.2 for recent changes in marriage and the family). Examples of such social forces include inflation, unemployment, and war. Inflation influences your choices by dictating what you can afford. Unemployment will dramatically affect the feelings you have about yourself and your spouse. And even though U.S. involvement in a new war is not imminent, couples are still reeling from Vietnam and military couples continue to experience the impact of separation.

Both the social variables of your immediate social context (the micro perspective) and in the larger society (macro perspective) influence your choices in relationships. Other influences include your family of origin, unconscious motivations, habit patterns, and individual personality. The family in which you were reared is a major influence on your attitudes, perceptions, and choices. For instance, many people in ACOA (Adult Children of Alcoholics) report that being reared in an alcoholic home influenced them to be distrustful, deceitful, and unable to make choices.

Unconscious motivations may also be operative in making choices. A person reared in a lower class home without adequate food and shelter may become overly concerned about the accumulation of money and make all decisions in reference to gaining higher income. An adult who, as a child, was sexually abused by a parent may reject subsequent sexual advances from a partner with whom he or she is emotionally involved.

Habit patterns also influence choices. A person who is accustomed to and enjoys spending a great deal of time alone may find it difficult to choose to become involved with a person who begins to make demands on his or her time.

Personalities (e.g., introvert, extrovert; passive, assertive) also influence choices. A person who is a risk taker is more likely to have an affair than someone who is comforted by stability and security.

At the end of each chapter we will review several choices relevant to the topic of the chapter. When making your own choices, you might consider the degree to which social forces, family of origin, unconscious motivations, habit patterns, and personality patterns influence you.

⠶ What Is Marriage?

Choices in the two major categories of relationships, marriage and the family, are the area of concern in this text. To begin, let's define and examine the various types of marriage.

Definition of Marriage

Marriage in the United States is a legal contract with the state that regulates the format for economic and sexual interaction between two heterosexual adults. The marriage between the partners is usually emotional, monogamous, protective of future children, and formal. These various elements are discussed in the following pages.

Legal Contract. Marriage in our society is a legal contract that may be entered into only by two people of the opposite sex and of legal age (usually 18 or older), who are not already married to someone else. The marriage license certifies that the individuals were married by a legally empowered representative of the state with two witnesses present. While common law marriages do exist, they are the exception.

| ▪ **DATA:** *About two and a half million marriage licenses are issued each year (National Center for Health Statistics, 1990).*

The license, as regarded by the laws of the state, means that all future property acquired by the spouses will be jointly owned and that each will share in the estate of the other. In most states, whatever the deceased spouse owns is legally

---

E X H I B I T   1.2

Factors Influencing Your Choices: Recent Changes in Marriage and the Family

Our society provides the social backdrop against which choices in marriage and the family are made—and our society is undergoing rapid change. The following attitudinal changes or societal events that are commonplace in your life were not true when your parents were growing up.

INDIVIDUALISM

Familism is getting increased competition from individualism (Painter, 1990). While family values are firmly entrenched in our society, some individuals are asking if their desires should supercede those of the family. Some families are becoming more adult centered (Glick, 1989).

AIDS

Contracting AIDS is a possibility all sexually active individuals are encouraged to take seriously. Both cultural support for "safe sex" and the use of condoms testify to the fact that we are now in a new sexual era.

ABORTION

A woman's right to have an abortion is becoming more tenuous. The Supreme Court and state legislatures are debating the conditions under which abortion should be made available. Some states are considering legislation to restrict abortion.

SINGLEHOOD

Although most people eventually marry, increasing numbers are delaying marriage to enjoy singlehood and to establish careers (Thornton, 1989). Some people will never marry, which is in part a function of musical chairs; there are more women than there are men to marry. Too few men is a particular problem for black women; there is only one eligible black man for every five black unmarried women.

"Young people today shy away from making serious commitments not because they're "free," but because they're afraid of making themselves vulnerable and then being abandoned" (interview with Gary Bauer by Pearcey, 1990).

LIVING TOGETHER

Living together is regarded by some as an extension of courtship. Unmarried couples who cohabit represent about 5 percent of all couples (married and unmarried)

---

transferred to the surviving spouse at the time of death. In the event of divorce, the property is usually divided equally regardless of the contribution of each partner. The license also implies the expectation of sexual fidelity in the marriage. In some states, infidelity is grounds for alimony. State law regulating marriage varies. Check with an attorney in your state to find out about the laws operating where you live.

CONSIDERATION

The marriage license entitles the spouses to file a joint income tax return, to receive payment by health insurance companies for medical bills if the partner is insured, and to collect social security benefits at the death of the spouse. While the definition of what constitutes a "family" is being reconsidered by the courts, the law is currently designed to protect spouses, not lovers and live-ins. An exception is common law marriage (recognized in some states) which means that if a couple cohabit and present themselves as married, they will be regarded as legally married.

(*Statistical Abstract of the United States: 1990*). A high divorce rate, a delay in women having their first child, and an increasing acceptance of the behavior have all contributed to the rise in the frequency of cohabitation among unmarrieds. Once considered a lower-class practice, living together is becoming more visible in the middle class.

EMPLOYED WIVES

Increasingly, spouses are choosing a two-income marriage. Although some couples need two incomes to survive, other couples have two incomes to afford a plush standard of living. In addition, more mothers with infants are working outside the home. The wife who stays at home to be with her children is becoming less frequent. Only 15 percent of all families consist of a breadwinning husband, a homemaking wife, and children (Merrick & Tordella, 1988).

CHANGING ROLES

Equalitarian role relationships between women and men have become more common. Choices about education, children, and chores are being made more frequently on an equalitarian basis by partners who have equal input into these decisions.

CHILDREN

For a growing number of people, children are no longer viewed as essential to personal or marital fulfillment. Although most couples continue to have children, having a childfree marriage is an option. For some single individuals, marriage is no longer considered a prerequisite to having children. Single Mothers by Choice is an organization for single women who want to have a baby.

DIVORCE

One in two marriages ends in divorce (Martin & Bumpass, 1989). Today, unhappy spouses are less willing to stay married for the sake of the children or what others may say.

TECHNOLOGY

Technology influences your life every day. Riding in a car to withdraw cash from a banking machine to buy food that has been heated in a microwave at a restaurant involves three technological innovations. Technology also influences your choices in relationships. Some examples include computers for computer dating, VCRs for the home viewing of video cassettes, video cameras to store your memories, satellite dishes for unlimited television home viewing, the separation of X and Y sperm to select a girl or a boy baby, artificial insemination for infertile couples, and penile implants for impotent males.

Emotional Relationship. Most people say they want to get married because they are in love.

■ **DATA:** *Ninety-five percent of 669 adults in a national sample agreed with the statement "People should not get married unless they are deeply in love" (Furstenberg, 1987, 47).*

This emotional prerequisite for marriages suggests that marriage (Western style) is a relationship sought by two people who care a great deal for each other, who enjoy being together, and who want to share their lives together. They want a lover, a friend, and a person they can trust and talk with in an otherwise competitive and sometimes impersonal world. Several researchers remarked that relationships in marriage and the family are "unique" in the nature of the affect and the intensity of the emotion they engender (Beutler et al., 1989).

Your movement toward an emotionally committed marital relationship may be measured in terms of the seriousness of the relationship. The Relationship Involvement Scale (see p. 13) is designed to help you assess the degree to which you

Most couples begin marriage with the commitment to sexual monogamy.

are close to getting married or establishing a high degree of commitment in your relationship.

It is as absurd to say that a man can't love one woman all the time as it is to say that a violinist needs several violins to play the same piece of music.
—HONORE DE
  BALZAC

Sexual Monogamy. In a marriage, the emotional commitment to each other is often thought to imply that each partner will be sexually faithful to the other. Although 50 percent of all husbands and almost as many wives eventually have intercourse with someone other than their partner during the marriage, they usually hide their extramarital encounters from the spouse. With the rare exception of couples who have sexually open relationships, sexual fidelity is expected.

Legal Responsibility for Children. Although individuals marry for love, fun, and companionship, the *real* reason (from the viewpoint of the state) for marriage is the legal obligation of a woman and man to nurture and support any children they may have. In our society, childrearing is the primary responsibility of the family, not of the state.

SELF ASSESSMENT

The Relationship Involvement Scale

This scale is designed to measure the degree to which you are seriously involved with your partner. There are no right or wrong answers.

Directions: After reading each sentence carefully, circle the number that best represents your feelings.

1 Strongly disagree
2 Mildly disagree
3 Undecided
4 Mildly agree
5 Strongly agree

	SD	MD	U	MA	SA
1. My partner and I have made it clear to each other that we love each other.	1	2	3	4	5
2. My partner and I know each other's families fairly well.	1	2	3	4	5
3. We have talked about spending the future together.	1	2	3	4	5
4. Our relationship is exclusive. We do not date other people.	1	2	3	4	5
5. We spend most of our free time together.	1	2	3	4	5
6. We have talked about getting married.	1	2	3	4	5
7. Our close friends know that we are very involved with each other.	1	2	3	4	5
8. My partner and I spend most holidays together.	1	2	3	4	5
9. My partner and I have purchased things that we jointly own.	1	2	3	4	5
10. My partner and I have told each other a great deal about ourselves.	1	2	3	4	5

Score_____

SCORING: Add the numbers you circled. The response that suggests the least involvement is 1 (strongly disagree), and the response that suggests the greatest involvement is 5 (strongly agree). Therefore, the lower your total score is (10 is the lowest possible score), the more likely you are to remain single for now; the higher your total score is (50 is the highest possible score), the closer you are to either getting married or establishing a high degree of commitment in your relationship. A score of 30 places you near the midpoint between a low level of involvement and a high level of involvement regarding your relationship.

NOTE: This Self-Assessment is designed to be fun and thought provoking; it is *not* intended to be used by students as a clinical evaluation device.

Marriage is a relatively stable unit that helps to ensure that children will have adequate care and protection, will be socialized for productive roles in society, and will not become the burden of those who did not conceive them. Thus, there is tremendous social pressure for individuals to be married at the time they have children. Even at divorce, the legal obligation of the father and mother to the child is theoretically maintained through child-support payments.

Formal Ceremony. The legal bonding of a couple is often preceded by an announcement in the local newspaper and a formal ceremony in a church or synagogue. Of their announcement one groom-to-be said, "The fact that Barbara and I were actually getting married was not real to me until I saw her picture in the paper and read the sentence that we were to be married on June third." The newspaper is not the only means of publicly announcing the private commitment. Telling parents, siblings, and friends about wedding plans helps to verify the commitment of the partners and also helps to marshal the social and economic support to launch the couple into marital orbit.

Types of Marriage

There are three major types of marriage: monogamy, polygamy, and group marriage. In *monogamy*, one wife and one husband have an exclusive sexual relationship. Monogamy is the only legal type of marriage in the United States. Although people in group and homosexual relationships may regard themselves as married, legally they are not. With 50 percent of all U.S. marriages ending in divorce (Martin & Bumpass, 1989) and 80 percent of these resulting in remarriage, we have a system of *serial monogamy* (individuals having several successive monogamous relationships).

Polygamy is a general term that refers to having several spouses. One form of polygamy is *polygyny,* in which one husband has several wives. Although illegal, polygyny is practiced by a few religious fundamentalist groups in the western United States (Arizona, New Mexico, Utah) that have splintered off from the Church of Jesus Christ of Latterday Saints. Officially, any member of this church who practices polygyny is excommunicated.

Albert Barlow, now 87, lives in Utah with his three wives, 34 children, 270 grandchildren, and 70 great-great grandchildren. These fundamentalists believe that they must create large earthly families so they will have large heavenly families. They also believe that polygyny is ordained and sanctioned by God as evidenced in Biblical history. From a worldwide perspective, many societies south of the Sahara Desert in Africa practice polygyny. Specific examples are the Yoruba of Nigeria and the Pokomo of Kenya.

> I'd rather have three husbands than one. I should have married more.
> —INGRID BERGMAN

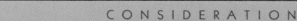

□   C O N S I D E R A T I O N   □

Although most American males view polygyny solely in terms of sexual pleasure with a variety of women, the reality in other societies is quite different. Additional wives are sought to produce heirs and to help with housework and are often en

continued on next page

couraged by first wives, who view several wives as a symbol of their husband's success (not to mention as helpers with domestic chores and childrearing). Much as a wife may encourage her husband to buy a new car or house to elevate her own status among her peers, so the wife in certain polygynous societies will want her husband to acquire additional wives. Such wives may also relieve first wives of sexual duty, and the husband of many wives is expected—indeed, obligated—to have sex with each wife on a regular basis.

Even though polygyny is permitted in a number of societies, most marriages in these societies are monogamous. Although additional wives produce heirs, they may also cost money—and only wealthy men can afford to support several wives and children. If a Pokomo man in Kenya has more than one wife, he must supply each with a house and help each cultivate a separate field.

In another form of polygamy, *polyandry,* one wife has several husbands, as do the Buddhist Tibetans. In some cases, these husbands may be brothers. Polyandry is functional economically. Several men can pool their resources and support one wife, a practice that not only distributes the economic burden among several men but also benefits the wife who may want several children (a husband may want no or only one child). Polyandry is a much rarer form of marriage than polygyny.

Group marriage, in which the men and women in the group consider themselves married to each other, is the third type of marriage. Although illegal, it was practiced in this country by the Oneida Community, a group of about 175 individuals who lived in communal fashion first in Putney, Vermont, and later along the Oneida Creek in New York State in the mid 1800s. According to their leader, John Humphrey Noyes, "It was natural for all men to love all women, and for all women to love all men. . . .any institution which flouted this truism was harmful to the human spirit" (Kephart, 1987, 68). In this community, a "go-between" committee arranged who would sleep with whom. Since falling in love with another person in the group was not acceptable, the committee would not allow people who did fall in love to sleep together again. External pressures resulted in the group disbanding in the late 1880s; Noyes feared prosecution for statutory rape and had already been deserted by many of his followers.

:: What Is Family?

As with marriage, the term family may be defined and typed.

Definition of Family

The United States Bureau of the Census defines family as a group of two or more persons related by blood, marriage, or adoption. According to this definition, married couples and their biological or adopted children as well as a parent and child/children are the only groups which constitute a family.

■ **DATA:** *There are over 55,000,000 white, 7,000,000 black, and 4,000,000 Hispanic families in the United States (Statistical Abstract of the United States: 1990).*

Other things may change us, but we start and end with family.
—ANTHONY BRANDT

Excluded in the Census definition of "family" are couples who live together (homosexual or heterosexual), stepfamilies, and foster families. More recently, the definition of what constitutes a family has been changing (see Exhibit 1.3).

Types of Family

Families may be typed according to an individual's function within the family and according to member inclusiveness.

Family of Orientation. The *family of orientation* is the family into which you were born or the family in which you were reared. This represents you, your parents, and your siblings. When you go to your parents' home for the holidays, you return to your family of orientation. We have emphasized the importance of your family of orientation (also called family of origin) in making choices throughout your life.

EXHIBIT 1.3

Gay and Lesbian Couples Constitute a Family

In the summer of 1989, the New York State Court of Appeals ruled 4 to 2 that a gay couple who had lived together for 10 years could be considered a family under the city's rent control regulations (*Newsweek,* 1989). In effect the court ruled that male and female homosexual couples may be considered families. At issue was whether a partner in a ten-year homosexual relationship could take over the couple's rent-controlled apartment when the leaseholding member dies. Since state law limits such takeovers to "family members," the partner would have been evicted without the court ruling (Beissert, 1989).

This ruling has enormous implications for how our society views family life. Currently, partners in homosexual relationships are not allowed to file a joint income tax, are denied health benefits if the partner's employer provides for family health coverage, are denied retirement benefits from the partner's employer, are denied leave time if the partner is sick, and are not permitted to collect on the partner's social security. These benefits are for married couples only. Since no state recognizes marriage between homosexual partners, homosexual couples are excluded from benefits that are provided for married couples.

Rather than view family members as partners related by blood, marriage, or adoption, increasingly the courts will be looking at the nature of the relationship between partners. Such issues to be considered include, "How long has the couple lived together?", "Do the partners in the relationship consider themselves a family?", and "Are the partners economically interdependent?" In effect, families will be defined by function rather than by structure. Seven cities (including Berkeley, Santa Cruz, and Seattle) already recognize "domestic partnerships" and provide health benefits for them (*Newsweek,* 1990).

One result of an expanded view of family will be a broadening of what is regarded as acceptable relationship patterns in our society. Once legal status is given to committed relationships, whether the partners are homosexual will carry less stigma than in the past. Heterosexual couples also benefit in that stepchildren, now denied health benefits from the stepparent, will more likely be covered.

Public opinion about gay relationships is ambivalent. When 1000 adult Americans were asked, "Do you think marriages between homosexual couples should be recognized by the law?", 69 percent said "No." However, when the respondents were also asked, "Do you think homosexual couples should be permitted to receive medical and life insurance benefits from a partner's policies?," 54 percent said "Yes" (Isaacson, 1989, 102).

Family of Procreation. The *family of procreation* represents the family you will begin if you marry and have children. More than 90 percent of us marry and establish our own family of procreation. We travel through time from the family of orientation to the family of procreation.

Nuclear Family. The *nuclear family* may refer to either your family of orientation procreation (if you decide to have children). Your nuclear family consists of you, your parents (or parent), and siblings or of you, your spouse, and your children (or just of you and your children). During the transition from your family of orientation to your family of procreation, you are in two nuclear families.

Extended Family. The *extended family* includes not only your nuclear family but other relatives as well. These relatives include your parents, grandparents, aunts, uncles, and siblings. An example of an extended family living together would be a husband and wife, their children, and the children's grandparents. Blacks, Hispanics, and Asian Americans are more likely to live with their extended families than whites. When a person's sex is taken into consideration, the chances of living in an extended family are greater for females than for males.

■ **DATA:** *Based on the national longitudinal survey of mature women, two-thirds of black middle aged women live in an extended family at least part of their middle years. One-fourth to one-third of middle aged white women live in an extended family for part of their middle years (Beck & Beck, 1989).*

> Marriage for human beings without extended families is a two-character play without a backstage crew and, far worse, without an audience out front that gives a damn.
> —KURT VONNEGUT

Most families enjoy playing together.

☐   C O N S I D E R A T I O N   ☐

There are numerous variations of these and other types of families that we discuss later in the text. Single-parent families headed by either a woman or a man, childfree families, communal families, and stepfamilies are examples. Awareness of these alternative family types expands the range of your choices.

The definitions and types of marriage and the family just described do not emphasize the important differences between these concepts. These differences are listed in Table 1.1.

Perspectives Other Than "Choices" in Viewing Marriage and the Family

Although we will focus on choices in relationships as the framework for viewing marriage and the family, there are other conceptual frameworks. These alternative marriage and family frameworks are examined in the following sections.

Structure and Function

The *structure-function view* of marriage and the family emphasizes the functions these institutions serve for the rest of our society. Just as the religious institution helps to explain the unknown, the economic institution ensures the production and distribution of goods and services, and the legal institution provides social control, so the institutions of marriage and the family have specific major functions.

TABLE 1.1 Some Differences Between Marriage and the Family

MARRIAGE	FAMILY
Usually initiated by a formal ceremony.	Formal ceremony not essential.
Involves two people.	Can be as few as two.
Ages of the individuals tend to be similar.	Individuals represent more than one generation.
Individuals usually choose each other.	Members are born or adopted into the family.
Ends when spouse dies or is divorced.	Continues beyond the life of the individual.
Sex between spouses is expected and approved.	Sex between near kin is neither expected nor approved.
Requires a license.	No license needed to become a parent.
Procreation expected.	Consequence of procreation.
Spouses are focused on each other.	Focus is diluted with the addition of children.
Spouses can voluntarily withdraw from marriage with approval from the state.	Spouses/parents cannot easily voluntarily withdraw from obligations to children.
Money in unit is spent on the couple.	Money is diverted from the couple to the children.

SOURCE: Axelson, 1990.

First, marriage and the family serve to replenish society with socialized members. Our society cannot continue to exist without new members, so we must have some way of ensuring a continuing supply. But just having new members is not enough. We need socialized members—those who can speak our language and know the norms and roles of our society. The legal bond of marriage and the obligation to nurture and socialize offspring help to assure that this socialization will occur.

Second, marriage and the family promote the emotional stability of the adult partners and give children a place to belong. Society cannot afford enough counselors to help settle us down whenever we have problems. Marriage provides an in-residence counselor who is, theoretically, a loving and caring partner. To have someone who loves and cares about us helps to keep us stable, so that we can adequately perform our work roles in society. Children also need people to love them and to give them a sense of belonging. The affective function of marriage and the family is one of its major strengths. No other institutions focus so completely on fulfilling our emotional needs as do marriage and the family.

One of the functions of marriage is the socialization of the young.

While replacement of societal members and the provision of emotional stability are the primary functions of marriage and the family for society, other functions include:

a) Physical care—Families provide the primary care for their infants, children, and aging parents. Other agencies (daycare, school, and nursing homes) may help but the family remains the primary caretaker.

b) Regulation of sexual behavior—Spouses are expected to confine their sexual behavior to each other which reduces the risk of having children who do not have socially and legally bonded parents and of spreading AIDS or other sexually transmitted diseases.

c) Status placement—Being born in a family provides social placement of the individual in society. One's social class, religious affiliation, and future occupation are largely determined by one's family of origin.

Family Life Cycles

That we are all moving forward in time is illustrated by the *family life cycle view* of marriage and the family. Examples of family life cycles (see Table 1.2) reveal what

---

▪▪ TABLE 1.2 **Alternative Family Life Cycles**

(A) FAMILY LIFE CYCLE OF THOSE WHO MARRY ONLY ONCE*	
LIFE STAGE	AVERAGE AGE
Marriage	Males: 26
	Females:23
First child born	Males: 28
	Females: 26
Last child born	Males: 34
	Females: 32
Last child leaves	Males: 52
	Females: 50
Grandparent	Males: 53
	Females:51
Widowhood	Females: 71
Death	Males: 72
	Females: 79

(B) FAMILY LIFE CYCLE OF THOSE WHO MARRY AND DIVORCE*	
LIFE STAGE	AVERAGE AGE
Marriage	Males: 26
	Females: 23
Divorce	Males: 32
	Females: 30
Remarriage	Males: 35
	Females: 34
Widowhood	Females: 71
Death	Males: 72
	Females: 79

*Ages are for white males and females and are taken from 1990 U.S. Vital Statistics data.

is happening to us at various ages. Cycle (A) is for people who marry only once and have two children. Cycle (B) is for people who get divorced and who remarry. Income, education, and age at marriage affect the chance of moving through the respective family life cycles. For example, having a low income, having completed fewer than 12 years of education, and having married during the teen-age years increases a person's chance of divorce. Other factors associated with divorce are discussed in Chapter 16.

Social-Psychological

The *social-psychological view* emphasizes the importance of psychological variables as they act on the individual in marriage and the family. Examples of these variables are self-concept and the self-fulfilling prophecy.

The *self-concept* is affected by family members who are social mirrors into which we look for information about who we are and how others feel about us. If we see approval in our parents and spouses, we develop and maintain a positive feeling about ourselves. Such a feeling allows us to believe that we are worthy of love and provides a positive basis for us to both love and be loved by others. Individuals who grow up feeling unloved by their parents find it more difficult to establish loving relationships with others.

The *self-fulfilling prophecy* implies that we behave according to the expectations of others. If our spouses expect us to be on time, faithful, and productive, we are likely to behave to make those expectations come true. On the other hand, if they expect us to be late, unfaithful, and lazy, we are likely to behave accordingly.

> To love oneself is the beginning of a life-long romance.
> —OSCAR WILDE

CONSIDERATION

What expectations do you have of your partner and what expectations does your partner have of you in regard to punctuality, faithfulness, and productivity? If these expectations are positive, then the behavior is also likely to be positive. In a sense, you find what you look for in your partner and your partner finds what he or she looks for in you.

It is particularly important for parents (and other child caregivers) to be aware of the self-fulfilling prophecy. Parents give children powerful messages that may become self-fulfilling prophecies. For example, parents who tell their children that they are "bad" are providing a negative label ("bad") that the children then internalize, or accept as true. The children then begin to view themselves as "bad" and act in a manner consistent with this view. In other words, children may act "bad" because they have been labeled "bad" by parents, teachers, or other child caregivers. Similarly, children may act "good" if they are labeled as such.

Social Class

Stratification, a term that has been borrowed from geology, refers to the differential ranking of people into higher or lower horizontal layers or strata. When individuals who occupy similar social positions on the scale of prestige are stratified, we say they are in the same *social class*. Students on your campus have been stratified into the academic classes of freshmen, sophomores, juniors, and seniors.

Marriages and families are also stratified into different social classes. The criteria used to define "social class" include education, occupation, and income and identify a family as belonging to the upper, middle, working, or lower social class. Families in these respective social classes reflect dramatic differences in attitudes, values, and behavior. For example, individuals from the upper class are more likely to attend the Episcopalian church and to marry in their twenties. In contrast, individuals from the lower class are more likely to attend the Pentecostal church and to marry in their teens.

☐   C O N S I D E R A T I O N   ☐

One way to assess social class is to define it in terms of acceptance—for example, who asks whom to dinner. If you want to know who your social class equals are, look across the table at your next meal.

Social class is associated with race. Table 1.3 reflects the racial composition of the population of the United States. Whites, blacks, Hispanics (Mexican Americans, Puerto Ricans), Asian Americans (Chinese, Japanese, etc.) and Native Americans (Indians, Eskimos, Aleuts) experience marriage and the family differently within their own racial group and between racial groups. For example, a larger percentage of the black and Hispanic population are more economically disadvantaged than whites, which increases marital stress and results in a higher divorce rate. Many Asian Americans also fall into lower income brackets than whites but are less likely to divorce than blacks or Hispanics due to a profamily and antidivorce value.

Black females are more likely than white females to be without a husband and to rear their children alone. A shortage of black males is a result of a lower life expectancy, a greater number of homicides, and a greater tendency to be in prison, mental institutions, or on drugs than is characteristic of whites. Black males also have fewer positive role models (many grow up without a father) and are sometimes stereotyped in the media as unemployed, irresponsible men who

---

▪▪ TABLE 1.3 **Racial Composition of the United States**

TOTAL POPULATION: 250,410,000

White: 210,616,000 = 84.1%
Black: 31,146,000 = 12.4%
Hispanic: 19,431,000 = 7%
Asian American: 6,534,000 = 3%
Native American: 1,400,000 = .5%

SOURCE: Adapted from Waldrop and Exter, 1990, and Schaefer, 1990. (Some Hispanics, Asian Americans, and Americans are also counted as whites which accounts for percentages adding up to over 100 percent)

exploit women. Such stereotypes fail to recognize employed, nurturing, loving black men who are devoted to their wives and children.

☐   C O N S I D E R A T I O N   ☐

Comparisons between blacks and whites often show that blacks have higher rates of unemployment, premarital pregnancies, divorce, and crime. However, social class seems to be a much more powerful influence and predictor of behavior than racial origin. Hence, lower class blacks and whites have high rates of unemployment, premarital pregnancies, divorce, and crime just as upper class blacks and whites have low rates of unemployment, premarital pregnancies, divorce, and crime. In looking at the comparisons between blacks and whites throughout this text, it is important to keep in mind that many presumed "racial" differences are really those of social class (Heiss, 1988).

In addition, one's opportunities are influenced more by class than by race. As Boston (1988) observed, "Class position instead of racial discrimination is the determining factor in the present status and future opportunities of blacks (p. 1).

Role

Marriage and family relationships may also be viewed from a role perspective. *Roles* are behaviors in which individuals are expected to engage. The more common roles in marriage and the family are those of wife, husband, parent, and child. *Role theory* emphasizes that one role does not exist without another (there is no wife without a husband), that roles are interactive (you say "hello" and someone else responds in kind), and that the greatest predictor of what you will do is to know what role you are playing. (As a fianceé, you will sit close to your partner when riding in a car; as a spouse, you will rarely do so.)

Crisis

Marriage and the family may also be viewed from a crisis perspective. A *crisis* may be defined as an event for which old patterns of adaptation are no longer helpful. Most individuals, spouses, and parents experience one or more crisis events in their lifetimes. Examples of crisis events include planned and unplanned pregnancy, divorce, widowhood, alcoholism, extramarital intercourse, incest, infertility, the birth of a child, unemployment, military separation, imprisonment of spouse, and spouse abuse. A crisis event may stem from an external source (for example, a recession may cause unemployment) or from an internal source (discovery of a spouse's affair may encourage alcoholism). The death of a newborn is one of the most devastating internal crisis events that happens to a couple (Callan & Murray, 1989). Couples who successfully respond to crisis events have high degrees of *cohesion,* or emotional bonding, and adaptability—which is the ability of the marital system to change its power structure, role relationships, and rules in response to new situations.

The six major perspectives on marriage and the family are summarized in Table 1.4.

■■ TABLE 1.4 **Six Major Perspectives on Marriage and the Family**

1. Structure-function perspective	Examines the ways in which marriage and the family help our society survive.
2. Family life cycle perspective	Identifies stages and transitions in families over time.
3. Social Psychological perspective	Examines how our personalities influence our relationships and how our relationships influence our personalities.
4. Social Class perspective	Examines how social class variables (education, income, occupation) influence marriages and families.
5. Role perspective	Examines the nature and interaction of roles (expectations of behavior) that are associated with various positions (e.g. spouse, parent, child).
6. Crisis perspective	Examines how individuals and families respond to crisis events.

■■ Information Sources for Marriage and the Family

This text is based on a comprehensive review of studies in the area of marriage and the family that have been reported in professional journals. The most important journals in the marriage and family field include the following:

Family Relations   *Journal of Divorce*
Family Process   *Journal of Family Law*
Journal of Family Issues   *Family Planning Perspectives*
Journal of Marriage and the Family   *Adolescence*
American Sociological Review   *Journal of Sex and Marital Therapy*
Journal of Family History   *Journal of Sex Research*
Journal of Family Therapy   *Journal of Family Welfare*
Sex Roles   *Journal of Marital and Family Therapy*
American Journal of Family Therapy   *Family Law Quarterly*
American Journal of Sociology   *Journal of Adolescence*

Although not specific to marriage and the family, the following professional journals frequently include studies on interpersonal relationships, divorce, and sexuality:

Journal of Home Economics   *Journal of Social Issues*
Child Development   *American Journal of Orthopsychiatry*
Journal of Gerontology   *SIECUS Report*
Studies in Family Planning   *Gerontologist*
Family Perspective   *Home Economics Research Journal*

Two weekly newsletters report the latest information in the marriage and family field:

Marriage and Divorce Today   *Sexuality Today*

:: Some Cautions About Research

Although the findings of the various studies presented in the publications just listed do furnish a basis for making choices in the area of marriage and the family, it is wise to be cautious about research. Some research limitations to be aware of are discussed in the following sections.

Sampling

Some of the studies published in the marriage and family journals just listed are based on random samples. Random sampling involves selecting individuals at random from an identified population. Studies which use random samples are based on the assumption that the individuals studied are similar to, and therefore representative of, the population that the researcher is interested in. For example, suppose you want to know the percentage of unmarried seniors (US) on your campus who are living together. Although the most accurate way to get this information is to secure an anonymous "yes" or "no" response from every US, doing so is not practical. To save yourself time, you could ask a few USs to complete your questionnaire and assume that the rest of the USs would say "yes" or "no" in the same proportion as those who did. To decide who those few USs would be, you could put the names of every US on campus on separate note cards, stir these cards in your empty bathtub, put on a blindfold, and draw 100 cards. Because each US would have an equal chance of having his or her card drawn from the tub, you would obtain what is known as a *random sample*. After

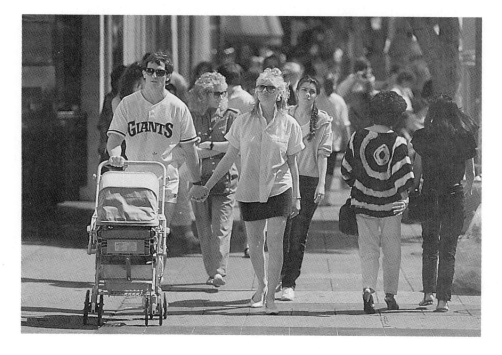

A researcher studies only a portion of a total group.

administering the questionnaire to this sample and adding the "yes" and "no" answers, you would have a fairly accurate idea of the percentage of USs on your campus who are living together.

Due to the trouble and expense of obtaining random samples, most researchers study subjects to whom they have convenient access. This often means students in the researchers' classes. The result is an overabundance of research on "convenience" samples consisting of white, Protestant, middle class college students.

☐   C O N S I D E R A T I O N   ☐

Today's college students, comprising only about 7 percent of all American adults, cannot be assumed to be similar to their noncollege peers or older adults in their attitudes, feelings, and behaviors.

Although the data presented in this text include those obtained from young unmarried college students, they also refer to people of different ages, marital statuses, racial backgrounds, lifestyles, religions, and social classes.

Control Groups

Experimental research involves randomly assigning subjects to two groups—the experimental group which is exposed to the experimental treatment, and the control group which is not exposed to the treatment and thus serves as a comparison group. Experimental research allows researchers to conclude that any differences between the two groups (experimental and control) are due to the experimental treatment.

In most marriage and family research, the experimental design cannot be used because researchers cannot randomly assign subjects to be in either the experimental or control group. For example, a researcher interested in studying the effects of divorce cannot select a sample and then randomly assign one-half of the subjects to the experimental group that gets divorced and the other half of the subjects to the group that stays married. Rather than select a sample and then randomly assign subjects to different groups, researchers must sometimes choose samples that are already grouped. For example, a researcher interested in the effects of divorce on children chooses subjects that are already in the category of "children of divorced parents." This type of research in which subjects cannot be randomly assigned to groups is known as *quasi-experimental research.*

In quasi-experimental research, it is difficult to determine if any differences between two groups are due to the research variable of interest or some other factor. For example, if children of divorced parents are being compared to children of parents who stayed married, any differences between the two groups may not necessarily be due to the fact that the parents are divorced. Perhaps the differences between the two groups are due to the fact that children of divorced parents are more likely to have fewer siblings than children of parents who stayed married (couples who stay married tend to have more children than couples who divorce).

Although we should be cautious in interpreting the results of quasi-experimental research in which the experimental and control groups are not based on random assignment, we should be even more cautious when research involves no control group at all. In a study of adult children of divorced parents, Wallerstein and Blakeslee (1989) found that many of these children reported entering adulthood as worried, underachieving, and self-deprecating. Forty percent between the ages of 19 and 29 were "drifting." These findings are of questionable value because no control group was used. Children from intact families may also be worried, underachieving, self-deprecating, and drifting. Hence, if we are to have any level of confidence in the interpretation of our research findings, we need to include a control group, even if the control group is not formed on the basis of random assignment.

Age and Cohort Effects

In some research designs, different cohorts or age groups are observed and/or tested at one point in time. One problem that plagues such research is the difficulty—even impossibility—of discerning if observed differences between the subjects studied are due to the research variable of interest, cohort differences, or to some variable associated with the passage of time (e.g., biological aging). A good illustration of this problem is found in research on changes in marital satisfaction over the course of the family life cycle. In such studies, researchers may compare the level of marital happiness reported by couples who have been married for different lengths of time. For example, a researcher may compare the marital happiness of two groups of people—those who have been married for fifty years and those who have been married for five years. But differences between these two groups may be due to either 1) differences in age (age effect), 2) the different historical time period that the two groups have lived through (cohort effect), or 3) being married different lengths of time (research variable).

Terminology

In addition to being alert to potential shortcomings in sampling and control groups, you should consider how the phenomenon being researched is defined. For example, in a preceding illustration of unmarried seniors (US) living together, how would you define *living together?* How many people, of what sex, spending what amount of time, in what place, engaging in what behaviors will constitute your definition?

| ■ **DATA:** *Researchers of living together have used more than 20 definitions.*

What about other terms? What is meant by marital satisfaction, commitment, interpersonal violence, and sexual fulfillment? Before accepting that most people report a high degree of marital satisfaction or sexual fulfillment, be alert to the definition used by the researcher. Exactly what is the researcher trying to measure?

Researcher Bias

Even when the sample is random and the terms are carefully defined, two researchers can examine the same data and arrive at different conclusions. In your study of living together, suppose you find that 25 percent of the students on your campus are living together. In discussing your findings, would you emphasize that fact or the fact that the majority of the students (75 percent) are not living together? You can focus on either aspect of the data to make the point you want to make. Many researchers tend to focus on selected aspects of the data they are reporting.

Also, the answer a researcher gets is related to the question she or he asks. In one *New York Times*/CBS poll, 30 percent of the respondents answered "yes" when asked, "Do you think there should be an amendment to the Constitution prohibiting abortions, or shouldn't there be such an amendment?" But when the same people were asked, "Do you believe there should be an amendment to the Constitution protecting the life of the unborn child?," 50 percent answered "yes."

Time Lag

There is typically a two-year lag between the time a research study is completed and its appearance in a professional journal. Because textbooks are based on these journals and take from three to five years from writing to publication, by the time you read the results of a study, other studies may have been conducted that reveal different findings. Be aware that the research you read in this or any text may not reflect current reality. Many of the journals listed earlier will be in your library; you might compare the findings of recent studies with the studies reported in this text.

Distortion and Deception

Researchers in all fields may encounter problems of sampling, terminology, lack of a control group, researcher bias, and time lag, but other problems specific to social science research—particularly to marriage research—are distortion and deception. Marriage is a very private relationship that happens behind closed doors, and we have been socialized not to reveal to strangers the intimate details of our marriages. Therefore, we are prone to distort, omit, or exaggerate information, perhaps unconsciously, to cover up what we may feel is no one else's business. Thus, the researcher sometimes obtains inaccurate information. Marriage and family researchers only know what people say they do, not what they actually do.

An unintentional and probably more frequent form of distortion is inaccurate recall. Sometimes researchers ask respondents to recall details of their relationships that occurred years ago. Time tends to blur some memories, and respondents may not relate what actually happened but only what they remember to have happened.

In addition to distortion on the part of the person being surveyed, outright deception on the part of the investigator is not unknown (Schacht, 1990; Kohn, 1987). In response to pressures to publish or a desire for prestige and recognition, some researchers have doctored their data. For example, the late British psychologist Cyril Burt was renowned for his research designed to test the relative importance of heredity and environment on a person's development. Burt studied identical twins who had been reared in separate environments since birth and presented data that seemed to indicate clearly that heredity was more important.

> You can fool some of the people all of the time, and all of the people some of the time, but you cannot fool all of the people all of the time.
>
> —ABRAHAM LINCOLN

Five years after Burt's death, evidence came to light that he had altered his data, that his coauthors had never existed, and that the investigations had never been conducted. Table 1.5 summarizes some potential weaknesses of any research study.

Other Research Problems

Nonresponse on surveys and the discrepancy between attitudes and behaviors are other research problems. In regard to nonresponse, not all individuals who complete questionnaires or agree to participate in an interview are willing to provide information about such personal issues as money, spouse abuse, family violence, rape, sex, and alcohol abuse. They leave the questionnaire blank or tell the interviewer they would rather not respond. Others respond but give only socially desirable answers. The implications for research are that data gatherers do not know the nature or extent to which something may be a problem because people are reluctant to provide accurate information. In general, males tend to give less information than females.

The discrepancy between the attitudes people have and their behavior is another cause for concern about the validity of research data. It is sometimes assumed that if a person has a certain attitude (for example, extramarital sex is wrong), then his or her behavior will be consistent with that attitude (avoid extramarital sex). However, this assumption is not always accurate. People do indeed say one thing and do another. This potential discrepancy should be kept in mind when reading research on various attitudes.

Finally, most research reflects information provided by volunteers. The question we must ask is, "Do volunteers represent nonvolunteers in terms of answer-

▪▪ TABLE 1.5 **Potential Weaknesses of Any Research Study**

WEAKNESS	CONSEQUENCES	EXAMPLE
Sample is biased	Inaccurate conclusions	Opinions of students in your marriage class do not reflect opinions of all college students.
Age and cohort effect	Inaccurate conclusions	Wallerstein study on the effects of divorce on children did not have a control group. Kids from intact families may also report having problems.
Unclear terms	Cannot measure what is not clearly defined	What is marital happiness? What is good communication?
Bias of researcher	Slanted conclusions	Heterosexuals conducting study on homosexuals.
Time lag	Outdated conclusions	Often quoted Kinsey research on sexuality is 45 years old.
Distortion	Unreliable conclusions	Research subjects exaggerate, omit information, and/or recall facts or events inaccurately.
Deception	Unreliable conclusions	British psychologist Cyril Burt altered his data on twins.

ing questions similarly?'' We do not know the answer which suggests that our research may be flawed.

□ C O N S I D E R A T I O N □

In view of the research problems outlined here, you might ask, ''Why bother to report the findings?'' The research picture is not as bleak as it may seem at first. A number of studies have been conducted that have none of these research drawbacks. The articles in *Journal of Marriage and the Family,* for example, illustrate the high level of methodologically sound articles that are being published. Even less sophisticated journals provide us with useful information about what is currently happening. The alternative to gathering data is relying on personal experience alone, and this is unacceptable to social scientists who study marriage and the family.

:: Trials

Trends

The farther backward you can look, the farther forward you are likely to see.
—WINSTON
    CHURCHILL

Being married and having children will continue to be goals for most people due to the interpersonal satisfaction that these relationships provide. Regarding such satisfactions, in one of his movies, Woody Allen tells his psychiatrist about his uncle who thinks he is a chicken. The psychiatrist asks, ''How long has he been thinking he is a chicken?'' ''Several years,'' Allen says, ''But why haven't you reported this before now?,'' asks the psychiatrist. Allen replies, ''It's because we need the eggs.''

For all the problems that interpersonal relationships may cause, we continue to seek them. Marriage and family relationships in particular feed the emotional part of ourselves. These relationships involve primary groups of intimate individuals. In contrast, we more easily tire of impersonal, secondary group relationships with those with whom we interact during the business day (the person who serves you a burger at McDonald's is in a secondary group relationship to you) and look forward to more personal interaction with primary group members at the end of the day. Marriage is here to stay.

Functional (applied) courses in marriage and the family will be in ever-increasing demand by students. Concern over a high divorce rate coupled with a desire that their marriages will be different will compel more students to take such courses in the hope of finding out what they can learn to help them increase the chance of their own marriage or remarriage being a success.

I don't think there *is* one, unless they stop taking car trips together.
—COLUMNIST DAVE
    BARRY, ASKED TO
    SPECULATE ON
    THE FUTURE OF
    THE AMERICAN
    FAMILY

Traditional definitions of what is considered a family will change. Couples who live together (whether heterosexual or homosexual), foster families, and stepfamilies may be given legal status in the years to come. The result will be benefits (health, retirement, social security) to those who are currently denied. Getting legal status will not come easy and lawsuits will be filed to gain them. For example, a lesbian couple in Minneapolis is suing the Minneapolis library for employee spousal benefits and a man is suing TWA to be allowed to join his partner on frequent flier trips (Beissert, 1989). In his preview of the family, Alan Carlson (1990) predicted, ''The decade ahead will not be friendly to traditional families. Traditional family no longer derives from imitation or conformity; rather it comes from choice and the exercise of will'' (p. 7).

:: Summary

Life is a series of choices. Deciding whether to marry, whether to have children, whether to have two incomes in one marriage, whether to be monogamous, and whether to view a situation positively are among the more important choices you will ever make in your lifetime. This text examines the nature and consequences of these and other choices relating to marriage and the family.

Although we tend to think of choosing as an act, if you decide not to choose, you have already made a choice by default. The theme of this text is to take charge of your life by making deliberate choices in your interpersonal relationships. Such choices, particularly in marriage and the family, are continual. While the single are contemplating whether to marry, the married are deciding whether to stay married and the divorced are considering whether to remarry.

As we will discuss in the choices section at the end of this chapter, the choices we make do not occur in a vacuum. Rather, they are influenced by the choices we see others make and the degree to which they approve of our choices. Such societal events as inflation, unemployment, and legislation also influence our choices. Choices are also influenced by the family into which we were born (family of orientation or family of origin), unconscious motivations, habit patterns, and individual personality differences.

Perspectives other than "choices" of marriage and the family include the structure-function, family life cycle, social-psychological, social class, role, and crisis views. The structure-function perspective emphasizes the benefits to society of the institutions of marriage and family. Marriage bonds a female and a male together in a legal relationship that obligates them to nurture and socialize any offspring they may have. Because society and its institutions depend on marriage and the family for new members, marriage will continue to be a valuable institution in our society.

Marriage in the United States is both an emotional relationship and a legal commitment. It usually includes a public announcement, a public ceremony, and sexual monogamy. It always provides for the transfer of property and the legitimizing of children. Marriage in other societies may be monogamous or polygamous. Polygamy may be polygynous when one man has several wives or polyandrous when one wife has several husbands. The latter is rare.

Family in the United States refers to a group of people who live together, cooperate economically, and reproduce. A wife, husband, and children represent the usual American family, although several variations (two spouses or two siblings or one parent and one child) also qualify as a family. The family of orientation is the one into which we are born; the family of procreation is the one we begin with our own spouse.

The research reported in this text should be viewed cautiously. Inherent in most research may be such methodological problems as the use of a small, unrepresentative convenience sample, lack of a control group, vague terminology, researcher bias, and distortion. These cautions do not imply that all research is problematic. Indeed, journals that report studies of marriage and family are becoming more sophisticated in their methodology and reflect some excellent research.

Although the form of marriage and the family will continue to change (for example, dual-income marriages and single-parent households will increase), the importance of marriage and the family as a set of relationships that meets our emotional needs for love and support will continue.

Questions for Reflection

1. What are the most significant choices you have made in reference to your interpersonal relationships?

2. If you knew that studying marriage and the family as a personal search would contribute to the break up of your relationship with your partner, would you still choose to study the subject from this perspective? (Questions 2 and 3 will become meaningful after reading the choices section that follows.)

3. Describe several decisions you have made by deciding not to decide.

References

Axelson, L. Department of Family and Child Development, Virginia Polytechnic and State University, Blacksburg, Virginia. Personal communication, 1990. Used by permission of Dr. Axelson.

Beck, Rubye W. and Scott H. Beck. The incidence of extended households among middle-aged black and white women. *Journal of Family Issues,* 1989, *10,* 147–168.

Beissert, Wayne. Gay family 'family' too, court rules. *USA Today,* July 7, 1989, p. 1.

Beutler, Ivan F., W. R. Burr, K. S. Bahr, and D. A. Herrin. The family realm: Theoretical considerations for understanding its uniqueness. *Journal of Marriage and the Family,* 1989, *51,* 805–816.

Boston, Thomas D. *Race, class and conservatism.* Boston: Unwin Hyman, 1988.

Callan, Victor J. and Judith Murray. The role of therapists in helping couples cope with stillbirth and newborn death. *Family Relations,* 1989, *38,* 248–253.

Carlson, Allan C. By the decades: The troubled course of the family, 1945–1990 . . . and beyond. *The Family in America,* 1990, *4,* 1–8.

Edgar, Don. Strengthening families in the 1990s. *Family Matters,* April 1989, 2–5.

Furstenberg, Frank F. Jr. The new extended family: The experience of parents and children after remarriage. *Remarriage and Stepparenting.* Edited by Kay Pasley and Marilyn Ihinger-Tallman, 1987, 42–61.

Glick, Paul C. The family life cycle and social change. *Family Relations,* 1989, *38,* 123–129.

Heiss, J. Women's values regarding marriage and the family. *Black Families.* 2d ed. Edited by Harriette Pipes McAdoo, 1988, 201–214.

Henry, W. A. III. Beyond the melting pot. *Time,* April 9, 1990, pp. 28–31.

Hochschild, A. *The second shift: Working parents and the revolution at home.* New York: Viking Press, 1989.

Isaacson, Walter. Should gays have marriage rights? *Time,* November 20, 1989, pp. 101–102.

Janofsky, Barbara J. Career options: A future without academia. *Family Relations,* 1989, *38,* 342–344.

John, Robert. The Native American family. *Ethnic families in America: Patterns and variations.* Edited by C. H. Mindel, R. W. Habenstein, and R. Wright, Jr. New York: Elsevier, 1988, 325–363.

Kephart, William M. *Extraordinary groups.* New York: St. Martin's Press, 1987.

Kohn, A. *False prophets.* New York: Basil Blackwell, 1987.

Lawson, A. *Adultery: An analysis of love and betrayal.* New York: Basic Books, 1988.

Martin, T. C. and L. L. Bumpass. Recent trends in marital disruption. *Demography,* 1989, *26,* 37–52.

Merrick, T. W. and S. J. Tordella. Demographics: People and markets. *Population Bulletin*, 1988, *43*, 1–48.

Mindel, C. H., R. W. Habenstein, and R. Wright, Jr., eds. *Ethnic families in America: Patterns and variations.* 3d ed. New York: Elsevier, 1988.

National Center for Health Statistics. 1990. Births, marriages, divorces, and deaths for 1989. *Monthly vital statistics report.* Vol. 38, no. 12. Hyattsville, Md.: Public Health Service.

Newsweek. Homosexual families and the law. July 17, 1989, p. 48.

Newsweek. The future of gay America. March 12, 1990, pp. 20–25.

Painter, K. Individuality is their claim. *USA Today,* February 2, 1990, pp. 1–2.

Pearcey, N. On the marriage front. *The World and I,* February 1990, 235–239.

Schacht, C. Fraud in science: An autobiographical case analysis. Paper, Eighteenth Annual Sociological Research Symposium, February 23, 1990, Greenville, N.C.

Schaefer, R. T. *Racial and Ethnic Groups.* Glenview, Ill.: Scott, Foresman/Little Brown Higher Education, 1990.

Schwartz, J. and T. Exter. All our children. *American Demographics,* 1989, *11*, 34–37.

Statistical Abstract of the United States: 1990. 110th ed. Washington, D.C.: U. S. Bureau of the Census, 1990.

Thompson, A. P. Extramarital sex: A review of the research literature. *Journal of Sex Research* 1983, 19, 1–22.

Thornton, A. Changing attitudes toward family issues in the United States. *Journal of Marriage and the Family,* 1989, *51*, 873–894.

Trotter, R. J. Stop blaming yourself. *Psychology Today,* February 1987, 31–39.

Wallerstein, Judith S. and Sandra Blakeslee. *Second chances: Men, women and children a decade after divorce.* New York: Tichnor and Fields, 1989.

Waldrop, J. and T. Exter. What the 1990 census will show. *American Demographics,* 1990, *12*, 20–34.

CHOICES

CHOOSING TO STUDY marriage and the family as an academic exercise or a personal search, consciously choosing between two alternatives or choosing by default, and choosing to be tolerant or condemnatory about the decisions of others are basic choices to be made in a marriage and family course.

Marriage and Family: An Academic, Personal, or Career Search?

Until your final grade for this course is posted, you will be involved in the systematic study of marriage and the family. One way to regard this course and the content of this text is as an academic exercise in which you come to class, take notes, skim the book, take tests, and go to the next course without ever becoming involved with the content. This is a legitimate choice. People take marriage and family courses for a variety of reasons and may do so to complete a social science requirement, to fill a transcript, or out of intellectual curiosity.

An alternative reason for studying marriage and the family is to explore the intimate relationship between you and your lover, spouse, parents, or children with the goal of making better decisions in your own life about marriage and family issues. As one student said:

A lot of people I know, including my parents and brother, are divorced or running around on their partners. I want to know all I can about why people do these things so I can help avoid similar things happening to me. My partner and I are taking this course together in hopes that we can beat the odds.

You may choose to regard the study of marriage and the family as an academic or personal search, or as both. Some people have mixed feelings:

Somehow I feel that some things should remain a mystery and maybe marriage, love, and sex are things you shouldn't "study"—it might take the spontaneity out of them if you do. On the other hand, I think of

marriage the same way I do a garden. Some things make it flourish, and some things make it wither. Knowing what those things are could make the differences in being happily married and being divorced three times.

You may also study marriage and the family in preparation for a career in the field. Being a marriage and family therapist, a family life educator, or a consultant (Janofsky, 1989) are among the career alternatives from which to choose. For those intrigued by interpersonal relationships, study or work with marriage and the family can be a rewarding career choice.

Choosing Carefully or Choosing by Default

Some of us believe we can avoid making decisions about marriage and the family. We cannot, because not to decide is to decide by default. Some examples follow:

- If we don't make a decision to pursue a relationship with a particular person, then we have made a decision (by default) to let that person drift out of our lives.
- If we don't decide to do the things that are necessary to keep or improve the relationships we have, then we have made a decision to let them slowly disintegrate.
- If we don't make a decision to be faithful to our dating partner or spouse, then we have made a decision to be open to situations and relationships in which we are likely to be unfaithful.
- If we don't make a decision to avoid having intercourse with a new partner early in the relationship, then we have made a decision to let intercourse occur.
- If we are sexually active and don't make a decision to use some form of birth control, then we have made a decision to conceive a child.

■ If we don't make a decision to break up with our dating partner or spouse, then we have made a decision to continue the relationship with him or her.

Throughout the text, we consider various choices with which we are confronted in the area of marriage and the family. It will be helpful for us to keep in mind that we cannot avoid making choices—that not to make a choice is to make one.

Tolerance or Condemnation for the Choices of Others?

Regardless of the choices we make about our own behavior and lifestyles, we must also make a choice about the rights of others to make choices that are different from ours. Most people are relatively tolerant of the choices others make. According to one woman:

One of my closest friends has started living with her partner. While I wouldn't want to do this myself, I feel it is okay for her to do what she wants.

Some people find it more difficult to be tolerant about homosexuality. The same woman remarked of another friend:

I couldn't believe she was gay when she told me. I can't handle her being gay and told her so. My tolerance stops when my friends want to be or do something that is unnatural. I guess I'd feel the same way if my boyfriend said he wanted to tie me up to have sex.

Impact of Social Influences on Choices

Earlier in this chapter, we noted that the decisions you make are influenced by the social context and social forces of those decisions. The degree to which you view the study of marriage and the family as an academic or a personal search may be influenced by the marriages of your parents, siblings, and friends, by a current partner, and by your level of involvement. For example, if your parents, siblings and most of your close friends are divorced, you may be more cautious about marrying and you may view the study of marriage and the family as more than a course on a transcript. Your awareness that 50 percent of all marriages end in divorce may further influence your study of marriage and the family.

Your perception of this course may also be influenced by a current partner. If she or he feels that the study of marriage and the family is silly because "you can't learn about real life from books," then she or he may not be interested in discussing these issues with you. Such lack of support for the study of marriage and the family may influence you to treat it only as "another course" and not to discuss it with your partner. Hence, the event of taking a marriage and family course will be perceived in reference to the marriages of those close to you and the opinions of those important to you.

Finally, your consideration of various personal choices may be related to the family in which you have been reared. For example, Asian American families are more likely than white families to believe in the importance of the family unit at the expense of the individual. Hence, the consideration of divorce and the subsequent decision to do so are much less likely to happen among Asian Americans than among whites.

Finally, all societies have a vested interest in the choices people make in reference to families. "No society has ever left separate families to their own devices, for families are social units, integral to the health and survival of every other social institution" (Edgar, 1989, 2). Through laws (age requirements for marriage; marriage license) and informal sanctions (social disapproval of divorce) societies are biased toward strengthening family life.

Love Relationships

CONTENTS

IS IT TRUE?

1. Women are more romantic than men.

2. High peaks of happiness don't seem to be as satisfying as a slightly lower but steady level of happiness over the long run.

3. Being in love is good for your health.

4. Love is more important than sex for human happiness.

5. Men are more likely to be jealous than women.

1 = researchers disagree; 2 = T; 3 = T; 4 = T; 5 = F

BEING IN LOVE, for many people especially in our society, is the ultimate experience in life. Just as falling in love often propels people toward commitment and marriage, falling out of love is sometimes a prelude to separation and divorce. Due to the importance of love in our (western) decision to marry and divorce, it is imperative that we try to understand the dynamics of love—how it develops, how it dies, and how to keep it alive and flourishing.

Although parent-child, sibling-sibling, and friend-friend relationships (same or opposite gender) often involve love, love feelings in adult pair bonded relationships is the focus of this chapter. Here, we will explore various definitions of love, the importance of love, and the relationship scripts men and women learn. We will conclude with an examination of the similarities and differences between love and sex.

:: Definitions and Dilemmas of Love

While social scientists have studied love (Sternberg & Barnes, 1988), there is no single definition of love. When students in the authors' classes were asked to define the meaning of love, some listed various qualities like "caring," "compassion," "respect," "sharing," and "commitment." One student said that "love is sacrificing because you want to;" another said that "love is being in a crowded room full of beautiful people of the opposite sex and wishing you were alone with your partner."

☐   CONSIDERATION   ☐

There is no one universally agreed upon definition of love. One reason why definitions of love are so varied is that love has emotional, physical, social, intellectual, and spiritual elements. Different definitions of love arise from placing varying degrees of emphasis on these elements.

Love may not only be defined differently; it may also be expressed in complicated ways that create dilemmas for us. One dilemma includes being in love with two people at the same time. "I know I love my husband," said one woman, "but I also love the man I work with." Such a dilemma is not unusual. The feelings are a consequence of being in two relationships at the same time that have engendered these feelings. It is possible to be involved in several relationships at the same time and to have love feelings for each of the people. But although it is possible to love two or more people at the same time, it is not possible to love them to the same degree (or in exactly the same way) at any particular moment because an individual must make a choice in terms of how to spend his or her time. If you choose to spend time with person X, then you value that person more than others—at least for that moment in time.

◻︎   C O N S I D E R A T I O N   ◻︎

Some people do not like the feeling of being in love with two people at once and try
to reduce their feelings for one of them. This is often accomplished by deciding to see
only one of the persons and by thinking negative things about the other. For example, Jan, who was in love with both her husband and her colleague, decided to stop
seeing her colleague socially. When she did think of him, she made herself think only
of what she perceived to be the negative aspects of being involved with him—he was
married, he drank heavily, he was 12 years older than she, and he had three children.

Another dilemma of love is being in love with someone who may not meet your
needs in the relationship, or who may have needs that you are unable or unwilling to meet. Someone who is radically different in age, who has severe problems
(alcoholism, drug addiction), who has radically different values, who criticizes
you continually, and who lies to you may not be a good partner for you. Nevertheless, you might love that person and feel that everything will turn out all right
in the end. Most marriage therapists would empathize with your love feelings and
suggest that you look at the payoffs for your loving this person. Does it upset your
parents? Do you feel this is what you deserve because you are "no good"? Do you
feel pity for the person and want to be her or his therapist? These questions imply
that the love relationship is based on some motivations that should be carefully
examined.

▪▪ Importance of Love

Although people disagree about the definition of love, people in Western societies rarely disagree about its importance. In American culture, love is important
both for one's physical and emotional health as well as for the quality of one's
relationship. Health may be adversely affected by trouble in one's love life. Physicians often report that many of the symptoms their patients have (sleeplessness,
significant weight gain/loss, nightmares, rashes, headaches) are sometimes related to stress in their interpersonal lives. In a study on love and health (Kemper
& Bologh, 1981), the respondents who had recently ended a love relationship had
the most negative health status. The authors concluded, "A relationship of long
duration that is going well appears to have a positive effect on one's health status"
(p. 86). Indeed, married people have a lower death rate than single people (Trovato & Lauris, 1989).

Regarding the emotional importance of love, Swanbrow (1989) conducted a
review of studies on what makes people happy and concluded that "of all the
circumstances happy people share, loving relationships seem the most characteristic and most important" (p. 39). Emotional relationships that are durable and
sustained seem to be the most rewarding. High peaks of happiness don't seem to
be as satisfying as a slightly lower but more consistent level of happiness over the
long run (Diener et. al., 1989). In a study on love and relationship satisfaction, an

Ain't no doubt in no
one's mind, love's the
finest thing around.
—JAMES TAYLOR

The world is a comedy
to those that think, a
tragedy to those who
feel.
—HORACE WALPOLE

intense love commitment was strongly associated with relationship satisfaction (Hendrick et al., 1988).

For some people, love is addictive (Peele & Brodsky, 1976). It produces a feeling of euphoria that a person learns to enjoy and depend on. Once we get accustomed to the euphoria of love, we need to be with our partner to feel the heightened sense of contentment and happiness. Withdrawal symptoms—depression, unhappiness, even somatic complaints—may begin when the love relationship is broken. According to these writers, the person suffering from a broken love relationship goes through withdrawal in much the same way as an alcoholic who has given up alcohol.

Persons who are ''love addicted'' and who have been dropped by their love partner may try to fall in love again as quickly as possible to relieve the pain of not

Sharing experiences together is one of the most wonderful aspects of a love relationship

being in love as well as the pain of rejection. The goal of "revenge love" is to show the former partner that a replacement can be found quickly and to prove that the person is lovable (Gullo & Church, 1988).

> ☐ C O N S I D E R A T I O N ☐
>
> Although love may be important for our emotional well-being, we all differ in the degree to which we need love relationships. For some of us, our support system of friends satisfies our need for connectedness. An intense one-on-one love relationship may not be necessary or desirable. "I don't like the obligations that creep into a love relationship," said one woman. "I have a lot of friends and enjoy being with them, but I don't need to be 'deeply in love' with a particular person to be happy or productive in my work." Other people may only feel content when in a love relationship and inordinately depressed if not.

▪▪ Conditions of Love

Love develops under various social, psychological, physiological, and cognitive conditions.

Social Conditions

Our society provides a basic context for love feelings to develop by emphasizing the importance of love. Through popular music, movies, television, and novels, the message is clear: love is an experience to enjoy and to pursue; you are missing something if you are not in love.

Peer influence is also important in creating the conditions for love to develop. Many of our peers establish love relationships and pair off. Their doing so makes love relationships normative and encourages us to seek the same experience. "All but one of my closest friends are involved in a steady love relationship," said one math major. "I'm wondering when I'm going to fall in love and be involved with someone."

Our society also links love and marriage. Couples who are about to get married are expected to be in love. If they are not, they would be ashamed to admit it. The fact that more than 90 percent of all Americans marry suggests that few escape the love feelings that are supposed to accompany courtship and marriage.

Psychological Conditions

Two psychological conditions are associated with healthy love relationships: a positive self-concept and the ability to self-disclose.

Positive Self-Concept/Self Love   The way you feel about yourself is your self-concept. If you have a positive self-concept, you like yourself and enjoy being who you are.

I am larger, better than I thought. I did not know I held so much goodness.

—WALT WHITMAN

A positive self-concept is important to the development of healthy love; once you accept yourself, you can believe that others are capable of doing so too. In contrast, a negative self-concept has devastating consequences for the individual and the people with whom he or she becomes involved. Individuals who cannot accept themselves tend to reject others. "My daddy always told me I was no good and would never amount to anything," said one man. "I guess I have always believed him, have never liked myself, and can't think of why someone else would either." Woody Allen has become famous for exploiting a negative self-concept. Groucho Marx once said, "I would never want to belong to an organization that would have me as a member."

In some cases, a positive self-concept is not a prerequisite for falling in love. People who have a very negative self-concept may fall in love with someone else as a result of feeling deficient. The love they perceive the other person having for them compensates for the deficiency and makes them feel better.

Self-Disclosure In addition to feeling good about yourself, it is helpful to disclose your feelings to others if you want to love and be loved. Disclosing yourself is a way of investing yourself in another. Once the other person knows some of the

A positive self-concept begins with feeling loved by a parent.

intimate details of your life, you will tend to feel more positively about that person because a part of you is now a part of them. Open communication in this sense tends to foster the development of an intense love relationship.

In a study (Rubin et al., 1980) of 231 couples who defined themselves as "going together," the researchers observed that the more the partners disclosed themselves to each other, the greater their love feelings for each other and the closer they regarded their relationship. As for what they disclosed, 70 percent of the women and men reported they had disclosed "fully" their feelings about their sexual relationship, and six in 10 had given full information about their previous sexual experiences. "Even in an area in which one would expect the greatest degree of reverse, 38 percent of the women and 35 percent of the men reported that they had revealed fully to their partners the things about themselves they were most ashamed of" (p. 313).

It is not easy for some people to let others know who they are, what they feel, or what they think. They may fear that if others really know them, they may be rejected as a friend or lover. To guard against this possibility, they may protect themselves and their relationships by allowing only limited access to their thoughts and feelings.

Trust is the condition under which people are willing to disclose themselves. To feel comfortable about letting someone else inside their head, they must feel that whatever feelings or information they share will not be judged and will be kept safe with that person. If trust is betrayed, a person may become bitterly resentful and vow never to disclose herself or himself again. One woman said, "After I told my partner that I had had an abortion, he told me that I was a murderer and he never wanted to see me again. I was hurt and felt I had made a mistake telling him about my intimate life. You can bet I'll be careful before I disclose myself to someone else."

Partners who are successful in disclosing to each other tend to feel better about their relationship—not only in courtship, but also in marriage. In a study of 120 couples (Jorgensen & Gaudy, 1980), those reporting the highest levels of satisfaction also reported the highest levels of self-disclosure. "Being open about fears, problems, self-doubts, feelings of anger or depression, and aspects of marriage perceived to be bothersome to one or both partners, as well as openly sharing positive feelings about the self and other" contributed to the happiness of the respective spouses (p. 286).

But disclosure must be equal to benefit the relationship. In one study (Davidson et al., 1983), the researchers found that those partners who were similar in affective disclosure had better adjustment than those who were dissimilar.

> "We both love each other at the same level," said one woman. "I tell him that I love him about as often as he tells me. I was once in a relationship where the guy loved me more than I loved him. He would always be telling me that he loved me. I got tired of hearing him say that, and it made me feel guilty when he did."

☐   C O N S I D E R A T I O N   ☐

Although it helps to have a positive self-concept at the beginning of a love relationship, sometimes this develops after becoming involved in a love relationship. "I've

continued on next page

> always felt like an ugly duckling," said one woman. "But once I fell in love with him and he with me, I felt very different. I felt very good about myself then because I knew that I was somebody that someone else could love."
>
> Other partners keep their disclosure at a very low level until after they define themselves as being in love. "I can't tell anybody anything that matters until after I feel that I can trust them," said one man. "When I start to love them, I usually tell them more than they want to know."

Physiological and Cognitive Conditions

After the social and psychological conditions of love are operative, the physiological and cognitive components of love become important. The individual must be physiologically aroused and interpret this stirred-up state as love (Schacter, 1964; Walster & Walster, 1978). For example, Carol was beginning her first year at a midwestern university. Being three states away from home in an unfamiliar environment, she felt lonely and bored. During registration, she met a good-looking junior. They exchanged pleasant glances and small talk and planned to go out together that night around 8:00. Carol became anxious when Brad had not shown up by 8:45. When he finally arrived at 9:00 (car trouble had delayed him), they went to a concert, drank some beer, and played video games at a local pub. Carol had a terrific time.

Two days went by before Carol heard from Brad again. He called to ask if she wanted to go home with him for the weekend. By the end of that weekend, Carol felt she was in love. Her loneliness, the fun they had when they were together, frustration (she never knew when Brad would call or come by), and sexual arousal (they had petted but had not yet had intercourse) were enough to induce an agitated, stirred-up state. Both her roommates were "in love," so Carol identified herself as being in the same condition.

There are many people who would never have been in love if they had never heard love spoken of.

—LA
    ROCHEFOUCAULD

CONSIDERATION

Social, psychological, physiological, and cognitive conditions are not the only factors important for the development of love feelings. The timing must also be right. There are only certain times in your life when you are seeking a love relationship. When those times occur, you are likely to fall in love with the person who is there and is also seeking a love relationship. Hence, many love pairings exist because each of the individuals is available to the other—not because they are particularly suited for each other.

The Lover Role

When all of the foregoing conditions are met, an individual may assume the role of lover. Like all roles, the role of lover suggests that the person will engage in certain behavior. First, the lover can be expected to idealize the partner. The lover will see qualities that are not there (perhaps the person is "never" selfish) and avoid seeing qualities that are there (such as the beginning of a drinking problem).

Such idealization is functional. It enhances the lover's self-esteem ("I must be a terrific person if I am in a love relationship with such a terrific person").

Another aspect of the lover role is that of suffering. The lover expects to endure a certain amount of pain, from either longing, unrequited love, or outright rejection. Pain may also result from being involved with an abusive and deceitful partner in an exploitative relationship. Some people stay in miserable relationships because they say they love the partner too much to leave.

A final element of the lover role is fantasy. The lover is allowed to spend a great deal of time envisioning a future that may be unrealistic. "The two of us together in a cottage by the sea" is a visual image of how some lovers think of marriage. The demands of working until 10:30 P.M. on the job or getting up three times a night with an infant who has colic is rarely part of the fantasy.

> In that strange unsettlement of love, we are always crazy.
> —SUSAN RICHARDS SHREVE

∷ A Triangular Theory of Love

Love may be viewed as consisting of three central elements—intimacy, passion, and commitment (Sternberg, 1986) as shown in Figure 2.1. *Intimacy* (the top vertex of the triangle) is the emotional connectedness that two people feel for each other. The partners feel bonded to each other in a context of emotional warmth. Intimacy is enhanced primarily as a consequence of open communication between the partners.

Passion (the left-hand vertex of the triangle) refers to the romantic and physical aspects of the relationship. The partners are physiologically aroused in reference to each other.

For some, an intimate, passionate, committed relationship is the ultimate human experience.

:: FIGURE 2.1
**Triangular
Theory of Love**

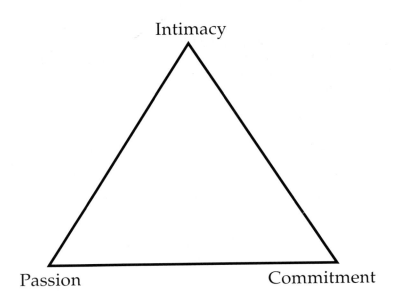

Commitment (the right-hand vertex of the triangle) is the desire to maintain the relationship. This is the cognitive aspect of the relationship over which the partners exercise the greatest conscious control.

Various kinds of love can be described on the basis of these three elements.

1. *Nonlove:* The absence of all three components in reference to another person.
2. *Liking:* The intimacy element of the relationship is present, but passion and commitment in the future are lacking.
3. *Infatuation:* The experience of passion without intimacy or commitment.
4. *Empty love:* The absence of both intimacy and passion but a commitment to love another.
5. *Consummate love:* A love resulting from a full combination of intimacy, passion, and commitment.

☐   C O N S I D E R A T I O N   ☐

To what degree are intimacy, passion, and commitment elements of the love relationship you have or have had? How important are each of these elements in terms of your satisfaction in a love relationship?

:: Romantic and Realistic Love

For some people, love is romantic; for others, it is realistic. *Romantic love* is characterized by such beliefs as "love at first sight," "there is only one true love," and "love conquers all." The symptoms of romantic love include drastic mood swings, palpitations of the heart, and intrusive thinking about the partner.

In contrast to romantic love, *realistic love*, or *conjugal love*, tends to be characteristic of people who have been in love with each other for several years. Partners who know all about each other yet still love each other are said to have a realistic view of love. The Love Attitudes Scale provides a way to assess the degree to which you are romantic or realistic about love.

Emotion has taught mankind to reason.
—MARQUIS DE VAUVENARGUES

☐   C O N S I D E R A T I O N   ☐

When you determine your score on the Love Attitudes Scale, be aware that you are merely assessing the degree to which you are a romantic or a realist. Your tendency to be one or the other is not good or bad. Both romantics and realists may be happy, mature people. However, being ultra-romantic is associated with a more difficult adjustment to having children (Belsky & Rovine, 1990).

Who Is Romantic? Who Is Realistic?

Using the Love Attitudes Scale, several studies have been conducted to find out the degree to which various categories of people are romantic or realistic. When 100 unmarried men and 100 unmarried women college students completed the inventory, the results revealed that men were more romantic than women and that freshmen were more romantic than seniors (Knox & Sporakowski, 1968). Comparable results were found in a similar study (Knox, 1982) in which 94 was the average score of 97 students; men and freshmen had more romantic scores, and women and seniors had more realistic scores. However, after analyzing the results of a romance survey of slightly less than 12,000 *Psychology Today* readers, the researcher concluded that "more women than men say that romance is important, and men rate their partners as being more romantic" (Rubenstein, 1983, 49).

I don't want realism, I want magic.
—TENNESSEE WILLIAMS

Another study (Knox, 1970) compared the love attitudes of 50 men and 50 women high school seniors with 50 husbands and 50 wives who had been married more than 20 years. Both the unmarried and married groups revealed a romantic attitude toward love. These findings were expected for the high school seniors but not for the older marrieds. It may be that partners who have been married for 20 years adopt attitudes that are consistent with such a long-term investment of their time and energy; that is, the belief that there is only one person with whom an individual can really fall in love and marry justifies those who have done so. Also, some older marrieds grow to love each other. One wife said:

> I knew when I married him I didn't love him. I was pregnant, and since you didn't get an abortion back then, I went through with the wedding. Our first years were rough, but we hung on to each other and have had a good marriage. My love for him is now stronger than I would have ever imagined. Love is something you grow into—not something that just happens.

When the high school seniors and older marrieds were compared with 100 couples who had been married less than five years, the last group proved to be very realistic. For them, moonlight and roses had become daylight and dishes.

The Love Attitudes Scale*

This scale is designed to assess the degree to which you are romantic or realistic in your attitudes toward love. There are no right or wrong answers.

Directions: After reading each sentence carefully, circle the number that best represents the degree to which you agree or disagree with the sentence.

1 Strongly agree
2 Mildly agree
3 Undecided
4 Mildly disagree
5 Strongly disagree

		SA	MA	U	MD	SD
1.	Love doesn't make sense. It just is.	1	2	3	4	5
2.	When you fall "head over heels" in love, it's sure to be the real thing.	1	2	3	4	5
3.	To be in love with someone you would like to marry but can't is a tragedy.	1	2	3	4	5
4.	When love hits, you know it.	1	2	3	4	5
5.	Common interests are really unimportant; as long as each of you is truly in love, you will adjust.	1	2	3	4	5
6.	It doesn't matter if you marry after you have known your partner for only a short time as long as you know you are in love.	1	2	3	4	5
7.	If you are going to love a person, you will "know" after a short time.	1	2	3	4	5
8.	As long as two people love each other, the educational differences they have really do not matter.	1	2	3	4	5
9.	You can love someone even though you do not like any of that person's friends.	1	2	3	4	5
10.	When you are in love, you are usually in a daze.	1	2	3	4	5
11.	Love "at first sight" is often the deepest and most enduring type of love.	1	2	3	4	5
12.	When you are in love, it really does not matter what your partner does because you will love him or her anyway.	1	2	3	4	5
13.	As long as you really love a person, you will be able to solve the problems you have with the person.	1	2	3	4	5
14.	Usually you can really love and be happy with only one or two people in the world.	1	2	3	4	5

	SA	MA	U	MD	SD
15. Regardless of other factors, if you truly love another person, that is a good enough reason to marry that person.	1	2	3	4	5
16. It is necessary to be in love with the one you marry to be happy.	1	2	3	4	5
17. Love is more of a feeling than a relationship.	1	2	3	4	5
18. People should not get married unless they are in love.	1	2	3	4	5
19. Most people truly love only once during their lives.	1	2	3	4	5
20. Somewhere there is an ideal mate for most people.	1	2	3	4	5
21. In most cases, you will "know it" when you meet the right partner.	1	2	3	4	5
22. Jealousy usually varies directly with love; that is, the more you are in love, the greater your tendency to become jealous will be.	1	2	3	4	5
23. When you are in love, you are motivated by what you feel rather than by what you think.	1	2	3	4	5
24. Love is best described as an exciting rather than a calm thing.	1	2	3	4	5
25. Most divorces probably result from falling out of love rather than failing to adjust.	1	2	3	4	5
26. When you are in love, your judgment is usually not too clear.	1	2	3	4	5
27. Love often comes only once in a lifetime.	1	2	3	4	5
28. Love is often a violent and uncontrollable emotion.	1	2	3	4	5
29. When selecting a marriage partner, differences in social class and religion are of small importance compared with love.	1	2	3	4	5
30. No matter what anyone says, love cannot be understood.	1	2	3	4	5

SCORING: Add the numbers you circled. 1 (strongly agree) is the most romantic response and 5 (strongly disagree) is the most realistic response. The lower your total score (30 is the lowest possible score), the more romantic your attitudes toward love. The higher your total score (150 is the highest possible score) the more realistic your attitudes toward love. A score of 90 places you at the midpoint between being an extreme romantic and an extreme realist.

NOTE: This Self-Assessment is designed to be fun and thought provoking; it is *not* intended to be used by students as a clinical evaluation device.

*From D. Knox, *The love attitudes inventory,* rev. ed. (Saluda, N.C.: Family Life Publications, 1983). Reprinted by permission.

This is not to suggest that recently married spouses do not love each other. However, their feelings about each other may change as a result of their movement from the role of lover to spouse. Lovers spend all of their time together and orient their day around each other. Spouses spend most of their time earning money and orient their day around their work. One husband said:

> My wife and I have been married for almost 10 months. The first six months were extremely gratifying, sexually and in all other aspects. Since then, we have begun working up to 10 or 12 hours per day, six days a week, trying to accumulate enough money to buy a new mobile home. This has put a lot of strain on us. Our sexual activities have been cut drastically to approximately once a week. We are more irritable toward each other, and we are overlooking some of each others' needs. I realize that we are losing our "romantic love," and I hope things will improve after I graduate and start working on a less demanding and more stable schedule.

From a racial and cross-cultural perspective, black and Japanese students view love differently from white students. When 327 black high school and college students completed the Love Attitudes Scale, the results revealed that black students had more romantic attitudes toward love than white students (Mirchandani, 1973). One explanation suggests that blacks are encouraged by their parents to be and to do the things that make them happy. This world view may lend itself to a less constrained, more positive "romantic" perspective.

Japanese students are more realistic than American students in their attitudes toward love. Japanese students are more likely to have been taught that love may follow rather than precede marriage. In addition, their parents are more involved in the selection and approval of the people they date than the parents of American students (Simmons et al., 1986).

It is impossible to love and be wise.
—FRANCIS BACON

Marrieds are more realistic about love than dating partners because the former see their partner in more realistic contexts.

CONSIDERATION

Is romantic love a sound basis for marriage? If the love you have for your partner is based primarily on physical attraction, little time together, and few shared experiences, marrying on this basis may be taking an unnecessary risk. To marry someone without spending a great deal of time with him or her (the minimum is one year) in a variety of situations (your home, your partner's home, four- or five-day camping trips, and so on) may be like buying a Christmas present without knowing what is inside.

▪▪ Greek Views of Love

In addition to viewing love on a romantic–realistic continuum, love may be conceptualized as *phileo, agape,* and *eros.* Introduced by the Greeks and reflected in the New Testament, *phileo,* or friendship love, may be in reference to siblings (*philadelphia*) or people in general (*philanthropia*).

Agape means a love of self-sacrifice that is spontaneous and unmotivated. This type of love is altruistic and requires nothing in return. The love of parents for their children is reflective of *agape* love.

Eros is a type of selfish love designed to get from another person what is valuable to the "taker." Dating someone because that person will type your term paper or will gratify your sexual needs is an example of eros love.

▪▪ Relationship Scripts

A social script defines the roles of the people in a social situation and predicts their behavior. For example, the social script of your marriage and family class dictates the situation (an academic learning experience), the roles (students and teacher), and the behavior (students are to attend class, take notes, and score well on exams; the teacher is to lecture, prepare tests, and give feedback on test performances). Relationship scripts identify how women and men are to view each other, what their roles are, and what they are expected to do. These scripts are learned from parents, peers, religion, novels, television, and movies, among other sources. Exposure to these influences allows people to develop a way of thinking and behaving in reference to romance. But the relationship scripts are different for women and for men, and they do not ensure a meaningful and lasting relationship:

> During the course of the courtship, the couples collectively manage to overcome a plethora of obstacles to their love and achieve the goal of making a lifetime commitment to each other. Abruptly, once the pair has been established as a couple, the story ends. The extent of the script provided for how to weather the remaining course of the relationship is a parsimonious "happily ever after" (Rose, 1985, 251).

The Relationship Script for Women

In the past, females were taught to be passive, to exchange sexual favors for commitment, and to prolong the arousal phase of an encounter. Although there were exceptions, women typically did not call men for dates. They were more likely to react rather than to be the acting agent. The relationship script for the woman was to "be" not to "do." In the classic fairy tale, Rapunzel used her long hair as a ladder so that her prince could climb up to see her in the tower.

Women have also learned that men want to have sex with them and that they could use sex to bargain for what they wanted—commitment. "I want a love that lasts past Saturday night," is the lyric from *A Sunday Kind of Love,* which emphasized the desire on the part of the woman to have sex only if it led to a stable relationship.

Because women were taught that they had the most control before they had sex with their partner, they were taught to prolong the encounter. In the romantic novel *Seaswept,* the heroine, Monica, kisses her partner once in a nine-page span but "also tells him 14 times that she isn't interested in him. In the interim, vivid descriptions of her passionate thoughts about him are detailed. What is symbolically satisfied here is the power to prolong and control the arousal phase of the sexual encounter" (Rose, 1985, 265).

The traditional script for American women has changed. The modern woman is assertive rather than passive, initiates rather than reacts to, and enjoys sex independent of her partner's interest. She does not feel that she has to be in a committed relationship before having sex. She may decide to have sex with or without a commitment.

The Relationship Script for Men

While women were being socialized to use one script in courtship, men were learning another script. The primary themes of this script were activity, conquest, and variety. Activity may be physical (lifting weights) or career success. Either produces the same outcome—approval from male peers and admiration from women. "There is no shortage of women for men at the top," noted one famous golfer.

Men were taught that success could occur independently, without regard to a relationship. Men viewed women as objects of conquest—as trophies or entities to obtain. Even though "getting a woman" (a phrase used in male peer groups) may have only a sexual connotation, it could also result in "getting a mate."

The relationship script for males also involves variety. Because males viewed females as sexual conquests, men believed that the more women they could conquer, the better.

The traditional script for American men has also changed. The modern man knows that the modern woman expects to be treated on equal terms and that sexism is not tolerated. Furthermore, women may be as reluctant to marry and to make a commitment as some men. In this regard, men can no longer use their commitment to marriage as a ploy to increase their power in the relationship.

> There is no greater or keener pleasure than that of bodily love—and none which is more irrational.
> —PLATO

▪▪ Love and Sex

> Sex without love is an empty experience.
> —DIANE KEATON

Love and sex are also involved in the developing relationship. There are a number of similarities and differences between love and sex.

Similarities between Love and Sex

Although we think of love and sex as being two different things, there are similarities between the two. These similarities include the following:

Both love and sex involve intense feelings. To be involved in a love relationship is one of the most exciting experiences an individual ever has. To know that another person loves us engenders feelings of happiness and joy. "No one ever really loved me until now," remarked one man, "and because of this love, I have a very good feeling inside."

Sex also involves intense feelings. Although sex involves more than orgasm, the latter is the epitome of intense pleasure.

Both love and sex involve physiological changes. When people are in an intense love relationship, their brain produces phenylethylamine, a chemical correlate of amphetamine, which may result in a giddy feeling similar to an amphetamine high (Liebowitz, 1983). When love affairs break up, people may "crash" and go through withdrawal because there is less phenylethylamine in their system. Some heartbroken lovers reach for chocolate, which contains phenylethylamine.

Further support for the idea that love has a physiological component has been suggested by Money (1980), who studied patients who had undergone brain surgery or suffered from a pituitary deficiency. Although they were able to experience various emotions, passionate love was not one of them.

The physiological changes the body experiences during sexual excitement have been well documented by Masters and Johnson (1966) in their observations of more than 10,000 orgasms. Such physiological changes include increased heart rate, blood pressure, and breathing.

Both love and sex have a cognitive component. To experience the maximum pleasure from both love and sex, the person must label or interpret what is happening in positive terms. For love to develop, each person in the relationship must define their interaction as enjoyable.

Positive labeling is also important in sex. Each person's touch, kiss, caress, and body type are different; sexual pleasure depends on labeling sexual interaction with that person as enjoyable. "I can't stand the way he French kisses" and "I love the way he French kisses" are two interpretations of kissing the same person. But only one of these interpretations will make the event pleasurable.

Both love and sex may be expressed in various ways. The expression of love may include words ("I love you"), gifts (flowers or candy), behaviors (being on time, a surprise phone call or visit), and touch (holding hands, tickling). Similarly, sex as well as love may be expressed through a glance, embracing, kissing, fondling, and intercourse.

The need for love and sex increases with deprivation. The more we get, the less we feel we need; the less we get, the more we feel we need. The all-consuming passion of Romeo and Juliet, perhaps the most celebrated love story of all time, undoubtedly was fed by their enforced separation. The following reflects a similar love-from-afar experience:

> I feel the thing that has affected me the most about love is that we broke up over a year and a half ago and I still think of him every day. I feel that if he walked in the door tomorrow we would start up where we left off—but that will never happen. A month after we became involved, he got a girl pregnant in his home town and married her. This destroyed me completely, and for a long time I wouldn't go out with anyone. The thing that bothered me most was when I saw him recently at a bar,

Yes, but as empty experiences go, it's one of the best.
—WOODY ALLEN

O love, thy kiss would wake the dead!
—TENNYSON

he told me that he still loved me but that he had to marry her because his parents found out she was pregnant.

Deprivation often has the same effect on the need for sex. Although the perceived need for sex varies among individuals and changes across time, in general, deprivation tends to increase one's perceived need for sex. But, this is not always the case.

Barbara Lockhart (1983), a competitive speed skater on the U.S. Olympic team, commented on sex:

> To me, channeling my energies in training was positive, exciting, and rewarding, and so is the channeling of sexual energy. I do not feel sorry for myself, nor do I feel deprived or depraved, not having any "outlet" for sexual feelings. I really enjoy not having sex in my life. It would be wonderful to be able to enjoy sexual intimacy, but as long as I am single, I am experiencing a far greater joy in my life by not having sex be a part of it. (p. 38).

Basic Differences between Love and Sex

There are several differences between love and sex. These include the following:

In our culture, *love is viewed as crucial for human happiness; sex is viewed as important but not crucial.* After analyzing the data from a study of more than 100,000 people about what makes them happy, one researcher concluded:

> Many people are unhappy with their sex lives, and many think this is an important lack, but almost no one seems to think that sex alone will bring happiness. Romance and love were often listed as crucial missing ingredients, but not sex; it was simply not mentioned. (Freedman, 1978, p. 56)

Love is pervasive whereas sex tends to be localized. Love is felt all over, but sexual feeling is most often associated with various body parts (lips, breasts, or genitals). People do not say of love as they do of sex, "It feels good here."

Love tends to be more selective than sex. The standards people have for a love partner are generally higher than those they have for a sex partner. Love wants *the* person rather than *a* person. Love also takes time to develop in a relationship; sexual feelings may occur instantaneously. Love necessarily involves the partners communicating with each other about themselves and their relationship. Sex can occur with little knowledge of the other and with limited verbal communication.

The standards for a love partner may also be different from those for a sexual partner. For example, some people form relationships with others to meet emotional intimacy needs that are not met by their sexual partners. A sexual component need not be a part of the love relationship they have with these people.

Gender Differences in Love and Sex

Although there are individual differences, women tend to be more interested in the emotional aspects of a relationship and men tend to focus more on the sexual aspects. Harlequin romance novels reflect this theme. One researcher has observed:

A surprising number of Harlequins employ the same vocabulary to describe the inner conflict of the heroine as she struggles against the hero on his own grounds where he has all the weapons. His main weapon in this idealized world is his powerful sexual attraction; her main weakness is her susceptibility to that attraction, which quickly becomes total love. Her struggle aims to prevent the hero from exploiting her love for his own sexual desires . . . (Rabine, 1985, p. 48) However, as gender roles are becoming more egalitarian, we may see less gender differences regarding love and sex in the future than in the past.

> The jealous are troublesome to others but a torment to themselves.
> —WILLIAM PENN

▪▪ Jealousy

Feelings of jealousy are not uncommon in love relationships. *Jealousy* is a set of emotional feelings that results when an individual perceives that the love relationship he or she has with a person is being threatened. The specific feelings are those of fear of loss or abandonment, anxiety, pain, anger, vulnerability, and hopelessness. Jealously has its basis in the obsession for an exclusive relationship rather than being based on a natural threat (e.g., the partner has cancer).

▪ **DATA:** *Of 103 women and men of varying ages and involvements in relationships, 75 percent reported feeling jealous. One-half of the respondents described themselves as "jealous" people (Pines & Aronson, 1983).*

Individuals who are more likely to be jealous are women: those who are not in a monogamous relationship, those who are dissatisfied with the sexual relationship with their partner, and those who are dissatisfied with their relationship in general (Hansen, 1983; Pines & Aronson, 1983).

Causes

Jealousy may be caused by external or internal factors. An external factor is the behavior of the partner that elicits jealousy. In the Pines and Aronson (1983) study of 103 respondents, most said they became jealous when they were at a party with their partner and their partner spent a great deal of time talking, dancing, and flirting with someone of the opposite sex. "I get to feeling very uncomfortable when I see him enjoying himself and putting his hands all over another woman," remarked one woman. Other behaviors of the partner that create jealousy include the partner expressing appreciation of and interest in someone else, having a close friend of the opposite sex, and involvement in a love or sexual relationship with someone else.

Jealousy may also be caused by internal factors, which exist independently of the partners behavior. For example, jealousy may arise because an individual has learned to be distrustful in previous situations. "I know my husband is faithful to me," said one wife, "but my ex-husband wasn't, and it's hard for me to trust men again."

Jealous feelings may also result from low self-esteem and lack of self-confidence (De Moja, 1986). People who feel inadequate in looks or personality may doubt their ability to get another person to love them and be faithful to them, so they are continually jealous of others whom they fear may take their partner away.

> Jealousy feeds on suspicion, and it turns into fury or it ends as soon as we pass from suspicion to certainty.
> —LA ROCHEFOUCAULD

Finally, jealousy is more likely to exist when an individual has no perceived alternatives. In a study of jealousy among spouses, the most jealous were those that felt that they could not get anyone else if their partner became attracted to someone else (Hansen, 1985).

☐   C O N S I D E R A T I O N   ☐

Sometimes the interaction of two people in a relationship may encourage the development of jealous feelings. Suppose John accuses Mary of being interested in someone else, and Mary denies the accusation and responds by saying "I love you" and being very affectionate. If this pattern continues, Mary will teach John the rewards of jealousy. John learns that when he acts jealous, good things happen to him—Mary showers him with love and physical affection. Inadvertently, Mary is reinforcing John for exhibiting jealous behavior. To break the cycle, Mary should tell John of her love for him and be affectionate when he is not exhibiting jealous behavior. When he does act jealous, she should say that she feels badly when he accuses her of something she isn't doing and to please stop. If he does not stop, she should terminate the interaction until John can be around her and not act jealous.

Consequences

Low levels of jealousy may be functional for a couple's relationship. Not only may jealousy keep the partner aware that he or she is cared for (the implied message is "I love you and don't want to lose you to someone else"), but also the partner may learn that the development of romantic and sexual relationships "on the side" is unacceptable. One wife said:

> When I started spending extra time with this guy at the office my husband got jealous and told me he thought I was getting in over my head and asked me to cut back on the relationship because it was "tearing him up" and he couldn't stay married to me with these feelings. I felt really loved when he told me this and drifted out of the relationship I was developing with the guy at the office.

Jealousy may improve a relationship in yet another way. When the partners begin to take each other for granted, involvement of one or both partners outside the relationship can encourage them to reevaluate how important the relationship is and can help recharge it.

In its extreme form, jealousy may have devastating consequences, including murder, suicide, spouse beating, and severe depression. "I turned into an alcoholic overnight," said one male. "I just didn't want to be sober because I would think about her and this other fellow. I almost drank myself into oblivion."

▪▪ Trends

The most predictable trend in love relationships is that romantic love will, in this society, continue to characterize each new love relationship. Although a person may have been disappointed in previous relationships, love feelings help to create the illusion that the current love relationship will be different. One person cannot convince another that love is something more than illusion, deception, and idealization. Such a perception is grounded in experience. Even those with extensive interpersonal experience are not immune to "falling in love" and riding the love wave.

Love will also continue to change in both feeling and expression as the relationship continues. Couples must inevitably encounter disillusionment of this romantic love and come to terms with the reality of day-to-day living where partners are sometimes exhausted and irritable. Learning to discuss issues, solve problems, and share their lives without the ever present "romantic love glue" is a feat for most couples.

▪▪ Summary

In American society, love is viewed as a crucial element in human happiness. It is also the feeling most Western people have when they say they want to get married. Most people agree on its importance, but they do not agree on the definition of love. Love is a feeling that people experience individually and privately.

Love occurs under certain conditions. Social conditions include a society that promotes the pursuit of love, peers who enjoy it, and a set of norms that link love and marriage. Psychological conditions involve a positive self-concept and a willingness to disclose one's self to others. Physiological and cognitive conditions imply that the individual experiences a stirred-up state and labels it "love." All of these conditions are important but not essential. What is essential is a high frequency of positive verbal and nonverbal behavior from the partner to furnish the basis on which love feelings may develop. It is easy for us to fall in love with someone who compliments us, is affectionate, and shares our value system. We are less likely to develop love feelings for those who criticize us, do not enjoy touching us, and do not respect our values.

A person who accepts the role of lover engages in predictable behaviors. Not only will the person idealize the partner, but she or he will also endure suffering and fantasize about the future with the beloved.

According to the Triangular Theory of love, three basic components of love are intimacy, passion, and commitment. Consummate love consists of all three components; infatuation consists of passion only.

Love may be viewed on a continuum from romanticism to realism. College freshmen, and never marrieds tend to be more romantic than college seniors, and young marrieds.

Relationship scripts specify how women and men view each other, what their roles are, and what they are to do. Women were taught to be passive, to exchange sex for commitment, and to prolong the arousal phase of an encounter (the condition of greatest control for the woman). Men were taught to be active, to view women as objects of conquest, and to seek sexual variety. These scripts are being replaced by more egalitarian scripts.

Love relationships in the future will be the same as those in the past—exciting. Each new love relationship often involves the same sense of exhilaration. In Western societies, love is the most sought after feeling in the human experience. In time, romantic love feelings change to a more comfortable though less intense set of feelings.

Questions for Reflection

1. To what degree are you comfortable disclosing yourself to others? How did you develop this level of comfort or discomfort?
2. To what degree do you feel the opposite gender is consistent with the relationship script discussed in this chapter?
3. To what degree are your decisions dominated by rational versus emotional concerns? (This question applies to the choices section that follows.)

References

Belsky, J. and M. Rovine. Patterns of marital change across the transition to parenthood: Pregnancy to three years postpartum. *Journal of Marriage and the Family,* 1990, *52,* 5–19.

Davidson, B., J. Balswick, and C. Halverson. Affective self-disclosure and marital adjustment: A test of equity theory. *Journal of Marriage and the Family,* 1983, *45,* 93–102.

De Moja, C. A. Anxiety, self-confidence, jealousy, and romantic attitudes toward love in Italian undergraduates. *Psychological Reports,* 1986, *58,* 138.

Diener, E., E. Sandvik, and W. Pavot. *The social psychology of subjective well-being* New York: Pergamon Press, 1989.

Freedman, J. L. *Happy people.* New York: Harcourt Brace Jovanovich, 1978.

Gullo, Stephen and Connie Church. Love survival: How to mend a broken heart. *Health,* 1988, *20,* 50–55.

Hansen, G. L. Marital satisfaction and jealousy among men. *Psychological Reports,* 1983, *52,* 363–366.

Hansen, G. L. Perceived threats and marital jealousy. *Social Psychology Quarterly,* 1985, *48,* 262–268.

Hendrick, S. S., C. Hendrick, and N. L. Adler. Romantic relationships: Love, satisfaction, and staying together. *Journal of Personality and Social Psychology,* 1988, *54,* 980–988.

Jorgensen, S. R. and J. C. Gaudy. Self-disclosure and satisfaction in marriage: The relation examined. *Family Relations,* 1980, *29,* 281–288.

Kemper, T. D. and R. W. Bologh. What do you get when you fall in love? Some health status effects. *Sociology of Health and Illness,* 1981, *3,* 72–88.

Knox, D. Conceptions of love at three developmental levels. *Family Life Coordinator,* 1970, *19,* 151–157.

Knox, D. *What kind of love is yours?* Unpublished study, Department of Sociology, Anthropology, and Economics. East Carolina University, 1982.

Knox, D. and M. J. Sporakowski. Attitudes of college students toward love. *Journal of Marriage and the Family,* 1968, *30,* 638–642.

Liebowitz, M. *The chemistry of love.* Boston: Little, Brown, 1983.

Lockhart, B. D. The "other" intimacy. *Family Perspective,* 1983, *17,* 35–39.

Masters, W. H. and V. E. Johnson. *Human sexual response.* Boston: Little, Brown, 1966.

Mirchandani, V. K. Attitudes toward love among blacks. Unpublished Master's thesis. East Carolina University, 1973.

Money, J. *Love and sickness.* Baltimore, Md.: Johns Hopkins University Press, 1980.

Peele, S. and A. Brodsky. *Love and addiction.* New York: New American Library, 1976.

Pines, A. and E. Aronson. Antecedents, correlates, and consequences of sexual jealousy. *Journal of Personality,* 1983, *51,* 108–109.

Rabine, L. W. Romance in the age of electronics: Harlequin enterprises. *Feminist Studies,* 1985, *11,* 39–60.

Rose, S. Is romance dysfunctional? *International Journal of Women's Studies*, 1985, *8*, 250–265.

Rubenstein, C. The modern art of courtly love. *Psychology Today*, July 1983, 40–49.

Rubin, Z., C. T. Hill, L. A. Peplau, and C. Dunkel-Schetter. Self-disclosure in dating couples: Sex roles and the ethic of openness. *Journal of Marriage and the Family*, 1980, *42*, 305–318.

Schacter, S. The interaction of cognitive and physiological determinants of emotional state. *Advances in experimental social psychology*. Edited by L. Berkowitz. New York: Academic Press, 1964, 49–80.

Simmons, C. H., A. V. Kolke, and H. Shimizu. Attitudes toward romantic love among American, German, and Japanese students. *The Journal of Social Psychology*, 1986, *126*, 327–336.

Statistical Abstract of the United States: 1990. 110th ed. Washington, D. C.: U. S. Bureau of the Census, 1990.

Sternberg, R. J. A triangular theory of love. *Psychological Review*, 1986, *93*, 119–135.

Sternberg, Robert J. and Michael L. Barnes, eds. *The psychology of love*. New Haven, Conn.: Yale University Press, 1988.

Swanbrow, D. The paradox of happiness. *Psychology Today*, July/August, 1989, 37–39.

Trotter, R. J. The three faces of love. *Psychology Today*, September 1986, 46–54.

Trovato, F. and G. Lauris. Marital status and mortality in Canada: 1951–1981. *Journal of Marriage and the Family*, 1989, *51*, 907–922.

Vannoy, R. *Sex without love: A philosophical exploration*. Buffalo, N.Y.: Prometheus Books, 1980.

Walster, E. and G. W. Walster. *A new look at love*. Reading, Mass.: Addison-Wesley, 1978.

CHOICES

CHOOSING TO LISTEN to one's heart or head when making decisions and choosing to have sex with or without love are two important decisions about love relationships. We will examine the consequences of each choice here.

Heart or Head: Which Should You Listen To?

Lovers are frequently confronted with the need to make decisions about their relationships, but they are divided on whether to let their heart or head rule in such decisions. In a marriage and family class, 120 students were asked whether they used their hearts or their heads in making such decisions. Some of their answers follow.

Heart

Those who relied on their heart (women more likely) for making decisions felt that emotions were more important than logic and that listening to your heart made you happier. One woman said:

In deciding on a mate, my heart should rule because my heart has reasons to cry and my head doesn't. My heart knows what I want, what would make me most happy. My head tells me what is best for me. But I would rather have something that makes me happy than something that is good for me.

Some men also agreed that your heart should rule. One said:

I went with my heart in a situation, and I'm glad I did. I had been dating a girl for two years when I decided she was not the one I wanted and that my present girlfriend was. My heart was saying to go for the one I loved, but my head was telling me not to because if I broke up with the first girl, it would hurt her, her parents, and my parents. But I decided I had to make myself happy and went with the feelings in my heart and started dating the girl who is now my fiancée.

Relying on one's emotions does not always have a positive outcome, as the following experience illustrates:

Last semester, I was dating a guy I felt more for than he did for me. Despite that, I wanted to spend any opportunity I could with him when he asked me to go somewhere with him. One day he had no classes, and he asked me to go to the park by the river for a picnic. I had four classes that day and exams in two of them. I let my heart rule and went with him. Nothing ever came of the relationship and I didn't do well in those classes.

Head

Most of the respondents (men more likely) felt that it was better to be rational than emotional.

In deciding on a mate, I feel my head should rule because you have to choose someone that you can get along with after the new wears off. If you follow your heart solely, you may not look deep enough into a person to see what it is that you really like. Is it just a pretty face or a nice body? Or is it deeper than that, such as common interests and attitudes? After the new wears off, it's the person inside the body that you're going to have to live with. The "heart" sometimes can fog up this picture of the true person and distort reality into a fairy tale.

. . .

Love is blind and can play tricks on you. Two years ago, I fell in love with a man whom I later found out was married. Although my heart had learned to love this man, my mind knew the consequences and told me to stop seeing him. My heart said, "Maybe he'll leave her for me," but my mind said, "If he cheated on her, he'll cheat on you." I got out and am glad that I listened to my head.

Some feel that both the head and the heart should rule when making relationship decisions.

When you really love someone, your heart rules in most of the situations. But if you don't keep your head in some matters, then you risk losing the love that you feel in your heart. I think that we should find a way to let our heads and hearts rule together.

Sex With and Without Love

Some individuals feel that sex is best in the context of a love relationship. Of 12,000 respondents in the

Psychology Today survey on romance, 30 percent of the men and more than 40 percent of the women said that sex without love was either unenjoyable or unacceptable. Half of those under the age of 22 felt this way (Rubenstein, 1983).

Here is an example of what some people have said about the importance of an emotional relationship as a context for sexual expression:

Sex is good and beautiful when both parties want it, but when one person wants sex only, that's bad. I love sex, but I like to feel that the man cares about me. I can't handle the type of sexual relationship where one night I spend the night with him and the next night he spends the night with someone else. I feel like I am being used. There are still a few women around like me who *need* the commitment before sex means what it should.

Other people feel that love is not necessary for sexual expression. Indeed, the theme of the book *Sex without Love* (Vannoy, 1980) is that sex should be enjoyed for its own sake. One person said:

You choose a lover according to how you wish to be loved, and you choose a sex partner according to how you wish to be laid. There is no guarantee whatever · that the person you love and the person whom you find most sexually desirable are one and the same. There are just certain things a lover may not be able to give you, and it may be good sex (p. 24).

The idea that sex with love is wholesome and sex without love is exploitive is a fallacious dualism. Two strangers can meet, share each other sexually, have a deep mutual admiration for each other's sensuous qualities, and go their separate ways in the morning. Their parting is not evidence that their sexual encounter was exploitation. Rather, it is a sign of their preference for independence and singlehood rather than permanent emotional involvement and marriage (Vannoy, 1980, 26).

Each person in a sexual encounter will undoubtedly experience different degrees of love feelings; and the experience of each may differ across time. One woman reported that the first time she had intercourse with her future husband was shortly after they had met in a bar. She described their firstsexual encounter as "raw naked sex" with no emotional feelings. But they continued to see each other over a period of months, an emotional relationship developed, and "sex took on a love meaning for us."

Sex with love can also drift into sex without love. One man said he had been deeply in love with his wife but that they had gradually drifted apart. Sex between them was no longer sex with love.

Both love and sex can be viewed on a continuum. Love feelings may range from nonexistent to intense, and relationships can range from limited sexual interaction to intense interaction. Hence, rarely are sexual encounters with or without love. Rather, they will exhibit varying degrees of emotional involvement. Also, rarely are romantic love relationships with or without sex. Rather, they display varying degrees of sexual expression. Where on the continuum one chooses to be—at what degree of emotional and sexual involvement—will vary from person to person and from time to time.

Impact of Social Influences on Choices

The degree to which you feel that sex and love always go together has probably been influenced by your gender. Many men in our society have been socialized to emphasize the importance of intercourse and orgasm. Male sexuality is sometimes *homosocial* in that some men engage in sex with women so that they can have something to tell their male peers about.

In contrast, many women in our society have been socialized to focus more on the relationship aspect of a sexual encounter. Some women only have intercourse in the context of a love relationship because they fear being used and/or dropped. Hence, the event of intercourse is perceived differently by men and women because each reports to and is evaluated by a different gender group. Male friends will want to know if their male peer "got any;" female friends will want to know, "Will you see him again?" ("Does he care about you?").

C H A P T E R

3

Gender Roles

CONTENTS

IS IT TRUE?

1. Even before the birth of their children parents relate differently to them according to whether their child is male or female.

2. The Sunday comics present women in a way which suggests that men do not want to be emotionally involved with women who have careers.

3. Women tend to see themselves as more overweight than men see themselves.

4. Men are more likely to express their emotions and to admit when they are depressed than women.

5. Most men are very supportive of women having careers and express this by sharing more of the childcare with their partners.

1 = T; 2 = T; 3 = T; 4 = F; 5 = F

ROSEANNE Barr, star of the highly successful television program, *The Roseanne Barr Show,* noted that one of her objectives is to provide a new role model for women:

> I see myself as a role model for people left of normal, a three-dimensional woman, not a token, not a supermom. I'm trying to show that there's a lot more to being a woman than being a mother . . . (Dutka, 1989, 82).

Barr provides one example of the changing role models for women and emphasizes that gender roles have a dramatic influence on who we are and how we feel. In this chapter we examine the terminology of gender roles, the biological basis of the sexes, and the social influences on gender role development. We focus on the consequences for socializing individuals as women and men and suggest trends for future female-male interaction.

:: Terminology

Sociologists, family specialists, home economists, and other family-life educators often have different definitions and connotations for the terms sex, gender, gender identity, and gender role. We use these terms in the following ways.

Sex refers to the biological distinction of being female or male. The primary sex characteristics that differentiate women and men include external genitalia (vulva and penis), gonads (ovaries and testes), sex chromosomes (XX and XY), and hormones (estrogen, progesterone, and testosterone). Secondary sex characteristics like the woman's larger breasts and the man's beard are additional distinctions.

The term *gender* includes not only our biological sex, but also social and psychological components that characterize us as female or male (Lips, 1988).

Gender identity is the psychological state of viewing one's self as a girl or a boy and later as a woman or a man. Such identity is learned and is a reflection of the society's conceptions of masculinity and femininity. Some individuals have difficulty in establishing a gender identity. For example, transsexuals may feel that they are psychologically the opposite of their biological sex.

Gender role, also called *sex role,* refers to the socially expected characteristics and behaviors that a social group imposes on its male and female members. In our society, the traditional concept of being female includes being emotional, dependent, and family-oriented, whereas the traditional concept of being male includes being nonemotional, independent, and career-oriented. The great majority of characteristics designated as feminine or masculine in any given culture are learned from the material and interpersonal environment in which we grow up. Gender-role prescriptions in our culture not only signal the color of the blanket in which an infant is to be wrapped but also strongly influence the choice of toys (doll or football), clothes (panties or briefs), and work roles (baby sitter or paper boy) for children. Gender roles also influence the type of greeting card a person will receive. Women are much more likely than men to receive cards with flowers on them (Brabandt & Mooney, 1989). These gender-role stereotypes are changing. Today, more parents are encouraging a wider range of behaviors in their children. Increasingly, women are being encouraged to be assertive and men are being encouraged to be nurturant. In addition, men today are expected to be egalitarian in their interactions with women, and women are expected to expect this pattern of interaction from men.

Whether gender roles are primarily a function of biological or social influences is a continuing controversy. Most researchers acknowledge that biological and social factors interact to produce an individual's personality. Although children are born female and male, they learn culturally defined feminine or masculine characteristics. In the following sections, we will review the biological beginnings of women and men and examine the ways in which the sexes are socialized.

Biological Beginnings

Although all human life begins with a *zygote*—a fertilized egg (see Figure 3.1)—all zygotes are not alike. They carry different *chromosomes* and *hormones* that result in women and men being housed in different bodies.

Chromosomes

Women and men have different genetic makeups. Every normal human *ovum* (egg) contains 22 "regular" chromosomes or *autosomes* (see Figure 3.2) and one sex chromosome. Every normal human sperm contains 22 "regular" chromosomes and one X *or* Y chromosome. The autosomes contain various genes that determine

■■ FIGURE 3.1
Fertilization
Fertilization occurs when a sperm penetrates an egg in a Fallopian tube.

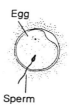

Egg

Sperm

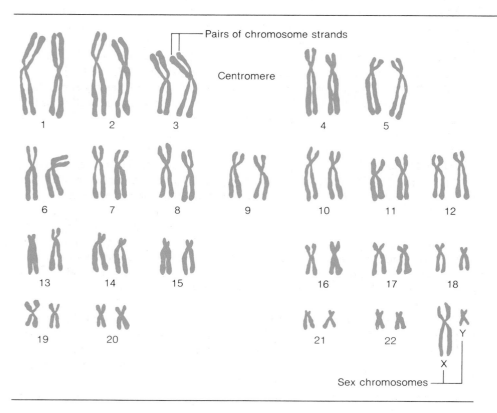

■■ FIGURE 3.2
Chromosome Pairs
Within each cell of a person's body are 23 chromosome pairs

the individual's eye color, hair color and body type. Because the sex chromosome in the ovum is *always* X (the female chromosome), the sex chromosome in the male sperm determines the biological sex of the child. If the sperm contains an X chromosome, the match with the female chromosome will be XX, and a female person will result. If the sperm contains a Y chromosome, the male chromosome, the match with the female chromosome will be XY, and a male person will result. Hence, the normal woman has 44 regular chromosomes (22 from each parent) plus an X chromosome from her mother and an X chromosome from her father. The normal man also has 44 regular chromosomes and an X chromosome from his mother but a Y chromosome from his father.

Hormones

Although the same hormones are in each sex, the release of these and other hormones into the bloodstream in varying amounts causes the development of a female or a male *embryo* (the human organism from conception until the end of the eighth week). Male and female embryos are indistinguishable from one another during the first several weeks of intrauterine life. In both, two primitive gonads and two paired duct systems form during the fifth or sixth week of development (see Figures 3.3 and 3.4). The male reproductive system develops from the Wolffian ducts, and the female reproductive system develops from the Müllerian ducts. However, both are present in the developing embryo at this stage.

If the embryo is genetically a male (XY), a chemical substance controlled by the Y chromosome stimulates the primitive gonads to develop into testes. The testes, in turn, begin secreting the male hormone testosterone, which stimulates the

■■ FIGURE 3.3
**Embryo Before
Six Weeks with
Undifferentiated
Sexual Structures**

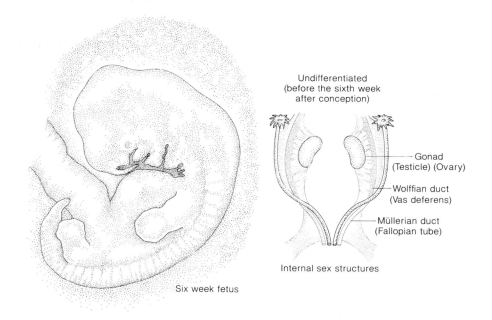

Undifferentiated
(before the sixth week
after conception)

Gonad
(Testicle) (Ovary)

Wolffian duct
(Vas deferens)

Müllerian duct
(Fallopian tube)

Internal sex structures

Six week fetus

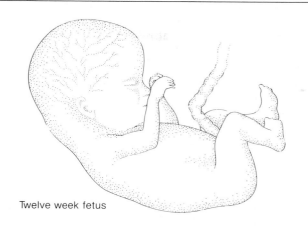

Twelve week fetus

Differentiated internal sex structures
(12 weeks after conception)

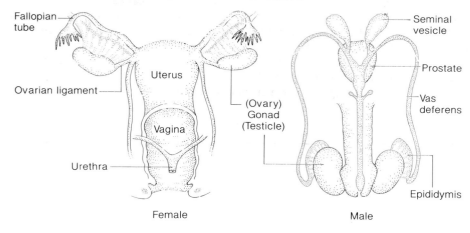

Fallopian
tube

Ovarian ligament

Uterus

Vagina

Urethra

(Ovary)
Gonad
(Testicle)

Seminal
vesicle

Prostate

Vas
deferens

Epididymis

Female

Male

development of the male reproductive and external sexual organs. The testes also secrete a Müllerian duct-inhibiting substance, which causes the potential female ducts to degenerate or become blind tubules. Thus, the development of male anatomical structures depends on the presence of male hormones at a critical stage of development.

The development of a female embryo requires that no (or very little) male hormone be present. Without the controlling substance from the Y chromosome, the primitive gonads will develop into ovaries and the Müllerian duct system into the Fallopian tubes, uterus, and vagina. Also without testosterone, the Wolffian duct system (epididymis, vas deferens, and ejaculatory duct) will degenerate or become blind tubules.

The impact of hormones becomes even more evident at puberty. The testes and ovaries release hormones that are necessary for the development of secondary sex

Twins emphasize the importance of heredity.

If I told you you had a beautiful body, you wouldn't hold it against me would you?
—DAVID FISHER

characteristics. Higher levels of testosterone account for the growth of facial hair in men and pubic and underarm hair in both men and women. Breast development, on the other hand, results from increasing levels of estrogen.

In addition to chromosomal and hormonal differences, a number of physical characteristics differentiate women from men. These differences begin before birth; the male *fetus* (the human organism from the eighth week of pregnancy until birth) is more likely than the female fetus to be miscarried during the early months of pregnancy. Male babies, children, and adults are also more likely to die each year than female babies, children, and adults.

■ **DATA:** *Persons who are white and female live six years longer than persons who are white and male. Persons who are black and female live eight years longer than persons who are black and male. (Statistical Abstract of the United States: 1990).*

Money (1987) summarized the following eight biological and social variables which are related to one's sex and gender.

1. Chromosomal gender: XX in the female; XY in the male.
2. Gonadal gender: Ovaries in the female; testes in the male.
3. Prenatal hormonal gender: Estrogen and progesterone in the female; testosterone in the male before birth.
4. Internal accessory organs: Uterus and vagina in the female; prostate and seminal vesicles in the male.

5. External genital appearance: Clitoris and vaginal opening in the female; penis and scrotum in the male.
6. Pubertal hormonal gender: At puberty, estrogen and progesterone in the female; testosterone in the male.
7. Assigned gender: The announcement at birth, "It's a girl" or "It's a boy," based on the appearance of the external genitals; the gender the parents and the rest of society believe the child to be; the gender in which the child is reared.
8. Gender identity: The person's private, internal sense of maleness or femaleness—which is expressed in personality and behavior—and the integration of this sense with the rest of the personality and with the gender roles prescribed by society.

People do not always fit neatly into the category of "male" or "female." In some cases, the gender indicated by one of the eight variables may disagree with the gender indicated by the other variables. For example, a person may have the external genital appearance of one gender but the chromosomes or hormones of another gender. Persons with these mixed characteristics are referred to as hermaphrodites or pseudohermaphrodites. Specifically, a *hermaphrodite* is an individual who has genitalia, gonads, and internal reproductive organs of both sexes. The term *pseudohermaphrodite* refers to an individual who has the chromosomes of one sex (XX or XY) and the external genitalia characteristic of the opposite sex.

:: Theories of Gender Role Acquisition

Most theorists agree that the environment has a profound effect on gender role development, but they do not agree on what the process is. Several different theories exist that explain how the environment influences gender role development. The four main theories about how female and male roles are acquired include social learning, sociobiological cognitive-developmental, and identification.

Social Learning Theory

Derived from the school of behavioral psychology, *social learning theory* emphasizes the role of reward and punishment in explaining how a child learns gender role behavior. For example, two young brothers enjoyed playing "lady." Each of them would put on a dress, wear high-heeled shoes, and carry a pocketbook. Their father came home early one day and angrily demanded that they "take those clothes off and never put them on again. Those things are for women," he said. The boys were punished for playing "lady" but rewarded with their father's approval for playing "cowboys," with plastic guns and "Bang! You're dead!" dialogue.

Reward and punishment alone are not sufficient to account for the way in which children learn gender roles. Direct instruction ("girls wear dresses," "men walk on the outside when walking with a woman") is another way children learn through social interaction with others. But there are too many gender rules to learn. They require the use of other mechanisms like modeling.

The eye's a better pupil
and more willing than
the ear;
Fine counsel is
confusing, but
example's always clear.
—EDGAR A. GUEST

The concept of modeling is important in understanding gender role acquisition from a social learning perspective. In *modeling*, the child observes another's behavior and imitates that behavior. On Monday afternoon, 8-year-old Bill helped his younger sister repair her tricycle. The Saturday before, Bill had observed his father putting spark plugs in their Dodge. His father was the "fix-it-man" in their home, and Bill, modeling after him, was the fix-it-man in his father's absence. Most parents are aware that their own roles were learned from their parents.

The impact of modeling on the development of gender-role behavior is controversial. For example, a modeling perspective implies that children will tend to imitate the parent of the same gender, but children are usually reared mainly by the woman in all cultures. Yet this persistent female model does not seem to interfere with the male's development of the behavior that is considered appropriate for his gender. One explanation suggests that boys learn early that our society generally grants boys and men more status and privileges than to girls and women and therefore devalue the feminine and emphasize the masculine aspects of themselves.

Women also do not strictly model their mothers' behavior. Although women who work outside the home usually have mothers who did likewise, their mothers may also be traditional homemakers.

In spite of the controversies over the impact of modeling on the development of gender role behavior, social learning theory has gained widespread support. Much research has contributed to this support. For example, in one study, 26 couples were assigned to a problem-solving, skills-training program after taking the Bem Sex Role Inventory—a test designed to assess the degree to which each person views herself or himself as masculine or feminine. The training consisted of learning how to disclose themselves to each other and to express feelings to each other. After completing the eight-week program, both the men and the women took the Bem Sex Role Inventory again and scored higher on the feminine

Children learn from
their parents through
modeling.

aspects. Similar changes were not observed in the control group of this experiment. Another study showed that men can learn empathy (Cleaver, 1987).

Both studies emphasize that self-disclosure and empathy—traits typically associated with women—can be learned. These traits are not innate but are acquired through social and cultural exposure to various learning experiences. Another study demonstrated that females display leadership skills similar to those of males when the situational context calls for such behavior (Koberg, 1985). Hence, the experiences a person is exposed to and the cues within a social context dictate the behavior that an individual expresses.

Another illustration of the degree to which gender roles are learned is the fact that spouses in different racial, ethnic, and social class groups reflect a variety of gender role patterns (see Exhibit 3.1). It is recognized that there are wide variations within, as well as between, the various groups.

Sociobiological Theory

Sociobiological explanations of gender roles emphasize that there are biological differences between males and females that account for differences in male and female gender roles. Sociobiologists (or biosociologists) do not view gender role behaviors as acquired, but rather as innate. Research, for example, has shown that there may be differences between the female and male brain. These differ-

---

E X H I B I T   3.1

Multicultural Differences in Sex Roles

GROUP	SEX ROLES
Whites	Traditional sex roles in lower class. More egalitarian as spouses move up the social class ladder.
Blacks	Similar to whites in all social classes with greater male domination at all levels. Mother-child bond tends to take precedence over wife-husband relationship.
Native Americans	Women concerned with kinfolk, family, marriage, and sexual relations. Men concerned with employment, money, success, and material matters.
Asian Americans	
Chinese	Mutual sharing of responsibility and authority in decision making, although the wife usually assumes the role of helper rather than equal partner.
Japanese	Priority given to husband-wife relationship over kinship ties with low instances of male dominance. Still a general tendency to view males as having primary responsibility for concerns outside the home and females for tasks inside the home.
Vietnamese	Male dominance. Female subordination.
Korean	Males do little household work, while females work outside the home in addition to caring for the home.

Source: Developed by Kim Tripp, Department of Sociology and Anthropology, East Carolina University, Specifically for This Text, 1990.

ences are believed to underlie females' superiority in manual dexterity and verbal and communication skills, and males' superiority in spatial-visual skills (Maccoby and Jacklin, 1974., Tavris and Wade, 1984).

From an evolutionary perspective, it has been argued that males had to develop spatial-visual skills for hunting and for leading migrations throughout hominid evolution. Females needed to develop language and communication skills in order to care for offspring (Levy, 1972), and manual dexterity was adaptive when women were responsible for gathering food.

Within the scientific community, there is much controversy regarding the issue of biologically-based gender role differences. Some researchers believe that these presumed differences do not exist or are insignificant (Springer and Deutsch, 1981).

☐   C O N S I D E R A T I O N   ☐

One of the concerns about biologically-based gender differences is that these presumed differences are used to justify sexism. For example, data that suggest that males have superior spatial-visual abilities may be used to justify assumptions that women cannot be competent engineers. Even if the presumed biological differences between the sexes exist, these differences may be overcome by learning. Alice Rossi (1977) said that "there are differences in the ease with which the sexes can learn certain things" (4). Her point is that biological sex differences mean that the sexes are different, but not unequal.

The view that at least some gender role behaviors are biologically based is deeply ingrained in our culture. For example, we tend to think of mothers as naturally equipped and inclined to perform the role of primary child caregiver. Chodorow (1978) argues that the role of child caregiver has been assigned to women, although there is no biological reason why fathers cannot be the primary caregiver or participate equally in child rearing activities.

Cognitive Developmental Theory

Male and female personalities are socially produced.
—MARGARET MEAD

The *cognitive-developmental theory* of gender role acquisition suggests that the mental maturity of the child is a prerequisite to such acquisition (Kohlberg, 1969). Although 2-year-olds can label themselves and each other as "girl" or "boy," they have superficial criteria for doing so. People who wear long hair are girls, and those who never wear dresses are boys. Thus, 2-year-olds believe they can change their gender by altering their hair or changing clothes.

Not until age 6 or 7 does the child view gender as permanent (Kohlberg, 1966, 1969). In Kohlberg's view, this cognitive understanding is not a result of social learning. Rather, it involves the development of a specific mental ability to grasp the idea that certain basic characteristics of people do not change. Once children learn the concept of gender permanence, they seek to become competent and proper members of their gender group. For example, a child standing on the edge of a school playground may observe one group of children jumping rope while another group is playing football. Her or his self-concept ("I am a girl" or "I am a boy") connects with the observed gender-appropriate behavior, and she or he joins one of the two groups. Once in the group, the child seeks to develop the behaviors that are socially defined as appropriate for her or his gender.

Cognitive-developmental theory also emphasizes that the moral development of men and women may be different. Gilligan (1982) observed that men make judgments on the basis of competing rights and abstract principles whereas women make judgments on their assessments of competing responsibilities. Gilligan's point is not only to demonstrate that men and women have different conceptions of morality but that the male conception is regarded as the universal standard by which both men and women are evaluated.

Identification Theory

The first psychologist to study gender role acquisition was Sigmund Freud. According to Freud, children take on the characteristics and behaviors of their same-sex parent through a process of identification. Boys identify with their fathers, girls identify with their mothers. Freud said that children identify with the same-gender parent out of fear (1925, 1933). Freud felt this fear could be one of two kinds: fear of loss of love or fear of retaliation. Fear of loss of love, which results in both girls and boys identifying with their mother, is caused by their deep dependence on her for love and nurturance. Fearful that she may withdraw her love, young children try to become like her to please her and to ensure the continuance of her love.

According to Freud, at about age 4, the child's identification with the mother begins to change, but in different ways for boys than for girls. Boys experience what Freud calls the "Oedipal complex." Based on the legend of the Greek youth Oedipus, who unknowingly killed his father and married his mother, the Oedipal complex involves the young boy's awakening sexual feelings for his mother as he becomes aware he has a penis and his mother does not. He unconsciously feels that if his father knew of the intense love feelings he has for his mother, the father

This photo illustrates the identification of the son with the father.

would castrate him (which may be what happened to his mother, because she has no penis). The boy resolves the Oedipal struggle—feeling love for his father but wanting to kill him because he is a competitor for his mother's love—by becoming like his father, by identifying with him. In this way, the boy can keep his penis and take pride in being like his father. According to Freud, the successful resolution of this Oedipal situation marks the beginning of a boy's appropriate gender-role acquisition.

While her brother is experiencing the Oedipal complex, the girl goes through her own identification process, known as the Electra complex. Around age 4, she recognizes that she has no penis, wishes she did (penis envy), and feels her mother is responsible for its absence. To retaliate, she takes her love away from her mother and begins to focus on her father as a love object. But her desire for a penis is gradually transformed into the need for a baby, and to get a baby from her father she recognizes that she must be more like her mother. So she identifies again with her mother. Her goal now is to be a woman like her mother and to be a mother herself. According to Freud, such gender-role identification is characteristic of a mature female.

Although Freud's identification theories are interesting to read, there is little scientific support for their validity as explanations for gender-role acquisition. Most 3- and 4-year-olds do not know the difference between males and females on the basis of their genitals. Also, it is possible that some women have status envy rather than penis envy. They may view the male role as offering more rewards, not because men have a penis, but because they tend to occupy social positions that are accorded status in our society (heads of corporations, senators, representatives).

In *The Reproduction of Mothering*, Chodorow (1978) uses Freudian identification theory as a basis for her theory that gender role specialization occurs in the family because of the *"asymmetrical organization of parenting"* (49).

> Women, as mothers, produce daughters with mothering capacities and the desire to mother. These capacities and needs are built into and grow out of the mother-daughter relationship itself. By contrast, women as mothers (and men as not-mothers) produce sons whose nurturant capacities and needs have been systematically curtailed and repressed (p. 7).

In other words, all activities associated with nurturing and child care are identified as female activities because women are the primary caregivers of young children. This one-sidedness (or assymmetry) of nurturing by women increases the liklihood that females, because they identify with their mothers, will see their own primary identities and roles as mothers.

Chodorow sees the "asymmetrical organization of parenting" as the basis for the continuing unequal social organization of gender. In order to change this social inequality, we must recognize "the need for a fundamental reorganization of parenting, so that primary parenting is shared between men and women" (1978, 215).

:: Agents of Socialization

The preceding discussion implies that gender roles are learned through interaction with the environment. In this environment are *agents of socialization,* which are individuals, groups, or organizations that influence a person's behavior, attitudes, and self-concept. Next, we look at how agents of socialization, specifically parents, teachers, peers, and the media influence gender roles and identities of developing children.

Parents

Parents are usually the first influence in a child's life. Even before the birth of their children, parents relate to their child on the basis of gender. In one study of expectant parents, 22 of 24 parents said that the way they related to their fetus depended on whether they thought it was a girl or boy. If they thought the fetus was a girl, they thought of it as "graceful and gentle." If they thought the fetus was a boy, they viewed its movement as "strong" (Stainton, 1985).

The type of toys children receive from their parents also depends on whether the child is a girl or a boy. Although there is a trend toward giving children sex-role-neutral toys (Robinson & Morris, 1986), parents tend to give their sons footballs and their daughters dolls. The toys parents give to their children are suggestive of the roles parents think are appropriate for the respective genders (football = aggression = toy for boy; doll = passive = toy for girl).

Fathers and mothers also differ in the way they play with their children. Researchers Ross and Taylor (1989) observed the parents (between the ages of 34 and 36) of eighteen boys as they played with their sons in playrooms behind a one-way mirror. They observed that the fathers "were more actively involved, took more initiative, and played more physically with their sons than did mothers" (p. 23).

Parents also have different expectations of daughters than sons. Daughters, more than sons, are socialized to be more family oriented, to be aware of who is having what birthday, and to want the family to be together for various holidays. Daughters are often expected to provide more care for ailing family members and relatives than their brothers (Spitze and Logan, 1990). In addition, parents often assign chores to their sons and daughters along traditional lines: mowing grass to sons, cleaning dishes to daughters (Lackey, 1989).

| ■ **DATA:** *Of 2,238 adult men and women, 45 percent socialize their children to adopt traditional roles in family settings (Lackey, 1989).*

The amount of surveillance parents give to children also differs by gender, with parents being more protective of their daughters (e.g., earlier curfew hour). One reason parents are more restrictive with their daughters is the fear that their daughters will be sexually molested. Excessive protectiveness may discourage girls from actively exploring their environment.

When girls and boys of feminist parents are compared with girls and boys in the general population, the former (particularly if they are boys) are less sex stereotyped than the latter. Quoss, Ellis, and Stromberg (1987) compared the scores on a masculinity-femininity test of 32 children whose mothers were dues-paying members of a "feminist" organization with the scores of 184 children (ages 3 to 6) in a rural university community. Although there were few differences between the girls, boys with feminist mothers were much more likely to feel that either sex could engage in almost any behavior. For example, girls could go fishing and boys could go shopping. This study illustrates that as the culture changes, so do parents, and so does the socialization of their offspring. In another study, women who worked outside the home had more liberal gender role attitudes than women who were full-time homemakers (Kiecolt & Acock, 1988). The gender role attitudes of parents presumably influence the socialization of their children.

Teachers

Although parents have the earliest and most pervasive influence on their children, teachers are a major influence outside the home. Teachers may inadvertently respond to boys and girls differently in the classroom. As two researchers have observed:

> When boys call out comments without raising their hands, teachers accept their answers. However, when girls call out, teachers reprimand this "inappropriate" behavior with messages such as, "In this class, we don't shout out answers; we raise our hands." The message is subtle but powerful: boys should be academically assertive and grab teacher attention; girls should act like ladies and keep quiet (Sadker & Sadker, 1985, p. 56).

The researchers also noted that boys tend to be called on wherever they sit in the classroom., girls tend to be called on if they sit in the first row or within close proximity to the teacher.

□   C O N S I D E R A T I O N   □

Even before reaching school age, many children, particularly those of single parents and dual income families, will spend most of their weekday hours in the care of paid caregivers. Although research has not yet assessed the specific gender role socialization effects of such caregivers, the effects are likely to be significant.

In the classroom setting, not only do teachers exhibit gender role expectations (e.g. boys are loud, girls are quiet), but students exhibit gender role expectations of their teachers as well. For example, university students feel that it is more appropriate for male teachers to make self-disclosing statements than for female teachers to do so. (Klinger-Vartabian & O'Flaherty, 1989).

Peers

Peers represent another pervasive influence outside the home. The individual looks to his or her peers to discover "the" appropriate language, dress, and interests. Parents often recognize the significance of peer group influence and try to encourage their children to have the "right friends."

A dramatic example of peer influence is evident when women attend male strip shows. Although women are sometimes characterized as being sexually passive rather than sexually aggressive, in the context of being surrounded by female peers at a male strip show, they teach and reinforce each other for being more sexually aggressive. From the male stripper's point of view, this display of assertiveness is viewed as "excessive, with women often becoming verbally and physically aggressive and sometimes engaging in behavior that dancers describe as lewd" (Petersen & Dressel, 1982, 204).

Media

Television also plays a significant role in gender socialization. It has been estimated that the typical child and teenager spend more time in front of the television than in school. Through television, the child is exposed to a male bias and stereotyped gender roles (Signorielli, 1989). News anchors are still primarily men, and narration voices on television specials are more often men than women. When commercials over the last 15 years are considered, 90 percent of all narrators are male (Bretl & Cantor, 1988). But changes are occurring. Increasingly, women are being portrayed on television as equals (e.g., Claire and Cliff in "The Cosby Show"), and assertive and independent (e.g., Roseanne Barr in *The Rose-anne Barr Show*). Also, television is more frequently casting women in roles that have traditionally been reserved for men, such as doctors, lawyers, and police. However, men are less often being cast in traditional female roles (e.g., nurse).

Ironically, many advertisements in mass media "women's" magazines (such as *Ms., Self, Working Mother,* and *Working Woman*) have portrayed women in stereotypical, sexist roles. In a study of 288 advertisements in these magazines, Ortiz and Ortiz (1989) observed that women were shown engaging in traditional female functions such as wives, mothers, secretaries, clerks, teachers, and nurses. The authors pointed out how paradoxical it was for the women's magazines, which exist to create a feminist message, to carry traditional, sexist advertisements (*Ms.* no longer accepts any sexist advertising).

Cartoons in the Sunday newspaper represent another form of media that influences gender role socialization. Two researchers (Mooney & Brabant, 1987) did a content analysis of six family-oriented Sunday cartoons (*Blondie, The Born Loser, Dennis the Menace, Hi and Lois, For Better or Worse,* and *Sally Forth*). One of the themes that the researchers identified in these comics was "if you are a woman and you want a happy home, do not have a career, and if you are a man, never marry a career woman" (p. 419).

Children's storybook fairy tales are another source of gender role socialization. For example, in the Grimms Fairy Tale "Hansel and Gretel," both Hansel and Gretel play an active role in escaping from the witch. However, only the role of Hansel is emphasized. Reflecting the gender stereotypes of male competence and female incompetence, Hansel says to Gretel: "Be quiet Gretel, do not distress yourself, I will soon find a way to help us" (Bottigheimer, 1986).

Heroines in fairy tales are presented in a way that associates goodness with beauty. "Good" girls and women are beautiful, whereas "bad" girls and women are portrayed as powerful or assertive. Hence, women are socialized to be beautiful rather than resourceful.

Some feminist writers have argued that fairy tales are "an unfortunate source of negative female stereotypes. The passive and pretty heroines who dominate popular fairy tales offer narrow and damaging role-models for young readers. . . ." (Stone, 1986, 229). Other feminists, however, suggest interpretations of fairy tales that reflect a more positive female image. For example, Cinderella may be viewed as a woman who gains freedom from household slavery. The "prince" that Cinderella longs for and is finally joined with at the end of the story may be viewed as a symbol for Cinderella's inner strength. Feminist writers have created fairy

Children spend more
time in front of the television than in school.

tales which do not reinforce stereotypical gender roles. In these fairy tales, the princess slays the dragon and rescues the prince.

Religion

Whether inadvertently or intentionally, some of the more traditional and conservative churches use the *Bible* to perpetuate the idea that the sexes are not to be regarded as equal.

> But I want you to understand that the head of every man is Christ, the head of every woman is her husband, and the head of Christ is God (I Corinthians 11:3).
> Neither was man created for woman but woman for man (I Corinthians 11: 7–11).
> Wives be subject to your husband, as to the Lord (Ephesians 5: 22–24).

More progressive churches avoid the issue of subjugation of women and emphasize role equality.

C O N S I D E R A T I O N

Notice the degree to which the feelings you have about your gender are influenced not only by your parents, peers, teachers, mass media, and religion but by the assumed dominance of men in the larger culture (Epstein, 1989). The Constitution is taught as being developed by Founding Fathers, presidents have always been men, and deities are described as male—Father. Corporate executives are also assumed to be male as are owners of national and international firms. Cultural male dominance continues to be pervasive.

Consequences of Female Role Socialization

Women and men are exposed to different socialization experiences as they grow up in our society. These experiences result in a number of consequences that are different for women than for men. Table 3.1 summarizes some of the positives and negatives of being socialized as a female member of our society. The question mark after each item denotes that this may or may not be true for a specific female individual. For example, a particular woman may not live longer than a particular man, and a particular woman may have a very positive self-concept as well as a happy marriage.

In the following section we discuss some of the consequences for female role socialization.

TABLE 3.1 **Consequences of Being Socialized as a Female**

ADVANTAGES	DISADVANTAGES
Live longer?	Negative self-concept?
Emotionally expressive?	Unhappy marriage?
Close family bonds?	Brief motherhood role?
Identity independent of career?	Overload of roles?
Custody of children?	No escape from children?

A Negative Self-Concept?

Feminists have observed that women in America live in a society that devalues them. "Women's natures, lives and experiences are not taken as seriously, are not valued as much as those of men" (Walker et al. 1988, 18). As a result, women may not only lack confidence in themselves, they may also be prejudiced against other women. In a study in which women and men were told that they were incapable of performing a cognitive task, the women were more likely than the men to believe that they were incapable (Wagner et al., 1986). When women are successful, they are more prone to attribute success to luck than to their own ability (Heimovics & Herman, 1988).

In another study, 180 females were asked to evaluate four academic articles. Their evaluations were less favorable if they thought the articles were written by a woman (Joan T.) than a man (John T.) (Paludi & Bauer, 1983).

Women even tend to view their own bodies less positively than men see their own bodies (Cash & Brown, 1989). Women tend to view themselves as overweight or slightly overweight (Hesse-Biber, 1989). Less positive attitudes toward one's body are related to lower levels of self-esteem (Mintz & Betz, 1986; Stake & Lauer, 1987).

Women also see more disadvantages associated with being a woman than with being a man (Fabes & Laner, 1986). When asked to identify some of the disadvantages of being female, 247 female college students gave responses such as having to wait to be asked for a date, being discriminated against, having to deal with menstruation, and having less money than men. Exhibit 3.2 reflects that more women than men live in poverty.

Disenchantment with being a woman may be related to *sexist* attitudes towards women. *Sexism* is defined as an attitude, action, or institutional structure which subordinates or discriminates against an individual or group because of their sex. Sexism against women reflects the tradition of male dominance and presumed male superiority in our society. Sexist attitudes exist not only in the U.S., but in the Soviet Union, China, India, Japan, and Latin America (Lindsey, 1990). The Sexist Attitudes Scale in the Self-Assessment section provides an informal way to assess the degree to which you may have sexist attitudes toward women.

Not all research demonstrates that women have a more negative self-concept than men. One researcher (Wright, 1987) compared the scores of 80 men and 65 women who completed a scale designed to assess self-esteem, and found no significant differences in the scores. In explaining that self-esteem may no longer be related to gender, Wright observed:

> This may be due to a lessened impact of the double standard and to the increased assertiveness of females in the 1980s—especially college educated females (Wright, 1987, 101).

Women also view themselves to be as capable as men in management roles. In a study by Schein et al. (1989), the researchers concluded, "Female management students do not sex type the managerial job, but see women and men as equally likely to possess characteristics necessary for managerial job success. As future managers, then, we might expect these women to treat men and women equally in the selection and promotion process" (p. 108).

E X H I B I T 3.2

The Feminization of Poverty

The "feminization of poverty" refers to the disproportionate percentage of poverty that is borne by women living alone or with their children (Bassi, 1988). There are over three million single mothers living below the poverty line, which represents about half of all single mothers *(Statistical Abstract of the United States: 1990)*. The reason for such poverty being specific to women is that they are more likely to have lower incomes than men—not only because they earn fewer academic degrees, but also because they tend to be employed fewer hours in order to be with and take care of their children. Even when women have the same job as men, their earning power is less than what men are paid.

As women move into certain occupations, such as teaching and nursing, a tendency toward increased segregation of women develops in the marketplace (women in one occupation, men in another) and the salaries of women in these occupational roles increases at a slower rate. The salaries of the teaching and nursing professions, which are predominantly female occupations, have not kept pace with inflation, resulting in a concentration of segregated women in lower-paid occupations. Poverty is primarily a feminine issue because more women than men have inadequate incomes. One of the consequences of being a woman is to have an increased chance of feeling economic strain throughout life.

Women with children who have held low-income jobs and who are divorced or widowed often drift into poverty. Those who were married to men who earn low incomes drift more swiftly into poverty. If they are also older, their movement into poverty can be dramatic (Bassi, 1988). Unless women attend to the fact that they cannot depend on the income of a mate, they become economically vulnerable. Women in professional careers are less vulnerable.

Single black females are particularly vulnerable to being economically disadvantaged. When black head-of-household women are compared with white head-of-household women, the former have about 60 percent of the income of the latter *(Statistical Abstract of the United States: 1990)*.

Frustrations With Marriage?

Wives seem to be under a lot of stress in marriage. More married women than married men feel that they are about to have a nervous breakdown, experience more psychological anxiety, and more often blame themselves for their own lack of adjustment (Caplan, 1985). Wives who do not share equally in decision making or household/childrearing chores with their husbands report higher levels of depression than wives who have equal power in the relationship (Whisman & Jacobson, 1988).

The explanation for the greater difficulty women experience in marriage compared to men is that women are expected to make their husbands, children, and employers happy, to keep the house clean, and to keep up correspondence with her parents (and his). To be superwives, moms, and workers is a cultural expectation that is unrealistic. Yet few husbands are willing to change their expectations (or to take the work load off their wives), with the result that wives stay stressed and wonder where are the satisfactions of marriage.

> Of fundamental importance is the fact that for women, marriage is no longer a stable, rewarding lifetime career.
> —MAGGIE SCARF

A Brief Motherhood Role?

Much of a woman's life may be spent preparing for and investing in the role of mother. When the children have left home, women are often faced with difficulty

SELF ASSESSMENT

The Sexist Attitudes Scale

Sexism against women is the belief that men are superior to women. This scale is designed to informally measure the degree to which you hold sexist attitudes towards women.

Note that in assessing sexism, this scale only measures sexism against women., it does not measure sexism against men. For example, answering "strongly disagree" to the statement "A man makes a better employer than a woman" does not reflect a sexist attitude against women. However, it does not rule out a sexist attitude against men, as a person who thought that a woman makes a better employer than a man (sexist attitude against men) would also answer "strongly disagree" to the above statement.

Directions: After reading each sentence carefully, circle the number that best represents the degree to which you agree or disagree with the sentence.
1 Strongly agree (definitely yes)
2 Mildly agree (I believe so)
3 Undecided (not sure)
4 Mildly disagree (probably not)
5 Strongly disagree (definitely not)

	SA	MA	U	MD	SD
1. Women are ruled by their hormones more than men.	1	2	3	4	5
2. Women tend to be less rational than men.	1	2	3	4	5
3. A man makes a better mechanic than a woman.	1	2	3	4	5
4. Women gossip more than men.	1	2	3	4	5
5. A man makes a better employer than a woman.	1	2	3	4	5
6. Women are better at taking care of a family than at any other role.	1	2	3	4	5
7. Women can't handle stress as well as men can.	1	2	3	4	5
8. Women have become too independent and career-oriented.	1	2	3	4	5
9. Women are not as good at making hard decisions as men.	1	2	3	4	5
10. A woman will get more satisfaction from her family than from her career.	1	2	3	4	5

SCORING: Add the numbers you circled. 1 (strongly agree) is most sexist response—you believe that women are inferior to men. 5 (strongly disagree) is the least sexist response—you do not believe that women are inferior to men. The lower your total score (10 is the lowest possible score), the more sexist you are; the higher your total score (50 is the highest possible score) the more sexist you are equals. A score of 30 places you at the midpoint on the continuum of believing in the equality of the sexes.
(Note: This Self-Assessment is intended to be thought-provoking., it should *not* be treated as a scientific measuring instrument.)

in refocusing their lives. Because men tend to be more involved in their careers, they may have less difficulty than their wives in adjusting to the children leaving home.

□	C O N S I D E R A T I O N	□

Why has American society socialized its female members to emphasize roles that are relatively short lived? One answer may lie in the benefit to male members. By emphasizing motherhood, men are able to escape much of the work of childcare, and at the same time minimize the stiff competition of women for their jobs.

Marriage and Motherhood: Achievement Barriers?

Being a wife and a mother may limit a woman's achievements in such areas as education and employment.

Education Women now constitute more than 50 percent of all students entering college. Although they earn more than one-half of all bachelor's and master's degrees, they earn only one-third of the Ph.D. degrees and fewer M.D. degrees. Whether the explanation is that women choose motherhood over long-term career preparation, lack educated female models, or believe there are not enough professional opportunities open to them, the result is the same—women tend to have other priorities than earning academic degrees.

This picture may be changing. As external barriers to professional schools (law, medicine, business) are removed and dual-career marriages increase, more academic degrees will be awarded to women. However, a study of the effects of marriage on education confirms that women who marry early radically reduce their chances of getting additional education (Haggstrom et al., 1986). And women who wait to marry after completing their education may end up not marrying at all.

Employment Marriage and motherhood may also interfere with a woman's economic potential. About half of American mothers drop out of the workforce during their children's preschool years (compared with almost zero percent for men). When they return to work, working mothers often select jobs with flexible hours so that they can be available to their children. Women's earnings are, in part, influenced by their level of education and their level of participation in the workforce. Women still earn only about 70 percent of what men earn (*Statistical Abstract of the United States: 1990*).

□	C O N S I D E R A T I O N	□

With the 50 percent chance of divorce, the likelihood of being a widow for seven or more years, and the almost certain loss of her parenting role midway through her

continued on next page

Women, like men, become more focused on their careers when they are not interrupted by children.

life, a woman without education and employment skills is often left high and dry. As one widowed mother of four said, ''The shock of realizing you have children to support and no skills to do it with is a worse shock than learning your husband is dead.'' In the words of a divorced, 40-year-old mother of three, ''If young women think it can't happen to them, they are foolish.''

Overload as an Employed Wife and Mother?

One of the factors contributing to the level of happiness of working wives is the degree to which their husbands help with the work load in the family. Most women are disappointed in the amount of help they get:

> Expectations that women will be involved in employment outside the home have not been accompanied by expectations that men will be involved in work inside the home. While liberal gender attitudes make women somewhat more sensitive to this issue, there is evidence of cultural lag (Morgan & Affleck, 1989, 213).

The belief that a woman can have everything—career, husband, children—is a delusion. It can't be done.

—BETTE DAVIS

Some research suggests that husbands are more likely to share the work load of the relationship in reference to the degree to which both spouses earn similar amounts of money. As a woman's income approaches that of her husband's, his domestic work participation increases proportionately (Kamo, 1988).

Benefits of Female Role Socialization

Although there may be some disadvantages of being a woman, there may also be some advantages of being a woman in our society. These include living longer, being able to express emotions easier, having a closer bond with children, having an identity independent of one's occupational role, and being more likely to get custody of the children in the event of a divorce. Women are awarded custody in 90 percent of divorce cases that go to court (some would regard this as a disadvantage).

CONSIDERATION

In an effort to eliminate the potential negative consequences of being socialized as a woman, parents might be alert to the societal bias against their daughters and attempt to minimize it. For example, parents might teach their daughters to view every occupation as an option for them, and to supplement marital and family roles with a meaningful worker role that will provide an independent source of income and identity. In addition, should a daughter not evidence an interest in getting married or having children, the parents should consider supporting her interests completely.

Consequences of Male Role Socialization

Male role socialization in our society is associated with its own set of consequences. ". . . The male sex role is a complex one to fulfill. It is fraught with contradictions which often lead to debilitating sex role strain for American men" (Franklin, 1988, 44). Table 3.2 summarizes the positives and negatives of being socialized as a male.

In the following section we discuss some of the consequences of male role socialization.

Required to Earn Money?

Just as women are more often channeled into the roles of wife and mother, men are tracked into the world of gainful employment to pay the basic bills of the family. Whereas women are viewed as having a choice regarding whether or not to be employed, men in our culture are expected to work.

Our culture not only expects men to earn money, but also equates money with success. This has implications for a man's self-esteem. Our society fosters the assumption that the man who makes $50,000 annually is more of a man than the one who makes $5,000. For men in our society, having a good self-concept is dependent on earning a good income.

TABLE 3.2 Consequences of Being Socialized as a Male

ADVANTAGES	DISADVANTAGES
Positive self-concept?	Required to earn money?
Less marital stress?	Identity tied to occupational role?
Greater income?	Adapt to changing woman?
Greater prestige?	Less emotionality?
Less discrimination?	Shorter life span?

Men derive their pri-
mary sense of worth
from their occupational
identity.

Identity Equals Occupational Role?

Ask men who they are, and some will tell you what they do. For some, their identity lies in their occupational role. Work is the principal means by which men confirm their masculinity and success. In studies of unemployment during the Great Depression, job loss was regarded as a greater shock to men than women, although the loss of income affected both.

The importance of the relationship between work and male identity makes it particularly difficult for black men, who have a much higher unemployment rate than white men. The result of not being able to fulfill a suitable economic role is considerable psychological stress (Kessler & Neighbors, 1986).

Mexican American men face a similar dilemma; they have a higher unemployment rate than whites, and they work in predominantly unskilled, blue-collar roles (see Exhibit 3.3). Moreover, access to education is more limited for Mexican Americans than it is for blacks or whites. In the United States, out of 25 million blacks, 2,200 have earned a Ph.D.; out of 9 million Mexican Americans, only 60 have earned a Ph.D. (Alvarez, 1985).

□   CONSIDERATION   □

Work may also involve an enormous toll on one's mental health (for both men and women). Dislike of one's work can cause anxiety, depression, rage, indecisiveness, psychosomatic illness, and excessive use of drugs and alcohol. Increasingly, people are seeking out therapists to help relieve the stress associated with their work (Sandroff, 1989).

continued on next page

EXHIBIT 3.3

Hey Man! Chicano Machismo

Chicano men are often stereotyped as being "macho" males. It is believed that they boss women around, beat them, and have numerous extramarital affairs. Although this image of *machismo* is widely held, it is not supported by consistent empirical data. Although some Chicano men do fit the stereotype, others are warm, nurturing, and egalitarian. The latter are more often found in marriages in which the wife is employed.

In cases in which Chicano men do display macho behavior, there are different interpretations as to why it occurs. A psychoanalytic interpretation views *machismo* as an *unconscious* attempt to overcompensate for feelings of inferiority, powerlessness, and inadequacy. According to this theory, the Chicano man unconsciously feels inferior because his Mexican forebearers were conquered by Spanish men who produced "the hybrid Mexican people having an inferiority complex based on the mentality of a conquered people" (Baca Zinn, 1980).

An alternative explanation—and a more acceptable one to sociologists—is that *machismo* behavior can be explained on the basis of the socially inferior position of the Chicano man and his *conscious* reaction to that position. As one researcher (Baca Zinn, 1980) notes:

> Men in certain social categories have had more roles and sources of identity open to them. However, this has not been the case for Chicanos or other men of color. Perhaps manhood takes on greater importance for those who do not have access to socially valued roles. Being male is one sure way to acquire status when other roles are systematically denied by the workings of society. This suggests that an emphasis on masculinity is not due to a collective internalized inferiority, rooted in a subcultural orientation (p. 39).

Hence, not only is the existence of the "macho" Chicano man a disputed phenomenon, but there are also different interpretations for its presumed existence. The implication of this sociological explanation suggests that any man in a similar inferior social position with limited opportunities to acquire status may resort to a "Hey man, do as I say" routine.

Adapted from Maxine Baca Zinn. Chicano men and masculinity. *The Journal of Ethnic Studies*, 1982, 10(2), 29–44. Used by permission.

The identification men have with their work role is changing. Some men are becoming less competitive and more family oriented. Some corporations are aware that today, in contrast to the past, men are less willing to move because of family considerations.

Emotional Stereotypes?

Some men feel caught between society's expectations that they be competitive, aggressive, independent, and unemotional and their own desire to be more open, caring, and emotional. Not only are men less likely to cry than women, but they are also less able to express feelings of depression, anger, fear, and sadness (Snell et al., 1988; Blier & Blier-Wilson, 1989).

The film *Tootsie* illustrated the degree to which men do not feel free to express the gentle side of their personalities. Near the end of the film, Dustin Hoffman (who had dressed up like a woman nicknamed Tootsie) said to Jessica Lange (with whom he had fallen in love), "I was more of a man with you as a woman than I have ever been with a woman as a man . . . I just need to learn to do it without the dress."

I loved the danger. He was so exciting. I can't describe it. He was a turn-on . . . there are times when a woman wants the man she's with to be . . . a man.
—ROBIN GIVENS, ON MIKE TYSON

Men also have fewer intense friendships than women. In interviews with 300 men and women, two-thirds of the men could not name a single best friend, in contrast to three-fourths of the women who had no trouble doing so (Rubin, 1985). Relationships between men tend to be characterized by competition which blocks their intimacy with each other. One man recalled:

The last time I had any really close relationships with guys was in high school, when we were still boys, not men. After that, the competition thing gets to you. You compete for grades in college so you can get into grad school. Then you compete for a job and a promotion and a woman and . . . Christ, it never ends (p. 82).

Donald Trump, one of the world's youngest billionaires, echoes the competitive theme: "I love to have enemies, I fight my enemies. I like beating my enemies to the ground" (Friedrich & McDowell, 1989, 48).

Adapting to Modern Women?

There is an emerging equality in relationships between women and men. Modern women, in contrast to traditional women, are more likely to challenge their partner's rationale and to suggest alternative explanations and preferences. Acquiescence and submission no longer necessarily characterize women in today's interpersonal relationships. Women who are married, have had a child, and who are employed are much more likely to have egalitarian expectations than women who are single and without a child or job (McBroom, 1986).

The egalitarian issue also expresses itself in couples' attitudes toward higher education. The man no longer asks, "Where will you work to put me through school?" but "How will we finance our educations?" or "Do you want to finish your education before I finish mine?" Because of women's increasing desire for education, career involvement, and economic independence, men can expect women today to be less interested in early marriage than before.

Also, when women do marry, they are likely to expect more from their partners in sharing childcare and housekeeping responsibilities. Some feel that liberation for men involves not only their freedom to cry but their willingness to share domestic work. Husbands who learn to share in the housework tend to report happier marriages (Antill & Cotton, 1980).

As women change, so must men. Some are reluctant to do so. In a study of over 500 college students, 82 percent of the men in contrast to 94 percent of the women said that they would be interested in an egalitarian relationship—a relationship in which the respective partners view each other as equals (Billingham & Sack, 1986). In interviews with over 300 men, Astrachan (1986) concluded in his book, *How Men Feel,* that there are no more than 5 to 10 percent of American men who fit the media's description of the enlightened "new age" men—those who support women in their work place and give equal time to new male roles such as childrearing.

Some men may resist the increasing power they feel women are trying to achieve. Goode (1982) suggested a *theory of marginal utility* as an explanation for such resistance.

Increasingly, women are occupying traditional male occupations.

Phrased in more theoretical terms, the underlying shift is toward the decreasing marginal utility of males, and this I suspect is the main source of men's resistance to women's liberation. That is, fewer people believe that what the male does is indispensable, nonsubstitutable, or adds such a special value to any endeavor that it justifies his extra "price" or reward. In past wars, for example, males enjoyed a very high value not only because it was felt that they could do the job better than women but also because they might well make the difference between being conquered and remaining free. In many societies, their marginal utility came from their contribution of animal protein through hunting. As revolutionary heroes, explorers, hunters, warriors, and daring capitalist entrepreneurs, men felt, and doubtless their women did too, that their contribution was beyond anything women could do. This earned men extra privileges of rank, authority, and creative services (p. 146).

The theory of marginal utility, then, suggests that men are losing status and power to women because women no longer rely on man's historical function as hunter, warrior, and more recently, business entrepreneur. Men are no longer indispensible.

Benefits of Male Role Socialization

As compared to women, men have a more positive self-concept, have greater confidence in themselves, and enjoy more status than women (Wagner et al., 1986). They also feel that they experience less discrimination and sexual harassment than women. Men (and women) see more advantages associated with being male than with being female (Fabes & Laner, 1986).

□   C O N S I D E R A T I O N   □

Males need to consider the potential trap of focusing on making money and pursuing a career to the exclusion of being able to care for themselves independently and developing relationships that provide meaning beyond work roles. In addition, parents should be aware that socializing their male children to be nurturant and competent in domestic work may be functional in their future interactions with women, who are socialized to expect these qualities in the men with whom they form relationships.

We have discussed some of the consequences of female and male role socialization. In the past, women reflected the characteristics of affection, tenderness, and sensitivity while men reflected the characteristics of aggressiveness, independence, and dominance. Increasingly, women and men are becoming more *androgynous* in that they reflect both feminine and masculine characteristics. Thousands of people have taken the Bem Sex Role Inventory (Bem, 1974) and have shown that both men and women can score high or low on either set of traits or have a combination of them (Lindsey, 1990).

:: Trends

Although we continue to recognize that biological heritage has a significant impact on human development, our society is becoming less rigid in its gender-role socialization. As a result, fewer roles will be closed to women and the roles of women and men will become more transferable.

As each gender begins to fill a wider range of roles, the trend toward *androgyny* will increase. For example, men will feel more free to be gentle and to express their emotions, whereas women will more often be assertive and competitive. Although gender role changes may be difficult for both women and men, movement toward these changes will be accelerated by women's greater participation in the labor force and men's greater involvement in childcare. However, these changes will be slow as men have not shown the same enthusiasm for domestic roles as women have shown for employment roles (Morgan & Affleck, 1989).

In the past 10 years, a number of social barriers to women's participation in formerly all-male activities have been removed. No longer are women barred from being vice-presidential candidates, Supreme Court justices, West Point cadets, or astronauts, and girls now play baseball on Little League teams. Today's woman is not only a married housewife with two children living in surburbia. She also may be a never married woman, a divorced woman, a married woman who works outside the home, or a childfree married woman. Stereotypes of who women are and what they do are fading.

The women's movement, which formerly focused on the passage of the Equal Rights Amendment (ERA) and abortion rights, will now turn its attention to the protection of working women who opt to become mothers. Because there is no government-sanctioned leave or childcare policy, a woman's income and job security nosedives when she has a child. Other countries (117 of them) have job-protected leaves of absence for pregnant women; the United States is moving toward such protection. The 1987 Supreme Court decision requiring states to provide job protection for pregnant women is an example of such movement.

Another trend that may develop is the recognition that the traditional male gender role is just as restrictive as the traditional female gender role. Edwin Schur asserts that:

> There is no denying that the gender system controls men too. Unquestionably, men are limited and restricted through narrow definitions of "masculinity" . . . They too face negative sanctions when they violate gender prescriptions. There is little value in debating which sex suffers or loses more through this kind of control., it is apparent that both do (1984, 12).

:: Summary

Sex refers to the biological distinction of being male or female based on biological differences in chromosomal and hormonal makeup. The term *gender* includes not only our biological sex, but also social and psychological components that characterize us as female or male.

A person's gender identity is her or his self-concept as a girl and later a woman or as a boy and later a man. Gender roles are the socially expected characteristics and behaviors associated with a person's sex. In our society, the traditional female role is to be emotional, dependent, and home oriented and the traditional male role is to be unemotional, independent, and career oriented. Today, these stereotypes are breaking down under the impact of changes in family structure and job participation.

Four explanations of how children acquire gender role behaviors are provided by social learning, sociobiological, cognitive-developmental, and identification theories. The social learning perspective states that children learn their roles through direct instruction, modeling, and reward and punishment. Sociobiological theory emphasizes biological differences between males and females as the basis for differences in gender roles. According to the cognitive-developmental view of gender role learning, children first reach the stage at which they understand that their gender is permanent and then actively seek to acquire masculine or feminine characteristics. Identification theory suggests that children take on the role of the same-gender parent either out of fear or love. Whereas biological differences may predispose people to behave in certain ways, society (represented by parents, teachers, peers, mass media, and religion) influences what people learn.

Being socialized as a woman or a man has varied consequences for the person. Women sometimes have less confidence in themselves than men do due to pervasive sexism. Marriage may be a disappointment if wives discover that husbands are more interested in work than in family. Women also pursue less education and earn less income than men. Those who do not develop an interest other than their husbands and children may feel a void when those roles terminate.

Men, on the other hand, feel an imperative to earn money and are looked down on by society if they do not. They are also less emotionally expressive and may place human relationships below their work in importance. Adapting to more assertive women and more egalitarian relationships is an increasing demand on the modern man.

The future of gender roles will include fewer barriers to women in various life options and a general movement toward androgyny. Another trend is the growing recognition that the traditional male gender role is just as restrictive as the traditional female gender role.

Questions for Reflection

1. Why is there little agreement about the precise way in which gender roles are learned?
2. To what degree do you feel free to exhibit behaviors that are typically associated with the opposite sex?
3. Do you think that men will ever participate equally in child caregiving? Why or why not?

References

Alvarez, R. The psycho-historical and socioeconomic development of the Chicano community in the United States. *The Mexican-American experience.* Edited by R. O. DeLaGarga, F. D. Bean, C. M. Bonjean, R. Romo, and R. Alvarez. Austin, Tex.: University of Texas Press, 1985, 32–56.

Antill, John K. and Sandra Cotton. Factors affecting the division of labor in households. *Sex Roles,* 1988, *18,* 531–553.

Astrachan, A. *How men feel.* New York: Anchor Press, 1986.

Baca Zinn, M. Gender and ethnic identity among Chicanos. *Frontiers,* 1980, *2,* 18–24.

Bassi, L. J. Poverty among women and children: What accounts for the change? *The American Economic Review,* May, 1988, 91–95.

Bem, S. L. The measurement of psychological androgyny. *Journal of Consulting and Clinical Psychology,* 1974, *42,* 155–162.

Billingham, R. E. and A. R. Sack. Gender differences in college students' willingness to participate in alternative marriage and family relationships. *Family Perspective,* 1986, *20,* 37–44.

Blier, M. J. and L. A. Blier-Wilson. Gender differences in self-rated emotional expressiveness. *Sex Roles,* 1989, *21,* 287–295.

Blumstein, P. and P. Schwartz. *American couples.* New York: Morrow, 1983.

Bottigheimer, Ruth B. "Silenced Women in the Grimms' Tales: The 'Fit' Between Fairy Tales and Society in Their Historical Context." In *Fairy Tales and Society: Illusion, Allusion and Paradigm,* edited by R. Bottigheimer. Philadelphia: University of Pennsylvania Press, 115–32. 1986.

Brabandt, Sarah and Linda Mooney. Him, her, or either: Sex of person addressed and interpersonal communication. *Sex Roles,* 1989, *20,* 47–58.

Bretl, Daniel J. and Joanne Cantor. The portrayal of men and women in U.S. television commercials: A recent content analysis and trends over 15 years. *Sex Roles,* 1988, *18,* 595–609.

Caplan, P. J. Single life and married life. *International Journal of Women's Studies,* 1985, *8,* 6–11.

Cash, T. F. and T. A. Brown. Gender and body images: Stereotypes and realities. *Sex Roles,* 1989, *21,* 361–373.

Chodorow, N. *The reproduction of mothering.* Berkeley, Calif.: University of California Press, 1978.

Cleaver, G. Marriage enrichment by means of a structured communication program. *Family Relations,* 1987, *36,* 49–54.

Cloninger, C. R. Is there a genetic predisposition to behavior?: Adoption study. *Marriage and Divorce Today,* 1986, *11,* no. 31, 3–4.

Dutka, E. Roseanne Barr: Slightly to the left of normal. *Time,* May 8, 1989, p. 82–83.

Epstein, C. F. *Deceptive distinctions: Sex, gender, and the social order.* New Haven, Conn.: Yale University and Russell Sage Foundation, 1989.

Fabes, R. A. and N. R. Laner. How the sexes perceive each other. *Sex Roles,* 1986, *15,* no. 3/4, 129–143.

Franklin, Clyde W., II. *Men and society.* Chicago: Nelson-Hall, 1988.

Freud, S. *New introductory lectures in psychoanalysis.* J. Strachey, ed. and trans. New York: W. W. Norton, 1965. Originally published in 1933.

Freud, S. Some psychological consequences of an anatomical distinction between the sexes (1925). *Women and analysis.* J. Strouse, ed. New York: Grossman, 1974.

Friedrich, Otto and Jeanne McDowell. Flashy symbol of an acquisitive age. *Time,* January 16, 1989, pp. 48–54.

Funk, Richard B. and Fern K. Willits. College attendance and attitude change: A panel study, 1970-81. *Sociology of Education,* 1987, *60,* 224–231.

Gilligan, C. *In a different voice* Cambridge, Mass.: Harvard University Press, 1982.

Gilmartin-Zena, Pat. Attitudes about rape myths: Are women's studies students different? *Free Inquiry in Creative Sociology,* 1989, *17,* 65–72.

Goode, William J. Why men resist. *Rethinking the Family.* Edited by Barrie Thorne with Marilyn Yalom. New York: Longman, 1982.

Haggstrom, G. W., D. E. Kanouse, and P. A. Morrison. Accounting for the educational shortfall of mothers. *Journal of Marriage and the Family,* 1986, *48,* 175–186.

Heimovics, Richard D. and Robert D. Herman. Gender and the attributes of chief executive responsibility for successful or unsuccessful organizational outcomes. *Sex Roles,* 1988, *18,* 623–635.

Hesse-Biber, Sharlene. Eating patterns and disorders in a college population: Are college women's eating problems a new phenomenon? *Sex Roles,* 1989, *20,* 71–89.

Hochschild, A. *The second shift: Working parents and the revolution at home.* New York: Viking Press, 1989.

Kamo, Yoshinoi. Determinants of household division of labor: Resources, power and ideology. *Journal of Family Issues,* 1988, *9,* 177–220.

Kessler, R. C. and H. W. Neighbors. A new perspective on the relationships among race, social class, and psychological distress. *Journal of Health and Social Behavior,* 1986, *27,* 107–115.

Kiecolt, K. J. and A. C. Acock. The long-term effects of family structure on gender role attitudes. *Journal of Marriage and the Family,* 1988, *50,* 709–717.

Klinger-Vartabedian, Laurel and K. M. O'Flaherty. Student perceptions of presenter self-disclosure in the college classroom based on perceived status differentials. *Contemporary Educational Psychology,* 1989, *14,* 153–163.

Koberg, C. S. Sex and situational influences on the use of power: A follow-up study. *Sex Roles,* 1985, *13,* 625–640.

Kohlberg, L. A cognitive-developmental analysis of children's sex-role concepts and attitudes. *The development of sex differences.* Edited by E. E. Macoby. Stanford, Calif.: Stanford University Press, 1966.

Kohlberg, L. State and sequence: The cognitive-developmental approach to socialization. *Handbook of socialization theory and research.* Edited by D. A. Goslin. Chicago: Rand McNally, 1969, 347–480.

Lackey, P. N. Adults' attitudes about assignments of household chores to male and female children. *Sex Roles,* 1989, *20,* 271–281.

Levy, J. Lateral specialization of the human brain., behavioral manifestations and possible evolutionary basis. In J. A. Kiger (Ed.), *The Biology of Behavior.* Corvallis, WA: Oregon State University Press, 1972.

Lindsey, L. L. *Gender roles: A sociological perspective.* Englewood Cliffs, N.J.: Prentice-Hall, Inc., 1990.

Lips, H. M. *Sex and Gender: An Introduction.* Mountain View, CA: Mayfield. 1988.

Maccoby, E. E., and C. N. Jacklin. *The Psychology of Sex Differences.* Stanford, CA: Stanford University Press, 1974.

Magner, Denise K. Decline in doctorates earned by black and white men persists study finds. *Chronicle of Higher Education,* 1989, 35.

McBroom, W. H. Changes in role orientation of women. *Journal of Family Issues,* 1986, 7, 149–159.

McLanahan, S. S. and J. L. Glass. A note on the trend in sex differences in psychological distress. *Journal of Health and Social Behavior,* 1985, 26, 328–336.

Mindel, C. H., R. W. Habenstein, and R. Wright, Jr., eds. *Ethnic families in America: Patterns and variations.* 3d. ed. New York: Elsevier, 1988.

Mintz, L. B. and N. E. Betz. Sex differences in the nature, realism, and correlates of body image. *Sex Roles,* 1986, 15, no. 3/4, 185–195.

Money, John. Sin, sickness, or status? Homosexual gender identity and psychoneuroendrocrinology. *American Psychologist,* 1987, 42, 384–399.

Mooney, Linda and Sarah Brabant. Two martinis and a rested woman: 'Liberation' in the Sunday comics. *Sex Roles, 1987, 17, 409–420*

Morgan, C. S. and M. Affleck. College women's expectations for work and family. *Free Inquiry in Creative Sociology,* 1989, 17, 207–212.

Ortiz, Jeanne A. and Larry P. Ortiz. Do contemporary women's magazines practice what they preach? *Free Inquiry in Creative Sociology,* 1989, 17, 51–55.

Paludi, M. A. and W. D. Bauer. Goldberg revisited: What's in an author's name? *Sex Roles,* 1983, 9, 387–396.

Petersen, D. M. and P. L. Dressel. Equal time for women: Social notes on the male strip show. *Urban Life,* 1982, 11, 185–208.

Powell, B., H. Takayama, and D. Benkoil. The end of the affair? *Newsweek,* July 19, 1989, pp. 22–23.

Quoss, Bernita, Godfry J. Ellis, and Frances Stromberg. Sex-role preferences of young children reared by feminist parents and by parents from the general population. *Free Inquiry in Creative Sociology,* 1987, 15, 139–150.

Robinson, C. C. and J. T. Morris. The gender-stereotyped nature of Christmas toys received by 36-, 48-, and 60-month old children: A comparison between nonrequested vs. requested toys. *Sex Roles,* 1986, 15, no. 1/2, 21–32.

Ross, H. and H. Taylor. Do boys prefer Daddy or his physical style of play? *Sex Roles,* 1989, 20, 23–34.

Rossi, Alice S. A Biosocial Perspective on Parenting. *Daedalus,* 106, 2, 1–31. 1977.

Rubin, Lillian B. *Just friends.,* New York: Harper & Row, 1985.

Sadker, M. P. and Sadker, D. M. Sexism in the Schoolroom of the '80s. *Psychology Today,* March 1985, 54–57.

Sandroff, R. Is your job driving you crazy? *Psychology Today,* 1989, July/August 41–45.

Schein, Virginia E., Ruediger Mueller, and Carolyn Jacobson. The relationship between sex role stereotypes and requisite management characteristics among college students. *Sex Roles,* 1989, 20, 103–110.

Schur, Edwin M. *Labeling Women Deviant: Gender, Stigma, and Social Control.* N.Y. C., NY: Random House. 1984.

Signorielli, Nancy. Television and conceptions about sex roles: Maintaining conventionality and the status quo. *Sex Roles,* 1989, 21, 341–360.

Snell, William E. Jr., Sharyn S. Belk, and Raymond C. Hawkins. The masculine and feminine self-disclosure scale: The politics of masculine and feminine self-presentation. *Sex Roles,* 1986, 15, 249–267.

Spitze, G. and J. Logan. Sons, daughters, and intergenerational social support. *Journal of Marriage and the Family,* 1990, 52, 420–430.

Springer, S., and Deutsch, G. *Left Brain, Right Brain*. San Francisco, CA: W. H. Freeman. 1981.

Stainton, M. C. The fetus: A growing member of the family. *Family Relations*, 1985, 34, 321–326.

Stake, Jayne and Monica L. Lauer. The consequences of being overweight: A controlled study of gender differences. *Sex Roles*, 1987, *17*, 31–48.

Statistical Abstract of the United States: 1987. 107th ed. Washington, D.C.: U.S. Bureau of the Census, 1987.

Statistical Abstract of the United States: 1990. 110th ed. Washington, D.C.: U.S. Bureau of the Census, 1990.

Stapley, J. C. and J. M. Haviland. Beyond depression: Gender differences in normal adolescents' emotional experiences. *Sex Roles* 1989, *20*, 295–308.

Stokes, Joseph P., and Judith S. Peyton. Attitudinal differences between full-time homemakers and women who work outside the home. *Sex Roles*, 1986, *15*, no. 5/6, 299–310.

Stone, Kay F. "Feminist Approaches to the Interpretation of Fairy Tales," In *Fairy Tales and Society: Illusion, Allusion, and Paradigm,* edited by R. Bottigheimer. Philadelphia: University of Pennsylvania Press, 229–36. 1986.

Tavris, C., and C. Wade. *The Longest War: Sex Differences in Perspective,* 2nd ed. San Diego, CA: Harcourt Brace Jovanovich, 1984.

Wagner, D. G., R. S. Ford, and T. W. Ford. Can gender differences in equality be reduced? *American Sociological Review*, 1986, *51*, 47–61.

Walker, Alexis J., Sally S. Kees Martin, and Linda Thompson. Feminist programs for families. *Family Relations*, 1988, *37*, 17–22.

Whisman, M. A. and N. S. Jacobson. Depression, marital satisfaction, and marital and personality measures of sex roles. *Journal of Marital and Family Therapy,* 1988, *15*, 177–186.

Wright, Mary. Gender, birth category and family structure as relating to self-esteem. *Free Inquiry in Creative Sociology*, 1987, *15*, 99–101.

CHOICES

THE RESULT OF our society becoming less rigid in its gender role expectations for women and men is a new array of choices of gender role behavior. Such choices are becoming increasingly available in dating, marriage, parenting, and employment.

Dating: Women Asking Men?

Traditionally, the only socially appropriate way for a woman and man to begin dating was for the man to call the woman up several days in advance and ask her if she would like to have dinner, see a movie, attend a concert, or whatever later in the week. Her role was passive. If she were asked, she could accept or reject. If a woman asked a man out for a first date, it implied that she was inappropriately aggressive; it was the man's role—not the woman's—to do the asking.

Some women are uncomfortable asking a new person for a date. Three women explain:

I just wouldn't feel right about it. I wouldn't want the guy to think I was too fast or pushy.

I couldn't take the rejection. Besides, nine out of ten guys I would want are already involved with someone else. Even the guys I just find attractive and talk to have steady girlfriends, so I don't want to humiliate myself by asking them out and being turned down.

We always had a phone rule in my house: *Never call a guy unless he has called and is expecting you to call him back.* I have three older sisters, and my parents have always made sure that my sisters never called their boyfriends (unless it was a serious relationship). Their reason was ''if he wants to go out, he'll call you.''

But more and more women are questioning their socialization and asking the man out, and such a choice is becoming more acceptable.

I say ''go for it'' simply because there are more advantages than disadvantages. The only disadvantage I can think of is the possibility of coming over as pushy. But on the advantage side: (1) Maybe he doesn't know if you're interested. If you wait around for him to ask you and he doesn't, you may never get together. (2)

Maybe he's shy. (3) Guys hate to say no to girls, so he'll probably go out with you and he may find that he likes you.

The boyfriend I have now I asked out over a year ago (he's shy). Things have been going great ever since. He told me about a month ago that if I had never asked him out, he would never have asked me out first because he thought I wasn't interested. I'm glad I let him know I was.

I wouldn't have much of a problem asking a guy out. Of course, I'd wait a little hoping that he would ask first. But some guys need a little push in the ''right direction''—my direction.

Women are sometimes interested in what men think about women who call them up. Most men feel positive about being asked for a date and do not regard the woman as too forward. The following are examples of what men in the author's class said when they were asked, ''How would you feel about a woman asking you out for a date if you have never dated her before?''

I'd love it. It makes me feel wanted, and I like for the female to be aggressive.

I prefer that the woman ask me out. I get tired of having to be the aggressor all the time.

I'm the traditional type. I'll do the asking.

If a woman decides to call a man for a date, what might she say? Does she call him up to borrow his class notebook or a record album and hope he will get the hint that she is interested in him? Or does she mention that there is a new movie in town that has had excellent reviews and wait for him to ask her? Both women who have asked men for dates and men who have accepted say that the direct approach is best. A woman might say ''Hi! This is Jill. I'm in your English literature class and am calling to ask if you would like to go out Saturday evening to see the campus movie.''

A woman who chooses to call a man for a date may experience what men experience who call a woman for a date—rejection. ''She won't get turned down much,'' said one woman. ''But it will happen, and she shouldn't feel bad about it when it does. I asked this one guy out who looked like

Richard Gere, and he told me he was involved with someone and couldn't go—I wasn't surprised."

Marriage: Role Sharing

The choices available to spouses regarding their role behavior in marriage are also increasing. More egalitarian relationships mean that either spouse may now be employed, cook supper, clean the house, and call out spelling words to the children. Such role flexibility increases the potential for experientially sharing the work required in marriage and provides the basis for each partner to better understand the feelings of the other. In essence, role sharing allows a greater range of sharing in all aspects of the relationship.

When only the husband worked outside the home and the wife stayed home to take care of the house and children, each spouse had a set of experiences that was unknown to the partner. He would be tired at the end of the day from working at the office; she would be tired from cleaning the house, preparing food, and listening to the bickering of two young children. Each one was sure that he or she was more tired than the other partner and regarded their own role as the most difficult and the partner's role as "easy and nothing to complain about." One outcome of both spouses choosing to engage in a greater range of roles is the increased understanding of what the other partner is experiencing. "Since I have been employed and my husband has taken over the meals and child care, we both know what it is like to be tired for different reasons," said one wife.

Employment: Occupational Choices

The general trend toward gender role flexibility is also having its impact on occupational role choices. Jobs traditionally occupied by one gender are now open to the other. Men may become nurses and librarians, and women may become construction workers and lawyers. A match between personality needs and occupational choices is not overridden by arbitrary social restrictions regarding who can and can't have a particular job or career.

Impact of Social Influences on Choices

The degree to which you want an equalitarian or role-sharing relationship (which translates into sharing in earning the income and in caring for the house and children) will be influenced by the roles of your parents and peers, your exposure to role-sharing ideas, and your partner's expectations of your behavior. If your parents and peers assume traditional roles in their respective relationships with you and if you have had limited exposure to role relationships beyond traditional ones, your desire for a role-sharing relationship will be influenced by the partner with whom you are involved.

One woman living with her partner told him that she loved him and wanted to continue to live with him but that he could leave if he was not interested in doing his share of the work—washing dishes, doing laundry, and vacuuming the apartment. He stayed, and both report a very satisfactory relationship.

C H A P T E R

4

Sexual Values and Behaviors

IS IT TRUE?

1. In one study of university students, both males and females reported that sexual infidelity is equally unacceptable in dating relationships as in marriage relationships.

2. Men and women have similar motivations for sexual intercourse.

3. Most people would feel guilty if they were involved with someone and had intercourse with someone else while their partner was away.

4. Most college students are changing their sexual behavior because of their fear of contracting AIDS.

5. In some states it is a felony to expose another person to the AIDS virus.
1 = F; 2 = F; 3 = T; 4 = F; 5 = T

O UR SEXUAL VALUES guide our sexual behavior. Think about the following situations.

Two people are slow dancing to romantic music. Although they met only two hours ago, they feel a strong attraction to each other. Each is wondering how much sexual involvement is appropriate when they go back to one of their apartments later that evening. How much sexual involvement is appropriate in a new relationship?

Two students have decided to live together, but they know their respective parents would disapprove. If they tell their parents, the parents will probably withdraw their financial support and both students will be forced to drop out of school. Should they tell?

While Mary was away for a weekend visiting her parents, the man with whom she is living had intercourse with an old girlfriend. He says he is sorry and promises never to be unfaithful again. How should she handle the situation?

A woman is married to a man whose career requires that he be away from home for extended periods of time. Although she loves her husband, she is lonely, bored, and sexually frustrated in his absence. She has been asked out by a colleague at work whose wife also travels. He too is in love with his wife but is lonely for emotional and sexual companionship. They are ambivalent about whether to see each other when their spouses are away. Should they see each other?

Lord give me
chastity—but not yet.
—SAINT AUGUSTINE

The individuals in these situations will all make decisions based on their personal value systems. Although we may not have experienced these particular encounters, we have confronted others that have required us to examine our own values. In this chapter, we will look at our sexual values and their behavioral expression in masturbation, petting, and sexual intercourse.

:: Types of Value Systems

Our sexual values become visible when we choose one course of action over another. This choice may be based on our feeling of what is right and wrong or moral and immoral or on a perception that one course of action will have more positive consequences than another. Sometimes a combination of factors affects our choice. A single woman who felt she was drifting into a love relationship with a married coworker stated:

Although I felt strongly about him, I thought it was wrong and immoral for me to get involved with him. He also had three kids, and the hurt it would cause them and his wife wouldn't be worth it, so I stopped flirting with him and was very careful about what I said to him.

Several value systems may offer guidelines to people who are making decisions about their sexual behavior. These systems include legalism, situationism, hedonism, asceticism, and rationalism.

Legalism. *Legalism*—a legalistic view of sexual ethics—involves making decisions on the basis of a set of laws or codes of moral conduct. The term "legalism" does *not* refer to laws of the state. In the example of the single woman and her married coworker, part of the woman's reasoning was legalistic: she felt that it is "wrong" to become involved with a married person.

■ **DATA:** *When asked about premarital sex, 13.6 percent of adult women under 30 and 7.6 percent of adult men under 30 agree that it is "always wrong"(Thornton, 1989).*

The official creeds of the Christian and Jewish religions reflect a legalistic view of sexual ethics. Intercourse between a man and a woman is a gift from God to be expressed only in marriage; violations (masturbation, homosexuality, and extramarital sex) are viewed as sins against God, self, and community. The person who adopts a legal set of sexual ethics is generally clear about what is appropriate, right, or moral. "I never wonder when I'm out with my fiancée if we're going to have intercourse or not—we won't," said a devoutly religious man.

Situation Ethics.   One of the most prevalent forms of contemporary sexual ethics is *situation ethics*. This perspective suggests that sexual decisions should be made in the context of the particular situation. Genuine love and good will should be the core motives for each decision, and the prediction of positive consequences should be a basic guideline.

The situationist believes that to make all decisions on the basis of rules is to miss the point of human love and to do more harm than good. Whereas the legalist would say it is right for married people to have intercourse and wrong for the unmarried to do so, the situationist would say "it depends" and would ask, "What if the married people do not love each other and intercourse is an abusive, exploitative act? Also suppose that the unmarried people love each other, and their intercourse experience is an expression of mutual concern and respect. Which couple is being more loving or ethical?"

The credibility of official religious creeds was brought into question with the exposure of Jimmy Swaggarts private life.

It is sometimes difficult to make sexual decisions on a case-by-case basis, "I don't know what's right anymore" reflects the uncertainty of a situation ethics view. Once a person decides that mutual love is the context justifying intercourse, how often and how soon should the person fall in love? Can love develop after two hours of conversation? How does one know that her or his own love feelings and those of a partner are genuine? The freedom that situation ethics brings to sexual decision making requires responsibility, maturity, and judgment. In some cases, individuals may deceive themselves by believing they are in love so they will not feel guilty about having intercourse.

The casual attitude toward sexuality that many young people hold today has greatly weakened the relationships they form as husbands and wives.
—GARY BAUER

Hedonism. A third value perspective—*hedonism*—suggests that one need not be concerned with moral or contextual issues but only with pleasure. "If it feels good, do it"emphasizes the hedonistic ethic that sexual desire is an appropriate appetite and its expression is legitimate. Like hunger and thirst, the sexual urge need not be subject to moral constraints.

Too much has been made, says the hedonist, of the sexual act; it should be regarded as one of the many pleasures we are capable of experiencing. Some conservative individuals feel that the hedonist has the potential to become a sexual addict who relates to sex as a drug—needing more and taking risks to get it.

Puberty showed up and that was it: I knew Catholicism wasn't for me. We were told it was a sin to think about sex, and meanwhile, you'd have these hormones racing through your body at five times the speed of light.
—KAREEM
    ABDUL–JABBAR

Asceticism. Monks, nuns, and other celibates have adopted the sexual value of *asceticism*. The ascetic believes that giving into what he or she considers to be carnal lust is unnecessary and calls us to rise above the pursuit of sensual pleasure into a life of self-discipline and self-denial. Accordingly, the spiritual life is the highest good, and self-denial helps us to achieve it.

Rationalism. *Rationalism*, a fifth view of contemporary sexual ethics, refers to the use of reason in determining a course of sexual action. Rationalism is concerned with the intellect rather than with the emotions. The rationalist makes a decision on the basis of the facts and/or the consequences of that decision. A rational perspective on deciding whether to have intercourse with a new partner will be discussed in the "Choices" section at the end of this chapter.

∷ Personal Sexual Values

You can clarify some of your own sexual values in several ways. One is a self-administered questionnaire, of which the following is an example.

Select one ending for each of the following statements, and consider why you chose that answer. You may wish to think of additional statements about sexual behavior that include a range of choices.

For me, it is most important that a sexual experience:

1. Be morally correct.
2. Be fun and pleasurable.

3. Increase the love feelings with my partner.
4. Improve my self-concept.
5. Result in orgasm.

In a sexual relationship, I would prefer that:

1. My partner be in love with me.
2. I be in love with my partner.
3. Sex means the same thing to both of us.
4. We are married to each other.
5. My partner is uninhibited.

If I am feeling the need for sexual release, I would rather:

1. Have intercourse.
2. Have my partner perform oral sex.
3. Engage in vigorous physical activity.
4. Masturbate.
5. Have a sexual dream resulting in orgasm.

Intercourse is appropriate under the following conditions:

1. The partners are married.
2. The partners are engaged.
3. The partners are in love.
4. The partners feel affection but not love for each other.
5. The partners feel no particular affection for each other.

The worst thing I could find out about my sexual partner is that she or he:

1. Has genital herpes.
2. Is homosexual.
3. Is unfaithful or has deceived me.
4. Is sterile.
5. Does not love me.

Another way of clarifying sexual values is to think of the degree to which you regard various behaviors as acceptable. Where would you place your feelings about sex on a continuum from total acceptance to total nonacceptance if the issues were sex without love, abortion, homosexuality, and extramarital sex?

Sexual values may also be assessed by identifying how guilty a person anticipates feeling after engaging in various sexual behaviors. Table 4.1 reflects the average level of guilt on a four-point continuum for various sexual situations reported by 175 university male students and 74 female students.

Still another exercise in values clarification is to develop an answer to a value dilemma. For example, Kathy and Bob are in love, and they plan to be married in June. Kathy is sterile and has been told by her physician that she can never have children. Bob has mentioned children, and Kathy knows he wants them. If she tells Bob of her sterility, she is certain that he will end the relationship with her. But she feels that he will not divorce her after they are married (although he could get an annulment) and that he will be willing to adopt. Should she tell him she cannot have children?

Idealism increases in direct proportion to one's distance from the problem.

—JOHN GALSWORTHY

:: TABLE 4.1 **Sexual Guilt**

HOW GUILTY WOULD YOU FEEL IF	AVERAGE SCORE
1. You have intercourse with someone 18 years older than you. Both of you are unmarried.	2.04
2. You decide not to tell the person you are about to marry any information concerning your previous affectional relationships because you believe it will have no bearing on your marriage.	2.18
3. The person you are about to marry learns of a previous sexual affair with another person you did not particularly care for prior to your present relationship.	2.29
4. You reveal to an associate that a person who had invited you to dinner was gay and there were to be no other guests.	2.48
5. Your mother discovers that you, at age 16, are having intercourse with a member of the opposite sex.	2.76
6. You concealed from the person you are about to marry that you had earlier contracted and was cured of gonorrhea.	2.88
7. Your parents learn of your sexual relationship with someone of another race and you know they disapproved.	3.03
8. As a student, you are in love with a teacher who is fired because your sexual relationship has been brought to the attention of the instructor's dean.	3.51
9. You are in a committed relationship with a person, yet you had intercourse with someone else.	3.52
10. Your fiancé learns that you had a sexual encounter with your fiancé's best friend while your fiancé was away visiting her/his grandmother.	3.66

1 = No guilt; 2 = Little guilt; 3 = Moderate guilt;
4 = Considerable guilt

SOURCE: ADAPTED FROM "MEASURING SEXUAL GUILT" BY DAVID KNOX AND JAMES WALTERS. EAST CAROLINA UNIVERSITY AND UNIVERSITY OF GEORGIA, UNPUBLISHED PAPER, 1990.

The goal in examining this and other value dilemmas is to explore our own sexual values. To assess the degree to which your sexual values are conservative or liberal, take the Sexual Attitude Scale (Hudson, Murphy, & Nurius, 1983) in the following Self–Assessment. According to the Sexual Attitude Scale, a liberal is one who feels that the expression of human sexuality should be open, free, and unrestrained; a conservative is one who feels that sexual expression should be considerably constrained and closely regulated. When 689 students (primarily seniors and graduate students) took the Sexual Attitude Scale, both sexes tended to score from borderline–low to high–grade liberal (Nurius & Hudson, 1982).

Whether your sexual values are liberal or conservative, they have been influenced by your family, peers, and society. Conservative parents and peers will have created a context conducive to the development of conservative sexual values. Liberal parents and peers will have created just the opposite context with a more liberal outcome. Societal influences are also involved. Our society is very liberal in terms of the sexual norms suggested in music, movie, and media. In contrast, strict sexual norms exist in Japan, where pornography is not readily available in the local convenience store and adolescents are expected to delay the expression of their sexuality.

Traditionally, males' major gratification from sexuality has not necessarily been from intercourse—often "the biggest pleasure has been the next day in the locker room".
–SYLVIA HACKER

Our society is sexually permissive.

∷ Gender and Racial Differences in Sexual Behavior

Are there differences between the sexual behaviors of men and women and between blacks and whites?

A team of researchers (Billingham et al., 1989) analyzed the questionnaires of 221 males and 220 females and observed that men reported higher rates of sexual aggressiveness and orgasmic behavior than females. The researchers concluded that biological factors provided the best explanation for the differences between the sexes. Alternatively, social learning theorists would argue that men learn to be more sexually aggressive and orgasmic than women.

Men and women also differ in their motivations for sexual intercourse. Men report the desire for sexual pleasure, conquest, and relief of sexual tension more often than women who emphasize emotional closeness and affection (Townsend and Levy, 1990). These sex differences appear in both heterosexuals and homosexuals (Leigh, 1989).

Finally, men and women differ in regard to their tolerance of sexual infidelity. When 370 university students were asked to indicate what sexual behaviors were acceptable at what levels of the relationship, men were more tolerant of a man's sexual infidelity than of a woman's (Margolin, 1989). Also, males in this study tended to say that sexual infidelity in dating or marriage relationships were "moderately unacceptable," whereas females tended to say that sexual infidelity is "very unacceptable" in both dating and marriage relationships.

While there are considerable differences between the sexes, there are considerable similarities between blacks and whites. In one study (Belcastro, 1985), of 565 unmarried undergraduates that compared blacks and whites on 25 sexual behaviors, only a few differences occurred. Some of these differences are discussed in the following paragraphs.

When black males were compared to white males at the same midwestern university, black males were significantly more likely to have had interracial in-

SELF ASSESSMENT

Sexual Attitude Scale

This questionnaire is designed to measure the way you feel about sexual behavior. It is not a test, so there are no right or wrong answers. Answer each item as carefully and accurately as you can by placing the most appropriate number beside each one as follows:

1 Strongly disagree
2 Disagree
3 Undecided
4 Agree
5 Strongly agree

	SD	D	U	A	SA
1. I think too much freedom is given to adults these days.	1	2	3	4	5
2. I think that the increased sexual freedom seen in the past several years has done much to undermine the American family.	1	2	3	4	5
3. I think that young people have been given too much information about sex.	1	2	3	4	5
4. Sex education should be restricted to the home.	1	2	3	4	5
5. Older people do not need to have sex.	1	2	3	4	5
6. Sex education should be provided only when people are ready for marriage.	1	2	3	4	5
7. Premarital sex may be a sign of a decaying social order.	1	2	3	4	5
8. Extramarital sex is never excusable.	1	2	3	4	5
9. I think there is too much sexual freedom given to teenagers these days.	1	2	3	4	5
10. I thing there is not enough sexual restraint among young people.	1	2	3	4	5
11. I think people engage in sex too often.	1	2	3	4	5
12. I think the only proper way to have sex is through intercourse.	1	2	3	4	5

tercourse (40 percent versus 13 percent) and to have avoided masturbation (44 percent versus 17 percent). In addition, black males were more likely to have experienced intercourse with a partner who was on birth control or who used post-coital foam.

More frequent interracial intercourse may result from black males socializing each other to try a "white woman" and white males socializing each other to avoid sex with a "black woman." Masturbation among black males has traditionally been viewed as an admission of not being able to seduce a woman for intercourse. Black males usually have sexual intercourse with more black females at younger ages than white males do with white females.

	SD	D	U	A	SA
13. I think sex should be reserved for marriage.	1	2	3	4	5
14. Sex should be only for the young.	1	2	3	4	5
15. Too much social approval has been given to homosexuals.	1	2	3	4	5
16. Sex should be devoted to the business of procreation.	1	2	3	4	5
17. People should not masturbate.	1	2	3	4	5
18. Heavy sexual petting should be discouraged.	1	2	3	4	5
19. People should not discuss their sexual affairs or business with others.	1	2	3	4	5
20. Severely physically and mentally handicapped people should not have sex.	1	2	3	4	5
21. There should be no laws prohibiting sexual acts between consenting adults.	1	2	3	4	5
22. What two consenting adults do together sexually is their own business.	1	2	3	4	5
23. There is too much sex on television.	1	2	3	4	5
24. Movies today are too sexually explicit.	1	2	3	4	5
25. Pornography should be totally banned from our bookstores.	1	2	3	4	5

SCORING: Reverse the scores for statements 21 and 22 in the following way; 1 = 5, 2 = 4, 4 = 2, 5 = 1. For example, if you wrote 1 for statement 21 ("There should be no laws prohibiting sexual acts between consenting adults"), change that number to five for scoring purposes. Reverse score statement 22 similarly.

Add the numbers you assigned to each of the 25 statements. Your score may range from a low of 25 (strongly disagreed with all items; 1 x 25 = 25) to a high of 125 (strongly agreed with all items: 5 x 25 = 125). If you score between 25 and 50, you may be regarded as a high-grade liberal; if you score between 50 and 75, a low-grade liberal. If you score between 100 and 125, you may be regarded as a high-grade conservative; if you score between 75 and 100, a low-grade conservative.

(NOTE: This Self-Assessment is included in this chapter for the purpose of being fun and thought-provoking for the student.)

SOURCE: Hudson, W.W., Murphy, G.J.,& Nurius, P.S. A short-form scale to measure liberal vs. conservative orientations toward human sexual expression. *Journal of Sex Research*, 1983, 19, 258–272. A publication of the Society for the Scientific Study of Sex. Reprinted by permission.

When black females were compared to white females, black females were significantly less likely to have performed fellatio (48 percent versus 82 percent) and less likely to have used coitus interruptus (withdrawal method of contraception) (48 percent versus 74 percent). However, black females were more likely to use birth control pills (77 percent versus 65 percent) than white females (Belcastro, 1985).

The infrequent reporting of fellatio among black females is probably largely due to their socialization that fellatio is an unclean and demeaning sexual act. Black woman may also feel that the best sex is "natural" (not oral or manual). Their slightly higher use of birth control pills may be a reaction to the high incidence of pregnancy among black unmarried women. In addition, white females report using fellatio as a method of birth control, which, along with black women's higher use of the pill, may contribute to the white women's higher frequency of fellatio.

:: Masturbation

Masturbation is defined as stimulating one's own body with the goal of experiencing sexual pleasure.

> ■ **DATA:** *In a study of 144 university males and 147 university females, 98.6 percent of the males and 70.1 percent of the females reported having masturbated (Alzate, 1989).*

In this section, we will review attitudes toward masturbation, who does it, and the benefits of masturbation.

Attitudes Toward Masturbation

Masturbation has traditionally had "bad press." Historically, it is almost as though the fields of religion, medicine and psychotherapy have "conspired" to give masturbation a bad name.

One boy, caught
masturbating by his
father and told that it
would cause him to go
blind, decided to
continue "until I have
to wear glasses."
—SYLVIA HACKER

Religion The Jewish and Catholic religions have been the most severe critics of masturbation, but Protestants have not been very positive about it either. Ancient Jews considered masturbation a sin so grave that it deserved the death penalty. Catholics once regarded masturbation as a mortal sin which, if not given up, would result in eternal damnation. Although Protestants felt that neither death nor eternal hellfire were appropriate consequences for masturbation, hell on earth (as a consequence of intense guilt) was.

□   C O N S I D E R A T I O N   □

The historical basis for the negative view of masturbation by religion is that masturbation is nonprocreative sex and that any sexual act that cannot produce children is a sin and an unnatural act. "Against nature" is a term that suggests an action is contrary to its essential purpose—or nature. For example, the essential purpose of eating is to sustain life. The essential purpose of sexual activity, according to Catholic thought, is to procreate.

Masturbation—it's sex
with someone I love.
—WOODY ALLEN

Medicine The medical community reinforced religion's prohibition of masturbation by bringing "scientific validity" to bear on the description of its physical and psychological hazards. In the mid-1700s, Samuel Tissot, a French physician, published a book in which he implied that the loss of too much semen, whether by intercourse or masturbation, was injurious to the body and would cause pimples, tumors, insanity, and early death (Tissot, 1766).

Adding to the medical bias against masturbation, American physician Sylvester Graham wrote that the loss of an ounce of semen was equal to the loss of several ounces of blood. Graham believed that every time a man ejaculated, he ran the risk of contracting a disease of the nervous system. His solution was Graham crackers, which was supposed to help the individual control the release of sexual energy (Graham, 1848). By the mid–nineteenth century, Tissot's theories had made their way into medical textbooks and journals. In spite of a lack of data, physicians added loss of hair, weak eyes, and suicidal tendencies to the list of disorders resulting from masturbation.

Psychotherapy In the early twentieth century, psychotherapy "joined" religion and medicine to convince people of the negative effects of masturbation. Psychotherapists, led by Freud, suggested that masturbation was an infantile form of sexual gratification. People who masturbated "to excess" were fixating on themselves as sexual objects and would not be able to relate to others in a sexually mature way. The message was clear. If you want to be a good sexual partner in marriage, don't masturbate; if you do masturbate, don't do it too often. This view is outdated and no longer considered valid.

CONSIDERATION

The result of religion, medicine, and psychotherapy taking aim at masturbation was devastating. Those who masturbated felt the shame and guilt they were intended to feel. The burden of these feelings was particularly heavy because there was no one with whom to share the guilt. In the case of a premarital pregnancy, responsibility could be shared. The "crime" of masturbation was committed alone. In recent years, the fields of religion, medicine, and psychotherapy have been more tolerant and supportive of masturbation.

Benefits of Masturbation

Although shame, guilt, and anxiety continue to be feelings associated with masturbation in our society, new attitudes are emerging. Although the attitudes of some religious leaders are still negative, most physicians and therapists are clearly positive about the experience. Masturbation is not only approved but recommended. Specific benefits of masturbation include:

1. *Self-knowledge.* Masturbation gives you immediate feedback about what you enjoy during sexual stimulation. You can tell another what turns you on sexually by exploring your own feelings, rhythms, and responses in private.
2. *More likely to orgasm.* In a study of 101 university females, 72.3 percent reported that they climaxed most of the time during masturbation; 51.1 percent during intercourse (Alzate, 1989).
3. *Pressure off partner.* When one partner in a relationship does not want to have intercourse or other sexual involvement, masturbation is a way of experiencing sexual pleasure without obligating the partner.

4. *No partner necessary*. Masturbation provides a way to enjoy sexual feelings if no partner is available.

5. *Unique experience*. When combined with one's own fantasies, masturbation is a unique sexual experience. It is different from petting, intercourse, mutual stimulation of the genitals, and oral sex.

6. *Avoidance of sexual involvement*. Extramarital or extrapartner entanglements can be avoided by masturbation. Sexual tensions can be released by one's self without risking sexual involvement with a partner external to the primary relationship.

□   C O N S I D E R A T I O N   □

In spite of the benefits of masturbation, it remains a private experience; the decision of whether to engage in the behavior is personal. Neither persons choosing not to masturbate nor those choosing to masturbate should feel guilty about their decision.

▪▪ Petting

Petting is the term that traditionally has been used to describe interpersonal physical stimulation that does not include intercourse. Other terms sometimes used synonymously with petting are "making out" and "necking."

> ▪ **DATA:** *Of 237 undergraduates in a probability sample, 61.3 percent reported that heavy petting was acceptable if the partners were casually dating; 90 percent if the partners were engaged (Sprecher et al., 1988).*

For some couples, petting acts as a substitute for intercourse. For example, a highly religious couple may engage in petting to orgasm and still see themselves as virgins. The petting behaviors discussed in this section include kissing, breast stimulation, manual genital stimulation, and oral sex.

Kissing

A kiss isn't just a kiss. There are different types of kissing. In one style of kissing, the partners gently touch their lips together for a short time with their mouths closed. In another, there is considerable pressure and movement for a prolonged time when the closed mouths meet. In still another, the partners kiss with their mouths open, using gentle or light pressure and variations in movement and time. Kinsey referred to the third style as "deep kissing" (also known as "soul kissing," "tongue kissing" or "French kissing").

One woman describes a good kiss:

> Variably soft and hard, but never rough. Tender touching of the lips, gentle parting— not too wide—playful archery and tactile explorations with the tongues. Letting emotions control the intensity of the contact—sucking, licking, and kissing.

Whoever called it necking was a poor judge of anatomy.
—GROUCHO MARX

A kiss is an intimate form of physical expression.

Kissing may or may not have emotional or erotic connotations. A good night kiss may be perfunctory or may symbolize in the mind of each partner the ultimate sense of caring and belonging. It may also mean different things to each partner.

Breast Stimulation

Breast stimulation, both manual and oral, was experienced by over 95 percent of female and male students in a study of sexuality at a Columbian university (Alzate, 1989). In both Columbian and American society, the female breasts are charged with erotic potential. A billion–dollar pornographic industry encourages the male to view the female's breasts in erotic terms. An array of adult magazines feature women with naked breasts in seductive poses.

```
☐          C O N S I D E R A T I O N          ☐

Male breasts have the same potential for erotic stimulation as female breasts. For
some males, breast stimulation by their partners is particularly important. Other
males are not socialized to be aware of or receptive to that form of stimulation.
```

Manual Genital Stimulation

Manual genital stimulation may be done by either partner. Once manual caressing begins, it may result in ejaculation or be a prelude to oral stimulation, intercourse, or both. Some people become aroused by observing their partner's erection and ejaculation as a result of their manual stimulation.

Some students think
genitalia is an Italian
airline.
—SYLVIA HACKER

The man who stimulates the woman's genitals may be readying her for intercourse, oral stimulation, or doing so as an end in itself. Regardless of the motive, the style of stimulation may vary. Some partners rub the mons veneris area (see Sexual Anatomy and Physiology in Part VI), putting indirect pressure on the clitoris. Others may apply direct clitoral pressure. Still others may insert one or several fingers into the vagina, with gentle or rapid thrusting, at the same time they stimulate the clitoris. Orgasm sometimes results.

■ **DATA:** *Ninety-six percent of 128 university males and 86 percent of 93 university females reported that they actively manually stimulated their partner's genitals (Alzate, 1989).*

Not all women enjoy the insertion of a finger or fingers into their vaginas during petting. The key to sexual pleasure for many women is pressure on and around the clitoris, not necessarily insertion.

Oral-Genital Sex

■ **DATA:** *Of 237 undergraduates in a probability sample, 37.1 percent reported that oral genital sex was acceptable if the partners were dating casually: 76.3 percent if the partners were engaged (Sprecher et al., 1988).*

Oral sex refers to both cunnilingus and fellatio. Cunnilingus is the stimulation of the woman's clitoris, labia, and vaginal opening by her partner's tongue and lips. Fellatio is oral stimulation of the male's genitals by his partner. Fellatio may involve sucking the penis, as well as licking the shaft and glans, frenulum, and scrotum. Couples engage in oral sex as a means of avoiding intercourse ("We want to save intercourse until we are older"), as a prelude to intercourse, or as a pleasurable activity independent of intercourse.

In spite of the relatively high frequency of cunnilingus and fellatio, particularly in engaged relationships, these subjects remain taboo. In some states, legal statutes prohibit these behaviors on the basis that they are a "crime against nature." In this case, "nature" refers to reproduction and "crime" refers to sex that does not produce babies.

⸬ Sexual Intercourse

Sexual intercourse, or *coitus*, refers to the sexual union of a man's penis in a woman's vagina.

■ **DATA:** *Ninety percent of 144 undergraduate males and 65 percent of 147 undergraduate females reported having had intercourse (Alzate, 1989).*

Sexual intercourse is also a means of communication that occurs for various reasons and in different contexts—before marriage, during marriage, outside marriage, and after marriage, as well as independently of marriage.

Intercourse is more than two bodies in motion. Each partner brings to the intercourse experience a motive (to express emotional intimacy, to have fun); a psychological state (contentment, excitement, hostility, boredom); and a physical state (aroused, relaxed, tense, exhausted).

□ C O N S I D E R A T I O N □

The combination of these motives and states may change from one sexual encounter to the next. Tonight, one partner may feel aroused and seek intercourse mainly for physical pleasure, but the other partner may feel tired and only have intercourse out of a sense of duty. Tomorrow night, both partners may feel relaxed and loving and have intercourse as a means of expressing their feelings for each other.

The verbal and nonverbal communication preceding intercourse may also give the partners information about out how each feels about the other. One woman said:

> I can tell how we're doing by whether or not we have intercourse and how he approaches me when we do. Sometimes he just rolls over when the lights are out and starts to rub my back. Other times, he plays with my face and kisses me while we talk and waits till I reach for him. Still other times, we each stay on our side of the bed so that our legs don't even touch.

If intercourse occurs, the afterplay is also revealing. Some couples feel closest to each other after lovemaking.

First Intercourse Experiences

Because people attach a great deal of emotional and social significance to intercourse, the first experience is likely to be memorable. Some confusion, anxiety, and frustration about the when, who, why, and how of first intercourse are typical. The following statements reflect such feelings: "I'd like to get it over with"; "My closest friend has intercourse regularly. I wonder when I'll be doing it?"; "I feel that I should already have had intercourse by now, but I haven't." Compounding these concerns are those about the partner ("Will my partner respect me?"), pregnancy ("How lucky will I be?"), and sexually transmitted diseases ("Will I become infected?"). Some couples use contraceptive methods during the first intercourse experience.

Orgasm during first intercourse occurs less often than might be expected. While 72 percent of 128 male undergraduate students reported having an orgasm during first intercourse, 23 percent of 93 undergraduate females reported having an orgasm during the first intercourse (Alzate, 1989).

Whether intercourse occurs in a particular relationship is influenced by the degree to which the partners regard themselves as being involved.

■ **DATA:** *Of 237 undergraduates in a probability sample, 41.3 percent reported that sexual intercourse was acceptable if the partners were casually dating; 81.93 percent if the partners were engaged (Sprecher et al., 1988; Sprecher, 1989).*

The degree to which a person is religiously devout also influences a person's decision about whether or not to have intercourse. Individuals who report having a strong religious faith are less likely to approve of premarital intercourse (Miller & Olson, 1988).

The age of the partner also has an effect on intercourse. Age 18 marks the time a person graduates from high school and leaves home and is regarded as the time sexual intercourse becomes socially approved. For college students, it is the time of "full premarital sexual rights" (Sprecher, 1989). However, the timing of first intercourse may vary. In one study of 126 males, the average age of first intercourse was 15.8. Of 93 females in the study, the average age of first intercourse was 19.1 (Alzate, 1989). In a national study males had first intercourse at 15.2; females at 16.2 (Zelnik & Shah, 1983).

:: Trends

The trend toward using a rational situation–ethics perspective in contrast to a rigid, legalistic one in making decisions about sexual behavior will continue. Individuals will rely more on their own judgment than on the rules of official religion.

However, our society wants to ensure that these individual decisions are not made at the expense of unwanted babies born to teenagers who cannot take care of them. The state of Wisconsin has passed a law that makes parents financially responsible for infants born to their unmarried children under age 18. Under this law, both sets of grandparents are required to support the infant if his or her parents cannot.

Masturbation will continue to become a more accepted behavior and topic in the media. Talk show hosts are no longer embarrassed to engage their guests in a discussion of masturbation (e.g., Johnny Carson talking with Dr. Ruth).

As the AIDS epidemic becomes more visible, people will be slightly more selective in their sexual partners and the use of condoms will increase considerably. Women, as well as men, will take initiatives in purchasing condoms and having them available for use. (Sexually transmitted diseases are discussed in Part VI.)

:: Summary

Sexual values are moral guidelines for appropriate behavior. Legalism, situationism, hedonism, asceticism, and rationalism are basic value frameworks within which an individual makes decisions.

Both liberal and conservative elements are reflected in our society's attitude toward sexuality. Sexual values are influenced by one's family, peers, and society.

In general, the sexual behaviors of blacks and whites are more similar than dissimilar. However, black males are more likely than white males to have interracial intercourse, to avoid masturbation, and to have intercourse with a partner who is on birth control. Black females are more likely than white females to avoid performing fellatio, to avoid manually stimulating their partner, and to use birth control pills.

Masturbation is sexual self–stimulation. Traditionally, masturbation has been viewed as immoral and harmful in the communities of religion, medicine, and psychotherapy. However, attitudes toward masturbation are changing. Although religious leaders may still express disapproval, most physicians and therapists are clearly positive about masturbation.

Petting is a frequent sexual behavior involving any sexual contact that does not include intercourse. Examples include kissing, breast stimulation, cunnilingus, and fellatio. There are different types of kissing, and kissing may or may not have emotional or erotic connotations. Cunnilingus is oral contact with the female genitals; fellatio is oral contact with the male genitals.

Sexual intercourse is a method of communication as well as a reproductive function. Intercourse also occurs in different interpersonal contexts before, during, outside, and after marriage.

Questions for Reflection

1. How have your sexual values and behaviors changed in the last five years? To what degree are these changes related to your education, peers, and love relationships?
2. What impact do you think having a number of sexual partners has on the individual involved? Is it positive or negative? Why?
3. Why do you feel blacks and whites view some sexual behaviors differently?

References

Alzate, H. Sexual behavior of unmarried colombian university students: A follow-up. *Archives of Sexual Behavior*, 1989, *18*, 239–250.

Belcastro, P. A. Sexual behavior differences between black and white students. *The Journal of Sex Research*, 1985, *21*, 56–67.

Billingham, Robert E., Kelly A. Smith, and J. Keller. The effect of chronological and theoretical birth order on sexual attitudes and behaviors. *Archives of Sexual Behavior*. 1989, *18*, 109–116.

Carroll, L. Concern with AIDS and the sexual behavior of college students. *Journal of Marriage and the Family*, 1988, *50*, 405–411.

Chase, Marilyn. Many who risk AIDS now weigh carefully whether to be tested. *The Wall Street Journal*, June 13, 1989, et passim.

Darling, C. A. and Sr. J. Davidson. Female sexual satisfaction: Effect of sexual experience. Paper, Southern Sociological Society, Knoxville, Tenn., 1984. Used by permission.

Fitzgerald, Michael. Falwell closes Moral Majority. *USA Today*, June 12, 1989, P. 3A.

Gordon, Barbara. *Jennifer Fever: Older men, younger women*. New York: Harper and Row, 1988.

Graham, S. *Lecture to young men, on chasity, intended also for the serious consideration of parents and guardians*. 10th ed. Boston: C. H. Pierce, 1848.

Hill, C. T., Z. Rubin and L. A. Poplau. Breakups before marriage: The end of 103 affairs. *Journal of Social Issues*, 1976, *32*, 147–168.

Hudson, W. W., G. J. Murphy, and P. S. Nurius. A short–form scale to measure liberal vs. conservative orientations toward human sexual expression. *Journal of Sex Research*, 1983, *19*, 258–272.

Katz, Roger C., Martin T. Gipson, Annette Kearl, and Melinda Kriskovich. Assessing sexual aversion in college students: The Sexual Aversion Scale. *Journal of Sex and Marital Therapy*, 1989, *15*, 135–140.

Leigh, Barbara Critchlow. Reasons for having and avoiding sex: Gender, sexual orientation, and relationship to sexual behavior. *Journal of Sex Research*, 1989, *26*, 199–209.

Haddock, J. W. Healthy family sexuality: Positive principles for educators and clinicians. *Journal of Applied Family and Child Studies*, 1989, *38*, 130–136.

Margolin, Leslie. Gender and the prerogatives of dating and marriage: An experimental assessment of a sample of college students. *Sex Roles*, 1989, *20*, 91–102.

Miller, Brent C. and Terrance D. Olson. Sexual attitudes and behavior of high school students in relation to background and contextual factors. *Journal of Sex Research*, 1988, *24*, 194–200.

Njeri, Itabari N. A new sexuality. *Essence*, January 1989, 66–68.

Notzer, N., D. Levran, S. Mashiach and S. Soffer. Effect of religiosity on sex attitudes, experience and contraception among university students. *Journal of Sex and Marital Therapy*, 1984, *10*, 57–62.

Nurius, P. S. and W. W. Hudson. A sexual profile of social groups. *Journal of Sex Education and Therapy*, 1982, *8*, no. 2, 15–30.

Randolph, L. B. The new black sexuality. *Ebony*, June 1989. 146–150.

Ratcliff, B. and D. Knox. University students motivations for intercourse. Paper, Southern Sociological Society, Memphis, Tenn., 1982. Used by permission.

Sprecher, S., K. McKinney, R. Walsh and C. Anderson. A revision of the Reiss Premarital Sexual Permissiveness Scale. *Journal of Marriage and the Family*, 1988, *50*, 821–828.

Sprecher, Susan. Premarital sexual standards for different categories of individuals. *Journal of Sex Research*, 1989, *26*, 232–248.

Staples, R. Black masculinity, hypersexuality, and sexual aggression. *The Black Family*. Edited by Robert Staples. Belmont, Calif.: Wadsworth Publishing Co., 1986, 57–63.

Statistical Abstract of the United States: 1990. 110th ed. Washington, D.C.: U.S. Bureau of the Census, 1990.

Thornton, A. Changing attitudes toward family issues in the United States. *Journal of Marriage and the Family*, 1989, *51*, 873–894.

Timberlake, Constance A. and Wayne D. Carpenter. Sexuality attitudes of black adults. *Family Relations*, 1990, *39*, 87–91.

Tissot, S. A. *Onania, or a treatise upon the disorders produced by masturbation*. A. Hume, Trans. London: J. Pridden, 1766. (Original work published in 1758).

Townsend, J. M. and G. D. Levy. Effects of potential partner's physical attractiveness and socioeconomic status on sexuality and partner selection. *Archives of Sexual Behavior*, 1990, *19*, no. 2, 149–164.

Williams, John, D. and Arthur P. Jacoby. The effects of premarital heterosexual and homosexual experience on dating and marriage desirability. *Journal of Marriage and the Family*, 1989, *51*, 489–497.

Zelnik, M., M. A. Koenig and Y. J. Kim. Sources of prescription contraceptives and subsequent pregnancy among young women. *Family Planning Perspectives*, 1984, *16*, 6–13.

Zelnik, M. and F. K. Shah. First intercourse among young Americans. *Family Planning Perspectives*, 1983, *15*, 64–70.

CHOICES

DECIDING WHETHER to have intercourse in a new relationship and what to do about the possibility of contracting AIDS are choices with which many are confronted.

Deciding About Intercourse

In each new relationship, a decision about whether to have intercourse must be made. From the first meeting, each partner thinks about this. You might consider the following issues when making this decision.

Personal Consequences

How do you predict you will feel about yourself after you have intercourse? An increasing number of individuals feel that if they are in love and have considered their decision carefully, the outcome will be positive:

I believe intercourse before marriage is okay under certain circumstances. I believe that when a person falls in love with another, it is then appropriate. This should be thought about very carefully for a long time, so as not to regret engaging in intercourse. I do not think intercourse should be a one-night thing, a one-week thing, or a one-month thing. You should grow to love and care for the person very much before giving that ''ultra'' special part of you to your partner. These feelings should be felt by both partners; if this is not the case, then you are not in love and you are not ''making love.''

Those who are not in love and have sex in a casual context sometimes feel badly about the experience:

I viewed sex as a new toy—something to try as frequently as possible. I did my share of sleeping around, and all it did for me was to give me a total loss of self-respect and a bad reputation. Besides, guys talk. I have heard rumors that I sleep with guys I have never slept with.

The first couple of guys I had sex with pressured me, and I regret it. I don't believe in casual sex; it brings more heartache than pleasure. It means so much more when you truly love the partner and you know your love is returned.

However, not all people who have intercourse within the context of a love relationship feel good about it:

The first time I had intercourse, I was in love and I thought he loved me. But he didn't. He used me, and I have always hated him for it.

Some also report positive consequences for casual sex:

We met one night at a mutual friend's party. We liked each other immediately. We talked, sipped some wine, and ended up spending the night together. Though we never saw each other again, I have very positive memories of the encounter.

The effect intercourse will have on you personally will be influenced by your religious values, your personal values, and the emotional involvement with your partner. Strong religious and personal values against intercourse plus a lack of emotional involvement usually mean guilt and regret following an intercourse experience. In contrast, values that regard intercourse as appropriate within the context of a love relationship are likely to result in feelings of satisfaction and contentment after intercourse.

Two researchers (Darling & Davidson, 1984) have compared the psychological and sexual satisfaction of 123 females who had intercourse with 79 females who had not had intercourse. Among the sexually experienced females, 75 percent were psychologically satisfied and 77 percent were physiologically satisfied with their sex lives. Among females who had not experienced coitus, only 46 percent reported psychological satisfaction and 47 percent reported physiological satisfaction with their sex lives.

Partner Consequences

Because a basic moral principle is to do no harm to others, it may be important to consider the effect of intercourse on your partner. Whereas intercourse may be a pleasurable experience with positive consequences for you, your partner may react differently. What are your partner's feelings about intercourse and her or his ability to handle the experience? If you suspect your partner will not feel good about it or be able to handle it psychologically, then you might reconsider whether intercourse would be appropriate with this person.

One man reported that after having intercourse with a woman he had just met, he awakened to the sound of her uncontrollable sobbing as she sat in the lotus position on the end of the bed. She was guilty, depressed, and regretted the experience. He said of the event, "If I had known how she was going to respond, we wouldn't have had intercourse."

Relationship Consequences

Does intercourse affect the stability of a couple's relationship? Apparently not. In a two–year follow–up on a study of the sexual behavior of 5,000 college sophomores and juniors who had ongoing sexual relationships (Hill et al., 1976), the researchers found that those who had had intercourse were no more likely to have broken up than those who had not. In another study (Ratcliff & Knox, 1982), less than 2 percent of 234 respondents said their relationship terminated as a result of their last intercourse. "Remained the same" was the most frequently chosen description of the effect intercourse had on the relationship.

Contraception

Another potential consequence of intercourse is pregnancy. Once a couple decides to have intercourse, a separate decision must be made as to whether intercourse should result in pregnancy. If the couple wants to avoid pregnancy, they must choose and effectively use a contraceptive method. But many do not. Among black women under age 20, 75 percent of all births are to unmarried women, compared to 25 percent of all births to young white women (Staples, 1986). In general, the interval between first intercourse and the use of a prescription method of birth control is about one year (Zelnik et al.,1984). Religiously devout individuals who have intercourse before marriage are particularly prone not to use contraceptives (Notzer et al., 1984). In most cases, the pregnancy was a surprise. One woman recalled:

It was the first time I had had intercourse, so I didn't really think I would get pregnant my first time. But I did. And when I told him I was pregnant, he told me he didn't have any money and couldn't help me pay for the abortion. He really wanted nothing to do with me after that.

Sexually Transmitted Diseases

Avoiding sexually transmitted diseases (STDs) is an important consideration in deciding whether to have intercourse. The result of increasing numbers of people having more frequent intercourse with more partners has been the rapid spread of the bacteria and viruses responsible for numerous varieties of STDs.

Although popular magazines suggest that there is less promiscuity among heterosexual persons (Randolph, 1989; Njeri, 1989), there is no conclusive documentation that people are actually changing their sexual behavior because of fear of AIDS. While over half of sexually active students claim that they have altered their sexual behavior, "there is no relationship between a reported decrease in the frequency of sex and reported coital frequency over the past year" (Carroll, 1988). Nevertheless, a sample of 382 college students reported being anxious about sexual activity because of the fear of contracting AIDS (Katz et al., 1989).

Although no method is completely safe, a sexually active person can reduce the chances of getting AIDS and other STDs by not having sex with someone who has multiple partners, by looking for sores or discharges and washing exposed areas after contact, and by urinating after sexual contact. Just as important is the use of a condom which is lubricated with non-oxynol 9 (the latter has been shown to kill the AIDS virus in laboratory animals). Foams, creams, or jellies may also be used as contraceptive agents in conjunction with condoms but the presence of non-oxynol 9 is most important. Read the labels on condoms and lubricants to insure that non-oxynol 9 is included.

Get Tested for AIDS?

There are two points of view about being tested for AIDS. An argument in favor of being tested is that drugs are now available (AZT) that can stave off the disease in infected individuals and prolong the lives of people who are already sick. In addition, knowing that one is infected would hopefully result in terminating sexual contact with others (there is no evidence that this actually occurs).

The argument against AIDS testing maintains that because there is no lasting cure for AIDS, testing for it is futile and only produces needless worry. Some people also fear that the results of such a test will be used against them (e. g., job discrimination).

Decisions

MORE THAN A century ago, young men and women faced great obstacles to spending time with each other. Not only were co-educational opportunities rare, but also the boy was expected to be introduced to the girl's parents before the partners could see each other socially. If her parents decided the boy was not suitable, no relationship would develop. If the partners did get together with their parents' approval, they were usually not alone. If they went out, the girl was often accompanied by a chaperone who would arrange the time, place, and events of the meetings between the partners. If they stayed inside, the boy would visit in the girl's house. They were expected to stay in the same room (usually the kitchen) with her parents. Private conversations were further limited because

there were no telephones and no cars to escape adult monitors.

Today, dating and mate selection decisions are made by the individual. While sitting in your marriage and family class, you might glance across the room and spot someone who is particularly interesting to you. You may envision developing a relationship with this person, including a number of dating events—dining together, going to parties, seeing movies, and attending concerts. The only obstacle to initiating the relationship is your instructor's lecture, which will be over in another 20 minutes. You may plan to approach this person after class and ask if you can borrow yesterday's class notes. If that person is not involved in another relationship and views you as a potential partner, your dating relationship will have begun.

The decisions regarding who to date, whether to live together, and who to select as a marital partner are among the concerns of Part Two. We begin by reviewing one of the most basic of all life choices—whether to stay single or get married.

5

Lifestyle Alternatives

CONTENTS

IS IT TRUE?

1. The ''real'' reason that society requires a marriage license is the physical care and economic support of children.

2. Women view ''loss of freedom'' as a major disadvantage of marriage as much as men do.

3. Married people live longer and are more healthy than single people.

4. More unmarried adults say that they are single by deliberate choice rather than by circumstances beyond their control.

5. Marriage will continue to be the dominant lifestyle choice for most Americans.

1 = T; 2 = F; 3 = T; 4 = T; 5 = T.

O NE WAY TO view your life is as a series of activities experienced alone or with other people. Eating, working, sleeping, seeing movies, attending concerts, and clipping coupons are all activities that occur within the context of a lifestyle choice. Although most people eventually marry, a small percent (5 to 10) remain single. An even smaller percentage live in communal or other alternative lifestyles.

:: Marriage

■ **DATA:** *Of all lifestyles, 95.7 percent of all American males (White, Black, Hispanic, and Asian) and 93.6 percent of all American females are married by age 75. Every year, about five million lovers become spouses (Statistical Abstract of the United States: 1990).*

As we noted earlier, marriage and the family have traditionally served several main functions in our society: to replace old members with new, socialized members; to regulate sexual behavior; and to stabilize adult personalities by providing companionship.

☐   C O N S I D E R A T I O N   ☐

The companionship-intimacy function of marriage has become more important as the form of marriage has changed. Unlike the traditional marriage, which was formal and authoritarian, emphasizing ritual and discipline, the egalitarian marriage pattern is delineated in terms of emotion, mutual affection, sympathetic understanding, and comradeship. The need for intimacy and companionship has become so strong that many couples consider divorce when they no longer feel "in love" or "able to communicate" with their partners. Other differences between the traditional and egalitarian marriage are presented in Table 5.1.

Recently, the traditional justifications for marriage have been questioned. There is little concern now that our society would "disappear" if people stopped marrying. Children would continue to be born, and the increase in single-parent families suggests that the wife and husband team is not the only pattern for rearing children.

The argument that marriage tends to regulate sexual behavior is true, as most spouses have intercourse with each other most of the time. But again, the issue is children, and the development of contraceptive technology has made it possible for individuals to make love without making babies. It is the use of contraceptives, not marriage, that now prevents unwanted children.

The emotional support each spouse derives from the marital relationship remains one of the basic functions of marriage. In our social world, which consists mainly of impersonal, secondary relationships, a sense of belonging may be particularly important. But proponents of singlehood are quick to point out that

I think I'd be really great for a guy. If it happens, it happens. If it doesn't, I'll get a kitten.

—OPRAH WINFREY

Married people report that they are happy more often than do singles, divorced and widowed people.

soaring divorce rates suggest that marriage does not offer much emotional support for some people and that an array of intimate friendships may be superior to the one-to-one marital relationship. Still, most of us have been socialized to believe that it is better to have one relationship for 50 years than to have 25 relationships of two-year durations.

Table 5.2 reflects that married people tend to be happier with their lifestyle than people who are never married, widowed, and separated/divorced. Although companionship and emotional support account for some of the increased happiness reported by married people, as a group, marrieds also have higher incomes (Oliver and Shapiro, 1990) and are more physically healthy (Feinson, 1985). These economic and health variables may contribute significantly to more positive ratings for those in the marital lifestyle.

▪▪ TABLE 5.1 **Traditional and Egalitarian Marriages Compared**

TRADITIONAL MARRIAGE	EGALITARIAN MARRIAGE
Emphasis on ritual and roles.	Emphasis on companionship.
Couples do not live together before marriage.	Couples may live together before marriage.
Wife takes husband's last name.	Wife may keep her maiden name.
Man dominant; woman submissive.	Neither spouse dominant.
Rigid roles for husband and wife.	Flexible roles for spouses.
One income (the husband's).	Two incomes.
Husband initiates sex; wife complies.	Sex initiated by either spouse.
Wife takes care of children.	Parents share childrearing.
Education important for husband, not for wife.	Education equally important for both.
Husband's career decides family residence.	Family residence decided by career of either spouse.

▪▪ TABLE 5.2 **Percent Reporting 'Very Happy' in a National Sample**

LIFESTYLE	MEN	WOMEN
Married	35.5	39.7
Never married	22.6	25.0
Widowed	21.1	29.0
Separated/divorced	17.7	19.3

SOURCE: GLENN AND WEAVER, *REASONS FOR MARRIAGE*, 1988, p. 319.

☐   C O N S I D E R A T I O N   ☐

Data that suggest that married people are happier, wealthier, and healthier may be interpreted in two different ways. Either marriage contributes to one's happiness, economic well-being, and health, or people who are happy, affluent, and healthy are more likely to marry. Perhaps both of these interpretations are operative.

▪ **DATA:** *When asked about the importance of marriage, 93 percent of adult women and 87 percent of adult men report that marriage is "extremely" or "quite" important (Thornton, 1989).*

Reasons for most of us being drawn to marriage include personal fulfillment, companionship, parenthood, and security.

Personal Fulfillment We are socialized as children to believe that getting married is what adult women and men do. Even if our parents are divorced, we learn that being married is what they wanted, but it didn't work out. Marriage often becomes a goal to achieve. Achieving that goal is assumed to give us a sense of personal fulfillment.

Companionship Many people marry primarily for companionship—for a *primary group relationship*. Primary groups are characterized by relationships that are intimate, personal, and informal. The family in which you grew up is a primary group.

Although marriage does not ensure it, companionship is the greatest expected benefit of marriage. Companionship is talking about and doing things with someone you love; it is creating a history with someone. "Only my husband and I know the things we've shared," said one wife. "The shrimp dinner at Ocean City, the walk down Bourbon Street, and the chipmunk in our backyard are part of our joint memory bank."

Just how many married people are there and what percent of our population do they represent?

■ **DATA:** *There are more than 110 million married people in our society. As a group, marrieds represent 63 percent of our population* (Statistical Abstract of the United States: 1990).

■ **DATA:** *Mexican Americans are more likely to be married than Blacks; Whites are more likely to be married than both groups* (Statistical Abstract of the United States: 1990).

Parenthood Some people marry to have children. Although some are willing to live with someone, it is rare that they express a desire for children outside of marriage. There is a strong presumption in our society that only spouses should have children. Role entry to parenthood is through marriage. One couple (both Ph.D.s) who had lived together for seven years said they decided to marry "so we could begin our family."

People get married for many reasons—love is only one of them.
—NATALIE CHILVERS

Over 90 percent of married people have children.

Security People also marry for the emotional and financial security marriage can provide. A 32-year-old single person remarked, "I've been through three relationships in the past year, and it's getting old. I want security. I want to get in a relationship where my partner and I will let ourselves completely go and commit ourselves to each other for the full trip."

☐   C O N S I D E R A T I O N   ☐

While some may marry for security, marriage is no longer a secure place to be. Since divorce in the United States can now be obtained by any spouse who wants one, marriage no longer provides the security—financial or otherwise—that it once did.

Some people view marriage as offering security for their old age. People don't want to grow old alone and have no one to care for or about them. One study of 76 older married couples in which one of the spouses was recuperating from being in the hospital supports this notion. The "well" spouse, regardless of gender, did provide physical care and psychological support for the sick spouse. The researcher (Johnson, 1985) concludes:

> The many years of shared experiences, of hardships as well as successes, are usually viewed as a source of cohesion. With the illness of one spouse, when additional demands are placed on the marriage, the interdependence that had developed over the years appears to provide the means to meet these needs, usually without reservations (p. 171).

If a person divorces, the desire to remarry is high. Five out of six divorced men and three out of four divorced women remarry. Regardless of the reason, marriage seems to offer what many people want and miss once they have experienced it.

☐   C O N S I D E R A T I O N   ☐

Although individuals may be drawn to marriage for reasons of security, companionship, etc., on the conscious level, unconscious motivations may also be operative. Individuals reared in a happy family of origin may seek to duplicate this perceived state of warmth, affection, and sharing. Alternatively, individuals reared in unhappy, abusive families may seek their own relationship to improve on what they observed in their parents' marriage.

:: Singlehood

We are witnessing a population explosion of "solos"—people who live alone, outside a family altogether.
—ALVIN TOFFLER

The lifestyle choice being considered by an increasing number of Americans is singlehood. Law separates people into "marrieds" and "singles." No matter how married a couple may feel, if they are not legally married by ceremony or common law, they are legally considered as two single individuals. Also, regardless of how single some married people may view themselves, they are still married.

Categories of Singles

There are about 48 million single adults over the age of 18 in the United States (*Statistical Abstract of the United States: 1990*), but they are not all alike. The different categories of singles include the never married, the separated or divorced, and the widowed.

Never Married Singles. The never marrieds represent the largest proportion of singles in the United States. Since 1970, there has been a dramatic increase in the percentage of men and women between the ages of 25 and 29 who are single. In 1970, 19 percent of the males and 11 percent of the females in these age ranges had never married; by 1988, these percentages had jumped to 30 percent and 43 percent, respectively (*Statistical Abstract of the United States: 1990*).

There is a larger percentage of single people at these ages now than in previous years for several reasons. These include a greater number of women in college, increased employment opportunities for women, more social support for single-hood (the women's movement, peers), the availability of effective contraception, and no available partner.

There is also a new wave of youth who feel that their commitment is to them-selves in early adulthood and to marriage only later, if at all. This translates into staying in school, establishing one's self in a career, and becoming economically and emotionally independent. The old pattern was to leap from school to mar-riage. The new pattern is to look, wait, and prepare before leaping.

Never marrieds are becoming happier with their lifestyle.

■ **DATA:** *Of never married males 25–39 in 1972–1976, 13.2 percent reported that they were "very happy" compared to 24.3 percent of never married males in 1982–1986. Similarly, of never married females 25–39 in 1972–1976, 13.7 percent reported that they were "very happy" compared to 24.4 percent of never married females in 1982–1986 (Glenn & Weaver, 1988, 319).*

> *It is true that I never should have married, but I didn't want to live without a man. Brought up to respect the conventions, love had to end in marriage. I'm afraid it did.*
> —BETTE DAVIS

☐　　　　C O N S I D E R A T I O N　　　　☐

In explaining why never marrieds are becoming happier with their lifestyle, Glenn and Weaver (1988) observed that regular sexual relations outside of marriage are more socially accepted and available, and less stigmatized than in the past.

Separated and Divorced Singles. There is a tendency to think of single people as only those who have never married. But statistics show otherwise.

■ **DATA:** *There are divorced men and women who are 'single again.' As a group, the divorced represent 7.8 percent of our adult population. In the United States, 7.7 percent of all white adults, 10 percent of all black adults and 7.4 percent of all adults of other races are divorced* (Statistical Abstract of the United States: 1990).

For many of the divorced, the return to singlehood is not an easy transition. The separated and divorced are the least likely to say that they are "very happy" with

People who are alone
are not necessarily
lonely.

their life: only 18 percent of divorced males compared to 36 percent of married males say they are "very happy." Only 19 percent of divorced females compared to 40 percent of married females say they are "very happy" (Glenn & Weaver, 1988, 319). The divorced are also more likely to commit suicide than the married (Stack, 1990).

After the initial impact of separation and divorce, most people remarry or adjust to and enjoy singlehood. One divorced man said, "I can stand being alone.

Perhaps I even have a gift for it. What I can't stand is taking what's available until something better comes along."

Widowed Singles   Whereas some separated and divorced people choose to be single rather than remain in an unhappy marriage, the widowed are forced into singlehood.

■ **DATA:** *There are widowed men and widowed women in our society. As a group, the widowed represent 7.6 percent of our population. In the United States, 7.5 percent of all white adults, 9 percent of all black adults, and 4.3 percent of all adults of other races are widowed* (Statistical Abstract of the United States: 1990).

As a group, the widowed are happier than the divorced but not as happy as the married. Twenty-one percent of widowed males in contrast to 18 percent of divorced males and 36 percent of married males report that they are "very happy." For females, 29 percent of the widowed compared to 19 percent of the divorced and 40 percent of the married report that they are "very happy" (Glenn & Weaver, 1988, 319).

Singlehood as a Lifestyle Choice

Singlehood has different meanings to the never married, the separated, the divorced, and the widowed, but there are two basic ways of viewing it—as a lifestyle or as a stage leading to marriage or remarriage. Table 5.3 reviews why people elect to stay single and to avoid getting married.

■ **DATA:** *When 482 adults were asked why they were unmarried, 46 percent said by deliberate choice (Austrom & Hanel, 1985).*

In interpreting the above data, it is important to recognize that some unmarried people who report that singlehood is their choice may be doing so in order to resolve cognitive dissonance. The term *cognitive dissonance* refers to a psychological state of conflict resulting from inconsistency between one's beliefs and one's actions. A person who has an underlying belief that marriage is a desirable state, yet has not married, may experience cognitive dissonance. In order to resolve this dissonance (or conflict) the person may adopt the position that singlehood is a choice.

TABLE 5.3 **Reasons To Remain Single**

BENEFITS OF SINGLEHOOD	DISADVANTAGES OF MARRIAGE
Freedom to have a variety of interpersonal relationships.	Restriction to one basic relationship.
Freedom to move from city to city.	Restriction of career mobility.
Freedom to travel.	Travel restricted by spouse and children.
Responsibility for oneself only.	Responsibility for spouse and children.
Not required to interact with others on an intimate basis.	Required to interact with others in household.
Spontaneous lifestyle.	Life sometimes too routine.

As of the time this book went to press, Arsenio Hall, Linda Ronstadt, and Eddie Murphy are examples of people in our society who have never married.

Exhibits 5.1 and 5.2 reflect the evaluation of being single as a lifestyle from the viewpoint of a woman and a man who have chosen to be single.

■ **DATA:** *When 482 adults were asked why they were unmarried, 23 percent said by circumstances beyond their control (Austrom & Hanel, 1985).*

One circumstance which accounts for singlehood is the lack of a marriageable partner. This is particularly true for black women. In a national survey of Black Americans, 35 and 38 percent of the females said that they were married or romantically involved in contrast to 53 and 49 percent of the males (Tucker & Taylor, 1989). Not only are there fewer single black males than single black females, the black males who are single often do not have the economic characteristics which encourage marriage. "Black men do not marry until they are capable of fulfilling the provider role" (p. 661).

EXHIBIT 5.1

::

My Life as a Never Married Woman

At this point in my life, I enjoy being single. Of course, there are disadvantages to singlehood, but I like the privacy and independence that it affords me.

Singlehood gives me a tremendous amount of freedom and time. Since I am responsible only for myself, I can decide to relocate and/or continue my education. This freedom allows me to change, grow, and develop as a person. Part of my growth is dependent on maintaining diverse relationships, including male friendships. Being single, I can consciously choose to become romantically involved with males who would not be threatened by my male friends. Singlehood permits all sorts of small but important freedoms. For example, I can sleep late, read in bed, travel, visit with friends after work, and eat odd meals at unusual times. I also have the option not to prepare meals, clean the house, or answer the phone.

Being single has made me more aware of the importance of developing a positive self-image and learning to "pat myself" on the back. It has been essential for my mental health to develop a good support system and to confide in close friends. I have also discovered the need to be competent in traditionally male areas of expertise, such as car and house repairs. Learning simple tasks like replacing a windowpane, repairing the lawn mower, and tuning the car engine increases my self-confidence and sense of independence.

I feel comfortable with my single status after listening to some of my married female friends discuss what is expected of them in terms of their role as a wife and mother. This is not a feeling of superiority because being comfortable with my choice does not prevent an occasional sense of ostracism for not being married. Also, feeling good about myself does not eliminate all the anxiety I have about singlehood. For example, I wonder if I am possibly missing something wonderful by not having children.

One of the most difficult aspects of singlehood to cope with is the attitude and behavior of a few of my peers. The belief that being single indicates a personality defect makes me defensive about my lifestyle. Occasionally, I feel that I am viewed as a threat to married females, particularly if I have a professional relationship with their husbands. Also, my family is not completely supportive of my single status. Although my father was pleased and proud of my independence, his death removed much of my family support, and I believe that my mother and sisters would be relieved if I married.

The fact that I am single does not mean that I do not want a serious long-term relationship. However, being single is a challenge because, to be independent and to be comfortable enough to live alone, I have to like myself. So even though there are times I am lonely, overall I enjoy being single.

Singlehood and Loneliness

It is sometimes assumed that most unmarried people are unhappy because they live alone—that to be alone is to be unhappy. But in one study, more than 400 older never married men and women said that their happiness depends not on whether they interact with others but on their standard of living and level of activity (Keith, 1986). Those who had adequate enough incomes to avoid having to always worry about money and who had enough things to do that they enjoyed (either through employment or self-generated activity) were happy.

However, other studies have suggested the importance of living with others. Anson (1989) analyzed data from the National Health Interview Survey and found that individuals who live with another adult have fewer acute conditions and a lower frequency of being ill. In the past, it was believed that being married somehow produced an immunity to illness. The research by Anson clearly indicated the importance of a "proximate adult," not necessarily a marriage partner.

> I love the freedom that I have. I don't have to worry about a man's wardrobe, or his relatives, or his schedule, or his menu, or his allergies. I would not be married again.
> —ANN LANDERS

Singlehood as a Stage

For some people, singlehood is not a permanent choice but a stage between various lifestyle choices they make throughout their lives. A fairly common pattern is for a person to experience singlehood, marriage, divorce (return to singlehood), living together, and remarriage. The decision to opt for any of these at any given time may be complex. Contributing to the selection of one lifestyle alternative is the perception of the positive and negative consequences of doing so compared to those of the other alternatives. The single person may be free but lonely and perceive marriage as worth the cost of lost freedom to gain companionship. The married person may be secure but bored and view the variety of singlehood as worth the cost of security. The person who lives with another may enjoy the spontaneity of "a relationship based on love, not law" but not like the lack of permanence of the relationship. Legitimizing the relationship through marriage may be worth risking the loss of some spontaneity.

☐   C O N S I D E R A T I O N   ☐

Decisions to end or maintain a specific relationship can be explained in terms of exchange theory. People enter and remain in relationships or lifestyles only as long as the individuals evaluate these relationships and lifestyles as profitable (profit in exchange terms is rewards minus costs). "I know it sounds crazy," said one 40-year-old bachelor, "but I feel it's time for me to be married because the advantages of this freedom don't mean anything anymore."

■■ Other Lifestyle Alternatives

Marriage or singlehood are two major lifestyle alternatives (see the Lifestyle Preference Inventory in the following Self-Assessment for a list of lifestyles). Other alternatives include living a heterosexual, homosexual, or bisexual lifestyle, living

EXHIBIT 5.2

My Life as a Never Married Man

I am not opposed to marriage. I am not opposed to courtship. I like women. I approve of women. I approve of men and women together. Despite much that I see to destroy my faith in old-fashioned love, I still believe in love—even if I have to admit I believe in that very outdated thing called "romantic love!"

I am 59 years old and I have never been married. I am an only child. I did not ever sit down and make a decision that I was never going to marry. I did not begin my life with the idea that I wanted to end it unmarried. I often think how nice it might have been had I married and had a family; but, perhaps I am something of a coward, for I often thank my lucky stars that I do not have a nagging "bitchy" wife and a house full of mean and ungrateful children! Somewhere along the line, I quietly decided that I did not wish to marry and I do not regret that decision. There is no history of divorce in my family. My parents and my grandparents were very happily married and well-adjusted people.

I do believe very much in the sacredness of marriage. I believe that marriage is a serious legal institution. I think of it as a legal commitment made by two people who have bonded themselves together—through vows or "oaths"—who have promised mutual respect, admiration, friendship and love.

I am appalled at people today who seem to consider marriage as nothing more than an amusing arrangement that can be broken, discarded, and forgotten. I am shocked at people who, after 25–30 years of marriage, are seeking separations and divorces. I am constantly amazed at parents and children who do not seem to have any avenue of communication.

I must confess that I often feel grateful that I do not run the risk of falling "out" of love with a married partner. I have observed that far too many husbands and wives are strangers to one another and to their children. I have observed that often, today, only a fraction of life is actually lived in the home. When I was young, people still thought of their home as their "castle." Today, alas, castles and homes do not seem to provide the security they once did. I am an "old fogey" for I am shocked at the growing number of abortions and out-of-wedlock births, and the acceptance of unromantic and permissive sex.

I see so much so-called "love" that seems to be merely infatuation or sexual excitement. I am certainly very much aware of the "facts of life" but I still find myself shocked at the openness of today's "sexual freedom." I was reared in a long-ago era when one was still taught that it was not a sin to have sexual intercourse with one's marriage partner but it was a sin to have sexual relations outside of marriage. I was taught that marital partners should always be true to one another.

I think one of my "problems" is that I am an incurable romantic and romantics find it hard to adjust to the cold hard facts of the real world! Just as people who have never had children often feel they can give advice to parents as to how to rear their children, perhaps I, who have never been married, might be presumptuous and share with you my extremely "old-fashioned" ideas about love, courtship and marriage.

In my own romantic, perhaps "foolish" way, I have always thought that courtship was a time when two people, attracted to one another, enjoyed each other's company and the company of their friends and if the friendship began to develop into love, then one began to think

in a commune, having a group marriage, being a single parent, and living together. We will discuss living together in Chapter 6. Here, we examine several other lifestyles.

Homosexual Lifestyle

While most single people are heterosexual, some are homosexual. In this section we review the definition and incidence of homosexuality and what homosexual relationships are like.

seriously of the other person as a lifetime mate and one gave careful consideration to mutual interests, backgrounds, goals in life, compatibility. One became increasingly aware of the possibility of uniting two lives, of trying to arrive at a complete understanding, a perfect partnership of democratic planning and mutual sharing. I have always felt that people who get married should be friends as well as lovers, that they should "like" one another as well as "love" or desire them.

I see many people (who are in marital situations) who take one another for granted. In my own romantic way, I have always felt that husbands and wives should remain affectionate, considerate, understanding, loving—even after the honeymoon is over. Somehow, I have thought that the "ideal" couple would always be as polite and courteous to one another as they were to their friends.

I look about me and see parents who are deeply pained and hurt by the indifference and the rudeness and embarrassing behaviour of their children and I am selfish enough to be glad that I will never have that problem. I see many parents as passive bystanders and others who are not sure how to go about being a parent. I see parents who work and sacrifice in order to provide their children with things the children often do not want or need or even appreciate and I am glad I will never have that experience.

I will never have to worry about dividing property—especially land and inherited possessions and I am glad I will not have to experience the bitterness, humiliation, and pain of divorce.

Philip Roth's autobiography relates that the author whistled on the way to his former wife's funeral and said at her casket: "You're dead and I didn't have to do it."

There was a time when a certain amount of pity and amused ridicule was felt toward the single person—the proverbial "old maid" or "sour old bachelor." Such people were thought of as eccentric and peculiar and "unwanted." The day of feeling sorry for the unmarried members of the family has long since passed away. Today, we see single people who lead perfectly happy and content lives, who maintain households and get along very well all alone. They have a freedom often envied by their married relatives. They have an affluence which is often a target of jealousy from those who have others to consider. It is not at all uncommon today to see a single man pushing a cart in a grocery store, washing clothes at a laundry mat, cooking a meal for guests, setting a table, cleaning with a vacuum, entertaining guests.

One of my favorite modern plays is Arthur Miller's *The Price*. The theme of that drama is that for every decision we make in life, we pay a price. I chose not to marry and I have paid a price for it. I do sometimes think how nice it would be to have a family and I often wonder what will become of the things which I cherish—those things left to me as family heirlooms and those things which I have acquired. Since I am an only child, I have no one to leave the family items to who would appreciate them from the family standpoint. What I have will, very likely, at my death be sold at auction or distributed by lawyers amongst largely indifferent cousins.

The irony, of course, is that I would not have been able to travel throughout Europe, into Africa and Asia, Mexico and throughout the United States or been able to do so many of the things I have been able to do had I had a family!

So, indeed a "price" has been paid.

Definition and Incidence *Homosexuality* refers to both emotional attachment and sexual attraction to those of one's own biological sex. Homosexual people, who are also called "gay" people, may be either men or women. When most people use the term *homosexual*, they mean a man who has an emotional and sexual preference for other men. The term *lesbian* refers to a woman who has an emotional and sexual preference for other women.

■ **DATA:** *In a study of 144 undergraduate males, 19 percent reported having had a homosexual contact; of 146 undergraduate females, 8 percent reported having had a homosexual contact (Alzate, 1989). It is commonly recognized that about 10 percent, or 25 million people in the United States are homosexual individuals.*

Lifestyle Preference Inventory

Below is a list of lifestyle choices. To indicate your preference, assign a number from 0 to 10 for each lifestyle (0 = no desire to experience this lifestyle; 10 = a strong desire).

Lifestyle	Preference
Sexually monogamous	_____
Sexually open	_____
Singlehood	
Single until meet "right" person	_____
Single until establish career	_____
Single forever	_____
Marriage	
Be married	_____
Traditional roles	_____
Shared roles	_____
One income or career	_____
Two incomes or careers	_____
Group marriage	_____
Sexual	
Heterosexual	_____
Homosexual	_____
Bisexual	_____
Children	
None	_____

Lifestyle	Preference
One	_____
Two	_____
Three	_____
Four or more	_____
Live Together	
To further assess relationship	_____
As a prelude to marriage	_____
As a permanent alternative to marriage	_____
For economic convenience	_____
Housing	
Live alone	_____
Live with someone of same sex	_____
Live with someone of opposite sex	_____
Live in commune	_____

Based on the preferences you selected, write a brief description of the lifestyle you prefer. If you are involved in a relationship, also ask your partner to indicate her or his preferences for each of these lifestyles.

Note: This Self-Assessment is intended to be fun and thought provoking, it is not a clinical or diagnostic instrument.

Rarely is anyone entirely homosexual or heterosexual in both attitudes and behavior. Rather, our sexual orientation can be placed on a continuum devised by Kinsey et al. (1953) and illustrated in Figure 5.1. Gay people are young and old, white and black, single and married, and from all social classes, occupations, and religions. The idea that a homosexual person is instantly recognizable is false. Although some effeminate men are homosexual, others are not.

In our society, there is a cultural bias against homosexuals. Students at Harvard and the University of North Dakota were very rejecting of partners who had had previous homosexual encounters. Such rejection (by both men and women)

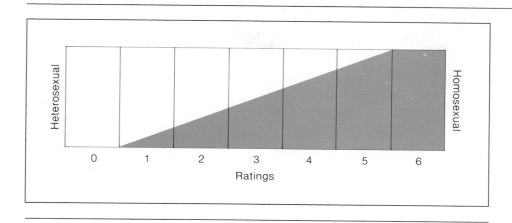

:: FIGURE 5.1
**The
Heterosexual-
Homosexual
Rating Scale**
SOURCE Kinsey, et al., 1953.

"seems to represent a generalized homophobia rather than a concern about AIDS" (Williams & Jacoby, 1989). Some research suggests that having a greater amount of contact with homosexuals is related to being less homophobic (Green, 1989).

Gay Male Relationships While many gay men establish lasting emotional and sexual relationships, they may have more difficulty in doing so, compared to "straight" (heterosexual) men. Several reasons may account for the tendency for gay males to have short-term relationships. First, men in our culture, in general, are socialized to be sexually active and to pursue a variety of sexual relationships.

Second, gay relationships also have few social and economic supports. When a heterosexual couple are in love, they can be public about their feelings and expect others to approve of their relationship. Many gay couples, particularly men, feel they must hide their expression of affection in public. In addition, their "marriage" is illegal, and their living together is suspect. Finally, gays cannot file joint tax returns, collect Social Security widowhood benefits, or be covered on each other's health insurance policies.

Some research suggests that gay men may be becoming more discriminating in their sexual relationships (Schechter et al., 1988). With public awareness of the fact that AIDS (acquired immune deficiency syndrome) kills and anyone who has sex with others is a potential victim, gay males have reduced the number of sexual partners they have.

■ **DATA:** *In 1985, 361 homosexual men reported a median of 8 sexual partners; in 1987, that number had dropped to a median of 5 (median means that half of the men had more and half less than the identified number) (Schechter et al., 1988).*

☐   C O N S I D E R A T I O N   ☐

In interpreting data on homosexual relationships, it is important to keep in mind that research on the homosexual population is often biased because of sampling difficul-

continued on next page

Gay males are the *least* likely to molest young children.

ties. For example, research on gay men may be based on samples that are easily accessible, such as those found in gay bars. Gay men who are in emotional, long-term pair-bonded relationships are underrepresented in such samples because they, like their heterosexual pair-bonded counterparts, are usually not found in bars, but rather are home with their partners. Therefore, the percentage of gay men in long-term pair-bonded relationships may be underestimated.

It [homosexuality] is not a new life style—just a more public one.

—VERN L. BULLOUGH

Gays have also increased the use of "safe sex" (use of a condom during anal intercourse, oral-genital contact without ejaculation, and mutual masturbation). "These shifts appear to attest to the efficacy of both public information and word-of-mouth in the 6 years since the onslaught of the AIDS epidemic began" (Siegel & Glassman, 1989). Previous researchers have also reported that homosexually active men have reduced sexual practices that put them at increased risk for acquiring or transmitting the AIDS virus (McCusker et al., 1988). In a study on condom use among gay and bisexual men, researchers found that not using condoms was associated with being "high" on drugs and/or alcohol during sex (Valdiserri et al., 1988).

Gay Female Relationships   Compared to homosexual males, lesbians have traditionally had fewer sexual partners and more emphasis on the emotional aspect of the relationship.

Although gay female relationships normally last longer than gay male relationships, long-term relationships (20 years or more) are rare. Serial monogamy (one relationship at a time) seems to be the dominant lesbian life pattern. Loss of romantic love or the inability to sustain feelings across time seem to be major reasons for the breakup of gay female relationships. Just as strong love feelings brought them together, their absence makes each person in a relationship question why they stay together. "I don't know what happened," said one woman. "I just wasn't in love with her anymore. And I couldn't fake my feelings any longer, so I left her."

Gay women also are typically denied the experience of rearing children; being parents can have a stabilizing effect on relationships. Prejudice against homosexuals being parents springs from the belief that their children will also become homosexual. But 36 of 37 children reared by lesbian or transsexual parents had heterosexual gender role preferences (Green, 1978).

When homosexual and heterosexual relationships are compared, which couples exhibit the greatest degree of satisfaction and commitment? In a comparison of the relationships of 25 lesbians, 25 homosexual males, 25 heterosexual females, and 25 heterosexual males, the researchers (Duffy & Rusbult, 1985/86) found that gender was more important than sexual preference in predicting relationship satisfaction. Both lesbians and heterosexual women reported investing more in their relationships and being more commited to maintaining their relationships than homosexual or heterosexual men. Greater commitment was also associated with greater satisfaction.

Gay couples enjoy the same emotional highs as heterosexual couples.

◻   C O N S I D E R A T I O N   ◻

Just as some people do not choose to be heterosexual but feel "naturally" inclined
toward those of the opposite sex, some people do not choose to be homosexual but
feel "naturally" inclined toward those of the same sex. In addition, human sexual
orientation is variable across time. Some individuals may feel very emotionally and
sexually attracted to those of the opposite sex at one point in their lives but equally
emotionally and sexually attracted to those of the same sex at another time in their
lives. Hence, some previously heterosexual individuals become involved in homosexual relationships and vice versa.

Communal Lifestyle

Historical analysis has shown communal movements are not randomly distributed across time and space but flourish only at points of relatively sharp social and cultural discontinuity.
—ANGELA AIDALA

Single individuals and married couples (with or without children) may choose a
lifestyle that includes an array of interpersonal relationships and join a *commune*.
Also referred to as an *intentional community*, a *collective*, or a *cooperative*, a commune
is a group of three or more adults with no legal or blood ties who live together by
free choice. Many groups have about six members; the Farm in Summertown,
Tennessee, has more than 300 members.

■ **DATA:** *There are over 1000 communes in the United States, Canada, and other countries (Springs, 1989).*

The Federation of Egalitarian Communities represents a network of communal
groups throughout North America. These communes include Twin Oaks in Louisa, Virginia; Sandhill in Rutledge, Missouri; and Mettanokit in Greenville, New
Hampshire. Individuals who join a commune usually adhere to a unique philosophy. The philosophy of communes in the Federation follows:

■ holding its land, labor, and other resources in common.
■ practicing nonviolence.
■ working to establish the equality of all people and not permit discrimination on
   the basis of race, class, creed, ethnic origin, age, sex, or sexual orientation.
■ acting to conserve natural resources for present and future generations while
   striving continually to improve ecological awareness and practice.
■ creating processes for group communication and participation and providing
   an environment that supports people's development (Federation of Egalitarian
   Communities, 1989, p.1).

Group Marriage

While the principles listed above are common to many communes, sexual sharing
is rare. When individuals in a group living arrangement agree to open sexual
access to each other, they are involved in a group marriage. As noted in Chapter
1, the Oneida Community featured group marriage. John Humphrey Noyes, its
founder, made clear his nonexclusive view of marriage:

We can enter into no engagements with each other which shall limit the range of our affections as they are limited in the matrimonial engagements by the fashion of this world (Noyes, 1931, 17).

In the 1870s there were about 300 adults in the Oneida Community each of whom was considered married to each other. They called their arrangement "complex marriage" and used withdrawal as a form of birth control. Unique pair bonding did not occur and the decision of who would bear children was decided by a committee. Being young and beautiful were the primary qualifications for getting permission to conceive as a woman; being spiritually mature was the chief qualification for being selected as a father. Stirpiculture ("the breeding of special stocks or races") was the term used to describe Oneida's eugenics program. Fifty-eight children were born under this system (Sill, 1990).

Because of dissatisfaction among some of the members preferring conventional marriage and pressure from the outside by local clergy, the idea of complex marriage was dropped. Many members subsequently married.

A modern day example of group marriage is the Kerista commune in San Francisco founded by Bro Jud in 1971. It currently has 28 members who practice what they call "polyfidelity."

It calls for a lifetime commitment not to one partner but to a group called a Best Friend Identity Cluster (B-FIC). The commune thus is not one large group marriage as the Oneida, but currently includes three Best Friend Identity Clusters as well as some persons not affiliated with any B-FIC. A new member of Kerista may apply for membership in a B-FIC. Membership in a cluster is granted only with unanimous agreement of B-FIC members. A three month period of Transitional Celibacy is observed by a new member before beginning sexual relations within the B-FIC. This period allows time for VD and AIDS tests (Sill, 1990, 24).

Eve, who helped in the development of the commune, observed the advantages of polyfidelity:

1. The combination of the best features of traditional marriage (lasting intimacy, trust, depth of relationships, secure home life) with the best features of the "open" lifestyle (variety and excitement).
2. It's a way for nonmonogamous persons to deal with AIDS (a screening process and fidelity within the group) (Sill, 1990, p. 24).

In spite of these presumed advantages, there seems to be little interest on the part of college students to participate in a group marriage.

■ **DATA:** *Out of 526 college students, 5 percent of the men and 1 percent of the women reported that they would be willing to participate in a group marriage (Billingham & Sack, 1986).*

Single Parenthood

Some individuals who are involved in neither a monogamous or group marriage choose to have and rear a child. We will discuss this topic in detail in Chapter 13 on Planning Children and Birth Control. Also, since most single-parent families result from divorce, we will discuss the nature of these families in Chapter 16 on "Divorce and Widowhood."

:: Trends

At least for the foreseeable future, marriage will continue to be the dominant lifestyle choice for most Americans. Although some people may delay getting married for educational or career reasons, there is no evidence of a major trend away from marriage.

However, marriage and family structures in the United States are becoming more "fragile, temporary and shrinking in size and importance" (John, 1988, p. 355). Increased singlehood, living together, childfree marriage, and divorce suggest that marriage may be a lifestyle most individuals sample at some time in their lifespan. But it is becoming increasingly more common that other lifestyles will be experienced in addition to marriage. Some researchers suggest that we will eventually stop thinking of marriage and lifestyle alternatives to it and develop a view of sexually-based primary relationships that are expressed in a variety of forms. (Scanzoni et al., 1989).

:: Summary

Traditionally, marriage has existed to replenish society with socialized members, to regulate sexual behavior, and to stabilize adult personalities. However, the problem of overpopulation and the availability of convenient, effective contraception have undermined the first two functions. Emotional support is the primary function of marriage today.

The decision to marry often involves assessing the advantages and disadvantages of marriage compared to singlehood. Marriage offers a potentially intense primary relationship over time and avoids the potential loneliness associated with singlehood. But singlehood offers freedom to do as one wishes and avoids the obstacles to personal fulfillment associated with marriage. For many Americans, the decision to marry or to be single is not permanent. Many singles contemplate marriage, and many marrieds ponder whether they should stay married and, indeed, many people eventually divorce.

About 25 million Americans are homosexual. These individuals are victims of considerable social ridicule and prejudice. Nevertheless, many homosexuals establish fulfilling emotional and sexual relationships with each other.

Communal living is another infrequently chosen lifestyle option. There are hundreds of communes to select from, including those that emphasize religion, ideology, or group marriage. The advantages of communal arrangements include living with several people in an intimate environment and sharing expenses.

Group marriage also has few followers. This lifestyle has limited social support and considerable legal sanctions against it.

While marriage continues to be the dominant choice for most Americans, a growing number of people will spend some amount of time in other lifestyles.

Questions for Reflection

1. Which lifestyle do you feel offers the most benefits? Why?
2. How would you defend your involvement in each lifestyle choice to your grandparents?
3. What do you think will be the dominant lifestyle in the year 2000? Why?

References

Alzate, H. Sexual behavior of unmarried Colombian university students: A follow-up. *Archives of Sexual Behavior,* 1989, *18,* 239–250.

Anson, Ofra. Marital status and women's health revisited: The importance of a proximate adult. *Journal of Marriage and the Family,* 1989, *51,* 185–194.

Austrom, D. and K. Hanel. Psychological issues of single life in Canada: An exploratory study. *International Journal of Women's Studies,* 1985, *8,* 12–23.

Billingham, R. E. and A. R. Sack. Gender differences in college students' willingness to participate in alternative marriage and family relationships. *Family Perspective,* 1986, *20,* 37–44.

Duffy, S. M. and C. E. Rusbult. Satisfaction and commitment in homosexual and heterosexual relationships. *Journal of Homosexuality,* 1985/86, *12,* 1–24.

Fay, R. E., C. F. Turner, A. D. Klassen, and J. H. Gagnon. Prevalence and patterns of same-gender sexual contact among men. *Science,* 1989, *243,* 338–348.

Federation of Egalitarian Communities. 1989. *Sharing the Dream,* Box FB4, Tecumseh, MO, 65760.

Feinson, M. C. Aging and mental health. *Research on Aging,* 1985, *7,* 155–174.

Glenn, N. D. and C. N. Weaver. The changing relationship of marital status to reported happiness. *Journal of Marriage and the Family,* 1988, *50,* 317–324.

Green, R. Sexual identity of 37 children raised by homosexual or transsexual parents. *American Journal of Psychiatry,* 1978, *135,* 692–697.

Green, S. K. Attitudes of family therapists toward AIDS, persons with AIDS, and homosexuals. Dissertation, School of Home Economics, Texas Tech, Lubbock, Tex., 1989. Used by permission of Shelly Green.

John, Robert. The Native American family. *Ethnic families in America: Patterns and variations.* Edited by C. H. Mindel, R.W. Habenstein, and R. Wright, Jr. New York: Elsevier, 1988, pp. 325–363.

Johnson, C. L. The impact of illness on late-life marriages. *Journal of Marriage and the Family,* 1985, *47,* 165–172.

Keith, P. M. Isolation of the unmarried in later life. *Family Relations,* 1986, *35,* 389–396.

Kinsey, A. C., W. B. Pomeroy, C. E. Martin, and P. H. Gebhard. *Sexual behavior in the human female.* Philadelphia: W. B. Saunders, 1953. Reprinted by permission of the Kinsey Institute for Research in Sex, Gender, and Reproduction, Inc. (Book reprinted in 1970 by Pocket Books).

McCusker, J., A. M. Stoddard, K. H. Mayer, J. Zapka, C. Morrison, and S. P. Saltzman. Effects of HIV antibody test knowledge on subsequent sexual behaviors in a cohort of homosexually active men. *American Journal of Public Health,* 1988, *78,* 462–467.

Noyes, G. W. 1932. *John Humphrey Noyes: The Putney Community.* (no publisher) Cited in Sill, John S. Utopian group marriage in the 19th and 20th centuries: Oneida community and Kerista commune. *Free Inquiry in Creative Sociology,* 1990, *18,* 21–28.

Oliver, M. L. and T. M. Shapiro. Wealth of a nation: A reassessment of asset inequality in America shows at least one third of households are asset poor. *The American Journal of Economics and Sociology,* 1990, *49,* 129–152.

Rice, Susan. Single, older childless women: Differences between never-married and widowed women in life satisfaction and social support. *Journal of Gerontological Social Work,* 1989, *13,* 35–47.

Scanzoni, J., K. Polonko, J. Teachman, and L. Thompson. *The sexual bond: Rethinking families and close relationships.* Newbury Park, Calif.: Sage, 1989.

Schechter, M. T. et al. Patterns of sexual behavior and condom use in a cohort of homosexual men. *American Journal of Public Health,* 1988, *78,* 1535–1538.

Siegel, K. and M. Glassman. Individual and aggregate level change in sexual behavior among gay men at risk for AIDS. *Archives of Sexual Behavior,* 1989, *18,* 335–346.

Sill, John. Utopian group marriage in the 19th and 20th centuries: Oneida community and Kerista commune. *Free Inquiry in Creative Sociology,* 1990, *28,* 21–28.

Springs, H. H. 1989. *New Age Community Guidebook.* Available from Community Bookshelf, Route 1, Box 155-F, Rutledge, MO, 63563.

Stack, Steven. New micro-level data on the impact of divorce on suicide, 1959–1980: A test on two theories. *Journal of Marriage and the Family,* 1990, *52,* 119–127.

Statistical Abstract of the United States: 1990. 110th ed. Washington, D.C.: U.S. Bureau of the Census, 1990.

Thornton, A. Changing attitudes toward family issues. *Journal of Marriage and the Family,* 1989, *51,* 878–893.

Tucker, M. Belinda and Robert J. Taylor. Demographic correlates of relationship status among Black Americans. *Journal of Marriage and the Family,* 1989, *51,* 655–665.

Valdiserri, R. O. et al. Variables influencing condom use in a cohort of gay and bisexual men. *American Journal of Public Health,* 1988, *78,* 801–805.

Williams, John D. & A. P. Jacoby. The effects of premarital heterosexual and homosexual experience on dating and marriage desirability. *Journal of Marriage and the Family,* 1989, *51,* 489–499.

CHOICES

BECAUSE OUR SOCIETY is becoming more tolerant of alternative lifestyles, a number of choices are realistic options for you. The basic choices and issues to consider follow.

Is Marriage for You?

The decision to marry or not might be based on the perceived consequences (positive and negative) of the respective lifestyles. The primary benefits of marriage include increased companionship, security, parenthood, and the development of a shared history. Although cohabitants may have made an emotional commitment to each other, spouses additionally have made a social and legal commitment. The blend of these commitments results in married people feeling more secure with each other and their relationship.

Marriage also furnishes the traditionally approved context for children. Although some individuals opt for single parenthood, most want to be married when they become parents. Persons who are not married and who choose parenthood will receive less social support than those who are married.

The experience of parenthood is one of numerous events spouses share over the course of their life together. Partners who don't get divorced may have 50 or so years of memories. One 40-year-old husband said:

My wife and I have been seeing a movie a week since we began dating more than 20 years ago. We have already seen close to 1,000 movies together, and some of them have become a part of us. We still enjoy *Casablanca.*

In his play *Chapter Two*, Neil Simon likened a relationship to the alphabet. People who have just met are in the As and Bs; those who have known each other for years are in the Rs and Ss. One of the frustrating aspects of divorce is that we lose the shared history with a person and must begin at the As and Bs with a new person.

The disadvantages of marriage include interference with the achievement of other goals and rela-

tionships, risk of becoming divorced or widowed, and financial responsibility for others. The person who travels fastest, travels alone. If you have a career goal or want career success, the involvement of another person in your life can hinder your achievement of that goal. Not only may marriage restrict your career mobility, it may also interfere with the development of other relationships.

At least 50 percent of all brides and grooms in the United States become divorced; by not marrying, individuals can avoid the traumatic experience of divorce. In addition, most women outlive their husbands by eight years or so, so most wives have inadvertently signed up for several years in the widow role.

Financial responsibility for children, for homes, and for all the things married people buy is part of the marital package. Some people don't like to get in debt or to be obligated to pay for things that someone else (the spouse) wants. If you marry, you will incur the financial obligations of your partner and vice versa.

The decision to marry may not be a one-time decision. Many of us will make the basic decision between marriage and singlehood many times throughout our lives. The single decide whether to marry, and the married decide whether to stay married. For the divorced, the question is whether to remain single or to remarry.

Is Singlehood for You?

Singlehood is not a unidimensional concept. There are many styles of singlehood from which to choose. As a single person, you may devote your time and energy to career, travel, privacy, heterosexual or homosexual relationships, living together, communal living, or a combination of these experiences over time. The essential difference between traditional marriage and singlehood is the personal and legal freedom to do as you wish.

Although singlehood offers freedom, single people must deal with the issues of loneliness, money, education, and identity.

Loneliness

For some singles, being alone is a desirable and enjoyable experience. "The major advantage of being single," expressed one 29-year-old man, "is that I don't have to deal with another person all the time. I like my privacy." Henry David Thoreau, who never married, spent two years alone on 14 acres bordering Walden Pond. He said of the experience, "I love to be alone. I never found the companion that was so companionable as solitude."

Others view solitude as an opportunity to become deeply involved in their work. A single-by-choice artist remarked:

Marriage would interfere with what I most enjoy—my work. I am most creative when I am alone. Fixing supper for someone else, changing a baby's diapers, or having to talk to someone else every night would be dreadful chores to me.

Economic Benefits

Having social relationships or developing an enjoyment for being alone are not the only prerequisites to successful single living. It takes money. Money is less likely to be a problem for a man who has been socialized to expect to work all of his life and who usually earns about one-third more than a woman. A woman who decides not to marry is giving up the potentially larger income her husband might earn. Also, both men and women who decide not to marry give up the possibility of a two-income family.

Education

Since higher incomes are often associated with higher education, the person who is considering singlehood as a lifestyle might stay in school. Women and men who complete four years of high school can expect to earn about 30 percent less than those who complete four years of college. "It earns to learn" is a phrase that is used to promote the importance of education.

Personal Identity

Single people must establish an identity—a role—that helps to define who they are and what they do. Couples eat together, sleep together, party together, and cooperate economically. They mesh their lives into a cooperative relationship that gives them the respective identity of being on their own marital team. On the basis of their spousal roles, we can predict what they will be doing most of the time. For example, at noon on Sunday, they are most likely to be having lunch together. Not only can we predict what they will be doing, their roles as spouses tell them what they will be doing—interacting with each other.

The single person must find other roles. A meaningful career is the avenue most singles pursue. A career provides structure, relationships with others, and a strong sense of identity ("I am an interior decorator"). To the degree that singles find meaning in their work, they are successful in establishing autonomous identities independent of the marital role.

In evaluating the single lifestyle, to what degree, if any, do you feel that loneliness would be a problem for you? What are your educational and career plans to ensure that you will be employed in your chosen field and maintain the standard of living you desire?

The old idea that you can't be happy unless you are married is no longer credible. Whereas marriage will be the first option for some, it will be the last option for others. One 76-year-old single-by-choice said, "A husband would have to be very special to be better than no husband at all."

Impact of Social Influences on Choices

Your decision to remain single or to marry is significantly influenced by your relationships with others—your parents, friends, and peers—and by the presence of a person in your life who wants to marry you.

The scenario most predictive of your wanting to marry includes your parents having a happy marriage, close friends having happy marriages, no employer making heavy demands on your time, being in your early thirties (your society expects you to be married by then), and being in love with a person who wants to marry you.

Alternatively, the scenario most predictive of

your remaining single includes your parents having an unhappy marriage, close friends being divorced or widowed and discussing the benefits of not marrying again, an employer making extensive demands on your time and leaving you little time for a relationship, and no one being currently available who wants to marry you and whom you want to marry.

Hence, whether you choose to remain single or to marry will very much depend on the social influences operative in your life.

C H A P T E R

6

Living Together

CONTENTS

IS IT TRUE?

1. Cohabitation rates in European countries are lower than cohabitation rates in the United States.

2. Couples who live together before marriage have a lower divorce rate than couples who do not live together before marriage.

3. Most people who are cohabitating are over the age of 25.

4. Less than one percent of those currently married lived together before marriage.

5. Individuals who live together have the same background characteristics as those who do not live together.

1 = F; 2 = F; 3 = T; 4 = F; 5 = F

NE OF THE major changes in our society has been the gradual acceptance of couples who live together before marriage. "The norms that once forbade premarital cohabitation have shifted to a more tolerant position" (White, 1989, 544). This new attitude toward living together has increased among people of all ages, races, and social classes. Some view living together as a necessary stage in a developing relationship before making a more permanent or legal commitment. In the 1920s, Judge B. B. Lindsey suggested the living together alternative out of his concern for the number of divorcing couples he saw in his court. He reasoned that if couples lived together before marriage, they might be better able to assess the degree to which they were compatible with each other. Similarly, Margaret Mead suggested a "two-stage marriage." The first stage would involve living together without having children. If the partners felt that their relationship was stable and durable, they would get married and have a family.

The idea of living together did not catch on until the early sixties, when half a million couples were living together. By the late eighties, the number had increased four times. Reasons for the increase include fear of marriage; career or educational commitments; increased tolerance from society, parents, and peers; and the desire for a stable emotional and sexual relationship without legal ties. "Cohabitation outside of marriage is no longer a deviant lifestyle alternative nor a clandestine arrangement apart from the larger context of courtship and marriage" (Spanier, 1989, 7).

In this chapter, we will examine the characteristics of those who live together, their motivations for doing so, and how they evaluate the experience. In addition, we will assess the potential benefits and disadvantages of becoming involved in a living-together relationship. Finally, because the courts are indicating increased concern, we look at the legal implications of living together as an unmarried couple.

The terms used to describe live-ins include *cohabitants* and POSSLQ (people of the opposite sex sharing living quarters), the latter term used by the U.S. Bureau of the Census.

⠿ Definition and Types of Living Together

We will define living together as two unrelated adults who live in the same household and have an emotional and sexual relationship.

DATA: *Four percent of our population is currently living with someone to whom they are not married; 17 percent of those who are currently married lived together before they were married; 25 percent of our population has lived with someone in the past (Bumpass & Sweet, 1989). Cohabitation rates are significantly higher in european countries. Two-thirds of 4,966 Swedish women reported that they had lived with their first husband prior to marriage (Bennett et al., 1988).*

The various types of living together relationships include individuals who are emotionally involved but are not ready for marriage, those who are waiting to get married, those who view living together as a permanent alternative to marriage, and those who live together for economic reasons (it is cheaper). Most individuals who live together have a strong emotional relationship with their partners, but they have not yet made a commitment to marry each other. In traditional terms, they are "going steady," but they have also moved in together. As one student expressed this "involved but not committed to marriage" pattern of living together:

> The only thing I know about is today. And today I'm happy with my partner. Tomorrow? Who knows? While we both intend to get married someday, we're not sure that it will be to each other.

Other couples are planning to marry each other and are living together until the time is right. Although they may not be officially engaged, they intend to be married and are consciously assessing their compatibility. "The idea of agreeing to spend the rest of your life with someone you've never lived with is nonsense," said one live-in partner. "We love each other very much and feel very secure with each other. But we want to see if we can pull it off on a day-to-day basis."

Some couples live together as a permanent alternative to marriage. Many of these individuals have been married and do not want to marry again but want a live-in lover relationship. Others are philosophically against marriage or are prohibited from marrying because of their sexual orientation (homosexual).

:: Characteristics of Live-In Partners

People who live together tend to differ from those who do not in their age, lack of children, and education. Cohabitants tend to be over the age of 25.

> There is no single answer to whether cohabitation is a late stage of courtship or an early stage of marriage.
> —LARRY BUMPASS
>   AND JAMES SWEET

■ **DATA:** *Based on a national study of cohabiting couples, 25 percent of people who are cohabiting are in the age category of 19–24 in contrast to 68 percent who are in the age category of 25–34 (Bumpass & Sweet, 1989).*

Cohabitants also tend not to have children living with them.

■ **DATA:** *About 70 percent of unmarried couples who live together do not have children under the age of 15 living with them (Statistical Abstract of the United States: 1990).*

Finally, cohabitants also differ by education with the highest rates of cohabitation among the least educated.

■ **DATA:** *Unmarried persons who have completed college are 64 percent less likely to cohabit than those who did not complete college (Bumpass & Sweet, 1989).*

In summarizing these and other characteristics of those who live together, Bumpass and Sweet (1989) observed:

> Cohabitation is most likely among those who did not complete high school, those whose family received welfare while growing up, and those who did not grow up in an intact family. Nonetheless, cohabitation before marriage has become common throughout society. For example, in spite of the large negative effect of education, over a quarter of college graduates have cohabited before marriage (p. 15).

▪▪ The Experience of Living Together

What is living together like on a day-to-day basis? In this section, we will explore the issue of the decision to live together in terms of the commitment, intimacy, and problems involved in such a situation.

Deciding to Move in Together

Sometimes, living together is the result of both partners making a conscious decision to do so. However, many partners become emotionally involved with each other, spend increasingly larger amounts of time together, and gradually drift into a living together arrangement. The typical pattern is to spend an occasional night together, then a weekend, then a night before or after the weekend, and so on. This escalation usually takes place over a period of months.

▪ **DATA:** *In one study of 40 spouses who had previously lived together, 73 percent of the partners had known each other for at least six months prior to moving in together; almost 50 percent had known each other for more than one year (Kotkin, 1985).*

"We just enjoyed spending time together and the more, the better. We weren't aware that we were gradually moving in together—but that's what was happening," an English major recalls.

Another couple remember their experience:

We were at his place fooling around when I said how nice it would be to have my stereo to listen to. We decided to go to my dorm and get it. Doing so was symbolic, because in the next few days we had moved my other stuff into his apartment. We never talked about living together, only "getting my stuff."

Crowded quarters is one price of living together.

Feelings about Marriage

What do couples who live together feel about marriage in general and about marriage to each other? When 40 college couples who were living together were asked these questions, 93 percent of the women and 85 percent of the men said they would eventually marry (Risman et al., 1981). "Just because we're living together doesn't mean we're anti-marriage," said one live-in partner.

Although most partners in living together relationships plan to marry eventually, they are less certain about whether they will marry each other. They do not begin to live together with the idea that they will marry at some later date.

> ■ **DATA:** *In one study, 50 percent of the men and 65 percent of the women who were living together said they did not consider their doing so to be a trial marriage (Kotkin, 1985).*
>
> *In another study, termination—not marriage, was the most likely outcome of living together (Yamaguchi & Kandel, 1985).*

Intimacy

When 40 couples who were living together were compared with 191 couples who were "going steady" (Risman et al., 1981), the living together couples were more intimate—they disclosed more to each other, indicated greater love for each other, had sexual intercourse more often, and viewed their relationship as closer. Hence, although the living together couples weren't sure about their future life together, they had drifted into very intimate relationships. Also, they were enjoying them. About 80 percent of both women and men reported they were satisfied with their relationships. These percentages were slightly above the satisfaction levels of partners who were "going steady."

Division of Labor

Who does the work in living together relationships?

> ■ **DATA:** *In a survey of the readers of Cosmopolitan magazine, of women who were living with their partners, 25 percent did all of the housework, 51 percent did most of it, and 20 percent split the chores (Bowe, 1986).*

Although many couples share the work in their relationships, there seems to be a drift toward traditional roles, the woman doing more of the work. This traditional division of labor may be the unconscious replication of the role relationships the respective partners observed in their parents' marriages. One woman who cooks, cleans, and does the laundry said, "I really don't mind. I'd rather be taking care of things around the apartment than just sitting around." One might predict that her mother also takes care of her father in a similar manner and feels guilty "just sitting around."

Some women feel frustrated and angry about the traditional drift toward conventional male-female roles in a living together situation. One graduate student who had recently moved in with her partner said:

> Moving in together has caused some unanticipated problems. Things prior to that had been quite egalitarian, and I liked the way Bob treated me. After we moved in,

Live-ins share the domestic work early in their relationship. Later, they tend to drift into traditional roles.

the boxes had not even been unpacked and I became a *housewife!* I worked all day on *our* house while he went to school. It was horrible, and I was miserable. We talked about it, and two days later I was the housewife again. I'm hoping that since we're moved in and things are unpacked and cleaned, this problem will be gone.

Problems

Liberty is the one thing you can't have unless you give it to others.
—WILLIAM ALLEN WHITE

Partners who live together report certain problems including parents, children, jealousy, and loss of freedom.

Parents. Most college students are reluctant to tell their parents they are living together. They fear their parents' disapproval and, in some cases, retribution. "My dad would cut off my money if he knew Mark and I were living together," said one junior.

Some live-in partners do not care if their parents know they are living together. Those who do hide it feel guilty about the deception. "I don't feel good about being dishonest with my folks, but I tell myself it would hurt them more if they knew," one partner said.

Still others are sorry they can't share their feelings about their companion with their parents. "I've never been happier than since I moved into Carl's apartment. But the fact that my folks don't know and would be disappointed if they did bothers me. Carl is a very important part of my life, and I feel sad that I can't share him with my parents," observed a music major.

Older, noncollege, divorced people who live together also have parental concerns. "No matter how old I am," said one 36-year-old woman, "I'm still my mother's child, and she thinks living together is wrong." Expecting parents to change their values is probably unrealistic. Most cohabiting couples who have disapproving parents are tolerant of their parents' values, yet respect their own values by continuing to live together.

Children. Youngsters of unmarried parents who live together may also create problems. These include rejecting the parent's new live-in partner by ignoring, direct attacks, or being disrespectful. These issues are similar to those experienced by partners in new stepfamilies.

Adult children of parents who cohabit may also be a problem. They may disapprove of the selection of their parent's partner and, like the youngster, ignore, attack, or be disrespectful. Whether a young child or older adult, children may affect the happiness of the partners who live together.

Jealousy. About 50 percent of the partners who live together are not committed to marrying each other, so it is not surprising that jealousy sometimes occurs. "When she doesn't come in until late and I know she's been with another guy, it hurts me terribly," said one partner. "I know I don't own her, but I can't help being jealous."

Loss of Freedom. Some partners complain that a live-in relationship restricts their freedom. One woman said:

> Last week I hit a new low point. I felt very trapped and that all my independence and freedom were gone. I had earlier insisted that we have an open relationship (sex with others allowed), but it didn't occur to me until now that I am part of a *couple* and no one's going to be interested in me. Also, I felt I'd have no alone time except when I'm working (we do not have separate bedrooms and we use one car to go back and forth to school). I've had nightmares about being married and even awakened one night terrified because I had rolled over and felt someone in bed with me (guess I'd been dreaming I was "single" again).

Living Together as Preparation for Marriage

One of the motivations for living together is the opportunity to screen out risky marriages. But do couples who live together before they get married have a greater chance of staying married than couples who do not live together before they get married? The answer is "No." Based on a comparison of national samples of couples who did and did not live together before they got married, "the proportion separating or divorcing within 10 years is a third higher among those who lived together before marriage than among those who did not—"36 versus 27 percent" (Bumpass & Sweet, 1989, 10). These results are similar to those reported by Balakrishnan and colleagues based on Canadian data (1987) and by Booth and Johnson for the U.S. (1988).

A Swedish study of 4,966 women found that "dissolution rates of women who cohabit premaritally with their future spouse are, on average, nearly 80 percent higher than the rates of those who do not live together" (Bennett et al., 1988, 132). The researchers suggested that persons who cohabit "may be unsure about, or ideologically opposed to, the institution of marriage itself, but who marry perhaps due to mounting external pressure" (p. 134). In other words, cohabitants may have a "weaker commitment to the institution of marriage" (p. 137).

These studies suggest that you should not live with a partner before marriage if your sole goal in doing so is to help to ensure a happy marriage with that partner. There is no data to support such a causal relationship.

In addition to a weaker commitment to marriage, there are at least three other reasons why cohabitation does not ensure a happy marriage.

1. *False image.* Live-ins may still be in courtship with each other in that they may selectively present their best "self." After marriage, their "real" self may emerge and be a shock to the partner. Cohabitants assume that because they are living with their partner that this is the way the partner is and will behave in marriage. This is not necessarily so.

2. *Role change.* When live-in lovers become spouses, they may find that their roles change. For example, cohabitants who had egalitarian role relationships may drift into traditional gender stereotyped roles after marriage. In addition, once live-ins assume the role of spouse, they may discover that they do not interact in the context of social and legal constraint as they did in a context of relative freedom.

3. *Norm breakers.* Cohabitants are people who are willing to break social norms and live together before they are married. Once they marry, they may feel less willing to stay married if they are unhappy than unhappily married persons who have no history of unconventional behavior.

:: Benefits of Living Together

Although having a successful marriage is not a predictable result of living with someone before marriage, some aspects of a living together relationship may be beneficial to a marriage. The most pervasive benefit is that most couples who live together report it is an enjoyable, maturing experience. There are other potential benefits as well.

Delayed Marriage

Individuals who marry in their middle and late twenties are more likely to stay married and to report higher levels of marital satisfaction than those who marry earlier. To the degree that living together functions to delay the age at which a person marries, it may therefore be considered beneficial. "I married when I was 20," remarked one woman, "because you just didn't live together in those days. I wish I had waited to get married and had had the option of living together in the meantime." Lana Turner, the Hollywood actress of the forties, said one of the reasons she had seven marriages was that when two people became involved, they were not expected to live together—they were expected to marry.

Ending Unsatisfactory Relationships Before Marriage

Even though ending a living together relationship may be just as traumatic as divorce, only the latter goes on your record. The legal system will record the number of divorces that you have but not the number of broken nonmarital relationships. Also, since living together may involve fewer legal ties, it may be easier to disengage from a living together relationship than a marriage.

Being with someone you love more often is a major benefit of living together.

CONSIDERATION

A team of researchers studied the termination of various premarital relationships and concluded, "The best divorce you get is the one you get before you get married" (Hill et al., 1976).

Less Idealization

You may have been to a dance and seen a ball made up of small square glass mirrors that cast reflections from a light shining on it as it turns. Traditional courtship usually gives information about a person in small units much like the light reflected from a couple of these mirrors. In contrast, living together may give you more information; you will see more facets of the person by being around her or him more of the time. You may or may not like what you learn about your partner from this increased exposure.

∷ Disadvantages of Living Together

"Never again" said a man who had formerly had a living together relationship. "I invested myself completely and felt we would eventually get married. But she never had that in mind and jut took me for a ride. The next time, I'll be married before moving in with someone." Living together does have negative consequences for some people—they feel used, tricked, and hostile.

Feeling Used

When levels of commitment are uneven in a relationship, the partner who is most committed feels used. "I always felt I was giving more than I was getting," said one partner. "It's not a good feeling."

Feeling Tricked

Some partners feel they have been deceived. "I always felt we would be getting married, but it turns out that she was seeing someone else the whole time we were living together and had no intention of marrying me," recalled one partner.

Developing Hostility

The feelings of being tricked and used often combine to create deep hostile feelings, not only against the live-in partner but also against others in general. Sometimes the person feels incapable of initiating or maintaining another relationship. "What's the use?" remarked one partner who had recently terminated a relationship, "I'm burned out on investing myself in people."

Relationships to Avoid

A team of researchers identified the types of living together relationships that had negative consequences for those involved (Ridley et al., 1978). These included the following.

1. *The "Linus blanket" relationship.* In this pattern, the individuals had an overwhelming need to be involved with someone—with anyone. The fear of breaking up caused the partners to defer to each other on almost every issue. As a result, the partners had no practice in problem solving and hid their real needs from each other. "We were always being nice to each other and never really disclosed ourselves to each other. . . . I guess that's why we broke up," said a business major.
2. *The emancipation relationship.* Often, one partner lives with someone to symbolize his or her independence from parents and rebellion against tradition. But feelings of guilt usually ensue, and the person soon withdraws from the relationship. Unless the person works out his or her ambivalent feelings about living together, the consequences of a live-in relationship are likely to be negative.
3. *The one-sided convenience relationship.* Although some live-in relationships involve mutual convenience, others do not. In a one-sided convenience relationship, one partner manipulates the other in order to fulfill sexual, domestic, or other needs while withholding any semblance of commitment. There is little reciprocity, and the relationship becomes exploitative.

To assess the degree to which living together may have a positive or negative outcome for you and your partner, you can rate yourself according to the Living Together Consequences Scale in the Self-Assessment.

:: Living Together as a Permanent Alternative

Whereas most people regard living together as a stage to a future marriage (although not necessarily with the person with whom they currently live), some people view living together as a permanent alternative to marriage. They enjoy living together, but they do not plan to marry anyone—ever.

Who Lives Together Permanently?

Those who select living together as a permanent alternative to marriage may have been married before and don't want the entanglements of another marriage. Others feel that the "real" bond between two people is (or should be) emotional. They contend that many couples stay together because of the legal contract, even though they do not love each other any longer. "If you're staying married because of the contract," said one partner, "you're staying for the wrong reason."

Some women reject marriage for philosophical reasons:

> I have enough trouble with my identity as a woman starting her own business that I don't need to confuse it with _____'s business. I don't like the stigma. . . . I don't want to be a "Mrs." in any way (Kotkin, 1985, 167).

Other individuals feel that living together permanently allows you to keep your own identity:

> . . . right now, we can take vacations separately; we can do things separately. It seems that once you're married, . . . the two of you become one identity—the way people look at you (Kotkin, 1985,).

Homosexual couples also live together as a permanent alternative to marriage. Our cultural bias against homosexuality is reflected in the law which prohibits homosexual couples from marrying. In some states, homosexual couples are being granted legal entitlements that have traditionally been reserved for married couples (see Chapter One, Exhibit 1.3). However, homosexual living together couples are still not allowed to be legally married, which gives them no choice but to live together as a permanent alternative to marriage.

He (William Hurt) told me that we had a spiritual marriage, that we were married in the eyes of God.
—SANDRA JENNINGS

	C O N S I D E R A T I O N	

Some living together homosexual couples may think of themselves as "married" in the sense that they view their relationship as a long-term, monogamous commitment. Homosexual couples may buy houses together, celebrate "anniversaries" together, and in some cases, rear children together.

Legal Rights of the Unwed

In recent years, the courts have become increasingly involved in living together relationships. Suits in reference to palimony, common law marriages, and child support have been filed by previous live-in partners.

Palimony. A take-off on the word "alimony," *palimony* refers to the amount of money one "pal" who lives with another "pal" may have to pay if the partners terminate their relationship. Palimony received national visibility in the early 1980s when Lee Marvin was ordered to pay Michelle Triola Marvin (with whom he had lived for seven years) $104,000 by the Los Angeles Superior Court for "rehabilitative purposes." Although the award was later overturned by the California Second District Court, a new era of palimony suits had begun.

In the past, partners in living together relationships had no legal rights in reference to each other. Today, such arrangements may be recognized as licit, and the parties can be held liable to each other and forced to pay money at the court's discretion. The primary factor in the court awarding palimony is the existence of a contract or agreement (written or implied) between the parties regarding their relationship. In 1989, Annie Bakes sued Dennis Rodman (Detroit Piston basketball player) for palimony asking him to share his income and property during their three-year relationship and to support their daughter. She contended that during their three-year relationship he promised to marry her and fathered her child.

Common law marriage. Thirteen states and the District of Columbia continue to recognize common law marriage. In these states (Alabama, Colorado, Georgia, Idaho, Iowa, Kansas, Montana, Ohio, Oklahoma, Pennsylvania, Rhode Island, South Carolina, and Texas), a heterosexual couple may be considered married if they are legally competent to marry and if there is agreement between the couple to live together with the intention of being husband and wife. A ceremony or compliance with legal formalities are not required. In 1989, Sandra Jennings contended that she and actor William Hurt were married by common law in the state of South Carolina where they lived for four weeks. As his common law wife, argued her lawyer, she would be entitled to half of his $10 million estate.

New York Yankees outfielder Dave Winfield was sued by Sandra Renfrom who contended that they were married by common law in Texas. She was awarded $13,500 a month in temporary alimony and child support.

Child Support. Tanena Love sued Chris Carson (the son of Johnny Carson) for the support of their daughter whom she contends he fathered. In New York the law states that the woman is due the same standard of living for her child that would have occurred had the relationship continued with the father. Ms. Love asked for $500 per week for her child.

☐   C O N S I D E R A T I O N   ☐

Couples who live together or have children together should be aware that laws traditionally applying only to married couples are now being applied to many unwed relationships. Palimony, distribution of property, and child support payments are all possibilities once two people cohabit or parent a child.

SELF ASSESSMENT

Living Together Consequences Scale

This inventory is designed to measure the degree to which living together may have positive or negative consequences for you and your partner. There are no right or wrong answers. After reading each sentence carefully, circle the number that best represents your feelings.

1 Strongly disagree
2 Mildly disagree
3 Undecided
4 Mildly agree
5 Strongly agree

	SD	D	U	A	SA
1. I have a fairly liberal background and living together is not against my values.	1	2	3	4	5
2. If we break up after living together without getting married, I will not be devastated.	1	2	3	4	5
3. I have thought a lot about the pros and cons of living together and feel that it is right for me and my partner.	1	2	3	4	5
4. I will not feel used if my partner breaks up with me and doesn't marry me.	1	2	3	4	5
5. I am not living with my partner so that I can get back at my parents.	1	2	3	4	5
6. I want to live with my partner out of love, not out of convenience.	1	2	3	4	5
7. My partner and I have known each other for a long time.	1	2	3	4	5
8. I am not counting on living together to help us have a stronger relationship.	1	2	3	4	5
9. My partner and I have discussed our future.	1	2	3	4	5
10. My parents would not disown me if they found out that I was living with my partner.	1	2	3	4	5

SCORING: Add the numbers you circled. 1 (strongly disagree) is the most negative response, and 5 (strongly agree) is the most positive response. The lower your total score (10 is the lowest possible score), the greater the negative consequences of living together; the higher your score (50 is the highest possible score), the greater the positive consequences of living together. A score of 25 places you at the midpoint between the positive and negative consequences of living together.

NOTE: This Self-Assessment is intended to be thought-provoking and fun; it is not intended to be used as a clinical diagnostic measuring instrument.

:: Trends

Living together will continue to increase. In 1970, 523,000 Americans reported that they were living together. By 1990, over two million were living together *(Statistical Abstract of the United States: 1990)*. The reasons for the increasing rate of living together include the delay in when people marry, the hesitancies about marriage in an age of divorce, and the increasing acceptance of living together by parents and institutions. As an example of institutional acceptance of cohabitating, Trinity College of Cambridge University has permitted unmarried students of the opposite sex to share two-bedroom apartments on campus. However, living together will probably not replace marriage, at least in the foreseeable future. Having children and being married are still very normative and many people who live together will most likely marry before they have a child.

Those who decide to live together will become more aware of the legal and economic implications of their doing so. This will be particularly true of those who live together for a considerable period of time or who suggest to others that they consider themselves "married" in a spiritual sense. In such relationships and depending on the state, implied agreements between the partners may be enforceable. William Hurt, Nick Nolte, and Alice Cooper have all been sued by their former live-in partners.

Increased legal rights will also be accorded to homosexual as well as heterosexual live-in partners. Cities such as Seattle give legal recognition to "domestic partnerships" which means that live-in partners have the same status as married couples. This means that live-in partners may benefit from the health insurance and retirement benefits of each other.

:: Summary

Living together may be defined as two unmarried adult lovers sharing a residence over an extended period of time. About 4 percent of all couples sharing a household are unmarried (this figure does not include homosexual couples, for which estimates of living together are difficult to obtain). Although most have a wait and see attitude about their relationships, others are committed to eventual marriage. Some couples view living together as a permanent alternative to marriage.

Couples who live together are more likely to be over 25, to be child free, and to have less education than couples who do not live together. Some live-ins drift into living together relationships; others formally discuss living together first. Live-in partners tend to report high levels of satisfaction in their relationships and often divide housework along traditional lines. Many seem troubled that their parents do not know of their relationship but feel they would be disappointed if they did know. Other problems that live-in partners may experience involve children, jealousy, and loss of freedom.

Living together before marriage may be associated with marital instability because those who live together may be more prone to breaking norms. People who are willing to break social norms by living together may also be more willing to break social norms by divorcing if their marriage is not working for them. In addition, those who live together may have a weaker commitment to marriage.

Potential benefits of living together include delaying marriage, ending unsatisfactory relationships before marriage, and reducing idealization. Potential disadvantages of living together include feeling used, tricked, and hostile toward the partner and toward others.

A small percentage of unmarried-couple households consist of those who are living together as a permanent alternative to marriage. These relationships may cause legal problems if they terminate, because the courts are increasingly willing to enforce implied agreements made by live-ins. Homosexual couples are prohibited by law to marry, and therefore have no choice but to view living together as a permanent alternative to marriage.

Trends in living together include an increase in the number of couples who live together, more legal benefits to those who live together (e.g., health insurance), and more lawsuits between those who live together and break up.

References

Balakrishnan, T. R., K. V. Rao, E. Lapierre-Adamyck, and K. J. Krotki. A hazard model analysis of the covariates of marriage dissolution in Canada. *Demography,* 1987, *24,* 395–406.

Bennett, Neil G., A. K. Blanc, and D. E. Bloom Commitment and the modern union: Assessing the link between premarital cohabitation and subsequent marital stability. *American Sociological Review, 1988,* 53, 127–139

Booth, Alan and D. Johnson, Premarital cohabitation and marital success. *Journal of Family Issues,* 1988, *9,* 255–272.

Bowe, C. What are men like today. *Cosmopolitan,* May 1986, 263 et passim.

Bulcroft, K. and M. O'Conner-Roden, Never too late. *Psychology Today,* June 1986, 66–69.

Bumpass, Larry and James Sweet. 1989. National estimates of cohabitation: Cohort levels and union stability. NSFH Working Paper No. 2, Center for Demography and Ecology, University of Wisconsin–Madison, 4412 Social Science Building, 1180 Observatory Drive, Madison, WI, 53706.

Hill, C.T., Z. Rubin and L. A.Peplau, Breakups before marriage: The end of 103 affairs. *Journal of Social Issues,* 1976, *32,* 147–168.

Kotkin, M. To marry or live together. *Life styles: A journal of of changing patterns, 1985, 7,* 156–170.

Ridley, C. A., D. J. Peterman, and A. W. Avery. Cohabitation: Does it make for a better marriage? *Family Coordinator,* 1978, *27,* 129–136.

Risman, B. J., C. T. Hill, Z. Rubin, and L. A. Peplau. Living together in college: Implications for courtship. *Journal of Marriage and the Family,* 1981, *43 No. 1,* 77–83.

Spanier, Graham B. Bequeathing family continuity. *Journal of Marriage and the Family,* 1989, *51,* 3–14.

Statistical Abstract of the United States: 1990. 110th ed. Washington, D.C.: U.S. Bureau of the Census, 1990.

Thornton, Arland. Cohabitation and marriage in the 1980s. *Demography,*1989, *25,* 497–508.

Trussell, James and K. Vaninadha Rao, Feedback: Premarital cohabitation and marital stability: A reassessment of the Canadian evidence. *Journal of Marriage and the Family,* 1989, *51,* 535–540.

White, James W. Reply to comment by Trussel and Rao: A reanalysis of the data. *Journal of Marriage and the family,* 1989, *51,* 540–544.

Yamaguchi, K., and D.B. Kandel, Dynamic relationships between premarital cohabitation and illicit drug use: An event-history analysis of role selection and role socialization. *American Sociological Review,* 1985, *50,* 530–546.

CHOICES

CHOICES ABOUT LIVING together include whether to live together, whether to maintain two residences, whether to tell parents, and how long to live together. Careful decision making may help to make living together a more positive experience.

Should I Live With My Partner?

There are three conditions under which you should probably not live together. First, if your values are such that you believe living together is wrong, the arrangement will probably have negative consequences for you. You may lose respect for yourself, your partner, and your relationship. Second, if you expect that marriage will result from living with your partner and you will be devastated if it does not, you should probably not live together. Living together is not equivalent to engagement, and it is not unusual for the partners who live together to have different goals about marriage. Even partners who view themselves as being engaged and who plan to marry may not do so after they have lived together. "I found out that I couldn't live with him," "I found out I didn't want to live with her," and "I found out I wasn't ready for marriage" are some of the comments made by those who live together but do not end up getting married. Third, it is unwise to live with someone you feel is exploiting you.

Aside from these three cautions, living together seems to have limited harmful effects and some beneficial ones. The primary benefit is that it may help partners to discover they are unsuited for marriage before they get married.

Should We Have One Residence or Two?

When partners drift into or decide to live together, they sometimes decide to maintain two residences. This arrangement furnishes a cover story for both sets of parents, a place for her to get her mail, and a haven to retreat to when conflict erupts in the relationship. One woman who maintained her own apartment said:

I needed a place I could go back to—to call my own—and to see my friends. Having a place of your own is expensive, but it gives you flexibility by not putting all your eggs into the living together basket. I ended up breaking up with my partner, and I'm sure the adjustment was a lot easier because I had a place to retreat to when I needed it.

The disadvantage of maintaining a separate place may be the flip side of the advantages. If you have a place to retreat to, the skills of managing conflict with your partner may not be as easily learned. You can walk out when you want to, and your motivation for working things out may be lower. "I'm sure we would be apart," said one cohabitant "if I had not given up my dorm room. But because I had no place to escape to, we worked out our differences and have a stronger relationship for it."

Should I Tell My Parents I Am Living With My Partner?

The decision to tell parents about the living together relationship will depend on the parents, the relationship with them, the values of honesty and kindness, and the ability to hide the living together experience.

Some parents are very conservative and are devastated to learn that their son or daughter is in a living together relationship. One mother said:

When we found out our daughter was living with her boyfriend, we were hurt more than we were shocked. We have a Christian home and always thought we had brought her up right. Her behavior was a slap in the face at everything that we had taught her.

Other parents don't approve of their children living together but view their doing so as part of the liberalization of our whole society. One father said:

We know that a lot of young folks are living together these days. Our son went to one of these liberal colleges and learned all sorts of things we don't approve of. But we trust his judgment and don't figure that living together will hurt him. Besides, we would rather he live with his girlfriend than get married as young as he is.

Just as some parents are conservative and others are more liberal, the relationships offspring have with their parents will vary. "I've always been fairly open with my parents no matter what it was," said one cohabitant. But another said, "I can't tell my parents anything without them criticizing me, so I've learned to live my life and let them know as little as possible." Whether you tell your parents about your living together relationship will depend not only on who they are but also on your relationship with them.

The values of honesty and kindness are often in conflict when it comes to making a decision about telling parents about a living together relationship. If you value being honest with your parents, you will tell them you are living with your partner. But doing so may hurt them and give them a problem to live with. As an alternative to being honest, you might choose to be kind and not tell them, sparing them the burden of living with such information.

Of course, your parents may already know of your living together or find out without your telling them. Keeping such a secret is difficult under the best of circumstances. The only way to ensure that your parents do not find out is to avoid the behavior. "I don't care whether my parents find out or not," said one person, "It's my life." But another said, "I couldn't do that to my parents."

How Long Should I Live With My Partner?

There is no evidence to suggest that living together before marriage for any length of time is predictive of a successful marriage relationship. However, it is known that any relationships in which the partners have known each other for at least a year have a higher chance of marital success than relationships of shorter duration.

Impact of Social Influences on Choices

Whether or not you live together with your partner will be influenced by your perception of the approval or disapproval of the persons you care about. If your primary group members (parents, siblings, children) would disapprove of your living together with a partner, then you may be less likely to do so (unless you are cohabitating out of rebellion).

Some partners want to live together very much, even though they know others will disapprove, so they hide their living together relationship. Lest we think that sneaking around is unique to young people, a study of courtship couples in their sixties reported ducking the eyes of their children. One 63-year-old retiree said, "Yeah, my girlfriend (age 64) lives just down the hall from me . . . when she spends the night, she usually brings her cordless phone . . . just in case her daughter calls" (Bulcroft & O'Conner-Roden, 1986). Another 61-year-old woman reported that she has been unable to tell her family that her 68-year-old boyfriend spends three to four nights a week at her house. "I have a tendency to hide his shoes when my grandchildren are coming over" (p.69).

C H A P T E R

7

Dating and Mate Selection

CONTENTS

IS IT TRUE?

1. Most people who join a videodating club say that they are looking for a lot of people to date casually.

2. People who are dating after a divorce have a shorter courtship to marriage than people who are dating for the first time.

3. Partners who have the same "body clock" in terms of being "morning" or "night" people are more likely to report being happy than partners who have different body clocks.

4. In America, the characteristics of the person you select as a mate are significantly influenced by those in your primary relationships.

5. Premarital counselors who use the PREPARE inventory can predict which couples are more likely to get divorced.

1 = F; 2 = T; 3 = T; 4 = T; 5 = T

Y OU WILL RECALL that a central goal of marriage from the viewpoint of society is to bond two people together who will produce, protect, nurture, and socialize children to be productive members of society. To ensure that this goal is accomplished, society must make some provision for sexually mature females and males to meet, interact, and pair off in permanent unions for eventual parenthood. The dating process serves this function and guides woman-man interaction through an orderly process toward mate selection.

There are different patterns of dating—in groups and in nonexclusive or exclusive relationships. Some people date by "hanging around" and "getting together" in groups of various sizes; others prefer one-to-one relationships. The latter may be "open" (each partner may date others) or "closed" (the partners date each other exclusively). Such exclusive dating may or may not be oriented toward marriage.

Even pairings that lead to marriage are not necessarily permanent. Rather, individuals are likely to pair with a number of others over the course of their lifetime. Also, the criteria for choosing a partner at one stage in life may be different from the criteria at another time. One divorced man said:

> The first time around, I wanted someone who was a visual knockout. I married a real beauty, and because we argued all the time, she began to look like Cyclops to me. The next time, I will choose in reference to similar values and goals, because I've found that looks become much less important after you get the person home.

After reviewing how the Industrial Revolution changed the dating relationships of women and men, we will examine the realities of dating, selecting a marriage partner, and using the engagement period. We end with a discussion of the conditions under which you might prolong your engagement with the goal of increasing the chance of having an enduring and happy marriage relationship.

:: Dating in Historical Perspective

In colonial America, a man who wanted to marry a woman had to ask the father's permission to do so. The following letter, written around 1705, is from William Byrd to Daniel Parke, asking his permission to marry his daughter (Woodfin & Tinling, 1942).

Having someone wonder where you are when you don't come home at night is a very old human need.

—MARGARET MEAD

> Since my arrival in this country, I have had the honour to be acquainted with your daughters, and was infinitely surpriz'd to find young ladys with their accomplishments in Virginia. This surprize was soon improv'd into a passion for the youngest, for whom I have all the respect and tenderness in the world. However, I think it my duty to intreat your approbation before I proceed to give her the last testimony of my affection. And the young lady her self, whatever she may determine by your consent, will agree to nothing without it. If you can entertain a favourable opinion of my person, I dont question but my fortune may be sufficient to make her happy, especially after it has been assisted by your bounty. If you shall vouchsafe to approve of this undertaking, I shall indeavour to recommend myself by all the dutiful regards to your Excellency and all the marks of kindness to your daughter. Nobody knows better than your self how impatient lovers are, and for that reason I hope youll be as

speedy as possible in your determination, which I passionately beg may be in favour of your & c.

The Industrial Revolution

The transition from a courtship system controlled by parents to the relative freedom of mate selection experienced today occurred in response to a number of social changes. The most basic change was the Industrial Revolution, which began in England in the middle of the eighteenth century. No longer were women needed exclusively in the home to spin yarn, make clothes, and process food from garden to table. Commercial industries had developed to provide these services, and women transferred their activities in these areas from the home to the factory. The result was that women had more frequent contact with men.

Women's involvement in factory work decreased parental control; parents were unable to dictate the extent to which their offspring could interact with those they met at work. Hence, values in mate selection shifted from the parents to the children. In the past, parents had approved or disapproved of a potential mate on the basis of their own values: Was the person from "good stock"? Did the man have property or a respectable trade? Did the woman have basic domestic skills? In contrast to these parental concerns, the partners focused more on love feelings. Finally, the Industrial Revolution created more leisure time for dating.

Parental Influence Today

As a result of the Industrial Revolution and the gradual loss of parental control, young American women not only became acquainted with young men outside the family circle but also felt free to consider them as possible mates. With the development of the automobile in the twentieth century came a radical change in the conditions of social interaction of unmarried men and women. Couples could now escape from their respective parents to do as they wished. Movies provided an additional place to share an evening away from friends. Within one generation, courtship had changed from parental to couple control.

Offspring of today are very careful in regard to what they tell their parents about their dating relationships. One researcher observed that they provide more information about persons they are more seriously involved with and try to change their parents' minds if they feel their parents do not approve of their choice.

■ **DATA:** *Of 159 college students in one study, 85 percent reported having tried to influence their mothers in regard to their relationships; 77 percent reported having tried to influence their fathers (Leslie et al., 1986).*

These respondents said that with rare exception, their parents approved of their dating relationships. In general, the parents lived in areas and their offspring attended schools in which the pool of available dates from which the offspring selected was consistent with the parents' wishes.

American parents have a moderate influence on the mate choice of their offspring; Asian American parents often wield a heavy influence. Some Chinese, Japanese, Korean, and Philippine men and women will not marry someone if their parents disapprove of their choice of a mate (Lindsey, 1990).

Parental interference sometimes drives dating partners to be together more often—even to marry. If your parents don't want you to date someone, try to separate the issue of why they disapprove of the person from the issue of whether you can see your partner. You can date and marry whomever you like. In a power struggle with your parents, you will win. The more important concern is why do they object? Your parents know you fairly well, love you, and probably have your best interests in mind. You may still decide to go against their wishes (it is your life), but do so because you genuinely disagree with their perceptions and concerns—not because you want to show them you can marry whomever you want whether they like it or not.

:: Contemporary Functions of Dating

It's what you learn after you know it all that counts.

—JOHN WOODEN

Because most people regard dating or "getting together" as a natural part of getting to know someone else, the other functions of dating are sometimes overlooked. There are at least five of these—confirmation of a social self; recreation; companionship, intimacy, and sex; socialization; and mate selection.

Confirmation of a Social Self

One of the ways we come to be who we are is through interaction with others who hold up social mirrors in which we see ourselves and get feedback on how others view us. When you are on a first date with a person, you are continually trying to assess how that person sees you: Does the person like me? Will the person want to be with me again? When the person gives you positive feedback through speech and gesture, you feel good about yourself and tend to view yourself in positive terms. Dating provides a context for the confirmation of a strong self-concept in terms of how you perceive your effect on other people.

Recreation

Dating, hanging around, or getting together is fun. These are things we do with our peers, away from our parents, and we select the specific activities because we enjoy them. "I get tired of studying and being a student all day," a straight-A major in journalism said. "Going out at night with my friends to meet guys really clears my head. It's an exciting contrast to the drudgery of writing term papers."

Companionship/Intimacy/Sex

Major motivations for dating are companionship, intimacy, and sex. The impersonal environment of a large university makes a secure dating relationship very appealing. "My last two years have been the happiest ever," remarked a senior in interior design. "But it's because of the involvement with my fiancé. During my freshman and sophomore years, I felt alone. Now I feel loved, needed, and secure with my partner." In a study on "Romance in the Personal Ads," Fischer (1990) observed that men were more interested in "companionship" while women were more interested in "a commitment."

Sharing recreational experiences together is a major function of dating.

Socialization

Before puberty, boys and girls interact primarily with peers of their same sex. A boy or girl may be laughed at if he or she shows an interest in someone of the opposite sex. Even when boy-girl interaction becomes the norm at puberty, neither sex may know what is expected of them. Dating offers the experiences of learning how to initiate conversation and developing an array of skills in human relationships, such as listening and expressing empathy. Dating also permits an individual to try out different role patterns, like dominance or submission, and to assess the "feel" and comfort level of each.

Sexual socialization is also a part of dating. Learning how to become physically close to another and to experience intimate encounters with different people is a typical pattern. "People make love differently. They hold you differently and have different preferences," said a drama major.

Mate Selection

Finally, dating may serve to pair two people off for marriage.

■ **DATA:** *Eighty-nine percent of 80 clients at a Videodating Service said that they were looking for a serious, permanent relationship rather than a casual relationship (Woll & Young, 1989, 485).*

Table 7.1 reflects the characteristics 443 university undergraduates identified as being preferred for their "ideal partner."

▪▪ TABLE 7.1 Preferred Characteristics of an "Ideal Partner" from Among 20 Competitive and 20 Noncompetitive Characteristics

"IN A CLOSE RELATIONSHIP, TOWARD ME, MY PARTNER . . ."	WOMEN (%)	MEN (%)
1. DISPLAYS HONESTY	95	89
2. IS TRUSTING	94	94
3. IS COMMUNICATIVE	89	82
4. IS SHARING	87	74
5. DISPLAYS THOUGHTFULNESS	84	74
6. SHOWS UNDERSTANDING (DISPLAYS EMPATHY)	83	75
7. displays intelligence, wit, knowledge	81	83
8. IS OPEN, STRAIGHTFORWARD	79	78
9. displays patience	74	68
10. DISPLAYS GENTLENESS	74	63
11. DISPLAYS KINDNESS	72	72
12. uses humor, irony	68	76
13. DISPLAYS CONFIDENCE (IS NONFEARFUL)	62	52
14. DISPLAYS OPTIMISM	58	55
15. IS OUTGOING	56	60
16. IS SELF-ACCEPTING (FEELS WORTHWHILE)	56	45
17. IS SPONTANEOUS	55	59
18. DISPLAYS HELPFULNESS	55	43
19. DISPLAYS GENEROSITY	53	50
20. displays flexibility	50	43
21. displays industriousness (works hard)	49	35
22. IS AT EASE, RELAXED	44	56
23. displays energy, stamina	40	52
24. acts enthusiastic, exuberant	40	47
25. acts calmly (maintains composure)	39	41
26. displays tolerance, endurance	36	36
27. SHOWS EVENHANDEDNESS (IS FAIR)	34	35
28. IS NONPOSSESSIVE	32	33
29. shows tenacity (sticks to things)	30	30
30. uses diplomacy, tact	29	30
31. displays self-reliance	28	28
32. displays self-awareness	26	32
33. displays courage	24	25
34. uses charm	22	28
35. IS NONDEFENSIVE (NOT SELF-PROTECTIVE)	22	23
36. uses careful planning	21	31
37. is persistent (perseveres)	20	21
38. acts like a "good sport"	15	27
39. displays expertise, competence	13	18
40. behaves stoically (avoids complaining)	13	26

[a]Noncompetitive behaviors are in upper case letters.

SOURCE: "Competitive vs. Noncompetitive Styles: Which is Most Valued in Courtship?" by Mary Riege Laner. *Sex Roles*, 1989, *20*, 168. Used by permission of Plenum Publishing Company.

∷ Dating Realities

One of the first concerns in dating is how to find someone to date. After discussing what is involved in finding a dating partner, we look at an issue that predominantly concerns women—coping with the threat of sexual harassment/rape on dates.

Finding a Dating Partner

There are a variety of mechanisms for meeting someone to date. Informal mechanisms involve meeting people through friends, at work, or in classes. Exhibit 7.1 provides a structured way for you to meet anyone in one of your other classes or on campus.

Three relatively new methods of meeting people involve advertising in magazines and newspapers, joining specialized dating clubs, and joining videodating clubs.

Magazines and Newspapers. While advertising in magazines or newspapers risks "the appearance of being 'desperate' for a date, self-advertisements provide an opportunity for singles to emphasize attributes they are most proud of—something difficult to do in the anonymity of a singles' bar or college dance" (LaBeff et al., 1989, 45).

In advertisements for dates, people most frequently mention their avocation, age, and personality characteristics. Seventy-eight, 77, and 34 percent respectively of one sample of students referred to these characteristics in their self-advertisements (Labeff et al., 1989). However, women were more likely to mention age and men were more likely to mention their personality characteristics. In regard to what they were looking for, both sexes were concerned about personality characteristics.

E X H I B I T   7.1

How to Meet Anyone On Your Campus

The following suggestion is a way for you to meet anyone on your campus.

Turn to page 00 on which you will see the Love Attitudes Scale. Hand the book to someone you are interested in meeting and say, "I'm enrolled in a marriage course on campus and have been requested to ask a person of the opposite sex to take this love test. Would you take a couple of minutes and complete it for me?"

Persons who are interested in some level of interaction with you will agree to complete the form. They may ask you questions about it ("What does the third statement mean?"), establish eye contact, and indicate (through smiles and gestures) a willingness to interact with you.

Not all persons will be receptive. The goal is to meet someone or to find out how others score on the Love Attitudes Scale—not for him or her to fall in love with you at first sight. If you ask 20 people to complete the inventory, expect only one to show an interest in you beyond the inventory.

Bars continue to be a favorite meeting place for some singles.

The creativity of the students was often evident in describing personality. For example, one male advertised for "a lady that loves to live but not too dangerously." Similarly, a female asked for a male who "must be clean, intelligent, have a good sense of humor, and willing to spend some money" (LaBeff et al., 1989, 46).

Advertising for someone to date is not unique to students. Fischer (1987, 1990) studied nonstudents in Washington D.C. and Roanoke, Virginia, who placed such advertisements in the *Washingtonian Magazine* and the *Roanoker.*

■ **DATA:** *Fifty women reported an average of 30 responses to their advertisements; 55 percent of these 50 women reported that "advertising is an effective method of meeting others" (Fischer, 1987).*

Specialized Dating Clubs. Rather than place an advertisement and in an attempt to narrow the people they select from, some people join a dating club that specializes in attracting people with specific characteristics. Below is a list of dating clubs which cater to a specific clientele:

■ Big Buddies (for large sized people) Contact Debby Mellen, 212–967–4628.
■ Vegetarian Dating Club (for people who are concerned about pairing with those who enjoy a vegetarian diet) Contact John Raworth, 619–281–2233.
■ DecMay Club (for partners who enjoy age-discrepant relationships) P.O. Box 2532, Beverly Hills, CA 90213.
■ Music and Art Lovers' Club for Singles, 3739 Nostrand Ave. Suite 333, Brooklyn, NY 11701.
■ Travel Companion Exchange Club, P.O. Box 833, Amityville, NY 11701.

Videodating Clubs. The newest method of finding a partner is to be interviewed on videotape and let others watch your cassette in exchange for your watching those already on file. Eighty clients of a videodating service said that the opportunity to watch the videotapes others had made of themselves was the most attractive feature of videotaping (Woll & Young, 1989). Once they saw someone that they liked, the person was contacted by the service and invited in to review the potential partner's videocassette. If the interest was mutual, the partners would meet.

■ **DATA:** *Great Expectations is the largest video dating service in the United States. It has over 21 centers and 65,000 clients nationwide. The cost for a lifetime membership (until you get married) in Los Angeles is $1850 (Goldberg, 1989).*

☐ C O N S I D E R A T I O N ☐

Most people used the videodating service as a way of finding a specific person (Mr. or Ms. "Right") rather than as a means of attracting a wide range of partners. One effect of this perspective is that "clients are led to rule out—and are themselves screened out by—individuals whom, under most circumstances, they might wish to pursue" (p. 488).

Becoming Involved With a New Partner

Once a dating partner is found, through friends, advertising in magazines/ newspapers, joining a specialized dating club, or joining a video club, the new partners may want to become involved. Such engagement involves establishing a mutually enjoyable relationship. Some prerequisites include a positive self-concept, open communication skills, and an optimistic prediction about the relationship (self-fulfilling prophecy). To the degree that each partner has a positive self-concept, the partners come to each other feeling that they are a person the other will find desirable. This feeling provides a sense of security in the interaction—neither partner fears rejection.

Confident interaction with each other may lead to open disclosure, reflective listening, and acceptance of the other person. As noted in Chapter 2 on Love Relationships, sharing one's self with another increases one's emotional bond to that person. Reflective listening, which we will discuss in more detail in Chapter 10 on Communication in Relationships, involves acknowledgment that you hear and understand what the person tells you. Acceptance involves not becoming judgmental about what the person shares with you.

An optimistic prediction for the future implies that each partner will want to continue the relationship and to see each other again. This self-fulfilling prophecy feeds on itself—by the partners expecting to enjoy each other, they do so, and end up wanting to spend more time together.

Partners who have negative self-concepts, disclose nothing, and predict that the person will never want to see them again are not likely to become emotionally involved with each other. The cycle then repeats itself—because the person does reject them, one's negative self-concept gets worse, and they predict rejection in the next relationship.

Sexual Harassment/Rape in Dating Relationships

Sometimes when partners begin to date, there is the unwelcomed threat of sexual harassment. Two hundred and fifteen university students (from a random sample) reported their experience with other students in dating contexts (Mazer & Percival, 1989).

■ **DATA:** *Twenty-five percent of the women reported that they had experienced unwanted attempts by another student to kiss and fondle them and to engage in sexual activities. No men reported unwanted pressure in regard to kissing or fondling; 3 percent of the men reported unwanted pressure to engage in sexual activities (Mazer & Percival, 1989, 12). Sexual harassment in dating situations which sometimes leads to violence is a universal problem regardless of ethnic background (Kiernan and Taylor, 1990).*

☐   C O N S I D E R A T I O N   ☐

Our society is ambivalent in how it views dating partners who claim they have been raped on a date. Part of this ambivalence is based on the knowledge that false accusations sometimes occur. Cathleen Crowell Webb publically declared that Gary Dotson, who was sent to prison in 1979 for rape, was not guilty. "In fact, she said, there was no rape; she made up the whole story out of fear that she might be pregnant by her boyfriend" (*Time*, 1989, 63).

More recently, Elizabeth Richardson of Lexington, Kentucky told authorities she was raped in 1988 by a painter who had visited her home inquiring about a job. Gary Nitsch was arrested on the charge. Mrs. Richardson later admitted that she made up the accusation to get attention from her husband, a truck driver who was often away from home ("False rape claim leads to apology," 1990).

But rapes do occur and with more than one male at a time. These are known as acquaintance gang rapes in which the girl goes with a trusted date to a fraternity party, is encouraged to drink large quantities of alcohol, and is taken to the room of one of the fraternity brothers and raped by several fraternity members. A member of a fraternity at Stetson University in Deland, Florida went on camera during a 20/20 interview and reported that "this happens about twice a month" ("Acquaintance Gang Rape," 1990).

Sexual harassment is not limited to heterosexual relationships. Twelve percent of gay men and 31 percent of gay women reported that they were victims of forced sexual advances by their current partners (Waterman et al., 1989). Lesbians reported a higher frequency of sexual harassment due to the fact that they were, generally, in relationships longer than men. Duration of a relationship is one variable that has been associated with harassment.

Sexual harassment on dates does occur. Potential victims may be female or male, young adults or older individuals. But, according to one study, most dates do not involve a disagreement concerning the level of sex in the relationship (Byers & Lewis, 1988). We will discuss violence in relationships in greater detail in Chapter 12.

∷ Dating the Second Time Around

Over two million Americans get divorced each year. Most people who divorce wish to become involved in another relationship, and so return to the dating scene to look for a new partner. Some differences between this population and those dating prior to the first marriage include:

- *Older*: Men are around age 32; women are around age 30. Men dating prior to the first marriage are 18–25; women, 18–23.
- *Fewer Available Partners*: Most men and women in their thirties find that there are fewer partners from which to choose than when they were dating prior to a first marriage. Not only are there more women than men in our society, but it is normative for men to date younger women. Hence, all the younger women are available to the older men but all the younger men are not available to the older women.
- *Greater AIDS Risk*: The older an unmarried person, the greater the likelihood of having had multiple sexual partners. Therefore, the person entering the dating market for the second time is likely to be having sex with individuals who have had a higher number of partners.
- *Presence of Children*: Over half of those "dating again" have children from a previous marriage. How these children feel about their parents dating, how the partners feel about each other's children, and how the partners' children feel about each other are complex issues that need attention. Deciding whether to have intercourse when one's children are in the house, what the children call the new partner, and how terminations of relationships are dealt with are other issues that are familiar to many people dating for the second time.
- *Presence of Ex-spouse*: The presence of an ex-spouse who still calls, alimony checks to or from an ex-spouse, and the psychological memory-experience of the partner's first marriage will have an influence on the new dating relationship.

■ *Shorter Courtship*: Divorced people who are dating again tend to have a shorter courtship period than first marrieds. In a study of 248 individuals who remarried, the median length of courtship was 9 months as opposed to 17 months the first time around (O'Flaherty & Eells, 1988).

Awkwardness of Dating Again

The divorced and widowed who re-enter the dating market comment that they feel awkward about "dating again." They are accustomed to being with one person at home every night and feel uncomfortable calling up someone for a date, going out on a date, and being in the role of a "date" rather than a "spouse." It may be helpful to keep in mind that the feeling is not uncommon and may be a topic to facilitate open communication with a new partner. "I'm not sure how to date anymore," when said to a new partner on a first date acknowledges the awkwardness of the situation, exposes one's vulnerability, and provides an opportunity for the partner to share similar feelings.

Dating in the Middle Years

Some of those dating the second time around are in their middle years (defined by the U.S. Bureau of the Census as age 45 to 65). In general, fewer norms guide the dating behaviors of middle-age partners. In their twenties, it was usually clear who would call whom, how soon or late sexual intimacy would occur, and when parents would be involved. But in middle age, the norms are in flux. While one of the partners may be operating on the "old" norms, the other partner may be behaving in reference to a new set of dating norms. The latter imply that either sex calls the other, sexual intimacy usually occurs sooner than later, and parents are not consulted about involvement with the new partner.

Children are often an important consideration and influence in the courtship progress of remarriages, either through direct involvement (taking the kids to the beach) or through their opinions ("I don't like her/him"). Financial obligations to previous spouses and children can also have an impact on the new couple.

Public disclosure in terms of announcements and a large wedding are more common in first than second marriages. The partners in a second marriage more often have a small wedding ceremony with a few selected friends. Announcements are less often sent out, and the couple are more likely to live together before getting married.

Dating in the Later Years

The older I grow, the more I listen to people who don't say much.
—GERMAIN G. GLIDDEN

The later years represent yet another dimension of dating. Senior citizens also date. In a study of 45 people, ranging in age from 60 to 92, who were divorced or widowed and dating again, two researchers observed that "when they fall in love, the older daters experience the same emotional somersaults, sweaty palms, and beating hearts as do younger couples" (Bulcroft & O'Conner-Roden, 1986, 68). Finding a partner may be particularly difficult for older women, as there are still more women than men in this age group.

The researchers also found that sexuality was an important part of dating in senior relationships, with a stronger emphasis on hugging, kissing, and touching. But not always. One 71-year-old widower said, "You can talk about candlelight dinners and sitting in front of a fireplace, but I still think the most romantic thing I've ever done is to go to bed with her" (p. 68).

These daters were also not too interested in marriage. They enjoyed their independence too much and wanted to avoid getting saddled with someone who might become ill and need a full-time caretaker. Nevertheless, dating relationships met an important emotional need in their lives that was not supplied by family or friends.

⠿ Mate Selection

■ **DATA:** *When asked if they would prefer to have a mate for most of their life, 63 percent of adult women and 55 percent of adult men said "Yes" (Thornton, 1989).*

The mutual selection of Connie Chung and Maury Povich, and Melanie Griffith and Don Johnson did not occur by chance. Various cultural, sociological, psychological, and—some sociobiologists say—biological factors combined to influence their meeting and marriage.

Cultural Aspects of Mate Selection

Cultural norms for mate selection vary. The degree of freedom individuals have in choosing a marriage partner depends on the culture in which they live. In some cultures, arranged marriages predominate; in others, including our own, "free" choice is the rule. But some arranging takes place in all cultures. A great many American marriages have been arranged up to modern times, both in poor rural areas and in high society (for example, the marriage of Consuelo Vanderbilt to the Duke of Marlborough in 1895). The Reverend Sun Myung Moon of the Unification Church personally matched and married 2,075 couples in a mass Madison Square Garden ceremony in New York in the early eighties.

Endogamous-Exogamous Pressures. Whereas some societies exert specific pressure on individuals to marry predetermined mates, other societies apply more subtle pressure. The United States has a system of free choice that is not exactly free. Social approval and disapproval restrict your choices so that you do not marry just *anybody*. *Endogamous pressures* encourage you to marry those within your own social group (racial, religious, ethnic, educational, economic); *exogamous pressures* encourage you to marry outside your family group (to avoid marriage to a sibling or other close relative).

The pressure toward an endogamous mate choice is especially strong when race is concerned. One white woman said, "Some of my closest friends are black. But my parents would disown me if I were to openly date a black guy." In contrast, a black man said, "I would really like to date a girl in my introductory psychology class who's white. But my black brothers wouldn't like it, and while my parents wouldn't throw me out of the house, they would wonder why I wasn't dating a black girl."

These individuals are oblivious to endoga- mous cultural pressure.

These endogamous pressures are not operative on all people at the same level or may not work at all. Those who are older than 30, who have been married before, and/or who live in large urban centers are more likely to be color blind in their dating and marrying. In Hawaii, interracial dating and marriage are norma- tive, and interracial marriage does occur throughout our society.

In contrast to endogamous marriage pressures, exogamous pressures are mainly designed to ensure that individuals who are perceived to have a close biological relationship do not marry each other. Incest taboos are universal. In no society are children permitted to marry the parent of the opposite sex. In the

United States, siblings and first cousins (in some states) are also prohibited from marrying each other.

Sociological Aspects of Mate Selection

There are several sociological factors at work in the attraction of two people to each other. The concepts "homogamy" and "propinquity" illustrate these factors.

Homogamy. The *homogamy* theory of mate selection states that we tend to be attracted to and become involved with those who are similar to ourselves in such characteristics as age, race, education, social class, intelligence, physical appearance, and body clock compatibility. There is particularly strong evidence for homogamy in reference to age, race, and education (Schoen & Woolredge, 1989). Research also suggests that the more similar you are to your partner, the better your chances are for achieving personal and marital happiness.

How old would you be if you didn't know how old you was?
—SATCHEL PAIGE

1. *Age.* When a friend gets you a date, you assume the person will be close to your age. Your peers are not likely to approve of your becoming involved with someone twice your age. A student who was dating one of her former teachers said, "He always comes over to my place, and I prepare dinner for us. I don't want to be seen in public with him. Although I love him, it doesn't feel right being with someone old enough to be my father." Such a concern for age homogamy is particularly characteristic of individuals who have never married. Those who have been married before are much more likely to become involved with someone who is less close to their age.

☐   C O N S I D E R A T I O N   ☐

One of the unique qualities of universities is that they provide an environment in which to meet hundreds or even thousands of possible partners of similar age, education, social class, and general goals. This opportunity will probably not be matched later in the work place or where one lives following graduation.

---

2. *Education.* The level of education you attain will also influence your selection of a mate. A sophomore who worked in a large urban department store during the Christmas holidays remarked, "The two weeks Todd and I spent selling record albums and tapes were great. But our relationship never gathered momentum. I was looking forward to my last two years of school, but Todd said college was a waste of time. I don't want to get tied to someone who thinks that way."

   This student's experience suggests that you are likely to marry someone who has also attended college. Not only does college provide an opportunity to meet, date, and marry another college student, but it also increases the chance that only a college-educated person will be acceptable. Education affects not only what you know but also what you are aware of. The very pursuit of education becomes a value to be shared.

3. *Social Class.* You have been reared in a particular *social class* that reflects your parents' occupations, incomes, and educations as well as your residence, lan-

guage, and values. If you were brought up in the home of a physician, you probably lived in a large house in a nice residential section of town. You were in a higher social class than you would have been if your parents were less educated and worked as clerks at K-Mart.

The social class in which you were reared will influence how comfortable you feel with a partner. "I never knew what a finger bowl was," recalled one man, "until I ate dinner with my girlfriend in her parents' Manhattan apartment. I knew then that while her lifestyle was exciting, I was more comfortable with paper napkins and potato chips. We stopped dating."

The tendency for men to marry down and women to marry up in age, social class, and education is referred to as the *mating gradient*.

■ **DATA:** *The median age at first marriage for American men is 25.1; for American women, it is 23.3 (U.S. Bureau of the Census, 1990).*

As a result of the mating gradient, some high-status women and low-status men remain single. Upper-class women typically receive approval from their parents and peers only if they marry someone of equal status. On the other hand, approval is less likely to be withheld from men who marry women who are younger and lower in social status. Educated, professional black females have a particularly difficult time finding black males of equal status.

☐   C O N S I D E R A T I O N   ☐

The mating gradient results in an oversupply of unmarried older, bright, educated, professional women. Men might consider the personal, social, and economic benefits of including such women in their pool of potential partners, and women might reconsider the idea that their mate must be older, educated, and professionally established. Solid happy relationships can result from a number of different pairings. The mating gradient may be an artificial restriction.

---

4. *Race.* Homogamy operates strongly in reference to race. In Chapter 8, we will discuss interracial marriages in detail. Here, we will merely point out that of the 50 million married couples in the United States, only 1.8 percent are interracial (*Statistical Abstract of the United States: 1990 Table 53*).

5. *Intelligence.* Intelligence was the number one characteristic that 122 male and 210 female undergraduates said they looked for in the opposite sex (Daniel et al., 1985). "There are plenty of bimbos on campus," said one student. "I need someone whose cortical cells are active and who thinks about things other than drinking Bud Lite." Another said, "I think intelligent guys are just more fun. They are never boring and seem to know what is coming down."

6. *Physical Appearance.* In general, people tend to become involved with those who are similar in physical attractiveness. However, a partner's attractiveness may be more important for men than for women (Sprecher, 1989). In one study, at least 50 percent of women said that "attractiveness" was what men were interested in, but only 13 percent of the men felt that this was important for women (Woll & Young, 1989, 485).

7. *Body clock compatibility.* Some of us are "morning people," some of us are "night people." Morning people arise early and feel most energetic in the morning.

Night people sleep late and feel most energy late at night. Night people like to go to sleep at dawn—just the time when morning people are getting up.

Research on partners who are matched or mismatched in terms of body clocks suggests that their happiness is related to the degree that they are matched. Couples who are on different body clock rhythms must work at this aspect of their relationship through compromise or accommodation to reduce its negative influence (Locitzer, 1989).

Love looks not with the eyes but with the mind.
—SHAKESPEARE

8. *Other Factors.* Marital status and religion are other factors involved in homogamous mate selection. The never married tend to select the never married, the divorced tend to select the divorced, and the widowed tend to select the widowed as partners to marry. In addition, although religious homogamy is decreasing because we are becoming increasingly pluralistic and secularized as a society, this factor is still operative (particularly among those of the Jewish faith).

CONSIDERATION

Even if all the homogamous factors discussed above were present in a couple's relationship, the couple would be unlikely to marry if they did not have love feelings. This is particularly true in the United States where couples are socialized to marry only those for whom they feel a deep emotional attachment. To marry without love, according to U.S. norms, is to begin a relationship with a missing psychological element.

This insistence on love before marriage is not true in all societies. In parts of rural China and India, marriages are still regarded as unions between families and are arranged by a matchmaker or go-between. Individuals are taught to expect love after, not before marriage (Lindsey, 1990).

Propinquity. Years ago, a sociologist found that one sixth of 5000 couples applying for marriage licenses in Philadelphia lived within one city block of each other. One third of the couples lived within five blocks of each other and half lived within 20 blocks (Bossard, 1932). This study illustrates the principle of residential propinquity, or the tendency to select marriage partners from among those who live nearby.

Propinquity, which means nearness or proximity, may also refer to the workplace and school. Propinquity may be related to mate selection because living, working, or going to school near someone provides an opportunity to meet that person. In addition, being at the same school, working at the same job, or living close to one another may be related to sharing similar interests, values, life experiences, and characteristics.

Psychological Aspects of Mate Selection

Psychologists have focused on complementary needs, exchanges, parental images, and personalities in regard to mate selection.

Complementary Needs Theory. "In spite of the women's movement and a lot of assertive friends, I am a shy and dependent person," remarked a transfer student.

"My need for dependency is met by Warren, who is the dominant, protective type." The tendency for a submissive person to become involved with a dominant person (one who likes to control the behavior of others) is an example of attraction based on *complementary needs*. Complementary needs theory states that we tend to select mates whose needs are opposite and complementary to our own needs. Partners can also be drawn to each other on the basis of nurturance versus receptivity. These complementary needs suggest that one person likes to give and take care of another, while the other likes to be the benefactor of such care. Other examples of complementary needs may involve responsibility versus irresponsibility and peacemaker versus troublemaker. The idea that mate selection is based on complementary needs was suggested by Winch (1955), who noted that needs can be complementary if they are different (for example, dominant and submissive) or if the partners have the same need at different levels of intensity. As an example of the latter, two individuals may have a complementary relationship when they both want to do advanced graduate study, but both need not get Ph.D.s. The partners will complement each other if one is comfortable with his or her level of aspiration, represented by a master's degree, but still approves of the other's commitment to earn a Ph.D.

Winch's theory of complementary needs, commonly referred to as "opposites attract," is based on the observation of 25 undergraduate married couples at Northwestern University. The findings have been criticized by other researchers who have not been able to replicate Winch's study. Two researchers said, "It would now appear that Winch's findings may have been an artifact of either his methodology or his sample of married people" (Meyer & Pepper, 1977).

Three questions can be raised about the theory of complementary needs:

1. Couldn't personality needs be met just as easily outside the couple's relationship rather than through mate selection? For example, couldn't a person who has the need to be dominant find such fulfillment in a job that involved an authoritative role, such as head of a corporation or an academic department?
2. What is a complementary need as opposed to a similar value? For example, is desire to achieve at different levels a complementary need or a shared value?
3. Don't people change as they age? Could a dependent person grow and develop self-confidence so that they may no longer need to be involved with a dominant person? Indeed, they may no longer enjoy interacting with a dominant person.

> How much you respect someone is more often determined by the balance of giving and getting between you than by old-fashioned standards like honor, talent, virtue.
>
> —ROBERT KAREN

Exchange Theory. *Exchange theory* suggests that mate selection is based on assessing who offers the greatest rewards at the lowest cost. Four concepts help to explain the exchange process in mate selection:

1. Rewards are the behaviors (your partner looking at you with the "eyes of love"), words (saying "I love you"), resources (being beautiful or handsome, having money), and services (driving you home, typing for you) your partner provides for you that you value and that influence you to continue the relationship.
2. Costs are the unpleasant aspects of a relationship. One man said, "I have to drive across town to pick her up, listen to her nagging mother before we can leave, and be back at her house by midnight."

3. Profit occurs when the rewards exceed the costs.
4. Loss occurs when the costs exceed the rewards.

Exchange concepts operate at three levels of the dating relationship—who can date whom, the conditions of the dating relationship, and the decision to marry. As for whom you date, two researchers (Schoen & Woolredge, 1989) noted a pattern of exchange based on "a female emphasis on male economic characteristics and a male emphasis on female noneconomic characteristics" (p. 465). Hence, females tend to trade their youth and beauty for the male's economic resources. However, as women have become more economically independent, this pattern of exchange has lessened.

Once you identify a person who offers you a good exchange for what you have to offer, other bargains are made about the conditions of your continued relationship. Forty years ago, two researchers (Waller & Hill, 1951) observed that the person who has the least interest in continuing the relationship can control the relationship. This *principle of least interest* is illustrated by the woman who said, "He wants to date me more than I want to date him, so we end up going where I want to go and doing what I want to do." In this case, the woman trades her company for the man's acquiescence to her choices.

Additional exchanges take place as the partners move toward marriage. They make a marital commitment when they both feel that they are getting the partner who offers the most rewards of all potential alternatives. A graduating senior and groom-to-be remarked, "It's easy. I've decided to marry Maria because sharing life with her is more fun than being with anyone else. And marriage is one way to help ensure that we will be together to share our lives across the years."

The cultural and sociological aspects of mate selection emphasize that two people do not arbitrarily select each other. Table 7-2 reflects the various filters operative in the process of two people dating and deciding to marry each other.

Another exchange occurring in relationships is that of information. As long as the information both partners learn about the other is consistent with their expectations of the other, the relationship will continue. One way to help become more secure in a relationship is to find out as much as possible about each other. If the relationship continues with full knowledge of each other's feelings on a variety of issues, it is more likely to be secure than if the partners stay together but know very little about each other. The Relationship Self-Assessment Inventory provides one way for partners considering marriage or living together to find out more about each other.

Parental Image. Whereas the complementary and exchange theories of mate selection are relatively recent, Freud suggested earlier that the choice of a love object in adulthood represents a shift in libidinal energy from the first love objects—the parents. This means that a man looks for a wife like his mother and a woman looks for a husband like her father. In a study of almost 7,000 spouses, Jedlicka (1984) has observed that selecting a partner similar to the opposite-sex parent occurs more often than can be expected by chance.

One of the reasons for selecting a person similar to the opposite-sex parent is the familiarity with the personality and values of the parent. Selecting someone who is similar to the parent provides a sense of comfort and predictability. Sharing similar values also helps to bond the partners to each other since most people like someone who agrees with them (Whyte, 1990).

■■ TABLE 7.2 **Cultural, Sociological, and Psychological Filters of Mate Selection**

CULTURAL FILTERS

For two people to consider marriage to each other,

Endogamous factors (same race, caste)	and ↓	Exogamous factors (not blood related)

must be met.
↓

After the cultural prerequisites have been satisfied, sociological and psychological filters become operative.

SOCIOLOGICAL FILTERS

Propinquity = the tendency to select a mate from among those who live, work, or go to school nearby.

Homogamy = the tendency to select a mate similar to oneself in regard to the following:

Age	Physical Appearance
Race	Body Clock Compatibility
Education	Religion
Social Class	Marital Status
Intelligence	

PSYCHOLOGICAL FILTERS

Love Feelings
Complementary Needs
Cost-benefit Ratio in Exchanges
Similarity to Opposite Sex Parent
Personality Characteristics

Personality Characteristics

In choosing a potential mate, we look for someone with particular personality characteristics that we find desirable. Someone who is viewed as being rude, irresponsible, unstable, and dull may not be as desirable as someone who is viewed as being polite, responsible, stable, and interesting.

There is subjectivity and individual variation in what people regard as desirable personality characteristics. Some characteristics, however, have been objectively shown to be undesirable in that they predispose an individual toward impaired functioning in marriage (Snyder and Regts, 1990). These characteristics include poor impulse control, hypersensitivity to perceived criticism, and exaggerated self-appraisal.

Sociobiological Aspects of Mate Selection

Sociobiology suggests that there is a biological basis for all social behavior—including mate selection. Based on Charles Darwin's theory of natural selection, which states that the strongest of the species survive, sociobiologists contend that men and women select each other as mates on the basis of their concern for producing offspring who are most capable of surviving.

According to sociobiologists, men look for an attractive, bright, sexually conservative woman who will care for their offspring. Men also look for young

S E L F   A S S E S S M E N T

The Relationship Assessment Inventory

The following questions are designed to increase your knowledge of how you and your partner think and feel about a variety of issues. Each partner should ask the other the following questions.

Careers and Money

1. What kind of job or career will you have? What are your feelings about working in the evening versus being home with the family? Where will your work require that we live? How often do you feel we will be moving? Where are the places you would refuse to move to? How much will your job require that you travel?

2. What are your feelings about joint versus separate checking accounts? Which of us do you want to pay the bills? How much money do you think we will have left over each month? How much of this do you think we should save?

3. When we disagree over whether to buy something, how do you suggest we resolve our conflict?

4. What jobs or work experience have you had in the past?

5. What is your preference for where we live? Do you want to live in an apartment or house? What are your needs for a car, compact disk player, video recorder, television, cable TV?

6. How do you feel about my having a career? Do you expect me to earn an income? If so, how much annually? To what degree do you feel it is your responsibility to cook, clean, and take care of the children? How do you feel about putting young children or infants in day care centers? When they are sick and one of us has to stay home, who will that be?

7. Do you want me to account to you for the money I spend?

8. How much money do you think we should give to charity each year?

Religion and Children

1. To what degree do you regard yourself as a religious person? What do you think about religion, a supreme being, prayer, and life after death?

2. Do you go to religious services? Where? How often? Do you pray? How often? What do you pray about? When we are married, how often would you want to go to religious services? In what religion would you want our children to be reared? What responsibility would you take to ensure that our children had the religious training you wanted them to have?

3. How do you feel about abortion? Under what conditions, if any, do you feel abortion is justified?

4. What do you think about children? How many do you want? Why? When do you want the first child? At what intervals would you want to have additional children? What do you see as your responsibility for childcare—changing diapers, feeding, bathing, playing with children, and taking them to piano lessons? To what degree do you regard these responsibilities as mine?

5. Suppose I did not want to have children or couldn't have them, how would you feel? How do you feel about artificial insemination, surrogate motherhood, in-vitro fertilization (see Chapter 14), and adoption?

6. To your knowledge, can you have children? Are there any genetic problems in your family history that would prevent us from having normal children?

7. Do you want our children to go to public or private schools?

8. How should children be disciplined? How were you disciplined as a child?

continued on next page

Sex

1. How much sexual intimacy do you feel is appropriate in casual dating, involved dating, and engagement?
2. What do you think about masturbation, oral sex, homosexuality, S & M, and anal sex?
3. What type of contraception do you suggest? Why? If that method does not prove satisfactory, what method would you suggest next?
4. What are your values regarding sex outside of marriage? If I were to have an affair and later tell you, what would you do? Why? If I had an affair, would you want me to tell you? Why?
5. What sexual behaviors do you most and least enjoy? How often do you want to have intercourse? How do you want me to turn you down when I don't want to have sex? How do you want me to approach you for sex? How do you feel about just being physical together—hugging, rubbing, holding, but not having intercourse?
6. What does an orgasm feel like to you? By what method of stimulation do you experience an orgasm most easily?
7. What is pornography and/or erotica to you? How do you feel about it?

Relationships with Friends/Coworkers

1. How do you feel about my spending one evening a week from 6:00 to 11:00 with my friends or coworkers?
2. How do you feel about my spending time with friends of the opposite sex during this time?
3. What do you regard as appropriate and inappropriate affectional behaviors with friends?

Recreation and Leisure

1. How do you feel about golf, surfing, swimming, boating, horseback riding, jogging, lifting weights, racquetball, basketball, football, baseball, tennis, soccer, wrestling, fishing-/hunting? How often do you engage in each of these activities? What recreational activities would you like me to become interested in?
2. What hobbies do you have?
3. What do you like to watch on TV? How often do you watch TV and for what periods of time?

4. What is the amount and frequency of your current alcohol and drug (i.e., marijuana, cocaine, crack, speed) consumption? What, if any, have been your previous alcohol and drug behaviors and frequencies? What are your expectations of me regarding the use of alcohol and drugs?
5. How often will you want to go on vacation? Where will you want to go? How will we travel? How much money do you feel we should spend on vacations each year?

Partner Feelings

1. If you could change one thing about me, what would it be?
2. What would you like me to do to make you happier?
3. What would you like me to say or not say to make you happier?
4. What do you think of yourself? Describe yourself with three adjectives.
5. What do you think of me? Describe me with three adjectives.
6. What do you like best about me?
7. Do you think I get jealous easily? How will you cope with my jealousy?
8. How do you feel about me emotionally?

Feelings about Parents

1. How often do you have contact with your father/mother? How do you feel about your parents?
2. What do you like and dislike about my parents?
3. What is your feeling about living near our parents? How would you feel about my parents living with us? What will we do with our parents if they can't take care of themselves?
4. How do your parents get along? Rate their marriage on a 0–10 scale (0-unhappy; 10-happy). What are your parents' role responsibilities in their marriage?

Other Questions

1. Do you have any history of abuse or violence, either with your being abused as a child or your being abused or being the abuser in an adult relationship?

2. If we could not get along, would you be willing to see a marriage counselor? Would you see a sex therapist if we were having sexual problems?
3. What is your feeling about prenuptial agreements?
4. What value do you place on the opinions or values of your parents and friends?

It would be unusual if you agreed with each other on all of your answers to the previous questions. You might view the differences as challenges and then find out the degree to which thedifferences are important for your relationship. You might need to explore ways of minimizing the negative impact of those differences on your relationship. It is not possible to have a relationship with someone where there is total agreement. Disagreement is inevitable; the issue becomes how you and your partner manage the disagreements.

NOTE: This Self-Assessment is intended to be thought-provoking and fun. It is not intended to be used as a clinical or diagnostic instrument.

women. It is advantageous for males to have good form vision for females between the ages of 15 and 40. It serves no advantage for men to deposit their sperm in matronly women, at least as far as procreation is concerned. Doing so increases the possibility of congenital aberrations (retardation, cleft palate, etc.) (Knox & Daniel, 1986).

Women, in contrast, look for an industrious man who has a good earning capacity to provide for her children. This pattern of men seeking physically attractive young women and women seeking economically ambitious men was observed in 37 groups of men and women in 33 different societies (Buss, 1989).

The sociobiological explanation for mate selection is extremely controversial. Critics argue that women may show concern for the earning capacity of men because the women have been systematically denied access to similar economic resources and selecting a mate with these resources is one of their remaining options. In addition, it is argued that both women and men, when selecting a mate, think more about their partners as companions than as future parents of their offspring.

:: Terminating a Dating Relationship

In dating relationships, just as in marital relationships, one or both partners may feel the need to terminate the relationship.

■ **DATA:** *About 30 percent of 104 nonmarried persons who were involved in a relationship terminated those relationships within a four-year period (Wheaton, 1990).*

A number of steps need to be considered in terminating a relationship.

Steps In Breaking Up With A Partner

1. Decide that terminating the relationship is what you want to do. In some cases, it may be possible to "fix" the relationship. Negotiating differences, compro-

Last night I wrote I loved you and your oatmeal cookies; tonight I write I hate you but I still love your oatmeal cookies.

—HAL J. DANIEL III

mising, changing expectations, and giving the relationship more time are alternatives to ending it. But in other cases, it may be wiser to terminate a wounded relationship than to try to keep it alive. As Rhett Butler says to Scarlett O'Hara in *Gone With The Wind*:

> I was never one to patiently pick up broken fragments and glue them together and tell myself that the mended whole was as good as new. What's broken is broken—I'd rather remember it as it was at its best than mend it and see the broken pieces as long as I lived. (Mitchell, 1977, 945)

Wheaton (1990) observed that persons who adjusted most easily to the termination of a relationship had a highly conflictual and stressful relationship from which they were withdrawing.

2. Acknowledge and accept that terminating a relationship may be painful for both partners. There may be no way you can stop the hurt. One person said, "I can't live with him any more, but I don't want to hurt him either." The two feelings are incompatible. To end a relationship with someone who loves you is usually hurtful to both partners.

3. After deciding that termination is the goal and accepting the inevitable pain, tell the partner that you do not want to continue the relationship for a reason that is specific to you ("I need more freedom," "I want to go to graduate school in another state," "I'm not ready to settle down," and the like). Don't blame your partner or give your partner a way to make things better. If you do, the relationship may continue because you may feel obligated to give your partner a second chance.

Although some people prefer to tell the partner in person, others feel that a

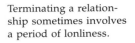

Terminating a relationship sometimes involves a period of lonliness.

letter is easier. "I know it's chicken," said one history major, "but I just can't tell her to her face. I've tried twice and she's talked me out of it both times." Still others prefer the phone. One person used a cassette tape. "I didn't want the coldness of a letter or to get trapped in a phone conversation and hear him start crying, so I made him a cassette tape and mailed it to him."

4. Cut off the relationship completely. If you are the person ending the relationship, you will be less involved in the relationship than your partner. Your lower level of involvement may make it possible for you to continue to see the other person without feeling too hurt when the evening is over. But the other person will have a more difficult time and will heal faster if you stay away completely.

5. Start new relationships. By going out with others you force your ex-partner to acknowledge that you are serious about ending the relationship. You should also encourage your ex-partner to see others. Time usually heals all wounds, but meanwhile another partner is an alternative source of reinforcement.

☐   C O N S I D E R A T I O N   ☐

Although you may not feel like initiating contact with others, it will eventually heal the pain to get back into the stream of life by doing so. Don't wait until you feel like seeing others; do it immediately. But watch the level of involvement in a new relationship. Because you have just come from a terminated relationship, you may be particularly vulnerable or susceptible to a new love. For now, the goal should be to see others and have fun—not to fall in love or find a new partner.

Individuals who report the easiest adjustment to the termination of a relationship are those who ended a very stressful relationship and became involved in a new relationship within a short time (Wheaton, 1990).

■■ Timing Your Decision to Marry

Launching a communications satellite into space requires precise timing. If liftoff occurs at other than the exact moment, the satellite will miss its orbit and be lost in space. (RCA once lost a multimillion dollar satellite in space.) Getting into a successful marital orbit also requires timing. Issues to consider in timing your commitment to marriage are age, education, and career.

Age

Your age and that of your partner at the time of marriage are predictive of your future happiness and stability. Individuals who get married in their early twenties (22–24) have the highest chance of being happy and staying together; those who marry in their teens or their late twenties (27–29) have the highest chance of divorce (Booth & Edwards, 1985). Very early marriages are associated with high rates of extramarital relationships, which are destructive to most marriages. Marriages in the late twenties may also be vulnerable to divorce because "later marriers may be wedding people who are quite different from themselves with respect to lifestyles and education" (p. 73). It is the fact of marrying someone different—not the fact of being "set in one's ways"—that contributes to marital instability in the twenties (Bitter, 1986). Another study found that those who delay first marriage until the age of 30 or beyond have an increased risk of getting divorced (Maneker & Rankin, 1985). Those who marry late must select from a smaller pool of partners.

□   C O N S I D E R A T I O N   □

Waiting until you have completed college seems to be an ideal time to get married in terms of having a low chance of divorce. According to divorce statistics, marrying in your teens is something to avoid. The teen divorce rate is two to three times greater than the divorce rate among people who marry in their twenties.

Education

How much education you have, when you were educated, and whether you or your partner has more education may also affect your marital happiness and the stability of your relationship. Men who complete college have a lower rate of divorce than men who complete only high school or who leave college without graduating. If you marry before you complete college, you will be likely to complete college. The reason for greater marital stability among college-educated men is not the education itself but the economic potential associated with increased education. The adage "The more you learn, the more you earn" is still true.

College graduates report higher incomes and higher marital satisfaction than high school graduates.

■ **DATA:** *The median income of family heads under age 30 with a college degree is four times greater than that of high school dropouts—$24,000 versus $6,240 (Cutler, 1989).*

Increased education for women is predictive of marital stability, but not if a wife has more education than her husband. This is particularly true if the wife is a college graduate and her husband is not (Glick, 1984).

The more educated person may put more "thought" into the selection of a partner. Finally, increased education may also involve enhanced communication and problem-solving skills.

Career Plans

The timing of your marriage will also depend on your career plans. Some individuals feel that they want to be established in a career for a couple of years and be economically independent before they get married. "My sister married a guy in college and threw her career plans to the wind," said one woman. "She's now divorced and is on the job market for the first time at age 31. I'm not going to let that happen to me."

Other people feel they have to make a choice between their career and their partner and fear losing the partner if they choose the career. "I can't put my partner on hold for two years while I find out what it is like in the business world," said another woman. "I'm confident that I'll be a great success in my work, but I don't know how much it will mean if I'm not married to Bill. It is a real dilemma."

▪▪ Becoming Engaged

An engagement to be married represents an intermediate stage between courtship and marriage. What are the implications of this stage, and how can you use it to increase future happiness?

> Engagement has two meanings—in war, it's a battle; in courtship, it's a surrender.
> —LAURENCE PETER

Implications of an Engagement

The engagement period is usually regarded as a serious, monogamous, public, and preparatory time for the wedding.

Serious. An engagement is a specific commitment to marry. Once the words "let's get married" are spoken and agreed to, the relationship assumes a different status.

The other person is no longer viewed as a casual partner but as a future spouse. Although a few regard engagement lightly, most take it seriously.

Monogamous. Engagements tend to carry the expectation that both partners refrain from engaging in romantic or sexual activity with other individuals. This informal expectation for engaged couples to be monogamous becomes a formal expectation once the couple is married, in that sex outside of marriage is a violation of the law.

Public. Some couples have the understanding that they are engaged, but choose to keep their engagement private and informal. For many couples, however, engagement involves a public, formal announcement of their intent to marry. Parents and peers become involved in the event and may communicate their evaluations of each partner's marital choice.

Preparations. Of first weddings, 80 percent take place in a traditional setting (a church or a synagogue) with bridesmaids and ushers. Such an event requires tremendous preparation and, for many couples, is a time of intense stress. "We were both under so much pressure preparing for the wedding," recalled one bride, "at one time we considered calling it off. My father told us if it was going to be that big of a hassle, to elope and he would give us the $2,500."

Using Your Engagement Period Productively

Marriage is a great institution, but I'm not ready for an institution yet.
—MAE WEST

"He's not the man I married," said a spouse, one year after her wedding. This is as often said of a wife. People frequently do not know the person they are marrying very well. "What you see is what you get" is not true of marriage partners. You really don't know what you have got until you relate to the person in the role of spouse over a period of time. But there are some things you can do to help minimize the surprises after marriage. These include systematically examining your relationship, recognizing dangerous patterns, visiting your future in-laws, and considering premarital counseling.

Examine Your Relationship. In a commercial for an oil filter, a mechanic says he has just completed a "ring job" on a car engine that will cost the owner over $400. He goes on to say that a $5.98 oil filter would have made the job unnecessary, and ends his soliloquy with, "Pay me now, or pay me later." The same idea applies to the consequences of using or not using your engagement period to examine your relationship. At some point, you will take a very close look at your partner and your relationship; but will you do it now—or later? Doing so now may be less costly than doing so after the wedding.

In examining your relationship, it may be helpful for you and your partner to take the Relationship Assessment Inventory presented earlier in this chapter. To what degree are you and your partner compatible, similar, or dissimilar in terms of the issues and values that matter to each of you?

Recognize Dangerous Patterns. As you examine your relationship, you should be sensitive to patterns that suggest you may be on a collision course. Three such patterns are breaking the relationship frequently, constant arguing, and inequality resulting from differences in education, social class, and the like. A roller-coaster engagement is predictive of a marital relationship that will follow the same pattern.

The same is true of frequent arguments in a relationship. Lovers' arguments become the married couple's fights. If arguing is a pattern, the engaged couple may want to consider learning more productive communication techniques (see Chapter 00 on Communication).

CONSIDERATION

A relationship pattern characterized by lack of communication may be just as unhealthy as a relationship pattern characterized by arguments. One divorced man said, "My wife and I never fought and never argued. We communicated very little of our real feelings to each other and over the years we drifted into separate lives."

Relationships in which the partners are regarded as being unequal to each other are precarious. Consider the case of Bill and Susan. He was a divorced physician with two children. She was a nurses' aide, and although she held him in awe, they had little in common. Although lovers may view each other with awe, spouses rarely do. Eventually, Bill may feel cheated because he does not have a companion equal to his life and educational experience. Susan may feel stress at continually trying to be what she is not to appease Bill. So persons who are radically different in age, education, social class, and values should be cautious about marrying. Friends select each other because they have something in common and will maintain their relationship for the same reason. Lovers may select each other on the basis of love feelings, but when these feelings dissipate, what they have in common is crucial in determining whether they maintain their interest in each other.

Observe Your Future In-Laws. Engagements often mean more frequent interaction with each partner's parents, so you might seize the opportunity to assess the type of family your partner was reared in and the implications for your marriage. When visiting your in-laws-to-be, observe their standard of living, the way they relate to each other, and the degree to which your partner is similar to your future in-laws. How does their standard of living compare with that of your own family? How does the emotional closeness (or distance) of your partner's family compare with that of your family? Such comparisons are significant because both you and your partner will reflect your respective home environments to some degree. If you want to know what your partner may be like in 20 years, look at his or her parent of the same sex. There is a tendency for a man to become like his father and a woman to become like her mother.

> Don't let your in-laws become out-laws.
> —ED HARTZ

Consider Premarital Counseling

Most clergy offer three premarital sessions before marrying a couple. These sessions may consist of information about marriage, an assessment of the couple's relationship, or resolving conflicts that have surfaced in the relationship. Those who do not plan to be married in a church or a synagogue or who do not choose to see a clergyman for premarital counseling sometimes see a marriage counselor. A professional can be helpful in assisting a couple to assess their relationship. Although the couple might deny the existence of a problem for fear that looking at it will break up the relationship, the counselor can help them examine the problem and work toward the goal of solving it.

Some premarital counselors use inventories to help identify couples who are likely to get divorced. Larsen and Olson (1989) developed an inventory (PRE-

A woman is likely to
turn out much like her
mother.

PARE) which assesses expectations, communication, conflict resolution skills, and
a host of other areas. They gave the inventory to 164 premarital couples and
conducted a follow-up three years later. They found that couples who had unrealistic expectations, poor communication patterns, absence of conflict resolution
skills, etc., were more likely to have separated than those scoring high in these
areas.

Prolong Your Engagement If . . .

Even though you and your partner may have examined your relationship, seen a counselor, and feel confident about your impending marriage, there are five conditions under which you might consider prolonging your engagement. In combination, these conditions argue against getting married at this time.

Age 18 or Younger. The strongest predictor of getting divorced is getting married as an adolescent. Individuals who marry in their teens may disrupt their ability "to resolve crises of intimacy and identity formation, and may thus lead to problems in the formation and maintenance of intimate relationships" (Teti & Lamb, 1989, 209). The effect is true for both whites and blacks.

Short Courtship. A short courtship is also associated with divorce. Partners who date each other for at least two years before making a marital commitment report the highest level of marital satisfaction (Grover, 1985). A short courtship does not allow the partners to observe and scrutinize the behavior of the other in a variety of settings.

☐   C O N S I D E R A T I O N   ☐

Suggestions to maximize learning about each other include taking a three-day "primitive" camping trip, taking a 15-mile hike together, wallpapering a small room together, and/or spending 24 hours together when one partner has the flu. Additionally, a dating couple may learn more about each other by spending time together during the woman's premenstrual period. Time should also be spent with each other's friends and family. If the couple plans to have children at some future point, they may want to observe how each other relates to infants and children.

Financial Stress. Two researchers (Johnson & Booth, 1990) observed that spouses who were economically stressed reported that it had a negative effect on their marital happiness and that they thought about divorce more often. Being economically stressed does not necessarily mean having a low income. Many couples with high incomes are under financial stress. A minister commented that "you can tell how big a couple's problems are by the size of their house." Two researchers suggest that marital satisfaction depends not on the income itself, but rather on the couple's feelings that their income is adequate (Berry & Williams, 1987).

Parental Disapproval. A parent recalled, "I knew when I met the guy it wouldn't work out. I told my daughter and pleaded that she not marry him. She did, and they are divorced." Such parental predictions (whether positive or negative) often come true. If the predictions are negative, they may contribute to stress and conflict once the couple marries.

Even though parents who reject the commitment choice of their offspring are often regarded as unfair, their opinions should not be taken lightly. The parents' own experience in marriage and their intimate knowledge of their offspring combine to help them assess how their child might get along with a particular mate. If the parents of either partner disapprove of the marital choice, the partners should try to evaluate these concerns objectively. The insights may prove valuable.

Premarital Pregnancy. Of unmarried women who become pregnant, what percent get married?

■ **DATA:** *Of the unmarried women who become pregnant, 48 percent of all unmarried white women and 10 percent of all unmarried black women marry before the birth of the child* (Statistical Abstract of the United States: 1990).

The spouses in such marriages have a higher risk of marital unhappiness and divorce than those who do not conceive children before marriage. Combined with adolescence, a short premarital period, lack of money, and parental or in-law hostility, premarital pregnancy represents an ominous beginning for newlyweds.

□   C O N S I D E R A T I O N   □

Should you call off the wedding? If you are having second thoughts about getting married to the person to whom you have made a commitment, you are not alone. About one-third of all engagements are broken. Although some anxiety about getting married is normal (you are entering a new role), constant questions to yourself, such as "Am I doing the right thing?," or thoughts, such as "This doesn't feel right," are definite caution signals that suggest it might be best to call off the wedding. Before marriage, you will be breaking an engagement; after marriage, you will be getting a divorce. Although calling off the wedding will create anxiety, calling off the marriage (divorce) will create even more. "When in doubt, don't go through with the wedding," says one marriage counselor.

Negative Reasons for Getting Married

In addition to premarital pregnancy, other questionable reasons for getting married include rebound, escape, psychological blackmail, and pity. Also, some couples may marry simply because they feel it is the next logical step to take in their relationship.

■ **DATA:** *In a survey of over 56,000* Woman's Day *readers, 41 percent said that they married for the wrong reasons (Lear, 1986).*

Rebound. A rebound marriage results when you marry someone immediately after another person has terminated a relationship with you. It is a frantic attempt to reestablish your desirability in your own eyes and in the eyes of the partner who just dropped you. One man said:

> After she told me she wouldn't marry me, I became desperate. I called up an old girlfriend to see if I could get the relationship going again. We were married within a month. I know it was foolish, but I was very hurt and couldn't stop myself.

☐   C O N S I D E R A T I O N   ☐

To marry on the rebound is questionable because the marriage is made in reference to the previous partner and not to the partner being married. In reality, you are using the person you intend to marry to establish yourself as the winner in the previous relationship. To avoid the negative consequences of marrying on the rebound, you might wait until the negative memories of your past relationship have been replaced by positive aspects of your current relationship. In other words, marry when the satisfactions of being with your current partner outweigh any feelings of revenge.

Escape. A partner may marry to escape an unhappy home situation in which the parents are often seen as oppressive and overbearing and their marriage as discordant. Their continued bickering may be highly aversive, causing the partner to marry to flee the home. A family with an alcoholic parent may create an escape situation. One woman said:

> I couldn't wait to get away from home. Ever since my dad died, my mother has been drinking and watching me like a hawk. "Be home early, don't drink, and watch out for those horrible men," she would always say. I admit it. I married the first guy that would have me. Marriage was my ticket away from that woman.

☐   C O N S I D E R A T I O N   ☐

Marriage for escape is a poor idea. It is far better to continue the relationship with the partner until mutual love and respect, rather than the desire to escape an unhappy situation, become the dominant forces propelling you toward marriage. In this way you can evaluate the marital relationship in terms of its own potential and not solely as an alternative to an unhappy situation.

Next Logical Step. Partners who have dated each other for several years may feel that marriage is the next logical step in their relationship. They may not be particularly enamoured with each other and may even have a very conflictual relationship, but feel that since they have already invested a significant amount of time into the relationship, they may as well marry each other. Partners might consider that marriage is optional, that it does not alter their relationship for the better, and that each feeling very positive about each other and their relationship is important before making a commitment to marry.

Psychological Blackmail. Some individuals get married because their partner takes the position that "I can't live without you" or "I will commit suicide if you leave me." Because the person fears that the partner may commit suicide, the wedding occurs. The problem with such a marriage is that the partner has learned to manipulate the relationship in such a way to get what he or she wants. Use of this power often creates resentment in the other partner who feels trapped in the marriage. Escaping from the marriage becomes even more difficult.

Pity. Some partners marry because they feel guilty about terminating a relationship with someone who they pity. The boyfriend of one woman got drunk one Halloween evening and began to light fireworks on the roof of his fraternity house. As he was running away from a Roman candle he had just ignited, he tripped and fell off the roof. He landed on his head and was in a coma for three weeks. A year after the accident his speech and muscle coordination were still adversely affected. The woman said she did not love him any more but felt guilty about terminating a relationship now that he had become physically afflicted. She was ambivalent. She felt it was her duty to marry her fiancé, but her feelings were no longer love feelings.

Pity may also have a social basis. For example, a partner may fail to achieve a lifetime career goal (for example, flunks out of medical school).

Delaying marriage until all of the "right" conditions are met may be extremely difficult. Most of us assume that *our* marriage will be different, that it will not end in divorce, and that love is enough to compensate for such factors as premarital pregnancy or financial stress.

Even if all of the indications for a successful marriage are present, either you or your partner may be reluctant to make a commitment. In this case, the individual may want to explore the source of the reluctance and remember that marriage is only one lifestyle option among several.

▪▪ Writing a Premarital Agreement

The primary purpose of a *premarital agreement* (referred to as an *antenuptial, prenuptial,* or *marriage contract*) is to specify ahead of time how property will be divided and who will be responsible for paying what to whom if there is a divorce. Persons who have been married before are often concerned that money and property be kept separate in a second marriage. One established widowed physician wanted his property and assets to go to his children. The woman he was to marry was also a widow and wanted her estate to go to her daughter.

They drew up an agreement stating that whatever property and assets they had would not become the spouse's in the event of death or divorce.

When only one party has assets, a prenuptial contract can have negative consequences for the other party. Sherry, a never married 22-year-old, signed such an agreement:

> Paul was adamant about my signing the contract. He said he loved me but would never consider marrying anyone unless we signed a prenuptial agreement stating that he would never be responsible for alimony in case of a divorce. I was so much in love, it didn't seem to matter. I didn't realize that basically he was and is a selfish person. Now, five years later, after a divorce, I go to the court begging for alimony while he lives in a big house overlooking the lake with his new wife.

Although most people who are marrying for the first time do not opt for a prenuptial agreement, a higher proportion of people in their second marriages do. Some agreements are designed to keep property separate. Other agreements are informal and designed to clarify expectations in the relationship. Exhibit 7-2 is a marriage agreement of spouses who have been married before. Most of the items in the agreement are about relationship issues and are not enforceable.

☐　　　C O N S I D E R A T I O N　　　☐

When the goal of a personal marital contract is to keep property separate, contact an attorney. The laws regulating marriage and divorce vary by state, and only an attorney can ensure that the document that is drawn up will be honored.

A premarital agreement has value beyond its legal implications. Its greatest value is probably the process of the partners discussing together their hopes and expectations of their relationship. In the absence of such an agreement, many couples may never discuss the issues they may later face.

▪▪ Predicting Your Marital Happiness

It is not possible to predict with 100 percent accuracy what your level of marital satisfaction will be even three days after your wedding. There are several reasons why.

Illusion of the Perfect Mate

The illusion that you have found the perfect partner—one who will be all things to you, and vice versa—will carry you through courtship. However, the reality is very different. You have not found the perfect mate—there isn't one. Anyone you marry will come with a minus quality, and the one quality that is lacking may become the only one you regard as important (sammons, 1990). When some people discover that their partner lacks something they think is essential ("the ability to communicate," "being faithful," "loves me"), they may consider a divorce.

We marry someone who is ideally suited to us NOW, in our present "headspace," present "need," and present environment. All are likely to change and it is expected that we accommodate to the changes and remain devoted to our partners.
—TIM BRITTON

EXHIBIT 7.2

Prenuptial Agreement

Pam and Mark are of sound mind and body, have a clear understanding of the terms of this contract and of the binding nature of the agreements contained herein; they freely and in good faith choose to enter into the PRE-NUPTIAL AGREEMENT and MARRIAGE CONTRACT and fully intend it to be binding upon themselves.

Now, therefore, in consideration of their love and esteem for each other and in consideration of the mutual promises herein expressed, the sufficiency of which is hereby acknowledged, Pam and Mark agree as follows:

NAMES

Pam and Mark affirm their individuality and equality in this relationship. The parties believe in and accept the convention of the wife accepting the husband's name, while rejecting any implied ownership.

Therefore, the parties agree that they will be known as husband and wife and will henceforth employ the titles of address: Mr. and Mrs. Mark Stafford, and will use the full names of Pam Hayes Stafford and Mark Robert Stafford.

RELATIONSHIPS WITH OTHERS

Pam and Mark believe that their commitment to each other is strong enough that no restrictions are necessary with regard to relationships with others.

Therefore, the parties agree to allow each other freedom to choose and define their relationships outside this contract, and the parties further agree to maintain sexual fidelity each to the other.

RELIGION

Pam and Mark reaffirm their belief in God and recognize He is the source of their love. Each of the parties have their own religious beliefs.

Therefore, the parties agree to respect their individual preferences with respect to religion and to make no demands on each other to change such preferences.

CHILDREN

Pam and Mark both have children. Although no minor children will be involved, there are two (2) children still at home and in school and in need of financial and emotional support.

Therefore, the parties agree that they will maintain a home for and support these children as long as is needed and reasonable. They further agree that all children of both parties will be treated as one family unit, and each will be given emotional and financial support to the extent feasible and necessary as determined mutually by both parties.

CAREERS AND DOMICILE

Pam and Mark value the importance and integrity of their respective careers and acknowledge the demands that their jobs place on them as individuals and on their partnership. Both parties are well established in their respective careers and do not foresee any change or move in the future.

The parties agree, however, that if the need or desire for a move should arise, the decision to move shall be mutual and based on the following factors:

1. The overall advantage gained by one of the parties in pursuing a new opportunity shall be weighed against the disadvantages, economic and otherwise, incurred by the other.
2. The amount of income or other incentive derived from the move shall not be controlling.
3. Short-term separations as a result of such moves may be necessary.

Mark hereby waives whatever right he may have to solely determine the legal domicile of the parties.

CARE AND USE OF LIVING SPACES

Pam and Mark recognize the need for autonomy and equality within the home in terms of the use of available space and allocation of household tasks. The parties reject the concept that the responsibility for housework rests with the woman in a marriage relationship while the duties of home maintenance and repair rest with the man.

Therefore, the parties agree, to share equally in the performance of all household tasks, taking into consideration individual schedules, preferences, and abilities.

The parties agree that decisions about the use of living space in the home shall be mutually made, regardless of the parties' relative financial interests in the ownership or rental of the home, and the parties further agree to honor all requests for privacy from the other party.

PROPERTY; DEBTS; LIVING EXPENSES

Pam and Mark intend that the individual autonomy sought in the partnership shall be reflected in the ownership of existing and future-acquired property, in the

continued on next page

characterization and control of income, and in the responsibility for living expenses. Pam and Mark also recognize the right of patrimony of children of their previous marriages.

Therefore, the parties agree that all things of value now held singly and/or acquired singly in the future shall be the property of the party making such acquisition. In the event that one party to this agreement shall predecease the other, property and/or other valuables shall be disposed of in accordance with an existing will or other instrument of disposal that reflects the intent of the deceased party.

Property or valuables acquired jointly shall be the property of the partnership and shall be divided, if necessary, according to the contribution of each party. If one party shall predecease the other, jointly owned property or valuables shall become the property of the surviving spouse.

Pam and Mark feel that each of the parties to this agreement should have access to monies that are not accountable to the partnership.

Therefore, the parties agree that each shall retain a mutually agreeable portion of their total income and the remainder shall be deposited in a mutually agreeable banking institution and shall be used to satisfy all jointly acquired expenses and debts.

The parties agree that beneficiaries of life insurance policies they now own shall remain as named on each policy. Future changes in beneficiaries shall be mutually agreed on after the dependency of the children of each party has been terminated. Any other benefits of any retirement plan or insurance benefits that accrue to a spouse only shall not be affected by the foregoing.

The parties recognize that in the absence of income by one of the parties, resulting from any reason, living expenses may become the sole responsibility of the employed party and in such a situation, the employed party shall assume responsibility for the personal expenses of the other.

Both Pam and Mark intend their marriage to last as long as both shall live.

Therefore the parties agree that should it become necessary, due to the death of either party, the surviving spouse shall assume any last expenses in the event that no insurance exists for that purpose.

Pam hereby waives whatever right she may have to rely on Mark to provide the sole economic support for the family unit.

EVALUATION OF THE PARTNERSHIP

Pam and Mark recognize the importance of change in their relationship and intend that this CONTRACT shall be a living document and a focus for periodic evaluations of the partnership.

The parties agree that either party can initiate a review of any article of the CONTRACT at any time for amendment to reflect changes in the relationship. The parties agree to honor such requests for review with negotiations and discussions at a mutually convenient time.

The parties agree that, in any event, there shall be an annual reaffirmation of the CONTRACT on or about the anniversary date of the CONTRACT.

The parties agree that, in the case of unresolved conflicts between them over any provisions of the CONTRACT, they will seek mediation, professional or otherwise, by a third party.

TERMINATION OF THE CONTRACT

Pam and Mark believe in the sanctity of marriage; however, in the unlikely event of a decision to terminate this CONTRACT, the parties agree that neither shall contest the application for a divorce decree or the entry of such decree in the county in which the parties are both residing at the time of such application.

In the event of termination of the CONTRACT and divorce of the parties, the provisions of this and the section on "Property; Debts; Living Expenses" of the CONTRACT as amended shall serve as the final property settlement agreement between the parties. In such event, this CONTRACT is intended to affect a complete settlement of any and all claims that either party may have against the other, and a complete settlement of their respective rights as to property rights, homestead rights, inheritance rights, and all other rights of property otherwise arising out of their partnership. The parties further agree that in the event of termination of this contract and divorce of the parties, neither party shall require the other to pay maintenance costs or alimony.

DECISION MAKING

Pam and Mark share a commitment to a process of negotiations and compromise that will strengthen their equality in the partnership. Decisions will be made with respect for individual needs. The parties hope to maintain such mutual decision making so that the daily decisions

continued on next page

affecting their lives will not become a struggle between the parties for power, authority, and dominance. The parties agree that such a process, while sometimes time consuming and fatiguing, is a good investment in the future of their relationship and their continued esteem for each other.

Now, therefore, Pam and Mark make the following declarations:

1. The are responsible adults.
2. They freely adopt the spirit and the material terms of this prenuptial and marriage contract.
3. The marriage contract, entered into in conjunction with a marriage license of the State of Illinois, County of Wayne, on this 12th day of June, 1990, hereby manifests their intent to define the rights and obligations of their marriage relationship as distinct from those rights and obligations defined by the laws of the State of Illinois, and affirms their right to do so.
4. They intend to be bound by this prenuptial and marriage contract and to uphold its provisions before any Court of Law in the Land.

Therefore, comes now, Pam Hayes Carraway, who applauds her development which allows her to enter into this partnership of trust, and she agrees to go forward with this marriage in the spirit of the foregoing PRENUPTIAL and MARRIAGE CONTRACT.

Therefore, comes now, Mark Robert Stafford, who celebrates his growth and independence with the signing of this contract, and he agrees to accept the responsibilities of this marriage, as set forth in the foregoing PRENUPTIAL and MARRIAGE CONTRACT.

This contract and covenant has been received and reviewed by the Reverend Ralph James, officiating.

Finally, comes Karen James and Bill Dunn, who certify that Pam and Mark did freely read and sign this marriage contract in their presence, on the occasion of their entry into a marriage relationship by the signing of a marriage license of the State of Illinois, County of Wayne, at which they acted as official witnesses. Further, they declare that the marriage licence of the parties bears the date of the signing of this PRENUPTIAL and MARRIAGE CONTRACT.

> ■ **DATA:** *Of 56,000 women responding to a Woman's Day survey, one-half said that they would not marry the same man again (Lear, 1986).*

Deception During the Premarital Period

Your illusion of the perfect mate is helped along by some deception on the part of your partner. At the same time, you are presenting only favorable aspects of yourself to the other person. These deceptions are often not deliberate but are merely attempts to withhold the undesirable aspects of yourself for fear that your partner may not like them. One male student said he knew he drank too much, but that if his date found out, she would be disappointed and might drop him. He kept his drinking hidden throughout their courtship. They married and are now divorced. She said of him, "I never knew he drank whiskey until our honeymoon. He never drank like this before we were married."

Courtship elicits the most positive aspects of an individual. Marriage elicits more (and sometimes less positive) aspects of the individual.

Life is like a dog-sled team. If you ain't the lead dog, the scenery never changes.
—LEWIS GRIZZARD

Confinement of Marriage

Another factor that makes it impossible to predict marital happiness is the different circumstances of the premarital period and marriage. Although premarital norms permit relative freedom to move in and out of relationships, marriage involves a legal contract. One recently married person described marriage as an iron gate that clangs shut behind you, and "getting it open is almost impossible." One's freedom to leave a relationship is transformed by the wedding ceremony. Thereafter, there is tremendous social pressure to work things out and a feeling of obligation to do so that was not previously present. The new sense of confinement may bring out the worst in partners who seemed very cooperative before marriage.

Balancing Work and Relationship Demands

Predicting marital happiness is also difficult because the partners must necessarily shift their focus from each other to the business of life. Careers and children emerge as concerns that often take precedence over spending time with each other, going to parties, and seeing movies. Time and energy spent on jobs and childrearing often leave marriage partners too tired to interact with each other. "I never see my partner" is a statement often heard by marriage counselors. Also, the more abrasive communication encouraged by conditions of stress has negative consequences for the way partners feel about each other. "Whenever we do get together, we fight," said one partner.

Inevitability of Change

One of the major themes of this text is that you are continually changing. Just as you are not the same person you were 10 years ago, you will be different 10 years from now. The direction and intensity of these changes are not predictable for you or for your partner. You, your partner, and your relationship will not be the same two years (or two days) in a row. Reflecting on change in her marriage, one woman recalled:

> When we were married we were very active in politics. Now I have my law degree and am enjoying my practice. But Jerry is totally immersed in meditating and taking health food nutrients. He also spends four nights a week playing racketball. I never imagined that we'd have nothing to say to each other after only three years of marriage.

Other spouses may maintain similar interests across years of marriage, but either or both may undergo a dramatic change in mental functioning. In recent years, Alzheimer's disease and its attendant problems for interpersonal relationships have been featured in the media (Wasow, 1986). One spouse said:

> We've lived together for 36 years, and now she has Alzheimer's disease. It means that the last of life we were looking forward to sharing has become a nightmare. She sometimes forgets my name and resents it when I try to help dress her. But if I don't she'll put her bra on backwards and she literally forgets where the bathroom is. I know that her brain has deteriorated and that the person I once knew is no longer inside, but it hurts me so much.

Though we were still happy with each other, we were growing in different ways.

—CYBILL SHEPERD OF HER EX-SPOUSE

☐   C O N S I D E R A T I O N   ☐

Whether or not you will be happily married after your wedding cannot be predicted. Although selecting a compatible partner is basic, other factors that are crucial to a successful marriage include giving up any illusions of finding a perfect mate, mini-

continued on next page

mizing premarital deception, accepting (and enjoying) the confinement of marriage, balancing work and relationship demands, and adapting to whatever changes occur.

:: Trends

The future of dating relationships will include more people spending more time in a number of such relationships, a gradual shift away from traditional dating practices, increased interracial, interreligious, and interethnic dating, and increased confusion about roles in dating relationships. As noted in the last chapter, both women and men are marrying later than in previous years. The result of such delay is that each person will have more time to become involved with a variety of people before marriage. More time spent dating also has implications for how dating is perceived—initially, more for recreation than for mate selection.

As a result of this shift in dating focus from mate selection to recreation, the traditional dating pattern, which is geared toward early marriage, will become less functional. "Hanging out" and "getting together," whereby individuals go where they can meet members of the opposite sex in informal ways without an introduction, will increase. The women's movement has been instrumental in making some women feel more comfortable about initiating relationships.

Other trends in dating will include greater use of mate-selection technology. As our society becomes more populated, urban, and industrial, there will be fewer personal networks within which to meet eligible mates. Increasingly, individuals who might not otherwise meet through traditional dating patterns will be linked through advertisements in newspapers or magazines and videotape dating clubs. The $40 billion dating service industry will also become more specialized. Individuals seeking a Jewish person, vegetarian, or music lover may use a specialized dating service to target these individuals (Kaplan, 1990). A list of some of these types of organizations can be found in Special Topics 4 at the end of this text.

With more than 50 percent of all marriages ending in divorce, some couples are becoming more cautious about entering into marriage. The growing possibility that "divorce may happen to me, too" may reduce the number of hasty, ill-conceived marriages. The fact that age at marriage is inching upward may reflect a greater determination to marry when the conditions are right, not when the emotions are ready. Also, the use of marriage agreements reflects a concern that each partner be aware of the other's expectations to prevent misunderstandings.

In addition to exercising greater caution in entering into marriage, alternatives to the traditional formal engagement are becoming more acceptable. Although the engagement ring and wedding announcement will continue to be the script for most people, a growing number, particularly those who live together, will bypass the formality of an engagement period.

It appears to me that finding someone one can truly enjoy is, to some extent, a happy accident.

—JAMES WALTERS

:: Summary

Dating is the primary mechanism by which men and women pair off into exclusive, committed relationships. Contemporary functions of dating involve confirmation of a social self, recreation, companionship, intimacy, sex, socialization, and mate selection.

Relatively new methods of finding dating partners include advertising, joining a specialized dating club, or joining a videodating club. Most people who use a videodating club do so as a way of meeting an exclusive mate rather than a means of attracting a wide range of partners.

Sexual harassment and attempted rape are issues 25 percent of females report they must contend with on dates. Acquaintance gang rape is a particularly disturbing sex violation that sometimes occurs in a dating context.

Persons who are dating "the second time around" are different from young people dating for the first time. These individuals are older, have fewer available partners, and over half have children from a previous marriage.

As dating moves toward mate selection, the partners are influenced by various cultural, sociological, pyschological, and perhaps biological factors. Although marriages in some cultures are arranged by parents or other relatives, our culture relies mainly on endogamous and exogamous pressures to guide mate choice.

Sociological aspects of mate selection include homogamy (people prefer someone like themselves) and propinquity (people are more likely to find a mate who lives in close proximity).

Psychological aspects of mate selection include complementary needs, exchange theory, parental image, and personality characteristics. Complementary needs theory suggests that people select others who have opposite characteristics to their own. They may also seek each other out if they both have the same need at different levels of intensity. Most researchers find little evidence for complementary needs theory.

Exchange theory suggests that one individual selects another on the basis of rewards and costs. As long as an individual derives more profit from a relationship with one partner than another, the relationship will continue. Exchange concepts influence who dates whom, the conditions of the dating relationship, and the decision to marry.

The parental image theory of mate selection says that a man looks for a wife like his mother and a woman looks for a husband like her father.

The sociobiological view of mate selection suggests that men and women select each other on the basis of their biological capacity to produce and support healthy offspring. Men seek young women with healthy bodies, and women seek ambitious men who will provide economic support.

You can use the engagement period productively by systematically examining your relationship, observing your future in-laws for clues about your partner's background and character, and going for premarital counseling. Conditions under which you might want to prolong your engagement include having known each other for less than two years, having an inadequate or unstable source of income, having parents who disapprove of your marriage, and being pregnant.

Some couples decide to write a marriage agreement to specify the understandings of their relationship. If these involve the disposition of property and assets, a lawyer should be asked to draw up the agreement. Otherwise, the document may not be in legal terms recognized by the courts.

Regardless of what you do, you will not be able to guarantee yourself and your partner a happy marriage. The illusion of the perfect mate, deception during the premarital period, the confinement of marriage, the demands of careers and children, and the inevitability of change make prediction of future marital happiness impossible.

Trends in dating relationships include a longer period of dating, a gradual shift from the traditional dating pattern to a more informal one, increased interracial, interreligious, and interethnic dating, and greater availability of technological means of finding dates. In addition, trends in marital commitments include the possibility of greater caution entering marriage (the fact that people are marrying later is some evidence for this) and the increasing use of prenuptial agreements.

Questions for Reflection

1. How does exchange theory help to explain your involvement in your most recent relationship? What specifically are or were the rewards and costs of that relationship?
2. What kinds of influence do your parents (or children) have on your dating relationships?
3. Do you feel that the happiest relationships are homogamous or complementary?

References

Acquaintance Gang Rape. *20/20*. American Broadcasting Company, April 13, 1990.

Berry, R. E., and Williams, F. L. Assessing the relationship between quality of life and marital income satisfaction: A path analytic approach. *Journal of Marriage and the Family*, 1987, *49*, 107–116.

Bitter, R.G. Late marriage and marital instability: The effects of heterogeneity and inflexibility. *Journal of Marriage and the Family*, 1986, *48*, 631–640.

Booth, A. and J. N. Edwards. Age at marriage and marital instability. *Journal of Marriage and the Family*, 1985, *47*, 67–75.

Bossard, James H.S. Residential Propinquity as a factor in marriage selection. *American Journal of Sociology*, 1932, *38*, 219–224.

Bulcroft, K. and M. O'Conner-Roden. Never too late. *Psychology Today*, June 1986, 66–69.

Buss, D. M. Sex differences in human mate preferences: Evolutionary hypotheses tested in 37 cultures. *Behavioral and Brain Sciences*, 1989, *12*, 1–13.

Byers, E. Sandra and Kim Lewis. Dating couples' disagreements over the desired level of sexual intimacy. *Journal of Sex Research*, 1988, *24*, 15–29.

Cutler, Blayne. Up the down staircase. *American Demographics*, 1989, *11*, 32–41.

Daniel, H. J., III, K.F. O'Brien, R.B. McCabe, and V.E. Quinter. Values in mate selection: A 1984 campus survey. *College Student Journal*, 1985, *19*, 44–50.

''False rape claim leads to apologies.'' *The Daily Reflector*, 1990, Greenville, NC, June 4, p. A-11.

Fischer, C. H. Advertising for love: Results and reactions to lonely hearts advertisements. Paper, Southern Society for Philosophy and Psychology, Atlanta, Ga., April 1987. Used by permission of Chet H. Fischer.

Fischer, C. H. Romance in the personal ads: A comparison of two metropolitan area male and female samples. Paper, Twentieth Annual Meeting of the Popular Culture Association, Toronto, Canada, March 9, 1990. Used by permission of Chet Fischer, Department of Psychology, Radford University.

Glick, P.C. How American families are changing. *American Demographics*, 1984, 620–27.

Goldberg, Bernard. Matchmaker. *48 Hours: Lonely Street*, CBS News, October 5, 1989.

Grover, K.J., C.S. Russell, W.E. Schumm, and L.A. Paff-Bergen. Mate selection processes and marital satisfaction. *Family Relations*, 1985, *34*, 383–86.

Jedlicka, D. Indirect parental influence on mate choice: A test of the psychoanalytic theory. *Journal of Marriage and the Family*, 1984, *46*, 65–70.

Johnson, D. R. and A. Booth. Rural economic decline and marital quality: A panel study on farm marriages. *Family Relations* 1990, *39*, 159–165.

Kaplan, Steven. Looking for love in all the right places. *The World and I,* February 1990, 224–229.

Kierman, J. E. and V. L. Taylor. Coercive sexual behavior among Mexican-American college students. *Journal of Sex & Marital Therapy,* 1990, 16, 44–50.

Knox, D. and H. J. Daniel, III. Gender differences in expressions of sexuality. *International Journal of Modern Sociology,* 1986, 16, 95–102.

LaBeff, Emily E., Hohn H. Hensley, Deborah A. Cook, and Christy L. Haines. Gender differences in self-advertisements for dates: A replication using college students. *Free Inquiry in Creative Sociology,* 1989, 17, 45–50.

Larsen, Andrea S. and David H. Olson. Predicting marital satisfaction using PRE-PARE: A replication study. *Journal of Marital and Family Therapy,* 1989, 15, 311–322.

Lear, M.W. How many choices do women have? *Woman's Day,* November 11, 1986, pp. 109 et passim.

Leslie, L.A., T. L. Huston, and M. P. Johnson. Parental reactions to dating relationships: Do they make a difference? *Journal of Marriage and the Family,* 1986, 48, 57–66.

Lindsey, L.L. *Gender roles: A sociological perspective.* Englewood Cliffs, N.J.: Prentice-Hall, Inc., 1990.

Locitzer, K. Are you out of sync with each other? *Psychology Today,* July/August 1989, 66.

Maneker, J.S., and R.P. Rankin. Education, age at marriage, and marital duration: Is there a relationship? *Journal of Marriage and the Family,* 1985, 47, 675–83.

Margolin, Leslie. Gender and the prerogatives of dating and marriage: An experimental assessment of a sample of college students. *Sex Roles,* 1989, 20, 91–101.

Mazer, Donald B. and Elizabeth F. Percival. Students' experiences of sexual harassment at a small university. *Sex Roles,* 1989, 20, 1–22.

Meyer, J.P. and S. Pepper. Need compatibility and marital adjustment in young married couples. *Journal of Personality and Social Psychology,* 1977, 35, 331–342.

Mitchell, M. *Gone With the Wind.* New York: Macmillian, 1977.

O'Flaherty, Kathleen M. and L.W. Eells. Courtship behavior of the remarried. *Journal of Marriage and the Family,* 1988, 50, 499–506.

Rubin, Z., L.A. Peplau, and C.T. Hill. Loving and leaving: sex differences in romantic attachments. *Sex Roles,* 1981, 7, 821–835.

Sammons, R.A., Jr. Personal communication. Mesa Behavioral Medicine Clinic, Grand Junction, Colo., 1990.

Schoen, Robert and John Woolredge. Marriage choices in North Carolina and Virginia, 1969–71 and 1979–81. *Journal of Marriage and the Family,* 1989, 51, 465–481.

Snyder, Douglas K. and J. M. Regts. Personality correlates of marital dissatisfaction: A comparison of psychiatric, maritally distressed, and nonclinic samples. *Journal of Sex & Marital Therapy.* 1990, 90, 34–43.

Sprecher, Susan. The importance to males and females of physical attractiveness, earning potential, and expressiveness in initial attraction. *Sex Roles,* 1989, 21, 591–607.

Statistical Abstract of the United States: 1990. 110th ed. Washington, D.C.: U.S. Bureau of the Census, 1990.

Teti, Douglas M. and Michael E. Lamb. Socioeconomic and marital outcomes of adolescent marriage, adolescent childbirth, and their co-occurrence. *Journal of Marriage and the Family,* 1989, 51, 203–212.

Thornton, A. Changing attitudes toward family issues. *Journal of Marriage and the Family,* 1989, 51, 873–893.

Time. DNA on trial. August 1989, 63.

U.S. Bureau of the Census. Marital status and living arrangements: March 1985. *Current Population Reports,* Series P-20, no. 410. Washington, D.C.: U.S. Government Printing Office, 1986.

Waller, W., and R. Hill. *The family: A dynamic interpretation.* New York: Holt, Rinehart & Winston, 1951.

Wasow, M. Support groups for family caregivers of patients with Alzheimer's disease. *Social Work*, 1986, *31*, 93–97.

Waterman, C. K., L. J. Dawson, and M. J. Bologna. Sexual coercion in gay male and lesbian relationships: Predictors and implications for support services. *The Journal of Sex Research*, 1989, *1*, 118–124.

Weaton, B. Life transitions, role histories, and mental health. *American Sociological Review*, 1990, *55*, 209–223.

Whyte, M.K. *Dating, mating, and marriage.* Hawthorne, New York: Aldine de Gruyter, 1990.

Winch, R.F. The theory of complementary needs in mate selection. Final results on the test of the general hypothesis. *American Sociological Review*, 1955, *20*, 552–555.

Woll, Stanley B. and Peter Young. Looking for Mr. or Ms. Right: Self-presentation in videodating. *Journal of Marriage and the Family*, 1989, *51*, 483–488.

Woodfin, M.H. and J. Tinling, eds. *Another secret diary of William Bryd of Westover, 1739–1741.* Richmond, Va., 1942.

CHOICES

SEVENTY STUDENTS IN a marriage and family class were asked if they would sign or ask their partners to sign a prenuptial agreement. About 40 percent said "yes."

Prenuptial Agreement: Yes

Those opting for a prenuptial agreement gave a variety of reasons:

I didn't have one in my previous relationship, and it caused a lot of problems because I didn't. I have a large inheritance, and my partner wanted to get his hooks into it.

Such a contract will make a divorce settlement less complicated.

If I brought something into the marriage, such as a savings account, I wouldn't want my partner to have one cent of it if we got divorced.

You know what happened to Johnny Carson. If he had had such an agreement, he would have gotten off easier in the settlement.

Although we may marry for love, we divorce in a state of hate. A contract about who gets what would come in handy at that time.

Although you marry when you are in love, feelings change and it's hard to predict the future. I am a very independent person, and I would like my husband to be independent also. Although our relationship will be based on emotional dependence on each other, I want each of us to be financially independent.

I am an only child, and I would hate for the money that my parents and grandparents worked so hard for to go to somebody outside the family.

Prenuptial Agreement: No

An equal number of students (40 percent) said they would not sign a prenuptial agreement or ask their partner to do so. Their reasons follow:

Asking your future spouse to sign such an agreement would mean that you don't trust them. I wouldn't marry someone unless I was absolutely positive that she was the one for me and that we would be together for the rest of our lives.

Signing a prenuptial agreement implies that your marriage won't last. It's a bad way to start a marriage.

It [a prenuptial agreement] would weaken the marriage from the start by making it easier to get out if something goes wrong. It also doesn't show complete trust, which is a core issue in any successful marriage relationship.

I wouldn't have the nerve to bring up a prenuptial agreement. It would be like slapping my partner's face.

A prenuptial agreement in my opinion is like saying that I want as much as I can get, and I just don't like the feel of such an agreement. In a marriage relationship, there should be a special trust—and if you don't have that, you're in trouble.

Marriage is an emotional commitment of each partner to the other that results from the love each feels for the other. If either partner asks the other to sign such an agreement, this takes all the emotion out of the relationship and you're headed toward a divorce.

Prenuptial Agreement: It Depends

About 20 percent of the respondents in the marriage and family class said that they would sign or ask their partner to sign such an agreement under certain conditions:

I would definitely consider a prenuptial agreement if I were a widow or a divorcé with children and had a considerable estate or money. While a prenuptial agreement would take a lot of the "glitter" and "romance" out of a second marriage, my first priority would be to protect my money for my children.

If I were making myself financially secure and found the girl of my dreams, I wouldn't ask her to sign such an agreement. But if I had already made my fortune and then found someone I loved, I would consider asking her to sign such an agreement.

No matter how much in love a couple is, whenever one owns anything of monetary value and the other one does not, that person should think with his head about keeping what is rightfully his. Some people do marry for money, and you need to watch out for them.

One student emphasized the importance of open communication.

I believe that both people must want a prenuptial agreement to alleviate some of the anxieties that might arise, such as distrust and misunderstanding. Moreover, I believe both people should communicate openly their fears, conceptions, and feelings about a prenuptial agreement. Further, I believe that if both have decided after lengthy dialogue that a prenuptial agreement is in order, both parties should sign on the dotted line. I want to emphasize that this must be a mutual decision with shared responsibility.

Should the Wife Keep Her Maiden Name?

Although the U.S. Census Bureau does not keep records on the extent to which married women are keeping their maiden names, more and more women are and the trend is increasing. Reasons include the delay of marriage, during which time a woman establishes a professional identity she does not want to lose, pride in one's own family name, and an awareness of the high divorce rate and the desire to avoid having a name to remind you of a bad marriage if it ends. Other women do not want to assume their husband's name because they feel that this tradition reflects the larger pattern of male dominance in our society. Options include the woman (for example, Mary Smith getting married to Mark Adams) keeping her last name (Ms. Mary Smith), hyphenating her last name (Ms. Mary Smith-Adams), or using her maiden name as her middle name (Ms. Mary S. Adams). Whatever the decision, it is important to use the same name consistently and to make sure that the name you are using is registered with the Social Security Administration and the Internal Revenue Service.

Impact of Social Influences on Choices

Whether or not the respective partners insist on a prenuptial agreement and/or the wife chooses to keep her maiden name are influenced by the social forces that operate on the man and the woman. Regarding a prenuptial agreement, if each partner has been married before and has children who will inherit from him or her, there is an increased probability that each partner will develop a prenuptial agreement. The social context of offspring has more to do with whether or not a couple has a prenuptial agreement than with whether or not the partners feel that such an agreement connotes a lack of love or commitment.

A woman who chooses to keep her own name after marriage has also probably been strongly influenced by peers who have done the same and/or by parents who support her doing so. Such decisions are rarely made independently of what others think.

Finally, the timing of your commitment to marriage is often related to completing a particular phase of education (for example, graduation) or establishing yourself in a career or some other goal or "rite of passage." Hence, a person becomes "ripe" and seeks a mate in reference to something external to the partner. People choose partners from a pool of potential partners who are available at the time the selection occurs. Sometimes two people are very compatible, but one or both of them is not ready to get married. They break up, years go by, and each marries someone else when he or she is ready. Social forces of readiness—not the occasion of actually finding a compatible and loving partner—often dictate when a person gets married.

P A R T

III

□

Realities

WHEN THE UNITED States was primarily rural, family members looked to each other to fulfill a variety of their needs—religious, recreational, educational, economic, and protective. Although people went to church, family members would gather around the open fire in the evening while father read from the Bible. Instruction in honesty, faithfulness, and obedience was part of the family's religious ritual. Education was also home-generated; although there was much work to do on the farm (milking cows, repairing fences, and tending crops), the family was the recreational unit, too. Finally, the rifle over the mantle was a symbol of family protection and sometimes a practical necessity.

Today, all of these needs can be met outside the family. Churches and synagogues com-

pete for membership. The state has taken over the education function. Recreation is no longer home-oriented; family members look to events outside the family for fun and to people outside the family to have fun with. Family members also earn their living outside the family by working for the government or for private industry or business. The spirit generated from working together as a family is gone. Finally, public police protection has replaced the need for a rifle over the mantle.

Although most of the needs of family members can be met outside the family, the need to feel emotionally connected to others, to be a part of others' lives, continues to be a major aspect that marriage and the family offer. Other realities of marriage involve work, sex, communication, and abuse.

C H A P T E R

8

Marriage Relationships

CONTENTS

IS IT TRUE?*

1. The rice thrown at the newly married couple by their guests signifies fertility.

2. Less than five percent of all marriages in the U.S. involve a bride who is older than the groom.

3. Marriage does not affect same or opposite sex friendships.

4. Husbands are more likely to help their wives with household chores after a year of marriage than in the early months of marriage.

5. The relationship with in-laws is likely to improve after marriage.

1 = T; 2 = F; 3 = F; 4 = F; 5 = T

The American family does not exist. Rather we are creating many American families, of diverse styles and shapes. In unprecedented numbers, our families are unalike.
—JERROLD K. FOOTLICK

After selecting the person to marry, the individuals make a marital commitment, get married, and move into their new roles as spouses. This transition involves various rites of passage and personal, social, and legal consequences. In this chapter we look at the transition that marriage involves. We also discuss an array of marriages of different groups and types—college marriages, mixed (interfaith, interracial, age-discrepant), black, Mexican American, Native American, Japanese American, and ''very happy'' marriages. The prevailing theme of this chapter is that there is no one marriage relationship. There are only marriage relationships, which differ by social class, ethnicity, religion, physical ability (or disability), presence or absence of children, degree of freedom or intimacy, and education of the spouses, among other variables. These differences imply that each marriage is unique.

:: Marriage as a Commitment

Maxim Gorky said, ''When a woman gets married, it's like jumping into a hole in the ice in the middle of winter; you do it once, and you remember it for the rest of your days.'' One of the reasons getting married leaves such an indelible memory is the significance of the commitment. Marriage represents a multi-level commitment—person to person, family to family, and couple to state.

Person to Person

Marital happiness is the most important determinant of overall happiness.
—MARY BENIN & BARBARA NIENSTEDT

Commitment may be defined as an intent to maintain a relationship. Saying ''I do'' in a marriage ceremony implies that you and your partner are making a personal commitment to love, support, and negotiate differences with each other. You are establishing a primary relationship with your partner. Although other existing relationships with parents and friends may continue to be important, they may become secondary.

☐   C O N S I D E R A T I O N   ☐

Despite the high divorce rate in our society, our cultural expectation of marriage is that it is a lifelong commitment. One hundred years ago, it was typical for married partners to stay together until one of them died. But the average life span then was only about 45. Today, because of an increased life span, ''till death do us part'' could mean being married for 50, 60, or more years. Because people today live longer than in the past, they have more years to grow and change in terms of their feelings and values. This is one reason why a lifelong commitment to marriage may be more difficult to achieve today than a hundred years ago.

Family to Family

Marriage also involves commitments by each of the marriage partners to the family members of the spouse. Married couples are often expected to divide their holiday visits between both sets of parents. In addition, each spouse becomes committed to help his or her in-laws when appropriate and to regard family ties as part of marital ties. For some older couples, this means caring for disabled parents who may live in their home. "We always said that no parent was ever going to live with us," said one spouse. "But my wife's father died, and her mother had no place to go. Her living here was an initial strain, but we've learned to cope with the situation quite well."

Not all couples accept the family to family commitment. Some spouses have limited contact with their respective parents. "I haven't seen my folks in years and don't want to," said one woman in her second marriage.

Couple to State

Finally, the spouses become legally committed to each other according to the laws of the state in which they reside. This means they cannot arbitrarily decide to terminate their own marital agreement.

■ **DATA:** *Around 2.5 million marriage licenses are issued to couples every year. These represent a legal bond—not only between the individuals, but also between the couple and the state (Statistical Abstract of the United States: 1990).*

Just as the state says who can marry (not close relatives, the insane, or the mentally deficient) and when (usually at age 18 or older), legal procedures must be instituted if the couple want to divorce. The state's interest is that a couple stay married, have children, and take care of them.

▪▪ Rites of Passage

The transition from one social status to another that is marked by some specific event is referred to as a *rite of passage*. The first day in school, getting a driver's license, and graduating from college are all events that mark major role transitions (to student, driver, and graduate). For two people in love, the marriage ceremony is a rite of passage to the role of spouse.

Weddings

In preparation for the wedding, some states require each partner to have a blood test to certify that neither has a sexually transmitted disease in the communicable stage. This document is then taken to the county courthouse, where the couple applies for a marriage license. Two-thirds of the states require a waiting period between the issuance of the license and the wedding. Eighty percent of the couples are married by a clergyman; 20 percent (primarily remarriages) go to a justice of the peace or judge.

I hope you will be as happy as we all thought we would be.
—SAID TO A BRIDE AT HER WEDDING RECEPTION.

□ CONSIDERATION □

Custom dictates that the bride wear something old, new, borrowed, and blue. The "old" (e.g., gold locket) is something that represents the durability of the impending

continued on next page

marriage. The "new," in the form of new unlaundered undergarments emphasizes the new life to begin. The "borrowed" (e.g., a wedding veil) is something that has already been worn by a currently happy bride, and the "blue" (e.g., ribbons) represents fidelity (those dressed in blue have lovers true). The bride throwing her floral bouquet signifies the end of girlhood; the rice thrown by the guests at the newly married couple signifies fertility.

It is no longer unusual for couples to have weddings that are neither religious nor traditional. Only friends of the couple and members of the immediate families may gather in the bride-to-be's back yard. Rather than the traditional white gown, the bride may wear her favorite dress. The groom may wear a suit (he just as well may not), and everyone else wears whatever they think is appropriate. In the exchange of vows, neither partner promises to obey the other, and their relationship is spelled out by the partners rather than by tradition. Vows often include the couple's feelings about equality, individualism, humanism, and openness to change.

Part of the preference for less lavish, less traditional weddings is economic. A couple can easily spend $20,000 on a wedding for the reception, rings, clothes, photographer, clergy person, and other related expenses. This amount does not include the honeymoon. As couples marry at a later age, more of them assume the financial responsibility of the wedding rather than the bride's parents paying for it.

■ **DATA:** *The average cost of a 200-guest wedding is between $15,000 and $30,000 (Cook, 1990).*

□   C O N S I D E R A T I O N   □

The alternative to spending such large sums on a wedding is elopement. Some couples make a deal with their parents either to elope or to have a small wedding in the back yard. One bride said, "The marriage license cost us $10, and we're using the $4,000 my dad gave us as a down payment on a mobile home." However, other couples want the experience of a big wedding. "I'm only going to get married once," said one bride-to-be. "And I want it to be a big church wedding with a horse-drawn carriage to take us away after the reception."

Honeymoons

Couples who live together before marriage are less likely to go on a honeymoon following their wedding. After brunch, dinner, or a party, they may return to their apartment or house, much as they would at the end of a normal day. "The newness is gone once you've lived with someone," remarked a new husband. "And while being married is supposed to be different, it doesn't *feel* that way."

Some couples choose camping and hiking in a National Park as their honeymoon site.

The honeymoon serves various social and personal functions. The social function of the honeymoon is to make it normative for the couple to isolate themselves from others. Although a few people will play pranks like tampering with the couple's car, hiding the luggage just after the wedding, or handcuffing the new husband to a doorknob, most people are socialized to view honeymooners as deserving of privacy.

This period of undisturbed privacy provides a personal function of the honeymoon—recuperation. Traditional weddings may include bridal showers, a rehearsal, a rehearsal dinner, and a long reception; the bride and groom often feel exhausted by the time they reach their first night's destination. The bride is usually more fatigued, since she has assumed greater responsibility for the wedding than her partner. "I was sick when we got to the motel room," recalled an exhausted bride. "I hadn't slept soundly in three days and had eaten only peanuts and cookies. I was a wreck." But the honeymoon dictates no responsibilities, plenty of sleep, and good food—the physician's prescription for fatigue.

Another function of the honeymoon is to provide a rite of passage to allow the partners to change their identity and self-perception from that of a single person to a married spouse. Hereafter, others will relate to the partners as a married couple and they to each other as spouses.

:: Changes after Marriage

After the wedding and honeymoon the partners begin to experience the stark realities of marriage. This involves learning that they have been taught certain myths (see Exhibit 8.1) about marriage. In addition, the partners become aware that changes occur in their personal, social, legal, and sexual relationship.

Personal Changes

One initial consequence of getting married may be an enhanced self-concept. Parents and friends may arrange their schedules to participate in your wedding and give gifts to express their approval. In contrast, there is no rite of passage for deciding to remain single, cohabit, or live in a commune. There is no ceremony, no fussing and excited parents or friends, no gifts—only the implied question, "Is something wrong with you?" As a married person, you are assumed to be "normal" and to have made the right decision. The strong evidence that your spouse approves of you and is willing to spend a lifetime with you also tells you that you are okay.

The married person also begins adopting new values and behaviors consistent with the married role. Although new spouses often vow that "marriage won't change me," it does. For example, rather than stay out all night at a party, which is not uncommon for singles who may be looking for a partner, spouses (who are already paired off) tend to go home early. Their roles of spouse, employee, and parent, force them to adopt more regular hours. The role of married person implies a different set of behaviors than the role of single person. Although there is an initial resistance to "becoming like old married folks," the resistance soon gives way to the realities of the role.

Another result of getting married is disenchantment. It may not happen in the first few weeks or months of marriage, but it is almost inevitable. Farrah Fawcett once said, "Marriage—that's when the blazing torch of love slowly turns into a pilot light." Whereas courtship is the anticipation of a life together, marriage is the day-to-day reality of that life together—and reality does not always fit the dream. Daily marital interaction exposes both partners as they really are: human beings

Almost all newlyweds like sex in the beginning.

—ELLEN FRANK & CAROL ANDERSON

E X H I B I T   8.1

Myths about Marriage

In their classic book, *The Mirages of Marriage,* Lederer and Jackson (1968) wrote that marriage is

> like taking an airplane to Florida for a relaxing vacation in January, and when you get off the plane you find you're in the Swiss Alps. There is cold and snow instead of swimming and sunshine. . . . After you buy winter clothes and learn how to talk a new foreign language, you can have just as good a vacation in the Swiss Alps as you can in Florida. But . . . it's one big surprise when you get off that marital airplane. . . ." (p. 39)

One of the reasons we are surprised by the actual experience of marriage is that we have a poor idea of what day-to-day living together in marriage is really like. Our assumptions are often distortions of reality. Some of the more unrealistic beliefs our society perpetuates about marriage are discussed here.

MYTH 1: OUR MARRIAGE WILL BE DIFFERENT

All of us know married people who are bored, unhappy, and in conflict. Despite this, we assume our marriage will be different. The feeling before marriage that "it won't happen to us" reflects the deceptive nature of courtship. If we are determined that our marriage will be different, what steps are we taking to ensure that it is? This question is relevant because many of us who enter marriage believing that it will be different for us blindly imitate the marriage patterns of others instead of making a conscious effort to manage our own relationship to make it as fulfilling as we expect it to be.

MYTH 2: WE WILL MAKE EACH OTHER HAPPY

We also tend to believe that we are responsible for each other's happiness. One woman recalls:

> When my husband tried to commit suicide, I couldn't help but think that if I had been the right kind of wife he wouldn't have done such a thing. But I've come to accept that there was more to his depression than just me. He wasn't happy with his work, he drank heavily, and he never got over his twin brother's death.

Although you and your partner will be a tremendous influence on each other's happiness, each of you has roles (employee, student, sibling, friend, son or daughter, parent, and so on) beyond the role of spouse. These role relationships will color the interaction with your mate. If you have lost your job or flunked out of school, your father has cancer, your closest friend moves away, or your mother can no longer care for herself, but is resisting going to a retirement home, it will be difficult for your spouse to "make you happy." Similarly, although you may make every effort to ensure your spouse's happiness, circumstances can defeat you. Also, waiting for someone else to make you happy is quite likely to be a lifelong wait.

MYTH 3: OUR DISAGREEMENTS WILL NOT BE SERIOUS

Many couples acknowledge that they will have disagreements, but they assume theirs will be minor and "just part of being married." However, "insignificant" conflict that is not resolved can't threaten any marriage. "All I wanted was for him to spend more time with me," recalls a divorced woman." But he said he had to run the business because he couldn't trust anyone else. I got tired of spending my evenings alone and got involved with someone else."

MYTH 4: MY SPOUSE IS ALL I NEED

All of us have needs that require the support of others. These needs range from wanting to see a movie with someone to needing someone to talk to about personal problems to needing the physical expression of a partner's love. Although it is encouraging to believe that our partner can satisfy all of our intellectual, physical, and emotional needs, it is not realistic.

A more optimistic way to think of these four beliefs about marriage is to recognize that our marriage *may* be different, that we will be *one* important influence on our partner's happiness, that our disagreements *may* not be serious, (or if they are serious, we may develop skills to resolve them) and that we will be able to satisfy many of our partner's needs.

who get tired and irritable. "Burt never snapped at me about anything when we were dating, but I never acted like a mean bitch (his term) before we were married either," expressed a wife of six months.

The disenchantment is also related to shifting the partners' focus of interest away from each other and toward their work. When children come, their focus extends to the children. In any case, each partner gives and gets less attention in marriage than in courtship.

Parents, In-Laws, and Friendship Changes

Marriage affects relationships with parents, in-laws, and the friends of both partners. Parents are likely to be more accepting of the partner following the wedding. "I encouraged her not to marry him," said the father of a recent bride, "but once they were married, he was her husband and my son-in-law, so I did my best to get along with him."

Just as acceptance of the mate by the partner's parents is likely to increase, interaction with the partner's parents is likely to decrease. This is particularly true when the newly married couple moves to a distant town. "I still love my parents a great deal," said a new husband, "but I just don't get to see them very often." Parents whose lives have revolved around their children may feel particularly saddened at the marriage of their last child and may be reluctant to accept the reduced contacts. Frequent phone calls, visits, invitations, and gifts may be their way of trying to ensure a meaningful place in the life of their married son or daughter (Goetting, 1990). Such insistence by the parents and in-laws may be the basis of the first major conflict between the spouses. There is no problem if both spouses agree on which set of in-laws or parents they enjoy visiting and the frequency of such get-togethers. But when one spouse wants his or her parents around more often than the partner does, frustration will be felt by everyone.

☐   C O N S I D E R A T I O N   ☐

Most marriage counselors believe that when the spouses must choose between their partner and parents, more long-term positive consequences are associated with choosing the partner rather than the parents. Ideally, of course, such choices should be avoided. For partners to try to deny their mate access to the mate's parents is risky. When a person marries, that individual inherits an already existing family; parent and in-law relationships come with the marriage.

Once I found the woman [Yoko], the boys became of no interest.
—JOHN LENNON

Marriage also affects relationships with friends of the same and opposite sex. Less time will be spent with friends because of the role demands from the spouse. In addition, friends will assume that the newly married person now has a built-in companion and is not interested in (or would be punished by the spouse for) going barhopping, to movies, or whatever. More time will be spent with other married couples, who will become powerful influences on the new couple's relationship.

☐   C O N S I D E R A T I O N   ☐

What spouses give up in friendships they gain in developing a close relationship with each other. "We still enjoy our friends, but we end up spending more time with each other than with anyone else. We like it that way," said an elementary school teacher.

However, it is a mistake to abandon friendships after getting married. The spouse cannot be expected to satisfy all social needs, and friends can often relieve some of the spouse's burden. Also, since 50 percent of all marriages end in divorce, friends who have been maintained throughout the marriage can become vital support systems when adjusting to a divorce.

Legal Changes

Unless the partners have signed a prenuptial agreement specifying that their earnings and property will remain separate, the wedding ceremony involves an exchange of property. Once two individuals become husband and wife, each spouse automatically becomes part owner of what the other earns in income and accumulates in property. In the event of divorce, the amount can be substantial. When Amy Irving and Steven Spielberg divorced, she reportedly received $100 million as her half of what he had earned during their marriage. Spouses are also legally entitled to inherit between a third and a half of the partner's estate at death, unless a will specifies otherwise.

Should the couple divorce after having children, each is legally responsible to provide for the economic support of their children. In the typical case, the wife assumes primary physical custody of the children and the husband is required by court order to pay one-fourth of his gross income if there are two children; 17% if there is one child. Failure to pay child support may lead to jail.

Sexual Changes

Sex will also undergo some changes during the first year of marriage. The frequency declines for most married couples, but the quality may improve. According to one wife:

> The urgency to have sex disappears after you're married. After a while you discover that your husband isn't going to vanish back to his apartment at midnight. He's going to be with you all night, every night. You don't have to have sex every minute because you know you've got plenty of time. Also, you've got work and other responsibilities, so sex takes a lower priority than before you were married.

Division of Labor Changes

One result of the feminist and women's movement is that an increasing number of couples share the domestic work in their relationship. In one study of 95 engaged couples, the men who accepted a feminist ideology anticipated they would be helpful and cooperative in the home, splitting the grocery shopping, cooking, cleaning, ironing, and other domestic duties when they were married. However, after one year of marriage, the partners had drifted toward a more traditional relationship in which the woman did more of the domestic work than the man (Koopman-Boyden & Abbott, 1985).

After the smoke of
passion cleared away,
we had two strangers
staring at each other.
—SYLVESTER
  STALLONE

Courtship is the preview of a marriage to come; marriage is the actual movie. It is not unusual for the preview to be different from the reality in terms of the division of labor, sex, friendships, and other factors.

▪▪ College Marriages

▪ **DATA:** *17.2 percent of all white, 15.0 percent of all black, and 12.6 percent of all Mexican Americans complete between one and three years of college* (Statistical Abstract of the United States: 1990 *Table 217*). *In general, about 20 percent of college students are married.*

This proportion of married college students is radically different from the proportions of earlier years. Before 1940, it was not uncommon for a college or university to deny admission to married students or to require enrolled students to drop out if they married. It was believed that married students would have an undesirable influence on other students. After World War II, the return of married veterans to college established the social legitimacy of the college marriage. (Even high school marrieds are acceptable now.)

Young Married College Students

Although most college students prefer to finish their degrees before getting married, others seem compelled by the desire to be married while still attending school. If they decide to marry, they will soon confront role conflict and economic issues.

Role Conflict.   Married students have two major roles to fulfill—student and spouse. In addition, the married student may also take on the role of parent and

About one in five col-
lege students are mar-
ried.

employee. Trying to fulfill all these roles may lead to *role conflict,* which exists when the expectations of one role are in conflict with the expectations of another role. For example, the role of student involves spending time writing term papers, studying for exams, and going to class. These role expectations may conflict with spending time with one's partner, caring for a child, or meeting one's job responsibilities.

CONSIDERATION

Although role conflict is not unique to the college marriage, one role is more likely to be added to another without sufficient time to adjust to the previous role. Stacking the roles of student, spouse, employee, and possibly parent requires a greater degree of adaptation than is required of the single college student, who has fewer roles to juggle. Aware of the role-stacking effect, most students opt to delay marriage until after graduation.

Money Problems. Some parents disapprove of their offspring getting married while still in college and stop financial support after the wedding. Lack of money is not unique to the young and newly married college couple, but it introduces a variable that was not present when they were single and engaged. A sophomore who married in his freshman year writes:

> We began our marriage without any help from our parents. The result was a tremendous strain on our once happy relationship. Not having enough money put us both under tensions that neither of us had known before. We struggled to make rent, utilities, tuition, and other payments. We squeezed our budget for money to buy food with. Our recreational lifestyle had changed drastically because we rarely had money to eat out or to see a movie. We bought no new clothes—birthdays were the only times we got new ones. The result was unhappiness which we would not let others know about because of our pride. We were both from middle-class families, but we were poor.

College professor—someone who talks in other people's sleep.
—BERGEN EVANS

Older Married College Students

A look around any college classroom reveals a number of older students, many of whom are married. In contrast to most of the younger college marrieds, many of these spouses have been or are employed in full-time jobs and have children.

How does returning to school affect the marriage relationship? In a study of 361 women age 26 and older who were married and had at least one child, one-half of those who dropped out before completing their degree and one-third of those who did complete their degree reported that their return to school had resulted in some strain on the marriage (Berkove, 1979). This showed itself in the husband's jealousy in competing with his wife's new interest and his annoyance over occasional late meals and a cluttered house. One student wife said of her husband:

> He mentions how much money my education is costing (even though I've worked part time off and on) and how much time I spend away from the family (he spends as much time away from the family as I do). He has stopped commenting on the state of the house, since I told him that if it was too dirty to suit him, he was welcome to clean it, because it suited me just fine.

Benefits also resulted from the wife's return to school. Most of the wives reported increased personal and intellectual development, and one-half reported that their husbands showed greater appreciation of, satisfaction with, and pride in the fact that they had returned to school (Berkove, 1979).

In another study (Van Meter & Agronow, 1982), married female students reported the least amount of role conflict when they "placed the family role first" and did not allow the role of student to interfere with that of wife and mother. Under these conditions, husbands were very supportive of wives going back to school. An additional finding was that husbands who had also attended college were much more supportive of their wives going to school. In general, wives are more supportive of the husband's return to school than husbands are supportive of the wife's return to school (Huston-Hoburg & Strange, 1986).

Student wives who are also mothers report positive benefits for their children. In a study of 40 such women (Kelly, 1982), more than half said the relationships with their children had improved since they had returned to school. Their children showed an increased interest in their own schoolwork, and there was a new mutuality of interest—both mother and child would talk about "having to get homework done."

Making good grades and spending time with family is often accomplished at the expense of the student wife's sleep. In essence, the wife and mother "added her study (sometimes a full-time student load) to her existing program, and what she cut back on was sleep and leisure time. It is little wonder that one of the main problems cited by mature-age female students is chronic tiredness" (Kelly, 1982, 291).

Although the personal, marital, and parent-child relationships tend to improve when the wife returns to school (assuming she continues to put her family role first), what happens when the older married husband returns to school? McRoy and Fisher (1982) studied 20 couples in which only the husband was in graduate school and compared them with 20 couples in which only the wife was in graduate school and 20 couples in which both spouses were in graduate school. Results showed that the husband being in school was associated with less money and less marital satisfaction than either of the other two groups. It seems that when the husband does not contribute economically to the marriage and family, everyone suffers. "But that's not true of us," says one student husband who is being supported by his wife. "I put her through school, and now it's her turn to earn the money. We both agreed on this plan, and it hasn't been a problem for either of us."

▪▪ Mixed Marriages

Interreligious, interracial, and age-discrepant marriages are examples of marriages in which the partners differ from each other in a particular way.

Interreligious Marriages

There has been a consistent trend toward increased willingness of people to marry someone who does not share their religious background. In the past, Jews have been the most prone to marry within their own faith.

■ **DATA:** *In the 1960s, 90 percent of Jewish marriages were between two persons of the Jewish faith. More recently, the percentage has dropped to 30 percent. The American Jewish committee estimates that there are 300,000 interfaith couples in the United States and more than 600,000 children with both Jewish and Christian parents (Kantrowitz & Witherspoon, 1987).*

Are people in interreligious marriages less satisfied with their marriages than those who marry someone of the same faith? The answer depends on a number of factors. First, people in marriages in which one or both spouses profess to "no religion" tend to report lower levels of marital satisfaction than those in which at least one spouse has a religious tie. Second, men in interreligious marriages tend to report less marital satisfaction than men in marriages in which the partners have the same religion. This may be due to the fact that children of interreligious marriages are typically reared in the faith of the mother, so that the father's influence is negligible. Third, wives who marry outside their faith do not seem any less happy than wives who marry inside their faith. Catholics who marry someone of a different faith are just as likely to report being happily married as Catholics who marry Catholics (Shehan et al., 1990).

□ C O N S I D E R A T I O N □

The impact of a mixed religious marriage may depend more on the devoutness of the partners than the fact that the partners are of different religions. If both spouses are devout in their religious beliefs, they may expect some problems in the relationship (although not necessarily). Less problematic is the relationship in which one spouse is devout but the partner is not. If neither spouse in an interfaith marriage is devout, problems regarding religious differences may be minimal or nonexistent.

Interracial Marriages

■ **DATA:** *Of the more than 50 million married couples in the United States, 1.8 percent are interracial (Statistical Abstract of the United States: 1990 Table 53).*

Interracial marriages may involve many combinations, including American white, American black, Indian, Chinese, Japanese, Korean, Mexican, Malaysian, and Hindu mates. In this first section, we will focus on black-white marriages in the United States.

Black-White Marriages

■ **DATA:** *Of the more than 50 million married couples in the United States, only 218,000 (less than 1 percent) are black-white couples (Statistical Abstract of the United States: 1990 Table 53). These spouses tend to have been married before and are more distant in age from each other (Tucker & Mitchell-Kernan, 1990).*

Problems. Disapproval by parents and discrimination by employers and land-lords is a problem for some black-white couples; such prejudices vary with the

We've not run into any problems. Some people may disagree, but we don't have to cope with them.

—HERSCHEL WALKER OF HIS INTERRACIAL MARRIAGE TO CINDY DEANGELIS

The trend in interracial dating apparently is not only on the increase, but the secretiveness previously associated with it is also declining.

—ERNEST PORTERFIELD

degree to which those who discriminate against people have been socialized to perceive interracial unions as appropriate or inappropriate. Rural, conservative, dogmatic individuals are likely to view interracial marriage negatively. Liberal people who live in large metropolitan centers are more likely to have a "live and let live" philosophy and to regard interracial marriage as appropriate.

Given the range of reactions, how are black-white couples actually treated by their parents, employers, and landlords? In general, although minority parents may be more accepting, both sets of parents tend to reject the interracial marriage of their son or daughter. One white husband says, "My parents have never accepted my marriage to a black woman. We have not visited or talked in nearly four years."

Such parental rejection springs from a concern about how the marriage will affect the parents' own status and their fear for the couple and the problems they must face. Hostility often disappears when the couple have a baby (the parents want access to their grandchild) or tragedy strikes (one partner becomes seriously ill). Difficulties with employers and landlords are less predictable. Some employers and landlords discriminate against an individual or a couple if they know that the marriage is interracial. Others, particularly those in larger cities, are indifferent to the marital status or choice of marriage partner of their employee or tenant.

Spouses in interracial marriages must also contend with problems concerning their children. Children of mixed marriages "will learn quickly that their lineage is a rarity that shapes friendships and futures, that white boys and white girls seldom date tan girls and tan boys, that color is not forgotten. That life in between is at once injustice and insight" (Harrington, 1982, 12). One resource for children of interracial parents is The Council on Interracial Books for Children (1841 Broadway, New York, NY 10023), which distributes a list of books designed to help the interracial child to develop a positive self-identity. At least one study of interracial offspring shows that they do not have more psychological problems than children born to parents of the same race (Johnson & Nagoshi, 1986).

Stability. In view of the problems experienced by some black-white couples, are they more likely to get divorced? Yes. When same-race and interracial marriages are compared, the latter are more likely to get divorced (Price-Bonham & Balswick, 1980). Lack of social support, overt hostility, and lack of similar backgrounds may contribute to a higher divorce rate for interracial couples. Black singer Lena Horne said of the divorce to her white husband, "We had a good life together and I loved him, but he didn't know what it meant to be black." Sammy Davis, Jr., and Mary Cunningham also divorced their respective spouses in earlier interracial marriages.

☐   C O N S I D E R A T I O N   ☐

Although individuals contemplating an interracial marriage might assess the degree to which different racial backgrounds will affect the relationship with their partners, divergent backgrounds are only one aspect of the decision-to-marry equation. Different racial backgrounds, in themselves, do not necessarily lead to subsequent divorce. Rather, this variable must be considered in the context of the total relationship.

Cross-Cultural Marriages

The number of international students studying at American colleges and universities is increasing.

■ **DATA:** *Over 350,000 foreign students study at more than 2,552 colleges and universities in the United States. The proportion of total students in the total enrollment at the Massachusetts Institute of Technology, Columbia University, and the University of Southern California is 20, 13, and 12 percent respectively (Open Doors, 1988).*

Since American students take classes with foreign students, it often happens that dating and romance lead to marriage. When the international student is male, more likely than not, his cultural mores will prevail and will clash strongly with his American bride's expectations, especially if they should return to his country.

One female American student described her experience of marriage to a Pakastani, who violated his parents' wishes by not marrying the bride they had chosen for him in childhood. The marriage produced two children before the four of them returned to Pakistan. She felt that her in-laws did not accept her and were hostile toward her. The in-laws also imposed their religious beliefs on her children and took control of their upbringing. When this situation became intolerable, she wanted to return to the United States. Because the children were viewed as being "owned" by their father, she was not allowed to take them with her and was banned from even seeing them. Like many international students, the husband was from a wealthy, high-status family and she was powerless to fight them. She has not seen her children in six years.

Some cross-cultural couples solve their cultural differences by making as complete a break as possible from their cultural past. In the above case, the girl could have accepted the traditions of her husband; alternatively, they could have stayed in America and reared their children here. Either way, the potential for problems is considerable and it may be advisable to spend time in the respective partner's cultural home before making a marital commitment.

Age-Discrepant Marriages

Although some women marry men who are younger than themselves (as examples, Olivia Newton-John is 11 years older than Matt Lattanz; Cher is 18 years older than Rob Cammilletti, the man she lived with), the most common age-discrepant marriage is between the younger woman and the older man. Celebrities and the number of years they are older than their spouses include, Hugh Hefner, 37; Johnny Carson, 26; and Dustin Hoffman, 18.

■ **DATA:** *Of marriages performed in the U.S., 67.1 percent are those in which the groom is older than the bride; 22.1 percent are those in which the bride is older than the groom; 10.8 percent are those in which the partners are the same age* (Statistical Abstract of the United States: 1990 *Table 130).*

Although there is an absence of hard data, some common issues in age-discrepant marriages revolve around motives, interests, children, sex, and early widowhood.

Motives. Instead of marrying a middle-aged woman with three children, the man in the May-December marriage often marries a young woman with whom he can start life over. From the young woman's perspective, she is marrying a man who has already made his mark in the world. She begins her marriage with instant status and probably an ample bank account. U.S. Supreme Court Justice William O. Douglas was 68 when he married a 23-year-old bride. Cary Grant was 48 years older than his last wife; Fred Astaire was 43 years older than his wife.

Interests. Although partners of very different ages may develop mutual interests, there is a greater potential for their interests to be different. The younger partner might enjoy Van Halen; the older partner, Glenn Miller. The younger partner may want to engage in strenuous recreation, such as skiing or hiking. Even if the older partner has an interest in such activity, this partner may be physically unable to engage in such recreation.

There are some places an older woman cannot go with a younger man. The office, for example, is one place to avoid.
—BARBARA
  REYNOLDS

Children. The May-December couple may experience difficulties concerning children. For example, the younger partner may want children, but the older partner may feel too old to be a parent to a young child. In addition, children from the older partner's previous marriage may require financial support, limiting the money available to the couple to start a new family.

Sex. An older man may not be able to meet the sexual demands of a much younger woman. As a consequence, she may seek a sexual companion outside the marriage. The husband may be threatened by such competition, and the marriage relationship may be jeopardized. Sex is not necessarily a problem, however. The younger partner may have a sex drive that is equal to (or even less than) that of the older partner. Also, partners with the lower sex drive (usually older partners) may learn to satisfy their mate's sexual needs in a variety of ways.

Early Widow. American men die approximately seven years earlier than American women. The younger wife in the May-December marriage is therefore more likely to be a widow longer than the wife who is married to someone closer to her age. Indeed, the woman married to a man older than herself is more likely to die at an earlier age than her counterpart who marries a younger man. Two researchers (Klinger-Vartabedian & Wispe, 1989) observed this phenomenon and speculated:

> Perhaps marital partners set their own social or biological clocks in accordance with their spouses' age, thus creating a mortality mean. In the hypothetical averaging of ages, the older person becomes "younger" and lives longer than expected, while the younger person becomes "older" and dies sooner than expected (p. 201).

□   C O N S I D E R A T I O N   □

None of these concerns is necessarily unique to the May-December marriage. Conflicts over sex, children, and recreation may occur in marriages in which the partners

continued on next page

are the same age, and no newlyweds are guaranteed that their spouse will be health-yand alive tomorrow. As for the success of age-discrepant unions, three researchers who compared various couples in age-discrepant marriages found them to be no more likely to report problems regardless of how close or far apart the spouses were in age (Vera et al., 1985).

:: Black Marriages

"The Bill Cosby Show" has captured the hearts of millions of white and black television viewers. Dr. Cliff Huxtable, an obstetrician/gynecologist, and Clare, an attorney, portray the difficulties, values, and lifestyle of a successful upper middle class black family.

| ■ **DATA:** *The black middle class (represented by the Huxtables on "The Bill Cosby Show") account for 15 percent of the black population (Boston, 1988, 8).*

The black middle class can be divided into two segments: the old and the new.

The old black middle class segment is distinguishable by the way it earns its means of livelihood: living mainly off its own effort through the ownership and operation of small businesses or services. In this category are self-employed people such as doctors, lawyers, shopowners . . . (p. 39).

The new black middle class consists of individuals who have special skills or training which they market at unusually high prices. Scientists, professional ath-

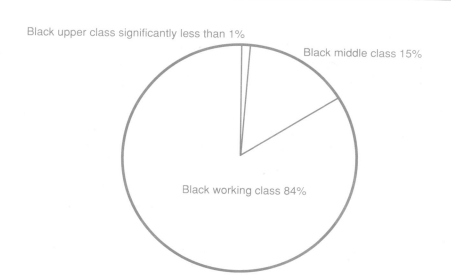

:: FIGURE 8.1
Relative Proportions of Black Social Classes

SOURCE: Thomas D. Boston. *Race, Class and Conservatism.* Boston: Unwin Hyman, 1988, p. 8. Used by permission.

Black upper class significantly less than 1%

Black middle class 15%

Black working class 84%

letes (Michael Jordan), and entertainers (Eddie Murphy) are examples of this class. Members of this new black middle class have also achieved their new status as a result of their own efforts in their own generation.

Middle class black marriages are few in comparison to the number of black families in the working and poor or lower class. The working class consists of individuals in blue collar trades involving manual labor, little prestige, and limited "fringe benefits" such as pensions and health insurance. However, the members of this class take pride in the fact that they work hard and are self-sufficient.

Poor or lower class individuals consist of those who are unemployed or underemployed. Many are illiterate and subsist on welfare. They do not like their status but feel powerless to change it. About 70 percent of the poor in our society are *white*. However, in proportion to their numbers, blacks are three times as likely as whites to be poor.

CONSIDERATION

The black family has often been described in negative terms such as low income, births to unmarried mothers, one-parent families, and spouses with limited education. In contrast, the black family may just as well be described in terms of its positive aspects or strengths. These include strong kinship bonds, favorable attitudes toward the elderly, adaptable roles, strong achievement orientations, strong religious orientation, and a love of children (Rice, 1990, 36).

The Context of Racism

Black marriages occur in the context of continued racism, discrimination, and economic insufficiency. *Racism* is the belief that some groups are, as a result of heredity, inferior to other groups. Blacks live in a white racist society in which

Black families are particularly noted for their strong kinship bonds.

whites, as a group, are prejudiced against blacks. This prejudice manifests itself in discrimination against blacks. Jaynes and Williams (1989) observed it is a myth that overt discrimination has virtually vanished in the last 20 years. They note that as soon as the workday ends, blacks and whites retreat to different worlds. Whites can, if they choose, buy their way into a world of racially homogeneous schools, shopping areas, and recreational facilities.

The figures on economic inequality emphasize the extent of discrimination. The median family income is about 40 percent less for blacks than whites (*Statistical Abstract of the United States: 1990* Table 40). Some of this economic strain is due to racial discrimination, which limits the employment opportunities and earning capacity of blacks.

> A racially integrated community is a chronological term timed from the entrance of the first black family to the exit of the last white family.
> —SAUL ALINSKY

Kinship Ties

Kinship was significantly important in the West African societies from which blacks were brought to be slaves in the United States. In these societies, an individual's social and economic status, as well as means of subsistence, depended on the maintenance of both nuclear and extended kinship ties. In spite of the efforts of slaveowners to sever kinship ties among blacks, the African pattern of family relationships, which consists of the cooperation and mutual support of mother, father, children, grandparents, brothers, nieces, nephews, and cousins, persisted and is regarded by scholars today as the major force contributing to the survival of black people in the United States.

As discrimination and economic insufficiency continued to plague black society, the need for kinship ties and community support became increasingly crucial and necessary to black survival. Today, black spouses continue to maintain close ties with their parents and kin after they are married. In some cases, they may live with their parents. Even if they do not, their parents continue to be important sources of emotional and economic support.

> Black America and black families can be understood only in the context of a white, racist America.
> —JOYCE E. WILLIAMS

> ■ **DATA:** *In a national study of Black Americans, 86.9 percent said that they sought informal assistance for a serious personal problem. Mothers and sisters were those most often asked for help (Chatters, 1989).*

Marital Roles

The strong emphasis on ties to one's parents and the larger kinship system seems to affect the black marriage relationship. In many cases, the mother-child relationship seems to take precedence over the wife-husband relationship. It is uncertain whether this tie is maintained because the black wife feels that her economically disadvantaged husband will not be able to support her or that he will not stay around to do so (desertion rates among black males are higher than among white males).

> Black Americans are still spatially segregated from the majority of the more affluent white citizenry, and certain cultural values distinguish their family life, in form and content, from the middle-class, white Anglo-Saxon model.
> —ROBERT STAPLES

Although not all black wives prioritize the mother role over the spouse role, the precedence seems well established. "In the colonial period of Africa, missionaries often observed and reported the unusual devotion of the African mother to her child" (Staples, 1988).

Black males also labor under negative stereotypes. Some of these stereotypes become self-fulfilling prophesies because the dominant society is structured in a way that prevents many black men from achieving socially approved goals. In spite of their disadvantaged socioeconomic status, most black males function in a way that gains the respect of their mates, children, and community (Staples, 1988, 312).

Marital Satisfaction

Compared to white spouses, black spouses tend to be less happy (Staples, 1988). Reasons for their lower sense of marital satisfaction are primarily in reference to economic and social discrimination. Black wives may be particularly unhappy because, with fewer partners to select from, they may be forced to settle for husbands who have less education than they do. The sense of inadequacy the black husband may feel, coupled with the black wife's feeling that she has selected someone who is less than her ideal mate, may have a negative impact on both partners (Ball & Robbins, 1986). Black husbands are also influenced by economic concerns: the higher the family income, the greater the satisfaction with family life (Staples, 1988). Finally, data from the National Survey of Black Americans reveal that black spouses who do not have children report being happier than black spouses who do have children (Broman, 1988).

■■ Mexican American Marriages

Approximately 21 million Mexican Americans (about 7 percent of our population) live in the United States, primarily in the five southwestern states close to Mexico (California, Texas, New Mexico, Arizona, and Colorado). The term "Mexican American" refers to those of Mexican origin or descent living in America. The term has no specific referent; Chicanos, Spanish Americans, Hispanics, Mexicanos, Californios, and Latin Americans may also regard themselves as Mexican Americans.

When America annexed Texas in 1845, Mexico became outraged and the Mexican War followed (1846–1848). In the Treaty of Guadalupe Hidalgo, Mexico recognized the loss of Texas and accepted the Rio Grande as the boundary between Mexico and the United States. Although the war was over, hostilities continued, and the negative stereotyping of Mexican Americans as a conquered and subsequently inferior people became entrenched. Such stereotyping and discrimination has had implications for the stress to which Mexican American spouses have been exposed. Compared to Anglos, Mexican Americans have less education, lower incomes, and work in lower-status occupations (Becerra, 1988).

The Husband-Wife Relationship

There is great variability among Mexican American marriages. What is true in one relationship may not be true in another, and the same relationship may not resemble itself at two different points in time. Nevertheless, some "typical" characteristics of Mexican American relationships are detailed here.

Role relationships between Mexican-American spouses are becoming more egalitarian.

Male Dominance. Although role relationships between women and men are changing in all segments of society, traditional role relationships between the Mexican American sexes are characterized by male domination.

> Male dominance is the designation of the father as the head of the household, the major decision maker, and the absolute power holder in the Mexican American family. In his absence, this power position reverts to the oldest son. All members of the household are expected to carry out the orders of the male head (Becerra, 1988, 148).

Female Submissiveness. The complement to the male authority figure in the Mexican American marriage is the submissive female partner. Traditionally, the Chicana is subservient to her husband and devotes her time totally to the roles of homemaker and mother. As more wives begin to work outside the home, the nature of the Mexican American husband-wife relationship is becoming more egalitarian (Becerra, 1988).

The divorce rate among Mexican Americans is lower than the rate for whites; this may be due to the strong family orientation and to the disproportionate number of Mexican Americans who are Catholic. Intermarriage is increasing as Mexican Americans move away from home to pursue lucrative jobs in urban areas. Although it is thought that most Mexican Americans live in rural areas, 85 percent of all Mexican American families reside in urban areas (Becerra, 1988).

The Parent-Child Relationship

In the past, Mexican Americans have valued close relationships with both nuclear and extended family members (*familism*). Although members of the extended

family (aunts, uncles, and grandparents) may still be regarded with great affection, Mexican Americans are becoming more Americanized and nuclear-oriented.
(Becerra, 1988).

The relationship between Mexican American children and their parents has
traditionally been one of respect. In addition, it is common for the younger generation to pay great deference to the older generation. When children speak to
their elders, they are expected to do so in a formal way.

:: Native American Marriages

About 1,534,000 individuals define themselves as Native Americans (*Statistical
Abstract of the United States: 1990* Table 44). The term refers not only to American
Indians but Eskimos and Aleuts. American Indians comprise over 95 percent of all
Native Americans and are the group to which we will refer.

Native Americans as a group are young (half are under 35), Protestant, and
Democrat (Hoffman, 1989). They are also more likely than other racial and ethnic
groups to live below the poverty line (*Statistical Abstract of the United States: 1990*
Table 44).

At the present time, there are approximately 300 federally recognized Native
American groups. Native American families are characterized by diversity. No
single form reflects *the* Native American family. When the various forms are
viewed across time, Native American families have been patrilineal (heritage
traced through males), matrilineal (heritage traced through females), monogamous, polygynous, and polyandrous. What is consistent is that tribal identity
takes precedence over family identity and the values of a family reflect those of
the particular tribe.

Given these caveats, John (1988) made some observations about Native American families:

1. Mate selection is based on romantic love.
2. There is little stigma attached to having a child whether the woman is married
   or not. Children are highly valued in the Native American community.
3. Intermarriage rates are the highest of any racial group. The most frequent
   intermarriage involving a Native American is between a white husband and an
   Indian wife.
4. Divorce among Native Americans is regarded as a less traumatic event and is
   usually not associated with guilt, recriminations, or adverse effects.
5. Elders are viewed as important and are looked up to. They are given meaningful economic, political, religious, and familial roles within the tribe.

What is certain about Native American families is that there is great cultural
conflict between their values and those of the larger American society. Native
Americans are very present oriented whereas mainstream (white) society is future
oriented and concerned with schedules and plans. John (1988) commented on the
outcome of the conflicts between the cultures:

> Despite the fact that Native American families are not immune to the larger, social
> structural forces in operation in the United States, I believe that Native American
> families continue to exhibit a unique character attributable to longstanding cultural

differences from American culture as a whole . . . they will adapt their family practices to meet their own needs (pp. 356, 358).

Japanese American Marriages—Then and Now

Japanese American marriages differ in regard to how long the spouses have lived in the United States. Issei or first generation Japanese Americans were born in Japan and immigrated to the United States in the early 1900s. They are now in their eighties and live with their children, in nursing homes, or in senior citizen housing projects such as the Little Tokyo Towers in Los Angeles. Their values, beliefs, and patterns reflect those of traditional Japanese families. These beliefs include (Kitano, 1988): 1. offspring not allowed to select their own spouse, 2. a stronger parent-child bond than the bond between husband and wife, 3. male dominance, 4. rigid division of labor by sex, and 5. precedence of family values over individual values.

The Nisei or second generation children "are products of a variety of influences—their Issei parents, Japanese American peers, other minorities, and the American mainstream" (p. 266.) The younger Nisei believe in romantic love, select their own mates, regard the husband-wife relationship as more important than the parent-child relationship, and have equalitarian sex roles. However, family gatherings of extended kin are common.

The Sansei are the third generation children and reflect even greater Americanization than the Nisei. The Sansei do not hesitate to marry someone who is not Japanese (about 60 percent of marriages are out-group marriages). Most of these interracial marriages are to whites. "The increase in out-group marriage rates is the result of the breakup of the ghetto, loss of family control over marital choices, changes in the law, and more liberal attitudes toward interracial unions on the behalf of both the ethnic and majority communities" (Kitano, 1988, 274).

Black, Mexican American, Native American and Japanese American marriages emphasize the diversity of marriage patterns in the United States. In the next section we focus on a goal which is common to very Americanized marriages—happiness.

Very Happy Marriages

Most people who marry do so with a common goal—to have a successful marriage. Marital success is measured according to marital stability and marital happiness. Stability refers to how long the spouses stay married whereas happiness is a more subjective term. In describing marital success, researchers have also used the terms satisfaction, quality, adjustment, lack of distress, and integration.

Marital happiness is often measured by asking spouses how happy they are, how much time they spend together, how successful they are at resolving conflicts, and how many areas of agreement they have (Krokoff, 1989). An example of an inventory that may be used to assess marriage happiness is illustrated in the Marriage Happiness Scale in the Self-Assessment.

One problem encountered in measuring marital happiness is that people tend to answer questions the way they think they should rather than the way things

Marriage Happiness Scale

This inventory is designed to measure the way you feel about your marital relationship. There are no right or wrong answers. After reading each sentence carefully, circle the number that best represents your feelings.

1 Strongly disagree
2 Mildly disagree
3 Undecided
4 Mildly agree
5 Strongly agree

	SD	MD	U	MA	SA
1. My partner and I enjoy spending our free time together.	1	2	3	4	5
2. My partner and I have never discussed separation.	1	2	3	4	5
3. My partner lets me know that I am loved.	1	2	3	4	5
4. I let my partner know that I love her or him.	1	2	3	4	5
5. My partner and I have a lot in common.	1	2	3	4	5
6. My partner and I are very affectionate with each other.	1	2	3	4	5
7. My partner and I have a good sex life.	1	2	3	4	5
8. My partner and I are able to talk about anything.	1	2	3	4	5
9. My partner and I respect each other's needs.	1	2	3	4	5
10. My partner and I are committed to make our marriage work.	1	2	3	4	5

SCORING: Add the numbers you circled. 1 (strongly the most negative feeling you can have, and 5 (strongly agree) is the most positive feeling you can have. The lower your total score (10 is the lowest possible score), the less happy you are in your marriage; the higher your score (50 is the highest possible score), the more happy you are in your marriage. A score of 30 places you at the midpoint between an unhappy and a very happy marriage.

(NOTE: This Self-Assessment is not intended to be used by students as a clinical diagnostic instrument.)

actually are. This tendency to give socially desirable answers (also referred to as conventionalization) keeps the marriage experience hidden and makes it difficult to determine the degree to which people are actually happy.

Nevertheless, 61 percent of 15,000 married respondents reported that they had "excellent"—27 percent, or "very good" marriages 34 percent—(Schwartz & Jackson, 1989). The respondents had been married an average of about six years, most in their first marriage, and had an average of 2.7 children living with them. These very happy marriages exhibited three primary characteristics.

1. *Quality Time Together.*

> ■ **DATA:** *Seventy percent of the respondents in excellent marriages spend more than 75 percent of their nonworking time together (Schwartz & Jackson, 1989).*

The spouses "had a close friendship and did all the little, daily things together. They were always there for each other" (p. 70).

2. *High Affection and High Sex Frequency.* Spouses in very happy relationships showed a great deal of affection in public. "We can't keep our hands off each other," said one respondent. Such affection reflects the delight the partners experience in each other.

The spouses also reported being sexually passionate in private with the happiest of spouses reporting the highest frequency of intercourse of all the couples—with 8 to 12 occasions of intercourse each month. One woman reported, "My husband satisfies my sexual needs; he is a sexually exciting partner" (p. 68).

3. *Equality of Respect for Each Other's Needs.* Very happy spouses also report fairness, cooperation, and sharing of cooking, cleaning, childrearing, and breadwinning. Each partner felt that they worked together and that neither was the dominant partner. The wives also reported that they shared equal financial authority. Decisions to purchase big ticket items such as cars and refrigerators were always discussed ahead of time.

> ■ **DATA:** *Eighty-eight percent of women who report having excellent marriages say that they share decision making equally (Schwartz & Jackson, 1989, 72).*

Equal decision making is important because it communicates to each partner that individual opinions and feelings are valued. Not to be consulted is to suggest that a partner regards the other's feelings as unimportant.

⠶ Trends

Marriage relationships in the United States will continue to be very diverse. No single family form, sex role relationship, or set of values will represent "the" American family. Racial, ethnic, and cultural differences will ensure that marital life is rich and varied.

Intermarriage (age-discrepant, religious, and racial) will continue to increase. This will result from a weakening of the influence nuclear families have over enforcing the norms of endogamy. That families have become more liberal with each succeeding generation was illustrated in the discussion of Japanese American marriages.

∷ Summary

All marriage relationships represent a commitment between the partners, between the respective families, and between the couple and the state. The wedding is a rite of passage signifying the change from the role of single individual to the role of married spouse. Marriage involves various personal, social, and legal changes for the spouses. Personal changes include an enhanced self-concept that results from entering into a committed, loving relationship. Society also approves of a couple's marriage and encourages them to feel good about their decision. But the reality of marriage also involves disenchantment—the gradual process whereby each spouse becomes aware that the other person in courtship is not always the same person in marriage.

Marrying while still in college may lead to role conflict. Trying to fulfill the roles of student, spouse, employee, and perhaps parent may introduce strain in some relationships.

An increasing number of marriages are interreligious. Although mixed religious marriages do not necessarily imply a greater risk to marital happiness, marriages in which one or both spouses profess no religion are in the greatest jeopardy. Also, husbands in interreligious marriages seem less satisfied because children are usually reared in the faith (or nonfaith) of the wife.

Divorce is greater among black marriages than white marriages. This is partly due to economic insufficiency and the social context of racism. It is a myth that overt discrimination has virtually vanished in the last 20 years. As soon as the workday ends, blacks and whites retreat to different worlds.

Mexican American marriages have traditionally been characterized by male dominance and female submissiveness. As more wives work outside the home, the power of the Chicana will increase and the balance of power will continue to shift.

Native American marriages are not so easily categorized. Since tribal identity supercedes family identity and the values and beliefs vary widely among and between the 300 federally recognized tribes, there are few fixed characteristics of Native American marriages.

Japanese American marriages differ depending on the degree of socialization of the spouses in the United States. Issei (first generation) marriages are very traditional in contrast to Sansei (third generation) marriages in which the spouses are very Americanized.

Marital happiness is assessed by examining the degree to which spouses spend time together, how they evaluate the time they spend together, the absence of conflict, and the similarity of values. Very happy spouses report that they spend the majority of their leisure time together, that they are affectionate in public and passionate in private, and that they value equality in their relationships.

Questions for Reflection

1. To what degree do you feel that marriage should be a legal relationship as well as an emotional relationship?
2. How do you feel about entering interreligious, interracial, and age-discrepant marriages?

3. How do the characteristics of your relationship compare with those of very happy marriages?

References

Ball, R. E. and L. Robbins. Marital status and life satisfaction among black Americans. *Journal of Marriage and the Family,* 1986, *48,* 389–394.

Becerra, R. M. The Mexican American family. *Ethnic families in America: Patterns and variations.* Edited by C. H. Mindel, R. W. Habenstein, and R. Wright, Jr. New York: Elsevier, 1988, pp. 141–159.

Berkove, G. F. Perceptions of husband support by returning women students. *Family Relations,* 1979, *28, no. 4,* 451–457.

Boston, Thomas D. *Race, class, and conservatism.* Boston: Unwin Hyman, 1988.

Broman, C. L. Satisfaction among blacks: The significance of marriage and parenthood. *Journal of Marriage and the Family,* 1988, *50,* 45–51.

Chatters, L. M, J. J. Taylor, and H. W. Neighbors. Size of informal helper network mobilized during a serious personal problem among Black Americans. *Journal of Marriage and the Family,* 1989, *51,* 667–676.

Cook, A. The $60,000 wedding. *Money,* May 1990, 118–132.

Cuber, J. F. and P. B. Harroff. *Sex and the significant Americans.* Baltimore, Md.: Penguin Books, 1965.

Feinson, M. C. Aging and mental health. *Research on Aging,* 1985, *7,* 155–174.

Fitzpatrick, Mary A. *Between husbands and wives: Communication in marriage.* Beverly Hills, Calif.: Sage Publications, 1988.

Glenn, N. D. Interreligious marriage in the United States: Patterns and recent trends. *Journal of Marriage and the Family,* 1982, *44, no. 3,* 555–566.

Goetting, A. Patterns of support among in-laws in the United States. *Journal of Family Issues,* 1990, *11,* 67–90.

Harrington, W. What color are our children? *Washington Post Magazine,* October 17, 1982, pp. 10 et passim.

Hoffman, Thomas J. Native Americans, public spending issues, incumbent support and political cynicism: A comparative analysis. *Free Inquiry in Creative Sociology,* 1989, *17,* 33–40.

Huston-Hoburg, L. and C. Strange. Spouse support among male and female returning adult students. *Journal of College Student Personnel,* 1986, *27,* 388–394.

Jaynes, Gerald D. and Robin M. Williams, Jr. *A common destiny: Blacks and American society.* Washington, D.C.: National Academy Press, 1989.

John, R. The native American family. *Ethnic families in America,* 3rd ed. Edited by C. H. Mindel, R. W. Habenstein, and R. Wright, Jr. New York: Elsevier, 1988, 325–367.

Johnson, M. P. and L. Leslie. Couple involvement and network structure: A test of the dyadic withdrawal hypothesis. *Social Psychology Quarterly,* 1982, *45, no. 1,* 34–43.

Johnson, R. C. and C. T. Nagoshi. The adjustment of offspring of within-group and interracial/intercultural marriages: A comparison of personality factors. *Journal of Marriage and the Family,* 1986, *48,* 279–284.

Kantrowitz, Barbara and D. Witherspoon. The December dilemma: How to reconcile two faiths in one household. *Newsweek,* December 28, 1987, p. 56.

Kelly, S. Returning to college. *Family Relations,* 1982, *31, no. 2,* 287–294.

Kitano, H. H. L. The Japanese American family. *Ethnic Families in America: Patterns and Variations,* 3rd ed. Edited by Charles H. Mindel, Robert W. Habenstein, and Roosevelt Wright, Jr. New York: Elsevier, 1988, 258–276.

Klinger-Vartabedian, Laurel and L. Wispe. Age differences in marriage and female longevity. *Journal of Marriage and the Family,* 1989, *51,* 195–202.

Koopman-Boyden, P. G. Expectations for household task allocation and actual task allocation: A New Zealand study. *Journal of Marriage and the Family,* 1985, *47,* 211–219.

Krokoff, Lowell J. Locke-Wallace Marital Adjustment Test. Used by permission of Lowell J. Krokoff, Child and Family Studies, University of Wisconsin-Madison, Madison, WI 53706, 1989.

Lederer, W. J. and D. D. Jackson. *The mirages of marriage.* New York: W. W. Norton, 1968.

McRoy, S. and V. Fisher. Marital adjustment of graduate student couples. *Family Relations,* 1982, *31,* no. 1, 37–41.

Open Doors, 1978–1988. Institute of International Education, 809 United Nations Plaza, New York, NY.

Price-Bonham, S. and J. O. Balswick. The noninstitutions: Divorce, desertion, and remarriage. *Journal of Marriage and the Family,* 1980, *42,* no. 4, 959–972.

Rice, F. P. *Intimate relationships, marriages, and families.* Mountain View, Calif.: Mayfield Publishing Co., 1990.

Schwartz, Pepper and Donna Jackson. How to have a model marriage. *New Woman,* February 1989, 66–74.

Shehan, C. L., E. W. Bock, and G. R. Lee. Religious heterogamy, religiosity, and marital happiness: The case of Catholics. *Journal of Marriage and the Family,* 1990, *52,* 73–79.

Staples, Robert. The Black American family. *Ethnic families in America: Patterns and variations.* Edited by C. H. Mindel, R. W. Habenstein, and R. Wright, Jr. New York: Elsevier, 1988, pp. 303–324.

Statistical Abstract of the United States: 1990, 110th ed. Washington, D.C.: U.S. Bureau of the Census, 1990.

Tucker, M. B. and C. Mitchell-Kernan. New trends in Black American interracial marriage: The social structural context. *Journal of Marriage and the Family,* 1990, *52,* 209–218.

Van Meter, M. J. S. and S. J. Agronow. The stress of multiple roles: The case for role strain among married college women. *Family Relations,* 1982, *31,* no. 1, 131–138.

Vera, H., D. H. Berardo, and F. M. Berardo. Age heterogamy in marriage. *Journal of Marriage and the Family,* 1985, *47,* 553–566.

CHOICES

MARRIAGE PARTNERS MAY be confronted with decisions about the type of marriage relationship desired, the partner's "night out," parents as live-ins, and who manages the money.

Type of Marriage Relationship Desired

Two researchers (Cuber & Harroff, 1965) interviewed 211 spouses and identified five types of marriage relationships:

1. *Conflict-habituated.* The spouses have a basic incompatibility and argue frequently. Their relationship is characterized by conflict.
2. *Devitalized.* The spouses don't argue; they are just bored. Their relationship is lifeless and apathetic.
3. *Passive-Congenial.* Whereas the devitalized spouses once shared good times together, the passive-congenial spouses have had a polite and stale relationship from the beginning. Their interests and energies are directed toward careers and children, not toward each other.
4. *Vital.* The mates share an emotional closeness and enjoy doing things together. Their central satisfactions in life are in their relationship.
5. *Total.* The total relationship is similar to the vital relationship except that it is more multifaceted. The "total" couple schedule their day around each other, meet for lunch, and anticipate every opportunity to be together.

It is not unusual for couples in courtship to begin with a total relationship and drift into a devitalized or conflict-habituated relationship after several years of marriage. If you choose to maintain a vital or total relationship, it will mean giving your relationship a high priority in terms of time and energy and developing relationship skills to effectively manage conflict.

Partner's Night Out?

Although recently married individuals may want to spend all of their time together, this need diminishes over the years and the need to spend time without the spouse increases. Frequently one or both partners want to spend time with their friends. This may mean going to happy hour on Wednesdays with their coworkers, bowling, shopping, playing bridge, fishing, or golfing.

Some spouses have a policy of trust with each other. One wife said:

I tell John to go anywhere he wants to with anyone he wants to just as long as he is emotionally and sexually faithful to me. I'm not going to try to restrict what John does. If he wants to be unfaithful to me, he will. But I have no reason to distrust him, and I'm sure he doesn't get involved with other women when we're apart.

Other spouses are very suspicious of each other. One husband said:

I didn't want her having lunch or after work drinks with her boss. I don't think it's a healthy situation. Before you know it they would be talking about getting together at the beach.

For partner's night out to have a positive impact on the couple's relationship, it is important that the partners maintain emotional and sexual fidelity to each other, that each partner have a partner's night out, and that the partners spend some nights alone with each other. Friendships can enhance a marriage relationship by making the individual partners happier; but friendships cannot replace the marriage relationship. Spouses must spend time alone to nurture their relationship.

Parents as Live-Ins?

As the parents of the spouses get older, a decision must often be made by the spouses about whether to have the parents live with them. Usually it is the mother of either spouse; the father is the most likely to die first. One wife said:

We didn't have a choice. His mother is 82 and has Alzheimer's disease. We couldn't afford to put her in a nursing home at $1,200 a month, and she couldn't stay by herself. So we took her in. It's been a real strain on our marriage, since I end up taking care of her all day. I can't even leave her alone to go to the grocery store.

Some elderly persons do have resources for nursing home care or the spouses can afford it. But even in these circumstances, some spouses decide to have their parents live with them. "I couldn't live with myself if I knew my mother was propped up in a wheelchair eating Cheerios when I could be taking care of her," said one spouse.

When spouses disagree about parents in the home, the results can be devastating. According to one wife:

I told my husband that mother was going to live with us. He told me she wasn't and that he would leave if she did. She moved in, and he moved out (we were divorced). Five months later, my mother died.

Who Will Manage the Money?

Marriage is a partnership of two people who cooperate economically. It is like a small business. Money comes in (income), and money goes out (expenses). Someone must be responsible for seeing that expenses do not consistently exceed income (to avoid going deeply into debt), bills are paid (to keep the lights and water on), and accurate records are kept (to pay taxes and for Internal Revenue Service audits). Couples differ in who manages the money. In some marriages, one spouse is responsible; in others, the partners may do so jointly. Joint bookkeeping works only if role responsibilities are clear and each person is disciplined enough to fulfill his or her responsibility.

How many checking and savings accounts to have is another issue. No pattern works best for all people. One couple may have one savings and one checking account; another may have three checking and three savings accounts. In an instance of the latter, the husband, wife, and child each had their own checking and savings accounts, and each was responsible for keeping the books for their accounts. "It is really easier if everyone keeps up with his or her own," said the wife.

Impact of Social Influences on Choices

The marriage relationship you develop with your spouse will be influenced by the marriage patterns the two of you have observed in your respective parents, friends, and other marital models. If you grew up in a home in which your parents demonstrated little affection toward each other, then you are likely to duplicate this pattern in your own marriage. Cartoons often picture marriage as a ball-and-chain, argumentative relationship. In the United States, the cultural image of courtship is all love and fun, but marriage is depicted as all work and hassle—from moonlight and roses to daylight and dishes.

Chinese, Japanese, and other Asian marriages focus on the functioning of the family unit and less on the happiness of the individual members. Happy spouses are viewed as less important than happy children, and keeping the spouses together is a strong goal. American marriages tend to focus more on individual happiness. If the spouses are not happy with each other, divorce becomes a consideration. Hence, the degree to which there is affection in your marriage and whether you stay married may be influenced by social forces that are beyond the control of you and your partner.

Two-Income Relationships

CONTENTS

IS IT TRUE?

1. Marriages in which the spouses have an equal say about how money is to be spent are more likely to remain intact than marriages in which one spouse determines how money is to be spent.

2. Wives are as likely to have a career as husbands.

3. Money was the most common problem identified by 15,000 spouses.

4. More than twenty percent of wives employed full time earn more than their husbands.

5. Only a few countries have job-protected leaves of absence during pregnancy and birth.

1 = T; 2 = F; 3 = T; 4 = T; 5 = F

W E MAY MARRY for love, but it is money that buys food, pays rent, and enables us to have some of the other things we want. Because our very survival depends on it, money is a powerful determinant of how we feel about ourselves and how we interact with others. After examining the ways in which money is significant in our lives and in our relationships, we will look at the implications of having two earners in one marriage.

▪▪ The Meanings of Money

Economists view money as the medium of exchange that makes possible the distribution of goods and services in our society. But money has more personal meanings, which relate to self-concept, power, security, freedom, social relationships, love—and to conflict in marriage.

Self-Concept

Money affects a person's self-concept because, in our society, human worth is sometimes equated with financial achievement. A young husband and father mused:

> I've been working for seven years, and I've got nothing to show for it. I can't even pay the light bill, let alone buy the things we want. My two closest friends are making good money in their own businesses. It makes me feel bad when I know that I can't provide for my family the way they provide for theirs. I'm a failure.

Money may also influence a person's self-concept in courtship. One 24-year-old said:

> I am not in school this semester because I had to drop out to earn some money. And finding a woman to date when you don't have any money is very difficult. Once a woman sees that I live in a trailer and that I'm broke, I never see her again. It has happened so many times I get depressed just thinking about asking someone out again. Money has a lot to do with the way a woman feels about you and the way you feel about yourself.

Power

Those who have money sometimes feel a sense of power, a sense of control over things, events, and people. Whereas the average shopper may say, "I can't afford that," the person with great means may not have to consider the price of things and may buy as desires dictate. This ability to purchase goods and services at will results in a feeling of power; power means getting what we want when we want it.

Money provides not only the power to possess things but also the power to control events. For the poor, a combination of subzero temperatures and high fuel prices is almost certain to mean discomfort and may mean death. For the wealthy, the high prices caused by a shortage of fuel are not even an inconvenience. No matter how high the price or how low the temperature, the rich will be snug and warm.

Money also means power over people—employers over employees, parents over offspring, and employed spouses over unemployed spouses. Anyone who

You can be young without money but you can't be old without it.
—TENNESSEE
   WILLIAMS

There are a lot of things that money can't buy—for example, what it bought last year.
—LAURENCE PETER

Money provides the opportunity for couples to do the things they enjoy.

has worked for someone else knows the power of employers. Unless the employee complies with the wishes of the employer, the employer may terminate the worker's job. Parents exercise power over their offsprings' private lives. The parents of one student threatened to withdraw financial support of a daughter if she continued to live with her boyfriend. She was committed to pursuing a business career and would be unable to pay tuition without her parents' help, so she moved out. Money gave her parents power, and they used it.

Money used as shared power by the spouses has positive consequences for the marriage. In a study of how married couples managed the money in their relationships, two researchers observed that when the wife had equal or greater influence in deciding how much cash to keep on hand, paying bills, and keeping track of expenditures, she reported being much happier in the relationship. When the husband dominated the economic decisions, wives were much more despondent about their relationships (Schwartz & Jackson, 1989).

☐   C O N S I D E R A T I O N   ☐

The woman who earns an income has more power in the relationship than the woman who does not earn an income. But unless she opens her own bank account, there is little gain in the degree to which she has control over the money she earns (Yoger & Brett, 1989).

Security

Oscar Wilde once said, "When I was young, I used to think that money was the most important thing in life; now that I am older, I know it is." Money represents security. People without money often feel that they live on the verge of disaster. "My car has four slick tires," said a single mother of two children who had returned to college, "and when one of those pops, I've had it. I don't have the money for new tires, and I can't walk to work."

Buying life insurance expresses the desire to provide a secure future for loved ones. "If something happens to me," one husband said, "my wife and children will need more than the sympathy they'll get at my funeral. They'll need money." Without money, there is no security—either present or future. Money also secures us against ill health. Because medical care often depends on the ability to pay for it, our health is directly related to our financial resources. Money buys visits to the physician, as well as food for a balanced diet.

Freedom

Money gives us the freedom to do the things we like to do. One husband recalls:

> When we were in school, we didn't have money to eat out or to see a movie. It was a terrible feeling being cooped up all the time with no money to do anything. Now we've graduated, and both of us have good jobs. We've got money in the bank (a little) and some in our pockets. We're free to do what we want when we want. It's a nice feeling—very nice.

Social Relationships

Money affects the relationship between spouses, between spouses and their parents, and between spouses and their peers. People are more likely to stay married under conditions of financial stress. Although most studies indicate that increased income is associated with increased marital stability (there is less conflict over the lack of money), in the Gary Income Maintenance Experiment, the probability of a divorce increased when the income available to low-income couples increased. "The wives could afford to leave," said the principal investigator (Maiolo, 1982).

As for the effect of money on spouse-parent relationships, married partners who are financially dependent on their parents often discover that the use of their parents' money is not free. In exchange for parental support, the couple is expected to visit frequently and, in some cases, to consult the parents before making major decisions. "You bet," said one parent. "After sending them $500 a month, I expect them to appreciate what I'm doing. And that means before buying a new car or taking a job out of state, they should consult me." Money also affects relationships with peers. One wife said:

> Our neighbors eat out every Friday night at an expensive restaurant and have asked us to join them. But we're on a tight budget and simply can't afford to spend $25 on a meal. We wave at them when we get the afternoon newspaper, but we haven't socialized with them in three months. If we had more money, it would be different.

Love

To some individuals, money may also mean love. While admiring the engagement ring of her friend, a woman said, "What a big diamond! He must really love you." The assumption is that big diamond equals high price equals deep love feelings.

Similar assumptions are often made when gifts are given or received. People tend to spend more money on presents for the people they love, believing that the value of the gift symbolizes the depth of their emotion. People receiving gifts may make the same assumption. "She must love me more than I thought," mused one man. "I gave her a record album for Christmas, but she gave me a cassette tape deck. I felt embarrassed." His feeling of embarrassment is based on the idea that the woman loves him more than he loves her because she paid more for her gift to him than he did for his gift to her.

Similarly, the withdrawal of money may mean the absence of love. When two people get divorced, aside from what the court may order in alimony and child support, it is assumed that their economic sharing is over.

Conflict

■ **DATA:** *Seventy-seven percent of 15,000 spouses reported that money was the greatest problem in their marriage—outranking sex, in-laws, or infidelity (Schwartz & Jackson, 1989).*

Money may also be a source of conflict between spouses when one spouse wants to buy something that would prevent the other spouse from buying something else. For example, Richard wanted to buy a videotape recorder and camera that cost around $1,500. Carol wanted to buy a piano and furniture for their empty living room, which would cost around $2,000. Richard thought that spending money on "a sofa and piano that nobody would play was foolish"; Carol thought that spending money on "movie stuff" was a "complete waste." Not all money conflicts in marriages may be over furniture and video recorders, but the issue is always the same—money spent for X can't be spent for Y.

Money can also be used to reduce marital conflict and stress. For example, partners who argue over who is to clean the house may hire a person to clean it for them once a week. Money also makes family vacations possible, allowing couples to escape day-to-day pressures and have fun together.

☐   C O N S I D E R A T I O N   ☐

To state the obvious, money is not the key to happiness. Although some assert that money helps, if you are rich but have nonexistent or negative relationships with your spouse and children, you can be emotionally bankrupt. Our society places a great deal of emphasis on making money and very little emphasis on meeting the human needs of love, intimacy, compassion for children, healthy home environments, and other important aspects of life. The relentless pursuit of money has its own price tag.

∷ Dual-Income Marriages

In the past, the typical American family consisted of a husband who earned the income and a wife who stayed home and took care of their children. This pattern has changed.

Working women and dual-wage-earner families have become a necessary response to the steady decline in the standard of living in the United States that has occurred over the last 15 years.
—ROBERT JOHN

■ **DATA:** *Sixty-one percent of 15,000 spouses reported that both the wife and husband work outside the home full-time. Eleven percent of the respondents reported that the wife was a full-time homemaker (Schwartz & Jackson, 1989). Only 15 percent of all families fit the traditional mold of the married couple with children and a wife not in the paid labor force (Merrick & Tordella, 1988).*

Couples who think in terms of a two-income marriage are not limited to whites. Black, Hispanic, Native American, and Asian American marriages are also characterized by two income earners. In the following section, we will focus on the motivations for employment.

Motivations for Employment

The traditional male role in our society is that of provider. No one asks a man if he is going to continue working after he gets married or after his partner has a child. Society expects men to work and most men have internalized this social expectation. Men who successfully fulfill the role of provider are more likely to be happy with themselves and to feel adequate as a husband and father than men who are not successful in that role (Osherson & Dill, 1983).

The traditional female role, on the other hand, has been that of child caregiver and homemaker. It is not unusual for a woman to be asked, "Are you going to work after you get married?" or "Are you going to continue working after you have a child?" Despite the increasing trend toward equalitarian role relationships between men and women in our society, husbands are still expected to work, whereas wives are viewed as having the option to work or not to work.

These traditional social expectations regarding male and female employment may be becoming less influential in the choices men and women make regarding their employment. Men and women today share the same motivations for working outside the home. These motivations include money, personal satisfaction, personal independence, and expansion of a social network.

Money. Regarding money, the costs of family living often require two incomes. For many couples, basic living expenses such as rent or mortgage, food, utilities, and car payment are not covered by one income. Indeed, it is not unusual for one or both partners to have a second job in order to meet monthly bills, pay off debts, save for a major purchase (house, car, boat), or pay for a vacation or college education of a child.

Personal Satisfaction. Another motivation for women and men to work outside the home is that it may provide personal satisfaction. For some individuals, having a job or career that is interesting, challenging, and meaningful is more important than having a job that is high-paying. For some men and women, working in the home caring for children and managing domestic responsibilities is more meaningful and challenging and provides more personal satisfaction than any form of outside employment.

Recent research concludes that "the majority of white married mothers who work outside the home do so because they want to work, not because they are compelled to work out of economic necessity" (Eggebeen & Hawkins, 1990, 57–58). These researchers suggest that the increase in wives in the labor force since

1960 is largely due to family decisions to earn more money so that the family can enjoy a higher standard of living.

☐   C O N S I D E R A T I O N   ☐

The term "high standard of living" may be misleading. One husband remarked:

> Pam and I live comfortably off our part-time incomes. We have a rich personal and social life and we enjoy our leisure time together. We live in a small apartment, drive an old car, eat a lot of peanut butter and jelly sandwiches, and wear second-hand clothes. But it is inaccurate to say that we have a low standard of living. We regard our standard of living as very high.

Once the desired standard of living is achieved, families may scale back their income needs to devote more time to family and recreation. But what is more likely to happen is that the family's standard of living continues to rise. America, after all, is a consumption society. The media bombards us daily with advertisements that increase our aspirations to have the things that money can buy. We may even get subtle messages suggesting that to spend money is to increase the economic health of our society. Thus, many couples get caught in a vicious circle of working to achieve the desired standard of living, only to find that the standard of living rises again.

☐   C O N S I D E R A T I O N   ☐

Some families choose to live with modest means because they recognize that "the benefits of an increased standard of living purchased with two incomes may fall below the social-psychological benefits of time devoted to family and personal leisure" (Eggebeen and Hawkins, 1990, 61). Others choose a modest lifestyle because they are concerned about the environmental pollution and depletion of the Earth's resources that result from America's overconsumption.

Personal Independence. Many spouses choose to work in order to be financially self-sufficient, rather than dependent on their partner's income. When each partner earns an income, they each may feel more personal independence in regard to how they spend their money. Due to the divorce rate and the probability that the husband will die before the wife, it is functional for the wife to develop her own job skills, employment history, and credit rating. Otherwise, she can quickly drift into poverty (see the "Feminization of Poverty" discussed in chapter 3) with no source of income.

Expanded Social Network. Employment usually involves an expanded social network. Spouses who are not involved in the labor force may feel socially isolated. Many work environments involve daily interaction with a variety of people. One young mother said she needed adult interaction to keep her brain from atrophying. "I had spent so much time around our son, I began to talk 'baby talk' to my husband. We agreed it was time for me to go back to my old job."

Men and women today expect to be involved in the work force. But this was not always the case for women. Next, we look at the transition from the traditional married woman's role in the home to her current role as employee.

Employed Wives: Past and Present

Before 1940, a married woman's place was in the home, and although she might sell her wares, sewing, laundry, and cooking skills (this work could be done without leaving home), she was not expected to earn an income working outside the home. The exception was the black, immigrant, rural woman, who has always tended to work outside the home out of economic necessity.

World War II marked the point at which employment became acceptable for all classes of women. Their participation in the labor force became a national necessity rather than a social request. While most middle-class, wartime, employed women were expected to return to the traditional roles of wife and mother after the war was over, a Women's Bureau survey conducted in 1944 and 1945 revealed that between 75 and 80 percent of all women war workers wanted to remain on the job after the fighting had stopped (Chafe, 1976). Although demobilization resulted in the loss of jobs for many women (and men), the trend toward increased participation of women in the labor force had been established.

■ **DATA:** *The proportion of employed married women increased from 20 percent just after World War II to 66.1 percent in 1989* (Statistical Abstract of the United States: 1990 Table 637).

Today's Employed Wives

Among all married women, those more likely to be employed are black, have not completed college, do not have preschool children, and have fewer children. Of course, white college-educated wives with several children are also employed, but there are proportionally fewer of them. In the past, a wife's and mother's employment pattern followed the development of her children; her times of peak employment were before her children were born and after they left home. But this pattern has changed; more mothers with children of all ages now work outside the home.

Wives tend to have traditionally "female" jobs: food-service worker, secretary, teacher, cleaning-service worker, and sales clerk. These are often part-time jobs that provide flexibility in working hours—an important benefit to women with children. Flexibility in work hours is usually an irrelevant issue to Chinese Americans, who have to cope with another set of problems to keep their families together and to survive economically (see Exhibit 9.1).

The Self-Assessment on "One or Two Incomes in Your Marriage?" is designed to assess whether you prefer a one or two income marriage.

❚❚ Job Versus Career

One of the choices individuals make in regard to employment is whether to have a "job" or a "career." Let's examine what a career typically involves.

E X H I B I T   9.1

Chinese Americans and Economic Survival*

Chinese spouses and their children have experienced one of three patterns of family relationships since immigration to America began in 1850.

SPLIT HOUSEHOLD

The split-household pattern—husbands leaving their wives and children in China while they came to America to work in the railroad, mining, and agricultural industries—existed primarily between 1850 and 1920. Employers needed an abundance of inexpensive labor, which these young, able-bodied Chinese males were willing to provide. The husbands sent money back to China to provide support for their wives and children. (Actually, the husband sent money to his kin—usually his parents—with whom his wife and children lived. This arrangement ensured that the wife would stay chaste and subject to the ultimate control of her husband).

The wives often preferred to stay in China—to live comfortably in their village on the money sent by their husbands. Some husbands had concubines in the United States. The marriage relationship lacked frequent nurturing, and the relationship between the father and his children was often formal and distant. The relationship between the mother and children was particularly strong, due to the husband's absence.

SMALL-PRODUCER FAMILY

As immigration laws were relaxed, more wives and children joined their husbands in America. From about 1920 to the mid-1960s, the typical Chinese American family functioned as a small producing unit:

> Some flavor of the close integration of work and family life is seen in this description of the daily routine in a family laundry, provided by a woman who grew up in Boston's Chinatown during the 1930s and 1940s. The household consisted of the parents and four children. The work day started

at 7:00 in the morning and did not end until midnight, six days a week. Except for school and a short nap in the afternoon, the children worked the same hours as the parents, doing their homework between midnight and 2:00 A.M. Each day's routine was the same. All items were marked or tagged as they were brought in by customers. A commercial laundry picked up the laundry, washed it, and brought it back wet. The wet laundry was hung to dry in a back room heated by a coal burner. Next, items were taken down, sprinkled, starched, and rolled for ironing. Tasks were allocated by age and sex. Young children of 6 or 7 performed simple tasks, such as folding socks and wrapping parcels. At about age 10, they started ironing handkerchiefs and underwear. Mother operated the collar and cuff press, while father hand-ironed shirts and uniforms. Only on Sunday did the family relax its hectic regime to attend church in the morning and relax in the afternoon (p. 40).

DUAL-INCOME FAMILY

Since 1965, over 20,000 Chinese have entered the United States each year. Unlike the earlier Chinese immigrants who came over one at a time, the new immigrants came to America in family groups—husband, wife, and children. At least 50 percent of these immigrants can be classified as working class. The husband usually works as a waiter, cook, or janitor; the wife, in a garment shop. Not unlike most American couples, Chinese American couples have come to consist of husbands and wives who work separate jobs. Chinese children are sometimes left unsupervised and complain that their parents are not around much to talk. One young student noted, "We can discuss things, but we don't talk that much. We don't have that much to say" (p. 42).

Our assumption that Chinese American families are always close-knit may not be true when we examine the degree to which the spouses are subjected to the strains of segregated employment and the children have limited interaction with their parents.

*Adapted from Evelyn N. Glenn. "Split Household, Small Producer, and Dual Wage Earner: An Analysis of Chinese American Family Strategies." *Journal of Marriage and the Family*, 1983, 45, 35–46. Used by permission of the National Council of Family Relations.

Criteria For a Career

Although there are many similarities between a job and a career, a career is more likely to require extensive training, commitment, continuity, and mobility. A clinical psychologist who is employed in a mental health center said, "I didn't get where I am just because I like to work with people. I went to school for 20 years,

One or Two Incomes in Your Marriage?

This scale is designed to assess the degree to which you want to be involved in a marriage in which both spouses earn an income. After reading each sentence carefully, circle the number that best represents your feelings.

1 Strongly disagree
2 Mildly disagree
3 Undecided
4 Mildly agree
5 Strongly agree

	SD	MD	U	MA	SA
1. Two incomes are necessary to pay for what a family needs.	1	2	3	4	5
2. The high divorce rate today necessitates both spouses developing job skills and a work history.	1	2	3	4	5
3. Being able to afford everything you want for your family is a very important goal.	1	2	3	4	5
4. Both spouses are really better off when both are earning an income.	1	2	3	4	5
5. Marriages are happier when both spouses are earning an income.	1	2	3	4	5
6. Each spouse should get as much education as possible to earn as much money as possible.	1	2	3	4	5
7. Children are really better off when they see that both spouses are employed.	1	2	3	4	5
8. It is best if both spouses work full time outside the home and share the cooking, cleaning, and taking care of the children rather than one spouse being responsible for earning the income and one spouse being responsible for household work and childcare.	1	2	3	4	5
9. Working outside the home is better for the spouse than staying home with children all day.	1	2	3	4	5
10. Dual income couples are happier than couples in which only one spouse works outside the home.	1	2	3	4	5

SCORING: Add the numbers you circled. 1 (strongly disagree) reflects that you feel that only one spouse should work outside the home, and 5 (strongly agree) reflects that you feel that both spouses should earn an income. The lower your total score (10 is the lowest possible score), the greater your preference for a one-income marriage. The higher your total score (50 is the highest possible score), the greater your preference for a two-income marriage. A score of 25 may suggest that you do not have a strong preference either way.

(NOTE: This Self-Assessment is intended to be fun and thought-provoking. It is not a scientific measuring instrument.)

read myself blind, and wrote a 230-page dissertation to get the Ph.D." A business major noted, "If you don't have your MBA [master's of business administration degree,] they won't talk to you."

In addition to formal training, a career also implies commitment in time and energy to pursue the goals of an organization or profession. An executive for a large insurance company observed, "The corporation wants your soul. If you are not willing to make phone calls in the evenings to your branch managers or to work on Saturdays—in general, work when the corporation needs you—you'll never be an executive and make $60,000 a year."

☐   C O N S I D E R A T I O N   ☐

Although corporations typically want the "souls" (the obligations are open-ended) of all of their employees at all levels, the career-minded person is more likely to meet their requests because the rewards are higher. In contrast, if too many demands (being asked to work overtime, cancel vacations) are made on employees who view their work as a job, the employees may conclude that the rewards are not worth the inconveniences and look for another job or quit working. "When my boss told me I would have to work on Saturday mornings, I said 'no way' " recalled one spouse. "That time belongs to me and my family." The fact that the obligations for both career and family are open-ended makes full investment in both difficult.

Related to career commitment is career continuity, which involves moving up the corporate ladder and remaining a full-time employee. In general, part-time workers tend to have jobs; full-time workers tend to have careers. Employed wives are more likely to have a job than a career; most do not work full time year-round. In addition, when employed wives are compared with employed husbands, the husbands more often are at the office on weekends, start their work earlier in the day, get off work later, work more hours per week, and hold second jobs (Pleck & Staines, 1985).

Mobility is a final element that helps to define a career. The trained, committed, full-time worker may be asked to move to another city. An air force officer observed, "Once you decide the air force is your career, you better decide to put up with the moving. We've moved 11 times in the last 20 years."

Some employers are reluctant to hire or promote women for fear they will give priority to their families and will not be willing to relocate if necessary. Felice Schwartz commented on how men in business view women:

Men continue to perceive women as the rearers of their children, so they find it understandable, indeed appropriate, that women should renounce their careers to raise families. Edmund Pratt, CEO of Pfizer, once asked me in all sincerity, "Why would any woman choose to be a chief financial officer rather than a full-time mother?" (1989, 67).

■ **DATA:** *Only 7 percent of all women who work outside the home hold anything remotely approaching an executive position (Hewlett, 1986).*

C O N S I D E R A T I O N

Careers and jobs have their respective advantages. Careers may involve more money and higher status, but jobs provide more employment flexibility. Jobs are easier to enter and leave and to adjust to different personal and family needs.

Although there are numerous exceptions, husbands tend to have careers and wives tend to have jobs (Bielby & Bielby, 1989). In the next section, we will examine why.

Obstacles to the Wife Pursuing a Career

There are at least three obstacles a wife may encounter as she pursues a career. These concern children, home, and husband.

It's not difficult for a woman to combine a family and a career—if she knows how to put both of them first.
—LAURENCE PETER

Responsibility for Children. More than 90 percent of all wives express a desire for children. Although there are exceptions, both wives and husbands tend to expect that the wife will be primarily responsible for childcare—an expectation that may block the wife's career advancement (Floge, 1989). The demands of home and family life may make it more difficult for women to compete with male colleagues who may not be encumbered with the daily responsibilities of homemaking and childrearing.

In general, wives tend to accommodate their work to their family rather than their family to their work. A large producer of consumer goods reports that one half of the women who take maternity leave return to their jobs late or not at all. For those who do return, part-time employment is "the provision women themselves most desire" (Schwartz, 1989, 73). One woman with three children remarked:

> There is tremendous social pressure on me to be responsible for my children. I don't have to be with them personally to take care of them, but I end up being responsible for arranging that someone takes Sandy from school to piano lessons, that Sam starts his homework after baseball practice, and that Melanie is picked up at the nursery. My husband is very willing to help with the kids, but he's trying to build his practice as an attorney, and I can't see bothering him with the details. If I did, it would soon cut into his career, and neither of us wants that. Of course, my career suffers, but I have the psychological comfort that I am taking care of my family.

Two researchers observed:

> In families with a traditional division of labor, wives take responsibility for household roles that obligate them to engage in specific behaviors. Thus, it is not surprising that the family is given priority in the distribution of role identities among working wives. In contrast, for husbands in traditional families, a strong family identity obligates them to very limited responsibilities outside of the 'provider' role (Bielby & Bielby, 1989, 786; Kalleberg and Rosenfeld, 1990).

■ **DATA:** *In a study of 204 physicians, parenthood significantly reduced the number of hours the woman worked. No reduction was observed for men (Grant et al., 1990).*

Employed mothers usually take greater responsibility for their children than employed fathers.

Responsibility for Home. Careers are also difficult for the married woman because she has no "wife" at home to do those things the traditional wife typically does. (Aware of this need, two California entrepreneurs have begun to offer a "Rent-A-Wife" service to working women and bachelors.) Keeping milk in the refrigerator, the clothes clean, the children cared for, and the meals prepared are chores that must be done. In most families, a wife who has a full-time job still does most of the domestic work when she gets home. Women who are employed come home to a *second shift* of work (Hochschild, 1989).

■ **DATA:** *Employed women may still spend three hours a day doing housework compared to their husbands who spend 17 minutes (Hochschild, 1989).*

Husbands also don't do much worrying about household responsibilities. One lawyer said it occurred to her in court that she would need to stop at the store on her way home and get some toilet paper because the family was down to the last roll. "I bet my husband has never had a thought like that when he is at work," she remarked.

One study looked at the relationship between men's attitudes about the provider role and their participation in domestic tasks. The researchers found that in dual-earner families, men who believed in the traditional male provider role were less involved in domestic tasks than men who viewed themselves as coproviders, rather than primary providers (Perry-Jenkins and Crouter, 1990).

☐ C O N S I D E R A T I O N ☐

This research suggests that if the goal is to achieve role sharing and equal responsibility in family domestic tasks, we must recognize the importance of changing men's attitudes toward family roles. Parents might consider socializing their sons to view husbands as coproviders.

The Husband's Disapproval. If the husband is not supportive of his wife's career, he can make it difficult for her to be successful and happy. Not only can he grumble about her working, but he can refuse to move if she has an opportunity for a promotion if she relocates to another city. Some men make it clear that they want a wife who does not work outside the home.

■ **DATA:** *In a survey of 999 college students on 104 college campuses, 15 percent of the men said that they wanted a marriage in which their wife did not work outside the home (Stewart, 1986).*

These data also make it clear that most men prefer that wives have careers and are supportive of their doing so.

☐ C O N S I D E R A T I O N ☐

Although an increasing number of American wives are demonstrating that it is possible to manage a job and a family, there is evidence to suggest that combining a career and a family is more difficult. Carol Orsborn says of the pressure:

> I began looking at ads and articles about working women, and it clicked. We all were expected to be wives, mothers, family providers, employees, and dynamic individuals—it was a complex trap we were falling for. I began talking about this with my friends, and they were as excited about it as I was (Edmondson, 1986, 18).

continued on next page

In response, Orsborn founded Superwomen Anonymous, which encourages women to stop seeking gratification from others, turn inward, discover what is most important, and reorganize their lives. The group's motto is "Enough is enough." (More information is available from the Orsborn Group: 1777 Union Street, San Francisco, California 94123, phone (415) 928-3600).

▪▪ Dual-Career Marriages

Dual-career marriages are not all alike. In this section, we will look at some of the variations in this lifestyle.

HIS/Her Career

Stan is a lawyer who specializes in criminal law. Barbara is a therapist who works with adolescents in a mental health center. Although each has a career, both Barbara and Stan regard his career as more important. Vacations, mealtimes, and social gatherings are more often scheduled around his work than hers. "It's not a problem for me," says Barbara. "He makes three times as much money as I do, so we feel it is more important to bend with his career than mine." This pattern in which the husband's career is given preeminence continues to be most common among dual-career couples.

HER/His Career

In other dual-career marriages, husbands and wives see the wife's career as more important.

▪ **DATA:** *Twenty-one percent of wives employed full time have higher earnings than their husbands (Crispell, 1989).*

Two researchers studied 46 spouses who were involved in marriages in which the wife's occupation was given priority over the husband's (Atkinson & Boles, 1984). Specific criteria for inclusion in the study included the husband's willingness to relocate to further his wife's career, the perception by the spouses that they would be more likely to move due to the wife's career, and the perception by the spouses that the family was organized around the wife's career. The spouses were in their forties and had been married an average of 12½ years. The men had flexible jobs; 42 percent were self-employed.

The wives and husbands in these marriages were asked to talk about the costs and rewards of this type of dual-career marriage. Wives said the costs included being responsible for the economic support of the family, being tired, feeling guilty over not being a good wife, lacking time to do things, and watching the husband suffer by comparison (for example, others viewing the husband as lazy, irresponsible, and unmasculine).

The major costs of this arrangement from the viewpoint of the husbands were sacrifices in their own careers and their wives being away from home. Also, occasionally, the husband would have to deal with a cryptic remark like the

The wife of one famous tenor says her husband does not make love for two days before a performance and for two days after it. And he gives a performance every four days.
—LUCIANO PAVAROTTI

Whoever said "money can't buy happiness" just don't know where to shop.
—JIM VARNEY

question addressed to the husband of an office manager: "Does she manage you, too?"

Both spouses saw more rewards than costs. Wives talked of the opportunity to pursue their careers, financial gain, independence, freedom from household chores, enhanced self-esteem, having emotional support from husbands, giving husbands time to spend with the children, additional resources for the children, and flexible gender role models for the children. One mother said:

> I think I show her (my daughter) that a woman can do things. I don't want my girl taking a back seat to a man. I know women who stayed with their husbands because they were afraid to leave . . . to go out on their own. Those women are trapped—like slaves. I don't want that kind of life for my girl. If she's going to live with a man, it's going to be because she wants to.

For husbands, the rewards of the her/his career pattern included being relieved of the major responsibility for the economic support of the family and having the freedom and resources to pursue their own interests. One attorney said, "Her job has allowed me to pick and choose cases. I only handle cases in my area of specialization. Most lawyers have to take cases they don't find interesting or challenging."

As for the happiness of these marriages, more husbands than wives felt their marriages were "very happy" or "somewhat happy." In contrast to 77 percent of the wives, 95 percent of the husbands selected one of these phrases to describe their marriage.

Not all research on marriages in which the wife has a higher-status job and earns more than the husband reflects as positive a picture as the Atkinson & Boles research. In a summary of three studies made on these marriages, another researcher (Rubenstein, 1982) concludes:

> When a wife has a job that outshines her husband's, sex lives may suffer and feelings of love may diminish. In addition, these couples run a high risk of mutual psychological and physical abuse, which leads to a significantly higher rate of divorce. Finally, for some underachieving husbands whose wives are overachievers, premature death from heart disease is 11 times more frequent than normal (p. 37).

A husband married to a physician may sometimes tire of the attention his wife gives to her career.

> Last night was the first night she was home before 7:30 in I don't know how long. Her schedule this rotation is incredible. The patients are really sick on her service, and I know she has to be there a lot. But last night I really wanted to be with her—to talk, to have sex, to enjoy ourselves. Well, she came home and said she just wanted to take a short nap first. Well, you can guess the rest. She didn't want to get up; she didn't want to talk; she didn't want sex (Gerber, 1983, 106–107).

Some husbands who are married to career-oriented women become "househusbands." One researcher (Beer, 1984) observes that househusbands tend to have had fathers who were a positive role model in terms of doing housework, tend to have an extraordinary sense of fair play regarding domestic work roles, and tend to be professionals who can more easily control their own time.

THEIR Careers

Sometimes spouses view each other as equals and their careers as equally important. "We respect each other's career commitment, try to support each other, and feel that we mutually benefit from keeping two strong careers going," said one spouse. In Exhibit 9.2, two people share their views of their dual-career marriage. Although career commitment may be equal, in only a few cases do the spouses earn the same amount of money.

One researcher compared 81 marriages in which both spouses were in professional or managerial positions and worked full time (more than 35 hours each week) to the marriages of 1,500 other families. The study indicated that the dual-career couples were more educated, had higher incomes, were younger, were childfree (60 percent) or had fewer children (75 percent of those with children had one or two), and tended to live in urban areas (Berardo, 1982).

Husbands in dual-career marriages did no more housework than other husbands. However, wives in dual-career marriages did less housework than wives

---

EXHIBIT 9.2

Two Views of One Dual-Career Marriage

Chris is a 40-year-old division chief at the New York Public Library in Manhattan. Janie is five years younger and is a full-time professional writer for national magazines. They have been married 14 years and have twins. They agree that the label "dual-career marriage" is an important part of their self-definition. Janie says:

> You know, it's like "tell me 10 words that describe you." . . . Dual-career couple is well up on the top of the list of phrases that describe us. A dual-career marriage is rigorous. It shapes everything.

But their feelings about their dual-career marriage are quite different.

CHRIS

We maintain this arrangement with my approval, but I have strong reservations. There are simply too many pieces in the puzzle. Our children live in a realm where time is beautifully unimportant. Parents with career lives are caught in time. Here we are, seeing ourselves as the radical left, institutionalizing our children in a nursery school from 9 to 3 and then farming them out to a sitter. Somebody else is raising our kids!

I would warn a couple contemplating a dual-career marriage in these terms: do you think your children are in a state of suspended animation from 8:00 A.M. to 7:00 P.M.? Look at my day outside the job. I wake everybody up, dress one child, and make the lunch boxes if I'm downstairs first. I try to leave Janie upstairs with the twins (age 4), so they can be relaxed together before she leaves.

Then I drive the children to their school (50 minutes round trip) before taking the commuter train into Manhattan. I'm home just before 7:00 P.M. Also, we're forced into everything ready made: frozen foods and coloring books instead of a game of cards that involves interacting as a family. I list all the negatives because Janie tends to see her job so rosily.

JANIE

Our happiness is work, love, and children. I feel I have everything—more than most people, more than I knew married life could contain. The many roles—wife, mother, worker, friend, editor, family arranger—are invigorating. My perfectionism has diminished. The stages of life have softened. Motherhood doesn't have to replace a professional career.

I feel a very positive model to my 4-year-old daughter. She helps me choose clothes each day . . . her ideas are (honestly) better on sartorial matters than mine. She loves her French-American school, and we share our delight in each other's days. The ache I feel is more with her twin, my son. Beneath his quiet, fun-loving, busy nature, is there a mirror of the loneliness I feel for him during the day? Does he need more alone time than his day allows?

Our intimacy as a married couple certainly does not suffer. Once a week Chris and I meet for lunch—our Thursday tryst—between our places of work. We are happy, so it is easy to be affectionate and generous-spirited toward each other.

In her novel *Happy Marriages*, Laurie Colwin says to her old-fashioned, stay-at-home mother, "Stop hectoring me—my children are arranged for, coddled, and loved." That's what I feel. The guilt is only fretting. What childrearing situation is perfect?

in other marriages. In another study, the researchers observed that as the status of the wife's work and her income increased, the husband was more likely to help with meal preparation, house cleaning, and childrearing (Kamo, 1988).

One researcher commenting on the phenomenon of physician-physician marriages noted that although the advantages include an affluent lifestyle and a companion who understands the language and work stress of a physician's life, the disadvantages are not being able to find the work environment to satisfy both partners, little time together, and no one to be the "wife" at home. "I know of no reliable data, but my experience, socially and professionally, indicates that these marriages tend to be considerably above average in stability" (Mathis, 1984, 196).

:: Commuter Marriages*

Increased commitment on the part of wives to pursue a career and an increased willingness on the part of husbands to be pair bonded with and supportive of a wife who is pursuing a career have resulted in the emergence of *commuter marriages*. One of the most visible commuter marriages in our society was between Phil Donahue (in Chicago) and Marlo Thomas (in New York), who commuted to and from one another for four years until Donahue moved his program to New York.

Characteristics of Commuter Marriages

There are at least four characteristics of commuter marriages: equal career commitment, distance, permanence, and a preference for living together (Gerstel & Gross, 1984).

Equal Career Commitment. In commuter marriages, both spouses are equally dedicated to the advancement and success of their respective careers. Her career is as important as his career. Like Brutus, who said of Caesar in Shakespeare's *Julius Caesar*, (Act III, Scene two) it's "not that I loved Caesar less, but that I loved Rome more," spouses in commuter marriages might say it's not that they love each other less but that they love their careers more.

The degree to which work represents a meaningful part of a commuter spouse's life is illustrated by a wife who said:

> I go to pieces when I don't work. I get bored when I am not working. We probably work too hard and occasionally feel guilty about it. But we're not the kind of people who can just relax. We think we have to do something (Gerstel & Gross, 1984, 33).

It's a real managing kind of ballet to get us together.
—MARLO THOMAS

Distance. In commuter marriages, the distance between the spouses is great enough to require the establishment of two separate households. Commuter spouses cannot live in the same place and commute to their separate work places. They must live near their work and commute to see each other. The distance can range from 1,000 miles for domestic marriages to 5,500 miles for bicoastal mar-

*Based on and reprinted by permission of the publisher of *Commuter Marriage* by N. Gerstel and H. Gross. Copyright © 1984 by The Guilford Press, New York.

riages. Gayle Oshima and Timothy Ome have the latter commuter marriage (Hammer and Gordon, 1989).

Permanence. Spouses in commuter marriages view pursuing their careers while living apart as a permanent arrangement. There is no specific time that they plan to live together. They focus on their careers, not on living together.

Preference For Living Together. Although separated in reference to their careers, spouses in commuter marriages wish they could be together. They are not separated because they are having marital problems or are drifting toward a divorce. They look forward to an undefined time in the future when they can have their careers and live together, too. In the meantime, they spend a lot of time, energy, and money traveling across the country so that they can be together.

> ■ **DATA:** *It is not unusual for commuter partners to spend about $6,000 per year traveling to be with each other (Gerstel & Gross, 1984).*

Commuters also recognize the costs of not pursuing their careers. Each spouse feels as though both partners, individually and as a couple, would suffer if they did not pursue their career interests independently. One commuting wife said:

> I'd be miserable if I knew I gave up the opportunity to reach my career potential. I was reared in a home in which my mother had a career, and I was taught to pursue my career goals to the fullest. My dad was always supportive of my mother's career, so I always expected my husband to be supportive of my career.

Unique Problems in Commuter Marriages

Like all relationships, commuter marriages have their share of problems. Some of them will be examined in the following sections.

Fragmented Conversations. Because commuters don't return to the same house each evening, their spouse is not there to share the intimate details of life and work. Most miss the presence of their partner and use the telephone as a substitute for face-to-face interaction.

> ■ **DATA:** *In one study, 42 percent of commuter spouses phoned each other every day, and 30 percent called every other day (Gerstel & Gross, 1984, 56).*

But just as spouses who live together don't always view their communication positively, neither do commuters. One husband recalls:

> Sometimes she will call me, and I'll be really tired. I just won't have any life in me. And she'll want something more from the call. There's a clashing. Or it happens the other way around. I'll feel good, and she'll be focused on something she's doing. It's hard to shift gears to get into someone else's mood when there is no forewarning and the phone call will soon be over (Gerstel & Gross, 1984, 58).

Lack of Shared Leisure. Each partner in a commuter marriage can talk with the other during the week, but going out to dinner, seeing a movie, or attending a concert or play with the spouse is not an option. Each spouse often misses not being able to spend leisure time with the other partner. Due to this high companionship need, most commuter spouses get together on weekends.

■ **DATA:** *More than 50 percent of 71 commuter couples get together every weekend (Gerstel & Gross, 1984).*

Marital Sex. Commuter spouses obviously are not sexually available to each other every evening. But even spouses who live together rarely have intercourse every night. In commuter marriages, however, the partners' options of when they can have sex get compressed into smaller time periods. Even when the partners are not in the mood, they may feel that they should have sex because the weekend will soon be over. This places the unrealistic burden on the relationship that the limited time the couple does spend together should be perfect.

Some commuting women and men also experience the "stranger effect," reporting that they need a period of time to reacquaint themselves with their partner before they feel comfortable about having sex. "It takes me at least a day to feel close to him again," said one woman.

Feeling Unproductive. Because commuter spouses may feel disconnected, disjointed, and lonely, they may not be able to concentrate and get their work done. According to one spouse:

> I end up goofing off a lot. It's like I can't get motivated or focused on what I know I should be doing. When my partner is around, I have no trouble getting on-task. It's really crazy how the absence of my partner makes me feel like doing nothing.

Children. Children may be an additional problem for the commuter couple. In most cases, young children will stay in the home of one parent, in effect making a single parent out of one spouse. Although some spouses enjoy the role of primary caregiver, others feel resentful of the spouse who is unhampered by the responsibilities of childrearing.

If the commuter couple are remarried and bring children from a previous marriage into the commuter marriage, then conflicts about how to spend holidays, with whom, and where may occur. Both spouses may want their own children and the partner to visit in their own home. There are only a limited number of holidays (there is only one Christmas Eve each year), so the competition for time can be enormous. One spouse said, "It would be nice if we liked each other's kids, but we don't. So vacation times always create real problems for us."

Benefits of Commuter Marriages

In spite of the problems, there are benefits to a commuter marriage. We will address some here.

Higher Highs. "I'd rather have two terrific evenings a week with my spouse than five average ones," illustrates the view that the time commuter spouses have for each other is, in some ways, like courtship time—more limited but definitely enjoyable. Each spouse makes a special effort to make the time they have together good time. Some commuter partners feel the periods of separation enhance the love feelings in their relationship. One woman said:

> It's added some romance. There are a lot of comings and goings. We give each other presents. When I come home, there's a huge welcome. And there are tears at parting. I usually arrive looking exhausted. Show up completely collapsed. And my husband has a bottle of wine, no kidding, with a bow around it and flowers or a bottle of Chanel. And he makes a bath for me (Gerstel & Gross, 1984, 76).

Limited Bickering. To ensure that the limited time is positive, commuters often make a point of avoiding petty bickering that sometimes creeps into the relationships of spouses who see each other every day. "We just don't want to argue over the laundry when we're together. We don't want to spoil the time we have together," said one commuter.

In summarizing the rationale and benefits for living in a commuter marriage, one spouse said:

> I want it all. A husband and a career. And while I would prefer for us to be together, it turned out that he was already established in his work in one city and I got a job offer I have been training for all my life in another city. I'd say the benefits are that I can get my work done (I work very well in an empty house) and enjoy him on the weekends. The drawbacks are that I'd like to have dinner with him and talk with him face-to-face every night. Someone asked me, "Why not just be single?" The answer is I loathe the problem of looking for a stable companion in my life and someone to spend holidays with. This way, I have a booked flight with the man I love every weekend and all holidays and I can enjoy my work in the in-between times. I know a lot of spouses who live with each other all the time, and the only time they look forward to is being away from each other.

□   C O N S I D E R A T I O N   □

Some of the conflict in living in a commuter marriage can be reduced by acknowledging to each other and to one's self that a career is important and that each partner values being married to a mate who has a high career commitment. The partners can focus on the benefits of their lifestyle decision and enjoy the very special times they have together.

∷ Job-Sharing Marriages

Job sharing is defined as a situation in which a permanent, full-time position is restructured to provide part-time employment for two people. Instead of both partners working all day at a particular job, each partner works some of the time. Two researchers (Mikitka & Koblinsky, 1985) studied 20 married couples who were job sharing a university position.

The primary reason for the decision to job share was the inability to find two full-time positions. Both spouses preferred to have their own position but that was not possible. Not all couples viewed job sharing as a last resort, however; 20 percent wanted a flexible lifestyle, which job sharing provides. When neither partner has to work all the time, the partners can share childcare and still have time for individual pursuits. Wives tend to work fewer hours than husbands in job-sharing marriages.

Both the husbands and the wives in this study expressed satisfaction with the emotional support they received from their spouses, childcare arrangements, and the division of domestic tasks. Spouses who job share may also share a common view of reality, which has been associated with marital satisfaction (Imig & Imig, 1985).

The disadvantages of job sharing were economic and political. The spouses earned less sharing one job than they would have earned if each spouse had had a separate job. About 50 percent of the sample felt exploited because they were given large amounts of committee work, received little economic support for research, and were expected to publish more articles in professional journals because they had reduced work loads.

■ **DATA:** *Only one couple in 20 saw job sharing as a permanent lifestyle; the other 19 found job-sharing salaries inadequate (Mikitka & Koblinsky, 1985).*

▖▖ Consequences of Two Incomes in One Marriage

Regardless of the type of dual-income marriage that couples have, there are various consequences for the spouses and their marriage.

Consequences for the Wife

Researchers disagree on the degree to which a woman's happiness increases as a result of working outside the home. In one study comparing homemakers and women employed outside the home, the homemakers were more satisfied. The explanation suggested by the researchers (Stokes & Peyton, 1986) for women who work outside the home being more dissatisfied was in reference to working in stressful jobs with low pay and limited potential for advancement. Wives who hold jobs with low prestige also report higher rates of depression (Saenz et al., 1989).

Other studies have shown that wives who work outside the home are happier than those who do not work outside the home (McLanahan & Glass, 1985) and that they feel happier about their marriages (Blumstein & Schwartz, 1983). Among the benefits that wives derive from outside employment are increased interaction with a variety of individuals, a broader base of recognition, enhanced self-esteem, and greater equality between self and spouse. One dual-income wife said:

> By having a career, you don't put all your eggs in the marriage-and-family basket. A career gives you another sphere in life to enjoy and in which to feel good about

Studies disagree on the degree to which employed wives are happier than homemakers.

yourself. You can bring more to your husband and children when you're happy doing what you like.

Employed women who receive social support from coworkers and who feel socially integrated into their work environment also report feeling more healthy and spending fewer days in the hospital (Hibbard & Pope, 1985). Housewives who are not involved in community activities seem to be the least healthy.

One cost associated with being a dual-income wife is having less time for self due to the tendency of the wife to extend herself in both roles (career and wife-mother) as a way of coping with the conflict between the roles. Thus, the working wife's major coping strategy is to "do it all." The result is that she experiences more stress than her husband is aware of (White et al., 1986).

As women reduce their reliance upon their husbands, they also reduce their services *to* their husbands. In other words, as women become less dependent upon their marriages to sustain them through their lifetimes, their marriages become less dependable.

—MAGGIE SCARF

A positive aspect about the woman's employment is that she experiences less anxiety and has better health when her children leave home than full time home-makers. Employment seems to provide an easy target for a shift in focus when the parenting role subsides (Adelmann et al., 1989).

CONSIDERATION

In a study of 697 married couples, the researchers (Hardesty & Bokemeier, 1989) observed that husbands tend to help with housework only when their wives demand that they do so. . . . "It is only when their wives hold liberal attitudes and demand a sharing of household tasks that men are encouraged to increase their participation in housework" (p. 264).

This study also suggests that husbands who choose not to participate with the domestic workload may be engendering unhappy feelings on the part of their partner and be planting seeds for an unhappy marriage. If the wife must pressure her husband to take responsibility for domestic work it will probably be at the expense of the couple's happiness. Alternatively, the couple might view the domestic work as a shared responsibility and discuss how they can manage it together. Indeed, with their joint incomes, they may elect to hire someone else to do the domestic work.

Consequences for the Husband

How do husbands feel about their wives being employed? In a study comparing 208 husbands whose wives were employed and 408 husbands whose wives were full-time housewives, the husbands of employed wives were less satisfied with their work and family lives than the husbands of women who stayed at home. These findings were true regardless of the husband's age, income bracket, or educational level. The researchers suggest that a husband's feeling about himself is related to his perception of his adequacy in the role of breadwinner. If his wife is employed, he feels he is not a good provider (Staines et al., 1986). Subsequent researchers have found that female labor force participation has a negative effect on the mental health of men married to women employed outside the home. One explanation for this is that men are very sensitive to home stress and such stress increases when wives take work outside the home (Bolger et al., 1989).

Husbands who grew up with a mother who worked outside the home are more supportive of their wives' occupational pursuits. Such an experience suggests that the wife's employment is normative.

Husbands whose wives have worked outside the home from the beginning of the marriage are more tolerant than husbands whose wives delay such employment. Husbands get accustomed to their wives preparing the meals, cleaning the house, and taking care of the children and miss these services when they stop. Husbands don't help much around the house, whether or not their wives work. True househusbands are rare (Beer, 1984). However, the husband of an employed wife does more than the husband of a full-time homemaker (Saenz et al., 1989). "Since women help bring home the bacon, they expect their husbands to help fry it," says Ann Landers. Also, husbands who have an egalitarian view of gender roles are more likely to take responsibility for meal preparation, cleaning, and childrearing (Bird et al., 1984).

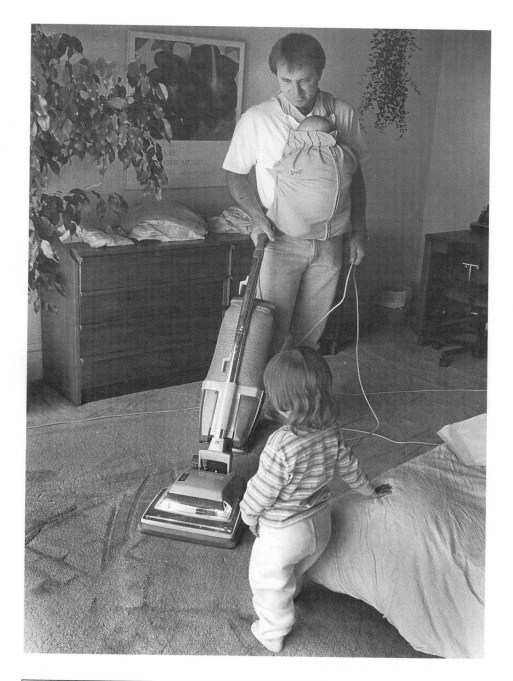

One effect of the wife's employment is for the husband to do more housework and child-care.

☐   C O N S I D E R A T I O N   ☐

These studies basically suggest that some men do not like for their wives to work outside the home. However, other data (Stewart, 1986) suggest that 85 percent of men prefer that their wives are employed outside the home. Benefits to the husbands

continued on next page

---

include a higher standard of living, a companion with whom to share the issues of employment, and, in some cases, a happier spouse.

In addition, a recent study of dual-career couples revealed that men are just as likely as women to cope with work and family demands by subordinating their careers. Their commitment to the relationship is reflected in their support for their wife's career and in their willingness to curtail their own careers (Schnittger & Bird, 1990).

Marital Consequences

What are the consequences for the marriage when the wife is employed? Results of studies differ. One study found that full-time employed mothers who had preschool children were very unhappy in their marriages. They felt overwhelmed with the demands of their job and taking care of their preschooler after work. Although they viewed their husbands as caring and understanding, they did not have time to discuss daily matters with him (Schumm & Bugaighis, 1986). One wife said:

> By 9 o'clock at night, there is nothing left of me. I'm completely worn out by my job and my kid. I don't even feel like talking to my husband. I just want to be by myself and sleep. I'll tell you—it's no good for your marriage.

Another study finds that employed wives are more likely to divorce because they can support themselves and end unhappy marriages (Canabal, 1990).

Other studies have found no effect of the wife's employment on the marriage. One researcher, who reviewed 27 studies covering a three-year period and involving 4,602 comparisons of marriages in which the wives did and did not work, concludes that "wife employment alone appears to have little or no effect on marital adjustment" (Smith, 1985).

Thomas (1990) studied 41 dual-career black couples in which both spouses were professionals. Most of these spouses reported being happy with their marriage.

■ **DATA:** *Ninety-eight percent of the husbands and 85 percent of the wives reported that they were happy with their marriage (Thomas, 1990, 175).*

☐　　　　　　C O N S I D E R A T I O N　　　　　　☐

These different conclusions suggest that the wife's employment by itself does not determine whether a couple's marriage will be happy. Issues that do influence happiness in the dual-income marriage are more likely to include the husband's support of his wife's employment, flexibility of roles, and commitment by each spouse to allocate time to their relationship. "The bottom line of making a dual-income marriage work," said one spouse, "is to help your partner and be committed to your relationship."

Employment of the wife alters the traditional pattern of the marriage relationship in the direction of equality, as the money she earns increases her power in the marriage. An interior designer said:

Now that I make a good income, my preferences are given equal weight by my husband. Whether we eat out or not, where we eat, and where we vacation are now joint decisions. Before, my husband would say, "We can't afford it . . ." and I would acquiesce.

The adage "He who pays the piper calls the tune" summarizes the relationship between money and power. In the dual-income marriage, there are two pipers contributing to the marital tune. The result is more joint decision making and more consensus on decisions (Godwin & Scanzoni, 1989).

Consequences for the Children

Most husbands and wives feel the wife's employment has more positive than negative personal and marital consequences, but they are more ambivalent about the consequences for their children. Most parents think it is best for their children for the mother to be with them when they are small.

Negative effects of a mother's employment on her children's self-concept, school achievement, and vocational development have not been verified. Rather, research shows that children of working mothers develop just as well emotionally, intellectually, and socially as children whose mothers stay at home (Berg, 1986). In addition, daughters of employed mothers also feel that women have much more career options than daughters of mothers who are not employed (Selkow, 1985). When children are asked about their parents' dual-career marriages, they are approving.

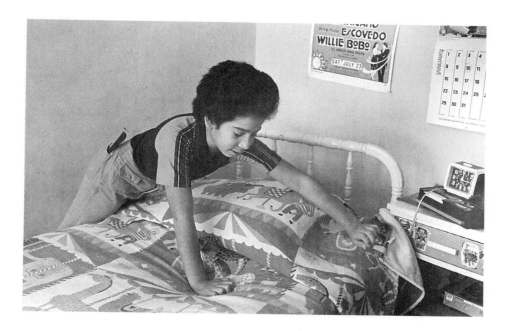

Children of employed parents do more housework than children whose parents are not employed.

■ **DATA:** *Out of 93 children, 96 percent said they were "satisfied" with the fact that both of their parents have careers (Knaub, 1986).*

But when mothers are asked the degree to which they feel their working outside the home is good for their children, only a few feel that it is.

■ **DATA:** *In a* Redbook *survey of almost 1,000 women, only 8 percent of the employed mothers agreed children are better off when the mother works outside the home (Gaylin, 1986).*

Mothers who work outside the home often feel guilty about doing so. One mother said:

> I'm very tired when I get home from teaching third grade all day, and I don't feel like going to Parents' Night at my child's school. But I ask myself, "What kind of a parent am I if I don't go to my own child's school functions?" and the guilt is usually enough to get me there.

Just as most children are not harmed by their mother's employment, most "self-care children," also referred to as "latch-key children," are not harmed either.

■ **DATA:** *About 7 percent (2.1 million) of the 28.6 million children aged 5 to 13 are not supervised by an adult for some period of time after school (Cain & Hofferth, 1989).*

It is commonly thought that self-care children are young children of low-income single parents who cannot afford stable childcare arrangements. More often, however, self-care children are older, white, middle class children who live in suburban or rural areas. These children are seen by their parents as responsible and mature.

However, some children may be at risk. These are the over 230,000 children ages five to seven who are left alone or in the care of a young sibling (Cain & Hofferth, 1989). Should these children get into an accident, getting prompt medical attention would be delayed.

To help allay children's fears, KIDLINE—a telephone support system—is available in Tucson, Arizona. KIDLINE aims to provide an interested and competent listener who will, if appropriate, teach children home safety and use of emergency service numbers, provide guidance for homework problems, accidents, illness, and make referrals to other community resources. Most of the calls received are from children who are lonely and want someone to talk to.

□   C O N S I D E R A T I O N   □

Children who must spend time alone at home should know the following:

1. How to reach their parents at work (the phone number, extension number, and name of the person to talk to if the parent is not there).
2. Their home address and phone number in case information must be given to the fire department or an ambulance service.

continued on next page

---

3. How to call emergency services, such as the police and fire departments.
4. The name and number of a relative or neighbor to call if the parent is unavailable.
5. To keep the door locked and not let anyone in.
6. Not to tell callers their parents are not at home. (They are busy or can't come to the phone.)
7. Not to play with appliances, matches, or the fireplace.

Aside from self-care children is the whole issue of day care. The effects of day care will be discussed in Chapter 15 on Rearing Children.

Other Consequences

Spouses in two-income marriages note that household chores, childrearing responsibilities, time priorities, and role overload are potential problems. Because each spouse's occupational role makes considerable demands on that partner, each spouse needs a "backup." In the traditional marriage, this is the nonworking wife. In the dual-income marriage, there is no backup.

Patterns of response to the "no wife at home" problem vary. As already noted, wives typically extend themselves and do much of the domestic labor and child-care in addition to their paid employment. Some husbands share the work. Other couples hire substitutes. One couple hires a person to come to the home Monday through Friday from 7:30 A.M. to 5:30 P.M. to take care of the couple's infant, clean the house, and prepare the dinner. Still other couples press their children into doing more housework. But daughters end up doing more. In a study of the amount of housework daughters and sons do whose parents work outside the home full time, daughters do 10 hours compared to sons who do less than three hours. The researchers (Benin and Edwards, 1990) explained:

> . . . the dependence of full-time dual-earner mothers on their daughters, but not their sons, may come from a stereotyped assumption that their daughters can perform housework tasks well, whereas their sons cannot (p. 371).

Regardless of how the work gets done, two-income couples complain that they have little time for each other. "We have to schedule Saturday from five till midnight for ourselves. If it weren't for the Saturday nights alone together, we would be divorced. If you don't spend time with each other, you grow away from your partner," remarked a real estate broker. Shift work has a particularly negative effect on marital relations (White and Keith, 1990).

Because they have limited leisure time and that is usually allocated to the children and each other, two-income couples may feel isolated from others. They have fewer friends. The friendships that do develop tend to be with other dual-income couples, which helps to validate the lifestyle.

Finally, cognitive restructuring is one of the mechanisms dual-career spouses use to cope with the role overload of a two-income marriage. This involves choosing to view their situation in positive terms—"Believing that our family life is better because both of us are employed," "Believing there are more advantages than disadvantages to our lifestyle," and "Believing that my career has made me a better wife/husband than I otherwise would be" (Schnittger & Bird, 1990, 201).

:: Trends

The number of married women employed in the labor force will continue to increase. Most women will continue to have jobs, but an increasing number will become involved in careers. For some brides, the understanding that they will pursue a career during their marriage is a nonnegotiable issue. "I want to be married," said one woman, "but I won't let it interfere with my career."

The war between the women who work outside the home and those who don't work outside the home will escalate. Known as the "mommy wars," Nina Darnton (1990) observed:

> Every so often a feud erupts that helps to define an era. In the '60s, it was hippies vs. rednecks. In the 70s, the decade of the women's movement, it was women against men. By the mid-'80s, and now into the '90s, it's mothers against mothers—more precisely, mothers who stay at home against mothers who work. This conflict is played out against a backdrop of frustration, insecurity, jealousy and guilt. And because the enemies should be allies, the clash is poignant (p. 64).

The percentage of husbands choosing to support their wife's employment will also increase. Economic benefits, male peers with working wives, and being reared by mothers who were employed outside the home will all contribute to this increase. Whether this support translates into an equal sharing of domestic and childcare tasks remains to be seen. Unless men take on more of the work load at home, women will continue to be burdened with the two major roles of employee and homemaker.

More mothers with young children will enter the work force. To encourage young parents to continue working, more companies will offer flextime (25 percent currently do so)—a system that permits workers to select the eight hours they will work. At Forecasting International in Arlington, Virginia, 50 percent of the employees work from 7:00 A.M. to 3 P.M. and 50 percent work from 9 A.M. to 5 P.M. Other accommodations by industry to family needs include the four-day work-week (four 10½-hour days), job sharing (two workers share one full-time job), and on-premise day care (about 2,000 companies provide day care for the mothers of small children who work there). All of these alternatives allow parents to continue to work by ensuring care for their infants and young children.

For the working parent with a sick child, a new industry is emerging. Day care programs for sick kids are now available. One such program—Sniffles 'N Sneezes at AMI Southeastern Medical Center in North Miami Beach, Florida—provides nursing care and a visit by a pediatrician for $30 per day.

Although the U.S. government is not likely to get into the day care business, federal policy may move toward protecting the jobs of parents who must take temporary leaves of absence from work due to their children.

> ■ **DATA:** *Family leave and maternity benefits are available in 135 countries and all but 10 mandate paid maternity leave. Four states (Connecticut, Rhode Island, Oregon, and Minnesota) currently have legislation providing for family leave (Wisensale & Allison, 1989).*

∷ Summary

Employed wives are becoming increasingly common, particularly in the middle class. Before 1940, female workers were primarily poor, black, and immigrant, but with World War II, middle-class wives flooded the labor force. At the end of the war, about 20 percent of all married women were employed; by 1990, that figure had jumped to almost 70 percent.

Motivations for working include money, personal satisfaction, personal independence, and expanded social network. The participation of wives in the labor force is related to the stage of their families' development. Wives with no children are the most likely to be employed, and those with preschool children are the least likely to work outside the home. Forty-four percent of mothers with children under the age of 6 are not employed outside the home.

When a career is defined in terms of training, commitment, continuity, and mobility, most wives seem to have jobs rather than a career. The obstacles married women must overcome in pursuing a career include responsibility for children and having no "wife" at home.

Dual-career marriages may be described as "his," "hers," or "theirs." When working wives are asked to evaluate the effect of their employment on themselves, their marriages, and their children, most report being happier individuals and happier in their marriages. Husbands report mixed feelings about their wives' employment. Although many husbands are delighted that their wives are happier and enjoy the economic benefits of a two-income marriage, they may miss the personal and domestic attentions of their wives and feel pressed into doing more housework themselves. Trends in two-income marriages include more two-income marriages, more mothers of small children working outside the home, and more companies offering flextime, leaves of absence, and day care facilities to working parents.

Questions for Reflection

1. Does the work role you foresee for yourself approximate a career or a job?
2. How much do you want the person you might marry to be involved in a career? In a job?
3. How does having or not having money influence your mood, your feelings about yourself, and your interaction with others?

References

Adelmann, P. K., T. C. Antonucci, S. E. Crohan, and L. M. Coleman. Empty nest, cohort, and employment in the well-being of midlife women. *Sex Roles,* 1989, 173–189

Atkinson, M. P. and J. Boles. WASP (Wives as Senior Partners). *Journal of Marriage and the Family,* 1984, *46,* 861–870.

Beer, W. R. *Househusbands.* South Hadley, Mass.: Bergin & Garvey, 1984.

Benin, M. H. and D. A. Edwards. Adolescents' chores: The difference between dual- and single-earner families. *Journal of Marriage and the Family,* 1990, *52,* 361–373.

Berardo, D. H. Dual-career families: A comparison with dual-occupation and traditional families. Paper presented at the National Council on Family Relations, Washington, D.C., 1982.

Berg, B. *The crisis of the working mother.* New York: Summit Books, 1986.

Bielby, W. T. and D. D. Bielby. Family ties: Balancing commitments to work and family in dual earner households. *American Sociological Review,* 1989, *54,* 776–789.

Bird, G. W., G. A. Bird, and M. Scruggs. Determinants of family task sharing: A study of husbands and wives. *Journal of Marriage and the Family,* 1984, *46,* 345–355.

Blumstein, P. and P. Schwartz. *American couples.* New York: William Morrow, 1983.

Bolger, Naill, A. DeLongis, R. C. Kessler, and E. Wethington. The contagion of stress across multiple roles. *Journal of Marriage and the Family,* 1989, *51,* 175–183.

Cain, Virginia S. and Sandra L. Hofferth. Parental choice of self-care for school-age children. *Journal of Marriage and the Family,* 1989, *51,* 65–77.

Canabal, M. E. An economic approach to marital dissolution in Puerto Rico. *Journal of Marriage and the Family,* 1990, *52,* 515–530.

Chafe, W. H. Looking backward in order to look forward: Women, work, and social values in America. *Women and the American economy: A look to the 1980s.* Edited by J. M. Dreps. Englewood Cliffs, N.J.: Prentice-Hall, 1976, p. 6–30.

Crispell, Diane. Dual disparity (earnings of working women). *American Demographics,* 1989, *7,* 16–18.

Darnton, N. Mommy vs. mommy. *Newsweek,* 1990, June 4, pp. 64–67.

Edmondson, B. Superwomen say enough is enough. *American Demographics,* 1986, *8,* 18.

Eggebeen, D. J. and A. J. Hawkins. Economic need and wives' employment. *Journal of Family Issues,* 1990, *11,* 48–66.

Floge, Liliane. Changing household structure, child-care availability, and employment among mothers of preschool children. *Journal of Marriage and the Family,* 1989, *51,* 51–63.

Galambos, Nancy L. Role strain in West German dual-earner households. *Journal of Marriage and the Family,* 1989, *51,* 385–389.

Garbarino, J. Can American families afford the luxury of childhood? *Child Welfare,* 1986, *65,* 119–128.

Gaylin, J. Do kids need a stay-at-home mom? *Redbook,* August 1986, 78–79.

Gerber, L. A. *Married to their careers.* New York: Tavistock Publications, 1983.

Gerstel, N. and H. Gross. *Commuter marriage.* New York: The Gilford Press, 1984.

Gilson, E. and S. Kane. *Unnecessary choices.* New York: William Morrow, 1987.

Glenn, E. N. Split household, small producer and dual wage earner: An analysis of Chinese-American strategies. *Journal of Marriage and the Family,* 1983, *45,* 35–46.

Godwin, D. D. and J. Scanzoni. Couple consensus during marital joint decision-making: A context, process, outcome model. *Journal of Marriage and the Family,* 1989, *51,* 943–956.

Grant, L., L. A. Simpson, X. L. Rong, and H. Peters-Golden. Gender, parenthood, and work hours of physicians. *Journal of Marriage and the Family,* 1990, *52,* 39–49.

Greenstein, T. N. Social-psychological factors in perinatal labor-force participation. *Journal of Marriage and the Family,* 1986, *48,* 565–571.

Hammer, J. and J. Gordon. The new bicoastals: Love on Tokyo time. *Newsweek,* February 13, 1989, p. 50.

Hardesty, Constance and Janet Bokemeier. Finding time and making do: Distribution of household labor in nonmetropolitan marriages. *Journal of Marriage and the Family,* 1989, *51,* 253–267.

Hewlett, S. A. *A lesser life: The myth of women's liberation in America.* New York: William Morrow, 1986.

Hibbard, J. H. and C. R. Pope. Employment status, employment characteristics, and women's health. *Women and Health,* 1985, *10,* 59–78.

Hochschild, Arlie. *The second shift.* New York: Viking, 1989.

Imig, David R. and G. L. Imig. Influences of family management and spousal perceptions on stressor pile-up. *Family Relations,* 1985, *35,* 227–232.

Johnson, D. R. and A. Booth. Rural economic decline and marital quality: A panel study of farm marriages. *Family Relations,* 1990, *39,* 159–165.

Kalleberg, A. L. and R. A. Rosenfeld. Work in the family and in the labor market: A cross-national, reciprocal analysis. *Journal of Marriage and the Family,* 1990, *52,* 331–346.

Kamo, Y. Determinants of household division of labor: Resources, power and ideology. *Journal of Family Issues,* 1988, *9,* 177–200.

Knaub, P. K. Growing up in a dual-career family: The children's perceptions. *Family Relations,* 1986, *35,* 431–437.

Maiolo, J. Department of Sociology and Anthropology, East Carolina University, Personal communication, 1982.

Mathis, J. L. Physician-physician marriages. *Medical Aspects of Human Sexuality,* January 1984.

McLanahan, S. S. and J. L. Glass. A note on the trend in sex differences in psychological distress. *Journal of Health and Social Behavior,* 1985, *26,* 328–336.

Merrick, T. W. and S. J. Tordella. Demographics: People and markets. *Population Bulletin,* 1988, *43,* 1–48.

Mikitka, K. F. and S. A. Koblinsky. Job-sharing couples in academia: Career and family lifestyles. *Home Economics Research Journal,* 1985, *14,* 195–207.

Norris, Phil E. *The job doctor.* Indianapolis, IN: Jist Works, Inc., 1990.

Osherson, S., and Dill, D. Varying work and family choices: Their impact on men's work satisfaction. *Journal of Marriage and the Family,* 1983, *45,* 339–346.

Perry-Jenkins, M. and Crouter, A. C. Men's provider-role attitudes: Implications for household work and marital satisfaction. *Journal of Family Issues,* 1990, *11,* 136–156.

Pleck, J. H. and G. L. Staines. Work schedules and family life in two-earner couples. *Journal of Family Studies,* 1985, *6,* 61–82.

Rubenstein, C. Real men don't earn less than their wives. *Psychology Today,* November 1982, 36–41.

Saenz, Rogelio, W. J. Goudy, and F. O. Lorenz. The effects of employment and marital relations on depression among Mexican American women. *Journal of Marriage and the Family,* 1989, *51,* 239–251.

Schnittger, M. H. and G. W. Bird. Coping among dual-career men and women across the family life cycle. *Family Relations,* 1990, *39,* 199–205.

Schumm, W. R. and M. A. Bugaighis. Marital quality over the marital career: Alternative explanations. *Journal of Marriage and the Family,* 1986, *48,* 165–168.

Schwartz, P. and D. Jackson. How to have a model marriage. *New Woman,* February 1989, 66–74.

Schwartz, Felice N. Management women and the facts of life. *Harvard Business Review,* January-February 1989, 65–76.

Selkow, P. Moms' jobs, kids' careers. Reported in *Psychology Today* by Diana Zuckerman. February 1985, 6.

Smith, D. S. Wife employment and marital adjustment: A cumulation of results. *Family Relations*, 1985, *34*, 483–490.

Staines, G. L., K. Pottick, and D. A. Fudge. Wives' employment and husbands' attitude toward work and life. *Journal of Applied Psychology*, 1986, *71*, 118–128.

Statistical Abstract of the United States: 1990. 110th ed. Washington, D.C.: U.S. Bureau of the Census, 1990.

Stewart, S. A. They see an upscale, happy future. *USA Today*, May 13, 1986, p. A-2.

Stokes, J. P. and J. S. Peyton. Attitudinal differences between full-time homemakers and women who work outside the home. *Sex Roles*, 1986, *15*, no. 5/6, 299–310.

Thomas, V. G. Determinants of global life happiness and marital happiness in dual-career black couples. *Family Relations*, 1990, *39*, 174–178.

White, P., A. Mascalo, S. Thomas, and S. Shoun. Husbands' and wives' perceptions of marital intimacy and wives' stresses in dual-career marriages. *Family Perspective*, 1986, *20*, 27–35.

White, L. and B. Keith. The effect of shift work on the quality and stability of marital relations. *Journal of Marriage and the Family*, 1990, *52*, 453–462.

Wisensale, Steven K. and Michael D. Allison. Family leave legislation: State and federal initiatives. *Family Relations*, 1989, *38*, 182–189.

Yoger, S. and J. M. Brett. Professional couples and money. *Family Perspective*, 1989, *23*, 31–38.

CHOICES

MAKING DECISIONS ABOUT a dual-income marriage involves different issues for the wife and the husband. How much to spend and how much to save may also become issues.

As a Wife, Do I Want a Dual-Career Marriage?

As a current or potential wife, personal needs, your husband's support, and your desire for children are issues you might consider in making a decision to pursue a career during your marriage. It is clear that some women are miserable in the sole roles of wife and mother. A newswoman for a television station said:

My employment offers me the chance to stay alive. When my children leave home or if my husband dies, I will still be a journalist. Otherwise I'd be nothing.

The husband's emotional support for his wife's employment is another important consideration. "I've got the best husband you could imagine," said one university professor. "He has always encouraged my involvement in whatever I wanted to do, and he struggled through the grind of a Ph.D program with me." Not all husbands are this supportive. Your husband's enthusiastic support is critical if your goal is to pursue a meaningful career and be a wife.

Finally, think about your desire for children. Unless your husband is willing to share the responsibility of rearing children fully (he takes the children to piano lessons or sees that someone else does; he calls out the spelling words; he helps with the math homework), your career advancement may suffer. It is common for wives to reduce the conflict between children and job demands by reducing job demands to meet family needs. This strategy will work as long as you are involved in a job, not in a career. If a career is your goal, consider the consequences of having children and a husband who does not support your career.

As a Husband, Do I Want a Dual-Career Marriage?

As a current or potential husband, you might assess the degree to which you want your wife to pursue a career. In general, husbands point to the empathy aspects, more money, and the knowledge that their wives are happier working than being at home as the primary benefits of a wife's employment. One husband said:

When your wife has a career, she understands what the stress of the work world is like. She knows what it is to meet deadlines, to have conferences that are boring, and to be exhausted by traveling. The empathy that each of you have for the other's work stress is a major benefit.

Increased money is also an advantage of a dual-income marriage from the husband's perspective. More money not only improves the couple's immediate life style (Home Box Office, new cars, a swimming pool), but it may also prolong the life of the man. One husband said:

My dad died of a coronary when he was 46. I'm sure that one of the reasons for his early death was the fact that he was totally responsible for earning all the money. Since my mother did not work outside the home, he worked himself crazy with the stress of two jobs. Since my wife earns a terrific income, I don't worry as much about money and certainly don't feel that I am responsible for sending our three kids to college on the money that I earn.

A final benefit to the husband of the wife's career involvement is her happiness. According to one husband:

I'm living with a happy woman. Although she is very busy and exhausted half the time, she loves her work. She's not the kind that can sit home and cut out the orange juice coupons all day long.

Husbands also point to several disadvantages of being married to a woman who has a career, especially missing the services of a domestic wife, feeling obligated to help more around the house, and feeling threatened by the wife's own income, increased power, and independence. Missing the services of the domestic wife is more characteristic of husbands whose wives were first homemakers and then career wives. Husbands who began marriage with the career wife don't know what they are missing.

The domestic obligation husbands feel increases as the career demands of the wife escalate. Some husbands respond to this feeling in a cooperative spirit and take over the cooking, cleaning, shopping, and laundry. Other husbands negotiate with their wives to hire a person to come in once or twice a week to take care of the house. Some dual-career spouses hire a full-time, live-in helper so that neither is burdened with housework.

The wife's economic independence is a problem for some husbands. Suddenly they recognize they are no longer needed economically. For the husband who has a low sense of self-esteem and needs his wife's constant adulation, her independence may be a threat.

In evaluating these advantages and disadvantages, questions husbands might ask include "Is the loss of domestic services counterbalanced by more income?", "Is my wife's absence from the home made up for by her greater fulfillment?", and "Am I willing to share the responsibility of parenting?"

Do Children Want Both Parents to Work Outside the Home?

As a result of the value parents place on money (in the case of the single parent, money is often necessary for survival), increasing numbers of preschool children are being reared in homes where they are taken to day care centers by day and live with parents who are too tired or irritable to spend time with them at night. When they reach school age, many of these children come home to an empty house to fend for themselves (self-care children) until their parents return from work. One child development expert asked, "Can American Families Afford the Luxury of Childhood?" (Garbarino, 1986) and commented:

The economic facts of the matter predict that parents will believe that young children are capable of assuming early responsibility for self-care and that early demands for maturity are in the child's best interest (and, by implication, there is something wrong with children if they cannot meet those demands). . . . it seems that many adults are taking the position that their families cannot afford to subsidize the child's experience of childhood as it has evolved in western culture as a desirable stage in life (p. 126).

Suppose preschool children were asked if they wanted a parent (father or mother) to stay home with them rather than have their parent work outside the home while the child is in day care. And suppose self-care children were asked to express their preference for being at home with a parent versus being home alone. Would the predictable answers influence the choices parents are making in reference to their employment and parenting?

Impact of Social Influences on Choices

As a woman, your desire to work outside the home in a job or career will be influenced by your mother's role, the degree to which your married female peers are employed, the presence of children, and the preference of your partner. If your mother worked outside the home, your peers work, you have no children, and your husband expects you to earn an income, the chance of your working is very high. However, if your mother did not work outside the home, your peers don't work, you have children, and your husband prefers that you stay at home, the likelihood of your not working outside the home may be equally strong. In effect, economic necessity may dictate whether you are employed outside the home—but always within the context of your relationships with others.

Women of today are the generation of the post-baby boomers who have been socialized to have it all—marriage, career, and children. While many will manage to do so through hard work, tremendous organizational skills, and supportive/cooperative mates, most probably will not, at least not all at the same time. Many women do have careers but usually before or after they have children.

As a man, the issue of working outside the home has such a strong cultural bias that you may not even consider staying home as an alternative. The employment patterns of your father and your male peers establish the norm that you are to have a career. Although some husbands and fathers are househusbands, they are still a rare phenomenon.

Communication in Relationships

CONTENTS

IS IT TRUE?

1. The content of effective communication is always positive.

2. Men are more likely to disclose feelings to a male friend than to their romantic partner.

3. Conflict in a relationship is sometimes good for the partners and the relationship.

4. Most states license or certify marriage and family therapists.

5. Telling everything you think and feel to your partner is probably better for a relationship than tempered honesty.

1 = F, 2 = F, 3 = T, 4 = F, 5 = F

O ne of the primary characteristics of all successful relationships is effective communication. All of us have some understanding of what communication is; fewer of us, however, feel certain that we know what effective communication is. In this chapter we define effective communication and look at its various components. Gender differences in communication and theories of communication are also explored. We end the chapter by reviewing the nature of marital conflict and how marital therapy may help.

:: Effective Communication in Relationships

Communication may be defined as the process of exchanging information between two individuals. Communication involves not only spoken words but implied messages. The latter are conveyed by tone of voice and body language. For example, assume two individuals are saying goodnight at the end of their first date. One says to the other, "I'll call you." Depending on the tone of voice (excitement or sullenness) and body language (looking into the eyes of the person and holding hands with the person or looking down and avoiding hand contact), the implied message will mean different things.

Effective communication may be defined as the exchange of timely and accurate information that is pleasing to each partner (Turner, 1990). Timely information means that you tell your partner information at a time that allows him or her to make an appropriate response. Suppose you want your partner to be aware that your birthday is a week from Saturday and that you would like to go out to dinner. Giving timely information, in this case, involves telling your partner *before* your birthday that you would like to go out to dinner on your birthday. If you wait until after your birthday to alert your partner to your desire to go out to dinner on your birthday, your partner is unable to respond to the request. Similarly, if you are resentful about something your partner has done or failed to do, telling your partner about your feelings and expectations when you are having these feelings provides an opportunity for effective change on the part of your partner.

Accurate information implies that you reveal precisely how you feel and what you want. If you have a particular place that you would like to go to dinner on your birthday, it is important that you make your wishes known. Otherwise, your partner may select a place you do not like.

It is not always easy to convey accurate information. For example, suppose you feel uncomfortable about your partner having long study sessions with someone of the opposite sex. It may be difficult to convey these feelings to your partner because you fear embarrassment at being jealous or because you fear your partner will think you are being too restrictive and unreasonable. But if you say that you don't care if your partner has study dates with someone of the opposite sex, when, in fact, you feel uncomfortable about it, your partner will be acting on inaccurate information.

In addition to being timely and accurate, effective communication involves an array of other factors. Partners who communicate effectively are those who:

1. *Prioritize Communication.* Communicating effectively implies making communication an important priority in a couple's relationship. When communication is a priority, partners make time for communication to occur in a setting without interruptions. Prioritizing communication results in more information be-

ing exchanged between the partners, which increases the knowledge each partner has about the other. In relationships where communication is a priority, partners may be more willing to communicate about difficult, but important topics.

2. *Provide Positive Feedback.* Everyone likes to hear others say positive things about them. Communication in any relationship feels better when it contains many positive references to the individuals involved. These positive references may be in the form of compliments. For example, a spouse who tells a partner that "You deserved a raise, you're the best!" or "You smell wonderful" is giving positive feedback to the partner. Positive feedback may also be in the form of words of gratitude. "I'm so glad you remembered to put gas in the car" and "Thank you for that delicious dinner" are examples of expressions of gratitude.

   By establishing a pattern of giving positive feedback, two people develop positive feelings about each other and about themselves. Hence, they enjoy and look forward to communicating with each other.

> *If you don't have time to nurture your relationship, do you have time to cope with a divorce?*
> —BOB SAMMONS

☐ C O N S I D E R A T I O N ☐

In order for spouses to give and receive positive feedback, they must engage in the behaviors that please their partner. For couples in which both partners work, spouses may please each other by helping with the responsibilities of home and family. Arlie Hochschild (1989) made the observation that,

> "what couples called 'good communication' often meant that they were good at saying thanks for one tiny form or another of taking care of the family. Making it to the school play, helping a child read, cooking dinner in good spirit, remembering the grocery list. . . .These were the silver and gold of the marital exchange" (p. 270).

---

3. *Make Positive Requests for Change.* In addition to telling their partner what pleases them, partners who communicate effectively give feedback about what displeases them. Communication is more effective when this type of feedback is expressed in terms of positive requests for future change. Rather than say, "Don't be late," it may sound better if the partner hears, "Please meet me at 4:00." Rather than say, "You always leave the bathroom a wreck," it may sound better if the partner hears, "Please hang up your towel after you take a shower."

4. *Make Specific Resolutions to Disagreements.* Couples who come up with a way to resolve issues on which they disagree are more likely to continue positive feelings for each other than couples who live with sustained conflict. Discussions about disagreements or problems in the relationship are often difficult and unpleasant. These discussions may be more productive if they focus on reaching an agreement of what each partner will do to prevent a recurrence of a particular problem.

5. *Use "I" Messages.* "I" messages take ownership of a feeling or perspective and reduce the chance that the partner will feel attacked. A statement like "I would like for us to take a vacation without your parents" rather than "You don't want to go anywhere without your parents" is easier for the partner to hear

since it is not presented as an attack (not to mention the possibility that the "attack" statement may be inaccurate).

6. *Give Congruent Messages.* A message is congruent when the verbal and non-verbal behavior match. A person who says, "O.K. You're right" and smiles as he or she embraces the partner with a hug is communicating a congruent message. In contrast, the same words accompanied by leaving the room and slamming the door communicate a very different message.

7. *Share Power.* Power is the ability to impose one's will on the partner and to avoid being influenced by the partner. Power is a subtle element in communication and is often operative without awareness. Partners exercise power by several means:

    Withdrawal—(Not speaking to the partner.)

    Guilt induction—("How could you ask me to do this?")

    Being pleasant—("Kiss me and help me move the sofa.")

    Being dependent—("Don't leave me—I need you.")

    Negotiation—("I'll go with you to your parents if you will let me golf for a week with my buddies.")

    Deception—(Running up bills on charge card.)

    Blackmail—("I'll tell your parents you do drugs if you do.")

    Physical Abuse—(or verbal threats)

As noted in Chapter 3 on Gender Roles, egalitarian relationships have the greatest capacity for satisfaction because neither partner feels exploited by the other nor guilty for taking advantage of the partner. Effective communication involves treating each other as an equal and not using power to gain one's own advantage.

▪▪ Communication: Content vs. Process

Communication involves both content and process. Content refers to the messages exchanged between individuals.

This couple has stopped the process aspect of their communication.

Content may be communicated verbally and nonverbally. Verbal communication involves transmitting the message content through spoken or written words. Additional nonverbal aspects of spoken verbal communication include tone of voice, volume, pitch, and rate of speech. Nonverbal aspects of written verbal communication include style of writing (handwritten, printed, typed, sloppy, neat) and medium (personal stationary, card, napkin).

There are many forms of nonverbal communication, which include the following (Argyle, 1988):

1. facial expression
2. gestures and bodily movements
3. spatial behavior (e.g. how close you stand to a person)
4. gaze and pupil dialation
5. bodily contact
6. nonverbal vocalizations (e.g. sighs, grunts)
7. clothes, and other aspects of appearance
8. posture
9. smell

Another form of nonverbal communication is gift giving (Brockman and Peterson, 1990). The number and type of gifts partners give to each other may contain intended messages about both the giver and the receiver.

☐   C O N S I D E R A T I O N   ☐

Nonverbal communication may be easily misinterpreted. For example, if your partner sighs, you may interpret that as boredom, whereas in reality, it may signify contentment. It is, therefore, important for partners to talk about their interpretations of each other's nonverbal communication.

Process refers to the way in which the content is delivered, received, and responded to. When we talk about the "flow" of communication, we are talking about the process of communication.

As discussed earlier, the process of effective communication involves conveying timely and accurate information from one partner to the other. When Mary tells Bob that she is upset with him because he stayed out too late she is giving him specific content about her feelings. Mary's comment to Bob is both timely and accurate. She told him the next morning (rather than three weeks later in the middle of a heated argument) and she told him exactly how she felt—angry. Even when the content may be difficult or unpleasant, it is important that the process of effective communication continue.

☐   C O N S I D E R A T I O N   ☐

Maintaining the process of effective communication is especially difficult when the content of what is being communicated is negative. In order to ensure that the process continues, partners should focus on the fact that the sharing of information

continued on next page

is essential and reinforce each other for keeping the process alive. For example, rather than Bob attacking Mary and justifying why he was out till 3:00 a.m., it is important that he let Mary know that he appreciates her telling him how she feels. If he berates her for telling him how she feels, she will stop giving him feedback, grow resentful, and begin to emotionally distance herself from him. His words might be, "I know it is difficult for you to tell me things you know I don't like to hear, but I appreciate your telling me how you feel. I need to know how upset you get when I do something you don't like." This statement will help to keep the process of communication alive in their relationship.

The Self-Assessment on "Communication Pattern Scale" may help to assess the degree to which your relationship is characterized by effective communication.

Gender Differences in Communication

Wives typically display more emotion in communicating with their husbands than vice versa. In one study, wives and husbands were videotaped as they discussed a "salient relationship issue." The tapes were then watched and coded for various aspects of positive (warm, tender, affectionate, cheerful) and negative (cold, impatient, sarcastic, blaming) communication. Wives were much more likely to display emotion (positive or negative) than their husbands (Notarius & Johnson, 1982). This finding is consistent with previous research indicating that men are less expressive of love, happiness, and sadness (Balswick, 1980), compared to women. Also, when men do display their emotions, they often do so in a more "forceful," "dominating," and "authoritarian" way than women do (Kramarae, 1981).

Another study of 166 women and 110 men revealed similar gender specific communication patterns. Women wanted empathy, and men wanted facts they could use when they were talking with someone. Because men are so focused on the facts, they "are relatively inaccurate decoders of their partners' nonverbal expressions" (Floyd, 1988, 531).

CONSIDERATION

The image of men as less expressive than women has become part of our cultural folk wisdom. Some research, however, suggests that the case for the "inexpressive male" may be overstated. One study showed that whereas men tend to inhibit their disclosure in conversations with men and women with whom they are not well acquainted, men do disclose at fairly high levels to their romantic partners (Reis et al., 1985).

Theories of Marital Communication

Various theories, or models, have been developed which help us understand the processes of communication in relationships. Four major theories of marital in-

SELF ASSESSMENT

Communication Pattern Scale

This scale is designed to predict the degree to which you and your partner have communication patterns that may be conducive to a positive relationship. There are no right or wrong answers. After reading each item carefully, circle the appropriate number:

1 Never
2 Rarely
3 Occasionally
4 Frequently
5 Very Frequently

	N	R	O	F	VF
1. When an issue is bothering one or both of us, we address it.	1	2	3	4	5
2. We are accepting of our partner giving us negative feedback.	1	2	3	4	5
3. We can state our feelings and attitudes about an issue.	1	2	3	4	5
4. We communicate to each other that resolving the problem is more important than being right.	1	2	3	4	5
5. We can discuss anything.	1	2	3	4	5
6. We are not violent when we have disagreements.	1	2	3	4	5
7. We do not need alcohol or drugs to lower our inhibitions so that we will talk about certain issues.	1	2	3	4	5
8. We have a good track record of resolving issues.	1	2	3	4	5
9. Our problem-solving discussions result in an agreement for each of us to engage in new behavior.	1	2	3	4	5
10. We do not put each other down but are supportive of each other during a disagreement.	1	2	3	4	5

SCORING: Add the numbers you circled. 1 (never) represents a pattern that does not reflect effective communication and 5 (very frequently) represents a pattern that reflects effective communication. The lower your total score (10 is the lowest possible score), the less effective is the communication between you and your partner. The higher your total score (50 is the highest possible score), the more effective is your communication pattern. A score of thirty places you at the midpoint between having ineffective and effective communication patterns.

(NOTE: This Self-Assessment is intended to be fun and thought-provoking. It is not intended to be used as a clinical diagnostic instrument).

teraction include behavioral exchange, behavioral competency, social learning, and relational control (Fitzpatrick, 1988).

Behavioral Exchange Model

The behavioral exchange model assumes that marital satisfaction is based on the ratio of rewards to costs in the relationship. Rewards are positive exchanges, such as compliments, compromises, and agreements. Costs refer to negative exchanges, such as critical remarks, complaints, and disagreements. According to this model, the greater the ratio of positive to negative exchanges, the happier the marriage is presumed to be.

The behavioral exchange model emphasizes the importance of positive interaction in marital satisfaction. However, it does not resolve the issue of whether positive interaction leads to marital happiness, or marital happiness leads to positive interaction.

Behavioral Competency Model

This model views marital unhappiness as resulting from the spouses' lack of skill in communication, conflict resolution, and stress management. This model views communication as a skill that can be learned and continually improved.

The behavioral competency model predicts that couples who have and use skill in arguing constructively will have a high level of marital satisfaction. But this model does not seem to apply to couples in courtship or in the early stages of a relationship. That is, inability to argue constructively in courtship does not seem to effect satisfaction with the relationship at the time, but it does predict unhappiness in the marriage after several years.

Social Learning Theory

Social learning theory focuses on how communication patterns between partners are learned through the reinforcement of behavior. Reinforcement refers to any response that strengthens a particular behavior. For example, a spouse may reinforce the partner for expressing affectionate feelings by reciprocating the behavior ("I love you too"). In this example, the spouse used positive reinforcement, which involves providing a pleasant stimulus after the partner has performed a particular behavior.

Negative reinforcement involves the termination of an aversive event. Nagging is an aversive event. A spouse who does what the nagging partner wants is, inadvertently, negatively reinforcing nagging.

Social learning theory also describes how partners decrease a behavior by punishing it. The wife who criticizes her husband's cooking is punishing her husband's cooking behavior, making him less likely to cook in the future.

☐   C O N S I D E R A T I O N   ☐

Sometimes people in relationships make the mistake of punishing the very behaviors they want to occur. The wife in the above example complained that her husband

continued on next page

> didn't do his share of the cooking. If she wants his cooking behavior to increase, she might consider reinforcing it ("It's so nice to come home and have dinner already made") rather than punishing it ("You overcooked the brocolli again," "Why didn't you put fresh garlic in the spagetti?")

Social learning theory is sometimes criticized for being too focused on observed behavior, and not attentive to internal states, such as thoughts and feelings. This model is particularly useful, however, not only in understanding behavior, but in changing it as well.

The relational control model views the communication between partners as reflective of the distribution of power in the relationship. One aspect of this model focuses on how the parties either assert or relinquish control through their communication. Hence, communication patterns reveal who has the power in the relationship and how this power is used. Power refers to the ability of individuals to carry out their will, even in the face of resistance by others.

This model may be criticized on two grounds. First, the "chicken and the egg" problem exists—does the power structure in a relationship determine the communication pattern? Or does the communication pattern in the relationship determine the power structure in that relationship? Second, this model does not acknowledge that one partner may have more power in some areas of the relationship, whereas the other partner may have more power in other aspects of the relationship. In addition, power in relationships is not fixed, but rather may change over time.

Each of these theories permit a unique focus when observing the interaction in your relationships. A summary of the basic perspective, key concepts, and criticisms of each theory is presented in Table 10.1.

:: Conflicts in Marriage

A professor in a marriage and family class said, "If you haven't had a disagreement with your partner, you haven't known him or her long enough." In this section, we will explore the inevitability, desirability, sources, and styles of conflict.

Inevitability of Conflict

If you are alone this Saturday evening from six o'clock until midnight, you are assured of six conflict-free hours. But if you plan to be with your partner, roommate, or spouse during that time, the potential for conflict exists. Whether you eat out, where you eat, where you go after dinner, and how long you stay must be negotiated. Although it may be relatively easy for you and your companion to agree on one evening's agenda, marriage involves the meshing of desires on an array of issues for up to 60 years.

We sleep in separate rooms, we have dinner apart, we take separate vacations—we're doing everything we can to keep our marriage together.

—RODNEY DANGERFIELD

▪▪ TABLE 10.1 **Theories of Marital Communication**

THEORY	PERSPECTIVE	KEY CONCEPTS	CRITICISMS OF THE THEORY
Behavior exchange	Ratio of positive to negative exchanges determines marital satisfaction.	Ratio of exchanges Rewards Costs	Causal direction is unclear. (Is positive interaction the cause or result of marital satisfaction?)
Behavior competency	Communication is a behavioral skill that can be learned	Expression of feelings Conflict resolution Negotiation	Does not apply to courtship or early stages of the relationship
Social learning	Positive verbal behavior must be rewarded to be maintained	Positive reinforcement Negative reinforcement Punishment	Focuses on behavior. Does not focus on internal thoughts & feelings.
Relational control	Communication between partners reflects the distribution of power in the relationship	Power	Causal direction is unclear (Is power in a relationship the cause or result of communication patterns?) Power structure changes over time Each partner may have power in some aspects of the relationship

Although most men and women reach agreement on many issues before marriage, new needs and preferences will arise throughout the marriage. Changed circumstances sometimes call for the adjustment of old habits. A wife of three years recalls:

> I can honestly say that before we got married, we never disagreed about anything, but things were different then. Both my husband and I got money from our parents and never worried about how much we spent on anything. Now I'm pregnant and unemployed, and Neal still acts like we've got someone to pick up the tab. He buys expensive toys like a computer and all the games and software he can carry. He thinks that because he uses VISA we can pay the monthly premium and still live high. We're getting over our heads in debt, and we're always fighting about it.

□   C O N S I D E R A T I O N   □

You and your spouse may not disagree on who spends how much on what, but the probability is zero that you will agree throughout your marriage on every issue related to sex, in-laws, recreation, religion, and children. Marital conflict is inevitable.

Conflict is both inevitable and desirable.

Desirability of Conflict

Not all conflict is bad (Altschuler & Krueger, 1986). One study found that confronting an issue may be healthy for the couple's marriage. When 138 divorced people were asked to talk about the communication patterns in their previous marriages, almost half of them said they seldom quarreled and only two in 10 said they constantly quarreled. The researchers concluded that "conflict was not an important variable because there often was no communication whatsoever occurring between the couple" (Hayes et al., 1981, 23).

In another study of how spouses cope with marital distress, ignoring and resigning one's self to a problem actually increased the stress level experienced by the spouses. Although negotiating differences may not reduce immediate stress (it is often upsetting and uncomfortable to discuss a conflict in the relationship), such discussions were associated with fewer problems at a later time among the 758 interviewed spouses (Menaghan, 1982).

☐   C O N S I D E R A T I O N   ☐

When you or your partner are concerned about an issue in your relationship, discussing it may have more positive consequences than avoiding it. You may not like what your partner has to say about the reason you are upset (and vice versa), but resolving the conflict becomes a possibility. Brooding over an unresolved issue may lead to further conflict.

By expressing your dissatisfactions, you alert each other to the need for changes in your relationship to keep your satisfactions high. One husband said he was "sick and tired of picking up his wife's clothes and wet towels from the bathroom floor." She, on the other hand, was angered by her husband talking on the phone during mealtime. After discussing the issues, she agreed to take care of her clothes in exchange for his agreement to take the phone off the hook before meals. The payoff for expressing their negative feelings about each other's behavior was the agreement to stop those behaviors. And confronting an issue may be good for your health. In one study, spouses with high blood pressure who suppressed their anger at their husbands or wives were twice as likely to die earlier than spouses who talked about what upset them (Julius, 1986).

Sources of Conflict

There are numerous sources of conflict. Some of these are easily recognized; others are hidden inside the web of marital interaction.

Behavior. The preceding example in which one spouse left dirty clothes on the bathroom floor and the other talked on the phone during mealtime illustrates how the behavior of the partner can sometimes create negative feelings and set the stage for conflict. In your own relationship, you probably become upset when your partner does things you do not like (is late or tells lies). On the other hand, when your partner frequently does things that please you (is on time, is truthful) you tend to feel good about your partner and your relationship.

There are always flowers for those who want to see them.
—HENRY MATISSE

Cognitions and Perceptions. Aside from your partner's actual behavior, your cognitions and *perceptions* of a behavior can be a source of satisfaction or dissatisfaction. One husband complained about the fact that his wife "was messy and always kept the house in a wreck." The wife suggested to her husband that rather than focus on the messy house, he might focus on the thought that she enjoys spending time with him rather than spending time cleaning the house. Thus, the husband replaces the cognition "What a messy house" with the cognition "Isn't it wonderful that my wife would rather go fishing with me than stay home and clean house.''

C O N S I D E R A T I O N

When dissatisfaction with your partner results from your partner engaging in behavior you do not like, consider if it may be easier for you to change your *perception* of the behavior rather than asking your partner to change the behavior.

Value Differences. Because you and your partner have had different socialization experiences, some of your values will be different. One wife, whose parents were both physicians, resented her mother not being home when she grew up. She vowed that when her own children were born she would stay home and take care of them. But she married a man who wanted his wife to actively pursue a career and contribute money to the marriage. This is only one value conflict a couple may have. Other major value differences may be about religion (one feels religion is a central part of life; the other does not), money (one feels uncomfortable being in debt; the other has the buy-now-and-pay-later philosophy), and in-laws (one feels responsible for parents when they are old; the other does not).

C O N S I D E R A T I O N

Value differences in a relationship are not bad in and of themselves. What happens depends less on the degree of difference in what is valued than on the degree of rigidity with which each partner holds his or her values. Dogmatic and rigid thinkers, feeling threatened by value disagreement, try to eliminate varying viewpoints and typically produce more conflict. But partners who recognize the inevitability of difference usually try to accept in each other what they cannot successfully compromise (Scoresby, 1977, 142).

Inconsistent Rules. Partners in all relationships develop a set of rules to help them function smoothly. These unwritten but mutually understood rules include what time you are supposed to be home after work, whether you should call if you are going to be late, how often you can see friends alone, and when and how you make love. Conflict results when the partners disagree on the rules or when inconsistent rules develop in the relationship. For example, one wife expected her husband to take a second job so they could afford a new car. But she also expected him to spend more time at home with the family.

Leadership Ambiguity. Unless a couple has an understanding about which partner will make decisions in which area (for example, the husband will decide over which issues to ''ground'' teenage children; the wife will decide how much money to spend on vacations), each partner may continually try to ''win'' a disagreement. All conflict is seen as an ''I win–you lose'' encounter because each partner is struggling for dominance in the relationship. ''In low-conflict marriages, leadership roles vary and are flexible, but they are definite. Each partner knows most of the time who will make certain decisions . . ." (Scoresby, 1977, 141).

Job Stress. When you are scheduled to take four exams on one day you are under a lot of pressure to prepare for them. The stress of such preparation may cause you to be irritable in interactions with your partner. A similar effect occurs when spouses are under job stress; they are less easy to get along with. When spouses are happy and satisfied with their employment, they are much more likely to report satisfaction in their marriages and in the relationships with their children (Belsky, et al., 1985). One husband said:

> If I've been on the road all week and haven't made any sales, I feel terrible. And I'm on edge when the wife wants to talk to me or touch me. I seem like I get obsessed with how things are at work, and if they aren't okay, nothing else seems okay either. But if I've made a lot of sales and the commission checks are rolling in, I'm a great husband and father.

Styles of Conflict

Spouses develop various styles of conflict. If you were watching a videotape of various spouses disagreeing over the same issue, you would notice at least three styles of conflict. These styles are clarified in *The Marriage Dialogue* (Scoresby, 1977).

Complementary. In the *complementary style* of conflict, the wife and husband tend to behave in opposite ways: dominant–submissive, talkative–quiet, active–passive. Specifically, one person lectures the other about what should or should not occur. The other person says little or nothing and becomes increasingly unresponsive. For example, a husband was angry because his wife left the outside lights of their house on all night. He berated her the next morning, saying she was irresponsible. She retreated in silence. Both partners should talk about how they feel and what they want the other partner to do.

Some evidence suggests that the complementary style of conflicts is more characteristic of "Southern" husbands and "Southern" wives than is true of "Northern" spouses. This is a potential result of the legacy of patriarchy in the Southern culture which suggests that wives accept rather than question (Wilson & Martin, 1988).

Symmetrical. In the *symmetrical style* of conflict, both partners react to each other in the same way. If she yells, he yells back. If one attacks, so does the other. The partners try to "win" their positions without listening to the other's point of view. In the preceding incident, the wife would blast back at the husband, stating he lived there too and was equally responsible for seeing that the lights were out before going to bed. An alternative would be to decide who was responsible for what household duties and to have each partner make a commitment to do specific chores. Soft discussions could replace loud arguments.

Parallel. In the *parallel style* of conflict, both partners deny, ignore, and retreat from addressing a problem issue. "Don't talk about it, and it will go away" is the theme of this conflict style. Gaps begin to develop in the relationship, neither partner feels free to talk, and both partners believe that they are misunderstood. Both eventually become involved in separate activities, rather than spending time together. In the outside-light example, neither partner said anything about the lights being left on all night, but the husband resented the fact that they were. A better alternative is for the partners to talk about what they want the other to do.

Condie (1989) identified three other styles of conflict. These include blowing off steam, alternating anger, and talking it out.

1. *Blowing Off Steam.* "Several couples indicated that the unfettered ventilation of emotions had been their preferred modus operandi for resolving differences" (p. 149).
2. *Alternating Anger.* Some couples have an agreement that if one of them gets angry, the other stays calm. One spouse said, "It is not good for two hotheads to be together" (p. 149).
3. *Talking It Out.* Couples agreed that this was the method they should use but that the "silent treatment" "was the fastest avenue to peaceful coexistence" (p. 149). The longer the couple was married, the more likely they were to talk things out rather than use the "silent treatment."

Conflicts in Black Marriages

Black marriages may have some unique features that make marital conflict more likely. These features include more educated black women than educated black men, black women having higher occupational status than black men, and black women being much closer in income to black men than white women are to white men (Hampton et al., 1989).

More Educated Black Wives. The result of black wives being more educated than their husbands is that they are likely to expect their husbands to be "more sensitive, more emotionally nurturant, and more companionable" (Secord & Ghee, 1986, 27). Less-educated black males with a traditional male-dominant orientation may be less likely to fulfill the expectations of the black female. Conflict results when the black female expects behaviors from her partner that are not forthcoming. Although white women may also expect their husbands to be nurturant and companionable, the higher percentage of white educated husbands may result in more white males who meet the gender role expectations of their partners.

Greater Occupational Status of the Wife. The fact that black wives tend to have greater occupational status than their husbands has implications for the marriage in that their husbands may feel threatened by this status. If the black male has been taught that his wife is to respect and admire him in his occupational role but he holds a lower-status job than his wife, then his self-concept may be negative. If he feels bad about himself, he may think that his wife shares his view. In an effort to deal with the discrepancy between what he is and what he thinks she wants him to be, the black husband may attempt to denigrate the black wife's status to make himself look better. Or he may want to disengage himself from her because she makes him feel bad by comparison.

Black Wife Almost an Equal Provider. The fact that black wives are likely to contribute a larger share of the family income than white wives may result in some black wives being dissatisfied with the performances of their partners as providers. "Other working black wives who slaken their demands on their husband as a provider are apt to substitute new demands for more companionship, emotional support, and sharing of domestic and childcare duties" (Secord & Ghee, 1986, 27). Although some black males willingly meet these expectations, others resent them and lose their interest in staying married.

▪▪ Productive and Nonproductive Communication

Beyond the information-giving ("I got the milk"), information-getting ("Did you get the wine?"), and sharing ("Look at that") functions, communication is essential for resolving difficulties as they crop up in a relationship. There are productive and nonproductive ways of communicating about conflict. Knowing which to use and which to avoid is one of the most valuable skills a spouse or couple can possess. In a study of almost 500 couples, the researcher noted that their marriage success had much more to do with their communication skills than with factors such as age at marriage or lack of money (Brandt, 1982).

Productive Communication

Productive communication increases the emotional closeness of the partners and brings their respective expectations and behaviors into alignment. Suppose one partner expects the other to be punctual, and the partners discuss the issue. Their communication will be productive to the degree that they feel closer as a result of the discussion and either one partner agrees to be more punctual or the other partner decides the issue isn't worth getting upset about and drops the expectation. Here is an example of productive communication:

Mary and Bob have been living together for about six months. When they first moved in together, they agreed that because they were both in school and had part-time jobs, they would share the housekeeping chores—cooking, washing dishes, doing laundry, and keeping the apartment neat. It seemed to Mary that she was gradually drifting into the role of housewife, which she thought was counter to her agreement with Bob. She felt Bob wasn't going to start doing his share of the housework unless she brought it up, so she mentioned the subject one evening as she was preparing dinner.

MARY: You know, I thought we agreed that we would do the cooking and other stuff together.

BOB: Well, I guess we did . . . [feeling somewhat guilty for not living up to his part of the deal]. What do you want me to do?

MARY: Since I've got classes Tuesday and Thursday nights, it would be nice for you to take care of the cooking and washing the dishes on those nights. I'll handle it Monday, Wednesday, and Friday, and we can worry about the weekend later."

BOB: Okay. I guess I'm cooking Thursday night, eh? What would you like?

Nonproductive Communication

Nonproductive communication increases the emotional distance between the partners and leaves the discrepancy between their respective expectations and behaviors unchanged. An example follows:

Alice and Jeff have the same problem as Mary and Bob. Jeff hasn't been helping around the apartment, and Alice is upset.

ALICE: Jeff, I'm really fed up with your lying around the apartment while I do all the work. Didn't we agree to do this stuff together?

JEFF: Maybe we did, but I've got all I can do with school and work, so you'll just have to do it yourself.

ALICE: You aren't being very sensitive to my needs—I go to school and work, too. You're so lazy.

JEFF: What would you know about sensitivity?

ALICE: You're being hateful and mean.

JEFF: I guess you're being real sweet when you talk like that aren't you? And when are you going to pay back the money you owe me, hypocrite?

ALICE: I'm not listening to this crap.

JEFF: Yeah! What are you going to do about it?

ALICE: Leave—that's what.

JEFF: Go ahead.

What began as a discussion about Jeff helping Alice around the apartment has escalated into a decision to terminate the relationship.

> An argument usually consists of two people each trying to get the last word—first.
> —LAURENCE PETER

Productive and Nonproductive Communication Compared

Mary and Bob did everything right in handling the housework issue; Alice and Jeff did everything wrong. Table 10.2 compares the two styles.

In a study of 40 married couples, the researchers observed what styles of communication were associated with marital happiness (Honeycutt et al., 1982). Spouses who were relaxed, friendly, and empathetic in relating to each other were happier than those who were rigid, distant, and cold. Mary and Bob's communication patterns reflect the former qualities.

Couples inadvertently establish unwritten rules governing the communication in their relationship. In one study, 16 couples identified 145 communication rules operative in their relationships (Jones & Gallois, 1989, 961–962). Some of these rules included:

1. Don't raise voice.
2. Don't talk down to the other person.
3. Acknowledge and try to understand the other person's point of view.
4. Don't make the other person feel guilty.
5. Don't interrupt.
6. Don't dominate the conversation.
7. Don't dismiss the other person's issue as unimportant.
8. Don't be sarcastic or mimic the other person.
9. Look at each other.
10. Don't exaggerate.

■■ TABLE 10.2 **Characteristics of Productive and**
Nonproductive Communication

PRODUCTIVE COMMUNICATION (MARY AND BOB)	NONPRODUCTIVE COMMUNICATION (ALICE AND JEFF)
1. Avoidance of behaviors in column 2.	1. Blaming: "... your lying around the house while I do the work."
2. Neutral statement rather than accusation: "I thought we agreed. . . ."	2. Name calling: "lazy," "hypocrite."
3. Acknowledgment of responsibility for partner's discomfort: "Well, I guess we did discuss my sharing the work."	3. Threatening: "I'm going to leave."
4. Expression of willingness to alleviate problem: "What do you want me to do?"	4. Using sarcasm: "What would you know about sensitivity?" "I guess you're being real sweet when you talk like that."
5. Positive labeling of suggestion—"It would be nice if. . . ."	5. Being judgmental: "You're being hateful and mean."
6. Reciprocity: "I'll handle it Monday, Wednesday, and Friday."	6. Changing issues: ". . . When are you going to pay back the money you owe me. . . ?"
7. Positive expression at end of conflict: "Okay. I guess I'm on for Thursday night, eh?"	7. No attempt to stop escalation of conflict.
8. Brief: Mary and Bob took two turns each speaking.	8. Lengthy: Alice and Jeff took six turns each speaking.

Good communication patterns also imply that each partner will participate in stopping negative interaction from escalating, in focusing on issues rather than on personalities, and in responding to each other with supportive comments. The last implies that each partner creates the context of positive regard for the other (Halford, et al., 1990). In addition, each partner being more concerned about the emotional quality of the relationship is more important than adapting a rational problem solving approach (Bowman, 1990).

Reflective listening—one of the most important aspects of effective communication—is the technique of paraphrasing how your partner feels about an issue rather than defending your own position. For example, suppose your partner wants the two of you to live together before you get married, but you are opposed to the idea. Rather than each of you becoming defensive and fixed in your own point of view, reflective listening implies that each of you explain to the other the other's point of view. Assuming that your partner has just told you why he or she wants to live together, reflective listening would involve your saying something like the following in response:

> As I understand it, you feel that we should live together before we get married because it would give us an opportunity to find out about each other. You also feel that there is nothing wrong with living together and that we should not have any misgivings about doing so. You also love me very deeply and want me to know that you simply want to be with me more of the time.

At this point, your partner should give you feedback on the degree to which you accurately understand how he or she feels about living together.

Then you should express how you feel about living together (in this example, you are opposed to it) and your partner would reflect back to you how you feel. In this case, your partner might say something like the following:

> You feel that living together is something that we should not do. Although you love me, you feel that living together would make you feel uncomfortable and would have a negative impact on our relationship. You also feel that your parents would object to our living together and would blame our living together on me.

In each of these examples, the focus is on reflecting back what the partner has said. The next time you are in a disagreement with someone, you might try reflective listening rather than continuing to defend your own point of view.

Be Aware of Defense Mechanisms

Defense mechanisms are unconscious techniques that function to protect individuals from anxiety. Defense mechanisms temporarily minimize anxiety and avoid emotional hurt, but they also interfere with conflict resolution.

Escapism. *Escapism* is the simultaneous denial and withdrawal from a problem. The usual form of escape is avoidance. The spouse becomes "busy" and "doesn't have time" to think about or deal with the problem, or the partner may escape into recreation, sleep, alcohol, marijuana, or work. Denying and withdrawing from problems in relations offer no possibility for confronting and resolving the problems.

I drink to make other people interesting.
—GEORGE JEAN NATHAN

Rationalization. *Rationalization* is the cognitive justification for one's own behavior that unconsciously conceals one's true motives.

These spouses are communicating even though they are not talking.

For example, one wife complained that her husband spent too much time at the health club in the evenings. The underlying reason for the husband going to the health club was to escape an unsatisfying home life. But the idea that he was in a "dead marriage" was too painful and difficult for the husband to face, so he rationalized to himself and his wife that he spent so much time at the health club because he made a lot of important business contacts there. Thus, the husband concealed his own true motives from himself (and his wife).

Projection. *Projection* occurs when one spouse unconsciously attributes their own feelings, attitudes, or desires to their partner. For example, the wife who desires to have an affair may accuse her husband of being unfaithful to her.

Projection may be seen in statements like "You spend too much money" (projection for "I spend too much money") and "You want to break up" (projection for "I want to break up"). Projection interferes with conflict resolution by creating a mood of hostility and defensiveness in both partners. The issues to be resolved in the relationship remain unchanged and become more difficult to discuss.

Displacement. *Displacement* involves shifting your feelings, thoughts, or behaviors from the person who evokes them onto someone else. The wife who is turned down for a promotion and the husband who is driven to exhaustion by his boss may direct their hostilities (displace them) onto each other rather than toward their respective employers. Similarly, spouses who are angry at each other may displace this anger onto someone else, such as the children.

Emotional Insulation. *Emotional insulation* interferes with conflict resolution by reducing the commitment of the partner to the relationship. One married person said:

> I was emotionally devastated by my first marriage because I let myself be vulnerable. I hid nothing and loved as fully as possible. But my partner took advantage of my love and did not reciprocate. I don't want it to happen again, so I am very guarded in my current relationship.

The partner has developed a protective posture to avoid being hurt. But the price of such protection may be high. A divorced person observed:

> Getting hurt sometimes happens when you get involved. And if you take your resentments with you into the next relationship, you've had it. You can't make your new partner responsible for something your previous partner did. I know; I would not drop my guard, become vulnerable, and let my love feelings go, and it cost me my second marriage.

☐ C O N S I D E R A T I O N ☐

By knowing about defense mechanisms and their negative impact on resolving conflict, you can be alert to their appearance in your own relationships. The essential

continued on next page

characteristics of all defense mechanisms are the same: they are unconscious, and they distort reality. When a conflict continues without resolution, one or more defense mechanisms may be operating.

A Plan to Communicate Successfully about Conflicts

Being sure that defense mechanisms are not operative, it is helpful to have an overall plan to resolve a conflict. Such a plan might include at least six stages.

Address Recurring, Disturbing Issues. If you or your partner are upset about a recurring issue, talking about it may help. Pam was jealous that Mark seemed to spend more time with other people at parties than with her. "When we go someplace together," she blurted out, "he drops me to disappear with someone else for two hours." Her jealousy was also spreading to other areas of their relationship. "When we are walking down the street and he turns his head to look at another woman, I get furious." If Pam and Mark don't discuss her feelings about Mark's behavior, their relationship may deteriorate due to a negative response cycle: he looks at another woman, she gets angry, he gets angry at her getting angry and finds that he is even more attracted to other women, she gets angrier because he escalates his looking at other women, and so on.

For some individuals, being upset interferes with their ability to communicate productively. One solution is for the partners to communicate about difficult issues at a time when they are feeling good rather than upset.

> Seldom, or perhaps never, does a marriage develop into an individual relationship smoothly and without crises; there is no coming to consciousness without pain.
> —CARL JUNG

Ask Your Partner for Help in Coping With an Issue. To bring the matter up, Pam might say something like "I feel jealous when you spend more time with other women at parties than me. I need some help in dealing with these feelings." By expressing her concern in this way, she has identified the problem from her perspective and asked her partner's cooperation in handling it.

When asking for help in coping with an issue, it is important to avoid attacking, blaming, or being negative. Such negative emotions reduce the motivation of the partner to talk about an issue and reduce the probability of a positive outcome (Forgatch, 1989).

Find Out Your Partner's View. We usually assume that we know what our partner thinks and why our partner does things. Sometimes we are wrong. Rather than assume how people feel about a particular issue, we might ask them to tell us how they see a particular situation. Pam's words to Mark might be, "What is it like for you when we go to parties?" "How do you feel about my jealousy?" Notice that both of these sentences are open-ended: Mark is asked to generate his own thoughts about the situation. Such questions are preferable to closed-ended questions, such as "Do you still like me when I'm jealous?" "Do you want to go alone to parties?" These questions require the other person to answer yes or no and make elaboration difficult—if not useless—once a single-word response has been given.

Nonjudgmentally Summarize Your Partner's View. Once your partner has shared his or her thoughts about an issue with you, it is important for you to summarize your partner's perspective in a nonjudgmental way. Summarizing serves three functions:

1. It ensures that you understand the situation from your partner's point of view. (If you don't summarize correctly, your partner will correct you.)
2. It lets your partner know that you know what his or her perspective is.
3. It validates the partner's right to view the situation as she or he does.

After Mark told Pam how he felt about their being at parties together, she summarized his perspective by saying, "You feel that I cling to you more than I should and that you would like me to let you wander around without feeling like you're making me angry." (She may not agree with his view, but she knows exactly what it is—and Mark knows that she knows.)

Examine Alternative Solutions. After both partners have told each other how they view the situation and have nonjudgmentally summarized each other's perspective, both partners should make various suggestions about how the problem can be resolved. Such "brainstorming" is crucial to conflict resolution because partners often feel upset when they know how their partner sees a situation. Brainstorming shifts the focus from criticizing each other's perspective to working together to develop alternative solutions. The partners suggest as many alternatives as possible, and no suggestion is "put down."

Alternatives suggested by Pam and Mark included the following:

1. Change cognitions—Pam might change the way she views Mark's interactions with others at parties. Rather than view him as neglecting and rejecting her at parties, she can view his desire to interact with others as evidence that he likes people and that he is socially skilled in interacting with others (both are positive qualities). She might also view his being across the room as an opportunity for her to meet new people or to talk with those she already knows. Finally, she might view his looking at other women as evidence that he has a strong sex drive and remind herself that he is always faithful to her (two more positive qualities).
2. Change behaviors—Mark might spend more time with Pam at parties, reduce the frequency with which he looks at other women, and point out good-looking men for Pam. Alternatively, Pam might begin to encourage Mark to talk with others at parties and initiate conversations with new people herself.
3. Stop going to parties.
4. Stop seeing each other for two weeks.
5. Stop talking about the issue.

Select and Execute a Plan of Action. After generating a number of solutions, one or a combination of them should be selected. Pam and Mark, for example, selected aspects from several alternatives from which they derived specific actions. They agreed that they would spend 45 minutes of each hour at a party talking and dancing together; Mark would be responsible for initiating and maintaining their time together, and Pam would be responsible for initiating their time away from each other. They also agreed that Pam would say nothing about the time they were apart unless Mark brought it up. They further agreed that it was okay for each of them to look at members of the opposite sex when they were with each other.

CONSIDERATION

Most of the agreements to resolve conflict that the partners feel good about are either compromises or contain elements of each partner's input. Both partners must be willing to assume responsibility for changing their own behavior first as a gesture of commitment and good faith toward each other and the relationship.

Here are some other examples of agreements reached by partners in conflict:

■ She wanted a half-carat diamond for her engagement ring; he thought it would be silly to spend $2,000 for a "rock." She put up half the money for the diamond; he put $1,000 on a down payment for a car for her.

■ He wanted to snow ski in Vermont on their honeymoon; she wanted to go to the Bahamas. They went to Disney World.

■ He wanted to buy Carnation Instant Breakfast because he likes its taste; she wanted to buy cereal because it would save them money. They bought both and alternated what they had for breakfast each morning.

■ He wanted her to get a job to put him through school; she wanted him to get a job and put her through school. They decided to work part time and go to school part time.

■ She wanted a baby; he didn't (he had two children from a previous marriage). He agreed to have a baby in exchange for her agreeing to wait two years. (She waited, and they had their baby.)

As we noted, some spouses view the resolution of their conflicts in win–lose terms rather than as compromises. In one study, 60 spouses (representing 30 marriages) were interviewed about relationship conflicts and their outcomes (Bell et al., 1982). The results showed that husbands "win most conflicts, regardless of the strategies they or their wives employ" (p. 111). Catholic and Mormon husbands were particularly likely to swing a disagreement their way. However, among couples in which the wife was a member of NOW (National Organization for Women), seven in 10 of the conflicts were "won" by the wife.

You cannot do a kindness too soon, for you never know how soon it will be too late.
—RALPH WALDO EMERSON

:: Marital Therapy

Sometimes it is difficult for spouses to resolve a conflict by themselves. Contacting a marriage therapist is an alternative. Examples of problems spouses bring to marriage therapy are described in Exhibit 10.1.

Questions about Marriage Therapy

If you decide to see a marriage therapist (see the Choices section at the end of this chapter), whom do you contact, how much will it cost, and what are the chances

---

E X H I B I T　10.1

Problems Couples Bring to Marriage Therapy

Communication
Don't feel close to spouse
Rarely alone with spouse
Spouse complains/criticizes
Don't love spouse
Not loved by spouse
Spouse is impatient
Too little time spent communicating
Nothing to talk about
Intellectual gaps
Unhappiness with type of conversation
Spouse is unhappy and depressed
Arguments end in spouse abuse/violence

Sex
Lack of sexual desire
Infrequent or no orgasm
Pain during intercourse
Vagina too tight for penetration
Premature ejaculation
Impotence
No ejaculation
Differences over how sex occurs:
　Too little foreplay

Spouse crude in approach
Oral sex
Positions
Too little affection
Disagreement about frequency of intercourse
Disagreement about when sex occurs
Extramarital affair

In-laws
Talking over the phone to in-laws
How often in-laws visit
Borrowing money from in-laws
Living with in-laws
How often to visit in-laws
In-laws' dislike of spouse
In-laws' interference in children's lives
Loaning/giving money to in-laws

Recreation
No sharing of leisure time
Desire of spouse for separate vacations
Competition (egos may be hurt if one spouse is, say, more athletic than partner)
Disagreement over amount of money to allocate for vacation
Spouse doesn't like family vacations
Disagreement over what is fun
Where to spend vacation

---

of a successful outcome? Your therapist should be a specialist with training in marriage therapy. Only one third of the states license or certify marriage therapists, so it is important to verify the training of your therapist. Don't be embarrassed to ask. You may prefer to select a therapist who is certified by the state or a clinical member of the American Association for Marriage and Family Therapy (AAMFT).

The cost of private marriage therapy is between $80 and $100 per hour. You can obtain a list of AAMFT members in your area by looking in the Yellow Pages or by writing to AAMFT at 1717 K St., N.W., Suite 407, Washington, D.C. 20006, (202) 429–1825. Members of AAMFT also conduct therapy in mental health centers, where the fee is considerably less.

Most marital therapy sessions last about 50 minutes, during which the spouses are usually seen together in what is referred to as *conjoint marriage therapy*. Some therapists (Gurman & Kniskern, 1986) feel strongly that it is important to see the spouses together; others (Wells & Giannetti, 1986) feel it is not harmful to see a spouse alone.

Children
Discipline of children
Care of children
Time with children
Number of children
Spacing of children
Infertility
Whether or not to adopt
Rivalry for children's love
Activities in which children should be involved
Sex education for children
Distress at children's behavior
Child abuse by one spouse
Retarded, autistic, or otherwise handicapped child
Stepchildren

Money
Too little money
Wife's job
Husband's job
Conflict over who buys what
Gambling
Borrowing
Excessive debts

Religion
Which church to attend
Wife too devout

Husband too devout
Wife not devout enough
Husband not devout enough
Religion for children
Church donations
Observance of religious holidays and
   rituals, such as circumcision
Breaking of vows

Friends
Too few friends
Too many friends
Different friends
Confidence to friends
Time with friends
Jealousy

Alcohol or Drugs
Spouse drinks too much
Spouse smokes too much marijuana
Spouse takes too many pills
Amount of money spent on
   alcohol/drugs
Flirting as a consequence of drinking
Influence of drinking/drug habits on
   children
Violence as a consequence of drinking

Whether two married people remain together will depend on their motivation to do so, how long they have been in conflict, the severity of the problem, and whether one or both partners is/are involved in an extramarital affair. Two moderately motivated partners with numerous conflicts over several years are less likely to work out their problems than a highly motivated couple with minor conflicts of short duration.

☐   C O N S I D E R A T I O N   ☐

Spouses most likely to benefit from marriage therapy come to therapy when they experience recurrent conflicts that they have been unable to communicate about and resolve. Spouses who wait until they are ready to divorce have usually waited too long.

To what degree does involvement in marriage therapy pay off?

> ■ **DATA:** *A total of 102 clients who had been involved in marriage and family therapy reported the degree to which they felt therapy had been effective. Of their marriages, 73 percent said they had "improved," 20 percent said "no change," and 7 percent said they had "deteriorated" as a result of the therapy (Crane et al., 1986).*

Styles of Marriage Therapy

All marriage therapists are not alike. Primarily they differ in the ways in which they identify the causes of marital problems and the ways in which they attempt to resolve these problems. The various approaches to marriage therapy include the following.

Systems Therapy. *Systems therapy* suggests that marriage problems can best be viewed and treated by examining the spouses in the larger context of their relationships with their children, in-laws, and friends—how spouses are connected to other people in their interpersonal system (Cottone, 1989). These connections and interactions are constantly changing (Constantine, 1989).

Problem marital behaviors, such as chronic drinking, are viewed in terms of how they serve to keep the couple functioning at a stable level. For example, does the wife protect the husband from the consequences of his drinking so that she can play the role of nurse? If he gets well, will he need her? In systems therapy intervention, the therapist explains to the spouses what "rules" they have developed to perpetuate their "co-dependent" problems. Spouses can then decide to adopt new rules to achieve new goals. For example, the wife of the alcoholic may decide to stop covering up her husband's alcoholism so that he may eventually seek treatment.

Behavioral Therapy. *Behavioral therapy* suggests that the cause of unhappiness between spouses is that each one engages in behavior that upsets the other. The behavioral therapist encourages each spouse to engage in behaviors of the kind and at a frequency desired by the partner and develops a behavior contract with each spouse to encourage new behavior. Exhibit 10.2 is an example of a behavior contract drawn up for a husband whose wife complained that he "leaves his clothes all over the house," "never helps me with meal preparation," "never says anything good about me," and "always criticizes me." Notice that the husband agrees to punish himself if he "forgets" to do what he agreed to do. By accepting a negative consequence, he teaches himself not to forget. A contract specifying what the wife will do for the husband (based on his requests) would also be developed. In this way, both spouses promise to change their behavior to be consistent with the expectations of the partner, so that each spouse will have a better behavioral basis for feeling positively about the other. Behavior contracts are one result of therapy, but a great deal of time is also spent on assisting the couple to develop positive communication and negotiation skills. Two researchers reported that behavioral marriage therapy not only improved marital satisfaction but reduced depression (Beach & O'Leary, 1986).

> Find out what a person will work for and what he or she will work to avoid, systematically manipulate these contingencies, and you can change behavior.
>
> —JACK TURNER

E X H I B I T 10.2

Behavior Contract

Name _Tom   Griffin_____   Date ____October 18_____

Behaviors	M	T	W	T	F	S	S

1. _Put clothes in closet or hamper by_
   8:30 am. every morning.   — — — — — — —

2. _Prepare and serve evening meal_
   Monday and Thursday at 7:00 p.m.   — — — — — — —

3. _Compliment Theresa twice daily._

   _____   — — — — — — —

4. _Make no negative statements_
   to Theresa.   — — — — — — —

Terms _If I fail to do any of the_
   above as specified, I forfeit reading
   the newspaper and watching T.V. news.   — — — — — — —

Cognitive Therapy. Based on the theories of Aaron Beck and Albert Ellis, cognitive therapy (sometimes known as rational-emotive therapy or cognitive-behavioral therapy) suggests that spouses are unhappy as a result of irrational beliefs they have about themselves and each other (Baucom & Epsten, 1989). The rational-emotive therapist encourages partners to examine their beliefs and to change them if they have a negative impact on the marriage. For example, the belief that "My spouse should care more about me than anything or anyone else" would be examined for its potential negative consequences on the relationship. Other beliefs that interfere with marital happiness include "I should always be happy with my partner," "We should be as happy as we were in courtship," and "I will be hurt if I get too close" (Israelstam, 1989; Burns, 1989).

Despite our celebration of openness, in the power struggle, it's the person who's most vulnerable, most generous, most committed who loses.

—ROBERT KAREN

Transactional Analysis. *Transactional analysis* (TA) suggests that spouses are un-happy because one spouse is interacting with the other as though the other spouse were someone else. As examples, a wife may act as if her husband were her father or a husband may relate to his wife as though she were his mother. The TA therapist encourages spouses to examine the ways in which their role rela-tionships with others have been problematic and how they may have introduced these unresolved conflicts into their marriage relationship.

Adlerian Therapy

Applying the theories of Austrian psychiatrist Alfred Adler, *Adlerian therapy* views marital discord as a result of power struggles between spouses. The individual is seen as trying to compensate for feelings of inferiority that began with the help-lessness of infancy. The Alderian therapist seeks to improve marital relationships by helping couples to feel secure and to regard their power struggles as unnec-essary.

Systems, behavioral, rational-emotive, transactional, and Adlerian therapy are only a few of the different approaches used by marriage therapists. Gestalt, psy-choanalytic, humanistic, reality, and paradoxical therapy are others. Although cognitive therapy is current attracting a new wave of therapists, no one therapy can be regarded as superior.

☐   C O N S I D E R A T I O N   ☐

All of the different styles of therapy can be placed into two basic categories—*directive* and *nondirective*. In behavioral, rational-emotive, and reality therapy, the therapist is more likely to be directive, which involves suggesting specific ways in which the spouses can improve their marriage. Therapists of the systems, transactional, Adle-rian, Gestalt, and psychoanalytic persuasions may or may not make specific recom-mendations. Whereas some clients want specific direction, others want to explore their relationships and develop insight into the dynamics of marital interaction. Should you decide to consult a therapist, you should seek the therapist who will offer the style of therapy you want. Regardless of particular orientation, the trained mar-riage therapist can be expected to express a genuine concern for your difficulty, to be nonjudgmental, and to regard all information as confidential.

⸬ Marriage Enrichment

Spouses who are having marital difficulties often see a marriage therapist as a last resort—their final choice before seeking a divorce. Marriage counselors are thought of as an emergency medical team at the bottom of a cliff that ministers to those who have fallen in the hope of reviving them—but why not a guardrail at the top to prevent couples from slipping off the edge? Such preventive interven-tion is the goal of marriage enrichment programs. More than 50 of these programs are currently operative, including Marriage Encounter, International Marriage Encounter, the Minnesota Couple Communication Program, Conjugal Relation-ship Enhancement (Pennsylvania), Training in Marriage Enrichment (TIME), and the Association of Couples for Marriage Enrichment (ACME).

One of the most well-known marriage enrichment programs is Marriage Encounter. (There are two rival branches—National and Worldwide.) As originally conceived by Gabriel Calvo, a Roman Catholic priest, Marriage Encounter is a 44-hour weekend program that attempts to teach "God's plan for marriage." A team of lay people and clergy present a series of talks designed to make couples aware that something is missing in their relationship. That something is *dialogue*. To correct the absence of dialogue, the group leader assigns the spouses a topic, asks them to write their respective feelings about the topic in a notebook, exchange their notebooks, and discuss the issue. The exercise focuses on sharing feelings, not on problem solving.

A number of couples have sought marriage enrichment through an encounter weekend.

■ **DATA:** *More than 1 million couples have participated in marriage encounter weekends (Doherty et. al., 1986).*

Most couples who attend marriage enrichment or marriage encounter weekends probably benefit from the experience. In one study, 80 percent of 200 couples who had attended a National Marriage Encounter weekend four years earlier reported they had a totally positive experience. The most positive aspect of the weekend was learning to express their feelings to each other. The most negative aspect was identifying needs during the weekend that were not subsequently fulfilled (Lester & Doherty, 1983).

For example, one wife said she wanted more frequent intercourse, which, at follow-up, had still not occurred. During this time, the husband had felt inadequate and the wife had felt frustrated.

Complete openness during an encounter weekend may be dysfunctional. One husband felt that to be honest he needed to disclose a previous affair to his wife. The encounter weekend was over before the effects of his disclosure were resolved by the couple. One respondent in a follow-up study (Doherty et al., 1986) said:

> The reason I feel the Encounter had a negative effect was that my husband indicated that he was not interested in working on any of the areas. This really made me question the stability of our marriage. I felt very upset, because I began to wonder how I could survive knowing there would be no changes—and wondering if I could accept this and live this way (p. 55).

☐   C O N S I D E R A T I O N   ☐

To minimize the negative effects of exposure to a marriage enrichment program, the partners should not regard the experience as an opportunity to solve problems or to deal with difficult issues in their relationship. Such issues should be dealt with alone or in marriage therapy. Instead a marriage enrichment program should be regarded as a place to improve communication skills between spouses who feel good about themselves and each other.

Couples who wish to experience a marriage enrichment program might consider enrolling in one in which the spouses are permitted to question and discuss the ideas and recommendations presented by the leaders of the group. In Marriage Encounter,

continued on next page

no such interaction is permitted during the sessions (Doherty et al., 1986). Spouses should also feel comfortable contacting a therapist after an encounter weekend if they feel worse as a result of the experience.

:: Trends

The most significant trend regarding communication in marriage is the increased willingness of couples to "go public" with their problems. The realization that it is normal for couples to be faced with problems in their relationships is replacing the old idea that happy couples don't have conflicts. The continuing popularity of marriage enrichment groups, encounter weekends, and marriage seminars reflects this trend.

When couples become involved in private therapy, they are more likely to look for a therapist specializing in short-term rather than long-term therapy (Bloomfield et al., 1989). The relief offered by cognitive behavioral approaches coupled with the fact that employers will pay for only a limited number of sessions has helped to solidify the trend toward short-term therapy.

A third trend concerns raising the standards that marriage and family therapists must meet. More states are enacting laws to create a classification of "certified marriage therapist" to denote that a counselor has the equivalent training and background required for admission to the American Association for Marriage and Family Therapy. This requires a minimum of a master's degree and specific training in marriage and family therapy, human sexuality, and ethics. Furthermore, the counselor must have conducted 1,500 hours of marriage and family therapy; at least 100 of these hours must be under the supervision of an approved supervisor. The hoped-for result will be a sufficient supply of highly trained and experienced marriage therapists to meet the growing demand for such services.

:: Summary

Communication may be defined as the process of exchanging information between two individuals. Communication involves both verbal and nonverbal communication. What partners say to each other and what they mean may be very different.

Effective communication includes giving priority to the communication aspect of the relationship, using "I" statements, and sharing power in the relationship. Effective communication also involves each partner encouraging the continuation of the dialogue between the parties (process) even when the words the partners say to each other may be uncomfortable to hear (content).

Communication is the core of any relationship. It involves the use of words and gestures to convey messages between two people. Productive uses of communication skills in conflict resolution include replacing accusations with neutral statements and sarcasm with positive labeling and not allowing a negative mutual-blame cycle to develop.

Marital conflict can erupt at any time. It is both inevitable and, under certain conditions, desirable. The causes of interpersonal conflict include behavior, perception, and value differences. Spouses also develop various styles of conflict—complementary (one dominant, the other submissive); symmetrical (both partners react the same way to each other); and parallel (both partners avoid confronting the problem).

Having a plan to communicate about conflicts is essential. Such a plan includes deciding to address recurring issues rather than suppressing them, asking the partner for help in resolving the issue, finding out the partner's point of view, summarizing in a nonjudgmental way the partner's perspective, brainstorming for alternative solutions, and selecting a plan of action. To the degree that the plan of action includes suggestions made by each partner, the potential for success in resolving the problem is maximized. When we participate in a solution, we are more committed to seeing it work.

Some couples who can't resolve a conflict by themselves contact a marriage therapist. These therapists are not regulated by law in all states, so care should be exercised in selecting one. Also, there are many theoretical approaches; it is important to select a therapist who offers the style of therapy the couple wants. Most spouses report positive outcomes from their involvement in marriage therapy.

Marriage enrichment programs are for couples who have good marriages and who want to keep them that way. However, some couples do report negative experiences from their involvement in these programs. Although such experiences are rare, couples should be careful about the type of marriage encounter program they select.

Trends in conflict and communication include an increasing number of couples becoming involved in marriage enrichment or marriage therapy. Ensuring the adequate training of therapists who provide the latter service has become a priority for some state legislatures.

Questions for Reflection

1. Have you been able to reinforce your partner for telling you things (process) even though you felt uncomfortable hearing the words (content)?
2. Which of the theories of communication process best describe the communication pattern you have with your partner?
3. Would you be willing to become involved in marriage enrichment or marriage therapy? Why or why not?

References

Altschuler, M. and D. W. Krueger. Game playing that destroys marriages. *Medical Aspects of Human Sexuality*, 1986, 20, 63–76.

Argyle, Michael. *Bodily Communication*. New York: Methuen, Inc. 1988.

Balswick, J. Explaining inexpressive males: A reply to L'Abate. *Family Relations*, 1980, 29, 231–233.

Baucom, D. H. and N. Epsten. *Cognitive-behavioral marital therapy*. New York: Brunner/Mazel, 1989.

Beach, S.R.H. and D. O'Leary. The treatment of depression occurring in the context of marital discord. *Behavior Therapy*, 1986, 17, 43–49.

Bell, D. C., J. S. Chafetz, and L. H. Horn. Marital conflict resolution: A study of strategies and outcomes. *Journal of Family Issues*, 1982, 3, 111–132.

Belsky, J., M. Perry-Jenkins, and A. C. Crouter. The work-family interface and marital change across the transition to parenthood. *Journal of Family Issues*, 1985, *6*, 205–220.

Bloomfield, H. H., S. VeHese, and R. B. Kory. Healthy love. *Health*, 1989, *21*, 24–26.

Bowman, M. L. Coping efforts and marital satisfaction: Measuring marital coping and its correlates. *Journal of Marriage and the Family*, 1990, *52*, 463–474.

Braiker, Harriet B. The power of self-talk. *Psychology Today*, December 1989, 23–27.

Brandt, A. Avoiding couple karate: Lessons in the marital arts. *Psychology Today*, October 1982, 38–43.

Brockman, C. T. and Y. Peterson. Marital gift giving. *Free Inquiry in Creative Sociology*, 1990, 18, 29–36.

Burns, David D. *The good feeling handbook*. New York: William Morrow & Co., 1989.

Condie, Spencer J. Older married couples. *Aging and the Family*, Edited by Stephen J. Bahr and Evan T. Peterson. Lexington, Mass.: Lexington Books, 1989, 143–158.

Constantine, Larry L. Furniture for firewood—Blaming the systems paradigm. *Journal of Marital and Family Therapy*, 1989, *15*, 111–113.

Cottone, R. R. Defining the psychomedical and systemic paradigms in marital and family therapy. *Journal of Marital and Family Therapy*, 1989, *15*, 225–235.

Crane, D. R., W. Griffin, and R. D. Hill. Influence of therapist skills on client perceptions of marriage and family therapy outcome: Implications for supervision. *Journal of Marital and Family Therapy*, 1986, *12*, 91–96.

Doherty, W. J., M. E. Lester, and G. Leigh. Marriage encounter weekends: Couples who win and couples who lose. *Journal of Marriage and Family Therapy*, 1986, *12*, 49–61.

Ellis, Albert. *How to stubbornly refuse to make yourself miserable about anything—Yes anything*. New York: Lyle Stuart, 1988.

Fitzpatrick, M. A. *Between husbands & wives: Communication in marriage*. Beverly Hills, Calif.: Sage Publications, 1988.

Floyd, F. J. Couples' cognitive/affective reactions to communication behaviors. *Journal of Marriage and the Family*, 1988, *50*, 523–532.

Forgatch, Marion S. Patterns and outcome in family problem solving: The disrupting effect of negative emotion. *Journal of Marriage and the Family*, 1989, *51*, 115–124.

Green, Shelley K. D. L. Sollie. Long-term effects of a church-based sex education program on adolescent communication. *Family Relations*, 1989, *38*, 152–156.

Gurman, A. S. and D. P. Kniskern. Commentary on Wells and Giannetti article on individual marital therapy. *Family Process*, 1986, *25*, 51–62.

Hampton, R. L., R. J. Gelles, and J. W. Harrop. Is violence in black families increasing? A comparison of 1975 and 1985 national survey rates. *Journal of Marriage and the Family*, 1989, *51*, 969–980.

Hayes, M. P., N. Stinnett, and J. DeFrain. Learning about marriage from the divorced. *Journal of Divorce*, 1981, *4*, 23–29.

Halford, W. K., K. Hahlweg, & M. Dunne. Cross-cultural study of marital communication and marital distress. *Journal of Marriage and the Family*, 1990, *52*, 487–500.

Hochschild, Arlie. *The second shift*. New York: Viking, 1989.

Honeycutt, J. M., C. Wilson, and C. Parker. Effects of sex and degrees of happiness on perceived styles of communication in and out of the marital relationship. *Journal of Marriage and the Family*, 1982, *44*, 395–406.

Jones, Elizabeth and Cynthia Gallois. Spouses' impressions of rules for communication in public and private marital conflicts. *Journal of Marriage and the Family*, 1989, *51*, 957–967.

Julius, M. Marital stress and suppressed anger linked to death of spouses. *Marriage and Divorce Today*, 1986, *11*, no. 35, 1–2.

Klagsbrun, F. *Married people: Staying together in the age of divorce*. New York: Bantam, 1985.

Kramarae, C. *Women and men speaking.* New York: Newbury House, 1981.

Lester, M. E. and W. J. Doherty. Couple's long-term evaluations of their marriage encounter experience. *Journal of Marriage and the Family,* 1983, *45*, 183–188.

Menaghan, E. G. Coping with marital problems: Assessing effectiveness. Paper presented at American Sociological Association Annual Meeting, 1982. Used with permission.

Notarius, C. I. and J. S. Johnson. Emotional expression in husbands and wives. *Journal of Marriage and the Family,* 1982, *44*, 483–489.

Reis, H., Senchak, M., and Soloman, B. Sex differences in interaction meaningfulness. 1985. *Journal of Personality and Social Psychology, 48,* 1204–1217.

Ryan, Barbara and Eric Plutzer. When married women have abortions: Spousal notification and marital interaction. *Journal of Marriage and the Family,* 1989, *51,* 41–50.

Scoresby, A. L. *The marriage dialogue.* Reading, Mass.: Addison-Wesley, 1977.

Secord, P. F. and K. Ghee. Implications of the black marriage market for marital conflict. *Journal of Family Issues,* 1986, *7,* 21–30.

Sherman, M. A. and A. Haas. Man to man, woman to woman. *Psychology Today,* June 1984, 72–73.

Turner, A. J. Communication in relationships. Paper, presented at 30th Annual Family Life Conference on Mediation in Relationships, East Carolina University, Greenville, N.C., September 28, 1989. Revised for this text in 1990. Used by permission of Dr. Turner.

U.S. Bureau of the Census, 1984. Marital status and living arrangements: March 1983. Current Population Reports P–20, No. 389, Washington, D. C., Government Printing Office.

Wells, R. A. and V. J. Giannetti. Individual marital therapy: A critical reappraisal. *Family Process,* 1986, *25,* 43–51.

Wilson, K. and P. Y. Martin. Regional differences in resolving family conflicts: Is there a legacy of patriarchy in the South? *Sociological Spectrum,* 1988, *8,* 197–211.

CHOICES

A BASIC CHOICE OF individuals in a relationship is deciding how honest to be in a relationship. After examining how much openness is productive for a relationship, we will consider the question of whether to consult a marriage therapist when relationship conflict becomes unmanageable.

Is Honesty Always the Best Policy?

Good communication often implies open communication, but how much honesty is good for a marital relationship? Does a "we tell each other everything" disclosure policy have more positive consequences than a "selective disclosure" policy? Two researchers (Ryan & Plutzer, 1989) compared wives who had had an abortion who told their husband with wives who had had an abortion who did not tell their husband. They found that "the unqualified generalization that notification and discussion promote marital harmony is not valid" (p. 49). In other words, telling the spouse about the abortion was not always a good idea in that the relationship suffered more stress by doing so.

One reason for being careful about what is disclosed is that sometimes total honesty may be too brutal, and might best be tempered with caring. A particular situation in which tempered honesty may be the best policy is when you are extremely upset. In this situation, you may honestly feel and think horrible things about your partner. If you express such thoughts and feelings, they may be difficult to retract later when you are calm. At such times it may be best to not be totally honest with your thoughts and feelings. Instead, admit you are upset and either wait until you are calm to talk about the problem or refrain from expressing thoughts that are hurtful to your partner.

Though honesty may be tempered with kindness in some situations, in others it is probably best to be completely honest. Specific information which should not be withheld from the partner include previous marriages and children, a sexual orientation different from what the partner expects, alcohol or drug addiction, having a sexually transmit-

ted disease, such as AIDS or genital herpes, and any known physical disabilities, such as sterility. Disclosures of this nature include anything that would have a significant impact on the relationship.

Should You Consult a Marriage Therapist?

Most people are reluctant to consult a marriage therapist. Most spouses have been taught that seeing a therapist about personal problems means they are mentally ill. "It's the crazy folks that see those counselors," said one woman. Other spouses feel that their marriage is private and nobody else's business. "You don't talk to strangers about those kinds of things," said another spouse. Still other spouses feel that if couples are really in love with each other, they will be able to work out anything. They assume it is only the people who don't love each other who can't work out their problems.

Each of these beliefs is a myth. Seeing a therapist does not mean that you are mentally ill. On the contrary, we are never more mentally and emotionally healthy than when we can acknowledge that we have a problem and seek help for it.

The fact that marriage is a personal and private affair does not mean we cannot discuss our concern with a specialist. Our bodies are also personal and private, but this does not stop us from seeing a physician when we have a physical problem. Our mental health is as important to our feeling good as is our physical health. Both physicians and marriage therapists can be expected to treat the information we share with them with strict confidentiality. This is required by their code of professional ethics.

Finally, as we have seen earlier in this chapter, love is not enough to ensure the resolution of all conflicts. Two people can love each other intensely and not be able to resolve their conflicts or to live together happily. "We loved each other," said one spouse, "but we just couldn't make a go of it together."

Signs to look for in your own relationship that suggest you might consider seeing a therapist include feeling distant and not wanting to or being unable to communicate with your partner, avoiding each other, drinking heavily or taking drugs, privately contemplating separation, being involved in an affair, and feeling depressed.

If you are experiencing one or more of these concerns with your partner, it may be wise not to wait until it reaches a stage beyond which repair is impossible. Relationships are like boats. A small leak will not sink it. But if left unattended, the small leak may grow larger or new leaks may break through. Marriage therapy sometimes serves to mend relationship problems early by helping the partners to sort out values, make decisions, and begin new behaviors so that they can start feeling better about each other.

However, in spite of the potential benefits of marriage therapy, there are some valid reasons for not consulting a counselor.

Not all spouses who become involved in marriage therapy regard the experience positively. Some feel that their marriage is worse as a result. Saying things the spouse can't forget, feeling hopeless at not being able to resolve a problem "even with a counselor," and feeling resentment over new demands made by the spouse in therapy are reasons some spouses cite for negative outcomes.

Therapists also may give clients an unrealistic picture of loving, cooperative, and growing relationships in which partners always treat each other with respect and understanding, share intimacy, and help each other become whomever each wants to be. In creating this idealistic image of the perfect relationship, therapists may inadvertently encourage clients to focus on the shortcomings in their relationship and to expect more of the therapist than is realistic. Couples in therapy must also be on guard against assuming that therapy is a quick and easy "fix." In order for therapy to be effective, a great deal of personal effort is required (Bloomfield et al., 1989).

Impact of Social Influences on Choices

Feeling free to consult a marriage therapist is often related to knowing someone who has done so and who reports that the experience was positive. In the absence of a social learning experience such as this, we are left with the stereotype of lying on a couch while someone asks us about our relationship with our mother. For most of us, the fear of being in a situation like that makes us too anxious to actually call and make the appointment.

One marriage therapist tells couples, who ask what they should tell their children about seeing a counselor, that it is healthy and productive for children to know that their parents are seeking help for a marriage problem. This communicates to a child not only that married couples have problems but also that they can do something about them by seeing a therapist. The fact that children know that their parents are seeking marriage therapy will make it easier for them to ask for help when they grow up, marry, and must face their own problems.

C H A P T E R

11

Sexuality in Relationships

CONTENTS

IS IT TRUE?

1. Sexual performance necessarily decreases with age.

2. Heavy drinking on the part of a woman increases her ability to have an orgasm.

3. Some medications can delay ejaculation.

4. Sexual addicts usually have very positive self concepts.

5. College students tend to disapprove of elderly people living together and having sex in nursing homes.

1 = F; 2 = F; 3 = T; 4 = F; 5 = F

In a study of over 9,000 spouses who rated their marriage as either "excellent" or "very good," physical affection in public and sexual passion in private were among the most important qualities in these relationships (Schwartz & Jackson, 1989).

In this chapter we review some unique aspects of marital sexuality, some facts about and prerequisites to sexual fulfillment, and various sexual problems couples experience. We also look at sexuality over the lifespan. We begin with a discussion of marital intercourse.

:: Marital Intercourse

In some ways, marital intercourse is different from intercourse before marriage. Marital intercourse is unique in terms of its social legitimacy and declining frequency over the course of the marriage. Marital intercourse also has varying degrees of importance to partners.

Social Legitimacy

In our society, marital intercourse is the most legitimate form of sexual behavior. Homosexual, premarital, and extramarital intercourse do not enjoy society's approval, although attitudes and laws are changing. It is not only okay to have intercourse when married, it is expected. People assume that married couples make love and that something is "wrong" if they do not.

Declining Frequency

Marital intercourse is also characterized by declining frequency.

■ **DATA:** *For couples who have been married between one month or 25 years, the frequency of intercourse decreases as marital duration increases (Jasso, 1985).*

Typically, a couple starts out having intercourse three to four times a week; 25 years later, the frequency is less than once per week. Reasons for declining frequency are careers or jobs, children, and satiation. Regarding the impact of employment, one spouse said:

> Exhaustion is a very big problem. I never thought it could happen. When I'm working and running my business, it is totally absorbing and it takes me a long time to decompress at night, by which time Jerry is usually sound asleep! And I guess Jerry, unlike when we first got married, has a lot of responsibility in his position—so it's work that's taking its toll on our sex life! (Greenblat, 1983, 296).

Children also decrease the frequency of intercourse by their presence and by the toll they take on the caregiver's energy. "After taking care of a 3-year-old and a 9-month-old all day, I'm in no mood for sex. I'll tell you that straight out," said one mother. Also, the mere fact that children are in the house and can walk into the bedroom or knock on the door at any time translates into the couple having intercourse late at night when the children are asleep or early in the morning before they are awake. "It shoots spontaneity in the neck," said one husband.

Satiation, in psychology, means that repeated exposure to a stimulus results in the loss of its ability to reinforce. For example, the first time you listen to a new cassette tape or cd, you derive considerable enjoyment and satisfaction from it. You may play it over and over during the first few days. But after a week or so, listening to the same music is no longer new and does not give you the same level of enjoyment that it first did. So it is with intercourse. The thousandth time that a person has intercourse with the same person is not as new and exciting as the first few times. Although intercourse can remain very satisfying for couples in long-term relationships, satiation may result in decreased frequency of intercourse.

Varying Importance

How important is intercourse to married couples? The range is very wide. Whether for physiological or psychological reasons, some married couples stop having intercourse. For them, sex is not a meaningful event. Yet they may love each other deeply and delight in the companionship they share.

Other couples regard sex as the only positive aspect of their relationship. One husband said that he and his wife had decided to separate, "and since we both knew that I would be moving out on Friday, we had intercourse twice a day that week." A year after the separation, he said, "Sex with us was the best there is. I don't miss the fights we had, but I do miss the sex." Some separated couples continue to have intercourse.

Between the extremes of "sex is nothing" and "sex is everything" is "sex is good but not everything." "It's the icing on the cake," said one man. "If you've got a good out-of-bed relationship, sex only makes things better. But sex can't make a bad marriage good."

∷ Sexual Fulfillment: Some Facts

Individuals who have a good sexual relationship with their partners are often aware of some basic facts about human sexuality. Some of these facts include those discussed in the following sections.

Sexual Attitudes and Behaviors are Learned

Whether you believe that "Sex is sinful" or "If it feels good, do it," your sexual attitudes have been learned. Your parents and peers have had a major impact on your sexual attitudes, but there have been other influences as well: school, church or synagogue, and the media. Your attitudes about sex would have been different if the influences you were exposed to had been different.

The same is true of sexual behavior. The words you say, the sequence of events in lovemaking, the specific behaviors you engage in, and the positions you adopt during intercourse are a product of the learning history you and your partner have had. The fact that learning accounts for most sexual attitudes and behaviors is important because negative patterns can be unlearned and positive patterns can be learned.

It is also important to be aware that you have been reared in American society and that your thoughts, feelings, attitudes, and behaviors are consistent with those of this culture. Had you been reared in another culture, your perceptions of sexuality would be different. For example, having intercourse with a brother or sister is likely to induce feelings of shame or disgust in our society, but the Dahomey of West Africa and the Inca of Peru have viewed such a relationship as natural and desirable (Stephens, 1982).

Also, from a cross-cultural perspective, sexual behavior that is punished in one society may be tolerated in a second and rewarded in a third. In the Gilbert Islands, virginity until marriage is an exalted sexual value and violations are not tolerated; premarital couples who are discovered to have had intercourse before their wedding are put to death. Our society tolerates premarital intercourse, particularly if the partners are "in love." In contrast, the Lepcha people of India believe that intercourse helps young girls mature; by the age of 12, most Lepcha women are engaging in regular intercourse.

There are also cultural variations in the frequency of intercourse. Although most couples throughout the world have intercourse between two and five times a week (Gebhard, 1972), the Basongye in the Kasai province of the former Belgian Congo, have intercourse every night even when they are in their fifties and sixties (Merriam, 1972). In contrast, a Cayapa man may go for several years without having intercourse; their Cayapan term for intercourse, *medio trabajo*, means "a little like work."

Sex Is a Natural Function

Although your sexual attitudes and behaviors are learned, your genital reflexes are innate. Males are not taught to have an erection, and females are not taught to lubricate vaginally. These are natural processes (Kolodny et al., 1986). Sex therapy is often aimed at minimizing the impact of negative learning experiences so that the natural physical processes can occur.

Effective Sexual Communication Takes Time and Effort

Most of us who have been reared in homes in which discussions about sex were infrequent or nonexistent may have developed relatively few skills to employ in talking about sex. Shifting to sex talk with our partner from, say, talking about current events may seem awkward. Overcoming our awkward feelings requires retraining ourselves so that sex becomes as easy for us to talk about as what we had for lunch. Some suggestions that may be helpful in developing effective sexual communication follow.

Say Sex Words. Effective sexual communication involves using words to refer to sexual anatomy and sexual behaviors. You might develop a list with your partner that contains all of the technical and slang words you can think of about sex. Then alternate with your partner, reading one word after the other from the list. As you read these sex words, take turns sharing your feelings about and reactions to each word. The goal is to find out which sex words you and your partner feel most comfortable using. Some individuals prefer technical terms for sexual acts and sexual anatomy. Others prefer certain slang terms. Many individuals are offended or uncomfortable with some slang terms because they have a negative connota-

A good sexual relationship often takes place in the context of a close emotional relationship.

tion. As a result of doing this exercise, you and your partner should know which sex words are preferred and which sex words are to be avoided.

☐   C O N S I D E R A T I O N   ☐

Some individuals do not like any of the technical or popular slang words for certain sexual anatomy or sexual behaviors. In this case, the partners may invent another word or term that they both feel good about. For example, one woman said she did not like any of the popular slang words for vagina. She also did not want her partner to use the word ''vagina'' in their sexual communication because it sounded too ''medical.'' The woman suggested that she and her partner invent another term to refer to ''vagina.'' They decided to use the word ''mango'' as their personal slang word for vagina.

Ask Open-Ended Questions.   Open-ended questions are questions that may elicit detailed answers, rather than one-word answers such as ''yes'' or ''no.'' To learn more about your partner, ask specific questions that cannot be answered with a yes or no. Examples include ''What does orgasm feel like to you?,'' ''Tell me about the sexual activities you like best,'' and ''How can I be a better sex partner?''

Give Reflective Feedback.   When your partner shares with you very intimate details concerning sexuality, it is important to respond in a nonjudgmental way. One way to do this is to reflect back what your partner tells you.

Suppose Mary tells Jim that the best sex for her is when he is holding and caressing her, not when they are actually having intercourse. An inappropriate response by Jim to her disclosure would be ''Something must be the matter with you.'' This would undoubtedly stop Mary from telling Jim anything more about her feelings. But Jim's reflective statement, "Our being close is what you like best in our relationship," confirms for Mary that he understands how she feels and that her feelings are accepted.

"Spectatoring" Interferes with Sexual Functioning

One of the obstacles to sexual functioning is spectatoring. Spectatoring involves mentally observing your sexual performance and that of your partner. When the researchers in one extensive study observed how individuals actually behave during sexual intercourse, they reported a tendency for sexually dysfunctional partners to act as spectators by mentally observing their own and their partners' sexual performance. For example, the man would focus on whether he was having an erection, how complete it was, and whether it would last. He might also watch to see whether his partner was having an orgasm. (Masters & Johnson, 1970).

CONSIDERATION

Spectatoring as Masters and Johnson conceived it, interferes with each partner's sexual enjoyment because it creates anxiety about performance; and anxiety blocks performance. A man who worries about getting an erection reduces his chance of doing so. A woman who is anxious about achieving an orgasm probably will not. The desirable alternative to spectatoring is to relax, focus on and enjoy your own pleasure, and permit yourself to be sexually responsive.

Spectatoring is not limited to sexually dysfunctional couples and is not necessarily associated with psychopathology. Spectatoring is a reaction to the concern that the performance of the sexual partners is consistent with their expectations. We all probably have engaged in spectatoring to some degree. It is when spectatoring is continual that performance is impaired.

Women and Men Have Different Sexual Response Cycles

As the spectatoring problem reveals, human sexuality has a psychosocial component. The other major component of human sexuality, the biophysical, includes the sexual response cycle. Masters and Johnson, who observed the sexual response cycles of more than 10,000 individuals, reported that women and men do not necessarily progress through the cycle in the same way (see Figures 11.1 and 11.2).

The four phases of the sexual response cycle are excitement, plateau, orgasm, and resolution. These phases represent what people report they experience when they have sexual intercourse. First, there is the period that extends from the beginning of sexual stimulation until a high degree of excitement is reached (excitement); then the level of excitement increases, but not to the point of orgasm (plateau); then one or both partners have a climax (orgasm); and this is followed by a period of relaxation and a return to the state that preceded sexual excitement (resolution).

The female alternative sexual response cycles are illustrated in Figure 11.1. Once sexual excitement begins, there may be three outcomes: (1) progression

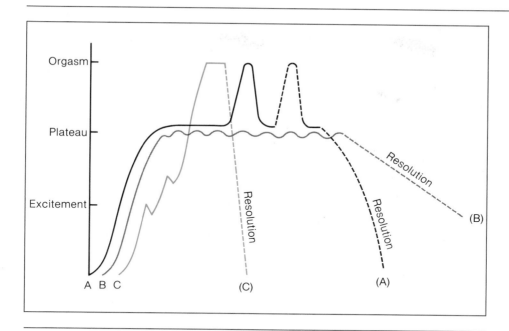

:: FIGURE 11.1

Female Alternative Sexual Response Cycles

The female may experience one of three patterns in her response to sexual stimulation: Pattern C, the typical response, involves moving from excitement to plateau to one orgasm to resolution. Pattern B involves becoming excited, stabilizing at the plateau phase, and moving toward resolution. Pattern A involves having an orgasm, returning to the plateau phase, and then back to another orgasm; this pattern may be repeated again and is referred to as multiple orgasm.

SOURCE: William H. Masters & Virginia E. Johnson, *Human sexual response.* Boston: Little, Brown, 1966. p. 5. Copyright © by Masters & Johnson, 1966.

from excitement to plateau to one orgasm to resolution (line C); (2) progression from excitement to plateau to orgasm to plateau to orgasm (or to a number of additional orgasms) to resolution (line A); or (3) progression from excitement to plateau to resolution without experiencing an orgasm (line B).

The male alternative sexual response cycles are illustrated in Figure 11.2. Once sexual response begins and assuming that both partners are willing for the male partner to complete the cycle, there is essentially only one outcome—progressing through plateau to orgasm to resolution. Although men may have additional orgasms, there is usually a considerable refractory (or recovery) period before doing so.

□   C O N S I D E R A T I O N   □

Observation of the sexual cycles of women and men reveals two essential differences. (1) The man usually climaxes once during sexual intercourse, but the woman may not climax at all or may climax several times. (2) When the woman does experience several climaxes, she is capable of doing so with only a brief time (seconds) between climaxes. In contrast, the man needs a considerable refractory period (minutes to hours) before he is capable of additional orgasms.

Physical and Mental Health Affect Sexual Performance

Effective sexual functioning requires good physical and mental health. Physically, this means regular exercise, good nutrition, lack of disease, and lack of fatigue. Regular exercise, whether walking, jogging, aerobics, swimming, or bicycling, is

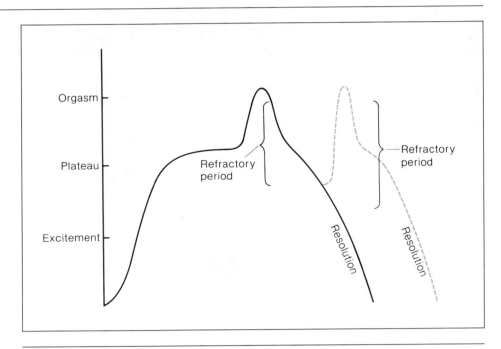

:: FIGURE 11.2

Male Alternative Sexual Response Cycles

The male typically experiences the pattern indicated by the solid line in his response to sexual stimulation. He becomes excited and moves through the plateau, orgasm, and resolution phases of the sexual response cycle. The dashed line describes the pattern in which, after a brief refractory period during which the male does not want additional stimulation, he enters the cycle at the plateau phase and has another orgasm, which is followed by another refractory period and resolution.

SOURCE: William H. Masters & Virginia E. Johnson, *Human sexual response.* Boston: Little, Brown, 1966. p. 5. Copyright © by Masters & Johnson, 1966.

related to higher libido, sexual desire, and intimacy (Ash, 1986). Performance in all areas of life does not have to diminish with age—particularly if people take care of themselves physically (Bronte, 1989).

Good health also implies being aware that some drugs may interfere with sexual performance. Alcohol is the most frequently used drug by American adults. Although a moderate amount of alcohol can help a person become aroused through a lowering of inhibitions, too much alcohol can slow the physiological processes and deaden the senses. Shakespeare may have said it best: ''It [alcohol] provokes the desire but it takes away the performance'' (Macbeth, Act II, Scene three). The result of the excessive intake of alcohol for women is a reduced chance of orgasm; for men, it is an increased chance of impotence.

The reactions to marijuana—a drug also used during sexual arousal—are less predictable than the reactions to alcohol. Some individuals report a short-term enhancement effect; others say that marijuana just makes them sleepy. In men, chronic use may decrease sex drive because marijuana may lower testosterone levels.

:: Sexual Fulfillment: Some Prerequisites

There are several prerequisites for having a good sexual relationship.

Self-Knowledge and Self-Esteem

Being sexually fulfilled implies having knowledge about yourself and your body. To be in touch with yourself and your own body is to know how you can best

Physically active people report having active sex lives.

experience sexual pleasure. "I've read all the books on how to get the most out of sex," said one man, "and I've concluded that the experts know a lot about what some people like sexually, but nothing about what *I* like. Good sex for me is more related to the context than to the technique. And I'm sure that for the next person it's something else."

Sexual fulfillment also implies having a positive self-concept. To the degree that you have good feelings about yourself, you will regard yourself as a person someone else would enjoy touching, being close to, and making love with. If you do not like yourself, you may wonder how anyone else would either.

A Good Relationship

A guideline among therapists who work with couples who have sexual problems is "Treat the relationship before focusing on the sexual issue." The sexual relationship is part of the larger relationship between the partners, and what happens outside the bedroom in day-to-day interaction has a tremendous influence on what happens inside the bedroom. The statement "I can't fight with you all day and want to have sex with you at night" illustrates the social context of the sexual experience.

The type of relationship the partners have may also be important. Two researchers observed that spouses who are androgynous (each person reflects a blend of masculine and feminine traits) in their sexual interaction report higher levels of sexual satisfaction (Rosenweig & Dailey, 1989).

So the effects of a couple's overall and sexual relationships are intertwined. According to an old adage, when sex goes well, it is 15 percent of a relationship, when it goes badly, it is 85 percent. Undoubtedly, many partners agree. The sexual relationship positively influences the couple's overall relationship in sev-

If you're not ready to get naked with your feelings, you're not ready to get naked with me.
—BLAZE STARR

Sex is not just intercourse but touching, closeness, and play.

eral ways: (1) as a shared pleasure, a positively reinforcing event; (2) by facilitating intimacy, as many couples feel closer and share their feelings before or after a sexual experience; and (3) by reducing tension generated by the stresses of everyday living and couple interaction (McCarthy, 1982).

☐   CONSIDERATION   ☐

Intercourse communicates how the partners are feeling and acts as a barometer for the relationship. Each partner brings to intercourse, sometimes unconsciously, a motive (pleasure, reconciliation, procreation, duty); a psychological state (love, hostility, boredom, excitement); and a physical state (tense, exhausted, relaxed, turned on). The combination of these factors will change from one encounter to another. Tonight the wife may feel aroused and loving and seek pleasure, but her husband may feel exhausted and hostile and only have intercourse out of a sense of duty.

continued on next page

Tomorrow night, both partners may feel relaxed and have intercourse as a means of expressing their love for each other.

The verbal and nonverbal communication preceding, during, and after intercourse also may act as a barometer for the relationship. One wife said:

I can tell how we're doing by whether or not we have intercourse and how he approaches me when we do. Sometimes he just rolls over when the lights are out and starts to rub my back. Other times, he plays with my face while we talk and kisses me and waits till I reach for him. And still other times, we each stay on our side of the bed so that our legs don't even touch.

Open Sexual Communication

Sexually fulfilled partners are comfortable expressing what they enjoy and do not enjoy in the sexual experience. Unless both partners communicate their needs, preferences, and expectations to each other, neither is ever sure what the other wants. In essence, the Golden Rule ("Do unto others as you would have them do unto you") is not helpful because what you like may not be the same as what your partner wants. A classic example of the uncertain lover is the man who picks up a copy of *The Erotic Lover* in a bookstore and leafs through the pages until the topic on how to please a woman catches his eye. He reads that women enjoy having their breasts stimulated by their partner's tongue and teeth. Later that night in bed, he rolls over and begins to nibble on his partner's breasts. Meanwhile, she wonders what has possessed him and is unsure what to make of this new (possibly unpleasant) behavior. Sexually fulfilled partners take the guesswork out of their relationship by communicating preferences and giving feedback. This means using what some therapists call the touch-and-ask rule. Each touch and caress may include the question "How does that feel?" It is then the partner's responsibility to give feedback. If the caress does not feel good, the partner can say what does feel good. Guiding and moving the partner's hand or body are also ways of giving feedback.

But open sexual communication is more than expressing sexual preferences and giving feedback. Women wish that men were more aware of a number of sexual issues. Some comments from students in the authors' classes follow:

- It does not impress women to hear about other women in the man's past.
- If men knew what it is like to be pregnant, they would not be so apathetic about birth control.
- Most women want more caressing, gentleness, kissing, and talking *before* and *after* intercourse.
- Some women are sexually attracted to other women, not to men.
- Sometimes the woman wants sex even if the man does not. Sometimes she wants to be aggressive without being made to feel that she shouldn't be.
- Intercourse can be enjoyable without a climax.
- Many women do not have an orgasm from penetration only; they need direct stimulation of their clitoris by their partner's tongue or finger. Men should be interested in fulfilling their partner's sexual needs.
- Most women prefer to have sex in a monogamous love relationship.
- When a woman says "no," she means it. Women do not want men to expect sex every time they are alone with their partner.

Good communication is as stimulating as black coffee, and just as hard to sleep after.

—ANNE MORROW LINDBERGH

- Many women enjoy sex in the morning, not just at night.
- Sex is *not* everything.
- Women need to be lubricated before penetration.
- Men should know more about menstruation.
- Many women are no more inhibited about sex than men.
- Women do not like men to roll over, go to sleep, or leave right after orgasm.
- Intercourse is more of a love relationship than a sex act for some women.
- The woman should not always be expected to supply a method of contraception. It is also the man's responsibility.
- Women tend to like a loving, gentle, patient, tender, and understanding partner. Rough sexual play can hurt and be a turnoff.
- Men should know that all women are not alike in what pleases them sexually.

Men also have a list of things they wish women knew about sex:

- Men do not always want to be the dominant partner; women should be aggressive.
- Men want women to enjoy sex totally and not be inhibited.
- Men enjoy tender and passionate kissing.
- Men really enjoy fellatio.
- Women need to know a man's erogenous zones.
- Oral sex is good and enjoyable, not bad and unpleasant.
- Many men enjoy a lot of romantic foreplay and slow, aggressive sex.
- Men cannot keep up intercourse forever. Most men tire more easily than women.
- Looks are not everything.
- Women should know how to enjoy sex in different ways and different positions.
- Women should not expect a man to get a second erection right away.
- Many men enjoy sex in the morning.
- Pulling the hair on a man's body can hurt.
- Many men enjoy sex in a caring, loving, exclusive relationship.
- It is frustrating to stop sex play once it has started.
- Women should know that all men are not out to have intercourse with them. Some men like to talk and become friends.

Realistic Expectations

To achieve sexual fulfillment, expectations must be realistic. A couple's sexual needs, preferences, and expectations may not coincide. It is unrealistic to assume that your partner will want to have sex with the same frequency and in the same way that you do on all occasions. It may also be unrealistic to expect the level of sexual interest and frequency of intercourse in long-term relationships to remain consistently high.

□   C O N S I D E R A T I O N   □

Sexual fulfillment means not asking things of the sexual relationship that it cannot deliver. Failure to develop realistic expectations will result in frustration and resentment.

A Healthy Attitude Toward Sex

Sexual fulfillment also depends on having a positive attitude toward sex. Incestuous or traumatic sexual experiences may create an intense negative attitude toward sex. Any sexual advance or contact can cause the individual to become anxious and engender the desire to escape or avoid the situation. Such negative reactions to sex are best dealt with through therapy.

The best way to hold a
man is in your arms.

—MAE WEST

Creativity

Couples who have an active sex life report that they have a range of ways to enhance the experience. The use of different positions, erotic clothes, and contexts (beach, bathtub, table) are examples. X-rated videos are also used by couples who rent the video and watch it on a VCR in their bedroom. Thirty percent of women in one study reported that an X-rated video had been used as a prelude to sexual intercourse (Lawrence & Herold, 1989).

■■ Female Sexual Dysfunctions

It is not uncommon for couples who are very satisfied with their relationship to have one or more sexual problems. Sex therapists refer to such problems as *sexual dysfunctions*. The existence of a sexual dysfunction implies that the partners want something to happen that is not happening (for example, orgasm) or want to stop something from happening that is happening (for example, vaginismus). In this section, we will examine lack of sexual desire, inability to achieve orgasm, pain during intercourse (dyspareunia), and inability to control constrictions of the vagina (vaginismus) as the major sexual dysfunctions among women.

□   C O N S I D E R A T I O N   □

Although we will discuss treatments for both female and male sexual dysfunctions in this chapter, these discussions are not a replacement for sex therapy. We recommend that partners experiencing sexual problems for a prolonged period of time who have been unable to resolve the concerns themselves consider consulting a marriage and family therapist or a sex therapist. The name of a certified sex therapist in your area can be located by calling 312–644–0828 or by writing to the American Association of Sex Educators, Counselors, and Therapists (435 North Michigan Avenue, Suite 1717, Chicago, IL 60611).

Lack of Sexual Desire

The person who lacks sexual desire—a problem also referred to as *inhibited sexual desire*—never initiates sexual activity and is rarely receptive to another who does (see Sex Interest Scale in the Self-Assessment section).

Lack of sexual desire may be primary (the person has never been interested in sex) or secondary (the person has demonstrated interest in sex with the same or a different partner in the past, but does not do so presently). Several reasons may account for a lack of sexual desire or low libido in women.

SELF ASSESSMENT

Sex Interest Scale

This scale is designed to assess the degree to which you have a low or high interest in sexual activity. There are no right or wrong answers. After reading each sentence carefully, circle the appropriate number.

1 Strongly Disagree
2 Mildly Disagree
3 Uncertain
4 Mildly Agree
5 Strongly Agree

	SD	MD	U	MA	SA
1. I think about sex often.	1	2	3	4	5
2. Others have told me that I like sex.	1	2	3	4	5
3. Masturbation is pleasurable.	1	2	3	4	5
4. I talk about sex often.	1	2	3	4	5
5. My partner feels that I am interested in sex.	1	2	3	4	5
6. I orgasm most of the time I have sex.	1	2	3	4	5
7. Sex is an important part of intimate relationships.	1	2	3	4	5
8. I like to have sex in different ways.	1	2	3	4	5
9. I sometimes wish I were having more sex than I am.	1	2	3	4	5
10. I think I am a good sexual partner.	1	2	3	4	5

SCORING: Add the numbers you circled. 1 (strongly disagree) represents a low interest in sex, and 5 (strongly agree) represents a high interest in sex. The lower your total score (10 is the lowest possible score), the lower your interest in sex. The higher your total score (50 is the highest possible score), the higher your interest in sex. A score of 30 places you at the midpoint between having no interest and a great deal of interest in sex.

(NOTE: This Self-Assessment is intended to be thought provoking and fun. It is not intended to be used as a clinical diagnostic instrument).

Relationship Dissatisfaction. It is important that the woman feel an emotional bond with her sex partner if she is to enjoy a satisfactory sex life with that person (Talmadge & Talmadge, 1986). Women who do not love or who have hostile feelings for their partners may not want to have any sexual encounter with their partners.

Restrictive Childrearing. The unresponsive woman may have been told as a child that sexual stimulation and sexual pleasure were sinful and dirty. As a result, she has learned to feel guilty and ashamed about her sexual feelings.

Passive Sexual Role. The woman with low libido has often been taught to be a passive and dependent sexual partner. The silent message of her socialization has been that women are not supposed to be sexual. Because sexual abandonment is incompatible with the passive feminine role, she does not permit herself to become sexually excited.

Physical Factors. Disease, drugs, fatigue, and infection may also erase a person's sexual responsiveness. A doctor said, "After I work the night shift at the hospital, sex is the last thing in the world I'm interested in. And when my partner touches me, I just have to tell him the truth—I'm not interested."

Sex therapy for low libido in a woman may involve rest and relaxation, reeducation, improving the relationship with her partner, the use of sensate focus, and masturbation or hormones. Reeducation includes systematically examining the thoughts, feelings, and attitudes the woman was taught as a child and reevaluating them. The goal is to redefine sexual involvement, so that it is viewed as a positive, desirable, pleasurable experience. Reeducation also means discarding the belief that one must feel interest in sex before one can engage in it. Rather, the therapist recommends that the woman become involved in sexual activity first. The premise is that "you can act yourself into a new way of thinking quicker than you can think your way into a new way of acting."

☐　　　　C O N S I D E R A T I O N　　　　☐

The woman's relationship with her partner may be central to her level of sexual desire and enjoyment. Is there trust, respect, and emotional closeness in the relationship? Unless the relationship with her partner is loving and reciprocal, gains in increasing sexual responsiveness may be minimal.

The woman and her partner are also encouraged to practice sensate focus exercises (see Figure 11.3). Introduced more than 25 years ago by Masters and Johnson, sensate focus is the mutual exploration and discovery of the partners through touch, massage, fondling, or tracing. Specific guidelines for the exercises include the following: (1) both partners are nude; (2) the partners are not to have intercourse or touch each other's genitals or breasts; (3) one partner is to give pleasure by touching and gently massaging the other; (4) the other partner is to pay attention to the pleasurable feelings of being touched and gently massaged and to let the first partner know when he or she does something that is or is not pleasurable; and (5) the partners are to switch roles, so that each gives and gets sensual pleasure. Sensate focus creates an environment in which the woman is permitted to explore her sexual feelings without having to perform for her partner.

The woman may be encouraged to masturbate—a suggestion also made to women who have difficulty climaxing. Some physicians recommend testosterone to increase a woman's interest in sex. Although unwanted facial hair may occur in 10—15 percent of the cases, it may heighten a woman's libido.

Finally, fantasy—one's own private video—can be a powerful aphrodisiac. Women who do not have sexual fantasies or who report feeling guilty about having them report higher levels of sexual dissatisfaction (Cado and Leitenberg,

■■ FIGURE 11.3
Sensate Focus

SOURCE: *Human Sexual Inadequacy* by William H. Masters and Virginia E. Johnson. Published by Little, Brown, and Company, Boston, Mass.: 1966, p. 300. Reprinted by permission.

1990). Individuals who have little sexual desire are encouraged to explore those fantasies which engender erotic feelings. These fantasies may focus on emotional as well as sexual encounters.

Inability to Achieve Orgasm

| ■ **DATA:** *Out of 365 college educated women, 13 percent said they had never experienced orgasm (Coleman et al., 1983).*

Masters and Johnson characterize women who have never had an orgasm as having *primary orgasmic dysfunction* (also known as *primary anorgasmia* or *preorgasm*). Those who have had an orgasm by any other means at any time in the past but who are unable to do so currently are regarded as having *secondary orgasmic dysfunction* (also known as *secondary anorgasmia*).

Some of the causes of inability to achieve orgasm are similar to the causes of lack of sexual interest (restrictive childrearing, passive sexual role, and so on). Other causes are included in the following sections.

Focusing on Partner. Many women have been taught to feel it is their duty to satisfy their partners sexually. But having an orgasm requires that a woman focus on the sexual sensations she is experiencing. If a woman is overly intent on pleasing her partner, she may do so at the expense of her own orgasm.

> Too much of a good thing can be wonderful.
> —MAE WEST

Negative Feelings about Mate. If the woman is angry at her partner or feels that he is using her sexually, she may "withhold" having an orgasm. "If I have an orgasm, he'll think I'm having a good time and really enjoying him," said one woman. "I wouldn't give him that kind of pleasure. I'm very mad at my partner now because I just found out he has been seeing other women when I'm not around."

Negative Feelings about Sexuality. When anorgasmic and orgasmic women were compared, the former had greater sex guilt and negative attitudes toward masturbation. They also believed in more sex myths and were uncomfortable talking with their partner about sex (Kelly et al., 1990).

Too Little Stimulation. The duration of stimulation is associated with whether a woman climaxes. In a study of about 1,000 wives, two-fifths reported climaxing after one to 10 minutes of foreplay. When foreplay lasted 21 minutes or more, three-fifths reported climaxing almost every time (Brewer, 1981). Similarly, the longer her husband's penis stayed erect and inside her, the greater the wife's chance of having an orgasm during intercourse. If penetration was one minute, one-fourth reported orgasm; between one and 11 minutes, one-half reported climax. If penetration lasted more than 15 minutes, two-thirds reported climax. A woman's orgasm is also related to how accurately her partner is aware of what gives her sexual pleasure (Kilmann et al., 1984).

Fear of Letting Go. Some women feel it would be too embarrassing to lose control in an orgasmic experience, so they deliberately block their sexual arousal.

Too Much Alcohol. While moderate drinking of alcohol (one or two mixed drinks) may induce relaxation and increase sexual arousal, heavy drinking has a depressant effect on the woman's orgasmic response.

Too Little Self-Knowledge. Some women have not discovered the kinds of stimulation that produce orgasm either through masturbation or with a partner. Most women report that stimulation on or around the clitoris is necessary for them to achieve orgasm.

Too High Expectations. Some women feel they should have an orgasm during every sexual encounter and that not doing so is evidence that they are not normal. Such expectations produce a great deal of anxiety, which blocks the ability of these women to have an orgasm even though they may try desperately to do so. It is sometimes helpful if the woman does not focus on orgasm as something to achieve but focuses on the pleasure of the moment.

Because the causes for primary and secondary orgasmic dysfunction are extremely variable, the treatment must be tailored to the particular woman. We have already discussed the use of sensate focus exercises to encourage a woman to explore her sexual feelings and to increase her comfort with her partner. In addition, the therapist may recommend that the woman masturbate to orgasm. Such self-stimulation provides direct feedback to the woman of the type of stimulation she enjoys, eliminates the distraction of a partner, and gives her complete control of the stimulation.

Sex therapists are reasonably successful in treating secondary orgasmic dysfunctions.

> ■ **DATA:** *A total of 289 sex therapists in the United States say they have successfully treated 56 percent of their secondary orgasmic dysfunction cases (Kilmann et al., 1986).*

After the woman has learned how to bring herself to orgasm through masturbation, she is encouraged to teach her partner how to stimulate her manually to orgasm first, while not having intercourse. Finally, if the partners prefer, the woman is taught how to have an orgasm during intercourse by using the "bridge method":

> The couple make love until the woman is aroused. Then the man penetrates, either in the female superior position or one of the variations of the side-to-side position. Then, with the penis contained, the man (or the woman) stimulates the woman's clitoris. When she nears orgasm, clitoral stimulation ceases at her signal, and the couple commence thrusting actively to bring about her orgasm (Kaplan, 1974, 138).

Pain During Intercourse

Pain during intercourse, or *dyspareunia,* occurs in about 10 percent of gynecological patients and may be caused by vaginal infection, lack of lubrication, a rigid hymen, or an improperly positioned uterus or ovary. Because the causes of dyspareunia are often medical, a physician should be consulted. Sometimes surgery is recommended to remove the hymen.

Dyspareunia may also be psychologically caused. Guilt, anxiety, or unresolved feelings about a previous trauma, such as rape or childhood molestation, may be operative. Therapy may be indicated.

Vaginismus

A less common sexual dysfunction in which the vaginal opening and outer third of the canal constricts involuntarily, making penetration impossible, is known as *vaginismus.* Like anorgasmia, vaginismus may be primary or secondary (Shortle & Jewelewicz, 1986). Primary vaginismus means that the vaginal muscles have always constricted to prevent penetration of any object, including tampons. Secondary vaginismus, the more usual variety, suggests that the vagina has permitted penetration in the past but currently constricts when penetration is imminent.

Vaginismus is most often found in women whose background has included traditional religious teachings suggesting that intercourse is dirty and shameful. Other background factors include rape, incest, repeated childhood molestation, or organic difficulties. Examples of the last are a poorly healed episiotomy (an incision in the perineum to prevent injury to the vagina during childbirth), a poorly stretched hymen, infections or sores near the vaginal opening, or a sexually transmitted disease. The woman who fears pain during penetration will try to avoid it, sometimes unconsciously.

Assuming that vaginismus is not caused by an organic or physical problem (for which a physician should be consulted), the treatment is first to have the woman introduce her index finger into her vagina while she relaxes. Then two fingers are introduced into the vagina, and this exercise is repeated until she feels relaxed enough to contain the penis. Once the woman learns that she is capable of vaginal containment of the penis, she is usually able to have intercourse without difficulty. Of course, therapy focusing on the woman's cognitions and perceptions about sex and sexuality with her particular partner precedes the finger exercises.

Another problem that some women experience is premenstrual syndrome. Although premenstrual syndrome is not a sexual dysfunction, it can be problematic for some women and their relationships with their sexual partners (see Exhibit 11.1).

■■ Male Sexual Dysfunctions

Sexual dysfunctions may also be experienced by male individuals. Men may experience sexual apathy, inability to achieve and maintain an erection (erectile dysfunction), inability to delay ejaculation as long as they or their partners would like (premature ejaculation), or inability to ejaculate at all (ejaculatory incompetence).

Sexual Apathy (Inhibited Sexual Desire)

It is a myth that men are always ready for sex. Some are apathetic or completely uninterested. "I just don't have any desire for sex," said one man. "And if I never have to do it again, I'll feel relieved."

There are many causes for a low sex drive in men: negative feelings about the partner, hormonal insufficiency, career fatigue, fear of parenthood, terror of intimacy, drugs, and a "too aggressive partner." In addition, the cultural expectation that men are always interested in sex may threaten a man's feelings of masculinity. Treatment for sexual apathy among men often begins with giving them permission not to be interested in sex. The therapist tells the male client not to masturbate or have intercourse until the next session. Then the contributing factors are explored.

Erectile Dysfunction

Erectile dysfunction, also known as *impotence,* is the lack or loss of an erection firm enough for intercourse, which may occur during foreplay, the moment of pene-

EXHIBIT 11.1

Premenstrual Syndrome

Also known as PMS, premenstrual syndrome refers to the physical and psychological problems some women experience from the time of ovulation to the beginning of, and sometimes during, menstruation. There are a number of symptoms, which may include the following:

Psychological
   Tension
   Depression
   Irritability
   Lethargy
   Altered sex drive
   Excessive energy

Neurological
   Migraine
   Epilepsy

Respiratory
   Asthma
   Rhinitis

Dermatological
   Acne
   Herpes

Orthopedic
   Joint pains
   Backaches

Physical
   Weight gain (due to increased appetite and water retention)
   Breast tenderness

But it is the experience of the woman that makes the syndrome real. Alice A., a 35-year-old housewife and mother, is usually a friendly and productive person, but two weeks out of each month she is overwhelmed by extreme irritability, tension, and depression.

It's as if my mind can't keep up with my body. I cook things to put in the freezer, clean, wash windows, work in the yard—anything to keep busy. My mind is saying slow down, but my body won't quit. When I go to bed at night, I'm exhausted. And everything gets on my nerves—the phone ringing, birds singing—everything! My skin feels prickly, my back hurts, and my face feels so tight that it's painful. I scream at my husband over ridiculous things like asking for a clean pair of socks. I hate myself even when I'm doing it, but I have no control. I can't stand being around people, and the only way I can even be civil at parties is to have several drinks.

This lasts for about a week, and then I wake up one morning feeling as if the bottom has dropped out of my life. It's as if something awful is going to happen, but I don't know what it is and I don't know how to stop it. I don't even have the energy to make the beds. Every movement is an effort.

I burst out crying for no reason at crazy times, like when I'm fixing breakfast or grocery shopping. My husband thinks I'm angry with him, and I can't explain what's wrong because I don't know myself. After about four days of fighting off the depression, I just give up, take the phone off the hook, and stay in bed. It's terrifying. I feel panicky—trapped.

Then one morning I wake up and suddenly feel like myself. The sun is shining, and I like life again.*

Between 5 and 10 percent of women experience PMS to the degree that Alice does. Some people have attributed instances of child abuse, alcoholism, divorce, and suicide to PMS. Recently, two British women introduced PMS as part of their legal defense for murder.

Other women experience a milder form of PMS, including different symptoms in varying degrees. But because more than 150 symptoms have been associated with PMS, there is little agreement about when a person is experiencing the phenomenon. The only agreement on premenstrual syndrome seems to be that the individual's specific symptoms occur together at regular intervals.

There also is no agreement on the causes of PMS and even less agreement on the cure. Hormones, diet, and culture are among the suggested causes. Some physicians treat the woman with PMS as though it is all in her head and will go away in a few days. Others view the problem as an imbalance of hormones and prescribe progesterone. Still others focus on nutrition and exercise. Diet changes include eliminating alcohol, sugar, salt, and caffeine. Eating several small meals every two to four hours is also suggested.

Increasingly, PMS is being recognized as a legitimate set of symptoms that require treatment. The Premenstrual Syndrome Clinic in Reading, Massachusetts, has treated more than 1,000 women. The clinic's approach to therapy is multidimensional, including diet, exercise, vitamins, and progesterone (if necessary). The clinic also assists women in diagnosing PMS and demonstrating its impact on their lives. Such diagnosis is facilitated by getting women to chart their physiological and psychological reactions as they progress through their cycles.

tration, or intercourse. Generally, a man who cannot get an erection feels humiliated and embarrassed.

Like some female sexual dysfunctions, erectile dysfunction may be primary (the man has never been able to have intercourse) or secondary (he is currently unable to have intercourse). Erectile dysfunction may also be situational. The man can get an erection in one situation (say, through masturbation) but not in another (such as intercourse). Occasional, isolated episodes of the inability to get an erection do not warrant the label of erectile dysfunction, nor is treatment necessary.

Primary or secondary impotence may be caused by organic or psychosocial (psychogenic) factors. Organic factors include endocrine malfunctions like diabetes, low testosterone levels, neurological disorders like multiple sclerosis, and medications, such as those for high blood pressure. In addition, venous leakage has been shown to be a major cause of erectile dysfunction.

■ **DATA:** *In a study of 44 men complaining of impotence, 68 percent showed a failure to trap blood in the penis to make it become erect (Rajfer et al., 1988).*

If organic causes are suspected, a urological examination by a physician is indicated.

If there is an organic problem, one alternative is a penile implant, which consists of either semirigid rods of silicone rubber that are surgically inserted into the penis to make it hard, resulting in a permanent semierection, or inflatable cylinders implanted in the penis. Although most males are satisfied with the result, it is important to assess the partner's attitude toward the prosthesis, the couple's relationship, and previous sexual frequency. Failure to consider these issues could result in a negative outcome for a penile implant (Meisler et al., 1988).

More often, particularly in the young male, erectile dysfunction is caused by psychological factors such as anxiety. Some relationships are particularly conducive to creating a problem with impotence. The woman makes it clear to the man that she expects him to have an erection and to have intercourse with her. Although some men find such an expectation to be a welcome situation, the man who has been impotent in the past begins to fear that he will not be able to get an erection and satisfy her. His anxiety about performing and his fear of her disapproval if he fails help to ensure that he will not get an erection. What follows is a devastating cycle of negative experiences locking the man into impotence at each sexual encounter: anxiety, impotence, embarrassment, followed by anxiety, impotence, and so on.

The man also has his own ideas of how he is supposed to perform as a male. Even if the partner is sympathetic and supportive, it may be his own self-imposed performance demands that create the anxiety that interfere with achieving an erection.

Anxiety may also be related to alcohol use. After more than the usual number of drinks, the man may initiate sex but fail to achieve an erection. He becomes anxious and struggles even more to get an erection, ensuring that he will not. Although alcohol may be responsible for his initial failure, his impotence continues because of his anxiety. Erectile dysfunction may also be associated with guilt. The man who is having an extra-partner sexual relationship may feel guilty. This guilt may lead to difficulty in achieving or maintaining an erection in sexual interaction with the primary partner.

Treatment for erectile dysfunction of psychosocial origin begins with the instruction that the couple not have intercourse. If there is no expectation for intercourse, the associated anxiety is minimized. The therapist then discusses with the couple how anxiety (and alcohol, if this is an issue) inhibits erection. The purpose of this information is to help the partners understand the man's erectile dysfunction rather than continue to be mystified by its occurrence.

The partners are also instructed to begin sensate focus exercises, and the man is encouraged to give pleasure to his partner through manual or oral stimulation. After several sensate focus sessions, during which there is no pressure to perform and the man learns alternative ways to pleasure his partner, he is more likely to have an erection.

But suppose the man cannot get and maintain an erection because he is anxious and has no sexual partner with whom to work on the problem? Or suppose the man has organically caused impotence and does not want a penile implant? One new alternative suggested by some sex therapists is Papavarine, a drug injected into the base of the penis to increase blood flow. Papavarine produces a sustained erection of from 45 minutes to three hours (Sidi et al., 1986). In some cases, another shot of a different drug is necessary to reduce the erection. The primary side effects are risk of infection and dependency on the shot to perform.

■ **DATA:** *Forty-six percent of patients who were given the option of using the injection method to resolve their erectile dysfunction either did not do so or discontinued doing so within two years. Reasons included an unwillingness to inject themselves and an intolerance of the side effects (Althof et al., 1989).*

Premature Ejaculation

Premature ejaculation, also known As *rapid ejaculation,* is the man's inability to control the ejaculatory reflex. Most men report times that they ejaculate too quickly. However, whether a man ejaculates too soon is a matter of definition, depending on his and his partner's desires. Some partners define a rapid ejaculation in positive terms. One woman said she felt pleased that her partner was so excited by her that he "couldn't control himself." Another said, "The sooner we get it over with, the better."

One cause of premature ejaculation lies in early learning experiences. Some men who ejaculate sooner than they want to report that their early masturbation and intercourse experiences were hurried. They felt pressure to ejaculate as soon as they could. One example is the male who had to masturbate quickly before his parents could discover what he was doing. Regardless of the reason, most males ejaculate relatively quickly.

■ **DATA:** *One researcher reported that the average duration of intercourse before ejaculation in men is two minutes (Hong, 1984).*

Use of the squeeze technique, developed by Masters and Johnson, is the most effective procedure for treating premature ejaculation. The woman stimulates her partner's penis manually until he signals her that he feels the urge to ejaculate. At his signal, she places her thumb on the underside of his penis and squeezes hard for three to four seconds. The man will lose his urge to ejaculate. After 30 seconds, she resumes stimulation, applying the squeeze technique again when her partner signals. The important rule to remember is that the woman should apply the squeeze technique whenever the man gives the slightest hint of readiness to ejaculate. (The squeeze technique can also be used by the man during masturbation to teach himself to delay his ejaculation.)

Another method in increasing the delay of ejaculation is for the man to ejaculate often. In general, the greater the number of ejaculations a male has in one 24-hour period, the longer he will be able to delay each subsequent ejaculation.

Medications have also been used to help men delay ejaculation. In a study of five males who took clomipramine, all ''reported significant delays and heightened control of ejaculation with a small nighttime dose'' (Assalian, 1988). Since ejaculation is dependent on the sympathetic component of the autonomic nervous system, clomipramine's effectiveness results from its ability to inhibit receptors in this area. Minor side effects include sleepiness, a dry mouth, and a tendency toward constipation.

The problem resulting from premature ejaculation is that the woman often does not have sufficient time to become aroused and have an orgasm before the man ejaculates. One way of dealing with this problem is for the man to work on delaying ejaculation, as we have already discussed. In addition, the man may devote more time to arousing his partner before intercourse. Such foreplay may be in the form of kissing, breast stimulation, and genital stimulation using the mouth, fingers, or vibrator. Alternatively, the man may use these same foreplay techniques to help his partner achieve orgasm after he has ejaculated. These techniques may be used in combination with the female stimulating herself. Another possibility is that the man may regain his erection and the couple may have intercourse again. Subsequent ejaculations usually involve longer ejaculatory delays.

Ejaculatory Incompetence

In contrast to the man who experiences rapid ejaculation, the man who experiences *ejaculatory incompetence* cannot ejaculate at all, even after prolonged stimulation. Also referred to as *retarded ejaculation, absence of ejaculation,* or *inhibited ejaculation,* ejaculatory incompetence may be primary or secondary. Primary ejaculatory incompetence describes the man who has never achieved orgasm and ejaculation. Secondary ejaculatory incompetence, the more common form, refers to the man's current inability to orgasm and ejaculate. It is not unusual for ejaculatory incompetence to be situational; it may occur with one partner but not another or with the same partner on one occasion but not on another.

☐   C O N S I D E R A T I O N   ☐

Most causes of ejaculatory incompetence are psychological. For example, one husband reported that for 33 years his wife would not let him ejaculate inside of her because she did not want to get pregnant. As a result, he learned to prolong his orgasm and to take his penis out of her vagina before ejaculating. After his wife's menopause, she wanted him to ejaculate inside of her but he could not

---

Lack of sexual excitement and feeling that the vagina is a disgusting place to ejaculate are other psychological causes of ejaculatory incompetence.

Treatment for psychologically based ejaculatory incompetence consists of exploring the emotions and cognitions that interfere with ejaculation. Some of the psychological issues that may be explored include negative attitudes toward sex, sex organs, the partner, or one's self. Fear of pregnancy, anxiety, and guilt may also interfere with a man's ability to orgasm and ejaculate.

:: Extramarital Encounters

Aside from specific performance problems, it is unusual when a relationship is not affected in some way by extramarital concerns. In this section, we review the definition, types, and motivations for extramarital involvements. Extramarital intercourse refers to having intercourse, while married, with someone other than one's own spouse.

> ■ **DATA:** *Studies differ on the extent of extramarital encounters. Seventy-three percent of the respondents in a British study reported that they had had extramarital intercourse (Lawson, 1988). In a review of the literature of extramarital intercourse, Thompson (1983) concluded that half of all husbands and wives have at least one extramarital intercourse experience. In regard to guilt, when asked if extramarital sex is always wrong or almost always wrong, 88 percent of adult women under 30 and 85 percent of adult men under 30 agreed (Thornton, 1989).*

All extramarital encounters are not alike.

Types of Extramarital Encounters

Extramarital intercourse may involve a brief encounter, a full-blown affair, or an event shared with the spouse.

The Brief Encounter. The lyrics to the song, "Strangers in the Night" describe two people exchanging glances who end up having intercourse "before the night is through." Although the partners may see each other again, their sexual encounter is a "one-night stand" more often than not.

It's hard for an old rake
to turn over a new leaf.
—LAURENCE PETER

> ■ **DATA:** *In one study, 28 percent of the men and 5 percent of the women said their last extramarital encounter was a one-night stand (Spanier & Margolis, 1983).*

The Affair. An extramarital affair implies an emotional and sexual relationship in which at least one of the partners is married. The various combinations of partners include married women-single men, married men-married women, and married men-single women. Single women may be increasingly willing to have affairs with married men not only because single men are scarce, but also because a relationship with a married man requires less commitment and leaves more time for the single woman to devote to her career. Single women are primarily motivated by the emotional attraction to the married man, but usually do not envision being married to the man they have an affair with. One single woman remarked:

Where else could I have exactly what I want from a relationship? I have my freedom and my own life separate from my life with him. I have certain wants and he meets those, and on my terms (Trotter, 1989, 215).

Intense reciprocal emotional feelings characterize most affairs. Such feelings are more a function of the conditions under which the relationship exists than any magical matching of the partners involved. For one thing, the time together is very limited. Like teenagers in love who are restricted by their parents, adult lovers are restricted by their spouses and other family responsibilities. Such limited access makes the time they spend together very special. In addition, the lover is not associated with the struggles of marriage—bills, children, housecleaning—and so is viewed in a more romantic setting.

Swinging. In the traditional affair, one or both of the spouses has intercourse with someone outside the marriage without the partner's knowledge. *Swinging,* also referred to as *comarital sex,* is another form of extramarital intercourse in which the spouses of one marriage or pair-bonded relationship have sexual relations with the spouses or partners of another relationship. Swinging differs from an affair in that it implies no deception (both partners are aware of the extramarital encounter) and both partners (rather than one) are usually involved. When 35 swinging couples were compared with 35 married couples who did not engage in swinging, the former group reported greater satisfaction with their marital sexual relationship. The researchers (Wheeler & Kilmann, 1983) commented:

> Thus, for comarital couples, engaging in recreational sexual activities with outside partners apparently does not interfere with each member's perception of a positive marital sexual relationship; for these couples, it may be that their marital sexual relationship is enhanced by agreed-on sexual contact with outside partners. This may not be the case for couple members who engage in covert extramarital sexual relationships, often as an "escape" from a dysfunctional marital relationship (p. 304).

Motivations for Extramarital Involvements

There are a number of reasons why spouses have intercourse with someone other than their mate. Some of these reasons are discussed here.

Variety. One of the characteristics of marital sex is the tendency for it to become routine. Before marriage, the partners cannot seem to get enough of each other. But with constant availability, the attractiveness and excitement of intercourse seems to wane.

The Coolidge Effect helps to explain the need for sexual variety:

> One day the President and Mrs. Coolidge were visiting a government farm. Soon after their arrival, they were taken off on separate tours. When Mrs. Coolidge passed the chicken pens, she paused to ask the man in charge if the rooster copulates more than once each day, "Dozens of times" was the reply. "Please tell that to the President," Mrs. Coolidge requested. When the President passed the pens and was told about the rooster, he asked, "Same hen every time?" "Oh no, Mr. President, a different one each time." The President nodded slowly and then said, "Tell that to Mrs. Coolidge" (Bermant, 1976).

Men seem more motivated by the desire for sexual variety than women.

I regret that I wasn't constituted, as some men are, to stay with one woman.

—JOHN HUSTON

■ **DATA:** *Some research suggests that twice as many men have extramarital intercourse for sex only (without an emotional component) than women (Thompson, 1984).*

☐ CONSIDERATION ☐

One sociobiologist (Symons, 1979) suggests an evolutionary reason for men having a greater desire for sexual variety than women. The male who achieved the greatest reproductive success—who had the most surviving progeny—would be the one who impregnated the greatest number of females. On the other hand, reproductive success for the female depended on mating with the most fit male to ensure that her offspring would have the greatest possible chance of survival. She did not need a variety of partners.

Friendship. Some people view intercourse outside their marriage as a natural consequence of a developing relationship. "It's not that I'm crazy about sex; it's just that I enjoy relationships with other men, and sex is only a part of that," is an expression that typifies this feeling. Such relationships usually develop when people work together. They share the same world 8–10 hours a day and over a period of time may develop good feelings for each other that eventually lead to a sexual relationship. As the interaction between David and Maddie on the hit television series, "Moonlighting" illustrates, flirting, friendship, and sometimes emotional attachment may develop out of a working relationship.

Apathetic or Unwilling Spouse. Some spouses have affairs because their partner is not interested in sex. "He doesn't like sex and never has," remarked one wife. "And it frustrates me beyond description to have intercourse with him when I know it's just a duty to him. So I've found someone who likes sex and likes it with me."

Although a spouse's lack of interest in intercourse is often a reason for an affair, some go outside the marriage because their spouses will not engage in other sexual behaviors they want and enjoy. The unwillingness of the spouse to engage in oral sex, anal intercourse, or sexual positions like rear entry sometimes results in the partner looking elsewhere for satisfaction.

Unhappy Marriage. It is commonly believed that people who have affairs are not happy in their marriage, but this is more likely to be true of wives than of husbands. Men who have affairs are usually not "dissatisfied with the quality of their marriage or their sex life with their wife" (Yablonsky, 1979), 15). Rather, men seem to seek extramarital relationships as an additional life experience.

Most wives "appear to seek extramarital sex when they experience some deficit—sexual, emotional, or, perhaps, economic—in their marriage, or perceive another man as being superior to (not merely different from) their husbands" (Symons, 1979, 238). Although trapped in a bad marriage, they may not want a divorce. "So they turn to an affair or a series of them as a means of treading water, keeping the marriage afloat for the time being until their children grow up or they (the wives) earn a degree, etc." (Schaefer, 1981).

You are only young once, but if you do it right—once is enough.
—LAURENCE PETER

Aging. A frequent motive for intercourse outside of marriage is the desire to reexperience the world of youth. Our society promotes the idea that it is good to be young and bad to be old. Sexual attractiveness is equated with youth, and having an affair may confirm to an older partner that he or she is still sexually desirable. Also, people may try to recapture the love, excitement, adventure, and romance associated with youth by having an affair. For some, it is viewed as the last opportunity to be young again.

One writer (Gordon, 1988) interviewed men who had left their wives for a younger woman. These men focused not on the physical youth of their partners, but on the youthful attitude of their new partners—the openness, innocence, unscarred emotions. They also emphasized the uncritical love they felt from their younger partner. Gordon labeled these men as having *Jennifer Fever*—they had developed a pattern of denying the aging process by seeking a youthful partner to create the illusion that they were not getting older. She further warned that they would seek another "Jennifer" as the current one aged. She pointed to the marriages of Benjamin Spock and Mary Morgan (41 years difference), Hugh Hefner and Kim (37 years difference) and John Derek and Bo Derek (30 years difference) as evidence for the existence of Jennifer Fever.

Absence from Spouse. Circumstances have more to do with some extramarital relationships than specific motives. One factor that predisposes a person to an extramarital encounter is prolonged separation from the spouse, which may make the partner particularly vulnerable to other involvements. Some wives whose husbands are away for military service report that the loneliness can become unbearable. Some husbands who are away say that it is difficult to be faithful. "You've almost got to be a saint to get through two years of not having intercourse if you're going to be faithful to your spouse," one air force captain said. "Most of the guys I'm stationed with don't even try."

Sexual Addictions

Having extramarital encounters may be related to the larger issue of sexual addictions.

■ **DATA:** *About 6 percent of Americans are sexual addicts (Sexual Addiction Survey, 1988).*

Sexual addictions are categorized according to two levels:

Level 1: Sexual behaviors that are viewed negatively, but are nevertheless tolerated by society—compulsive masturbation frequently combined with excessive expenditure on pornography, prostitutes, affairs, and anonymous homosexual sexual encounters.

Level 2: Sexual behaviors which are nuisance crimes such as voyeurism, exhibitionism, and frottage.

Sexual addicts, like other addicts, typically believe that they are not worthwhile, that no one would love them for themselves, and that the object of their addiction is their most important need (Carnes, 1983).

In a study of 50 married couples who identified themselves as a sexual addict and coaddict, treatment involved the addict giving up sex for 1 to 3 months (including masturbation) to provide an opportunity to learn that sex is optional and to learn how to relate in nonsexual intimacy (Schneider, 1989). The partner (coaddict) must learn how to trust the sexual addict again via building his or her own self-confidence and not centering life around the addict. Couple and individual therapy is suggested for the sexual addict and partner. For help and information, sexual addicts may contact the National Association for Sexual Addiction Problems, NASAP, P.O. Box 696, Manhattan Beach, CA 90266.

⁞⁞ Sexual Enrichment Programs

It is not unusual for couples who have a good relationship and who are not experiencing any specific sexual dysfunctions to attend a sexual enrichment program designed to further enhance their sexual relationship. One such program, Enhancing Marital Sexuality, consists of 11 hours (seven on Saturday and four on Sunday) during which the couples hear lectures, watch films regarding sexual enhancement, and participate in overnight "homework assignments."

Respondents who have participated in such programs reported that they felt better about themselves as sexual partners and more knowledgeable about what their partners wanted and that they derived increased pleasure from their sexual relationships. These benefits were maintained three months after they participated in the workshops. The researchers suggested that these results are a strong recommendation for similar couples (happy and not sexually dysfunctional) to participate in such programs (Nathan & Joanning, 1985). Unhappy couples or those with sexual dysfunctions are more likely to benefit from sessions with a therapist.

⁞⁞ Sexual Fulfillment in the Later Years

■ **DATA:** *Twelve percent of all Americans (over 25 million whites; over 2 million blacks) are over the age of 65. By the year 2000, people over 65 will represent about 14 percent of our population (Statistical Abstract of the United States, 1990 Table 18).*

We used to think that both children and the elderly were asexual. Now we know that sexuality lasts "from erection to resurrection, from sperm to worm."
—SYLVIA HACKER

The way a society views the elderly influences the expression of their sexuality. Although our society tends to expect people to reduce their sexual activities as they age, this expectation is not characteristic of all societies. In one study, 70 percent of one group of societies had expectations of continued sexual activity for their aging males (Winn & Newton, 1982). Among the Tiv in Africa, many older men "remain active and 'hot' for many years after they become gray-haired" (p. 288); among the Taoist sects of China, there are records of men retaining their sexual desires past 100 years of age. Similar reports of continued sexual activity and interest among aging women have been found in 84 percent of the societies for which data on this age group are available. The researchers conclude "that cultural as well as biological factors may be key determinants in sexual behavior in the later part of life" (p. 283).

Our society has perpetuated the myth that growing old and remaining sexual are incompatible. If we are not aware this expectation is culturally induced, the self-fulfilling prophecy may take effect—because we believe that we should not be sexual when we are old, we stop being sexual.

Sexuality of the Elderly: Some Facts

Growing old need not mean an end to a person's sex life. On the contrary, sex may continue into the eighties and beyond.

■ **DATA:** *In a study of 60-80 year old women and men in Sweden, researchers (Bergstrom & Nielsen, 1990) found that 61% of the 509 respondents express their sexuality through intercourse, mutual sexual stimulation, and masturbation.*

■ **DATA:** *In a study of 100 white men and 102 white women ranging in age from 80 to 102, a significant number were still sexually active: 88 percent of the men and 71 percent of the women still fantasized or daydreamed about being close, affectionate, and intimate with the opposite sex. Touching and caressing without sexual intercourse was the most common activity for 82 percent of men and 64 percent of women (Bretschneider & McCoy, 1988, 125).*

Acceptance of Sexuality Among the Elderly. Two hundred and ninety undergraduate students completed questionnaires about the degree to which they approved of sexuality among the elderly. Overwhelmingly, they approved of the elderly (those over 70) having unmarried sexual intercourse, living together, and having sex in nursing homes. However, as emotional closeness to elderly relatives increased, there were decreases in acceptance of sexual activity for the elderly (Pratt & Schmall, 1989).

Frequency of Intercourse Declines With Age. The longer a couple is married the less likely they are to engage in intercourse.

■ **DATA:** *In one study, 62 percent of the men and 30 percent of the women in their eighties, nineties, and older reported that they still have sexual intercourse (Bretschneider & McCoy, 1988, 116). Newly married couples have intercourse 3 to 4 times per week.*

Reasons for this decline include societal expectations, physical problems, and satiation. The elderly are sometimes forced into mandatory retirement from sexual activity; sexuality among the elderly in our society is not expected.

Physical problems also take their toll. In men, diabetes, malfunctions of the thyroid and pituitary glands, and alcoholism may impair the man's ability to get and keep an erection.

■ **DATA:** *Of 100 men between the ages of 80 and 102, 37 percent reported a fear of performance, 28 percent reported impotence, and 28 percent reported an inability to achieve orgasm. Of 102 women of similar age, 30 percent reported that orgasms do not occur frequently enough, 30 percent said that they lacked vaginal lubrication, and 25 percent said that they did not have enough sexual encounters (Bretschneider & McCoy, 1988, 118).*

Frequency of Intercourse: Age 20-40—Tri-weekly; Age 40-60—Try weekly; Age 60-80—Try weakly.

—UNKNOWN

Although physical changes in older women result from a decrease in estrogen, the primary factor affecting the declining frequency of intercourse in an elderly woman is the waning interest or the absence of a sexual partner. The presence of a culturally approved sexual partner (husband) is often regarded as a prerequisite for heterosexual expression among elderly women—and many do not have a partner.

Masturbation Declines With Age. As individuals age, the reported frequency of their masturbation declines. In the study of individuals in their eighties, nineties, and older, 28 percent of the men and 60 percent of the women reported that they do not currently masturbate. These percentages are lower than those given when asked about their masturbatory patterns in the past. Fifteen percent of the men and 53 percent of the women said that they never masturbated in the past (Bretschneider & McCoy, 1988).

Sexual Fulfillment Among the Elderly

There are several things people can do to achieve sexual fulfillment in the later years: doing what they want to do sexually (including nothing), relabeling their "losses" as "transitions," and adapting as necessary. It is important that the elderly not view the publicity about sex in the later years as an obligation to enjoy an active sex life. Sexual fulfillment is individually defined. Elderly persons, like others, should decide what behaviors and frequencies make them feel comfortable. There are no normal or abnormal definitions.

☐   C O N S I D E R A T I O N   ☐

Rather than viewing partial erection, impotence, lack of vaginal lubrication, or pain during intercourse as sexual losses, the elderly might see them as inevitable transitions. We expect change in all other areas of life and should not be dismayed to discover that our bodies change too (Olds, 1985). Adaptation to change is likely to be a more satisfying response.

Adaptation does not necessarily mean resignation. It may mean finding substitute techniques for sexual expression. For example, for partial erection or impotence, some couples use the "stuffing technique" (manually pushing the penis into the vagina). This often stimulates the penis to erection, which can be followed by intercourse. Another problem that can be helped is pain during intercourse, which was reported by slightly more than 10 percent of the women in the Starr and Weiner study (1982). Pain may be caused by decreased vaginal lubrication, a smaller vaginal opening, and friction against the thinner walls of the vagina. A liberal use of K-Y jelly, a sterile lubricant, is helpful in minimizing the pain. Applied to both the penis and vagina, it helps the penis slide in and out with less friction.

:: Trends

Trends in sexual fulfillment include greater access to information about sexual fulfillment, a wider range of expression of sexual fulfillment, and increased exploration of sexual alternatives. Magazines like *Cosmopolitan, Redbook, Ladies Home Journal, McCall's,* and *Family Circle* regularly feature articles on sexual aspects of the woman-man relationship. Research on sexuality is no longer available only to academics. It is available to every person who stands in line to pay for groceries. Such visibility of sexual topics is not limited to magazines but includes movies, television, and radio. The openness with which the media treats sex will continue.

One consequence of this visibility is an awareness of the widening range of sexual behaviors expressed by different people. "Donahue" and "Geraldo" once featured discussions on "safe" topics only; more recent programs have included such topics as polygamy, bisexual marriage, celibacy, and transsexuality. Exposure to media-mediated sex alerts us to the tremendous variations in sexual experience.

Because our population is gradually getting older, there may be a gradual trend away from a focus on sexuality in youth to sexuality in the middle and later years. A life-span focus on sexuality will replace the overconcern with teenage sexuality. A dominant theme of the television sitcom, "The Golden Girls," is sexuality in the middle and later years.

:: Summary

Spouses who report having an "excellent" or "very good" relationship also report a great deal of affection in public and sexual passion in private. While a good sexual relationship often depends on a good emotional relationship, other variables include open communication, realistic expectations, and creativity.

Sexual dysfunctions are also a concern in many relationships. Lack of sexual responsiveness, inability to achieve orgasm, pain during intercourse (dyspareunia), and involuntary constrictions of the vagina (vaginismus) are the main female sexual dysfunctions. Men may be troubled by sexual apathy or the inability to get and maintain an erection (erectile dysfunction), to delay ejaculation (premature ejaculation), or to ejaculate at all (ejaculatory incompetence).

Growing old need not lead to the end of a person's sex life. Persons in their eighties, nineties, and older still report sexual activity. The aged can also do several things to achieve sexual fulfillment in the later years, including doing what they want to do sexually (including nothing), relabeling their losses as transitions, and adapting as necessary.

Trends in sexual fulfillment include greater access to sexual information, increased visibility of sexual variations, and a greater concern for sexuality in the middle and later years.

Questions for Reflection

1. How do you define sexual fulfillment?
2. What physical changes, if any, are you experiencing which suggest to you that you are aging?
3. How willing would you be to consult a sex therapist for a sexual problem?

References

Althof, Stanley E., Louisa A. Turner, Stephen D. Levine, Candace Risen, Elroy Kursh, Donald Badner, and Martin Resnick. Why do so many people drop out of auto-injection therapy for impotence? *Journal of Sex and Marital Therapy*, 1989, *15*, 121–129.

Ash, P. Healthy sexuality and good health. *Sexuality Today*, 1986, *9*, no. 24, 1.

Assalian, Pierre. Clomipramine in the treatment of premature ejaculation. *Journal of Sex Research* 1988, *24*, 213–215.

Barbach, L. and M. Flaherty. Group treatment of situationally orgasmic women. *Journal of Sex and Marital Therapy*, 1980, *6*, 19–29.

Bergstrom, Maj-Briht and H. H. Nielsen, Sexual expression among 60-80 year old men and women: A sample from Stockholm, Sweden. *The Journal of Sex Research*, 1990, *27*, 289–295.

Bermant, G. Sexual behavior: Hard times with the Coolidge Effect. *Psychological Research: The Inside Story*. Edited by M. H. Siegel and H. P. Zeigler. New York: Harper & Row, 1976.

Bretschneider, Judy G. and Norma L. McCoy. Sexual interest and behavior in healthy 80- to 102-year olds. *Archives of Sexual Behavior*, 1988, *17*, 109–129.

Brewer, J. S. Duration of intromission and female orgasm rates. *Medical Aspects of Human Sexuality*, 1981, *15*, no. 4, 70–71.

Britton, T. Lenoir Community College, Kinston, N.C. Personal communication, 1984.

Bronte, Lydia. *Head first: The biology of hope*. New York: E. P. Dutton, 1989.

Cado, S. and H. Leitenberg. Guilt reactions to sexual fantasies during intercourse. *Archives of Sexual Behavior*, 1990, *19*, 49–63.

Carnes, P. *Out of the shadows: Understanding sexual addition*. Minneapolis: CompCare Publications, 1983.

Coleman, E., A. Listiak, G. Braatz, and P. Lange. Effects of penile implant surgery on ejaculation and orgasm. *Journal of Sex and Marital Therapy*, 1985, *11*, 199–205.

Duddle, C. M. and A. Ingram. Treating sexual dysfunction in couple's groups. *Medical sexology*. Edited by R. Forleo & W. Pasini. Littleton, Mass.: PSG Publishing, 1980, 598–605.

Gebhard, P. H. Human sexual behavior: A summary statement. In *Human sexual behavior*. Edited by D. S. Marshall and R. C. Suggs. Englewood Cliffs, N.J.: Prentice-Hall, 1972, 206–217.

Golden, J. S., S. Price, A. G. Heinrich, and W. C. Lobitz. Group vs. couple treatment of sexual dysfunctions. *Archives of Sexual Behavior*, 1978, *7*, 593–602.

Gordon, B. *Jennifer Fever*. New York: Harper & Row, 1988.

Greenblatt, C. S. The salience of sexuality in the early years of marriage. *Journal of Marriage and the Family*, 1983, *4*, 289–299.

Hong, L. K. Survival of the fastest: On the origin of premature ejaculation. *Journal of Sexual Research*, 1984, *20*, 109–122.

Humphrey, F. G. and L. D. Strong. A comparison of the effects of husband's versus wife's extramarital relationships upon the process and outcome of marital therapy. Unpublished manuscript, University of Connecticut, 1978. Used with permission.

Jasso, G. Marital coital frequency and the passage of time: Estimating the separate effects of spouses' ages and marital duration, birth and marriage cohorts, and period influences. *American Sociological Review*, 1985, *50*, 224–241.

Kaplan, H. The classification of the female sexual dysfunctions. *Journal of Sex and Marital Therapy*, 1974, *1*, no. 2, 124–138.

Kelly, M. P., D. S. Strassberg, J. R. Kircher. Attitudinal and experiential correlates of anorgasmia. *Archives of Sexual Behavior*, 1990, *19*, 165–177.

Kilmann, P. R., K. H. Mills, C. Caid, B. Bella, E. Davidson, and R. Wanlass. The sexual interaction of women with secondary orgasmic dysfunction and their partners. *Archives of Sexual Behavior*, 1984, *13*, 41–49.

Kilmann, P. R., J. P. Boland, S. P. Norton, E. Davidson, and C. Caid. Perspectives of sex therapy outcome: A survey of AASECT providers. *Journal of Sex and Marital Therapy,* 1986, *12,* 116–138.

Kolodny, R. C., W. H. Masters, and V. E. Johnson. *Sex and human loving,* Boston, Mass.: Little, Brown, 1986.

Lawrence, Kelli-an and Edwards S. Herold. Women's attitudes toward and experience with sexually explicit materials. *Journal of Sex Research,* 1988, *24,* 161–169.

Lawson A. *Adultry: An Analysis of Love and Betrayal* New York: Basic Books, 1988.

Masters, W. H. and V. E. Johnson. *Human sexual inadequacy,* Boston, Mass.: Little, Brown, 1970.

McCarthy, B. W. Sexual dysfunctions and dissatisfactions among middle-years couples. *Journal of Sex Education and Therapy,* 1982, 8, no. 2, 9–12.

Meisler, A. W., M. P. Carey, D. J. Krauss, and L. J. Lantinga. Success and failure in penile prosthesis surgery: Importance of psychosocial factors. *Journal of Sex and Marital Therapy,* 1988, *14,* 108–119.

Merriam, A. P. Aspects of sexual behavior among the Bala (Basongye). *Human Sexual Behavior.* Edited by D. S. Marshall & R. C. Suggs. Englewood Cliffs, N.J.: Prentice-Hall, 1972, 71–102.

Nathan, E. P. and H. H. Joanning. Enhancing marital sexuality: An evaluation of a program for the sexual enrichment of normal couples. *Journal of Sex and Marital Therapy,* 1985, *11,* 157–164.

Olds, S. W. *The eternal garden: Seasons of our sexuality.* New York: Random House, 1985.

Peter, L. *Peter's almanac.* New York: William Morrow, 1982.

Pratt, Clara C. and Vicki L. Schmall. College student's attitudes toward elderly sexual behavior: Implications for family life education. *Family Relations,* 1989, *38,* 137–141.

Rajfer, J., A. Rosciszewski, and M. Mehringer. Prevalence of corporeal venous leakage in impotent men. *Journal of Urology,* 1988, *140,* 69–71.

Rosenzweig, Julie M. and Dennis M. Dailey. Dyadic adjustment/sexual satisfaction in women and men as a function of psychological sex role self-perception. *Journal of Sex and Marital Therapy,* 1989, *15,* 42–56.

Schaefer, L. Women and extramarital affairs. *Sexuality Today,* 1981, *4,* no. 13, 3.

Schneider, J. P. Rebuilding the marriage during recovery from compulsive sexual behavior. *Family Relations,* 1989, *38,* 288–294.

Schwartz. P. and D. Jackson. How to have a model marriage. *New Woman,* February 1989, 66–74.

Sexual Addiction Survey Results Released. *Siecus Report,* 1988, *17,* 20.

Shortle, B. and R. Jewelewicz. Psychogenic vaginismus. *Medical Aspects of Human Sexuality,* 1986, *20,* 82–87.

Sidi, A. A., J. S. Cameron, L. M. Duffy, and P. H. Lauge. Intracavernous drug-induced erections in the management of male dysfunction: Experience with 100 patients. *Journal of Urology,* 1986, *135,* 704–706.

Spanier, G. B. and R. L. Margolis. Marital separation and extramarital sexual behavior. *Journal of Sex Research,* 1983, *19,* 23–48.

Statistical Abstract of the United States: 1990. 110th ed. Washington, D.C.: U.S. Bureau of the Census, 1990.

Starr, B. D. and M. B. Weiner. *The Starr-Weiner report on sex and sexuality in the mature years.* New York: McGraw-Hill, 1982.

Stephens, W. N. *The family in cross-cultural perspective.* Washington, D.C.: University Press of America, 1982.

Symons, D. *The evolution of human sexuality.* New York: Oxford University Press, 1979.

Talmadge, L. D. and W. C. Talmadge. Relational sexuality: An understanding of low sexual desire. *Journal of Sex and Marital Therapy,* 1986, *12,* 3–21.

Thompson, A. P. Emotional and sexual components of extramarital relations. *Journal of Marriage and the Family,* 1984, *46,* 35–42.

Thompson, A. P. Extramarital sex: A review of the research literature. *Journal of Sex Research,* 1983, *19,* 1–22.

Thornton, A. Changing attitudes toward family issues in the United States. *Journal of Marriage and the Family*, 1989, *51*, 873–893.

Trotter, S. Single women/married men. *Free Inquiry in Creative Sociology*, 1989, *17*, 213–217.

Wheeler, J. and P. R. Kilmann. Comarital sexual behavior: Individual and relationship variables. *Archives of Sexual Behavior*, 1983, *12*, 295–306.

Winn, R. L. and N. Newton. Sexuality in aging: A study of 106 cultures. *Archives of Sexual Behavior*, 1982, *11*, 283–298.

Yablonsky, L. *The extra-sex factor: Why over half of America's married men play around.* New York: Times Books, 1979.

CHOICES

SOME COUPLES WHO are unable to resolve the sexual problems in their relationship become involved in sex therapy. Once the decision is made to consult a sex therapist several choices must be made, including whether one or both partners should attend sex therapy and whether to have private or group therapy.

Therapy: Alone or With a Partner?

Should just the person experiencing the sexual problem or the person and sexual partner become involved in sex therapy? It depends. Some people prefer to go alone. One woman said:

If I ask him to go to therapy with me, he'll think I'm more emotionally involved than I am. And since I don't want to encourage him, I'll just work out my problems without him.

Other reasons why a person might see a sex therapist alone are if no partner is available, if the partner won't come, or if the person feels more comfortable discussing sex in the partner's absence.

However, there are also several reasons why a person might want her or his partner to become involved in sex therapy: to work on the problem *with* someone, to share the experience, and to prevent one partner from being identified as the "one with the problem." Although there are exceptions, a greater proportion of sexual problems can be more effectively treated by engaging in sex therapy with a partner.

Therapy: Privately or in a Group Setting?

Once the decision to pursue therapy (with or without a partner) is made, another choice is whether to see the therapist in private or in groups with other people who are experiencing similar problems. There are advantages and disadvantages of each treatment pattern.

Although being seen privately helps to ensure that therapy will be tailored to fit the specific needs of the client, the cost is considerably higher for private therapy than it is if the client is treated in a group setting. Private therapy may cost $100 an hour; therapy in a group of five members may only cost $15 for the same amount of time.

Another advantage of group therapy is that being surrounded by others who have similar problems helps to reduce the feeling that "I'm the only one." One woman who had difficulty achieving orgasm said, "When I heard the other women discuss their difficulty with climaxing, I knew I wasn't abnormal." The empathy of a group of peers can be extremely effective in helping a person feel less isolated.

A group setting also furnishes the opportunity to try new behaviors. For example, some sexual problems may be part of a larger problem, such as the lack of social skills to attract and maintain a partner. Fear of rejection can perpetuate being alone. But group members, with the help of their therapist, can practice making requests of each other and getting turned down. Such an exercise helps to develop the social skill of approaching others while learning to deal with rejection. Practicing with other group members is safe and gives a person the necessary confidence to approach someone outside the group.

There are at least two disadvantages of group therapy. The first is the possibility that not enough time will be spent on the individual's own problem. The second is the risk to the relationship with the partner, who may not be involved in the group. In one study of women in group therapy for lack of orgasm, one in four reported a negative effect on their partner (Barbach & Flaherty, 1980).

Comparative Effectiveness

What is the comparative effectiveness of couples being treated in a group or in private therapy? In one study, when group-couple therapy for premature ejaculation and orgasmic dysfunction was compared with therapy for the same problems treated in private, there were no differences in outcome. Both treatment patterns were effective. Men reported satisfaction with their ability to prolong intercourse, and women reported satisfaction with their orgasmic ability. (Golden et al., 1978). Other researchers have found similar results: couples in groups are as successful in achieving their goals as couples in private therapy (Duddle & Ingram, 1980).

This suggests that *couples* can be treated effectively in either a private or a group setting. The selection of a therapy setting is therefore a matter of preference. But group therapy for *individuals* may not be as effective as therapy with a partner in private or in a couples group. However, most individuals in group sex therapy without a partner do benefit from the experience.

Extramarital Sex? No

As noted earlier, about 50 percent of husbands and wives report they have had intercourse with someone other than their spouse. Conversely, about 50 percent of husbands and wives do not have an affair (or report that they do not).

Some of those not having an affair feel that it causes more trouble to themselves and their partners than it is worth. "I can't say I don't think about having sex with other women, because I do—a lot," said one husband, "But I would feel guilty as hell, and if my wife found out, she would kill me."

Although his wife probably wouldn't "kill him," she probably would express her pain and disillusionment by asking, "How could you do this to me?" Extramarital intercourse is still regarded as adultery in an emotional sense. Like conspiring with a thief to rob their home, the adulterer is seen as conspiring with another to invade the privacy of the marriage. As a result, the partner may develop a deep sense of distrust, which often lingers in the marriage long after the affair is over. "I can forgive you," said one husband, "but I'll never forget what you've done." A wife said that whenever her husband is away on a business trip, she has visions of him being in bed with another woman. "I just don't trust him anymore."

In addition to guilt and distrust as outcomes of an affair, another danger is the development of a

pattern of having affairs. "Once you've had an affair, it's easier the second time," said one spouse. "And the third time, you don't give it a thought." Increasingly, the spouse looks outside the marriage for sex and companionship.

A spouse who establishes a pattern of affairs also invests increasing amounts of time and energy in someone other than the marriage partner. Although this commitment of self to the new person helps to build the relationship with that person, it does nothing to improve the relationship with the spouse.

Of 108 marriages, in which one of the spouses had an affair, 30 percent ended in divorce (Humphrey & Strong, 1978). One spouse said:

When you have an affair, you are playing with a ticking time bomb. I was able to hide mine for three years before she found out, but when she did, she threw me out of the house. When I think about what I actually did, I traded something good for something new. It was a terrible mistake.

If a divorce occurs subsequent to the partner finding out about the affair, the "adulterer" may also pay an economic price. In some states, adultery is grounds for alimony.

Another potential danger in having extramarital sex is the potential to contract a sexually transmitted disease. The AIDS epidemic has increased the concern over this possibility. A spouse who engages in extramarital sex may not only contract a sexually transmitted disease, but also transmit the disease to their partner (and potentially their unborn offspring). In some cases, extramarital sex may be deadly.

Furthermore, spouses who engage in extramarital relationships risk the possibility of their partner finding out and going into a jealous rage. Jealousy may result in violence and even the death of the unfaithful spouse and/or the lover involved (violence in relationships is the subject of the next chapter).

Extramarital Sex? Yes

A small percentage of spouses who have an affair feel that it has positive consequences for them, their marriage, and their partners.

One woman, whose husband constantly denigrated her, said of her extramarital relationship, "He made me feel loved, valued, and worthwhile again." This woman eventually divorced her husband, but said she would not have had the strength to go through a divorce had it not been for her lover's support.

Benefits to the marriage may also occur. Some partners become sensitive to the fact that they have a problem in their marriage. "For us," one spouse said, "the affair helped us to look at our marriage, to know that we were in trouble, and to seek help." Couples need not view the discovery of an affair as the end of their marriage; it can be a new beginning.

A final positive effect of a partner discovering an affair is that the partner may become more sensitive to the needs of the spouse and more motivated to satisfy them. The partner may realize that if spouses are not satisfied at home, they will go elsewhere. One husband said his wife had an affair because he was too busy with his work and did not spend enough time with her. Her affair taught him that she had alternatives—other men who would love her emotionally and sexually. To ensure that he did not lose her, he became intent on satisfying her.

Although an affair is dangerous for most marriages, one researcher (Britton, 1984) interviewed 276 spouses who had had an affair and identified the conditions under which an extramarital encounter is least likely to have negative consequences:

1. The spouses have a solid marriage relationship. The one who has the affair has a strong emotional commitment to the mate. The lover is viewed as short-term only—not as a potential replacement for the mate.
2. The spouses compartmentalize easily. The one who has the affair can keep the lover and the mate separated in time, place, and thought. Memories of the experiences with the lover are not allowed to blend into the relationship with the spouse so that behavior is adversely affected.
3. The spouses avoid disclosure. Disclosure is like a rattlesnake in the relationship; it strikes the spouse, and introduces a deadly venom. Few spouses can tolerate the information that their partner had or is having a sexual relationship with someone else.
4. The spouses limit contacts. Frequent contacts with one or more lovers take the energy away from the marriage and increase the chance of getting caught.
5. The spouses seek recreation only. Sexual experiences solely for spontaneous recreation do the least damage. Those that are carefully orchestrated for emotional impact take time and energy away from the mate.

Impact of Social Influences on Choices

Your willingness to go public with your sexual problems is related to society's openness about sexuality, your having friends who have consulted a sex therapist, and your income. With the advent of Dr. Ruth Westheimer on television and radio and in newspapers, the discussion of sexuality has become normative. Problems of lack of orgasm, premature ejaculation, and impotence are now openly discussed by "Dr. Ruth" as well as "Dear Abby." As a result of such societal openness, you will be more much likely to consult a sex therapist than your parents were.

Having friends who consult a sex therapist increases the likelihood that you will if you and/or your partner need to do so. Individuals who live in large urban centers are more likely to be involved in sex therapy than people who live in small towns and rural areas. Also, sex therapy is expensive, so your income will influence whether you seek a sex therapist.

Therefore, although we might assume that involvement in sex therapy is an individual decision, contacting a sex therapist in reality is more related to societal openness about sexuality, to friendships, and to income.

C H A P T E R

12

Violence and Abuse in Relationships

CONTENTS

IS IT TRUE?

1. Men abuse women at a much higher rate than women abuse men.

2. Cross-cultural studies support the popular belief that alcohol consumption causes violent and aggressive behavior.

3. Elderly victims of abuse are typically financially dependent on their abuser.

4. Having an abusive spouse arrested usually results in less frequent future abuse.

5. Stepparents are more likely to abuse their stepchildren than biological parents are to abuse their biological children.

1 = F; 2 = F; 3 = F; 4 = T; 5 = T

The terms *abuse* and *violence* are not easily defined. Although we may feel certain that particular acts constitute abuse (e.g., intentionally breaking a child's finger), we may be uncertain as to whether other acts constitute abuse. For example, some individuals think that spanking a child is abusive, whereas others regard spanking as appropriate discipline. Among the factors that influence our individual perceptions of what constitutes abuse and violence are the beliefs and values of our culture, religion, and family of orientation.

In this chapter, we focus on abuse in dating, cohabitation, and family relationships. We define abuse as any physical or mental injury, sexual abuse, or negligent treatment that threatens an individual's health or welfare.

▪▪ Abuse in Dating, Cohabitation, and Marital Relationships

Shakespeare said, "The course of true love never did run smooth" (*A Midsummer Night's Dream*, Act 1, Scene one). For some dating, cohabiting, and married couples, this means that one or both partners may experience abuse in the form of physical violence, verbal attacks, and/or sexual assaults.

Abuse in Dating and Cohabitation Relationships

Because it has been the object of much media attention, spouse abuse is a concept familiar to most of us. News specials and documentaries, newspaper and magazine articles, and television movies and talk shows have all portrayed spouse abuse as a compelling social problem. But much less attention has been given to abuse in dating relationships. The popular belief in our culture is that during the dating phase of a relationship, partners are on their best behavior and so abuse is unlikely. In reality, this is not always the case.

> ▪ **DATA:** *In a study of 5,768 couples, 20 percent of the dating couples had experienced a physical assault during the previous year, compared to 15 percent of the married couples (Stets & Straus, 1989).*

Other studies also support the conclusion that violence in dating relationships is a widespread phenomenon. Thirty percent of the women and 25 percent of the men in one study reported that they had been victims of courtship violence (McKinney, 1986). In another cross-cultural study of college students, 48.8 percent of the women reported that they had experienced at least one kind of physical violence or threat in dating situations. The authors concluded that "violence in dating situations is a universal problem on campuses regardless of ethnic background" (Kiernan & Taylor, 1990).

Makepeace (1989) found that among three different categories of dating among college students (first dates, casual dates, and steady dates), violence was most intense on first dates. His findings revealed that physical injury, emotional trauma, and forced sex were more likely to occur on a first date than on a date in which the partners have been dating on a casual or steady basis. Furthermore, Makepeace found violence that occurs in different stages of courtship is precipitated by different types of disagreements. Violence in steady dating relationships is likely to be precipitated by arguments over jealousy. In casual dating relation-ships, violent episodes are likely to be precipitated by arguments over sex or jealousy. On first dates, violence is likely to be precipitated by disagreements over sex or alcohol/drugs. (See Chapter 7 on Dating and Mate Selection for further discussion on forced sex in the context of dating.)

Violence and abuse also occurs in cohabitation relationships.

■ **DATA:** *In a study of 5,768 couples, 35 percent of the cohabiting couples had experi-enced a physical assault during the previous year, compared to 20 percent of the dating couples and 15 percent of the married couples (Stets & Straus, 1989).*

Not only is the rate of assault highest among cohabiting couples, the severity of violence is greater among cohabiting couples compared to dating and marital partners (Stets & Straus, 1989). In living together relationships that experience violence, the precipitating disagreement is likely to be about jealousy or sex (Makepeace, 1989).

One explanation for the greater violence among cohabitors is the lack of secu-rity in such relationships. Spouses have made a legal commitment to each other; singles don't expect much commitment from their dating partners. But cohabitors are in limbo. And when a partner is late or evidences interest in another relation-ship, jealousy, anger, and violence can follow. Alcohol and drug use also seems to be higher among cohabitors. They have reported being either drunk or stoned and having intercourse unknowingly more often than either singles or marrieds (Lane & Gwartney-Gibbs, 1985).

☐   C O N S I D E R A T I O N   ☐

Because anger (sometimes jealous anger) and alcohol are two precipitating factors in the expression of violent behavior, partners who want to avoid such violence might be sensitive to the combined effects and carefully monitor not only their alcohol intake but also the escalation of their anger (and that of their partner's). By doing so, they can withdraw from each other before the violence erupts. One couple who had had problems with violence in their relationship agreed to withdraw from each other (one partner would leave the apartment) when either of them felt their anger had climbed above a level of 3 on a 10-point scale. If arguments over drinking alcohol are frequent, treatment by a substance-abuse counselor may be indicated. In some in-dividuals, alcohol often creates the context for violence.

Violence and abuse in committed relationships are not specific to heterosexuals. Most of the 100 battered lesbians who participated in a study reported that they had lived with their partners. Half of these said that "having no place to go" created an outburst of violence. One respondent said:

I was afraid of leaving because she'd tried to kill me three times, each as more of a threat than an attempt, but I thought she'd be more serious if she knew I was serious about going (Renzetti, 1989, 161).

■ **DATA:** *Twenty-five percent of 100 battered lesbians reported that they had been phys-ically abused by a female partner in a committed relationship (Renzetti, 1989, 157).*

Violence is usually pre-
ceded by a verbal argu-
ment.

Nothing multiplies
more easily than force.
—NORMAN COUSINS

Once abuse occurs, it is not unusual for it to recur. When the abuse happens after the partners have become emotionally as well as sexually involved, the partners are less likely to view it as a reason for terminating the relationship. Later in this chapter, we look at why some people stay in relationships with abusive partners.

□ CONSIDERATION □

If you have experienced violence in the relationship with your dating partner, be aware that such expressions are likely to become a pattern in your relationship. Couples who do not make a conscious attempt to stop such violence are making an unwritten agreement that such behavior is going to be tolerated in their relationship. The Partner Abuse Scale in the Self-Assessment exercise (p. 362) is designed to help you predict the possibility of abuse becoming a part of your current relationship.

Abuse in Marriage Relationships

Estimates of spouse abuse are difficult to obtain, as husbands and wives are often reluctant to report being either the victim or perpetrator of marital violence. Nevertheless, we know that spouse abuse is not a rare phenomenon.

■ **DATA:** *About one quarter of spouses have experienced violence in their relationships. In about one half of these relationships that have experienced violence, both the husband and the wife were violent (Flynn, 1990).*

The pattern of both partners in a relationship participating in violent behavior is true not only of married partners, but of dating and cohabiting partners as well. Stets and Straus (1989) found that for dating, cohabiting, and married couples, the most frequent pattern is for both partners to be violent, followed by female only, and the least frequent pattern is male only violence.

■ **DATA:** *The results of a national family survey revealed that women direct as much violence toward men as men do toward women—although women are usually more severely injured (Straus et al., 1980).*

□ CONSIDERATION □

Although much public attention has been given to women and children who are victims of abuse, very little attention has been given to the problem of men who are abused by women. One reason that "man battering" is less visible than woman or child battering involves the traditional gender stereotype of women as weak and nonaggressive. Any physically violent act that women commit cannot possibly (according to the stereotype) be harmful. Men, who are stereotyped as being strong and tough, are assumed to be immune from any harm a woman (who is supposedly weak) could inflict. Men who are beaten and harmed by women are often reluctant to seek help out of fear that they may be viewed as weak and "unmasculine."

Physical harm to one or both spouses is a serious consequence of marital violence. Much more serious, however, is the frequency that spousal abuse leads to death.

■ **DATA:** *Among all female murder victims in 1988, 31 percent were murdered by husbands or boyfriends; 5 percent of all male murder victims were killed by wives or girlfriends (U.S. Dept. of Justice, 1989).*

SELF ASSESSMENT

Partner Abuse Scale

This scale is designed to predict the potential for violence and abuse in your current relationship. There are no right or wrong answers. After reading each sentence carefully, circle the appropriate number.

1 Never;
2 Rarely;
3 Occasionally;
4 Frequently;
5 Very frequently

	N	R	O	F	VF
1. I get irritated easily.	1	2	3	4	5
2. At least one of my parents was abusive to the other.	1	2	3	4	5
3. I was abused as a child.	1	2	3	4	5
4. I have had the urge to hit my partner.	1	2	3	4	5
5. I sometimes feel out of control.	1	2	3	4	5
6. I am under a lot of pressure most of the time.	1	2	3	4	5
7. I drink a lot of alcohol.	1	2	3	4	5
8. I lose my temper when I drink.	1	2	3	4	5
9. My partner and I argue.	1	2	3	4	5
10. It is hard for me to control my temper.	1	2	3	4	5

Scoring: Add the numbers you circled. 1 (never) represents the lowest probability for potential abuse; 5 (very frequently) represents the highest probability for potential abuse. The lower your total score (10 is the lowest possible score), the lower the chance of abuse in your relationship; the higher your total score (50 is the highest pos-sible score), the higher the chance of abuse in your relationship. A score of 30 places you at the midpoint between a nonabusive and an abusive relationship.

Note: This scale is for self evaluation and is not intended to be used as a clinical diagnostic instrument.

Women who kill their partners are likely to do so in self-defense. It is estimated that 3 out of 4 women who kill their partners do so in self-defense (Gelles & Straus, 1988, 133).

This level of violence is one reason why police officers may be reluctant to intervene in domestic disputes. About 20 percent of police officers killed each year meet their death while trying to intervene in a family dispute. More than 25 percent of assaults on police officers occur during family fights (Jaffe, 1990).

Five issues that are related to spousal abuse are housekeeping, sex, social activities, money, and children (Straus et al., 1980). Housekeeping is the most frequent source of conflict and "conflict over children . . . is most likely to lead a couple to blows" (p. 171). It is not surprising that marital violence is associated with unhappy marital relationships (Bowman, 1990).

□   C O N S I D E R A T I O N   □

Stets (1990) suggests that verbal aggression often precedes physical aggression in episodes of marital violence. This finding suggests that one way to avoid physical violence in a relationship is for partners to withdraw from interaction that involves verbal aggression, before it escalates into physical abuse.

Understanding Violence

It seems ironic that those individuals who care about each other are also the most likely to physically hurt each other. Why do people in intimate relationships behave violently toward each other?

Previous Family Learning. Violence is learned primarily in the home. This cycle of violence in which children observe, experience, and inflict violence in their own adult relationships is sometimes difficult to stop, as each generation tends to learn from the preceding one.

■ **DATA:** *In a study of 328 couples in which there had been abuse between the partners, 75 percent of the women and 80 percent of the men reported being hit by their parents (Malone et al., 1989).*

Socialization. Men are socialized to be more aggressive than women. They are also less likely to define aggressive acts against women in negative terms. In general, men are more approving of sexual aggression against women than are women (Margolin et al., 1989).

Men have traditionally been socialized to have sexist attitudes toward women. Men who feel that they are superior to women may justify aggression toward women on the grounds that "women need to be put in their place."

Traditional gender role socialization may also explain some instances of physical aggression of women toward men. Shupe et al. (1987) explain how "reverse sexism" may be operative in women becoming violent toward men. The logic goes something like this:

1. Men are bigger and stronger than women.
2. Thus, men have a special responsibility to be protective and morally restrained toward women and treat them like ladies. Sometimes men misbehave so that women are justified in physically slapping or threatening them to correct their actions.
3. Because of their physical advantage in an actual fight, men are supposed to accept the slap without resistance as a reminder of their responsibility. To retaliate in kind would be unfair (Shupe et al., 1987, 57).

In effect, society perpetuates a double standard that says it is acceptable for a woman to hit a man, but not acceptable for a man to hit a woman.

Ownership. Some individuals feel that they own the person to whom they are married. Historically, men have viewed women (and children) as property. Prior to the late nineteenth century, it was a husband's legal right and marital obligation to discipline and control his wife through the use of physical force.

☐ C O N S I D E R A T I O N ☐

The expression "rule of thumb" can be traced to an old English law which permitted a husband to beat his wife with a rod not thicker than his thumb. This "rule of thumb" was originally intended as a humane measure to limit how harshly men could physically abuse their wives.

Low Self-Esteem. When 20 abusive husbands were compared with nonabusive husbands in both happy and unhappy marriages, the abusive husbands had lower self-esteem. Whether low self-esteem is a cause or an effect of spouse abuse is unknown. However, abusive husbands also reported that they viewed their wives as threatening to their self-esteem (Goldstein & Rosenbaum, 1985).

> Argument is the worst sort of conversation.
> —JONATHAN SWIFT

Displacement of Tension. Sometimes being violent may have nothing to do with winning an argument or getting one's way. Rather, the partner may feel frustrated by unemployment or limited income, irritated by the bickering of children in a crowded house, or angered by the boss at work. Any of these factors can produce a feeling of anxious tension, which is released on the spouse out of displacement (discussed in Chapter 10). The spouse may be blamed for the partner's unhappy, frustrated feelings, and the partner may see violence toward the spouse as a way of getting back.

Some data suggest that while there are no differences in the proportion of black and white women who are victims of marital violence, black middle class women experience more violence than their white counterparts. This may be due to the stress on middle class blacks who are often isolated from a support network and who are under pressure to maintain their middle class status (Lockhart, 1987; Stets, 1990).

Reinforcement of Violence. The law of *reinforcement* states that any behavior followed by a reward will increase the frequency of that behavior in the future. When spouses get their way as a result of being violent, the odds increase that they will use violence in the future. "I've found that I can control by wife by beating her up now and then," said one husband. "She's due for another beating soon."

Violence in Society. Social models for violence on television create a norm of violence in our society.

| ■ **DATA:** *By age 16, the typical child has witnessed 200,000 acts of violence on television (Toufexis, 1989).*

When violence occurs in the home, our legal system—for the most part—looks the other way. Not only are the police reluctant to arrest an abusive spouse (police prefer to stay out of what they call "domestic trouble"), but when they do make an arrest, the abusive spouse is often released within one hour. It is extremely rare for spouses to be arrested, tried, found guilty, and sentenced to jail on the charge of assault and battery of their marital partner.

In addition to the factors described above, alcohol use is also associated with domestic violence (and violent behavior in general). Although it is commonly believed that alcohol consumption causes violent behavior, some research suggests otherwise (see Exhibit 12.1).

Rape in Marriage

Violence in marriage sometimes includes rape.

> ■ **DATA:** *Ten percent of married women in a Boston survey reported that they had been raped by their husbands (Finkelhor & Yllo, 1988).*

Sexual assault may have included not only intercourse but also other types of sexual activities in which the wife did not want to engage, most often fellatio and anal intercourse. Rape is a crime of violence, not a crime of passion.

Two researchers have identified several types of marital rape (Finkelhor & Yllo, 1988).

> In the scale of the destinies, brawn will never weigh as much as brain.
> —JAMES RUSSELL LOWELL

Battering Rape. These rapes occur in the context of a regular pattern of verbal and physical abuse. The husbands yell at their wives, call them names, slap,

---

E X H I B I T   12.1

Does Alcohol Consumption Cause Violent Behavior?

One of the popular beliefs about alcohol use is that it often leads to aggressive or violent behavior. Indeed, research done on domestic violence reveals that almost half of all couples who engage in marital or parental violence report that it is associated with drinking by either the one who is violent, the victim, or both (Gelles & Straus, 1988). But does the consistent relationship between alcohol and violence mean that alcohol is the *cause* of violent behavior? Some evidence suggests that the answer is "no."

If the chemical property of alcohol acts on the human organism in such a way as to produce violence, then drinking would produce violence in all people, no matter what culture they lived in. But a classic anthropological study on drinking patterns in various cultures suggests that this is not the case. In *Drunken Comportment* (1969), researchers Craig MacAndrew and Robert Edgerton report that drunken behavior varied considerably across cultures. In some societies, drinking would lead to violence and sexual promiscuity. In other societies, however, drinking would lead to other behaviors, such as passivity and withdrawal. The implication of these findings is that behaviors that are associated with alcohol consumption are learned from the culture. In American culture, we learn that drinking is associated with physical and sexual aggressiveness. Although alcohol no doubt has specific physiological effects on the human central nervous system, the behavioral manifestations of alcohol consumption are learned and culturally determined.

shove, and beat them. These husbands are angry, belligerent, and frequent alcohol abusers. An example follows:

> One afternoon she came home from school, changed into a housecoat, and started toward the bathroom. He got up from the couch where he had been lying, grabbed her, and pushed her down on the floor. With her face pressed into a pillow and his hand clamped over her mouth, he proceeded to have anal intercourse with her. She screamed and struggled to no avail. Her injuries were painful and extensive. She had a torn muscle in her rectum, so that for three months she had to go to the bathroom standing up (pp. 144–145).

Nonbattering Rape. These rapes occur in response to a long-standing conflict or disagreement about sex. The violence is not generalized to the rest of the relationship but specific to the sexual conflict. An example follows:

> Their love making on this occasion started out pleasantly enough, but he tried to get her to have anal intercourse with him. She refused. He persisted. She kicked and pushed him away. Still, he persisted. They ended up having vaginal intercourse. The force he used was mostly that of his weight on top of her. At 220 pounds, he weighs twice as much as she. "It was horrible," she said. She was sick to her stomach afterward. She cried and felt angry and disgusted. He showed little guilt. "He felt like he'd won something" (p. 145).

Obsessive Rape. These rapes may also be categorized as bizzare. The woman is used as a sex object to satisfy an atypical need of the husband. An example follows:

> "I was really his masturbating machine," one woman recalled. He was very rough sexually and would hold a pillow over her face to stifle her screams. He would also tie her up and insert objects into her vagina and take pictures, which he shared with his friends. The interviewee later discovered a file card in her husband's desk which sickened her. On the card, he had written a list of dates—dates that corresponded to the forced sex episodes of the past months. Next to each date was a complicated coding system which seemed to indicate the type of sex act and a ranking of how much he enjoyed it (p. 146).

☐ CONSIDERATION ☐

As of 1990, fewer than half the states viewed marital or cohabiting rape as a crime. But even in the 24 states that do view it as a crime, the law may be of little help. Wives are extremely reluctant to press charges. And those who do press charges are, in effect, challenging a large segment of society that still tends to view sex as the right of men in a pair-bonded relationship with a woman. In essence, "the marriage license is a raping license" (Finkelhor & Yllo, 1988, 150).

Impact of Marital Rape

Being raped by a husband can be more devastating than being attacked by a stranger. The primary effect is to destroy the woman's ability to trust a man in an intimate interpersonal relationship. In addition, the woman raped by her husband lives with her rapist and may be subjected to repeated assaults. Most of the women in the preceding study were raped on multiple occasions.

Raped wives are also likely to have low self-esteem and more negative attitudes toward their marriages. Other symptoms experienced by marital rape victims include anger, shame, inability to concentrate or express themselves, and withdrawal (Pagelow, 1988). While some raped wives leave the marriage, others stay in the relationship.

Why People Stay in Relationships With Partners Who Rape or Abuse Them

Why do partners who experience abuse in a relationship stay together? Some stay because they see the violence as only a small part of the relationship. One woman said:

> Even though he slapped me around a lot, I never left him because when he wasn't hurting me he was so gentle and sweet. He would tell me that he loved me and that I was the only one in the world that really understood him. Besides, he never *really* hurt me, always told me he was sorry, and was good to me right after the violence.

Others continue the relationship because there is no perceived alternative. "If I leave him because he's rough with me now and then," said one woman, "I don't know what I would do. He's such a part of my world that I can't imagine life without him." Still others stay because they label the abusive acts as expressions of love. Much like children who were told when they were about to be punished, "I'm doing this because I love you; it hurts me more than you," so the dating partner, cohabitant, or spouse interprets the violent acts as those only a person who loves him or her would engage in.

Some partners remain in an abusive relationship because they perceive violence to be a legitimate part of an intimate relationship. This is particularly true if they grew up in homes in which their parents, whom they viewed as loving each other, abused each other. One person in an abusive relationship said:

> I grew up watching my dad get drunk and hit on my mother. I don't think it's right to hit a woman, but it happens and it's not the end of the world. Folks who live together are bound to hit each other sometime.

Some partners may continue a relationship after they have been abused because they feel they deserve such abuse ("I deserve to be pushed around and beaten; I'm no good") or they caused the abuse ("It was my fault he got angry and beat me . . . I was just asking for it"). Those who use this rationale for continuing to subject themselves to abuse often have negative self-concepts, which receive an additional blow with each violent episode. This inability to move away from an abusive relationship also suggests that some people are extremely psychologically dependent and will stay with an abuser rather than be alone.

Related to these reasons is that the women believe that they have no alternative—no place to go, nobody to go to. With no options, they take the view of "appeasement rather than massive resistance" (Finkelhor & Yllo, 1988, 147).

Being the victim of abuse is a horrifying experience.

He [Ike] tortured me with phones, shoes, and coat hangers.
—TINA TURNER

Furthermore, women (particularly those with young children) who do not have employment outside the home and who are not economically independent are more constrained to put up with their husbands' abusive behavior. The patriarchal structure of traditional, one-income marriages also helps to perpetuate the continued abuse of wives.

Men may also stay in abusive relationships for economic reasons. Even though men, as a group, have more economic resources than women, if a husband leaves a family he is still responsible for a certain amount of economic support of the family, in addition to the cost of maintaining a separate residence for himself.

A man's decision to stay in an abusive relationship may also be influenced by his children. Some abused men fear that if they leave the family, further violence will be directed at the children. Hence, "men feel that by staying they are providing some protection for their children" (Steinmetz & Lucca, 1988).

Finally, both men and women may stay in an abusive relationship because they want the relationship to work. Abused spouses who have been married for several years because they feel committed to make the marriage work "no matter what" are likely to continue to stay in the relationship (Strube & Barbour, 1983). One woman who was abused weekly by her partner said, "I have always felt that 'you just don't get divorced.'"

Most of the wives who do decide to leave their abusing husbands go to their parents or relatives, an apartment of their own, a motel or car, or just wander. The fewest number go to shelters for battered women, which are available in more than 1,000 communities to furnish protection from further violence. These shelters provide individual assistance to help the woman decide what to do and give her a safe place to stay in the meantime. However, in some cases, by going to a shelter, the wife may inadvertently encourage retaliation on the part of the husband (Berk et al., 1986). Because the problem of abused men has less visibility and is not regarded as serious in nature, abused men have virtually no social supports to assist them in dealing with abuse.

☐   C O N S I D E R A T I O N   ☐

Spouses who are abused by their partners should consider calling the police and having their partners arrested. Although there is the risk of making the abusive partner angrier, there is some evidence that abusers may be less likely to be abusive if they know their partners will have them arrested if they are. In addition to having the abuser arrested, it is helpful to have the abuser involved in individual or group therapy. Family therapy, with both spouses present, does not seem to be as effective as the abusing spouse meeting alone with a therapist or with other abusing spouses in a group setting (Willbach, 1989). Unless individuals in abusive relationships take action (police, therapy, termination of the relationship), they are likely to experience the abuse again.

Help for Spouse Abuse

From a larger perspective, decreasing spouse abuse will require sweeping public policy shifts. These include outlawing family violence (as the Swiss have done) and providing supports for families in the form of day care, health care, full employment, and the end of sexism in the workplace and in the home (Gelles & Straus, 1988).

⠶ Child Abuse

Violence in relationships is not limited to violence between dating partners, co-habitants, and spouses. In January, 1989, Joel Steinberg was convicted of second degree manslaughter for the death of six-year-old Lisa and sentenced to prison for eight to twenty years. The case brought nationwide attention to the reality and horror of child abuse.

Child abuse may be defined as any interaction or lack of interaction between a child and his or her parents or caregiver that results in nonaccidental harm to the child's physical or developmental well-being. The definition includes what a parent may do (beat, burn, scald) and may fail to do (feed the child, provide a caretaker for a young child, take the child to the doctor) to either bring physical harm to the child or negatively affect the child's development. The parents who refuse to take their ill and suffering children to the doctor are just as guilty of child abuse and neglect as the parents who poison their infant by putting arsenic into the baby bottle. The number of abused children is staggering.

■ **DATA:** *It is estimated that between 669,000 and two million children are victims of abuse each year. Only one in seven incidents of child abuse is reported (Knudsen, 1989).*

There are twice as many cases of child neglect than of child abuse. Mothers are somewhat more likely to neglect their children; fathers, to abuse them. The children are most often normal (for example, not retarded, emotionally disturbed, or physically handicapped) and require some form of treatment for bruises, welts, lacerations, burns, and bone fractures in about 20 percent of the cases. In about 5 percent of the cases, skull fracture, bleeding within the skull, and severe burns require hospitalization.

□   C O N S I D E R A T I O N   □

Some students who take marriage and family courses have the professional goal of social worker, psychologist, or marriage and family therapist. It is important to be aware that persons in any one of these professional roles are required in all states to report to the Department of Social Services any suspicion of child abuse or neglect.

Various researchers have identified those conditions which are predictive of child abuse (Oates et al., 1983; Krugman et al., 1986):

1. The pregnancy is unplanned, and the father does not want the child.
2. The birth is complicated and unpleasant.
3. Mother-infant bonding is lacking.
4. Childrearing techniques are strict and harsh and include little positive reinforcement for the child.
5. The child is compared unfavorably with other children, and the parents have an unhappy relationship.
6. The parents are unemployed.

Causes of Child Abuse

There is little agreement on the cause or causes of child abuse. A number of theories follow:

Parent Psychopathology.   Child abuse has been associated with parents who are prone to anger, are rigid, are domineering, are dependent on alcohol or drugs, have low self-esteem, and have difficulty with self-control and handling stress. Some parents who abuse their children have thought disorders and "may attribute unrealistic feelings and motivations to their behavior . . . for example, persistent crying might be viewed as harassment rather than as a genuine need for attention" (Dubowitz & Egan, 1988, 40).

Parents Modeling on Abusive Parents.   Parents who were themselves abused or the victims of harsh physical punishment tend to duplicate these patterns in their own families (Herrenkohl et al., 1983). One father said:

> My father beat on me as long as I can remember. And for no reason at all. One time, it was because I walked over a newspaper in the living room and didn't pick it up. He got up from the couch and shoved me against the wall while yelling obscenities at me. Then he proceeded to sock me with his fists. He did that for years until I was finally old enough to leave home. I never want to go back. But when I had my own kids, I noticed that I had the impulse to do like my dad. I am able to control it most of the time, but at other times, it gets the best of me.

☐   C O N S I D E R A T I O N   ☐

A man who attended a lecture on child abuse approached the speakers after the lecture ended. With tears in his eyes, the man told the speakers that he could not get married. He said to the lecturers, "You said that people who are abused grow up to be abusers. Well, I was an abused child. I don't want to get married and grow up to abuse my children, so I will not get married" (Gelles & Straus, 1988, 49). Although data suggest that children who were abused tend to grow up to be abusers, this does not mean that ALL people who are abused as children become abusers as adults. Indeed, some adults who were abused as children are dedicated to nonviolent parenting techniques precisely because they were abused as children and have experienced the firsthand physical and psychological consequences of abuse.

Displacement of Aggression.   One cartoon shows several panels consisting of a boss yelling at his employee, the employee yelling at his wife, the wife yelling at their child, and the child kicking the dog who chases the cat up a tree. Some child abuse can be explained by our social norm that the strong dominate the weak. Of women's aggression, Washburne (1983) observes, "Women's abuse of children stems directly from their own oppression in society and within the family. . . . some women displace their frustration and anger on their children, the family members who are less powerful than they" (p. 291).

It is estimated that only 1 in 7 incidents of child abuse is reported.

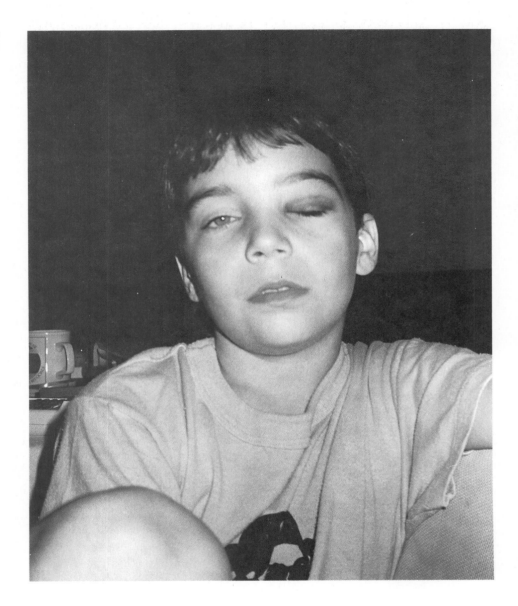

Social Isolation.   Unlike most societies of the world, many Americans rear their children in closed and isolated nuclear units. In extended kinship societies, other relatives are always present to help with the task of childrearing. Isolation means that there is no relief from the parenting role as well as no supervision by others who might interfere in child abusing situations.

In a national survey of family violence, there was no difference between blacks and whites in the rate of abusive violence toward children (Gelles & Straus, 1988). This puzzled the researchers, as blacks in the United States have higher rates of unemployment and lower annual incomes compared to whites. Both unemployment and low income are associated with child abuse. The researchers concluded that, while blacks did suffer more economic problems and life stresses than whites, they were also more involved in family and community activities than whites, who tend to be more isolated from kinship networks. According to Gelles and Straus,

> Blacks reported more contact with their relatives and more use of their relatives for financial support and child care. . . . The extensive social networks that black families develop and maintain insulate them from the severe economic stresses they also experience, and thus reduce what otherwise would have been a higher rate of parental violence (p. 86).

The Stepparenting Factor. Children are much more likely to be abused if they are being reared in a home where there is a stepparent.

■ **DATA:** *In one study, preschoolers living with one natural and one stepparent were 40 times more likely to become child abuse cases than were like-aged children living with two natural parents (Daly & Wilson, 1985).*

The researchers suggest that because stepparents do not have a biological tie with the stepchildren, they are less tolerant and altruistic toward them. This lack of tolerance, when coupled with stress in the marital and parental relationship, may result in abuse (Daly & Wilson, 1985).

☐   C O N S I D E R A T I O N   ☐

Although stepparents do not have a biological tie to their stepchildren, they may nevertheless develop strong, affectionate bonds with them. On the other hand, some stepparents may want a close emotional bond with their stepchildren, but are not accepted by the stepchildren. This lack of acceptance is, in some cases, related to the negative attitudes of divorced parents toward their ex-spouse's new partner. In order for children to develop strong bonds with their stepparent (and hence, reduce the likelihood of abuse by the stepparent), it is important that divorced parents encourage their children to have positive feelings for their stepparent.

Agency Response to Child Abuse

Social worker Patricia Capps has furnished the following information on how one state (North Carolina) responds to reported child abuse. Child abuse is normally discovered by a school counselor, neighbor, or physician who calls the local social service department, which is responsible for investigating the abuse. A social worker is required by law to visit the home of the alleged abused child within 24 hours if the abuse is physical and within 48 hours if the abuse is neglect. Parental response to these visits ranges from denial ("What are you talking about?") to anger ("Get off my porch!") to apology ("We're sorry it happened"). If the parents are cooperative, the caseworker discusses the nature and context of the abuse and ways to prevent it from recurring. Weekly visits are then made by the social worker to ensure that the abuse or neglect has been eliminated. If the parents are not cooperative, the social worker gets a court order to remove the child from the home temporarily. In some cases, the child is placed in a foster home.

Treatment for the Child Abuser

The most effective way to treat child abuse is to train parents to behave more appropriately with their children. Several clinicians have observed that the best setting for such learning may be small groups of parents that meet for eight sessions twice weekly to examine self-control, alternative actions, and effective childrearing procedures (Barth et al., 1983).

Self-Control. Parents are shown a videotape of parental reactions to a child spilling milk. In one scene the reaction is volatile; in the other, self-controlled. After the first scene, parents identify factors that may have made the parent vulnerable to abuse—fatigue, frustration over work, hunger, and impending illness. The second tape shows the parent talking aloud to identify these factors that create "vulnerability to provocation" (p. 317). After the child's accident, the parent stops, takes a deep breath, and consciously responds appropriately. After the video demonstration, first the group leader and then the members assume parent and child roles. "Initially guided by the script, then progressively without prompts, group members rehearse the use of self-talk, impulse delay, and relaxation to the 'spilled milk' situation" (p. 317).

Alternative Reactions. Group leaders and parents determine alternative behaviors to expressing anger aggressively—telephoning another parent, vacuuming the house, doing aerobic exercises, or looking in the mirror while smiling and saying positive things. Parents learn to yell "stop" subvocally and to engage in one of these behaviors overtly instead. An additional alternative is for parents to relax by means of deep breathing exercises and tranquil fantasies.

Childrearing Procedures. Harsh physical punishment has negative consequences for children and their parents. It teaches children to fear and sometimes to hate their parents. Although punishment may be effective in suppressing behavior temporarily, it does not teach the child appropriate behavior.

Positive reinforcement and time out are two alternative techniques parents can use to encourage the behavior they want in their children. "Catch children doing good" and praise them—thus reinforcing positive behavior—rather than waiting until they drift into expressing negative behavior that angers the parent is one of the most effective childrearing techniques parents can engage in. Parents are encouraged to systematically praise and compliment their children every day whenever the parents approve of the things their children do.

"Time out," also known as "time out from reinforcement," is an effective way of punishing children for negative behavior that avoids long-term negative consequences for the parent-child relationship. When the child misbehaves, the parent instructs the child to go to an isolated place in the home (for example, the bathroom) for about five minutes. Children usually do not like "time out;" it mildly punishes the behavior they were engaging in, so that the behavior is less likely to recur.

CONSIDERATION

If abusing parents learned self-control skills, alternatives to aggression, and "time out" as a childrearing tool, the frequency of child abuse would be reduced. However, for any treatment program to be effective, the abusing parents must be motivated. One factor that predicts motivation for therapy is the degree to which parents are emotionally bonded with their children.

Prevention of Child Abuse

The ultimate solution to child abuse and neglect is the early socialization of parents. Three steps can be taken to execute this solution (Dubowitz & Egan, 1988). First, educate the public, through the mass media, that child abuse and neglect do occur and that these behaviors are unacceptable. Second, provide community adult education programs on marriage and family relationships, including interpersonal communication, coping with stress, and parent skills training. More one-on-one training might involve a health visitor program at home for *all* new parents for one to two years after the birth of their firstborn. Three, provide quality, low-cost day care to help alleviate adult stress in reference to rearing children. "Good quality, affordable day care is needed particularly by lower-income families" (Dubowitz & Egan, 1988, 48).

For parents who discover that they are abusive, Parents Anonymous (6733 South Sepulveda Blvd. Suite 270; Los Angeles, CA 90045; 800–421–0353) is a national organization with 1,500 local chapters that have been created to provide immediate help and support. One of the goals of P.A. is to teach parents about child development. Often the cause of child abuse is that the parent is unaware of how children develop and, consequently, places unrealistic expectations upon a child.

The National Committee for the Prevention of Child Abuse also emphasizes that parents can control their behavior in reference to children. They recommend several alternatives to lashing out at one's child. These include remembering that they are the responsible adult, removing themselves from the situation with the child, phoning a friend, or taking a bath.

⁞ Incest

A variation of child abuse is incest. *Incest* is defined as sexual relations between close relatives, such as father and daughter, mother and son, and brother and sister. Although "sexual relations" may imply intercourse, it may also include fondling of the breasts and genitals and oral sex. "Relatives" usually implies biologically related individuals but may also include stepparents and stepsiblings. Sexual abuse is not unusual.

■ **DATA:** *In a national survey of adults concerning their childhood sexual abuse, 27 percent of the women and 16 percent of the men reported being victims (Finkelhor et al., 1990).*

Incest, particularly parent-child incest, is an abuse of power and authority. It is usually coercive and is therefore considered a form of family violence. A child is not in a position to consent to a sex act instigated by an adult. The experience of a black woman who, as a child, was forced to have sexual relations with her father is described here:

> I was around 6 years old when I was sexually abused by my father. He was not drinking at that time; therefore, he had a clear mind as to what he was doing. On looking back, it seemed so well planned. For some reason, my father wanted me to go with him to the woods behind our house to help him saw wood for the night. I went without any question. Once we got there, he looked around for a place to sit and wanted me to sit down with him. In doing so, he said, "Susan, I want you to do something for daddy." I said, "What's that daddy?" He went on to explain that "I want you to lie down, and we are going to play mama and daddy." Being a child, I said "okay," thinking it was going to be fun. I don't know what happened next because I can't remember if there was pain or whatever. I was threatened not to tell, and remembering how he beat my mother, I didn't want the same treatment. It happened approximately two other times. I remember not liking this at all. Since I couldn't tell mama, I came to the conclusion it was wrong and I was not going to let it happen again.
>
> But what could I do? Until age 18, I was constantly on the run, hiding from him when I had to stay home alone with him, staying out of his way so he wouldn't touch me by hiding in the corn fields all day long, under the house, in the barns, and so on, until my mother got back home, then getting punished by her for not doing the chores she had assigned to me that day. It was a miserable life growing up in that environment.

Although white women are sexually abused, too, it is not as unusual for a black woman to have had this kind of experience during her childhood.

■ **DATA:** *In a study of 60 sexually abusive families, 95 percent of the victims were female, 65 percent of the victims were black, and 80 percent of the offenders were the significant male in the household (Estroff, 1986).*

Twenty-three child victims of sexual abuse revealed the stages that were involved in their being victimized (Berliner & Conte, 1990):

■ *Sexualization of the relationship.* This stage took place gradually and began with the adults engaging in normal affectional contact or typical physical activities such as bathing or wrestling. Gradually these behaviors became more sexual.
■ *Justification of the sexual contact.* The victims were encouraged to perceive that the contact was not really sexual or to regard the sexual contact as appropriate.
■ *Maintenance of the child's cooperation.* In order to continue the sexual molestation with the child's cooperation, the adults threatened, or intimidated the child. Other adults exploited the child's need to be feel loved, valued, and cared for by an adult.

Father-Daughter Incest

Father-daughter incest has received the most attention in our society. Unlike the experience of the 6-year-old girl just described, incest may begin by affectionate cuddling between father and daughter. The father's motives may be sexual; his daughter's are typically nonsexual. More often, the daughter is innocent of the sexual connotations of her behavior; her motive is to feel acceptance and love from her father. Ambivalent feelings often result:

> My daddy never touched me unless he wanted to have me play with his genitals. I didn't like touching him there, but he was affectionate to me and told me how pretty I was. I was really mixed up about the whole thing.

Because of her ambivalence, the daughter may continue to participate in sexual activity with her father. Not only may she derive attention and affection from the relationship, but also she may develop a sense of power over her father. As she grows older, she may even demand gifts as the price of her silence.

Father-daughter incest may begin by force. There are a few cases of fathers having raped their daughters when there were very small—even as babies—injuring them badly. Baby incest is difficult for the wife to overlook, but she may sanction the sexual relations of her husband and her older daughter in her desire to preserve the family unit. One woman said that her "nerves" were about to "snap" because her husband and daughter were having sex. But she did not say anything about it because if she did, her husband, on whom she depended economically, might leave her alone with the children. "At least," she said, "his playing around is kept in the family."

What does the mother do when she finds out her husband has been molesting their daughter?

> ■ **DATA:** *In a study of 43 mothers whose daughters were sexually abused by their fathers, 56 percent sided with their daughters and rejected their mates, 9 percent denied the incest and took no action, and 35 percent sided with their mates at the expense of their daughters (Myer, 1985).*

Research suggests that a girl is more likely to be sexually abused by her step-father than by her natural father.

> ■ **DATA:** *Among women whose principal male parent was a stepfather, about 1 in 6 had been sexually abused by him before she reached the age of 14. In comparison, 1 in 43 women whose principal male parent was a biological father had been sexually abused by him (Russell, 1986).*

Russell suggests that stepfathers are more likely to sexually abuse stepdaughters than biological fathers are to abuse daughters for the following reasons.

1. Because there is no biological tie, the incest taboo is weak in the stepfather-stepdaughter relationship.
2. Stepfathers have a weaker parent-child bond compared to biological fathers.
3. Stepfathers may have greater opportunity to commit the offense, as mothers in remarriages are more likely to be employed fulltime.

Mother-Son Incest

Incest between mothers and sons occurs even less frequently than father-daughter incest. It rarely includes intercourse but is usually confined to various stimulating behaviors. The mother may continue to bathe her son long after he is capable of caring for himself, during which time she stimulates him sexually. Later, she may stimulate her son to ejaculation. The mother may also sleep with her son. Although no specific sexual contact may occur, she may sleep in the nude; this behavior is provocative as well as stimulating.

Brother-Sister Incest

One of the most common and least visible forms of incest occurs between siblings. Siblings are peers. Their incest may seem natural to them, and they may wonder why there is a taboo against it.

Whether brother-sister incest is a problem for siblings depends on a number of factors. If the siblings are young, of the same age, have an isolated sexual episode, engage only in exploratory, nonintercourse behavior, and both consent to the behavior, there may be little to no harm. But a change in any of these factors increases the chance that such incest will have negative consequences for future relationships.

If the siblings are young (age 4 to 8), they will have had less exposure to the idea that sexual behavior among siblings is inappropriate. Although they may have vague feelings that their parents would not approve of their sexual behavior, they will probably not feel the guilt usually associated with such behavior. As they grow older, they may relabel their former behavior as "child's play" to offset its impact.

Being of the same age will minimize the negative consequences of sibling incest. Although in most cases the siblings are of the same age, it is not uncommon for an older brother to seduce his younger sister into having intercourse with him. It is less common for an older sister to become sexually involved with a younger brother. A difference in age increases the chance that the sexual relationship will be exploitative.

A childhood sexual experience with a sibling that occurs once or twice is also less consequential than a series of such experiences that takes place over a number of years. Most incestuous experiences are limited, but some develop into a pattern and continue for years.

The nature of the sexual behavior is also important. Playing doctor, strip poker, or "you show me; I'll show you" probably has minimal impact on siblings. Siblings learn that these are common childhood experiences. But intercourse may increase the potential for negative effects.

▐ ■ **DATA:** *In one study, 18 percent of the brother-sister incest experiences in which the siblings were over the age of 13 involved intercourse. Half of the reactions to the experiences were positive; half were negative (Finkelhor, 1980).*

Consent is important if the negative consequences are to be minimal. Particularly when one sibling is older than the other, a brother or sister may use blackmail, bribery, or force to get the sibling to comply, as in the case of Jim, age 15, and his sister, Michelle, age 12:

> Michelle had stolen money from her mother to buy some marijuana. Jim threatened to tell their mother if Michelle did not let him fondle her when she was naked. After Michelle consented, Jim threatened her repeatedly over a period of three years. The parents never knew.

Impact of Incest

Two researchers (Morrow & Sorell, 1989) studied adolescent females who had been sexually abused and observed that the most devastating effects occurred when the sexual behavior was intercourse. These effects include lower self-esteem, higher levels of depression, and greater numbers of antisocial (e.g., running away from home, illegal drug use) and self-injurious (e.g., attempted suicide) behaviors. "This finding supports the contention that sexual intercourse in a tabooed incestuous relationship, which is likely to involve the loss of virginity, is viewed as extremely negative by adolescent incest victims" (p. 683).

Case studies of eight adult males who were molested as children by their nonpsychotic mothers revealed several problems the males had as adults. These problems include difficulty establishing intimate relationships with significant others (100 percent), depression (88 percent), and substance abuse (63 percent) (Krug, 1989).

Both women and men who have experienced incest as children experience a set of symptoms which fit the diagnosis of Post Traumatic Stress Disorder, a classification used by psychologists and psychiatrists. These symptoms include reexperiencing the trauma in terms of recurrent and invasive thoughts and emotions, feeling detached and feeling numb to the external world, and feeling compelled to avoid situations which remind them of the original trauma (Edwards, 1989).

□   C O N S I D E R A T I O N   □

If you have been the victim of sexual abuse and the event or events have resulted in thoughts of suicide, drug abuse, or low self-esteem, you might contact your local mental health center or student counseling center and schedule an appointment with a therapist to discuss these issues. To keep the feelings inside of you may be destructive.

Treatment for Incest Abusers and Victims

More than 4,000 children and their families have been treated by the Child Sexual Abuse Treatment Program in Santa Clara County, California. In a typical case, a girl will tell a school nurse or counselor that she is being sexually molested by her father. The mother is called, apprised of the situation, and asked to come get the child. The police department is also called, and an officer is sent to obtain an initial statement from the girl. If the investigation suggests there is sufficient evidence to warrant an arrest and referral to the district attorney for prosecution, the father is arrested and placed in jail or released on his own recognizance. But he is not allowed to make contact with the daughter or to return to the home; if he does return home, the child is removed to a foster home or care shelter.

Counseling begins immediately. According to one therapist:

> Incestuous families are badly fragmented as a result of the original dysfunctional family dynamics, which are further exacerbated on disclosure to civil authorities. The child, mother, and father must be treated separately before family therapy becomes productive (Giarretto, 1982, 263).

The mother and father are also contacted by telephone by a member of Parents United (P.O. Box 952; San Jose, CA 95108–0952; 408–453–7616) who has been through a similar experience and who becomes their "sponsor." In addition to personal contacts, the sponsor invites the clients to Parents United and prepares them for the initial group sessions in which other parents will discuss the incest that has occurred in their homes.

Meanwhile, depending on the circumstances and the recommendation of the social worker, the father might face criminal proceedings. If he is charged with a felony (usually for child molestation or statutory rape), two court appointed psychiatrists determine if he is a mentally disturbed sex offender. If he is, he is sent to the state psychiatric facility for chronic sex offenders. If he is not, he may be sent to prison or receive a suspended sentence if he agrees to participate in a treatment program of individual, group, and family counseling. The average length of treatment is about nine months.

While one school of thought suggests that the child abuser can be treated via individual and family therapy, another suggests that the abuser is a pathological offender (chronically pedophilic), is "dangerous," and should be permanently incarcerated. Mass media have reported incidents of abusers being released from prison who commit similar crimes. These incidents are used to suggest that the abuser cannot be rehabilitated.

Help for sex abuse victims is available nationwide through Childhelp USA. Once a victim calls 1–800–422–4453, the counseling process begins immediately.

Prevention of Incest

Their body belongs to them, and they can decide who touches it.
—JUDITH HOOPER

The Committee for Children (P.O. Box 15190, Wedgewood Station; Seattle, WA 98115; 206–524–6020) is an organization that helps children acquire knowledge and skills to protect them from sexual abuse. Through various presentations in the elementary schools, children are taught how to differentiate between appropriate and inappropriate touching by adults or siblings, to understand that it is okay to feel uncomfortable if they do not like the way someone else is touching them, to say "no" in potentially exploitative situations, and to tell other adults if the offending behavior occurs.

□   C O N S I D E R A T I O N   □

Edwin Schur (1988) emphasizes that traditional male gender role socialization may perpetuate child sexual abuse. Schur suggests that "our culture promotes sexual victimization of children when it encourages males to believe that they have overpowering sexual needs that must be met by whatever means available" (p. 173). Schur says that this belief, and the association of sexual conquest with masculinity, enables men to think of using children for their own sexual gratification. The implication here is that one way to discourage child sexual abuse is to change our traditional notions of masculinity and male sexuality.

:: Parent and Sibling Abuse

Children are not only victims of family abuse, they are also perpetrators. In this section we examine abuse that involves children harming their parents and their siblings.

Parent Abuse

The other side of child abuse is parent abuse. Some people assume that because parents are typically physically and socially more powerful than their children, they are immune from being abused by their children. But parents are often targets of their children's anger, hostility, and frustration. It is not uncommon for teenage and even younger children to physically and verbally lash out at their parents.

■ **DATA:** *In one survey of family violence, almost 10 percent of the parents reported that they have been hit, bit, or kicked at least once by their children (Gelles & Straus, 1988).*

The same researchers found that three percent of parents report that they had been victimized at least once by a severe form of violence inflicted by a child age eleven or older.

Children are capable of violent behavior that is as devastating as violence inflicted by adults. Children have been known to push parents down stairs, set the house on fire while their parents are in it, and use weapons such as guns and knives to inflict serious injuries or even kill a parent.

Parents who are physically abused by their children may suffer psychologically as well. They may feel like they failed in the role of parent and may blame themselves for their children's behavior. Abused parents may not reveal to others that their children mistreat them, for they may fear that they will be publicly blamed for their children's violent behavior. There are virtually no social programs for battered parents.

Sibling Abuse

Observe a family with two or more children and you will likely observe some amount of sibling violence. Even in "well-adjusted" families, some degree of fighting among the children is expected. In the television series, *The Wonder Years,* Kevin Arnold is constantly being bullied by his older brother, Wayne. Most incidents of sibling violence consist of slaps, pushes, kicks, bites, and punches. However, serious and dangerous violent behavior between siblings occurs as well.

■ **DATA:** *It is estimated that each year about 3 percent of children in the United States use a weapon towards a brother or sister (Gelles & Straus, 1988).*

:: Elder Abuse

Another form of family abuse involves abuse of the elderly. Although the definitions regarding what constitutes elder abuse vary, some forms of abuse include the following (White, 1989):

1. Physical abuse: infliction of bruises, lacerations, fractures, or burns.
2. Psychological abuse: threats, insults, harrassment, withholding affection.
3. Nutritional neglect: failure to provide adequate nutrition.
4. Medical neglect: failure to provide appropriate medical care for an elderly person.
5. Financial exploitation: manipulating an elderly person to sign resources away to the caregiver.

Psychological abuse is the most frequent form of elder abuse (Lucas, 1989).

As is true of all forms of domestic violence, reliable estimates of the prevalence of elder abuse are difficult to obtain.

■ **DATA:** *Estimates of elder abuse vary from 1 to 10 percent of the elderly population (Pillemer & Suitor, 1988).*

The abusers of the elderly tend to be either children or spouses of the victim. Research suggests that it is more often a spouse, rather than a child, who victimizes an elderly person.

■ **DATA:** *One study revealed that nearly two-thirds of elderly victims were abused by their spouses, while less than one-fourth were abused by their children (Pillemer & Finkelhor, reported in Gelles & Straus, 1988).*

It is commonly believed that spouses and adult children who are burdened with the responsibility of caring for an elderly spouse or parent may abuse the elderly person out of frustration and stress. While this pattern does occur, the more typical abuser is not responsible for the care of the elderly person, but rather is dependent on the elder. In one study, Pillemer (1985) found that 64 percent of the abusers in his sample were financially dependent on their elderly victims, and 55 percent were dependent on the victims for housing. Pillemer found the abusers to be very dependent individuals, including spouses who were disabled or cognitively impaired and children who were unable to separate themselves from their parents. One explanation of why this pattern occurs is that abusive acts compensate for the abuser's perceived lack or loss of power.

Adult children who are most likely to abuse their parents tend to be under a great deal of stress and to use alcohol or drugs. They also tend to be white, middle-aged, and lower-middle or upper-lower class (White, 1989). In some cases, parent abusers are "getting back" for their parents' maltreatment of them as children. In still other cases, the children are frustrated with the burden of having to care for their elderly parents. For the last category of parent abusers, local agencies throughout the nation provide such services as Meals on Wheels and elderly day care to help children with their aging parents. The name of the agency nearest you may be obtained by writing the National Association of Area Agencies on Aging (600 Maryland Avenue, S.W., Suite 208; Washington, D.C.

20024). A newsletter, *Advice for Adults with Aging Parents*, is also available from Helpful Publications, Inc. (310 West Durham Street; Philadelphia, PA 19119–2901)

:: Family Violence: A Cross-Cultural Perspective

David Levinson (1988) described the results of an extensive cross-cultural study of family violence that looked at family violence in 90 non-Western societies. These societies represent the major cultural and geographical regions of the world. In this section, we look at the results of this study in order to gain a cross-cultural perspective on family violence.

Cross-cultural Family Violence Statistics

Levinson reports that wife beating is the most common form of family violence, occurring in 84.5 percent of the 90 societies. Husband beating, on the other hand, occurs in only 26.9 percent of the 90 societies. In 15.5 percent of the societies, wife beating is rare or unheard of. In contrast, husband beating is rare or unheard of in 73.1 percent of the 90 societies. Adultery or sexual jealousy is a major reason for spouse abuse of both men and women.

In reference to child abuse, some form of physical punishment is used in 74.4 percent of societies. Physical punishment of children is rarely or never used in 26.5 percent of societies.

In our society, fighting among siblings is expected and common. However, physical violence between non-adult siblings is rare or absent in 56.2 percent of societies.

Societies with Minimal or No Family Violence

Out of the 90 societies in Levinson's study of family violence, 16 societies are virtually free of family violence. In these societies, spouse, child, and sibling abuse are rare or nonexistant. Levinson suggests that four factors explain the low rates of family abuse in these 16 societies.

1. Spouses have equal decision-making power in household and financial matters, equal freedom to divorce for both men and women, and no double standard regarding premarital sex.
2. Marriage is monogamous and the divorce rate relatively low, which suggests marital stability and emotional and economic dependence between spouses.
3. Disagreements between adults are resolved peacefully through mediation, disengagement, or avoidance of conflict situations.
4. Family members who are victims or are threatened with physical harm by a family member are offered immediate help by neighbors who intervene or provide shelter.

:: Trends

Trends in handling violent and abusive relationships include greater public awareness that such behavior occurs in intimate relationships, an increased number of shelters for battered women, and a less punitive and more rehabilitative approach to sexually abusive fathers. Regarding the latter, the current trend is putting the father on probation, thereby keeping the family together, and involving family members in individual and group counseling. Imprisonment only further loosens the family members' emotional ties and, in many cases, economically devastates the family. One social worker commented:

> Once you take the father out of the home, even though the mother may work, she can't produce the income two of them would produce. Also, it is assumed that every daughter wants her father to be sent to prison because of what he did to her. But that simply isn't so. I was in a courtroom when a judge sentenced a father to 15 years in prison for molesting his 15-year-old daughter. The daughter was in the courtroom at the time of the sentencing and went absolutely berserk. After regaining her composure, she pleaded with the judge not to "send my daddy to prison."

The Institute for the Community as Extended Family (P.O. Box 952; San Jose; CA 95108–0952; 408–280–5055) will continue to train professionals to develop child sexual abuse treatment programs like the one in Santa Clara County, California. The Institute has also developed another organization, Adults Molested as Children, to provide help to adults who are still adversely affected by earlier sexual abuse experiences.

Until recently, spouse abuse has been synonymous with woman battering. Definitions and popular conceptions of domestic violence will likely change in the coming years to reflect the degree to which women participate in violent behavior.

:: Summary

Violence may occur in dating relationships, and is especially likely and intense in the context of first dates. Such violence includes pushing, slapping, threatening, and punching. Either or both partners may be the abuser. It is not unusual for couples to continue their relationship after violence has occurred. For some individuals, violence is viewed as part of a love relationship. Others have no alternative to the primary relationship. Still others feel they deserve the abuse.

Violence may also extend into cohabiting and marriage relationships. Such violence may be explained by traditional gender role socialization, previous family learning, the perceived reinforcement following violence, and the modeling of violence in the larger society.

Rape occurs in marriage as well as outside of it. Marital rape may be part of a larger context of violence in the relationship or a specific conflict over sex. This type of rape is potentially more devastating than rape by a stranger because the woman lives with the rapist. Having the husband arrested for violence and abuse seems to reduce the frequency of such abuse. Therapy that focuses on communication and conflict resolution are alternative responses to marital violence.

Child abuse is any action that results in nonaccidental harm to the child's physical or developmental well-being. Child abusers may be found in all races, and all income and educational levels. A primary predictive factor of the child abuser is a lack of emotional bonding with the child. Although there is no single cause of child abuse, the factors involved are lack of impulse control, parental experience of abuse as children, displacement of aggression, and environmental stressors. Successful treatment of child abuse includes teaching parents to exercise self-control and to use "time out" and positive reinforcement for good behavior as alternatives to harsh punishment for bad behavior.

Incest may be between father and daughter, mother and son, or brother and sister. Although brother-sister incest is probably most prevalent, parent-offspring incest is the most destructive. Parents or stepparents may use their authority to coerce the child into a pattern of sexual relations.

Treatment for incest should involve the whole family in individual, marital, and family therapy for several months. Teaching young children that it is not okay to let other adults touch them in ways that make them uncomfortable and to tell another adult if someone tries to do so is an incest prevention technique.

Children may also abuse their parents and each other (sibling abuse). Abusers of elderly persons are more likely to be the victim's spouse rather than child and are likely to be dependent on the elderly victim for money or housing.

Cross-culturally, family abuse patterns vary. The most common form of family violence is wife beating. In some societies, family violence is rare or nonexistent.

Trends in handling violence and abuse include greater visibility of the subject, more shelters for abused wives, and a less punitive approach to parents who abuse their children. In addition, more attention will be given to abusive situations in which men are victimized by women.

Questions for Reflection

1. Have you experienced violence or abuse in your intimate relationships? If so, how has this behavior affected your relationships?
2. To what degree would you be willing to continue a relationship in which you were abused?
3. What are your feelings about criminally prosecuting parents who have sex with their children versus putting parent sexual abusers on probation and immersing them in individual, marital, and family therapy?

References

Barth, R. P., B. J. Blythe, S. P. Schinke, and R. F. Schilling, II. Self-control training with maltreating parents. *Child Welfare*, 1983, *72*, 313–324.

Berk, R. A., P. J. Newton, and S. F. Berk. What a difference a day makes: An empirical study of the impact of shelters for battered women. *Journal of Marriage and the Family*, 1986, *48*, 481–490.

Berliner, Lucy and J. R. Conte. The process of victimization: The victims' perspective. *Child Abuse and Neglect,* 1990, *14,* 29–40.

Bowman, M. L. Measuring marital coping and its correlates. *Journal of Marriage and the Family,* 1990, *52,* 463–474.

Daly, M. and M. Wilson. Child abuse and other risks of not living with both parents. *Ethology and Sociobiology,* 1985, *6,* 197–210.

Dubowitz, H. and H. Egan. The maltreatment of infants. *Abuse and Victimization Across the Life Span.* Edited by Martha B. Straus. Baltimore, MD.: The Johns Hopkins University Press, 1988, 32–53.

Edwards, Patrick. Assessment of symptoms in adult survivors of incest: A factor analytic study of the responses to childhood incest questionnaire. *Child Abuse and Neglect,* 1989, *13,* 101–110.

Estroff, S. Kinship and conflict: Child sexual abuse as a family problem. *Social Science,* 1986, *71,* 11–15.

Finkelhor, D., G. Hotaling, I. A. Lewis, and C. Smith. Sexual abuse in a national survey of adult men and women: Prevalence, characteristics, and risk factors. *Child Abuse and Neglect,* 1990, *14,* 19–28.

Finkelhor, D. Sex among siblings: A survey on prevalence, variety and effects. *Archives of Sexual Behavior,* 1980, *9,* 171–194.

Finkelhor, D. and Yllo, K. Rape in marriage. *Abuse and Victimization Across the Life Span.* Edited by Martha B. Straus. Baltimore, Md.: The Johns Hopkins University Press, 1988, 140–152.

Flynn, C. P. Relationship violence by women: Issues and implications. *Family Relations,* 1990, *39,* 194–198.

Gelles, R. and M. Straus. *Intimate violence.* New York: Simon and Schuster, 1988.

Giarretto, H. A comprehensive child sexual abuse treatment program. *Child Abuse and Neglect,* 1982, *6,* 263–278.

Goldstein, D. and A. Rosenbaum. An evaluation of the self-esteem of maritally violent men. *Family Relations,* 1985, *34,* 425–428.

Herrenkohl, E. C., R. C. Herrenkohl, and L. J. Toedter. Perspectives on the intergenerational transmission of abuse. *The Dark Side of Families: Current Family Violence Research.* Edited by D. Finkelhor, R. J. Gelles, G. T. Hotaling, and M. A. Straus. Beverly Hills, Calif.: Sage, 1983, 305–316.

Jaffe, N. *Spouse abuse.* New York Public Affairs Committee, 1990.

Kierman, J. E. and V. L. Taylor. Coercive sexual behavior among Mexican-American college students. *Journal of Sex & Marital Therapy,* 1990, *16,* 44–50.

Knudsen, Dean D. Duplicate reports of child maltreatment: A research note. *Child Abuse and Neglect,* 1989, *13,* 41–43.

Kohn, A. Shattered innocence. *Psychology Today,* February 1987, 54–58.

Krug, Ronald S. Adult male report of childhood sexual abuse by mothers: Case descriptions, motivations, and long-term consequences. *Child Abuse and Neglect,* 1989, *13,* 111–119.

Krugman, R. D., M. Lenherr, B. A. Betz, and G. E. Fryer. The relationship between unemployment and physical abuse of children. *Child Abuse and Neglect,* 1986, *10,* 415–418.

Lane, K. E. and P. A. Gwartney-Gibbs. Violence in the context of dating and sex. *Journal of Family Issues,* 1985, *6,* 45–59.

Levinson, David. Family violence in cross-cultural perspective. *Handbook of Family Violence.* Edited by V. B. Van Hasselt, R. L. Morrison, A. S. Bellack, and M. Herson. New York: Plenum Press, 1988, 435–455.

Lockhart, L. L. A reexamination of the effects of race and social class on the incidence of marital violence: A search for reliable differences. *Journal of Marriage and the Family,* 1987, *49,* 603–610.

Lucas, Emma T. Elder mistreatment: Is it really abuse? *Free Inquiry in Creative Sociology,* 1989, *17,* 95–101.

MacAndrew, C. and R. Edgerton. *Drunken comportment: A social explanation.* Chicago: Aldine, 1969.

Makepeace, James. Dating, living together, and courtship violence. *Violence in Dating Relationships.* Edited by M. A. Pirog-Good and Jan E. Stets. New York: Greenwood Press, 1989, 94–107.

Malone, J., A. Tyree, and K. D. O'Leary. Generalization and containment: Different effects of past aggression for wives and husbands. *Journal of Marriage and the Family,* 1989, *51,* 687–697.

Margolin, L., M. Miller, and P. B. Moran. When a kiss is not just a kiss: Relating violations of consent in kissing to rape myth acceptance. *Sex Roles,* 1989, *20,* 231–243.

McKinney, K. Measures of verbal, physical, and sexual dating violence by gender. *Free Inquiry in Creative Sociology,* 1986, *14,* 55–60.

Morrow, R. B. and G. T. Sorrell. Factors affecting self-esteem, depression, and negative behaviors in sexually abused female adolescents. *Journal of Marriage and the Family,* 1989, *51,* 677–686.

Myer, M. H. A new look at mothers of incest victims. *Journal of Social Work and Human Sexuality,* Spring 1985, *3,* 47–58.

Oates, R. K., A. A. Davis, and M. G. Ryan. Predictive factors for child abuse. *International Perspectives on Family Violence.* Edited by R. J. Gelles and C. P. Cornell. 1983, 97–106.

Pagelow, Mildred D. Marital rape. *Handbook of Family Violence.* Edited by V. B. Van Hasselt, R. L. Morrison, A. S. Bellack, and M. Hersen. New York: Plenum Press, 1988, 207–232.

Pillemer, Karl A. and David Finkelhor. The prevalence of elder abuse: A random sample survey. Paper presented at the annual meetings of the Gerontological Society of America, Chicago, November 1986. Reported in R. J. Gelles and M. A. Straus, *Intimate Violence.* New York: Simon and Schuster, 1988, 63.

Pillemer, K. The dangers of dependency: New findings on domestic violence against the elderly. *Social Problems,* 1985, *33,* 146–158.

Pillemer, K. and J. Jill Suitor. Elder abuse. *Handbook of Family Violence.* Edited by V. B. Van Hasselt, R. L. Morrison, A. S. Bellack, and M. Hersen. New York: Plenum Press, 1988, 247–270.

Renzetti, Claire M. Building a second closet: Third party responses to victims of lesbian partner abuse. *Family Relations,* 1989, *38,* 157–163.

Roscoe, B. and N. Benaske. Courtship violence experienced by abused wives: Similarities in patterns of abuse. *Family Relations,* 1985, *34,* 419–424.

Russell, Diana E. H. *The secret trauma: Incest in the lives of girls and women.* New York: Basic Books, 1986.

Schur, Edwin. *The Americanization of sex.* Philadelphia: Temple University Press, 1988.

Shupe, A., W. A. Stacey, and L. R. Hazlewood. *Violent men, violent couples.* Lexington, Mass.: D.C. Heath and Co., 1987.

Steinmetz, S. K., and J. S. Lucca. Husband battering. *Handbook of Family Violence.* Edited by V. B. Van Hasselt, R. L. Morrison, A. S. Bellack, and M. Herson. New York: Plenum Press, 1988, 233–246.

Stets, J. E. Verbal and physical aggression in marriage. *Journal of Marriage and the Family,* 1990, *52,* 501–514.

Stets, J. E. and M. A. Straus. The marriage as a hitting license: A comparison of assaults in dating, cohabiting, and married couples. *Violence in Dating Relationships.* Edited by M. A. Pirog-Good and Jan E. Stets. New York: Greenwood Press, 1989, 33–52.

Straus, M. A., R. Gelles, and S. K. Steinmetz. *Behind closed doors: Violence in the American family.* Garden City, N.Y.: Doubleday, 1980.

Strube, M. J. and L. S. Barbour. The decision to leave an abusive relationship: Economic dependence and psychological commitment. *Journal of Marriage and the Family,* 1983, *45,* 785–793.

Toufexis, A. Our violent kids. *Time,* June 12, 1989, pp. 52–58.

U.S. Dept. of Justice, Federal Bureau of Investigation, *Crime in the United States,* 1988, Washington, D.C., 1989, p. 13.

Washburne, C. K. A feminist analysis of child abuse and neglect. *The Dark Side of Families: Current Family Violence Research.* Edited by D. Finkelhor, R. J. Gelles, G. T. Hotaling, & M. A. Straus. Beverly Hill, Calif.: Sage, 1983. 289–292.

White, Melvin. Elder abuse. *Aging and the Family.* Edited by Stephen J. Bahr and Evan T. Peterson. Lexington, Mass.: Lexington Books, 1988, 261–271.

Willbach, Daniel. Ethics and family therapy: The case management of family violence. *Journal of Marital and Family Therapy,* 1989, *15,* 43–52.

CHOICES

CHOICES ABOUT ABUSIVE relationships involve basically the decision to terminate or to continue such relationships.

Terminate an Abusive Dating Relationship?

People disagree on whether to terminate an abusive courtship relationship. In a marriage and family class, 70 students were asked if they would continue a relationship with someone they were dating who hit and kicked them. Their answers follow.

End Dating Relationship

Most said they would end the dating relationship, because such violence is intolerable in an intimate relationship, because they would lose respect for their partner, or because they would fear that the abuse would recur.

If my partner hit me out of anger or jealously, it would be the first and last time. I would absolutely terminate the relationship—my reasoning being that if a person hits you once, he will more than likely hit you again and again.

I would terminate the relationship immediately because I am totally against any type of violence. Striking anyone is an inhumane gesture, especially if it is done out of anger.

If a problem arises, I feel we should be able to discuss it in an adult manner. Hitting me would be uncalled for. If my partner hit me, I would hit him back and the relationship would be over.

If he feels that he could do it once and get away with it, he might do it again. If we were to marry, he would probably do it even more, so I would get out of such a relationship while I could.

I would have no desire to nurture a violent relationship and would leave the bum.

I would lose all respect for that person and couldn't trust her again. Besides, if she hit me, she might hit our child

Continue Dating Relationship

A few said they would continue the dating relationship with the partner but that it would depend on the circumstances.

If the infraction was not severe and if the person was "sorry" for his actions and if he thought he had lost control for a split second, I would want us to continue our relationship. But if he hit and kicked me on a regular basis and showed no remorse, I would end the relationship.

I would not terminate a dating relationship if my partner hit or kicked me because I would want to find out my partner's rationale for her behavior. Maybe it was something that I did that provoked her anger.

It would really depend on the situation or the severity of the blows. If the violence was minimal, I would stick around. But violence is not the kind of thing I would put up with too often.

I would probably let it slide the first time, yet I would tell him that he had one and only one more chance. If it ever happened again, I would probably leave him. It also would depend on how long I had been dating him. If it was a second date, I'd leave him in a heartbeat, because there are other fish in the sea. If I had been dating him for a long time, I could tell if his outburst was intentional or emotional.

Terminate Abusive Marriage Relationship?

These students were also asked if they would end their marriage if the spouse hit and kicked them. Although some said they would seek a divorce, most felt that they should try to work it out.

Seek a Divorce

Those opting for divorce basically felt they couldn't live with someone who had or would abuse them.

I abhor violence of any kind, and since a marriage should be based on love, kicking is certainly out of the norm. I would lose all respect for my mate and I could never trust him again. It would be over.

Continue Marriage Relationship

Most felt that marriage was too strong a commitment to end if the abuse could be stopped.

I would not divorce my spouse if she hit or kicked me. I'm sure that there's always room for improvement in my behavior although I don't think it's necessary to assault me. I recognize that under certain circumstances, it's the quickest way to draw my attention to the problems at hand. I would try to work through our difficulties with my spouse.

The physical contact would lead to a separation. During that time, I would expect him to feel sorry for what he had done and to seek psychiatric help. My anger would be so great, it's quite hard to know exactly what I would do.

I wouldn't leave him right off. I would try to get him to counseling. If we could not work through the problem, I would leave him. If there was no way we could live together, I guess divorce would be the answer.

I would not divorce my husband because I don't believe in breaking the sacred vows of marriage. But I would separate from him and let him suffer!

I would tell her I was leaving but that she could keep me if she would agree for us to see a counselor to ensure that the abuse never happened again.

Impact of Social Influences on Choices

Part of the reason people stay in or leave abusive relationships is their perception of how others view them. One woman said that she couldn't bring herself to tell her mother that her husband was beating her up, so she endured the beatings for five years. Finally, the beatings became so frequent and painful that she no longer cared how her mother would respond. She had reached the point at which she had to leave her husband to survive. She went to see a close girlfriend, who had also been abused by her husband and who had left him. The friend strongly encouraged her to leave and pointed out that there is a life beyond abuse. In this example, just as one social influence (the mother) kept this wife in an abusive relationship, another social influence (the friend) helped her to leave her abusive husband.

Gender role socialization also influences people in their decision regarding whether to stay in an abusive relationship. Men have traditionally been socialized to view themselves as "the stronger sex." A man who is abused may feel that to leave the relationship is to admit that he is "weaker" than his partner, which may threaten his masculine identity. Traditional female role socialization has emphasized female passivity and dependency, which may influence a woman to stay in an abusive relationship. As traditional gender stereotypes are being replaced with egalitarian role relationships, both men and women may be more likely to leave abusive relationships.

P A R T

IV

□

Families

ONE HUNDRED YEARS ago, technology had very little impact on the family. The automobile and the television were nonexistent, and medical technology was relatively primitive. Family members spent most of their time working on the farm. Travel was by horse-drawn buggy, and information sources were limited to word of mouth and the printed page.

Today, automobiles of every color, style, and option are available to take courtship partners away from the watchful eyes of parents and families on extended, cross-country vacations. Television news provides instant exposure to the happenings of the day throughout the United States and the world. Situation comedies comment on a variety of lifestyles, values, and behaviors.

Medical advances such as artificial insemination, test-tube fertilization, ovum transfer, amniocentesis, and chorion biopsy offer infertile couples a way to increase the probability of pregnancy and help to ensure a healthy fetus and infant. In addition, new contraceptives (subdermal implants for women, a "pill" for men) are being developed to provide increased control over family size.

C H A P T E R

13

Planning Children and Birth Control

CONTENTS

IS IT TRUE?

1. Childfree couples often go out at night and are frequently on vacation.

2. Middle-age couples whose children have left home are more satisfied than couples who never had children.

3. Only children have different personalities than children who have siblings.

4. Men with stable incomes are more interested in having children than unemployed men.

5. Most unmarried women who attend the "thinkers' group" sponsored by Single Mothers by Choice to contemplate whether to have a baby decide not to have a baby.

1 = F; 2 = T; 3 = F; 4 = T; 5 = T.

P ARENTHOOD SHOULD BEGIN with planning. Before each academic term as a student, you decide how many courses you want to take and when you want to take them. You probably try to avoid overloading your schedule and feel pleased when you get the sequence of courses you want. Successful family planning means having the number of children you want when you want to have them. Although this seems to be a sensible and practical approach to parenthood, many couples leave the number and spacing of their children to chance.

Family planning has benefits for the mother and the child. Having several children at short intervals increases the chances of premature birth, infectious disease, and death for the mother or the baby. Parents can minimize such risks by planning fewer children at longer intervals.

Both parents may also benefit from family planning by pacing the financial demands of parenthood. "We spaced our three children every four years," said one father, "so we would have only one child in college at a time."

Conscientious family planning may also reduce the number of children born to parents who do not want them. A child born to rejecting parents is a tragic situation—but a preventable one.

> ■ **DATA:** *Six million women become pregnant each year. Of these pregnancies, 3.3 million or 54 percent are not planned (Koop, 1989). Of all births to white women, 17% are to unmarried women. Of all births to black women, 62% are to unmarried women (Statistical Abstract of the United States: 1990, Table 90).*

Family planning also benefits society by enabling people to avoid having children they cannot feed and clothe adequately—children whose rearing may have to be subsidized by the taxpayer. Finally, family planning is essential to halting the continuing expansion of the world population and the consequent drain on limited environmental resources.

In this chapter you are encouraged to consider four basic questions: Do you want to have children? How many? When do you want to get pregnant? What form of birth control will you use to ensure the family size that you want?

▪▪ Do You Want To Have Children?

In this section, we examine the social influences that affect our decision to have children. We also look at reasons that individuals give for wanting children.

> ■ **DATA:** *Over 95 percent of wives ages 18–34 expect to have children (Statistical Abstract of the United States: 1990, Table 98).*

Positive Aspects of Parenthood

In their book *Parents in Contemporary America,* researchers LeMasters and DeFrain (1989) write that "rearing children is probably the hardest and most thankless job in the world" (p. 21). Yet most Americans express a desire to have this experience. Some of the benefits parents report from having children include play, companionship, and having a "real" family.

Play. Children give you an excuse to express the child in yourself that society assumes you have outgrown. One parent said, "I like to ride an inner tube down a river with my kids in the summer and swing off a rope into the water, as I did when I was a kid. I can't ask my friends to play like that; they'd think I was nuts. With your own kids, you've got the chance to play, really play, again." It is also fun to observe and join in the spontaneity that children bring to their activities. Children have no internal schedule that tells them what they should do next. Being tickled, playing hide and seek, and flying a kite always have the potential of leading to another, perhaps more surprising, adventure.

Companionship. In a study of 610 married couples, researchers found that children are viewed as important sources of love and affection (Neal et al., 1989). Children often provide emotional nurturance to their parents, as well as protection against loneliness.

Parents also feel that they have a sense of immortality in their children. "There will be a part of me left when I die," said one parent.

Play is something both parents and children can agree on.

Family Relationships. Many young married couples view children as necessary for "having a real family life" (Neal et al., 1989). The emotional bond that each parent forms with their child may provide an additional marital bond.

A parent may also value the relationships that form between their child and other family members, such as the child's grandparents, aunts, uncles, and cousins.

Negative Aspects of Parenthood

The positive aspects of parenthood have a flip side. Research findings suggest that the primary disadvantages of having a first or additional child consist of the financial costs of children, the increased work demands for the employed mother, and the drastic changes in lifestyle that are required (Neal et al., 1989). Children may also have a negative impact on the marriage relationship. We will review this latter issue in Chapter 14 on Having Children.

Financial Costs. Demographers estimate that couples will spend $5,774 on their baby the first year (Cutler, 1990). Up to age 18 (college expenses are not included), one child costs $133,000. When couples have more than one child, they spend less on each child. A middle-class married couple with three children will spend $86,000 on each child to age 18 for a total of $258,000. These figures assume that the wife works part time (Crispell, 1989).

New Role Demands for Employed Mother. For single mothers, getting ready for work means not only getting one's self ready, but also getting the child(ren) ready for school or day care. Although teenagers may not require parental assistance in getting ready for school, younger children must be awakened, dressed, groomed, and fed breakfast. For infants and toddlers, a diaper bag must be packed and bottles and/or food prepared.

Working mothers who are married or cohabiting may share these morning childcare responsibilities with their partners. However, because the traditional female role is that of primary caregiver, the woman often takes on more of the childcare responsibility than her male partner.

Another difficulty involves making childcare arrangements (or staying home from work) when children are sick, have teachers' workdays, or are on school vacation. The issue of childcare is explored in more detail in Chapter 15.

Children, from a strictly economically rational viewpoint, are unalloyed economic liabilities for an entire lifetime.

—ROBERT JOHN

Changes in Lifestyle. Children influence the total lifestyle of the couple, who must adjust to new routines. Changes include more frequent visits by and to parents and in-laws, less sleep (sometimes chronic exhaustion), family-focused entertainment (G-rated movies), less lovemaking, and loss of discretionary income. Having children also restricts a couple's social life.

"Before you have a baby," said one father, "you assume that you can always get a baby sitter when you want to and that your social life won't change. The reality is that when you spontaneously decide to go out, it's too late to find a sitter. You have to plan every social event at least three days ahead. The result—you go less often."

Another father who had been married 10 years before his child arrived expressed bitter resentment about the baby's interference with the sailing weekends he and his wife usually enjoyed from April through late fall each year. "You can't take a baby on a sailboat, and being with Carol was part of the fun. We fought it for three months but finally sold the boat. If we had known that a baby equals a blackout on our sailing together, we would have reconsidered having a child."

☐   C O N S I D E R A T I O N   ☐

Parents experience these aspects of parenthood to a different extent at different times throughout the family life cycle. Parenthood is neither positive nor negative all the time but is a mixture of these experiences over the years.

Social Influences on Deciding to Have Children

We live in a pronatalistic, or prochild producing society. Unless the members of a society have children, the society will cease to exist. The Shakers, also called the United Society of Believers, provide an example of the consequences of a social deemphasis on procreation. Founded in New York in 1787, the Shakers were a religious community that grew to more than 5,000 members by winning others to their faith. Their doctrine included an emphasis on celibacy, which resulted in no marriage, no sexual intercourse, and no children. The effect of prohibiting reproduction was to ensure that the Shaker community would eventually cease to exist. Today, only a few members remain who were recruited into the community.

Aware of the importance of reproduction for its continued existence, our society tends to encourage childbearing, an attitude known as *pronatalism*. Our family, friends, religion, government, and schools help to develop positive attitudes toward parenthood. Cultural observances also function to reinforce these attitudes.

So I've realized there are other things grown-ups should be and need to be concerned with—such as kids.

—DAVID LETTERMAN

Family. The fact that we are reared in families encourages us to have families of our own. Our parents are our models. They married; we marry. They had children; we have children. Some parents exert a much more active influence. "I'm 73 and don't have much time. Will I ever see a grandchild?," asked the mother of an only child. Other remarks parents have made include "If you don't hurry up, your younger sister is going to have a baby before you do," "We're setting up a trust fund for your brother's child, and we'll do the same for yours," "Did you know that Nash and Marilyn (the child's contemporaries) just had a daughter?" "I think you'll regret not having children when you're old," and "Don't you want a son to carry on your name?"

Friends. Our friends who have children influence us to do likewise. After sharing an enjoyable weekend with friends who had a little girl, one husband wrote to the host and hostess, "Lucy and I are always affected by Karen—she is such a good child to have around. We haven't made up our minds yet, but our desire to have a child of our own always increases after we leave your home." This couple became parents 16 months later.

Religion. Religion may be a powerful influence on the decision to have children. Catholics are taught that having children is the basic purpose of marriage and gives meaning to the union. Although many Catholics use contraception and reject their church's emphasis on procreation, some internalize the church's message. One Catholic woman said, "My body was made by God, and I should use it to produce children for Him. Other people may not understand it, but that's how I feel." Judaism also has a strong family orientation. Couples who choose to be childfree are less likely than couples with children to adhere to any set of religious beliefs.

Government. The tax structures imposed by our federal and state governments support parenthood. Married couples without children pay higher taxes than couples with children, although the reduction in taxes is not large enough to be a primary inducement to have children.

Governments in other countries have encouraged or discouraged childbearing in different ways. In the 1930s, as a mark of status for women contributing to the so-called Aryan race, Adolf Hitler bestowed the German Mother's Cross on Nazi Germany's most fertile mothers—a gold cross for eight or more children, a silver cross for six or seven, and a bronze cross for four or five.

China has a set of incentives to encourage families to have a maximum of one child. Couples who have only one child are given a "one-child glory certificate," which entitles them to special priority housing, better salaries, a five-percent supplementary pension, free medical care for the child, and an assured place for the child in school. If the couple has more than one child, they may lose their jobs, be assigned to less desirable housing, and be required to pay the government back for the benefits they have received.

Special Observances. Our society reaffirms its approval of parents every year by allocating special days for mom and dad. Each year on Mother's Day and Father's Day, parenthood is celebrated across the nation with gifts and embraces. There is no counterpart, such as a Childfree Day.

☐   C O N S I D E R A T I O N   ☐

Many pronatalism influences operate without our conscious awareness. For example, while growing up in a family, rarely are we told by our parents that children are a benefit and we should have them when we grow up. Rather, the experience of growing up in a family encourages us to duplicate the behavior of our adult models.

Personal Reasons for Having Children

The impact of pronatalism influences is reflected in the reasons people give for having children. Some of these reasons follow.

Social Expectations. A sociologist and father of two daughters said, "Having children was never a deliberate decision. It was more of a feeling that one ought to have a family." A mother of two expressed a similar feeling: "All my friends were having babies, and I never questioned whether I would too." Our society expects its members to conform to certain conventions, not the least important of which is having children. Conforming to society's expectations assures a degree of acceptance from peers and places us in the mainstream of American life.

Personal Fulfillment. Some parents encourage their daughters to anticipate having children of their own. Giving them dolls and a dollhouse as playthings reinforces this. In some cases, the socialization is so strong that womanhood is equated with motherhood. "I suppose I felt I had to get pregnant to verify that I was a real woman," a young mother said.

Men also derive personal fulfillment from children. Paternalism—taking pride in meeting the needs of their offspring and showing affection for them—is a strong motive for some men. Men may also feel they affirm their masculinity by proving that they can conceive children.

Personal Identity. Related to the quest for personal fulfillment is the feeling that a baby gives the parent an identity. As one woman explained, "Before my son, Benny, I had nothing. I was bored, I hated my job, and I didn't have any goals or focus to my life. Now I know who I am—a mother—and I feel that I am needed." Some fathers express the same feeling. "Having my child is the meaning of life," remarked the father of a newborn. "I am a lousy employee, but I'm a great father. For the first time in my life, I really feel like somebody."

Influence of Spouse. Some spouses have children primarily to please their mates. "I wasn't wild about the idea of having children but decided to go along with it

> You can learn many things from children. How much patience you have, for instance.
> —FRANKLIN P. JONES

Daughters are socialized early to look forward to having their own children.

because my husband wanted one. As it turns out, I'm glad we did,'' one mother said. When husband and wife feel differently about having children, the disagreement is not always resolved in favor of having them. The woman bears the child, and her preference is usually given more weight.

Accident. Many couples have children without intending to. "I was out of pills and we didn't have any condoms," recalls a young wife, "but we wanted to have intercourse and decided to take a chance. An eight-pound baby was the result." Such accidents are not unusual. They sometimes also occur before marriage.

Whatever reasons parents give for having children, the rewards of parenthood are basically intangible. Parents often speak of the delight of seeing children discover their world for the first time, the joy of holding a baby in their arms and realizing it is a part of them and their partner, and the pleasure of following their children's development through the years and of relating to them as adults. A clinical psychologist and mother of three said, "The real problem with children is not their coming but their going. My first daughter will soon be married and will move six states away. I used to feel that babies were not worth the trouble, but now I know the joy of an adult relationship with them. I'm not only losing a daughter but my best friend."

> Some people try to achieve immortality through their offspring or their works. I prefer to achieve immortality by not dying.
> —WOODY ALLEN

CONSIDERATION

Psychologist B. F. Skinner once said that if there were not two of us the question of why would never occur. The reasons for having children are basically explanations given to someone else to justify the person's own behavior. Often we do not know why we do what we do. We just know it is something we want to do and develop reasons when asked. As Freud said, "We do not want a thing because we have reasons for it; we find reasons for it because we want it."

:: The Childfree Alternative

> ■ **DATA:** *Five percent of U.S. wives ages 18–34 do not expect to have children* (Statistical Abstract of the U.S.: 1990, *Table 98*).

Wanting to remain childfree is related to racial and ethnic background. Whites are most likely to consider marriage without children. Blacks, Native Americans, and Mexican Americans are more likely to be family-oriented and to consider children an important part of marital life (Mindel et al., 1988).

Some couples do not decide to remain childfree. About 20 percent of American couples are unable to have children and feel relegated to a life of involuntary childlessness. Billie Holiday, a blues singer of the 1930s, was devastated because she could not get pregnant and was turned down (because of her alleged drug abuse) when she tried to adopt.

Other couples do not initially decide to be childfree. They put off having children ("we'll wait till we're out of school . . . until we get a house . . . until our careers are established . . . until we have more money") and become satisfied

> Being a housewife and a mother is the biggest job in the world, but if it doesn't interest you, don't do it. It didn't interest me, so I didn't do it. Anyway, I would have made a terrible parent. The first time my child didn't do what I wanted, I'd kill him.
> —KATHARINE HEPBURN

with the childfree lifestyle and decide to continue it. However, those who never have children voluntarily are in the minority.

But how do couples who don't have children feel about their decision later in life? Two researchers (Bell & Eisenberg, 1985) have contrasted the life satisfaction of midlife, childless couples with empty-nest couples (couples with children who have left home). Empty-nest individuals were more satisfied than childless persons with regard to their decisions regarding children; however, the childless individuals were not unhappy with their decisions. In another study comparing couples in their seventies who did and did not have children, the researcher (Rempel, 1985) concluded:

> . . . today's childless elderly have levels of well-being that match and sometimes exceed those of parent elderly. . . . It is erroneous to assume that the elderly have children who can and will look after them. We have learned from this examination that family is not necessarily the crucial element in determining high-quality life in old age. (pp. 346–347)

☐   C O N S I D E R A T I O N   ☐

Is the childfree lifestyle for you? If you get your primary satisfactions from interacting with adults and from your career and if you require an atmosphere of freedom and privacy, perhaps the answer is yes. But if your desire for a child is at least equal to your desire for a satisfying adult relationship, career, and freedom, the answer may be no. The childfree alternative is particularly valuable to persons who would find the demands of parenthood an unnecessary burden and strain. You can assess the degree to which you want to have children by completing the Attitudes Toward Children Scale.

Childfree spouses can spend a lot of time sharing adult recreational activities.

:: How Many Children Do You Want?

If you decide to have children, how many do you want? Most people are reluctant to have an only child and prefer to have at least two.

One Child

■ **DATA:** *Twelve percent of U.S. wives ages 18–34 expect to have one child* (Statistical Abstract of the U.S.: 1990, *Table 98*)

The number of children a couple choose to have is influenced by the society in which the couple lives. In the United States, the two-child norm exerts enormous social pressure on parents of one child to have a second child. In China, the one-child family is actively encouraged and has resulted in a drop in the country's birth rate. Although most only children are stereotyped as being spoiled, selfish, and lonely, data suggest that they are happy, bright, and socially skilled (Falbo & Polit-O'Harra, 1985).

Two Children

■ **DATA:** *Fifty percent of U.S. wives expect to have two children* (Statistical Abstract of the U.S.: 1990, *Table 98*)

One mother was asked the difference between having one and two children. She said that when her first child swallowed a quarter, they took him to the hospital to have his stomach pumped out. When the second child swallowed a coin, he was told, "It will come out of your allowance."
—ANONYMOUS

The most preferred family size in the United States is the two-child family. How does having two children differ from having one? In one study, 144 mothers who had two children and whose second child was less than 5 years old revealed their motivations for having a second child and the consequences of doing so (Knox & Wilson, 1978). About one-half of these mothers said they enjoyed their first child and wanted to repeat the experience. More than one-quarter stated they wanted a companion for the first child. Other reasons included the husband wanting another child, personal fulfillment, and wanting a child of the opposite sex.

These mothers also commented on the consequences of having a second child. Almost half (49 percent) said the first child made a greater personal impact on them than the second child. Specific comments included "I lost my freedom to truly enjoy life and do what I wanted with the first child. Once I began forgetting myself, my second child had little effect;" "Childbirth and responsibility for a baby were new experiences with the first child. I felt more confident with the second child;" and "I got used to never being alone after my first child was born" (p. 24).

Although the second child had less personal impact than the first, the mothers reported that their marriages were more affected by their second child than by their first. One mother remarked, "The main difference I noticed with the second child was that I was more exhausted, since I had to relate emotionally to two children throughout the day." Another woman said:

> After I had listened to incessant pleading such as "I need a fork," "Can I have some more apple juice?" and "I don't like oatmeal," there was little left of me for my husband. And when the children were finally in bed, I needed to use the rest of the

Although negatively stereotyped, more often only children are happy, bright, and socially engaging.

evening to catch up on the housework I was unable to do during the day because of the constant interruptions (p. 15).

Three Children

Some couples want three children.

■ **DATA:** *Twenty-three percent of U.S. wives expect to have three children* (Statistical Abstract of the United States: 1990, *Table 98). Six million families have three or more children (Crispell, 1989).*

The Attitudes Toward Children Scale

This scale is designed to measure the way you feel about having and rearing children. There are no right or wrong answers. After reading each sentence carefully, circle the number that best represents your feelings.

1 Strongly disagree
2 Mildly disagree
3 Undecided
4 Mildly agree
5 Strongly agree

	SD	MD	U	MA	SA
1. I will be more fulfilled as a person if I have children.	1	2	3	4	5
2. If I couldn't have children, I would consider adopting.	1	2	3	4	5
3. Holding a baby is a very enjoyable experience.	1	2	3	4	5
4. Whatever children cost, they are worth it.	1	2	3	4	5
5. Children provide a type of satisfaction you get nowhere else in life.	1	2	3	4	5
6. Children may require a married couple to make more adjustments, but those adjustments are worth the experience of having children.	1	2	3	4	5
7. Childfree couples are really missing a worthwhile experience.	1	2	3	4	5
8. Most childfree couples will regret not having children when they are old.	1	2	3	4	5
9. Children may tie you down more, but they are worth it.	1	2	3	4	5
10. Children are worth sacrificing whatever career goals are necessary to have them and rear them properly.	1	2	3	4	5

Having a third child creates a "middle child." This child may be neglected, because parents of three children may focus on "the baby" and the firstborn and only rarely on the one in between.

But some middle children see their position in the family in positive terms:

I feel that being a middle child has turned out to be a great advantage for me. I received the love, but not the overattention, that was given my older brother and younger sister. Although I have at times been envious of my siblings, I am very close to them (even though they cannot get along with each other). I feel that I am capable

	SD	MD	U	MA	SA
11. Parenthood is more of an enriching experience than a burden.	1	2	3	4	5
12. I would consider marrying someone who already has children.	1	2	3	4	5
13. I wouldn't mind doing the work that taking care of a baby requires—feeding, changing diapers, giving baths, reading stories at bedtime.	1	2	3	4	5
14. Children make a lot of noise and tear up the house, but these are minor concerns in deciding to have children.	1	2	3	4	5
15. The happiest couples are those who have children.	1	2	3	4	5
16. Even if I were single, I would want to be a parent.	1	2	3	4	5
17. I enjoy the experience of taking care of a helpless infant.	1	2	3	4	5
18. Rearing children through the teen years would be a challenging experience rather than an experience to avoid.	1	2	3	4	5
19. Children usually appreciate what you do for them when they get older.	1	2	3	4	5
20. I can't imagine not having children.	1	2	3	4	5

SCORING. Add the numbers you circled. 1 (strongly disagree) is the most negative feeling you can have, and 5 (strongly agree) is the most positive feeling you can have. The lower your total score (20 is the lowest possible score), the more pessimistic you feel about parenthood; the higher your score (100 is the highest possible score), the more optimistic you feel about parenthood. A score of 60 places you at the midpoint between having negative and positive feelings about children.

(NOTE: This Self-Assessment is designed to be fun and thought-provoking, it is not a scientific or clinical measuring device).

of being responsive and caring for others when they need someone. All things considered, it's great to be a middle child!

I have one older brother and one younger sister, and they are loved very much along with myself. However, I am the one to be spoiled out of the three of us. I get whatever I want—not only from my parents, but also from my grandparents. (My grandparents gave me a new Ford Mustang for graduation.) At Christmas, I get very unhappy because I can see that my brother and sister resent me very much, and I have been told by their best friends that they resent me. But what can I do?

Four or More Children

In contrast to having only a few children or a childfree marriage, some couples want a child-full marriage.

Some children feel displaced by their younger siblings.

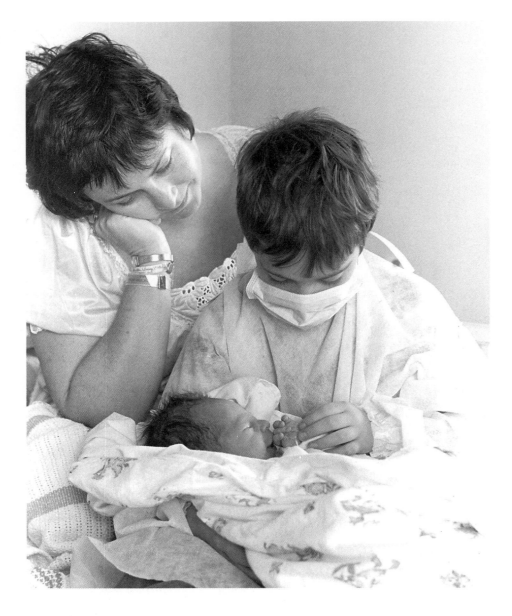

| ■ **DATA:** *Nine percent of U.S. wives expect to have four or more children* (Statistical Abstract of the U.S.: 1990, *Table 98)*

Men are more likely to want four or more children than women. Blacks and Mexican Americans are more likely to want larger families than whites (Mindel et al., 1988).

Larger families have complex interactional patterns and different values. The addition of each subsequent child dramatically increases the possible relationships in the family. For example, in the one-child family, four interpersonal relationships are possible: mother-father, mother-child, father-child, and father-mother-child. In a family of four, 11 relationships are possible; in a family of five, 26; and in a family of six, 57.

In addition to relationships, values change as families get larger. Whereas members of a small family tend to value independence and personal development, large-family members necessarily value cooperation, harmony, and sharing. A parent of nine children said, "Meals around our house are a cooperative endeavor. One child prepares the drinks, another the bread, and still another sets the table. You have to develop cooperation, or nobody gets fed."

☐   C O N S I D E R A T I O N   ☐

When people think about and plan for the size family they want, they rarely take into consideration the possibility of divorce. In deciding how many children you want (if you want any at all), ask yourself the following question: How would you care for the child(ren) if you became divorced and either had primary custody of the child(ren) or had to make child support payments?

Another possibility that affects family size is remarriage. When divorced people with children remarry, they often find themselves in families that are larger than what they had originally planned. For example, a woman with two children who marries a man with 3 children suddenly has five children in her family unit. Given the high rate of divorce (50 percent) and remarriage (80 percent), it is not unrealistic to consider these issues when thinking about the number of children you want to have.

∷ Timing the Birth of Your Children

Having decided how many children you want, when is the best time to have them? There are at least three issues to consider in planning the first pregnancy.

Mother's Age

The age of the mother is related to the baby's birth weight. Birth weight is the greatest single predictor of the baby's current and future health. The more weight the woman gains during pregnancy (up to 35 pounds), the lower the risk of a low-weight baby.

■ **DATA:** *Mothers aged 25–34 tend to have the lowest risk (about 6 percent) of having a low birth weight baby (defined as a baby weighing less than 5 pounds, 8 ounces). The median weight of all babies at birth is 7 pounds, 7 ounces. The median weight for white babies is 7 pounds, 9 ounces; for black babies, 7 pounds exactly (National Center for Health Statistics, 1989).*

Risks to the baby's life also increase with the mother's age. The chance of a chromosomal abnormality is 1 percent if the woman is in her early twenties, 2 percent at ages 35–39, 3 percent at 40, and 10 percent at 45 (Seashore, 1980). A higher proportion of babies born to older mothers die or have Down's syndrome (sometimes improperly called mongolism), a genetic defect caused by an extra chromosome. A Down's syndrome baby is physically deformed, mentally retarded, and has a shorter life span. Having a Down's syndrome baby is a particular concern of women who become pregnant after age 40. Many physicians recommend amniocentesis (described in Exhibit 13.1) for these women to determine the presence of this and other chromosomal abnormalities.

Amniocentesis is not without risks. In rare cases (about 2 percent of the time), the fetus may be damaged by the needle even though an ultrasound scan (sound waves beamed at the fetus which produce a detailed image) has been used to identify its position. Congenital orthopedic defects, such as clubfoot, and premature birth have been associated with amniocentesis. Also, if no specific abnormality is detected (as is the case 97.5 percent of the time), this does not guarantee that the baby will be normal and healthy otherwise (Hogge et al., 1986).

An alternative to amniocentesis is chorion villus sampling. Also risky, the procedure involves placing a tube through the vagina into the uterus. Chorionic tissue, which surrounds the developing embryo, is removed and analyzed in the laboratory to assess the presence of genetic defects. The procedure can be performed in a physician's office as early as the eighth week of pregnancy, and

---

EXHIBIT 13.1

Sex Selection

In addition to wanting a specific number of children, some couples are concerned about the biological sex of their children. In his desire to have a male heir, King Henry VIII discarded several wives because they delivered only female children. The hapless Anne Boleyn was beheaded. But only the third of his six wives, Jane Seymour, gave him a son, who died in childhood. Although few American men and women feel the same desperation to have a child of a certain sex, some do express a preference for either a male or female child.

Enter *gametrics*—the application of biological-mathematical theory to gamete separation. The biological part is the knowledge that Y chromosomes determine a male child and X chromosomes determine a female child. The mathematical part is increasing the probability of a male child by isolating the sperm carrying the Y chromosomes, putting them together, and artificially inseminating the woman.

The Y sperm are isolated by putting all of the sperm from an ejaculation on top of a thick substance in a test tube. Since Y sperm are stronger and swim faster, those sperm going through the substance and swimming to the bottom first are more often male sperm. These are collected from several ejaculations and are used for the ar-

tificial insemination procedure. The probability of conceiving a male child using the procedure is 80 percent. If left to chance, the probability is 50 percent.

An alternative to the gametrics procedure is to separate the X sperm and Y sperm on the basis of their molecular properties. This process has also proved to be 80 percent effective in isolating X sperm to produce female offspring (Uzzell, 1985).

The method of amniocentesis and abortion may be used in gender selection. Fluid from the uterus in which the fetus floats contains fetal cells. These cells can be analyzed by inserting a needle into the pregnant woman's abdomen and withdrawing a sample of fluid to see if the cells carry XX (female) or XY (male) chromosomes. (This procedure is commonly used to test for certain genetic defects, such as Down's syndrome and sickle-cell anemia.) If the fetus is the gender desired by the parents, it is allowed to develop. Otherwise, it may be aborted. In one case, amniocentesis was used to preclude the possibility of a male birth because a lethal inherited disease was characteristic of male babies in that family.

Although amniocentesis has been used for the purpose of having a baby of the desired sex, it is unlikely to become routine. Not only are there moral objections to this procedure (some regard abortion as murder, and others see sex selection as sexist and biologically maladaptive), but there are also risks to the mother and the baby.

results are available in two to three weeks. (Amniocentesis is not performed until the sixteenth week, and results are not known for three to four weeks.)

□ C O N S I D E R A T I O N □

An increasing number of women are waiting until their thirties and forties (examples include Connie Chung, Farrah Fawcett, Bette Midler, and Meryl Streep) to have their children. For these women, the risks taken by delaying conception may be insignificant compared with the joy derived from motherhood. Michelle Strada had her first child just before her 42nd birthday. She said of her daughter, "She's been so wonderful that we're even thinking about squeezing in another one, believe it or not" (Painter, 1990, D1).

Dr. Luella Klein, chairperson of gynecology and obstetrics at Emory University, Atlanta, said that older women who decide to start their families are ideal obstetric patients: "These are planned pregnancies and the women take very good care of themselves. They eat right and they don't smoke" (Painter, 1990, 2D).

Father's Age

The father's age is also a consideration in deciding when to have the first child. Down's syndrome is associated with increased paternal as well as maternal age. Other abnormalities that may be related to the age of the father include achondroplasia (a type of dwarfism), Marfan syndrome (height, vision, and heart abnormalities), Apert syndrome (facial and limb deformities), and fibro-dysplasia ossificans progressiva (bony growths). Such congenital defects are rare (2 percent of all births).

To help reduce birth defects of genetic origin, older couples and those whose family histories show evidence of hereditary defect or disease should consider genetic counseling. Such counseling helps the potential parents to be aware of the chance of having a defective child.

A variable related to age is economic stability. Men who are earning a stable income are more willing to plan a first birth than men who have no economic security. This finding is true for both whites and blacks (Teachman & Schollaert, 1989).

Number of Years Married

Although most spouses are confident about their decision to have children when they are in their twenties or early thirties, they are somewhat ambivalent about how long it is best to be married before having a baby.

■ **DATA:** *The average length of time between marriage and the first birth is two years (Bloom & Bennett, 1986).*

One viewpoint suggests that newlyweds need time to adjust to each other as spouses before becoming parents. If the marriage is dissolved, at least there will not be problems of child custody, child-support payments, and single-parent status.

But if couples wait several years to have a baby, they may become so content with their childfree lifestyle that parenthood is an unwelcome change. "We were married for seven wonderful years before Helen was born," recalls one mother. "The adjustment hasn't been easy. We resented her intrusion into our relationship."

In one study, more than 5,000 parents were interviewed on the effect of delaying children versus having them soon after the marriage. Results indicated that marital satisfaction after children was about the same regardless of the length of time the parents waited before having children (Marini, 1980).

Your degree of commitment to your career is also an issue to consider in timing your first child. Although couples have different agreements about childcare, many couples prefer that the wife be primarily responsible for the child on a daily basis. Such allocation of responsibility will be a major barrier to the woman who wants to pursue a full-time career with its demands of training, commitment, mobility, and continuity. Career-oriented women often decide to get their career going before beginning their family or to have their children first and then launch a career. Unless the partners opt to truly coparent, having a child while pursuing a career will be difficult. An alternative is for the wife to have a job rather than a career.

Increasingly, couples are deciding to have children in their late thirties and forties. In addition to having their careers established, they experience parenthood at a time when they no longer wonder what the childfree lifestyle would be like. Many have traveled extensively and feel that they now prefer to stay home to rear a family.

Timing Subsequent Births

Assuming you decide to have more than one child, what is the best interval between children?

Most couples space their children within three years of each other with younger women tending to have longer intervals between births than older women (Wineberg and McCarthy, 1989). This interval allows parents to avoid being overwhelmed with the care of two infants, but is short enough so that the children can be companions. In addition, subsequent children conceived within a year of the last birth exhibit a much higher mortality rate than children conceived at greater intervals.

⠿ Contraception

Having decided not to have children or to delay having them, the choice of which type of contraception to use becomes important. Prior to 1870 (when condoms were first mass-marketed), abstinence was the only way a couple could ensure that the woman would not get pregnant. Today, couples can separate their lovemaking from their babymaking with a variety of birth control procedures. After reviewing the available array of contraceptives, we will examine sterilization and abortion as ways of controlling family size. Most women have no problem getting pregnant. But many get pregnant when they do not want to because they do not use contraception. "I was a freshman and unmarried. The last thing I wanted at that time in my life was a baby,'' recalls one woman. *Contraception,* the prevention of pregnancy by one of several methods, is an alternative to pregnancy.

All contraceptive practices have one of two common purposes—to prevent the male sperm from fertilizing the female egg or to keep the fertilized egg from implanting itself in the uterus. In performing these functions, contraception permits couples to make love without making babies.

Although contraception is not always used, both sexes feel it is their responsibility to provide birth control.

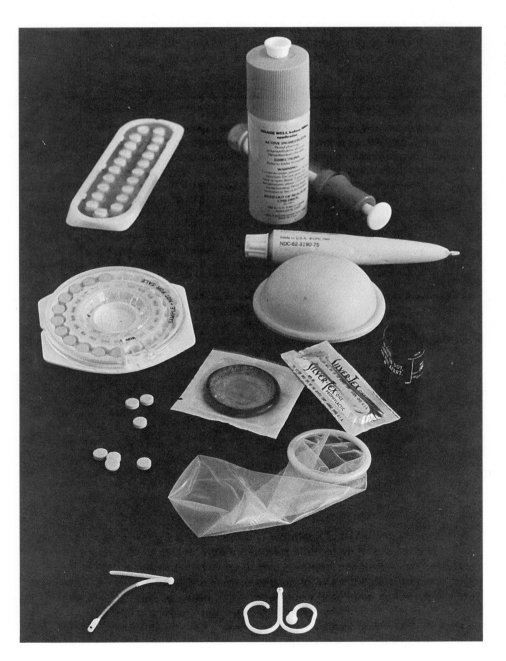

The condom is the only contraceptive which provides some protection against contracting sexually transmitted diseases.

■ **DATA:** *More than 91 percent of both male and female undergraduates in one study said that it was their independent responsibility to ensure that contraception was used when they had intercourse (Sheehan et al., 1986).*

Oral Contraceptives

The birth control pill is the most commonly used method of all the nonsurgical forms of contraception.

The most effective contraception for parents is to spend an hour with their children before going to bed.

—ROSEANNE BARR

■ **DATA:** *Nineteen percent of all never married women and 13 percent of married women use the pill (Statistical Abstract of the United States: 1990, Table 99).*

Although there are more than 40 brands available in North America, there are basically two types of birth control pills—the combination pill and the minipill.

The combination pill contains the hormones estrogen and progesterone (also known as progestin), which act to prevent ovulation and implantation. The estrogen inhibits the release of the follicle-stimulating hormone (FSH) from the pituitary gland, so that no follicle will develop. In effect, an egg will not mature. In other words, A (estrogen) blocks B (FSH), which would have produced C (egg).

The progesterone inhibits the release of luteinizing hormone (LH) from the pituitary gland, which during a normal cycle would cause the mature ovum to move to the periphery of the follicle and the follicle to rupture (ovulation). Hence, there is no ovulation. In this case, A (progestin) blocks B (LH), which would have caused C (ovulation).

The progesterone serves as a secondary protection by causing the composition of the cervical mucus to become thick and acidic, thereby creating a hostile environment for the sperm. So even if an egg were to mature and ovulation were to occur, the progesterone would ward off or destroy the sperm. Another function of progesterone is to make the lining of the uterus unsuitable for implantation.

The combination pill is taken for 21 days, beginning on the fifth day after the start of the menstrual flow. Three or four days after the last pill is taken, menstruation occurs, and the 28-day cycle begins again. To eliminate the problem of remembering when to begin taking the pill every month, some physicians prescribe a low-dose combination pill for the first 21 days and a placebo (sugar pill) or an iron pill for the next seven days. In this way, the woman takes a pill every day.

The second type of oral contraceptive, the minipill, contains the same progesterone found in the combination pill, but in much lower doses. The minipill contains no estrogen. Like the progesterone in the combination pill, the progesterone in the minipill provides a hostile environment for sperm and inhibits implantation of a fertilized egg in the uterus. In general, the minipill is somewhat less effective than other types of birth control pills and has been associated with a higher incidence of irregular bleeding.

Either the combination pill or the minipill should be taken only when prescribed by a physician who has detailed information about the woman's previous medical history. Contraindications—reasons for not prescribing birth control pills—include hypertension, impaired liver function, known or suspected tumors that are estrogen-dependent, undiagnosed abnormal genital bleeding, pregnancy at the time of the examination, and a history of poor blood circulation. The major complications associated with taking oral contraceptives are blood clots and high blood pressure. Also, the risk of heart attack is increased in women over age 30, particularly those who smoke or have other risk factors. Women over 40 should generally use other forms of contraception, because the side effects of contraceptive pills increase with the age of the user. Infertility problems have also been noted in women who have used the combination pill for several years without the breaks in pill use recommended by most physicians.

Although the long-term negative consequences of taking birth control pills are still the subject of research, short-term negative effects are experienced by 25 percent of all women who use them. These mild side effects include increased susceptibility to vaginal infections, nausea, slight weight gain, vaginal bleeding between periods, breast tenderness, mild headaches, and mood changes (some women become depressed and experience a loss of sexual desire).

Finally, women should be aware that pill use is associated with an increased incidence of chlamydia and gonorrhea. In one study, women using the pill had a 73 percent higher rate of chlamydia and a 70 percent higher rate of gonorrhea compared with nonusers (Witwer, 1989). The researcher concluded that women using oral contraceptives should be screened more actively than nonusers of oral contraceptives for both gonorrhea and chlamydia.

□   C O N S I D E R A T I O N   □

In spite of the negative consequences associated with birth control pill use, numerous studies involving hundreds of thousands of women show that the overall risk of pill use is less than the risk of full-term pregnancy and giving birth.

Immediate health benefits are also derived from taking birth control pills. Oral contraceptives tend to protect the woman against breast tumors, ovarian cysts, rheumatoid arthritis, and inflammatory diseases of the pelvis. They also regularize the woman's menstrual cycle, reduce premenstrual tension, and may reduce menstrual cramps and blood loss during menstruation. Finally, oral contraceptives are convenient, do not interfere with intercourse, and most important, provide highly effective protection against pregnancy.

Whether to use birth control pills remains a controversial issue. Some women feel it harms their body to take birth control pills; others feel it harms their body not to take them. Whatever a woman's choice, it should be made in conjunction with the physician who knows her medical history.

Condom

Also referred to as a "rubber," "safe," or "prophylactic," the condom is currently the only form of male contraception. The condom is a thin sheath, usually made of synthetic material or lamb intestine, which is rolled over and down the shaft of the erect penis before intercourse. When the man ejaculates, the sperm are caught inside the condom. When used in combination with a spermicidal, or sperm-killing, agent that the woman inserts in her vagina, the condom is a highly effective contraceptive.

■ **DATA:** *Four percent of all never married women and 10 percent of all married women report that their partners use condoms* (Statistical Abstract of the United States: 1990, Table 99).

In pre-World War II pharmacies, women typically bought cigarettes openly but were ashamed to ask for condoms. Now it's the other way around.
—SYLVIA HACKER

□   C O N S I D E R A T I O N   □

The condom is the only contraceptive that provides some protection against sexually transmitted diseases. With the spread of AIDS in our society (see the Special Topics section on AIDS and Other STDs) it is especially important for sexually active individuals to use condoms (particularly those condoms with nonoxynol-9 which is effective in killing the AIDS virus). Yet, only about half of sexually active males in a national survey of adolescents reported using the condom the last time they had intercourse (Sonenstein et al., 1989).

Some men say they do not like to use a condom because it decreases sensation. Others say that having the woman put the condom on their penis is an erotic experience and that the condom actually enhances pleasurable feelings during intercourse.

Like any contraceptive, the condom is effective only when properly used. It should be placed on the penis early enough to avoid any seminal leakage into the vagina. In addition, latex condoms with a recessed tip are preferable, as they are less likely to break. Finally, the penis should be withdrawn from the vagina soon after ejaculation. If the penis is not withdrawn and the erection subsides, semen may leak from the base of the condom into the vaginal lips. Alternatively, when the erection subsides, the condom will come off when the male withdraws his penis if he does not hold on to the condom. Either way, the sperm will begin to travel up the vagina to the uterus and fertilize the egg.

In addition to furnishing extra protection, spermicides also provide lubrication, which permits easy entrance of the condom-covered penis into the vagina. If no spermicide is used and the condom is not of the prelubricated variety, K-Y jelly, a sterile lubricant, may be needed. Vaseline or other kinds of petroleum jelly should not be used because they may increase the risk of vaginal infection. While the term condom usually refers to a male contraceptive, a female condom is being developed (see Exhibit 13.2).

E X H I B I T 13.2

∷

A Woman's Condom?

Not yet approved for use in the United States but already being tested in England, Germany, Denmark and Sweden, the "woman's condom" resembles a man's condom except that it fits in the woman's vagina to protect her from pregnancy, AIDS, and other STDs. There is a flexible plastic ring at the closed end of the sheath that fits loosely against the cervix, like a diaphragm. Another ring encircles the labial area. Like the male version, the condom is not reusable.

Women report that they have orgasm more often with the sheath. Researchers suggest this is because the polyurethane transfers heat better than traditional latex condoms and because the device creates more friction in the labia. The female condom is as effective as the male condom in preventing pregnancy. The woman's condom will be tested in the United States (Wolinsky, 1988).

Intrauterine Device (IUD)

■ **DATA:** *Two percent of all never married women and 5 percent of married women use the IUD as their method of contraception* (Statistical Abstract of the United States: 1990, *Table 99*).

The intrauterine device, or IUD, is a small object that is inserted by a physician into the woman's uterus through the vagina and cervix. Although 60 million women use the IUD worldwide (40 in China alone), use of the IUD in the United States is minimal. Due to problems (infertility, miscarriage) associated with IUDs and subsequent lawsuits against manufacturers by persons reporting that they were damaged by the device, only two types remain on the market. The Progestasert releases progesterone directly into the uterus and must be replaced every year by the physician. The Progestasert has the effect of reducing menstrual flow which reduces the risk of anemia.

The newer Copper T (T-380A) is thought to alter the functioning of the enzymes involved in implantation. It was introduced in the late 80s and preliminary studies show that it has a failure rate as low as the pill (Thomas, 1988).

It is thought that the IUD works by preventing implantation of the fertilized egg in the uterine wall. The exact chemistry is unknown, but one theory suggests that the IUD stimulates the entry of white blood cells into the uterus, which attack and destroy "invading" cells—in this case, the fertilized egg. Implantation may also be prevented by the IUD mechanically dislodging the egg from the uterine wall.

Side effects of the IUD include cramps, excessive menstrual bleeding, and irregular bleeding, or spotting, between menstrual periods. These effects may disappear after the first two months of use. Infection and perforation are more serious side effects. Users of the IUD have a higher incidence of pelvic inflammatory disease, which infects the uterus and Fallopian tubes and may lead to sterility. In addition, the IUD may cut or perforate the uterine walls or cervix, resulting in bleeding and pain.

> Whenever I hear people discussing birth control, I always remember that I was the fifth.
> —CLARENCE DARROW

+---+
| □   C O N S I D E R A T I O N   □ |
| |
| Due to these potential side effects, women should consider |
| using a method of contraception other than the IUD. |
+---+

Some women are unable to retain the IUD; it irritates the muscles of the uterus, causing them to contract and expel the device. To make sure that the IUD remains in place, a woman should check it at least once a month just after her period. The Progestasert is particularly vulnerable to expulsion.

The fact that the IUD does not prevent conception is its greatest advantage and disadvantage. The advantage is that the IUD does not interfere with the body's normal hormonal and physiological responses. The disadvantage is that it permits conception and then destroys the fertilized egg, which is morally repugnant to some people. "It's the same as abortion," said one devout Catholic. Also, women who do get pregnant (tubal pregnancies with the Progestasert do occur) while using the IUD must make a decision about whether to leave it in or remove it.

There is a 50 percent chance of miscarriage if the IUD is left in and a 25 percent chance of miscarriage if the IUD is taken out. In most cases, the IUD is removed. However, there are no reports of birth defects if the IUD is left in and the baby is carried to a term delivery.

Diaphragm

■ **DATA:** *Five percent of both never married and currently married women report using the diaphragm as their method of contraception* (Statistical Abstract of the United States: 1990, *Table 99*).

The diaphragm is a shallow rubber dome attached to a flexible, circular steel spring. Varying in diameter from 2 to 4 inches, the diaphragm covers the cervix and prevents sperm from moving beyond the vagina into the uterus. This device should always be used with a spermicidal jelly or cream.

To obtain a diaphragm, the woman must have an internal pelvic examination by a physician or nurse practitioner who will select the appropriate size of diaphragm and instruct the woman how to insert it. She will be told to apply one teaspoonful of spermicidal cream or jelly on the inside of the diaphragm and around the rim and to insert it into the vagina no more than two hours before intercourse. The diaphragm must also be left in place for 6 to 8 hours after intercourse to permit any lingering sperm to be killed by the spermicidal cream.

After the birth of a child, a miscarriage, abdominal surgery, or the gain or loss of 10 pounds, a woman who uses a diaphragm should consult her physician or health practitioner to ensure a continued good fit. In any case, the diaphragm should be checked every two years for fit.

A major advantage of the diaphragm is that it does not interfere with the woman's hormonal system and has few, if any, side effects. Also, for those couples who feel that menstruation diminishes their capacity to enjoy intercourse, the diaphragm may be used to catch the menstrual flow.

On the negative side, some women feel that use of the diaphragm with the spermicidal gel is messy and a nuisance. For some, the use of the gel may produce an allergic reaction. Furthermore, some partners feel that the gel makes oral-genital contact less enjoyable. Finally, if the diaphragm does not fit properly, pregnancy can result.

Vaginal Spermicides

■ **DATA:** *Less than 1 percent of never married women and 2 percent of currently married women report using foam as their method of contraception* (Statistical Abstract of the United States: 1990, *Table 99*).

Spermicidal foam contains chemicals that kill sperm. The foam must be applied near the cervix (appropriate applicators are included when the product is purchased) no more than 20 minutes before intercourse. Each time intercourse is repeated, more foam must be applied. Spermicidal creams also kill sperm; each application comes individually packaged, and the packaging can be disposed of after use.

Foams are advantageous because they do not manipulate the woman's hormonal system and they have few side effects. These include allergic reactions in some men and women (their genitals may become irritated by the chemicals in the foam). The main disadvantage of contraceptive foam is that some regard its use as messy and its taste unpleasant if oral-genital contact is enjoyed.

☐   C O N S I D E R A T I O N   ☐

Contraceptive foams, such a Delfen and Emko, should not be confused with vaginal deodorants, such as Summer's Eve. The latter has no contraceptive value. Spermicidal foams should also not be confused with spermicidal gels that are used in conjunction with a diaphragm. These gels should never be used alone because they do not stick to the cervix as well as foam does.

Vaginal suppositories also contain spermicide. They are inserted about 30 minutes before intercourse. Also known as pessaries, vaginal suppositories provide protection by killing sperm and weakening sperm motility.

Vaginal Sponge

One of the newest contraceptives to win approval by the Food and Drug Administration is the vaginal sponge. The sponge is 2 inches in diameter, 1¼ inches thick, and contains spermicide that is activated when the sponge is immersed in water before insertion into the vagina. A small loop allows for easy removal of the sponge. Like condoms and spermicidal foams, the sponge is available in drugstores without a prescription. The brand name for the sponge is Today. It prevents fertilization, not only by releasing spermicide to kill sperm but also by blocking the cervix to prevent the sperm from entering and by absorbing sperm into the sponge.

■ **DATA:** *Women who use the sponge report using it more consistently than women who use the diaphragm (Harvey et al., 1989).*

A major advantage of the sponge is that it allows for spontaneity in lovemaking. It can be inserted early in the day, may be worn for up to 24 hours, and may be used for more than one act of intercourse without requiring additional applications of spermicide. According to FDA tests on 1,582 sponge users, the sponge is comparable to the diaphragm in effectiveness.

☐   C O N S I D E R A T I O N   ☐

Difficulty in removing the sponge and toxic shock syndrome when the sponge is used during the menstrual period have been reported by women using the sponge. The first problem has not been significant, but the second may be dangerous. The sponge should not be used during the menstrual period (Greenberg et al., 1986).

Rhythm Method

Also referred to as the "natural family planning" method, the rhythm method is based on the premise that fertilization cannot occur unless live sperm are present when the egg is in the Fallopian tubes. Sperm usually live two to three days, whereas an egg lives 24 hours. Women who use the rhythm method must know their time of ovulation and avoid intercourse just before, during, and immediately after that time. There are four ways of predicting the presumed safe period: the calendar method, the basal body temperature method, the cervical mucus method, and the hormone-in-urine method.

■ **DATA:** *Less than 1 percent of never married women and about 3 percent of married women use the rhythm method of contraception* (Statistical Abstract of the United States: 1990, *Table 99).*

Calendar Method.   When using the calendar method to predict when the egg is ready to be fertilized, the woman keeps a record of the length of her menstrual cycles for eight months. The menstrual cycle is counted from day one of the menstrual period through the last day before the onset of the next period. She then calculates her fertile period by subtracting 18 days from the shortest cycle and 11 days from the longest cycle. The resulting figures indicate the range of her fertility period. It is during this time that the woman must avoid intercourse.

For example, suppose that during an eight-month period, a woman had cycle lengths of 26, 32, 27, 30, 28, 27, 28, and 29 days. Subtracting 18 from her shortest cycle (26) and 11 from her longest cycle (32), she knows the days that the egg is likely to be in the Fallopian tubes. To avoid getting pregnant, she must avoid intercourse on days 8 through 21 of her cycle.

☐   C O N S I D E R A T I O N   ☐

The calendar method of predicting the "safe" period is unreliable for two reasons. First, the next month the woman may ovulate at a different time from any of the previous eight months. Second, sperm life varies; they may live long enough to meet the next egg in the Fallopian tubes.

Basal Body Temperature (BBT) Method.   This method is based on temperature changes that occur in the woman's body shortly after ovulation. The basal body temperature is the temperature of the body at rest on waking in the morning. To establish her BBT, the woman must take her temperature for three months at this time before she gets out of bed. Just before ovulation, her temperature will drop about 0.2° F. Between 24 and 72 hours later, there will be a rise in temperature of about 0.6-0.8° F. above her normal BBT, signaling the time of ovulation. Intercourse must be avoided from the time the woman's temperature drops until her temperature has remained elevated for three consecutive days. Beginning on the night of the third day after the temperature shift is observed, she may resume having intercourse.

Cervical Mucus Method. The cervical mucus method is based on observations of changes in the mucus cycle from no perceptible mucus for several days after menstruation to sticky to very slippery mucus during ovulation to a cloudy discharge after ovulation ends. The mucus becomes thin and slippery, very similar to raw egg white, during ovulation to create a favorable environment for sperm. The woman should abstain from intercourse as soon as mucus appears before ovulation and continue to do so for four complete days after the peak of cervical mucus. A woman can check her cervical mucus by wiping herself with toilet paper several times a day before she urinates and observing the changes. This method requires the woman to distinguish between mucus and semen, spermicidal agents, lubrication, and infectious discharges. Also, the woman must not douche because she will wash away what she is trying to observe.

Other labels for the cervical mucus method are natural family planning and the Billings method (named after Evelyn and John Billings). Associated with the Billings method is the woman's observation of the *Mittelschmerz*—the mid-cycle abdominal pain or ''ping'' sometimes associated with ovulation.

Hormone-in-Urine Method. A hormone is released into the bloodstream of the ovulating female 12 to 24 hours prior to ovulation. Women can purchase First Response and Ovutime, two variations of the same test, in drugstores to ascertain if they have ovulated.

Nonmethods

Some people erroneously regard withdrawal and douching as effective methods of contraception. They are not.

Withdrawal. Withdrawal, also known as *coitus interruptus*, is the practice of the man taking his penis out of the vagina before he ejaculates. Not only does this technique interrupt sexual pleasure, but it is also an unreliable means of contraception. Even before ejaculation, the man can, without his awareness, emit a small amount of fluid from the Cowper's gland, which may contain sperm. In addition, the man may delay his withdrawal too long and inadvertently ejaculate some semen near the vaginal opening of his partner. Sperm deposited here can live in the moist vaginal lips and make their way up the vagina to the uterus.

Douching. Douching refers to rinsing or cleansing the vaginal canal. After intercourse, the woman fills a syringe with water or a spermicidal agent and flushes (so she assumes) the sperm from her vagina. But in some cases, the fluid will actually force sperm up through the cervix. In other cases, a large number of sperm may already have passed through the cervix to the uterus, so that the douche may do little good.

Morning After Pill

Some women who have engaged in unprotected intercourse in the middle of their cycle elect to take a morning after pill, which contains high levels of estrogen to prevent implantation of the fertilized egg on the uterine wall. This is an emergency form of birth control, is potentially dangerous, and is available only by prescription from a physician.

Diethylstilbestrol (DES) is the most commonly used morning after pill. The first of ten 25 milligram doses must be taken within 72 hours after intercourse (preferably, within 12 to 24 hours). Normally, the pills are taken twice a day for five days.

A new drug—RU-486—has no significant side effects and can end a pregnancy 95% of the cases if taken with prostaglandin within seven weeks of conception. The drug is legal and has been used (as of August 1990) by an estimated 55,000 women in fifteen European countries, but it is not available in the United States. Table 13.1 summarizes the methods of contraception available in our society.

:: Avoiding Sexually Transmitted Diseases and Pregnancy

A condom that is put on before the penis touches the other person's body will make it difficult for sexually transmitted diseases or STDs (including genital herpes and AIDS) to pass from one person to another (see the Special Topics section on AIDS and Other STDs).

It isn't very romantic to talk about STDs with a partner you are about to have sex with, but to ignore STDs one minute is to risk contracting one the next. Contraception should also be discussed before sexual intercourse. Not to do so involves the risk of unwanted pregnancy.

What might a person say about the issues of sexually transmitted diseases and protection from pregnancy before having a sexual experience with a new partner?

▪▪ TABLE 13.1 **Contraception Alternatives***

CONTRACEPTIVE METHOD	HOW IT WORKS	FAILURE RATE PER 100 WOMEN**	ADDITIONAL COMMENTS
Abstinence	Not having sex	0	The only method that offers 100% protection against pregnancy and diseases that are transmitted through sexual intercourse.
Withdrawal	Withdrawal of the penis from the vagina prior to ejaculation	20	Although the male withdraws before ejaculation, pregnancy can still occur because of semen released from the penis during foreplay. This method is not recommended.
Natural Family Planning, "Rhythm Method"	Female identifies her most fertile time of the month and abstains from sexual intercourse at that time	14-47	A health care provider must instruct a woman how to determine fertile periods by noting changes in body temperature and cervical mucous.
Spermicidal Foams and Jellies	A chemical that contains sperm-killing agents is inserted into the vagina prior to sexual intercourse	4-29	Spermicides that contain the active ingredient "Nonoxynol-9" offers additional protection against AIDS and other STDs.
Condoms	Thin latex sheath worn over erect penis to prevent sperm from entering into the vaginal area	2-10	Next to abstinence or mutual monogamy with an uninfected partner, condoms, combined with spermicidal forms and jellies, are the best available means to prevent the spread of AIDS and other STDs.
Diaphragm	Thin rubber device that is inserted into the vagina and fits over the cervix to prevent sperm from entering the uterus.	5-10	Must be used with a spermicidal foam or jelly.
Oral Contraceptive Agents, "The Pill"	A combination pill made up of synthetic hormones that prevents the ovary from releasing an egg	1	Take pill at approximately the same time each day. Follow directions of health care provider. Smokers should not use the pill since it increases the chance of a stroke or a blood clot.

*Developed by Suzanne Kellerman, M.A. Health Educator, Student Health Services, East Carolina University, Greenville, NC. Used by permission of Suzanne Kellerman.
**Based on data from "Facts About Birth Control," Planned Parenthood Federation of America, January 1989.

Maggie Hayes at the University of Oklahoma asked her students how they would handle the situation if they were on an isolated moonlit beach with a person they wanted to have sex with. Some of their responses follow:

In a situation like this, you have to be open and discuss the consequences. If this "messes up the mood," maybe that's the best thing—better than ending up diseased or pregnant. You can't let your feelings and your hormones [urges] control this situation.

Even in the heat of passion, one still has to be concerned about AIDS and pregnancy. I would first ask if he was going to share something with me that he knew I wouldn't want him to share. I would definitely clarify if necessary. I would also state that I am not ready to be a mother and that some sort of birth control is necessary to continue.

The discussion of protection against pregnancy could be entwined into the romance of the evening, perhaps even made part of verbiage in sexual play. The discussion would probably not be purely sensual—rather one in which feelings of care and love are conveyed. The discussion of STD would not be nearly as simple. It would be next to impossible to keep this subject within the mood of the evening. One of the parties will probably be offended. Nonetheless, this topic is of vital importance to discuss—mind you, lightly, but it must be done. Perhaps after putting it into perspective for "our future," not to hurt each other, the ground lost can be recovered later in the evening.

I would just have to come right out and question my partner point blank about the subjects. If she had no protection, I'd make a quick trip to the convenience store to buy a condom if possible or abstain if not. If she had an STD, I would take her back to her place and ride off into the sunset as quickly as possible, never to return.

Bringing up a subject like herpes or contraception would seem to detract from the mood more than would abstinence. This fact, along with the guilt feelings I would have to deal with after the experience, with or without protection, has been enough incentive in this situation in the past to get me to stop short of intercourse, so that the beauty of the memory is as great as the beauty of the moment. I'll keep it that way.

"Since this is a new experience for us, we would probably both be more comfortable if we completely leveled with each other about protection. This includes birth control as well as sexually transmitted disease. Is this agreeable with you?" If the partner doesn't want to discuss it, I'd be wary of the partner. I'd also be aware that complete honesty is not always forthcoming in such situations. Open communication enhances any relationship—sexual or otherwise.

People most likely to discuss condoms and contraception with a sexual partner are involved in an ongoing relationship with the partner and has established a pattern of open communication with the partner (Fullilove et al., 1990). In addition, they are also comfortable with and accepting of their own bodies and sexuality.

Persons most likely to use condoms or some other form of contraception have partners who actively support their use (Whitley, 1990) and have relationships in which alcohol or other drugs are not used (Leigh, 1990). Taking a course designed to provide specific information about STDs and fertility does not seem to affect behavior. While students are more knowledgeable about STDs and birth control, such knowledge does not translate into use of condoms or other forms of contraception (Baldwin et al., 1990). Similarly, students who viewed a film on sex with condom use reported more positive attitudes about using a condom during sex. However, it is not known if such attitude change translates into behavioral change (Kyes, 1990).

Teenage Pregnancy

Wll your child learn to multiply before she learns to subtract?
—ANTI-TEEN PREGNANCY POSTER

Teenage pregnancy is associated with dropping out of high school, poverty, and low birth weight for the baby. The latter is associated with poor health for the baby. About 13 percent of all low birth weight babies are born to teenage mothers (Statistical Abstract of the United States: 1990, *Table 91*).

■ **DATA:** *Over one million American teenagers (ages 15–19) become pregnant annually. Of these pregnancies, 46 percent elect to have their offspring; 41 percent elect to have an abortion; the remaining percentage have a miscarriage or stillbirth. The teen pregnancy rate among nonwhites is twice as high as among whites (Henshaw & Van Vort, 1989). Three-quarters of the pregnancies among young white mothers and 95 percent of those among young black mothers were unplanned (Hardy et al., 1989).*

Teenage girls become pregnant for a number of reasons (Chilman, 1990; Butler & Burton, 1990):

1. Low educational/occupational achievement and goals.
2. High fertility values and desiring a pregnancy.
3. Attitudes of risk-taking.
4. Poor communication skills about sex and contraception.
5. Lack of partner cooperation.
6. Lack of information about contraception.
7. Seeking independence, attaching themselves to a safe partner, or fleeing from an unhappy home situation.
8. Being a member of a society that does not adequately encourage the use of contraception.

The teenage pregnancy rate for the United States is almost twice that of France, England, and Canada, three times that of Sweden, and seven times that of the Netherlands. Teenagers in these countries are as sexually active as U.S. teenagers but have easier access to sex education and contraception (Hyde, 1990).

The abstinence approach to teenage sexuality does not appear to be effective in reducing the number of teenage pregnancies. In one study, 191 teenagers who were exposed to six program sessions on self-esteem, communication skills, peer pressure, and teaching the value that sex should be confined to marriage were compared with 129 teenagers who were not exposed to the sessions. An "increase in premarital sexual activity" on the part of those who took the course was the only change observed by the researchers (Christopher & Roosa, 1990).

Gordon (1986) suggested that our approach to sex education should be the same as our approach to alcohol: Don't drink, but if you do drink, don't drive. Don't have intercourse as a teenager, but if you do have intercourse, use a reliable form of contraception.

The American Academy of Pediatrics has adopted a policy which includes prescribing birth control for sexually active teens without telling the parents. "Pediatricians have the obligation to protect the health of these children, which includes protecting them against venereal diseases and pregancy," reported Dr. Roberta Beach of the Academy (Elias, 1990, 1).

∷ Sterilization

Unlike the temporary and reversible methods of contraception just discussed, sterilization is a permanent surgical procedure that prevents reproducing. Sterilization is losing its stigma as an extreme and undesirable method of birth control. It may be a contraceptive method of choice when the woman should not have more children for health reasons or when individuals are certain about their desire to have no more children or to remain childfree. Most couples complete their intended childbearing in their late twenties or early thirties, leaving more than 15 years of continued risk of unwanted pregnancy. Due to the risk of pill use at older ages and the lower reliability of alternative birth control methods, sterilization has become the most popular method of contraception among married women who have completed their families.

Slightly more than half of all sterilizations are performed on women. Although male sterilization is easier and safer than female sterilization, women feel more certain they will not get pregnant if they are sterilized. "I'm the one that ends up being pregnant and having the baby," said one woman. "So I want to make sure that I never get pregnant again."

Female Sterilization

■ **DATA:** *Of women ages 15–44, 28 percent of white women and 24 percent of black women have been sterilized* (Statistical Abstract of the United States: 1990, *Table 99).*

Although a woman may be sterilized by removal of her ovaries (oophorectomy) or uterus (hysterectomy), these operations are not normally undertaken for the sole purpose of sterilization because the ovaries produce important hormones as well as eggs and because both procedures carry the risks of major surgery. But sometimes there is another medical problem requiring hysterectomy.

The usual procedures of female sterilization are the salpingectomy, or tubal ligation, and a variant of it, the laparoscopy. Salpingectomy, also know as "tubal ligation" or "tying the tubes," is often performed under a general anesthetic while the woman is in the hospital just after she has delivered a baby. An incision is made in the lower abdomen, just above the pubic line, and the Fallopian tubes are brought into view one at a time. A part of each tube is cut out, and the ends are tied, clamped, or cauterized (burned). The operation takes about 30 minutes. About 700,000 such procedures are performed annually. The cost is around $1,500.

A less expensive and quicker (about 15 minutes) form of salpingectomy, which is performed on an outpatient basis, is the laparoscopy. Often using local anesthesia, the surgeon inserts a small, lighted viewing instrument (laparoscope) through the woman's abdominal wall just below the navel through which the uterus and the Fallopian tubes can be seen. The surgeon then makes another small incision in the lower abdomen and inserts a special pair of forceps that carry electricity to cauterize the tubes. The laparoscope and forceps are then withdrawn, the small wounds are closed with a single stitch, and small bandages are placed over the closed incisions. (Laparoscopy is also known as "the band-aid operation").

As an alternative to reaching the Fallopian tubes through an opening below the navel, the surgeon may make a small incision in the back of the vaginal barrel (vaginal tubal ligation).

These procedures for female sterilization are highly effective, but sometimes there are complications. In rare cases, a blood vessel in the abdomen is torn open during the sterilization and bleeds into the abdominal cavity. When this happens, another operation is necessary to find the bleeding vessel and tie it closed. Occasionally, there is injury to the small or large intestine, which may cause nausea, vomiting, and loss of appetite. The fact that death may result, if only rarely, is a reminder that female sterilization is surgery and, like all surgery, involves some risks.

Male Sterilization

| ■ **DATA:** *About 300,000 men have vasectomies every year (Keen, 1988).*

Vasectomies are the most frequent form of male sterilization. They are usually performed in the physician's office under a local anesthetic. Vasectomy involves the physician making two small incisions one on each side of the scrotum so that a small portion of each vas deferens (the sperm-carrying ducts) can be cut out and tied closed. Sperm are still produced in the testicles, but since there is no tube to the penis, they remain in the epididymis and eventually dissolve. The procedure takes about 15 minutes and costs about $350; the man can leave the physician's office within a short time.

Since sperm do not disappear from the ejaculate immediately after a vasectomy (some remain in the vas deferens above the severed portion), another method of contraception should be used until the man has had about 20 ejaculations. He is then asked to bring a sample of his ejaculate to the physicians' office so that it can be examined under a microscope for a sperm count. In about 1 percent of the cases, the vas deferens grows back and the man becomes fertile again. In other cases, the man may have more than two tubes, which the physician was not aware of.

A vasectomy does not affect the man's desire for sex, ability to have an erection, orgasm, amount of ejaculate (sperm comprise only a minute portion of the seminal fluid), or health. Although in some instances a vasectomy may be reversed, a man should get a vasectomy only if he never wants to have a biological child.

While over a quarter of a million men have vasectomies annually, the number of vasectomies has dropped to less than half of the number over a decade ago. Possible reasons include: men still view sterilization as primarily an option for women; they are aware that reversal of a vasectomy is successful less than half the time; men fear a negative impact of sterilization on their desire for sex.

:: Abortion

What if an unwanted pregnancy occurs? Seven hundred and four college students were asked by two researchers (Ryan & Dunn, 1988) to order their preference of five possible options for handling an out-of-wedlock, unintended pregnancy: having the child and keeping it as a single parent; having the child and allowing the grandparents to raise it; having the child and placing the child for adoption; marrying the father; and getting an abortion.

The preferences follow:

Getting married	37.5%
Abortion	30.5%
Keep child	13.9%
Adoption	12.7%
Grandparents rear child	5.4%

An abortion is defined as the removal of an embryo or fetus from the woman's uterus early in pregnancy before it can survive on its own (91 percent of all abortions are obtained within the first 12 weeks of gestation).

■ **DATA:** *Of the 1.6 million abortions performed annually in the United States, half are obtained by women who are young (age 24 or younger), white (59 percent of all abortions), and unmarried or never married (80 percent of all abortions) (Kochanek, 1990).*

The woman with an unwanted pregnancy may be beset by a number of strong feelings: fear ("What will I do now?"); self-anger ("How could I let this happen?"); guilt ("What would my parents think if they knew I was pregnant?"); ambivalence ("Will I be sorry if I have an abortion? Will I be sorry if I don't?"); and sometimes desperation ("Is suicide a way out?").

There is no conclusive evidence that abortion does or does not cause or contribute to psychological problems. There is evidence that abortion may lead to infertility, a damaged cervix, miscarriage, and low birth weight babies (Koop, 1989).

■ **DATA:** *About 10 percent of female college students have had an abortion (Leatherman, 1989).*

☐　　　　　C O N S I D E R A T I O N　　　　　☐

One of the best decisions during this period of crisis is to talk with an abortion counselor or a counselor at a local mental health center. These professionals are trained to help women look at alternatives to unwanted pregnancy and to help them decide what course of action is best for the individual woman. Perhaps most important, they can help the pregnant woman to make her decision with care and deliberation rather than under pressure.

Methods of Induced Abortion

An abortion may be spontaneous (by miscarriage) or induced. Methods of inducing an abortion include the following.

Suction Curettage. In suction curettage, a hollow plastic rod attached to a suction aspirator is inserted into the woman's uterus through the cervix, which has been dilated and anesthetized. The device draws the fetal tissue and surrounding matter out of the uterus. Suction curettage can be performed in a physician's office and takes about 10 minutes. If done within eight weeks of the last menstrual period, the dilation and anesthesia may not be necessary and the procedure is referred to as a menstrual extraction. Ninety-six percent of all abortions involve the suction curettage method (Kochanek, 1990).

Dilation and Curettage (D and C). In place of the suction curettage, a metal surgical instrument is used to scrape the fetal tissue and placenta from the walls of the uterus. A general anesthetic is usually administered. This more traditional procedure is regarded as inferior to the suction curettage method.

Dilation and Evacuation (D and E). Used in the second trimester, D and E is a combination of the vacuum curettage and D and C methods. However, greater dilation of the cervical opening is required.

Saline Injection. As pregnancy progresses, the fetus becomes too large to be removed safely by any of the preceding methods. Abortion by saline may be performed by inserting a long needle containing a concentrated salt solution through the abdominal and uterine walls into the amniotic cavity. This kills the fetus. From six to 48 hours later, the uterus contracts until the fetus is pushed out. Only one percent of abortions are performed using this method (Kochanek, 1990).

☐   C O N S I D E R A T I O N   ☐

Because saline injection is a major surgical procedure, earlier termination of pregnancy is desirable.

A variation of the saline method of abortion is the use of prostaglandins— hormonelike substances that cause the uterus to contract. When introduced into the vagina as a suppository or injected into the amniotic sac, they induce labor and the fetus is aborted.

As noted earlier, RU-486 (mifepristone) is used in Europe (it is not available in the United States) to bring about a very early abortion. When taken with prostaglandin up to seven weeks after conception, it is 95% effective. French researchers refer to this drug as the "month after pill."

Abortion Legislation

In 1973, the U.S. Supreme Court, in its famous Roe vs. Wade case, ruled that during the first three months of pregnancy, a woman has the constitutional right to obtain an abortion from a licensed physician without interference from the state. From the fourth through the sixth month, the decision to have an abortion belongs to the woman and her physician, but because an abortion at this later stage of pregnancy is more dangerous, the state may require that the abortion be performed in a hospital. During the last three months of pregnancy, the state may prohibit abortion except in those cases where the life or health of the mother is in danger. Neither a woman's husband nor her parents may veto her decision. In effect, the Supreme Court ruled that the fetus is a *potential* life and not a "person." It is generally agreed that before six months there is little chance for the fetus to survive on its own.

In the summer of 1989, the Supreme Court, in a split 5–4 decision, voted to give states the right to impose new restrictions on abortions. Referring to this decision, Justice Blackmunn said, "I fear for the liberty and equality of the millions of women who have lived and come of age in the 16 years since Roe was decided."

Elaine Bingham, an anti-abortion activist, hailed the decision as "the first step in overturning Roe vs. Wade" (*News and Observer*, 1989, 1). In the summer of 1990, the Supreme Court upheld an Ohio statute that required a one-parent notification before a minor could obtain an abortion. Some of the other restrictions that states may impose on abortion include the following:

1. States may ban any public employee—doctor, nurse, or other health care provider—from performing or assisting in most abortions.
2. States may ban the use of any public hospital or other facility for performing most abortions.

Linda Ellerbee, journalist and author, had an abortion at age 20 and feels that the choice is a private issue. Of legislation surrounding the issue, she states, "What's of interest is *who* will make this choice."

> "Making abortion illegal won't stop it," she adds. "What we're talking about is keeping it safe and available to women who don't have a lot of money to fly to another state, and keeping it out of the hands of every state legislature or small, vocal power group" (Trost, 1989, 2).

Public opinion on the abortion issue is mostly pro-choice. A *Wall Street Journal-/NBC* poll shows that the public, by a 2 to 1 margin, believes that abortion should be legal. A higher percentage believe that abortion should be legal if the woman's health is endangered, if the baby is defective, or if the pregnancy results from rape (Trost, 1989).

Abortion continues to be a very debated issue.

Abortion legislation is sometimes pro-choice. In May, 1990, the Supreme Court ruled that anti-abortion groups could not block the entrances to clinics that performed abortions.

:: Trends

The future of family planning will include less social obligation to have children. Twenty-five years ago, 85 percent of a national sample of women responded that almost all married women "ought" to have children; today, only 43 percent responded this way (Thornton, 1989). The one-child family will also become more prevalent as current concerns about inflation, personal freedom and growth, and the woman's career influence young couples to limit family size.

A greater number of women will delay childbearing until their thirties due to later age at marriage and a desire to pursue their careers. Because the risks to the baby increase with the mothers age, amniocentesis and chorion biopsy will be used more often to diagnose genetic abnormalities. Of women in their thirties, an increasing number will be willing to have a baby without being married. This issue is discussed in the Choices section.

Trends in birth control include the development of new contraceptive methods. One new contraceptive method is a subdermal implant (Norplant 2) of levonorgestrel (a synthetic progestin) under the skin of the women's arm. The procedure (minor surgery performed with a local anesthetic) takes about five minutes and furnishes protection against pregnancy for five years or more. Fertility returns after the implants are removed. Also being tested is an implant that is effective for one year and that is biodegradable and therefore does not require surgical removal.

For men, hormonal contraceptives such as MPA (medroxyprogesterone acetate) and TO (testosterone oenanthate) have been tested in Toronto, London, and Santiago, but have not received FDA approval for use in the United States. Gossypol, an extract of cottonseed oil, has also been tested in China as an oral contraceptive. U.S. research firms are now testing the long-term safety of gossypol. A major problem in male contraceptives has been to develop one that reduces sperm count without reducing sexual interest or making the man permanently sterile.

Drug awareness education will sensitize pregnant women to the potential negative effects of drugs during pregnancy. Alcohol can have harmful effects on the fetus and cocaine has been associated with babies born with enlarged kidneys and gross deformities that cannot be corrected (Chavez et al., 1989).

:: Summary

The decision whether to become a parent is one of the most important decisions you will ever make. Unlike marriage, parenthood is a role from which there is no easy withdrawal. Individuals may try out marriage by living together, but there is no such trial run for would-be parents.

Spouses, children, and society all benefit from family planning. These benefits include less health risk to mother and child, fewer unwanted children, decreased economic burden for the parents and society, and population control.

The decision to become a parent is encouraged (sometimes unconsciously) by family, peers, religion, government, education, and cultural observances. The reasons people give for having children include social expectations, influence of spouse, accident, a sense of immortality, personal fulfillment and identity, and the desire for a close affiliative relationship.

Some couples opt for the childfree lifestyle. Reasons wives give for wanting to be childfree are more personal freedom, greater time and intimacy with their spouses, and career demands. Husbands also are motivated by the desire for more personal freedom. They mention disinterest in being a parent and the desire to avoid the responsibilities of parenthood as reasons for choosing a childfree lifestyle.

The most preferred family size in the United States is the two-child family. Some of the factors in a couple's decision to have more than one child are the desire to repeat a good experience, the feeling that two children provide companionship for each other, and the desire to have a child of each sex.

The primary methods of birth control are contraception, sterilization, and abortion. With contraception, the risk of becoming pregnant can be reduced to practically zero, depending on the method selected and how systematically it is used. Contraception includes birth control pills, which prevent ovulation; the IUD, which prevents implantation of the fertilized egg; condoms and diaphragms, which are barrier methods; as well as vaginal spermicides and sponge, and the rhythm method. These methods vary in effectiveness and safety.

Sterilization is a surgical procedure that prevents fertilization, usually by blocking the passage of eggs or sperm through the Fallopian tubes or vas deferens, respectively. The procedure for female sterilization is called salpingectomy, or tubal ligation. Laparoscopy is another method of tubal ligation. The most frequent form of male sterilization is vasectomy.

Abortion is one alternative if an unwanted pregnancy occurs. Methods of inducing abortion include suction curettage, dilation and curettage (D and C), and dilation and evacuation (D and E), all of which are used in the earlier stages of pregnancy; saline and prostaglandin injection are used when the pregnancy is more advanced.

Questions for Reflection

1. What impact have your experiences in the family in which you were reared had on your desire for children? If you want children, how does the number of siblings you have influence the number of children you want?
2. To what degree do the only children you know fit the stereotype of being lonely and spoiled?
3. To what degree are you pro-choice or pro-life regarding abortion?

References

Baldwin, J. J., S. Whiteley, and J. D. Baldwin. Changing AIDS and fertility related behavior: The effectiveness of sexual education. *The Journal of Sex Research*, 1990, *27*, 245–262.

Bell, J. E. and N. Eisenberg. Life satisfaction in midlife childless and empty-nest men and women. *Lifestyles: A Journal of Changing Patterns*, 1985, *7*, 146–155.

Billingham, R. E. and A. R. Sack. Gender differences in college students' willingness to participate in alternative marriage and family relationships. *Family Perspective,* 1986, *20,* 37–44.

Bloom, D. E. and N. G. Bennett. Childless couples. *American Demographics,* 1986, *8,* no. 8, 23 et passim.

Butler, J. R. and L. M. Burton. Rethinking teenage childbearing: Is sexual abuse a missing link. *Family Relations,* 1990, *39,* 73–80.

Chavez, G. F., J. Mulinare, and J. F. Cordero. Maternal cocaine use during early pregnancy as a risk factor for congenital urogenital anomalies. *Journal of the American Medical Association,* 1989, *262,* 795–798.

Chilman, C. S. Promoting healthy adolescent sexuality. *Family Relations,* 1990, *39,* 123–131.

Christopher, F. S. and M. W. Roosa. An evaluation of an adolescent pregnancy prevention program: Is "Just say No" enough? *Family Relations,* 1990, *39,* 68–72.

Crispell, D. Three's a crowd. *American Demographics,* 1989, *11,* 34–38.

Cutler, Blayne. Rock-a-buy baby. *American Demographics,* 1990, *12,* 21–34.

Dawson, D. A. The effects of sex education on adolescent behavior. *Family Planning Perspectives,* 18, no. 4, 162 170.

Elias, M. Doctors call for teen birth control. *USA Today,* May 11, 1990, p. A1.

Falbo, T. and D. F. Polit-O'Harra. Only children: What do we know about them? *Pediatric Nursing,* 1985, *11,* 356–360.

Fullilove, M. T., R. E. Fullilove, K. Haynes, and S. Gross. Black women and AIDS prevention: A view towards understanding the gender rules. *The Journal of Sex Research,* 1990, *27,* 47–65.

Gordon, S. What kids need to know. *Psychology Today,* 1986, *20,* no. 10, 22–27.

Greenberg, J. S., C. E. Bruess, and D. W. Sands. *Sexuality: Insights and issues.* Dubuque, Ia.: William C. Brown, 1986.

Hanson, S. H. and M. J. Sporakowski. Single parent families. *Family Relations,* 1986, *35,* 3–8.

Hardy, J. B., A. K. Duggan, K. Masnyk, and C. Pearson. Fathers of children born to young urban mothers. *Family Planning Perspectives,* 1989, *21,* 159–163.

Harvey, S. M., L. J. Beckmna, and J. Murray. Factors associated with use of the contraceptive sponge. *Family Planning Perspectives,* 1989, 21, 159–163.

Hyde, J. S. *Understanding Human Sexuality.* 4th ed. New York: McGraw-Hill, 1990.

Height, D. Black families. *USA Today,* September 25, 1986, p. 7–A.

Henshaw, Stanly K. and Jennifer Van Vort. Teenage abortion, birth and pregnancy statistics: An update. *Family Planning Perspectives,* 1989, *21,* 85–88.

Hogge, W. A., S. A. Schonberg, and M. S. Golbus. Chorionic villus sampling: The experiences of 1,000 cases. *American Journal of Obstetrics and Gynecology,* 1986, *154,* 1249–52.

Johnson, Jeanette H. Weighing the evidence on the pill and breast cancer. *Family Planning Perspectives,* 1989, *21,* 89–92.

Keen, H. A decline in vasectomies. *Maclean's,* May 2, 1988, p. 10.

Knox, D. and K. Wilson. The differences between having one and two children. *Family Coordinator,* 1978, *27,* 23–25.

Kochanek, K. D. Induced terminations of pregnancy: Reporting states, 1985 and 1986. *Monthly Vital Statistics,* April 28, 1989, *37,* no. 12. Hyattsville, Md.: Public Health Service: National Center for Health Statistics.

Kochanek, K. D. Induced terminations of pregnancy: Reporting states, 1987. *Monthly Vital Statistics Report,* 38, no. 9, suppl. Hyattsville, Md.: Public Health Service: National Center for Health Statistics, 1989.

Kochanek, K. D. Induced terminations of pregnancy: reporting states, 1987. *Monthly Vital Statistics Report,* 38, no. 3, suppl. Hyattsville, Md.: Public Health Service: National Center for Health Statistics, 1990.

Koop, C. Everett. A measured response: Koop on abortion. *Family Planning Perspectives*, 1989, *21*, 31–32.

Kyes, K. B. The effect of a "Safer Sex" film as mediated by erotophia and gender on attitudes toward condoms. *Journal of Sex Research*, 1990, *27*, 297–303.

Leatherman, C. Only 1 in 10 female college students has had an abortion. *The Chronicle of Higher Education*, May 31, 1989, p. A23.

Leigh, B. C. The relationship of substance use during sex to high-risk sexual behavior. *The Journal of Sex Research*, 1990, *27*, 199–213.

LeMasters, E. E. and J. DeFrain. *Parents in contemporary America*. Belmont, California: Wadsworth Publishing Co. 1989.

Marini, M. M. Effects of the number and spacing of children on marital and parental satisfaction. *Demography*, 1980, *17*, 225–242.

Marsiglio, W. and F. L. Mott. The impact of sex education on sexual activity, contraceptive use, and premarital pregnancy among American teenagers. *Family Planning Perspectives*, 1986, *18*, no. 4, 151–162.

National Center for Health Statistics. Advance report of final natality statistics, 1987. Monthly Vital Statistics Report, *38*, no. 3, suppl. Hyattsville, Md.: Public Health Service, 1989.

Mindel, C. H., R. W. Habenstein, and R. Wright Jr., eds. *Ethnic families in America: Patterns and variations*, 3rd. ed. New York: Elsevier, 1988.

Neal, A. G., H. T. Groat, and J. W. Wicks. Attitudes about having children: A study of 600 couples in the early years of marriage. *Journal of Marriage and the Family*, 1989, *51*, 313–328.

News and Observer. Court OKs State Abortion Limits. July 4, 1989, p. 1.

Painter, K. Joys override obstacles for late bloomers. *USA Today*, May 11, 1990, p. D1, D2.

Rempel, J. Childless elderly. *Journal of Marriage and the Family*, 1985, *47*, 343–348.

Renvoize, J. *Going solo: Single mothers by choice*. London: Routledge and Kegan Paul, 1985.

Rind, P. Vasectomy proves to be preferable to female sterilization. *Family Planning Perspectives*, 1989, *21*, 191.

Rivara, E. P., P. J. Sweeney, and B. F. Henderson. A study of low socioeconomic status, black teenage fathers, and their nonfather peers. *Pediatrics*, 1985, *75*, no. 4, 648–656.

Rogers, C. C. and M. O'Connell. Child-spacing among birth cohorts of American women (1905–1959). U.S. Bureau of the Census, Series P-20, no. 385. U.S. Government Printing Office, Washington, D.C., 1984.

Roper Organization. *The 1985 Virginia Slims American Women's Opinion Poll*. New York, 1985.

Ryan, I. J. and P. C. Dunn. Association of race, sex, religion, family size, and desired number of children on college students preferred methods of dealing with unplanned pregnancy. *Family Practice Research Journal*, 1988, *7*, 153–161.

Seashore, M. R. Counseling prospective parents about possible genetic disorders in offspring. *Medical Aspects of Human Sexuality*, 1980, *14*, no. 11, 97–98.

Sheehan, M. K., S. K. Ostwald, and J. Rothenberger. Perceptions of sexual responsibility: Do young men and women agree? *Pediatric Nursing*, 1986, *12*, 17–21.

Sonenstein, F. L., J. H. Pleck, and R. C. Ku. Sexual activity, condom use, and AIDS awareness among adolescent males. *Family Planning Perspectives*, 1989, *21*, 152–158.

Stark, E. Young, innocent, and pregnant. *Psychology Today*, 1986, *20*, no. 10, 28–35.

Statistical Abstract of the United States: 1989, 109th ed. Washington, D.C.: U.S. Bureau of the Census, 1989.

Statistical Abstract of the United States: 1990, 110th ed. Washington, D.C.: U.S. Bureau of the Census, 1990.

Stewart, S. A. They see an upscale, happy future. *USA Today*, May 13, 1986, p. A-2.

Teachman, Jay D. and Paul T. Schollaert. Economic conditions, marital status, and the timing of first births: Results for whites and blacks. *Sociological Forum*, 1989, *4*, 27–46.

Thomas, P. Contraceptives: Break due after decade of drought. *Medical World News*, March 14, 1988, pp. 49–68.

Thornton, A. Changing attitudes toward family issues in the United States. *Journal of Marriage and the Family*, 1989, *51*, 87–893.

Trost, Cathy. Women who've had abortions speak out, but hardly in unison. *The Wall Street Journal*, June 13, 1989, p. 1 et passim.

Uzzell, O. Family planning: The artificial control of gender. *Family Perspective*, 1985, *19*, 279–282.

Webster-Stratton, Carolyn. The relationship of marital support, conflict, and divorce to parent perceptions, behaviors, and childhood conduct problems. *Journal of Marriage and the Family*, 1989, *51*, 417–430.

Whitley, B. E. College student contraceptive use: A multivariate analysis. *Journal of Sex Research*, 1990, *27*, 305–313.

Wineberg, Howard and James McCarthy. Child spacing in the United States: Recent trends and differentials. *Journal of Marriage and the Family*, 1989, *51*, 213–228.

Witwer, M. Oral contraceptive use linked to chlamydial, gonococcal infections. *Family Planning Perspectives*, 1989, *21*, 190.

Wolinsky, H. A woman's condom? *American Health Magazine*, June 1988, p. 10.

CHOICES

IN ADDITION TO the choices of whether to have children and, if so, how many, there is the choice on the part of some who are not married whether to have a child without a spouse. Because there are more men than women and because men tend to marry women much younger than themselves, there are women in their thirties who want a baby but who have no husband. Other women are lesbians and do not want a husband. Still others, prefer to have a child without a spouse even though their sexual preference is heterosexual and potential marital partners are available. Regardless of the reason, the question remains the same.

Having a Child Without a Spouse?: The Biological-Clock Issue

Of the 9 million parents rearing children by themselves, 8 million are mothers and 1 million are fathers. Although most of these parents are separated or divorced, about twenty percent of them are never married mothers (*Statistical Abstract of the United States: 1990*, Table 96). Most of the children born to these unmarried mothers were unplanned and were born when the mother was between the ages of 18 and 24. However, an increasing number of children are being conceived by single women over 30. Many older women feel that their biological clock doesn't allow them much more time. In a Roper Poll, four in ten women said that it is all right for adults to have children without getting married (1985). One woman said:

I'm 37 and feel that I need to make a decision. I've always wanted a baby, and I always thought that someday I was going to meet the right guy and we would find a house and start our family. But each year, I meet fewer prospects, and the ones I'm dating aren't what you would call the pick of the litter. Because it looks like I may never get married, I'm looking seriously at getting pregnant and rearing a child on my own.

Jean Renvoize (1985) interviewed over 30 unmarried women who made the conscious decision to have a baby with the intent of rearing their baby alone. Of these women, the researcher said;

I expected to find a group of tough-minded, militant women somewhat on the defensive; instead I found mostly happy, fulfilled, strong, but gentle individuals who gave out warmth and a readiness to share with others. These were women who had made their choice after much deliberation, mostly at a mature age, and who knew in advance that nothing in life comes free (p. 5).

One single mother by choice said:

I felt I could go through life without being married, I could be fulfilled without a man in my life, but I knew I couldn't be fulfilled without at least having experienced a pregnancy and raising a child (p. 91).

In making the conscious decision to raise a child as a single parent, several issues might be considered:

1. *Satisfaction of the emotional needs of the child.* Perhaps the greatest challenge for single parents is to satisfy the emotional needs of their children—alone. Children need love, which a parent may express in a hundred ways—from hugs and kisses to help with homework. But the single parent who is tired from working all day and who has no one else with whom to share parenting at night may be unable to meet the emotional needs of a child.

2. *Satisfaction of adult emotional needs.* Single parents have emotional needs of their own that children are often incapable of satisfying. The unmet need to share an emotional relationship with an adult can weigh heavily on the single parent. Most single parents seek such a relationship.

3. *Satisfaction of adult sexual needs.* Most single parents regard their role as interfering with their sexual relationships. They may be concerned that their children will find out if they have a sexual encounter at home and frustrated if they have to go away from home to enjoy a sexual relationship. They may have asked themselves such questions as "Do I wait

until my children are asleep and then ask my lover to leave before morning?," "Do I openly acknowledge my lover's presence in my life to my children and ask them not to tell anybody?," and "Suppose my kids get attached to my lover, who may not be a permanent part of our lives?"—and deal with the answers. (Most single parents hide their sexual relationships from their children and make them aware of another person in their life only if the other person is of significant emotional importance to the single parent.)

4. *Childcare and supervision.* Because the single parent is likely to be employed, adequate childcare arrangements must be made. Using a relative or hiring a baby sitter are the most frequent arrangements for the preschool child of a single parent. Commercial day care centers are also available, but paying for childcare services may take a large slice out of the single parent's often modest income.

When single mothers are compared with mothers living with their partners, single mothers report more stress and more behavior problems with their children. These single mothers also reported more conflict with their daughters than their sons (Webster-Stratton, 1989).

5. *Money.* Lack of money is one of the most difficult aspects of single parenthood. The problem may be particularly acute when the single parent is a woman. The mean income for female-headed, single-parent families is less than half the mean income for two-parent families. Male-headed, single-parent families are less economically stressed because men typically make more money than women.

6. *Guardian.* The single mother needs to appoint a guardian to take care of her baby in the event of her death or disability.

An organization for women who want children and who may or may not marry is Single Mothers by Choice (1642 Gracie Square Station; New York, NY 10028; 212–988–0993). The organization has more than 1,000 members and provides support for women who make this decision. The organization also has "thinkers' groups" for women who are contemplating whether to have a child outside of marriage. Most women attending these groups decide not to have children after they have been presented with all the facts. Other women can't envision a life without children even though they are aware of some of the difficulties:

I knew that rearing my kids alone wasn't going to be easy. But I can also tell you that we have a wonderful, loving, sharing family that makes me swell with love. Yes, I am exhausted, and we don't have much money, and the kids get on my nerves. But we are a family unit and care about each other and that makes up for all the problems.

Impact of Social Influences on Choices

The combined factors of a shortage of men, peers who talk about having a child without a spouse, and social pressure to have a child account for the willingness of some women to have a child without being married. There are not enough single men for every woman who wants to get married and have a baby to do so. One alternative for a single woman who wants a baby is to get pregnant by a man she does not intend to marry. (Adoption is another alternative.) Women who do so are responding to one set of social pressures (have a baby) but resisting another (only married people should have babies). Those who discount the latter social pressures often develop friendship networks such as Single Mothers by Choice with other women who have the same plan of action.

C H A P T E R

14

Having Children

CONTENTS

IS IT TRUE?

1. Artificial insemination is more acceptable than adoption to college students if they are confronted with a problem of infertility.

2. Black students are more willing to use artificial insemination than whites.

3. If a couple adopts a child through a state agency, the biological mother can change her mind within 30 days and ask to have her baby back.

4. Black fathers have traditionally been absent from their homes—a pattern which began during slavery.

5. Studies agree on how children influence marital happiness.

1 = F; 2 = F; 3 = T; 4 = F; 5 = F.

WHEN A COUPLE or individual decides to have a child, getting pregnant becomes a goal. Becoming pregnant through sexual intercourse is one of several alternatives. Other alternatives include artificial insemination, in-vitro fertilization, and embryo transfer. Once a baby begins to develop, by whatever means, role transitions begin: wife to mother, husband to father, and couple to family. We will address these issues in this chapter.

▪▪ Fertilization

Fertilization takes place when a woman's egg, or ovum, unites with a man's sperm. This may occur through sexual intercourse or artificial insemination, or more recently, through the methods of test-tube or in-vitro fertilization and embryo transfer.

At orgasm, the man ejaculates a thick white substance called semen, which contains sperm.

| ▪ **DATA:** *About 300 million sperm are expelled during the average ejaculation (Greenberg et al., 1986).*

Once the semen is deposited in or near the vagina, the sperm begin to travel up the vagina, through the opening of the cervix, up the uterus, and into the Fallopian tubes. If the woman has ovulated (released a mature egg from an ovary into a Fallopian tube) within eight hours, or if she ovulates during the two or three days the sperm may remain alive, a sperm may penetrate and fertilize the egg. About 30 percent of fertilized eggs die. Although popular usage does not differentiate between the terms "fertilization" and "conception," conception refers to a fertilized egg that survives through implantation on the uterine wall.

If the goal of an individual or a couple is to get pregnant, it is important to be patient about doing so, to time intercourse to coincide with ovulation, and to use the most efficient position during intercourse. In general, a woman in her twenties should allow herself about six months to conceive. A woman in her thirties should allow about a year, with the probability of conception dropping as the woman gets older.

☐   C O N S I D E R A T I O N   ☐

A woman who gives herself time to get pregnant will be less anxious about doing so. This is important because anxiety may affect ovulation. Social workers in adoption agencies have noted that women, frustrated and despairing over their attempts to get pregnant and seeking to adopt a child, frequently become pregnant soon after they obtain a child and their anxiety disappears. "It was only after we had completed all the red tape and finally had our adopted daughter in the bassinet that I became pregnant," recalls one mother.

When is the best time to have intercourse to maximize the chance of pregnancy? Since a woman is fertile for only about 48 hours each month, the timing of sexual intercourse is important. In general, 24 hours before ovulation is the best time. There are several ways to predict ovulation. Many women have breast tenderness, and some experience a "pinging" sensation at the time of ovulation. Also, a woman may record her basal body temperature and examine her cervical mucus. After menstruation, the vagina in most women is without noticeable discharge because the mucus is thick. As the time of ovulation nears, the mucus thins to the consistency of egg white, which may be experienced by the woman as increased vaginal discharge. Intercourse should occur during this time. In essence, the "technology" of the rhythm method to avoid pregnancy can be used to maximize the potential for pregnancy.

During intercourse, the woman should be on her back and a pillow should be placed under her buttocks after receiving the sperm so a pool of semen will collect near her cervix. She should remain in this position for about 30 minutes to allow the sperm to reach the Fallopian tubes. "She may get tired of lying there," said one woman, "but if she wants to get pregnant, it's the thing to do."

:: Infertility

Some couples are unable to get pregnant. Infertility is defined as the inability to achieve a pregnancy after at least one year of regular sexual relations without birth control, or the inability to carry a pregnancy to live birth.

> ■ **DATA:** *Infertility affects between 15 and 20 percent of married couples in the United States (Higgins, 1990).*

Some of the more common causes of infertility in men include low sperm production, poor semen motility, effects of sexually transmitted diseases such as gonorrhea and syphilis, and interference with the passage of sperm through the genital ducts due to an enlarged prostate. The causes of infertility in women include blocked Fallopian tubes, endocrine imbalances that prevent ovulation, dysfunctional ovaries, chemically hostile cervical mucus that may kill sperm, and effects of sexually transmitted diseases. About half of all infertility problems can be successfully treated so that a pregnancy will result.

☐   C O N S I D E R A T I O N   ☐

Not being able to get pregnant is a grievous experience for many couples. "Yet this is a different kind of grief. A death has finality to it, but infertility can go on indefinitely. It is like having a chronic illness; there is the continuing reminder of loss coupled with continued hope for a cure. Each month there is a new hope, the fantasy of being pregnant, the conviction that this time it just has to work" (Lasker & Borg, 1987, 20).

Higgins (1990) reported changes couples experience when confronted with infertility—their sexual relations may no longer be spontaneous but scheduled and regimented, they may avoid friends who have children, and they may begin to consider alternatives to having children the traditional way.

Artificial Insemination of Wife

When the sperm of the husband is low in count or motility, it sometimes helps to pool the sperm from several ejaculations and artificially inseminate the wife. This procedure is known as AIH (artificial insemination by husband). There is widespread acceptance of this method of fertilization.

■ **DATA:** *Out of more than 700 university students, 76 percent said artificial insemination of the wife with the husband's sperm was acceptable (Dunn et al., 1988).*

In other cases, sperm from an unknown donor (AID, or artificial insemination by donor) is used. There is less acceptance for AID than for AIH.

■ **DATA:** *Out of more than 700 university students, 20 percent said artificial insemination of the wife by an unknown donor was acceptable (Dunn et al., 1988).*

☐　　　　　　　C O N S I D E R A T I O N　　　　　　　☐

The American Fertility Society has issued a set of guidelines for donor insemination clinics and physicians. These include:

The donor's sperm should be screened for genetic abnormalities and sexually transmitted diseases.
All semen should be quarantined for 180 days and retested for the AIDS virus.
Fresh semen should never be used. The donor should be under age 50 in order to diminish hazards related to aging (Foreman, 1990, 7A).

Sometimes the donor's and the husband's sperm are mixed, so that the couple has the psychological benefit of knowing that the husband may be the biological father. One situation in which the husband's sperm is not mixed with the donor's sperm is when the husband is the carrier of a genetic disease, such as Tay-Sachs disease.

Although there are about 85 sperm banks in the United States, some couples have sought sperm from the Repository for Germinal Choice. This controversial sperm bank in Escondido, California, specializes in providing sperm from men of known intellectual achievement. Among their donors have been three Nobel prize winners in science. No donor to the sperm bank has an IQ under 140.

In the procedure of artificial insemination, a physician or the husband who has been trained by the physician deposits the sperm through a syringe in the wife's cervix and places a cervical cap over her cervix, which remains in place for 24 hours. On the average, it takes about three such inseminations before fertilization occurs.

■ **DATA:** *In the United States, about 30,000 infants are conceived each year through the use of artificial insemination (Foreman, 1990, 7A).*

One couple's experience with artificial insemination by donor follows:

Because of my need to get pregnant, my husband and I decided after long, hard thinking and sleepless nights to try artificial insemination. But I wasn't sure if that was what I wanted. I was very afraid that after the baby was born my husband would resent the child because it would be from another man's sperm. He tried to assure me that he would not feel that way. He wanted a baby almost as much as I did. So we began the procedures.

The first thing we had to do was to turn in my basal body temperature chart, so the physicians could determine the exact time I ovulated. Then we had to give them a picture of my husband and his personal and biological traits (they also categorize donors according to these characteristics). Then they tried to find a donor with the characteristics that matched those of my husband.

The injections of the donor semen cost $100 and were done the day before and the morning of ovulation. The actual procedure was very humiliating. I had to lay on the examination table after I received the injection with my feet up in the air at a 90° angle for 30 minutes.

I became pregnant after the first set of injections. It was really hard to believe that we were finally going to have a child. My husband was as excited as I was.

I carried the child full term and had no complications. It was hard to believe that after all those years of failing, some other man's sperm got me pregnant. Actually, I don't think about that now. We have a beautiful boy named Mark who is the joy of our lives. He is named after my husband, is very healthy, and we feel lucky to have him. As long as both parents agree, I feel that artificial insemination is the best answer to the problem of sterility. At least he is a part of one of us in flesh and bone! Our marriage is closer than ever now.

☐   C O N S I D E R A T I O N   ☐

Like this couple, most AID couples report having a positive experience. Although couples feel severe emotional pain when they learn of the husband's inability to impregnate the wife, they decide on AID because, as the wife in the narrative noted, it allows at least one-half of them as a couple to be biologically related to the prospective child. This fact is often kept secret, and neither their friends nor the child are told.

This secrecy sometimes leads to negative consequences. Annette Baran, a clinical social worker, cited the following example:

The mother and father have divorced and father's new girlfriend is taunting the ex-wife with the knowledge that she knows the children aren't really his because she knows he's sterile. Mother becomes panicked and wakes the children up in the middle of the night to tell them for fear that his new girlfriend will reveal the secret (Foreman, 1990, 7A).

■ **DATA:** *The average cost for each artificial insemination is between $100 and $150; between 2 and 5 inseminations are usually needed before conception occurs (Foreman, 1990, 7A).*

Before AID is carried out, the parents-to-be agree that any child produced by this procedure will be their own and their legitimate heir. The potential legal problems with AID have not been worked out. Only 18 states have laws pertaining to artificial insemination. For example, a couple could charge a physician with negligence if the child was born with a severe defect.

Artificial Insemination of Surrogate Mother

I had very easy pregnancies, and I didn't think it would be a problem for me to carry another child. I figured maybe I could help someone.

—VALERIE, A SURROGATE MOTHER

Sometimes artificial insemination does not help a woman to get pregnant (for example, her Fallopian tubes may be blocked or her cervical mucus may be hostile to sperm). The couple who still wants a child and who has decided against adoption may consider parenthood through a surrogate mother—a woman who is impregnated with the husband's sperm and carries the child to term. As with AIH, the motivation of the prospective parents is to have a child that is genetically related to at least one of them. For the surrogate mother, the apparent motivation is to help involuntary childless couples achieve their aspirations of parenthood and to make money (the surrogate mother is paid about $10,000).

The concept of surrogate pregnancy is not new. The Bible reports that Abraham and his wife Sarah could not conceive a child. Their solution was for Abraham to have intercourse with Sarah's Egyptian maid, Hagar, who bore a child for them.

There is limited acceptance among university students for surrogate motherhood.

■ **DATA:** *Out of more than 700 University students, 15 percent said having a baby via a surrogate mother was acceptable (Dunn et al., 1988).*

□   C O N S I D E R A T I O N   □

Legally, there are few guidelines to protect involuntary childless couples who engage a surrogate mother for procreative services. The surrogate could change her mind and decide to keep the child, as did a New Jersey surrogate mother. Mary Beth Whitehead decided she wanted to keep her baby, even though she had signed a contract to give up the baby for $10,000. William and Elizabeth Stern, the would-be parents, sued Whitehead for and eventually won custody of the child. Surrogate mothers who want to keep their babies are rare, however. Only 4 of 500 have sought custody (Sharpe, 1987).

Engaging a surrogate mother is expensive.

■ **DATA:** *The cost of having a baby via surrogate motherhood is between $25,000 and $30,000. This pays for the legal, medical, and counseling fees as well as the fee for the surrogate mother (Lasker & Borg, 1987).*

In-Vitro Fertilization

About 2 million couples cannot have a baby because the woman's Fallopian tubes are blocked or damaged, preventing the passage of the eggs to the uterus. In-vitro or test-tube fertilization is an additional option to parenthood for infertile couples.

Using a laparoscope (a narrow, telescope-like instrument inserted through an incision just below the woman's naval to view the tubes and ovaries), the physician is able to see a mature egg as it is released from the woman's ovary. The time of release can be predicted accurately to within two hours. When the egg emerges, the physician uses an aspirator to remove the egg, placing it in a small tube containing a stabilizing fluid. The egg is taken to the laboratory, put in a culture dish, kept at a certain temperature-acidity level, and surrounded by sperm from the husband. After one of these sperm fertilizes the egg, it divides and is implanted by the physician in the wall of the wife's uterus. Usually, several fertilized eggs are implanted in the hope that one will survive. Occasionally, some fertilized eggs are frozen and implanted at a later time, if necessary. This procedure is known as *cryopreservation*.

In the meantime, the couple may get divorced and disagree over who owns the frozen embryos. Such was the case of Mary Sue Davis and Junior Davis who took their disagreement to court. The court awarded the embryos to Ms. Davis (Fitzgerald, 1989).

■ **DATA:** *The average cost for in-vitro fertilization until conception is between $4,000 and $7,000* (Consumer Protection Issues Involving In-Vitro Fertilization Clinics, *1989).*

Student acceptance of in-vitro or test-tube fertilization is much greater than student acceptance of surrogate motherhood.

■ **DATA:** *Out of more than 700 university students, 55 percent said having a baby via in-vitro or test-tube fertilization was acceptable (Dunn et al., 1988).*

Louise Brown of Oldham, England, was the first baby to be born by in-vitro fertilization. After her birth in 1978, there have been over 14,000 attempts by a total of 146 clinics in the United States. About 150 live births have resulted from the procedure.

■ **DATA:** *Between 6 and 15 percent of couples who use in-vitro fertilization subsequently give birth to a baby* (Consumer Protection Issues Involving In-Vitro Fertilization Clinics, *1989).*

Among the clinics reporting the highest success rates are Norton Hospital at the University of Louisville, Brookwood Women's Medical Plaza in Birmingham, Alabama, and the Department of Ob/Gyn at the University of Utah in Salt Lake City (*Consumer Protection Issues Involving In-Vitro Fertilization Clinics,* 1989).

Ovum Transfer

An alternative to test-tube fertilization for the infertile couple is ovum transfer.

■ **DATA:** *Out of more than 700 university students, 26 percent said having a baby via ovum transfer was acceptable (Dunn et al., 1988).*

The husband allows his sperm to be placed by a physician in a surrogate woman. After about five days, her uterus is flushed out (endometrial lavage) and the contents are analyzed under a microscope to identify the presence of a fertilized ovum, which is inserted into the uterus of the otherwise infertile partner. The embryo can be frozen and implanted at a later time.

Infertile couples opt for ovum transfer, also called embryo transfer, because the baby will be half theirs (the man is the biological father) and the partner will have the experience of pregnancy and childbirth. The surrogate woman participates out of her desire to help an infertile couple.

Gamete Intrafallopian Transfer

The newest discovery in helping women with blocked or damaged Fallopian tubes is gamete intrafallopian transfer or GIFT. Using this procedure, the woman's ovum is fertilized by the man's sperm within the woman's body rather than in a glass dish. The success rate using this procedure is about 20 percent compared with the 6-15 percent success rate of in-vitro fertilization.

▪▪ Miscarriage

A miscarriage is the spontaneous abortion of an embryo too young to live outside the womb—usually due to a chromosomal abnormality (Wilcox et al., 1988). In spite of the effort that may be involved in the woman becoming pregnant, as many as one in three may have a miscarriage. Until recently, there was little recognition that the woman (and her partner) may experience profound grief for the loss of the fetus. Remarks such as "Don't worry, you'll try again soon," or "It's only Nature's way," are intended to minimize the impact of the miscarriage. In a study of 65 women who had miscarried anywhere from 2 to 21 weeks after conception, a sense of sadness was universal; 30 percent of the women reported feelings of frustration, disappointment, or anger (Cole, 1988). Many women blamed themselves for the miscarriage; some felt that they were being punished for something they had done in the past.

CONSIDERATION

Miscarriage may produce marital stress caused by the different ways that men and women react to the event. Men tend to be action-oriented, to seek distraction in movies or vacation while women tend to relive the miscarriage over and over again. "In this dynamic, the wife may perceive her husband's suggestions to go out as unhelpful or uncaring, while the husband may see his wife's desire to talk about the event as obsessive. The two withdraw from each other, and other unresolved strains in the marriage may surface" (Cole, 1988, 65).

A miscarriage can be just as tough as a death in the family.
—KIM WILEY

Individuals may seek assistance in adjusting to a miscarriage through SHARE (St. Elizabeth's Hospital, National Share Office, Belleville, Ill. 62222, 618–234–2415), which is a nationwide organization with 200 chapters. SHARE gives validity to the woman's grief, encourages her to give her miscarried fetus a name, to get footprints, and to have a ceremony recognizing the death of the fetus. Rather than try and minimize the event, SHARE encourages the woman to process all of

:: Choosing a Childbirth Method

Couples who give birth to a child have several methods from which to choose, including Lamaze, Dick-Read, Bradley, LeBoyer, regional anesthesia, and Cesarean births.

Lamaze Method

Preferred by an increasing number of couples, the Lamaze method of childbirth, often called "natural" or "prepared" childbirth, was developed by French obstetrician Fernand Lamaze. The method is essentially a preparation for childbirth, in which the woman and her partner take six one-and-a-half-hour classes during the last trimester of pregnancy, usually with several other couples. The goal of these sessions is to reduce the anxiety and pain of childbirth by viewing it as a natural process, by educating the couple about labor and delivery, and by giving them specific instructions to aid in the birth of their baby.

There are several aspects of the Lamaze method:

1. *Education about childbirth.* The instructor explains the physiology of pregnancy, stages of labor, and delivery.
2. *Timed breathing exercises.* Specific breathing exercises are recommended for each stage of labor to help with the contractions by refocusing the laboring woman's attention and keeping the pressure of the diaphragm off the uterus. These exercises are practiced between sessions, so that the couples will know when and how to use them when labor actually begins.
3. *Pain control exercises.* The woman is taught to selectively tense and relax various muscle groups of her body (for example, her arm muscles). She then learns

"Lamaze" is one of the most popular "prepared" childbirth methods.

how to tense these muscle groups while relaxing the rest of her body, so that during labor she can relax the rest of her body while her uterus is contracting involuntarily.

4. *Husband's involvement*. A major advantage of the Lamaze method is the active involvement of the husband in the birthing event. His role (or that of a coach substitute if the father is not available) is to tell his wife when to start and stop the various breathing exercises, give her psychological support throughout labor, and take care of her in general (get ice, keep her warm, and so on).

Most couples report that the sharing of the labor and delivery is one of the most significant and memorable events of their lives. Many husbands who are with their wives during labor and delivery take photographs or videotape the event.

Dick-Read Method

Grantly Dick-Read introduced his concept of prepared childbirth in the 1930s, about a decade before Lamaze. He believed it was a woman's fear of childbirth that produced the physical pain during delivery and the pain could be avoided by teaching the woman to relax. Similar to the Lamaze method, Dick-Read classes emphasize breathing and relaxation exercises, basic information about the birth event, and the husband's support. In addition, they focus on preparation for parenthood.

Bradley Method

Another lesser known method of childbirth than the Lamaze method was developed by a Denver obstetrician, Robert Bradley. Also known as "husband-coached childbirth," the Bradley method focuses on the couple—their marital communication, sexual relationship, and parental roles—as well as on relaxation exercises and proper nutrition during pregnancy. An important aspect of the Bradley method is the couple's relationship with their physician. They are encouraged to deal with issues such as the kind of delivery they want (hospital or home birth) and breast feeding well in advance of the birth. The Bradley method emphasizes a couple's freedom to choose the type of birth experience that is desired. If the physician is reluctant to cooperate, the couple is encouraged to seek another physician.

LeBoyer Method

The LeBoyer method of childbirth is named after its French founder, Frederick LeBoyer, who has delivered more than 10,000 babies using his own method. The goal of a LeBoyer birth experience is to make the infant's transition to the outer world as nontraumatic as possible. The delivery room into which the baby is born is quiet and dimly lit. After emerging from its mother, the baby is placed on the mother's abdomen, where she gently strokes and rubs her child. The umbilical cord is cut only after it stops throbbing in the belief that this will help the newborn's respiratory system adjust to its new environment.

After a few moments, the baby is immersed in water that is the approximate temperature of the amniotic sac which has housed the baby for the past nine months. The infant is allowed to relax and enjoy the bath. Then the baby is wrapped in layers of cotton and wool and placed next to the mother. Placing babies on their backs is avoided because it is felt the spine should not be stressed this soon after birth.

To what degree is the LeBoyer method of childbirth beneficial to infants and mothers? A study comparing babies born LeBoyer style with babies born by conventional hospital procedures revealed no differences in responsiveness or irritability during the first three days of life (Nelson, 1979). Mothers delivering by the LeBoyer method did not see the experience any differently or make a different postnatal adjustment than mothers delivering by a conventional method.

The preceding methods emphasize drug-free deliveries. But not all pregnant women have the interest or the time to devote to childbirth preparation according to these methods and prefer to rely on more traditional methods of birthing their children with the least amount of pain. Two commonly used procedures for administering anesthesia are the caudal and epidural. Both involve introducing drugs into the spinal column, which eliminates the pain typically involved in childbirth. The caudal involves placing a needle at the base of the tailbone; the epidural involves placing the needle further up the backbone. The result—a pain-free delivery—is the same.

Other women prefer medications, which are usually administered intravenously, to alleviate labor pain at the onset of three to five contractions. These analgesics reduce the pain but allow the woman to be aware of the childbirth process. A woman should not view herself as a "failure" if she feels the need for medication.

Cesarean Births

Regardless of which method of childbirth a couple chooses, most anticipate that the baby will be born by passing through the vaginal canal. As a result they receive little information about cesarean births. In cesarean section, an incision is made in the woman's abdomen and uterus and the baby is removed. The term does not derive from the Roman emperor Caesar being delivered in this way but from a law passed during Caesar's reign that made it mandatory for women dying in the advanced stages of pregnancy to have their babies removed by surgical means.

Cesareans are not uncommon.

■ **DATA:** *About twenty-five percent of all births are by cesarean section. This represents about a million deliveries each year* (Statistical Abstract of the United States: 1990, *Table 89*).

Cesarean deliveries are most often performed when there would be risk to the mother or baby through normal delivery; as examples, the fetus may be positioned abnormally, the head may be too large for the mother's pelvis, or the woman may have diabetes or develop toxemia during pregnancy. The woman is put to sleep with general anesthesia or given a spinal injection, enabling her to remain awake and aware of the delivery.

Although Cesareans are major surgery, the risk of death to the mother is less than 2 percent. When death occurs, it is usually the result of a preexisting condition, such as severe toxemia or heart disease—not a result of the surgery itself.

The cesarean section is regarded as one of the safest of all abdominal surgeries and holds the record for the fewest postoperative problems.

☐   C O N S I D E R A T I O N   ☐

There has been considerable criticism of physicians who routinely perform cesarean surgery even when it is not medically indicated. Until recently, a woman who had a C-section had to have all subsequent births by C-section, and physicians were accused of creating a market for cesarean surgery. But due to advances in surgical techniques, the American College of Obstetricians and Gynecologists reversed its 75-year-old policy and said that some women who have a Cesarean delivery for their first child can have subsequent vaginal deliveries. More than 30,000 such deliveries have taken place. However, due to mothers being older when they give birth and to more conservative medical care in response to past litigation, the number of Cesarean deliveries is on the rise again.

:: When a Woman Becomes a Mother

A mother is not a person to lean on, but a person to make leaning unnecessary.
—DOROTHY
   CANFIELD FISHER

About four million babies are born each year in the United States. But this number does not reflect the individual experiences of the respective mothers. In general, motherhood results in a more profound change for the mother than for the father (Wilkie & Ames, 1986). What are the nature of these changes and how do women adjust to their new role as mothers?

Reaction to Childbirth

Although childbirth and the labor preceding it are sometimes thought of as a painful ordeal, some women describe the birthing experience as "fantastic," "joyful," and "unsurpassed." One woman said, "Having a baby come out of me was literally the grandest experience I have ever had."

Once her baby is born, the mother often feels an enormous sense of pride. This pride is heightened as parents and friends come to view the baby, give gifts, and assure the new mother that she has accomplished a miracle. A mother of three days explained, "I love to hear people tell me how beautiful my baby is. I immediately project into the future and count them lucky to have seen a baby who is destined for greatness."

The strong emotional bond between mother and baby develops early, so that mother and infant resist separation. Sociobiologists suggest that there is a biological basis for the attachment between a mother and her offspring. The mother alone carries the fetus in her body for nine months, lactates to provide milk, and produces oxytocin—a hormone excreted by the pituitary gland during the expulsive stage of labor that has been associated with the onset of maternal behavior in lower animals.

Not all mothers feel immediate joy, however. Emotional bonding may be temporarily impeded by a mild depression, characterized by irritability, crying, loss of appetite, and difficulty in sleeping.

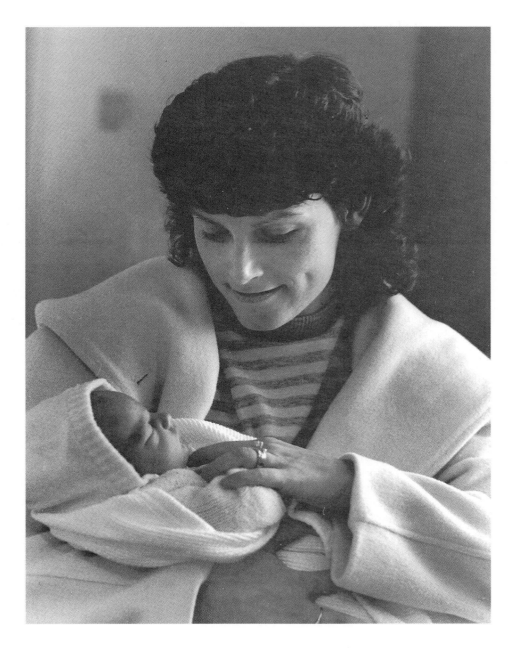

Most mothers feel a strong emotional bond with their infant.

■ **DATA:** *From 50 to 70 percent of all new mothers experience the "maternity blues"—transitory symptoms of depression 24–48 hours after the baby is born. About 10 percent experience postpartum depression—a more severe reaction than "maternity blues" (Kraus & Redman, 1986).*

Postpartum depression is believed to be a result of the numerous physiological and psychological changes occurring during pregnancy, labor, and delivery. Although the woman may become depressed in the hospital, she more often experiences these feelings within the first month after returning home with her baby. Most women recover within a short time; some (about 5 percent) seek therapy to speed their recovery.

☐   C O N S I D E R A T I O N   ☐

To minimize "maternity blues" and postpartum depression, it is important to recognize that having misgivings about the new infant is normal and appropriate. The danger in these thoughts is not that they occur but that they are labeled by others as inappropriate, so that the woman begins to feel like an awful person for having such thoughts. In addition, the woman who has negative feelings about her new role as mother should elicit help with the baby from her husband or mother so that she can continue to keep up her social contacts with friends.

Adjustments to Motherhood

"You can read about motherhood, watch your friends as they become mothers, and fantasize about having your own baby, but until you've done it, you can't really evaluate how you feel about motherhood," reflected a young mother. Whereas people can try out living together, they cannot try out being a parent.

Every woman goes into motherhood naively, and every woman has widely differing experiences in managing the role. For some women, motherhood is the ultimate fulfillment; for others, the ultimate frustration. Most women report mixed emotions during their mothering experience. Whatever a woman's attitude before the birth of her baby, she is not likely to take her role lightly. From the time she knows she is pregnant (or about to become an adoptive mother), no woman's life is ever the same (McKim, 1987).

Motherhood brings with it changes in a woman's daily routine, an increased feeling of responsibility, worry, and often a need to balance the demands of job or career and family. To adapt to all of these changes, she develops coping strategies. We will now examine each of these adjustments.

Routine Work. The new mother finds herself with a new set of tasks. Feeding, diapering, and bathing the infant are added to the responsibilities she already has. "Extra work to care for the baby" and "loss of sleep" are common problems mentioned by mothers of two-month-old infants. "Having less time for yourself" and "feeling physically tired and fatigued" are other common changes for first-time mothers. New mothers may also feel less interested in sex and less sexually responsive during intercourse.

Mother, I want you to be with me always.
—AGE 4, TRACY ELLIS

Responsibility. Most mothers contend that the actual day-to-day work of childcare is not the factor that makes motherhood difficult; it is the incessant and unrelenting responsibility. Even when the husband and wife say they will share the responsibility for childcare, this duty more often falls on the wife.

The responsibility of motherhood is long-term. A middle-class woman with two children observed:

People tend to think of having children only in terms of the baby period. While it may seem like an eternity, the baby-toddler stage of a child is short compared with the 12 or 16 years of the school-age child. Parents may not be legally responsible for a child beyond 21, but morally and emotionally, once a parent, always a parent.

Worry. "You can make them go into their rooms, but you can't get them out of your mind," said the mother of three daughters. Her observation reflects that children are an emotional as well as physical drain. First, a child's safety is a major concern. "I look at the clock at three and know that my child will soon be crossing the street from school," one mother said, "and although there is a police officer there, I don't relax until I see her when I get home from work." When mothers do not worry about busy streets, it is money (Will there be enough for them to complete college?) or peer persecution (Will they make fun of her because she has one crossed eye?) or health (Does a sore throat warrant a trip to the doctor?) or her own employment (Will my children suffer because I'm too involved in my career?)

The Employed Woman as Mother. For the traditional housewife who stays at home, adding the role of mother may be relatively easy. She may have the time and resources (with her husband's economic support) to cope with her infant's demands. Indeed, for some women, being at home with their baby is a dream come true. But more and more women are working outside the home and dropping out of the labor force only long enough to have their children.

■ **DATA:** *Fifty-seven percent of all mothers (husband present) with preschool children are employed outside the home* (Statistical Abstract of the United States, 1990, *Table 636).*

To the demanding role of employee and wife, she must add that of mother. Even with her husband's support, the employed woman must find ways to fit the demands of motherhood into her busy schedule. The term "role overload" is used to characterize this often difficult situation.

Priorities must be established. When forced to choose between her job and family responsibilities (the baby sitter does not show up, the child is sick or hurt, or the like) the employed woman and mother generally responds to the latter role first. "Sarah, my 2-year-old, fell and cut her lip as I was about to leave for the office," remarked a young systems analyst. "Instead of dropping her at the day care center, I took her to the doctor who stitched her up. I didn't have to think about whether I was going to be late for work. My child is more important to me." Many employed women use their sick leave when their child is sick.

But other employed women have different priorities in a time of crisis. The managing editor for a local newspaper said, "My work comes first. I will see that my child is taken care of, but I took him to the sitter anyway. Of course, there are occasions I will let my work go, but they are rare."

Some employed women give up their work completely. "No job is so fulfilling, no experience so rich as that of being with my baby," said one woman. "Your employed friends with children don't like it. They think you are a traitor. But many of them feel guilty about not being with their children."

I'll be with you always, and even when you don't want me to be with you.
—MOTHER, DIANA ROSS

▐ When a Man Becomes a Father

Unlike the woman who feels the presence of her developing fetus months before the baby is born, the father has his first real exposure to fatherhood at the time of the baby's birth. Many fathers take Lamaze or similar childbirth classes with their wives and are present in the delivery room. Even before the birth, their perceptions of fatherhood may begin to take form. In this section, we look at how men view parenthood.

How Men View Parenthood

Bill Cosby, in his role of father in the television sitcom, *The Cosby Show,* has reemphasized the role of father in our society. Among the perceptions fathers have of their role include those of provider, teacher, playmate, companion, caregiver, and nurturer.

Provider. Men have traditionally conceptualized their role of father in terms of economic responsibility. While most men still feel obligated to provide for their children, the career may be losing its priority and family considerations may be gaining in importance. Some men would rather be with their children than spend another hour at the office. One father said, "My kids would rather I watch them perform in athletics or in school plays than make an extra buck."

The role of father is gaining increased emphasis in our society.

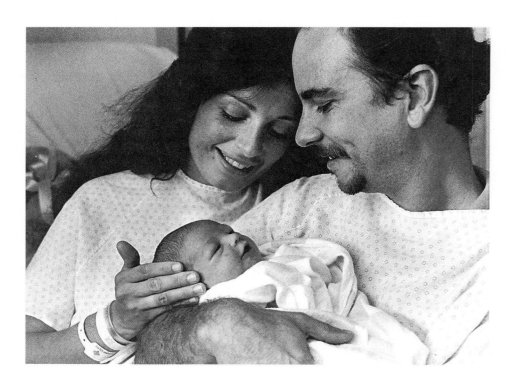

Teacher. Some fathers enjoy the role of teacher and regard their role as important in teaching their children to be independent, self-sufficient, and self-reliant. "I taught all my kids," said one father of three, "that there is always room at the top and the only way to get there is good morals and discipline."

■ **DATA:** *One myth of the black family is that black males have been absent from their homes since the days of slavery. An examination of black fathers in 13 American cities between 1850 and 1880 revealed that the proportion of black fathers present in families ranged from 70 to 90 percent (McAdoo, 1985–1986).*

Companion. As children continue to mature, some fathers begin to relate to them on the level of companion. "Regardless of how busy my dad was, he always spent some time with me in the evening and on weekends. We would talk about everything from football to what really matters in life. I've always felt my dad cared about me, and I've tried to be the same kind of father to my children," said the father of two youngsters.

Some fathers like to think of themselves as a friend or companion to their offspring, although the relationship varies with the age and sex of the children. For example, a father may relate quite differently to his son and daughter during their childhood and adolescence. "I've always been closer to my son, even when he was a kid," observed one father. "We just had more in common. When he was an adolescent, we worked on cars together and did some hunting. Now we're in business together. I love my daughter but have never had much in common with her."

But a father of two daughters said, "I can't imagine what it would be like to have a son because I've always related to my two children as people, not girls. I have enjoyed them since they were babies, and while we had our differences when they were teenagers, we are friends."

Increasingly, fathers are experiencing both the responsibility and joy of taking care of their children.

Caregiver. The new image of fatherhood in our society suggests that fathers are actively involved in the parenting role. However, the reality is that the work of parenting is usually performed by the mother.

■ **DATA:** *In regard to who is actually accountable for the child's welfare and care, mothers appear to carry 90 percent of the load (LaRossa, 1988).*

Fathers who do become actively involved in the care of their children are often middle class professionals such as educators, artists, physicians, and social workers. Hence, the image of the father involved in the parenting role may be specific to only a unique segment of fathers (LaRossa, 1988, 451).

Nurturer. Fathers are becoming increasingly visible in the new role of nurturer. Some men are excellent at providing warmth, affection, acceptance, and love for their children. When their child skins a knee, some men enjoy and are good at comforting the frightened child while washing and putting a bandaid on the open sore. Some evidence suggests that black fathers are more nurturing, warm, and loving toward their infants and children than white fathers (McAdoo, 1985–1986).

Television is helping to provide a positive model for nurturing fathers. In a study of all family-oriented television programs shown on the three networks between 7:00 and 9:00 P.M., the researchers concluded, "Clearly, males are being portrayed as active, nurturant parents" (Dail & Way, 1985, 497).

Transition to Fatherhood

The fatherhood role begins with the woman's pregnancy as the husband relates to his wife as a mother-to-be. This means sharing her excitement about the pregnancy with parents and close friends. "It was like telling people that we were getting married," said one father. "We delighted in breaking the news to people who were as excited as we were."

Men who actively participate in caring for their newborns evidence a more favorable adjustment to parenthood than fathers who neglect or avoid changing diapers and feeding and bathing their babies. Not only do participating fathers feel better about their infants, they feel better about their wives and marriages, too (Goldberg et al., 1985).

□	C O N S I D E R A T I O N	□

To ease the transition to fatherhood, new fathers might consider becoming actively involved in the care of their infants. Not to do so is to increase the chance of feeling more disgruntled and despondent about the entrance of a child into the marriage.

The Self-Assessment on "What Kind of Parent Will You Be?" provides a way for you to assess the degree to which you might be a good parent. While what constitutes a "good" parent is difficult to define, a high score on the self-assessment may suggest a propensity toward being a good parent.

∷ When a Couple Becomes a Family

How does the prospect of having a child affect a couple's relationship, and what happens to their relationship after the baby is born? In this section, we will examine what happens when women and men have less time to be wives and husbands as they fit the demands of mother and father into their already busy schedules.

The Couple During Pregnancy

As soon as the woman becomes aware that she is pregnant, the couple begin to address issues that are entirely new to them—talking to parents and friends about the pregnancy, allocating existing space for the baby (or getting a larger house or apartment), furnishing a nursery, choosing names for the child, and deciding whether to attend parenthood classes.

Pregnancy may also be a time when husbands feel as though they are being moved to second place in the wife's priorities and may react by reducing their emotional involvement in the relationship (Shapiro, 1987). The sexual behavior of the couple is also affected. Most couples report a decreased frequency of intercourse throughout the pregnancy. Some view it as a time to explore alternatives to intimacy. Two researchers (Bryant & Collins, 1985) observed:

> Ed and Linda had had an active sex life together which primarily involved traditional lovemaking methods. During pregnancy, they found a decrease in their interest in intercourse but an increase in touching and holding each other. They found these activities to be satisfying which brought a closeness and unity that they had not felt in the pre-pregnancy state (p. 109).

CONSIDERATION

Does having intercourse during pregnancy involve a risk to the baby? Generally not. Women who have had a previous miscarriage or who are experiencing vaginal bleeding, ruptured membranes, or threatened premature labor should consult their physician about intercourse during pregnancy. In the absence of these complications, most couples can continue intercourse as late in pregnancy as they desire.

The Baby's Impact on the Couple's Marriage

After the birth and return home from the hospital, how does the baby's presence affect the marital happiness of the spouses, who are now mother and father? The answer is unclear (Belsky & Rovine, 1990). Some studies suggest that children increase marital happiness; others suggest the opposite.

SELF ASSESSMENT

What Kind of Parent Will You Be?

This scale is designed to measure the degree to which you have the qualities that are characteristic of being a good parent. It is recognized that "good parent" is a subjective term and criteria for this label are debatable. In this regard, the scale is suggestive. After reading each sentence, circle the number that best represents your feelings.

1 Strongly disagree
2 Mildly disagree
3 Undecided
4 Mildly agree
5 Strongly agree

	SD	MD	U	MA	SA
1. I am a nurturing person.	1	2	3	4	5
2. I am, basically, not a selfish person.	1	2	3	4	5
3. The sound of a crying baby does not really bother me.	1	2	3	4	5
4. I like taking care of children.	1	2	3	4	5
5. I love children.	1	2	3	4	5
6. I was not abused as a child.	1	2	3	4	5
7. My parents were good parents to me.	1	2	3	4	5
8. I feel that family considerations should take precedence over individual considerations.	1	2	3	4	5
9. I enjoy spending time with infants and young children.	1	2	3	4	5
10. The work of parenting (feeding, diapering, etc.) is something I will not mind doing.	1	2	3	4	5

SCORING: Add the numbers you circled. 1 (strongly disagree) reflects a strong dislike for the role of parent, and 5 (strongly agree) reflects a strong enthusiasm for the role. The lower your total score (10 is the lowest possible score), the greater the chance that you will not be a good parent. The higher your total score (50 is the highest possible score), the greater the chance that you will be a good parent. A score of 30 places you at the midpoint between being a questionable and an excellent parent.

(NOTE: This Self-Assessment is intended to be thought-provoking and suggestive, it is not a clinical diagnostic instrument).

Children Increase Marital Happiness. Some studies report that having a baby is associated with improving the marital relationship. Out of a total of 30,000 parents, 43 percent said they felt closer to their spouses after they had children (Greer, 1986). In another study of 75 fathers and 115 mothers, one researcher observed that couples who reported a high degree of marital satisfaction prior to the birth of their baby were more likely to experience positive changes as a result of the baby than spouses who reported a low degree of marital satisfaction prior to the birth (Harriman, 1986). Children seem to stabilize marriages. Or, do stable couples have more children? (See Figure 14.1)

□   C O N S I D E R A T I O N   □

The researcher said of the timing of one's children, "Adding the parenting role when there is stress in one's marital life may only compound the difficulties and the amount of stress experienced" (p. 238).

Children Decrease Marital Happiness. Other parents feel that their marital satisfaction decreases after the birth of their baby. These feelings are particularly true of women who are married to men who do not share the childcare/housekeeping responsibilities brought on by the new infant (Ruble et al., 1988). Temperamental babies who sleep and eat irregularly are also associated with a decrease in marital happiness (Belsky and Rovine, 1990).

Marks (1989) observed that the effect of a new baby is to separate the spouses in terms of their activities. The wife becomes consumed with her role of mother in caring for the infant while the husband spends more time at the office developing his career (or escaping from childcare?). Spouses who experience difficulties during a pregnancy often continue to experience difficulties in adjustment after the baby is born (Snowden et al., 1988; Wallace & Gotlib, 1990).

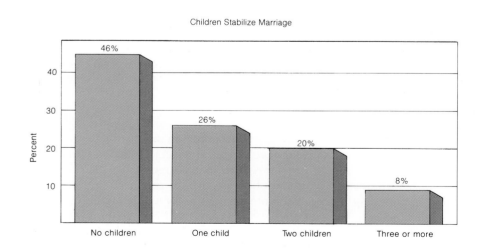

■■ FIGURE 14.1
Percent of couples getting divorced by number of children

Regardless of how children affect the feelings spouses have about their marriage, children are associated with marital stability (National Center for Health Statistics, 1989). Figure 14.1 reflects that the more children a couple have, the more likely they are to stay married. Reasons for this include the unwillingness of one spouse to be separated from the children if the other spouse gets custody and the expense of two separate households.

Children Do Not Affect Marital Happiness. Some research suggests that children neither increase nor decrease marital happiness. In a study comparing married couples who had children with those who did not have children, the researchers (MacDermid, Huston, and McHale, 1990) observed that the spouses in both groups reported declines in love feelings, marital satisfaction, doing things together, and positive interactions. Although the parents become more child oriented, they were no less happy in their marriages than those who did not become parents. The researchers concluded: "In short, our results are consistent with those of some previous research that suggests that the transition to parenthood is not an inescapable detriment to marital quality" (p. 485).

∷ Trends

Artificial insemination, in-vitro fertilization, and ovum transfer will be used by an increasing number of people who cannot conceive a child through sexual intercourse. In spite of the cost and low rate of actual births, most couples are socialized to have children and will explore all options before giving up the goal.

The legal issues raised by these developments will be numerous. Does a surrogate mother have a right to her baby if she changes her mind after delivery? If a deformed child results from an artificial insemination in a surrogate mother, do the parents who paid for the child have a right to reject it? What are the responsibilities of a sperm bank to provide sperm that is free of defects? Do frozen embryos have inheritance rights from the people who produced them?

Genetic engineering (also called biotechnology)—manipulating an organism's genes so that the "good" genes are passed on and the "bad" genes disappear—is not likely to be used on humans in the near future. Genetic engineering has been used to create plants that are resistant to frost, disease, and herbicides, leaner pigs, and cows that produce 25 percent more milk, but altering human genes is illegal.

More fathers will actively participate in the birth of their children, in taking care of their children and in taking off work to be with their children. The precedence for paternity leave has been established by the Equal Opportunity Employment Commission. Stephen Onera of Chicago was granted a six-month paternity leave to be with his new daughter. In addition, the House of Representatives passed a family leave bill which would offer both fathers and mothers 12 weeks of job-protected leave each year for births, adoptions, or family illness. The bill applies to employers with 50 or more employees and would cover 44 percent of all workers (Phillips, 1990). Such legislation would help to protect the right of family members to participate as necessary in family matters (the Bill was vetoed by George Bush on the grounds that it would be too costly to industry).

:: Summary

Fertilization is the result of the union of an egg and a sperm. Pregnancy may occur through sexual intercourse, artificial insemination of the wife by husband (AIH) or donor (AID), artificial insemination of a surrogate mother by the husband, in-vitro or test-tube fertilization, ovum transfer, or gamete intrafallopian transfer. Artificial methods of conception are being used increasingly by couples when one of the spouses cannot or should not conceive.

Some expectant parents, who are dissatisfied with traditional, hospital-managed deliveries, are choosing alternative childbirth methods, including the Lamaze, Dick-Read, Bradley, and LeBoyer methods. When there is a risk to the mother or baby through vaginal delivery, a cesarean section may be performed.

A woman's reactions to childbirth may include temporary feelings of depression as well as a developing emotional bond with her infant. Motherhood brings with it changes in the woman's daily routine, an increased feeling of responsibility, worry, and often the need to balance the demands of a job or career and family. For some women, motherhood is the ultimate fulfillment; for others, it is the ultimate frustration. Most women experience mixed emotions during their mothering experience.

The impact of becoming a parent is sometimes less profound for the man than for the woman because his daily routine doesn't change much after the baby is born. Most men are guided by certain impressions they have of the father's role. They tend to view the father as provider, teacher, playmate, companion, care-giver, and nurturer. Although fathers participate less in childcare than mothers, they are interested and capable and, if given opportunity and encouragement, do become involved.

Having a baby affects the marriage relationship during as well as after pregnancy. During pregnancy, the couple may have to adjust to a new division of labor and an altered sexual relationship. After the baby is born, rosy expectations of parenthood give way to reality, as the couple begins to adjust to the new family constellation.

The future of fertilization includes the implantation of previously frozen human embryos and the legal unraveling of the complex issues involved in surrogate motherhood.

The future of parenthood includes a greater understanding of the parenting role, an increased sharing of the childbirth and childrearing experience by the spouses, and a questioning of traditional childbirth procedures (to be discussed in the Choices section that follows).

Questions for Reflection

1. To what degree are artificial insemination, surrogate mothers, in-vitro fertilization, and ovum transfers options you would consider if you and your partner were having difficulty becoming pregnant and wanted a baby?
2. As a woman, to what degree would you expect your husband to share the work of parenting if you had a baby?
3. As a man, to what degree would you want to share the work of parenting with your wife if you decided to have a baby?

References

Baran, A. Artificial insemination: Remove clock of secrecy. *USA Today,* March 26, 1990, p. 7A.

Belsky, J. and Rovine, M. Patterns of marital change across the transition to parenthood: Pregnancy to three years postpartum. *Journal of Marriage and the Family,* 1990, *52,* 5–19.

Bryant, N. B. and C. J. Collins. Human sexuality and feminism: A new approach to perinatal social work. *Journal of Social Work and Human Sexuality,* Spring 1985, *3,* 103–117.

Consumer Protection Issues Involving In-Vitro Fertilization Clinics. Hearing before Subcommittee on Regulation, Business Opportunities, and Energy of the Committee on Small Business. House of Representatives, 101st Congress, Washington, D.C., March 9, 1989.

Dail, P. W. and W. L. Way. What do parents observe about parenting from prime-time television? *Family Relations,* 1985, *34,* 491–499.

Donovan, P. New reproductive technologies: Some legal dilemmas. *Family Planning Perspectives,* 1986, *18,* 57–60.

Dunn, P. C., I. J. Ryan, and K. O'Brien. College students' level of acceptability of the new medical science of conception and problems of infertility. *Journal of Sex Research,* 1988, *24,* 282–287.

Fitzgerald, M. Couples fawn over frozen embryos, expert says. *USA Today,* August 9, 1989, p. 3A.

Foreman, S. Risk is small in hiding the identity of donor. *USA Today,* March 26, 1990, p. 7A.

Gibbs, Nancy. The baby chase. *Time,* October 9, 1989, pp. 86–89.

Goldberg, W. A., G. Y. Michaels, and M. E. Lamb. Husbands' and wives' adjustment to pregnancy and first parenthood. *Journal of Family Issues,* 1985, 6, 483–504.

Greenberg, J. S., C. E. Bruess, and D. W. Sands. *Sexuality: Insights and Issues.* Dubuque, Ia. William C. Brown, 1986.

Greer, K. Today's parents: How well are they doing? *Better Homes and Gardens,* October 1986, 36–46.

Harriman, L. C. Marital adjustment as related to personal and marital changes accompanying parenthood. *Family Relations,* 1986, *35,* 233–239.

Higgins, B. S. Couple infertility: From the perspective of the close-relationship model. *Family Relations,* 1990, *39,* 81–86.

Holmes, P. Squeeze on alternatives to hospital births. *New Statesman,* 1988, *116,* 6.

Hyde, J. S. *Understanding human sexuality.* New York: McGraw-Hill, 1990.

Kaye, Kenneth. Turning two identities into one. *Psychology Today,* 1988, *22,* 46–50.

Kraus, M. A. and E. S. Redman. Postpartum depression: An interactional view, *Journal of Marital and Family Therapy,* 1986, *12,* 63–74.

LaRossa, R. Fatherhood and social change. *Family Relations,* 1988, *37,* 451–457.

LaRossa, R. The transition to parenthood and the social reality of time. *Journal of Marriage and the Family,* 1983, *35,* 579–589.

Lasker, J. N. and S. Borg. *In search of parenthood.* Boston: Beacon Press, 1987.

Lumley, J. Preschool siblings at birth: Short-term effects, *Birth Issues in Perinatal Care and Education,* 1983, *10,* 11–16.

MacDermid, S. M., T. L. Huston, and S. M. McHale. Changes in marriage associated with the transition to parenthood: Individual differences as a function of sex-role attitudes and changes in the division of household labor. *Journal of Marriage and the Family,* 1990, *52,* 475–486.

Marks, Stephen R. Toward a systems theory of marital quality. *Journal of Marriage and the Family,* 1989, *51,* 15–26.

McAdoo, J. L. A black perspective on the father's role in child development. Robert A. Lewis and Marvin B. Sussman, eds. *Marriage and Family Review,* 1985/1986, *9,* 117–133.

McKim, M. K. Transition to what? New parents' problems in the first year. *Family Relations,* 1987, *36,* 22–25.

National Center for Health Statistics, Advance report, final divorce statistics—1986. Monthly Vital Statistics report; *38,* no. 2, suppl. Hyattsville, Md.: Public Health Service, 1989.

National Center for Health Statistics. 1989. Perinatal mortality in the United States: 1981–85. *Monthly Vital Statistics Report 37,* no. 10. suppl. DHHS Pub. No. (PHS) 89-1120. Hyattsville, Md.: Public Health Service.

Phillips, L. House OKs guaranteed family leave. *USA Today,* May 11, 1990, p. 4A.

Riche, M. F. The adoption story. *American Demographics,* 1986, *8,* 42–45.

Ruble, D. N., L. S. Hackel, A. S. Fleming, and C. Stangor. Changes in the marital relationship during the transition to first time motherhood: Effects of violated expectations concerning division of household labor. *Journal of Personality and Social Psychology,* 1988, *55,* 78–87.

Sacks, S. R. and P. B. Donnerfeld. Parental choice of alternative birth environments and attitudes toward childrearing philosophy. *Journal of Marriage and the Family,* 1984, *46,* 469–475.

Shapiro, J. L. The expectant father. *Psychology Today,* January 1987, 36–42.

Sharpe, R. Baby M case good advertising. *USA Today,* February 17, 1987, p. 1.

Snowden, L. R., T. L. Schott, S. J. Awalt, and J. Gillis-Knox. Marital satisfaction in pregnancy: Stability and change. *Journal of Marriage and the Family,* 1988, *50,* 325–333.

Statistical Abstract of the United States. 1990, 110th ed. Washington, D.C.: U.S. Bureau of the Census, 1990.

Wallace, P. M. and I. H. Gotlib. Marital adjustment during the transition to parenthood: Stability and predictors of change. *Journal of Marriage and the Family,* 1990, *52,* 21–29.

Wilcox, Allen J., C. R. Weinberg, J. F. O'Connor, D. D. Baird, J. P. Schlatterer, R. E. Canfield, E. G. Armstrong, and R. C. Nisula. Incidence of early loss of pregnancy. *The New England Journal of Medicine,* 1988, *319,* 189–194.

Wilkie, C. F. and E. W. Ames. The relationship of infant crying to parental stress in the transition to parenthood. *Journal of Marriage and the Family,* 1986, *48,* 545–550.

CHOICES

SOME COUPLES WANT to have their baby at home. But should they? What issues need to be considered when deciding to have a child in the hospital or in the home? In addition, some fathers are making choices about the time they spend with their children. How should they allocate time to career and family?

Home or Hospital Birth?

At the turn of the century, about 95 percent of all babies were born at home. Because there were few physicians and fewer hospitals, a midwife was usually summoned to assist the laboring mother-to-be with her delivery. Birthing was a family event, with father, mother, and children competing to hold the new infant.

But because of infant and maternal mortality, the developing political strength of the medical profession, and the development of hospital facilities to handle difficult deliveries, home births became less common. Today more than 99 percent of all births take place in a hospital. When the woman experiences uterine contractions that are regular and intense, she checks into the hospital, is prepped (may have her pubic hair shaved, an enema, and her vaginal area cleaned), and completes labor in a special room near the delivery room. Depending on whether the couple has taken preparation for parenthood classes and also on hospital policy, her partner may or may not be allowed to remain with her during labor and delivery.

Some expectant parents are concerned that traditional childbirth procedures are too impersonal, costly, and potentially dangerous. Those who opt for home birth are primarily concerned about avoiding separation from the new infant, maintaining control over who can be present at the delivery, and avoiding "excessive obstetrical management" (Sacks & Donnenfeld, 1984, 471).

Safety is a primary concern in deciding to have a baby at home. Most physicians view home births as unsafe and do not support the movement toward home births. However, some physicians feel that it is usually possible to predict a dangerous delivery because high-risk mothers (such as those with hypertension or diabetes) can be identified early in the pregnancy. Some proponents of the home birth movement feel that for the mother without prenatal complications, there is greater risk in having a baby in the hospital than at home.

The nurse-midwife is most often asked to assist in home births. Some nurse-midwives are certified members of the American College of Nurse-Midwives and have successfully completed a master's degree in nurse-midwifery offered at various universities, including Georgetown, Emory, St. Louis, and Columbia. Two organizations—ACAH (Association for Childbirth at Home) and HOME (Home Oriented Maternity Experience)—help couples prepare for home births.

What is the relative safety of home versus hospital birth? A study designed to answer this question revealed that except in special cases, at home births involve no extra risks than births in hospitals. However, the researchers warned that in cases of delayed labor, breech birth, or fetal distress, a hospital is the safer environment (Holmes, 1988).

Sometimes preschool siblings observe the home births of their sisters and brothers. Some advocates of hospital births suggest that such observations have negative consequences for the children. But Lumley (1983) compared the short-term effects on preschool siblings who observed their brothers and sisters being born with preschool siblings who were not allowed such observations and found no significant differences.

For Fathers: Career or Family?

Women have traditionally been socialized to give priority to their children over their careers, whereas men have been socialized to do the opposite. With the advent of preparation for parenthood classes, Lamaze births, and most wives working outside the home, men have been given the opportunity to rethink their socialization and make conscious choices on an individual basis. Some men still opt for their career. One man said:

I love my children but I really am not happy being around them for more than a weekend. By Monday, I'm ready to go back to work and see them for a few minutes before bedtime during the week. I enjoy the competitive struggle of my work and making money is what I do best. I guess I'm lucky to be married to a woman who enjoys taking care of the kids.

But other men feel differently. One said:

I make about all the money I need, and I've learned that it is a dead-end trail. Here I am at middle age— . . . my last child will be leaving for college in September, and I hardly know him. I've got money, but I don't have my boy. I think I've gotten my priorities mixed up.

Men might be aware that although they may be subject to enormous pressures to be successful in a career, attaining such success without taking time to "smell the roses" with their children may be less than fulfilling.

Impact of Social Influences on Choices

Home births and the resocialization of men in the father role have only recently become issues in our society. The desire for home birth is a result of general questioning of the medical profession and a feeling that prospective parents should be given all the data and allowed to make their own decision regarding where their baby will be born, rather than have the physician dictate the place of birth.

Industries reward men for career success—not for the time they spend with their children. Such an emphasis on career achievement makes it difficult for a father to switch from external to internal reinforcers in reference to spending time with his children. To do so requires a conscious and deliberate choice.

However, the changing gender roles and the high divorce rate may influence more men to emphasize their family life. More men are being socialized into male gender role expectations that include more parental involvement. Also, because more women are employed, there is a greater need for shared parenting. Women are placing more expectations on their partners regarding the management of domestic responsibilities—including childrearing.

The high divorce rate results in many divorced men having responsibility for childcare through shared or sole physical custody or during visitation. One divorced man said that he spent less time with his children before the divorce, as his wife primarily took care of them. "Now that I am divorced," he said, "I actually spend more time doing things with my kids, even though I see them every other weekend."

C H A P T E R

15

Rearing Children

CONTENTS

IS IT TRUE?

1. Your children will turn out okay if you just
   love them enough.

2. About 10 percent of young adults return to
   their parent's home to live at least once.

3. Taking urine samples of your adolescent
   who has abused drugs is an alternative in
   your attempt to help your adolescent stop
   using drugs.

4. Most parents want their adult children to
   continue to live with them.

5. Most parents say that their marriage
   improves when their children return to live
   with them.

1 = F; 2 = F; 3 = T; 4 = F; 5 = F

M OST PARENTS LOOK forward to bringing up their children. They view childrearing as a process of teaching and instilling in their children the values and behaviors that will make the children happy. In this chapter, we will examine realities of parenthood, the folklore that surrounds childrearing, and various approaches to childrearing. We also focus on communication between parents and teenagers and look at how parents might respond to teenage drug abuse and other issues concerning parents.

∷ Childrearing in Perspective

Although rearing children is a major undertaking, it is helpful to keep it in perspective. In this section, we will make some generalizations about the realities of parenthood.

Parenthood Is Only One Stage in Life

Children are a great comfort in your old age—and they help you reach it faster, too.
—LIONEL KAUFFMAN

Parents of newly adult children often lament, "Before you know it, your children are grown and gone." Although parents of infants sometimes feel that the sleepless nights will never end, they do end. Unlike the marriage relationship, the parent-child relationship inevitably moves toward separation. Just as the marital partners were alone before their children came, they will be alone again after their children leave. Except for occasional visits with their children and possibly with grandchildren, the couple will return to the childfree lifestyle.

Typical parents are in their early fifties when their last child leaves home. Since the average woman and man can expect to live until she is 78 and he is 72, spouses in a continuous marriage will have a minimum of about 20 years together after their children leave home. Hence, parenthood might be perceived for what it is—one stage in marriage and in life.

■ **DATA:** *Assuming individuals marry at age 24, have 2 children at 3-year intervals, and die at age 77, they will have children living with them about 30 percent of their lifetime and 40 percent of their marriage.*

One mother said:

We had three kids, and I loved taking care of all of them. I think the happiest time in my life was when my husband and I would wake up in the morning and they would all be there. But that's changed now. They are married and have moved several states away. I know they still love me and they call to stay in touch, but I rarely see them anymore.

Parents Are Only One Influence in Their Children's Development

Although parents often take the credit—and the blame—for the way their children turn out, they are only one among many influences on child development. Peers, siblings, teachers, relatives, and the mass media are also influential. Although parents are the first significant influence, peer influence becomes increas-

The influence of teachers begins early.

ingly important and remains so into the college years. During this time, children are likely to mirror the values and behaviors of their friends and agemates.

Siblings are not necessarily peers, but they too have an important and sometimes lasting effect on each other's development. One adolescent said:

> I can remember walking up to my mother (I was about 5) after my little baby brother was born. My mother was nursing him while she was sitting in the chair in the den. I wanted to sit in her lap, but she said she couldn't hold both of us. I felt as though my mother had replaced me with my brother. It wasn't a good feeling; my brother and I have always been competitive.

Sibling influences may also be positive. "I've always been close to my sister," remarked one woman. "She's the best friend I have."

Relatives, particularly grandparents, may be significant childrearing agents.

■ **DATA:** *Eighty-nine percent of 179 college students reported that they had an emotional attachment to their grandparents. Ninety-three percent said that they had learned from them (Sanders & Trygstad, 1989).*

One graduate student said, "My grandmother is the one that reared me. She was a very polite person, and although I resented her nagging me to be polite when I was a kid, I am very much the way she would have wanted me to turn out."

Teachers become influential once a child begins school, and they remain so as long as the child is exposed to the educational system. Most teachers are middle class and tend to stress the values of achievement and discipline. (Fabes et al., 1989). But teachers have another effect on their students. They may teach offspring things parents do not want them to know. One conservative parent told his

Parents are not really interested in justice. They just want quiet.
—BILL COSBY

son that he was more concerned about him getting a B.A. as a born-again Christian than a B.A. from the university he was attending. "You've got some liberal professors down there that are threatening your very soul," he said.

Television is another influence that parents may not approve of. Television is a major means of exhibiting language, values, and lifestyles to children that may be different from those of the parents. One father had Home Box Office and Showtime disconnected because he did not want his children seeing the movies and specials on those channels. Another parent went through the television guide each week and marked the programs he would not allow his children to watch. The guide was left on top of the television, and the children were to look at what programs had been approved before they turned it on.

Not all television viewing may have negative consequences.

■ **DATA:** *In a study of 116 households, the average amount of time spent viewing television together as a family unit was 2–3 hours daily Monday through Friday and 4–6 hours on the weekend (Schroeder & Brocato, 1983).*

These researchers concluded that the more time a family spent watching television together, the greater their interaction, discussion of individual problems, and feeling of having a "close, loving, and supportive family relationship" (p. 64).

In addition to being influenced by peers, siblings, relatives, teachers, and the mass media, children are affected by different environmental situations. An only daughter adopted into an urban, Catholic, upper-class family will be exposed to a different environment than a girl born into a rural, Southern Baptist, working-class family with three male children. Some of the potentially important environmental variables include geographic location, family size, how authoritarian or permissive the parents are, the family's social class, religion, and racial or ethnic background, and whether the children and parents are mentally and physically healthy.

Internal physiological happenings in the developing child will also influence the child's behavior. Particularly during pubertal development, hormones that may influence social behavior are released into the bloodstream of both sexes.

☐   C O N S I D E R A T I O N   ☐

Because parents are only one of many influences on their children, they should be careful about taking the credit or the blame for the way they turn out. "It's not in the books," said a professor of psychology. "My wife and I have modeled a relatively conservative but ambitious life for our children and had hoped that they would want to become professionals. But they met a group in college and decided to drop out and join this commune. That was 10 years ago. It's not what we wanted for them, but they're happy."

Parenthood Demands Change as Children Grow Up

The demands of parenthood change as the children move through various developmental stages. Infants, toddlers, preschoolers, pre-adolescents (8–11), new adolescents (12–15), middle adolescents (15–18), and older adolescents (18–22) all exhibit different behaviors and require different emotional, social, and psychological resources from parents. Over time the child is growing from a state of total dependence to one of total independence. Knowing how much freedom to give at what age for what events is a challenge for most parents. During adolescence, effective childrearing has been likened to flying a kite—the string must be let out to give the kite height; if the string is kept too tight, it will snap and the kite will plummet.

The best way to keep children home is to make the home atmosphere pleasant—and let the air out of the tires.
—DOROTHY PARKER

Each Child Is Different

Children differ in their tolerance for stress, in their capacity to learn, in their comfort in social situations, in their interests, and in innumerable other ways. Parents soon become aware of the specialness of each child—of her or his difference from every other child they know and from children they have read about. Parents of two or more children are often amazed at how children who have the same parents can be so different. Some differences between children may be due to differences in sex differences and differential gender role socialization. Parents who have only male children report more conflict in the family than parents who have only female children (Falconer et al., 1990).

Parenthood is Sometimes Scary

While being tolerant of individual differences, parents must be alert to signs of serious disturbance in their adolescent. This is the time when risk of suicide is high. Danger signs include:

■ Adolescent is withdrawn for long periods of time and shows no interest in social interaction. The adolescent has few or no friends.

The time needs of children vary with their age.

- Adolescent abuses alcohol or drugs. He or she frequently gets "high."
- Adolescent has no respect for authority—parents, teachers, or police.
- Adolescent engages in indiscriminate sex with numerous sexual partners. No emotional bonds are established with sexual partners.

Parenting Styles Differ

Parents in different social classes rear their children differently. In general, middle class parents tend to be concerned about their children being independent and creative while working class parents tend to emphasize the importance of conformity. Middle class parents who value self-direction function in a supportive parental role. Working class parents who value conformity adopt a parental role which emphasizes imposing constraints on their children (Luster, Roades, & Haas, 1989). Specific parenting styles are presented in the Choices section at the end of the chapter.

Looking at childrearing through a wide-angle lens, other societies provide still different contexts and styles. For example, Polynesian children learn to view not only their mother and father but also their grandparents and all relatives of equivalent age as parents. In practice, multiple parenting in Polynesia means that a number of people will be involved in the life-transition ceremonies, that the children will have a number of houses they regard as home, and that they will have an array of adults who nurture them, love them, and protect them.

Among the Chinese, "mother-child relations tend to be close and affectionate, in contrast to father-child relations marked by greater affectional distance, perhaps even tension and antagonism" (Ho, 1989, 160). Exhibit 15.1 provides more information about childrearing among the Chinese.

> The crux of parenthood is emotional grunt work. It's: No, you can't have a third cookie; no, you may not interrupt others while they're talking.
> —JANET BARLOW

:: Folklore About Childrearing

To encourage adults to rear children, certain folklore romanticizing the experience has arisen. Two researchers (LeMasters & DeFrain, 1989) have identified some widely held beliefs about parenting that are not supported by facts.

Myth 1: Rearing Children Is Always Fun

> To grow up to be healthy, very young children do not need to know how to read, but they do need to know how to play.
> —FRED ROGERS ("MR. ROGERS")

Would-be parents see television commercials of young parents and children and are led to believe that drinking Pepsi in the park with their 4-year-old is what childrearing is all about. Parenthood is portrayed as being a lot of fun. The truth is somewhat different than the folklore:

> The idea of something being fun implies that you can take it or leave it, whereas parents do not have this choice. Fathers and mothers must stay with the child and keep trying, whether it is fun, or whether they are enjoying it or not. Any comparison to bowling, listening to jazz records, or sex is strictly coincidental. . . . Rearing children is hard work; it is often nerve-racking work; it involves tremendous responsibility; it takes all the ability one has (and more); and once you have begun, you cannot quit when you feel like it (pp. 22, 23).

E X H I B I T   15.1

Childrearing—Chinese Style

Even though Chinese Americans are the largest of the Asian groups in the United States (812,000) they comprise less that half of one percent of the total U.S. population. Twenty-one percent of Chinese Americans are children age 14 or younger. They live in families with an average size of four (*Statistical Abstract of the United States: 1989*, Table 44).

Although not all Chinese American families are alike, some of the patterns of childrearing that are characteristic of Chinese American families include the following:

1. *Father Dominance*. Chinese families have traditionally been patriarchal whereby males, particularly the father and eldest son have had dominant roles. Chinese American children are taught that the source of authority in their family is the father. The father maintains his authority and respect in the family by means of emotional distance. Chinese children do not question their father's authority.

2. *Punishment*. Physical punishment is generally not used for children in Chinese American families (Wong, 1988a). Rather, the mechanism of social control in Chinese families involves creating a sense of shame. Children who disobey are taught to feel that they bring disgrace not only to themselves but to their family and whole collective group. This pattern may account for the low level of juvenile delinquency among Chinese Americans.

3. *Sibling Modeling*. Older siblings are expected to care for younger siblings and to be good role models. Children are not allowed to be aggressive with other siblings. Children spend most of their time around adults and older children and are expected to behave as adults.

4. *Value for Education*. Chinese children learn early that education is important. The source of this value is from the Confucian respect for learning, the parents' belief that education is the way to security and a better life, and the desire of parents to receive social status from the Chinese community for having a college educated or professional child (Wong, 1988a).

5. *Care for the Elderly*. Chinese children are also socialized to respect and take care of their elderly. This norm is embedded in the tradition of male dominance—in exchange for being given a dominant role in the family, eldest sons were to ensure the care of their parents. Today, "studies suggest that family members are the primary source of assistance for the elderly Chinese and that assistance from social service agencies and professional persons is almost nonexistent" (Wong, 1988a, 250).

6. *Intermarriage*. While two-thirds of Chinese Americans marry other Chinese, increasingly they are crossing racial lines to marry whites (Wong, 1988b). A major reason for such a trend is the dissatisfaction of acculturated (Americanized) Chinese females who want a more egalitarian partner than the traditional Chinese male is prepared to be.

■ **DATA:** *In one study, 47 percent of the parents polled said that rearing children was more difficult than they had imagined it would be (Greer, 1986).*

Myth 2: Good Parents Inevitably Produce Good Kids

It is assumed that children who turn out wrong—who abuse drugs, steal, and the like—have parents who really did not do their job. We tend to blame parents when children fail. But good parents have given both their emotional and material resources to their children and the children have not turned out well. One mother said:

We live in one of the finer suburbs of our city, our children went to the best schools, and we spent a lot of time with them as a family (camping, going to the beach, skiing). But our son is now in prison. He held up a local grocery store one night and got shot in the leg. We've stopped asking ourselves what we did wrong. He was 23 and drifted into friendships with a group of guys who just decided they would pull a job one night.

A corollary to the belief that good parents will produce good kids is the idea that parents know what kind of kids they are producing. But a study comparing what parents thought their children's attitudes and values were on religion, drugs, and sex with what their children's beliefs actually were showed that parents had inaccurate perceptions (Thompson et al., 1985).

Myth 3: Love Is the Essential Key to Effective Childrearing

Parents are taught that if they love their children enough, they will turn out okay. Love is seen as the primary ingredient, which if present in sufficient quantities, will ensure a successful child. But most parents love their children dearly and want only the best for them. Love is not enough and does not guarantee desirable behavior. One parent said:

We planned our children in courtship, loved them before they got here, and have never stopped loving them. But they are rude, have despicable table manners, and hardly speak to us. We are frustrated beyond description. We've done everything we know how to do in providing a loving home for them, but it hasn't worked.

Myth 4: Children Are Always Appreciative

Most parents think of childrearing in terms of love, care, and nurturing—and also in terms of giving their children things. These parents assume their children will appreciate their tender loving care and the material benefits, like stereos, computers, and cars they bestow. That assumption may be wrong. Children often think parents are supposed to love them and give them things. They view material benefits as their birthright.

> ☐   C O N S I D E R A T I O N   ☐
>
> It is a mistake for would-be parents to embark on the adventure of having children with the expectation that they will always be appreciated. For the most part, parenting involves a lot of selfless giving with no thought of a return. One parent said, "The best part about being a parent is loving your children. If they love you back or appreciate what you are doing, you get a bonus. But don't expect it."

■**DATA:** *In spite of the problems of parenting, 90 percent of 30,000 parents say having children is worth the sacrifice (Greer, 1986).*

⠸⠆ Approaches To Childrearing

Beyond the folklore of parenthood, there are several theoretical approaches to rearing children (see Table 15.1). In examining these approaches, it is important to keep in mind that no single approach is absolutely superior to another. What works for one child may not work for another. Any given approach may not even work with the same child at two different times.

Developmental-Maturational Approach

For the past 60 years, Arnold Gesell and his colleagues at the Yale Clinic of Child Development have been known for their ages-and-stages approach to childrearing. Their *developmental-maturational approach* has been widely used in the United States. Let's examine the basic perspective of this approach, some considerations for childrearing, and some criticisms of the approach.

Basic Perspective.   Gesell theorizes that what children do, think, and feel are the result of their genetic inheritance. Although genes dictate the gradual unfolding of a unique person, every individual passes through the same basic pattern of growth. This pattern includes four aspects of development: motor behavior (sitting, crawling, walking); adaptive behavior (picking up objects and walking around objects); language behavior (words and gestures); and personal-social behavior (cooperativeness and helpfulness). Through the observation of hundreds of normal infants and children, Gesell and his coworkers have identified norms of development. Although there may be large variations, these norms suggest the ages at which an average child displays various behaviors.

▌ ■ **DATA:** *On the average, children begin to walk alone (although awkwardly) at age 13 months and use simple sentences between ages 2 and 3.*

Considerations for Childrearing.   Gesell suggests that if parents are aware of their children's developmental clock, they will avoid unreasonable expectations. For example, a child cannot walk or talk until the neurological structures necessary for those behaviors have matured. "Parents who provide special educational lessons for their babies are wasting their time," because the infants are not developmentally ready to profit from the exposure (Scarr, 1984, 60). Also, the hunger of a 4-week-old must be immediately appeased by food, but at 16 to 28 weeks, the child has some capacity to wait because the hunger pains are less intense. In view of this and other developmental patterns, Gesell suggests that the infant's needs be cared for on a demand schedule; instead of having to submit to a schedule imposed by parents, infants are fed, changed, put to bed, and allowed to play when they want. Children are likely to be resistant to a hard and fast schedule because they may be developmentally unable to cope with it.

In addition, Gesell alerts parents to the importance of the first years of a child's life. In Gesell's view, these early years assume the greatest significance because the child's first learning experiences occur during this period.

■■ TABLE 15.1 **Theories of Childbearing**

THEORY	MAJOR CONTRIBUTOR	BASIC PERSPECTIVE	FOCAL CONCERNS	CRITICISMS
Developmental-Maturational	Arnold Gesell	Genetic basis for each child passing through predictable stages	Motor behavior Adaptive behavior Language behavior Social behavior	Overemphasis on biological clock Inadequate sample to develop norms Demand schedule questionable Upper-middle class bias
Behavioral	B. F. Skinner	Behavior is learned through operant and classical conditioning	Positive reinforcement Negative reinforcement Punishment Extinction Stimulus Response	Deemphasis on cognitions of child Theory too complex to be accurately/ appropriately applied by parent Too manipulative/ controlling Difficult to know reinforcers and punishers in advance
Parent Effectiveness Training	Thomas Gordon	The child's world view is the key to understanding the child.	Change the environment before attempting to change the child's behavior. Avoid hurting the child's self-esteem. Avoid win-lose solutions.	Parents must sometimes impose their will on the child's. How to achieve win-win solutions is not clear.
Socioteleological	Alfred Adler	Behavior is seen as attempt of child to secure a place in the family	Insecurity Compensation Power Revenge Social striving Natural consequences	Limited empirical support Impractical Child may be harmed taking "natural consequences"
Reality	William Glasser	Behavioral problems children develop result from inability to cope with stress	Irrational narcissism Emotional precociousness Vicarious living	Parental love not sole determinant of outcome Children have large numbers of socialization agents Child may be endangered if approach is followed

Criticisms of the Developmental-Maturational Approach. Gesell's work has been criticized because of (1) its overemphasis on the idea of a biological clock; (2) the deficiencies of the sample he used to develop maturational norms; (3) his insistence on the merits of a demand schedule; and (4) the idea that environmental influences are weak.

Most of the children who were studied to establish the developmental norms were from the upper-middle class. Children in other social classes are exposed to different environments, which influence their development. So norms established on upper-middle class children may not adequately reflect the norms of children from other social classes.

Whereas parents may not be too concerned about the way in which developmental norms have been established, they may be quite concerned about the suggestion that they do everything for the infant when the infant wants it. Rearing an infant on the demand schedule can drastically interfere with the parents' personal and marital interests. As a result, most American parents feed their infants on a demand schedule but put them to bed to accommodate the parents' schedule (Shea, 1984).

Behavioral Approach

The *behavioral approach* to childrearing, also known as the *social learning approach*, is based on the work of B. F. Skinner. We will now review the basic perspective, considerations, and criticisms of this approach to childrearing.

> In nature there are neither rewards nor punishments—there are consequences.
> —ROBERT GREEN INGERSOLL

Basic Perspective. Behavior is learned through classical and operant conditioning. *Classical conditioning* involves presenting a stimulus with a reinforcer. For example, infants come to associate the faces of their parents with food, warmth, and comfort. Although initially only the food and feeling warm will satisfy the infant, later just the approach of the parent will soothe the infant. This may be observed when a father hands his infant to a stranger. The infant may cry because the stranger is not associated with pleasant events. But when the stranger hands the infant back to the parent, the crying may subside because the parent represents positive events and the stimulus of the parent's face is associated with pleasurable feelings.

Other behaviors are learned through *operant conditioning*, which focuses on the consequences of behavior. Two principles of learning are basic to the operant explanation of behavior—reward and punishment. According to the reward principle, behaviors that are followed by a positive consequence will increase. If the goal is to teach the child to say "please," doing something the child likes after he or she says "please" will increase the use of "please" by the child. Rewards may be in the form of attention, praise, desired activities, or privileges. Whatever consequence increases the frequency of something happening is, by definition, a reward. If a particular reward doesn't change the behavior in the desired way, a different reinforcer needs to be tried.

The punishment principle is the opposite of the reward principle. A negative consequence following a behavior will decrease the frequency of that behavior; for example, the child could be isolated for five or ten minutes following an undesirable behavior. The most effective way to change behavior is to use the reward and punishment principles together to influence a specific behavior. British psychiatrist Michael Rutter (1984) comments:

> Not just stopping children from doing things—that doesn't seem to me to be the way, and in any case it doesn't work in the long run. You have to provide children with alternatives, to teach them what they should be doing, rather than what they should not be doing (p. 64).

If a child is rewarded (gets to watch television) every time she or he makes the bed and punished (can't watch television for 24 hours) every time she or he doesn't, it is likely that the bed will get made most of the time. In addition, children of parents who use a behavioral approach to discipline perceive their parents as being congruent—doing what they say they will do. This perception may result from parents backing up rules with consequences (Haffey & Levant, 1984).

Considerations for Childrearing.   Parents often ask, "Why does my child act this way, and what can I do to change it?" The behavioral approach to childrearing suggests the answer to both questions. The child's behavior has been learned through being rewarded for the behavior; the child's behavior can be changed by eliminating the reward for the undersirable behavior and rewarding the desirable behavior.

The child who cries when the parents are about to leave home to go to dinner or see a movie is often reinforced for crying by the parents' staying home longer. To teach the child not to cry when the parents leave, the parents should reward the child for not crying when they are gone for progressively longer periods of time. For example, they might initially tell the child they are going outside to walk around the house and they will give the child a treat when they get back if he or she plays until they return. The parents might then walk around the house and reward the child for not crying. If the child cries, they should be out of sight for only a few seconds and gradually increase the amount of time they are away. The essential point is that children learn to cry or not to cry depending on the consequences of crying. Because children learn what they are taught, parents might systematically structure learning experiences to achieve specific behavioral goals.

Criticisms of the Behavioral Approach.   Professionals and parents have attacked the behavioral approach to childrearing on the basis that it is deceptively simple and does not take cognitive issues into account. Although the behavioral approach is often presented as an easy-to-use set of procedures for child management, many parents do not have the background or skill to implement the procedures effectively. What constitutes an effective reward or punishment, presented in what way, in what situation, with what child, to influence what behavior are all decisions that need to be made before attempting to increase or decrease the frequency of a behavior. Parents often do not know the questions to ask or lack the training to make appropriate decisions in the use of behavioral procedures. One parent locked her son in the closet for an hour to punish him for lying to her a week earlier—a gross misuse of learning principles.

Behavioral childrearing has also been said to be manipulative and controlling, thereby devaluing human dignity and individuality. Some professionals feel that humans should not be treated like rats in a cage and given food pellets for pressing a bar.

Finally, the behavioral approach has been criticized because it de-emphasizes the influence of thought processes on behavior. Too much attention, say the critics, has been given to rewarding and punishing behavior and not enough attention has been given to how the child perceives a situation. For example, parents might think they are rewarding a child by giving her or him a bicycle for good behavior. But the child may prefer to upset the parents by rejecting the bicycle and may be more rewarded by their anger than by the gift.

Parents who must cope with severe behavior problems may find practical help in Toughlove, described in Exhibit 15.2.

E X H I B I T   15.2

::

Toughlove

Although not based on a specific childrearing theory, TOUGHLOVE is a self-help organization of parents (none of whom profess to have "professional qualifications" other than experience) who have difficulty controlling severe problem behaviors of their teenage children, including drug abuse, physical abuse of parents, staying away from home without explanation, using obscene language to parents, and stealing from other family members. These parents feel overwhelmed with the magnitude of their child's unacceptable behavior and helpless to cope with it. They may have had "good kids" up until the teen years but are now experiencing behaviors in their children that they never imagined could occur.

TOUGHLOVE parents meet weekly with other parents in groups of about 10 to discuss their children and potential solutions to their behavior problems. The typical format is for each parent to tell what problems she or he is experiencing. Other group members will comment on having had a similar problem, what they did, and how it worked out. Although there is no pressure to talk about one's problems or to take action, once a parent decides to discuss a problem and becomes committed to a course of action, the group members will ask at the next meeting if the parent followed through and what the consequences were. TOUGHLOVE parents are very supportive of each other.

The group setting eliminates the parents' feeling that they are the only parent whose children have gotten out of control, that they are embarrassed at their inability to

cope with the situation, and that they have some reason to be ashamed. TOUGHLOVE parents take the position that they are people too and that they have a right to expect their children to behave appropriately. The TOUGH part becomes operative in the withdrawal of family resources when children consistently disregard parental requests. "The way you get cooperation from unruly young people is to withdraw the family resources that allow them to exploit their parents" (York & York, 1982, 114). For example, a child who says, "I am going to smoke dope whether you like it or not," may, as a last resort, be asked to find somewhere else to live. The child who is arrested for drunk driving for the third time is left in jail for three days even though his parents could bail him out.

The larger community consisting of teachers, probation officers, social workers, therapists, and citizens may also be involved in helping parents in TOUGHLOVE. For example, a child who takes drugs and has a history of lying about doing so may be taken to school by the parents, watched carefully at school by the teacher, have weekly meetings with a caseworker, and be taken home by another member of the TOUGHLOVE group. The community pulls together to try to help the parents control their child's negative behavior. The emphasis is not on blaming anyone but on correcting the behavior problem. There are more than 500 chapters of TOUGHLOVE in the United States (York & York, 1982). Information about a chapter in your community can be obtained from the co-founders of TOUGHLOVE, David and Phyllis York, (P.O. Box 1069; Doylestown, PA 18901; 215-348-7090).

Parent Effectiveness Training Approach

As B.F. Skinner is to behavior modification, so Thomas Gordon is to parent effectiveness training (PET).

Basic Perspecitve. Parent effectiveness training focuses on what children feel and experience in the here and now—how they see the world. The method of trying to understand what the child is experiencing is active listening, in which the parent reflects the child's feelings. For example, the parent who is told by the child, "I want to quit taking piano lessons because I don't like to practice" would reflect, "You're really bored with practicing the piano and would rather have fun doing something else."

PET also focuses on the devleopment of the child's positive self-concept. Such a self-concept is the result of other people reflecting positive images to the child— letting the child know he or she is like, admired, and approved of.

Considerations for Childrearing. To assist in the development of a child's positive self-concept and in the self-actualization of both children and parents, Gordon makes a number of recommendations. These include managing the environment rather than the child, engaging in active listening, using "I messages," and resolving conflicts through mutual negotiation. An example of environmental management is putting breakables out of reach of young children but towel racks and toy boxes within reach. It is sometimes easier and safer to manage the enviornment—not just the child.

The use of active listening becomes increasingly important as the child gets older. When Joanna is upset with her teacher, it is better for the parent to reflect the child's thoughts than to take sides with her. Saying "You're angry that Mrs. Jones made the whole class miss play period because Becky was chewing gum," rathar than saying "Mrs. Jones was unfair and should not have made the whole class miss play period," shows empathy with the child without blaming the teacher.

Gordon also suggests using "I" rather than "you" messages. Parents are encouraged to say "I get upset when you're late and don't call," rather than "You're an insensitive, irresponsible kid for not calling me when you said you would." The former avoids damaging the child's self-concept but still encourages the desired behavior.

Gordon's fourth suggestion for parenting is the no-lose method of resolving conflicts. He rejects the use of power by parent or child. In the authoritarian home, the parent dictates what the child is to do and the child is expected to obey. In such a system, the parent wins and the child loses. At the other extreme is the permissive home, in which the child wins and the parent loses. The alternative, Gordon syas, is for the parent and the child to seek a solution that is acceptable to both and to keep trying until they find one. In this way, neither parent nor child loses and both win.

Criticisms of the Parent Effectiveness Training Approach. Although much is commendable about PET, parents may have problems with two of Gordon's suggestions. First, he recommends that because older children have a right to their own values, parents should not interfere with their dress, career plans, and sexual behavior. Some parents may feel they do have a right (and an obligation) to "interfere."

Second, the no-lose method of resolving conflict is sometimes unrealistic. Suppose a 16-year-old wants to spend the weekend at the beach with her boyfriend and her parents do not want her to do so. Gordon says to negotiate until a decision is reached that is acceptable to both. But what if neither the parents nor the daughter can suggest a compromise or shift their position? The specifics of how to resolve a particular situation are not always clear.

Socioteleological Approach

Alfred Adler, a physician and former student of Sigmund Freud, saw a parallel between psychological and physiological development. When a person loses her or his sight, the other senses (hearing, touch, taste) become more sensitive—they compensate for the loss. According to Adler, the same phenomenon occurs in the psychological realm. When individuals feel inferior in one area, they will strive to compensate and become superior in another. Rudolph Dreikurs, a student of Adler, has developed an approach to childrearing that alerts parents as to how their children might be trying to compensate for feelings of inferiority. Dreikurs's suggestions are based on Adler's theory.

Basic Perspective. According to Adler, it is understandable that most children feel they are inferior and weak. From the child's point of view, the world is filled with strong giants who tower above him or her. Because children feel powerless in the face of adult superiority, they try to compensate by gaining attention (making noise, becoming disruptive), exerting power (becoming aggressive, hostile), seeking revenge (becoming violent, hurting others), and acting inadequate (giving up, not trying). Adler suggested that such misbehavior is evidence that the child is discouraged or feels insecure about her or his place in the family. The term *socioteleological* refers to social striving or seeking a social goal—in the child's case, the goal of a secure place within the family.

Considerations for Childrearing. When parents observe misbehavior in their children, they should recognize it as an attempt to find security. According to Dreikurs, parents should not fall into playing the child's game by, say, responding to a child's disruptiveness with anger, but should encourage the child, hold regular family councils, and let natural consequences occur. To encourage the child, the parents should be willing to let the child make mistakes. If John wants to help Dad carry logs to the fireplace, rather than Dad saying "You're too small to carry the logs," John should be allowed to try and encouraged to carry the size limb or stick that he can manage. Furthermore, Dad should praise John for his helpfulness.

Along with constant encouragement, the child should be included in a weekly family council. During this meeting, such family issues as bedtimes, the appropriateness of between-meal snacks, assignment of chores, and family fun are discussed. The meeting is democratic; each family member has a vote. Such participation in family decision making is designed to enhance the self-concept of each child.

> The best way to make children is to make them happy.
> —OSCAR WILDE

Finally, Dreikurs suggests that the parents let natural consequences occur for their child's behavior. If a daughter misses the school bus, she walks or is charged "taxi fare" out of her allowance. If she won't wear a coat and boots, she gets cold and wet. Of course, parents are to arrange suitable consequences when natural consequences will not occur or would be dangerous if they did. For example, if a child leaves the video games on the living room floor, they could be taken away for a week. "If we are not exposed to the natural consequences of our behavior, we will never learn the hardworking, cooperative behaviors that lead to social, economic, or personal success" (Love & McVoy, 1981, 13).

Criticisms of the Socioteleological Approach.   The socioteleological approach to childrearing has been criticized because it lacks supportive empirical research and is occasionally impractical. It is fair to say that some of the other childrearing approaches already discussed also lack solid empirical support.

The impracticality of the socioteleological approach is sometimes illustrated by letting children take the natural consequences of their action. This may be an effective childrearing procedure for most behaviors, but it can backfire. Letting children develop sore throats in the hope that it will teach them the importance of wearing a raincoat in the rain is questionable.

Reality Therapy Approach

Based on the work of William Glasser and his parent involvement program (PIP), the *reality therapy* approach to childrearing focuses on the developing child and teenager.

Basic Perspective.   Glasser suggests that the young child is irrationally narcissistic, emotionally precocious, and incapable of coping with frustration and stress. These qualities cause the behavioral problems children exhibit—from not cleaning their rooms to taking drugs. By irrational narcissism, Glasser means the child is completely self-centered and views everything in terms of "what's in it for me." Emotional precociousness means that the child is insensitive to the needs of others and seeks to manipulate others' emotions to serve the child's own ends. But Glasser sees the child's greatest character flaw as not being able to cope with stress and quitting rather than working through a problem. Children do not have the confidence in themselves to figure out what to do when something goes wrong or the perseverance to make a bad situation better.

Television is the villain behind these flaws. The hours children spend in front of this "mindless tube," according to Glasser, are destructive—not because the content of television is so awful, but because children are not using this time to interact with others, to develop social skills, and to learn about life by experiencing it. They are living vicariously.

Considerations for Childrearing.   Glasser suggests that nothing parents can do for their children is more valuable than spending time with them. This communicates to children that they are loved and valued, which is a prerequisite for developing their confidence to persevere in spite of setbacks. Spending time with children also helps them to learn social skills, to learn another person's point of

In bringing up children, spend on them half as much money and twice as much time.

—LAURENCE PETER

view, and to learn to share with others. Participation in family rituals, such as Christmas, birthdays, vacations, Easter, and Sunday dinner, also may have the effect of bonding family members to each other.

The reality therapy approach to childrearing also emphasizes the right of children to make their own choices. Parents are urged to give children responsibility for their choices and to let them take the consequences. This principle is similar to the Adlerian principle of natural consequences. "My child has a right to fail in school," said one parent. This viewpoint acknowledges that only the child can decide what course of action to take (for example, whether to study or not) and that accepting the consequences for decisions is an effective way of learning how to make decisions.

Criticisms of the Reality Therapy Approach. Like most childrearing approaches, the reality therapy approach looks good on paper. Spending time with children, giving children the right to make their own decisions, and letting natural consequences follow are suggestions with which parents might find it easy to agree. However, the basic premise of the reality therapy approach is that the love relationship between the parent and the child is the critical variable that determines the way the child turns out. This premise is suspect. One parent said:

> I've spent half my life with my son, including regular fishing trips when he was a small boy and working with him in Scouts when he was older. His teacher told me the reason he is doing poorly in school is because I haven't spent enough time with him to show my love for him. Baloney!

Children are subject to a wide variety of influences, and parent behavior—regardless of how loving or stable it is—is only one aspect of the child's socialization.

In addition, as with the socioteleological approach, some parents may have a difficult time standing by waiting for children to learn from their own decisions. For example, does a parent allow a 15-year-old to buy a motorcycle and learn through experience that turning curves too fast can cost a leg? Does a parent permit his or her child to be unconcerned about grades to the point of not being able to graduate?

Although you may not adhere to any one particular approach to childrearing, you probably do have a perspective on the permissiveness or strictness of child discipline. The Child Discipline Scale in the Self-Assessment is designed to help you identify this perspective.

▪▪ Communication Between Parents and Teenagers

There is a saying that "The trick of talking with adolescents is to find their reason without losing yours." The wisdom of this adage suggests that the core of communication with adolescents is to try to see the world from their point of view rather than to impose the adult point of view on them. Some other techniques which may be useful include:

1. Catch them doing what you like rather than criticizing them for what you don't like. Adolescents are like everyone else—they don't like to be criticized but do like to be noticed for what they do that is good.

Child Discipline Scale

This inventory is designed to measure the degree to which you have a permissive or strict view of childrearing. There are no right or wrong answers. After reading each sentence carefully, circle the number that best represents your view.

1 Strongly disagree 2 Mildly disagree 3 Undecided 4 Mildly agree 5 Strongly agree

	SD	MD	U	MA	SA
1. When you spare the rod, you spoil the child.	1	2	3	4	5
2. It is better for your children to view you as an authority than as a friend.	1	2	3	4	5
3. Parents let their children get away with too much.	1	2	3	4	5
4. One of the most important qualities a child can have is to be obedient.	1	2	3	4	5
5. Children should do as they are told without asking why.	1	2	3	4	5
6. If you aren't strict with children, they won't respect you.	1	2	3	4	5
7. The only thing children really understand is a good spanking.	1	2	3	4	5
8. Parents who try to be buddy-buddy with their children lose their respect.	1	2	3	4	5
9. When children have done something bad, punishing them is more effective than talking with them about doing better the next time.	1	2	3	4	5
10. The Bible is a good guidebook for child discipline.	1	2	3	4	5

SCORING: Add the numbers you circled. 1(strongly disagree) is the most permissive response you can make, and 5 (strongly agree) is the most strict response you can make. The lower your total score (10 is the lowest possible score), the more permissive your childrearing view; the higher your total score (50 is the highest possible score), the more strict you are about child discipline. A total score of 30 total places you at the midpoint between being permissive and being strict.

(NOTE: This Self-Assessment is intended to be thought-provoking and suggestive; it is not a clinical diagnostic instrument).

2. Ignore some things. One adult said that when he was 13, he stayed up late, stole one of his father's cigarettes, and smoked it while watching television. Although he thought that his father was asleep, he was surprised by his father who walked into the room where he was smoking. When his father saw his teenager smoking, he said nothing, turned around, and went back to bed. The father never spoke of the incident. The effect on the adolescent was to feel the tolerance for experimentation from his father that he wanted. After finishing the cigarette, he never smoked again.

3. Provide information rather than answers. When teens are confronted with a problem try to avoid making a decision for them. Rather, it is helpful to provide information on which they may base a decision. What courses to take in high school and what college to apply for are decisions that should be made primarily by the adolescent. The role of the parent might best be that of providing information.

4. Be tolerant of high activity levels. Some teenagers are constantly listening to loud music, going to each other's homes, and talking on the telephone for long periods of time. Parents often want to sit in their easy chair and be quiet. Recognizing that it is not realistic to expect teenagers to be quiet and sedentary may be helpful in tolerating their disruptions.

5. Engage in some activity with your teenagers. Whether it is renting a video, eating a burger, or taking a camping trip, it is important to structure enjoyable activities with your teenagers. Such activities permit a context in which to communicate with them. One parent goes on a three day hiking/camping trip with each of his three children every summer. "It gives us an opportunity to connect," he notes.

∷ Responding to Teenage Drug Abuse

One of the fears of today's parents is that their child will abuse drugs.

> ■ **DATA:** *In a Gallup poll, 23 percent of youth ages 13–17 (4.5 million) had been offered illegal drugs in the previous 30 days. Nineteen percent say that they had friends who use drugs regularly (Kelley, 1989).*

Various factors associated with the use of drugs include peers who use drugs, alcoholic parents, poor relations with parents, poor school performance, low IQ, inadequate moral development, and being male (Carpenter et al., 1988). For the drug abuser, the use of drugs or alcohol ultimately causes a problem in all areas of life—health, school, work, home, and social relationships. Parents *can* help to prevent their son or daughter from abusing drugs. If their prevention efforts fail, however, they should be ready to respond.

Drug Prevention—The Best Medicine

It is easier to do everything possible to ensure that your child does not begin to use drugs than it is to try to stop the drug use once it has begun. Some specific things that parents can do to ward off drug abuse in their children have been recommended by Louis Meador (1990), a drug-abuse specialist who works with teenagers and their families.

Be a Good Example

Parents who come home from a day at the office and drink liquor until bedtime are teaching their children that alcohol is used to relieve stress—the more alcohol, the better. Regardless of what you say, your children will attend to what you do.

Just as getting drunk models abuse of alcohol, moderate use of alcohol models drinking control. Children who are reared in homes in which their parents drink alcohol in moderation are most likely to avoid becoming alcoholics. On the other hand, children who are reared in homes in which one or both parents abuse alcohol or in homes in which alcohol is forbidden are most likely to become alcoholics. An alcoholic from a nondrinking home said, "My folks made a big thing out of never drinking alcohol and told me I was never to do it. I rebelled against them, started drinking at 17, and haven't quit."

Parents who use marijuana, cocaine, or other illegal drugs serve as role models for teenagers to use these same drugs. If your goal is for your child not to use any of these drugs, you should not use them yourself. To do so is to teach your child that drug use is acceptable behavior. And your saying "I'm older and know what I'm doing" won't mean much to your teenager.

Misuse of prescription drugs carries the same caveat. Although your physician may have prescribed tranquilizers to relieve stress, your taking more than the recommended dosage is similar to drinking more than a couple of cocktails or beers. If your children see you taking aspirin for a headache, valium for your nerves, and Dalmane to sleep, the message is clear—drugs are the answer to pain, stress, and insomnia.

There may also be a genetic link to the potential to abuse drugs. Individuals whose parents, grandparents, or siblings have a history of substance abuse or major depression are much more likely to abuse drugs themselves.

☐   C O N S I D E R A T I O N   ☐

Some parents who once abused drugs but no longer do so wonder if they should tell their teenager of their earlier drug use. Two issues are at stake in such a situation. One, is it appropriate to lie to your teenager under any conditions? And two, what impact will the knowledge of your drug use have on your teenager's drug use? In regard to the first issue, one parent said that she "would never lie to her child because she would lose faith in me." But another parent said, "Everybody lies about something, and there may be some good reasons to lie to your kids about drugs." One of these "good" reasons follows:

> If you tell your children that you use or have used drugs, they may use the fact that you did to justify their doing so. And while you may be able to handle marijuana or cocaine or whatever, your teenager may not be able to do so. People have different biochemical makeups, and the drug a parent may not get addicted to the child might. So think carefully before you tell your children that you use or have used drugs. The drug may have an entirely different (and possibly addictive) effect on them.

An alternate perspective is to tell the truth. If you have used drugs, say so but explain the context of your doing so, the hazards, and the reasons you feel it is unwise to take drugs.

Keep Communication Channels Open. Teenagers who are troubled about school, work, and social relationships are more vulnerable to drug use than teenagers who make good grades, enjoy their after-school jobs, and have meaningful social relationships. The best way for parents to recognize that their teenager is becoming despondent is to keep the channels of communication open.

Open communication translates into less drug use. Children who enjoy their parents' approval are less likely to do something (drink, take drugs) if they know their parents will disapprove of the action. Good communication does not eliminate the possibility that children will drink or take drugs, but it does reduce the chance that they will. Parents can learn how to listen reflectively, respond empathetically, and help their children make wise decisions (Tebes et al., 1989). Training seminars designed to teach parents these skills are sometimes offered in local mental health centers.

When Drug Abuse Is Already Happening

A parent who becomes aware that a son or daughter is already involved in drugs should assess the situation. Drinking a beer at a party is not the same as getting drunk before school; taking a draw on a marijuana cigarette is not the same as having a bag of dope in a sock drawer. The parent should be careful not to overrespond to the smell of alcohol or something different from cigarette smoke in a child's room, for example. It is appropriate to ask, "What do I smell?," rather than accuse a son or daughter of drinking alcohol or smoking marijuana.

Assuming that the teenager admits to having had a beer or smoked some "dope," the parents' response will differ depending on their values. Some parents absolutely abhor the use of any alcohol or drugs; in these cases, they will tell the teenager this is completely unacceptable behavior, withdraw privileges ("you can't have the car for a month"), and encourage the teenager to recognize that alcohol and marijuana are drugs that are better left alone.

Other parents are more liberal and feel that moderate drug use is acceptable. "I've been using drugs since I was 18," said one 50-year-old parent. "And I've never missed a day at work. Nor has my efficiency dropped one iota. I am just very careful in terms of what drugs I take, how much, how often, and in what context. I think these are the more important issues."

If, however, a teenager has gone overboard and becomes a drug abuser (drugs are affecting his or her health, grades, and social relationships), the following steps, directed toward the parent, are indicated.

Confront Your Teenager. Armed with evidence (the teenager is drunk or in possession of a bag of dope, a container of cocaine, pills, or some other drug), make your teenager aware that you know of the drug use. Cutting through your teenager's denial that he or she uses drugs is difficult for both teenager and parent.

Ask for Your Teenagers' Point of View. Be careful not to criticize or belittle your teenager, but ask for an explanation of why he or she drinks, smokes, snorts, or whatever. It is not unusual for teenagers to feel very guilty about what they are doing; once confronted by their parents, some teenagers are anxious to stop. "I drifted in over my head," said one teenager to her parents, "and I really am sick of it and want to stop."

Alcohol is the most abused drug in our society.

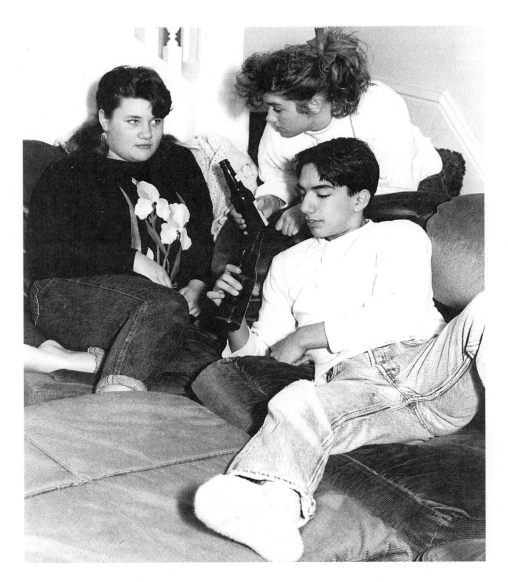

Consult a Professional Drug-abuse Counselor. Drug abuse can be a difficult family problem, and there are no quick and easy solutions. Family therapy, in which the whole family is involved, is the treatment of choice when drug abuse surfaces (Lewis, 1989). In addition, individual therapy for the abuser is indicated and should focus on teaching the adolescent to cope with the stress of life without drugs as well as how to say no to friends who offer drugs. Improving the adolescent's self-esteem should also be a focus of therapy (Rosenberg et al., 1989). Both family and individual treatment are available through local mental health centers.

Make Your Position Clear. If your teenager is willing to stop drinking or using drugs, offer your love and support. Ask what you can do to make it easier for him or her to stop abusing alcohol or drugs.

But if your teenager is defiant and says that he or she is going to do whatever he or she wants, fight back. Drug abuse can ruin a life in terms of debilitating health, making it difficult to keep a job, and souring social relationships. As long as you have some control over your teenager's life, use it.

Make an Agreement. One alternative is to make it clear to your child that you will not tolerate drug use. One parent told her 16-year-old:

> Your father and I know that you get tired of us butting into your life. But we feel that drugs can harm you, and we ask that you stop as long as you are living with us. To ensure that you are not using drugs, we want you to have your urine analyzed weekly. If drug use has occurred, we are going to send you to an in-patient drug rehabilitation center.

If the teenager can stay drug-free without being admitted to an institutional environment, he or she should be encouraged to attend Narcotics Anonymous at least once weekly.

Narcotics Anonymous. Former drug abusers meet weekly in local chapters of Narcotics Anonymous (NA), patterned after Alcoholics Anonymous, to help each other continue to be drug-free. The premise of NA is that the best person to help someone who is abusing drugs is someone who once abused drugs. NA members of all ages, social classes, and educational levels provide a sense of support for each other to remain drug-free.

If the substance-abuse problem is alcohol, Alcoholics Anonymous (AA), is an appropriate support group (national headquarters mailing address: AA General Service Office; P.O. Box 459, Grand Central Station; New York, NY 10017). There are over 15,000 AA chapters nationwide; the one in your community can be contacted by looking in the Yellow Pages of your local telephone directory. Al-Anon is an organization that provides support for family members of drug abusers. Such support is often helpful to parents coping with a teenage drug abuser.

▪▪ Other Issues Concerning Parents

Getting children to avoid abusing drugs is only one of many issues that concern most parents. Other issues include infant death, day care, quality education, healthy adolescent sexuality, automobile accidents, and children leaving home.

Death of a Child

The number of infant deaths is shocking and the event is devastating.

▪ **DATA:** *Almost 14,000 children 1 year old and younger die each year (Statistical Abstract of the United States: 1990,* Table 111).

Of the death of her baby, one mother wrote:

> When Thomas died at the age of seven months, he died a baby—a very lovable, cuddly baby. The crisis of his death stripped away our coping skills . . . In a heart-beat, we had become a bereaved family. Once again, our emotions took roller-coaster rides . . In the aftermath of intense grief, new values emerged. No, I would never

have chosen this way, but I want to survive. Desire to survive is the necessary ingredient for healing to begin (Farnsworth, 1988, 1).

Adjusting to the death of one's child involves a similar pattern to adjusting to the death of any person we love. The typical sequence involves denial, intense grief, followed by anger, numbness and mourning, followed by recognition that life must go on, followed by a new level of functioning. Waves of grief may still return on the anniversary of the death, on the birthday, and on other special occasions. Over time, the wounds may heal but are never forgotten.

> Somewhere in my journey, I became aware of my choices. I could spend the rest of my days bitter and angry over my plight. Or I could choose to forgive life, to remember that I am not the only one who has had pain. In forgiving, I opened the door to life and love and new possibilities. I feel rich again (Farnsworth, 1988, 60).

In the grieving process, men may heal more quickly than women. Based on a study of 33 couples who had experienced the death of a child, the researcher (Bohannon, 1990) observed that husbands generally experienced lower levels of grief intensity than did their wives and that these levels were consistently lower across time.

Day Care

While most parents do not dwell on the possibility that their child will die, they do spend an enormous amount of time thinking about who will take care of their children when both parents are earning an income. Day care is defined as any of the many different types of arrangements that are used to provide supervision and care to children when the parents are unable to do so. For the employed mother, the care of her child in her absence is of critical and primary concern.

■ **DATA:** *Nearly 8 million employed women depend on baby sitters, relatives, pre-schools, or day care centers to look after their children* (Statistical Abstract of the United States: 1990, *Table 616). Day care costs parents an average of $53 per child per week (Cutler, 1990).*

When the child is an infant or toddler, the preferred child care arrangements are (in order of preference) leaving the child with a parent or other relative, having a sitter come to the home, or taking the infant to someone else's home. As the child gets older (four years and over), parents are more likely to put them in a day care center.

■ **DATA:** *Three percent of employed mothers with children age 2 and under preferred that their children were in day care; fifty-percent preffered day care when their children were between the ages of 4 and 5 (Mason & Kuhlthau, 1989).*

Good quality care is a critical concern. "When parents can't tend to their children themselves, good quality care, not cost, is their biggest worry" (Cheskis-Gold, 1988, 47). Quality day care is often lacking. Staff are usually inexperienced, poorly paid, and overworked.

Centers that once required staff to have college degrees in child development have dropped educational requirements and still have trouble filling vacancies.

Wages in child care are usually minimum wage. And so most centers hire 18-year-olds with no experience, and no interest in working longer than a few months until they find something else (Coniff, 1988, 22).

CONSIDERATION

Before enrolling their child in a day care facility, parents might ask: What are the licensing requirements in the state in which the facility is located and is the license current? Are the caregivers educated in child psychology and development and/or early childhood education? Is there 35 square feet of space per child indoors and 75 square feet per child in outside areas? Does the center take care of sick children? Is a pediatric nurse practioner or pediatrician on call at all times? What is the ratio of children to staff for the respective age groups? The ratio recommended by the National Association of Pediatric Nurse Associates and Practitioners follows (McGuire, 1989, 5):

Infants to 18 months	4:1
18 Months to 2 years	5:1
2–3 years	8:1
3–4 years	10:1
5–6 years	15:1
7 years and older	20:1

What are the effects of day care on children? While the data are inconsistent, it seems that day care does not necessarily adversely affect the infant-mother bond and tends to facilitate positive preschool social behavior (Field et al., 1988). The risks are highest for infants in day care for more than 20 hours a week during their first year. Parents are advised to be very selective about the day care they provide for their child during the first year (Belsky, 1988).

Some parents tire of traditional day care and hire an *au pair*. These are usually European women (age 18 to 25) who help with childcare duties 5½ days a week for one year in exchange for room and board and the right to attend classes in their spare time. About 1,000 *au pairs* enter the United States annually. *Au pair* means "on par," or "equal"—the hosts must be willing to treat them as part of the family. The popularity of *au pairs* has also resulted in the training and hiring of American-born nannies. Families with children under the age of 3 are particularly interested in hiring an *au pair* or a nanny. (See Childcare in Resources and Organizations on page 604 for more information.)

For parents who cannot afford day care, an *au pair*, or a nanny, help from the government is needed. The National Research Council of the National Academy of Sciences has recommended that the federal government and the states should expand subsidies to help make quality childcare available to low-income families. In addition, the Council recommended that the federal government should require employers to provide unpaid, job-protected leave for parents of infants under age one.

Quality Education

Parental concern continues when the children move beyond day care and into public education.

■ **DATA:** *When parents are asked to give a grade reflecting the efectiveness of the schools in the U.S., 22 percent give an* A *or* B *(Ordovensky, 1989).*

Considerable media attention has been given to the problems of public school education. Some graduates of public high schools can't read, work simple math problems, or write an intelligible sentence. Parents feel frustrated when their children don't learn such basic skills. One parent said, "For all the money that is pumped into education, you would think high school graduates could read."

Parental involvement is a necessary part of quality education.

Healthy Adolescent Sexuality

Most parents are hopeful that their adolescent will develop healthy attitudes about sex. One researcher (Chilman, 1990) defined healthy adolescent sexuality as follows:

> . . . adolescent sexual health is based on esteem and respect for the self and other people of both sexes. It embraces the view that both males and females are essentially equal, though not necessarily the same. Sexually healthy adolescents take pleasure and pride in their own developing bodies. As they mature, they have an increasing ability to communicate honestly and openly with persons of both sexes with whom they have a close relationship. They accept their own sexual desires as natural but to be acted upon with limited freedom within the constraints of reality considerations, including their own values and goals and those of 'significant others' (p. 124).
>
> It (healthy sexuality) does not include the concept of complete freedom to behave as one wishes so long as contraceptives, including condoms, are used and so long as this behavior is in private with consenting partners. In short, I challenge the notion that so-called recreational sex is fine so long as it doesn't become procreational sex. My chief objection to recreational sex is that it tends to trivialize the depth and meaning of the exceptional intimacy and potential involvement of the total self through intercourse (p. 124).

Fatal Automobile Accident

Another primary concern for parents is the fear that their son or daughter will be involved in a fatal automobile accident. Of the over 62,000 automobile deaths which occur annually (*Statistical Abstract of the United States: 1990*, Table 1041), about 20 percent are caused by drivers (age 15–21) who had been drinking alcohol. A strategy parents can implement involves restricting the amount of time their children have access to a car, particularly late at night.

■ **DATA:** *Although only 20 percent of the total mileage of teen drivers is accumulated between 9 PM and 6 AM, over 50 percent of fatalities occur during those hours (Williams, 1985).*

Children Leaving Home—The "Empty Nest" Syndrome

While researchers disagree on the definition of the "empty nest," this term typically refers to the period when the children have left home (for college, marriage, or work) and the spouses are alone as they were before the children were born. The children's leaving is usually a gradual process and is associated with their emotional and economic independence (Barber, 1989).

While marital happiness increases when children leave home (White and Edwards, 1990), most parents have mixed emotions about their children leaving home. Having an "empty nest" means relief from the relentless responsibility of caring for children, more privacy, and freedom to do as one wishes. But to many parents, an empty nest also creates feelings of sadness over not having spent enough time with their children, lonliness, and worry about how the children are doing.

The degree to which parents have negative feelings about their children leaving is related to the degree of investment in the parental role. Women who have been full-time mothers with no external career may experience the greatest impact. But fathers who are emotionally close to their children may also experience a deep sense of loss. As Barber (1989) notes, "there is little support for the notion that the empty nest syndrome is widespread or pertains solely to women" (p. 20).

There may be ethnic differences in the empty nest syndrome. Blacks and Mexican American women in traditional families may experience the syndrome to a lesser degree because they usually have economic roles outside the family. In addition, their large extended family system results in an overlap between the rearing of their own children and the rearing of grandchildren.

■■ Trends

New parents will continue to enter their childrearing role more or less naively, which suggests that most couples wait until they have a child to begin talking about their concerns about the childrearing role. Of course, no book, lecture, or course can adequately prepare a person for what it means to rear a child. Those who have had a great deal of responsibility for the care of younger siblings probably have a better idea than most.

A national day care program will receive an increasing amount of attention. While Sweden has day care centers that are operated by the state, parents in the United States must find day care for their children themselves. With an increasing number of dual-income and single parent families, the need for a national day care program has become critical.

Working parents today are tending to use a wider range of options for childcare than their parents, who left their children with their own parents. These options include day care, flex-time, job-sharing, and nannies. Working parents may also indulge their children more than parents in previous generations because they have less time to spend with their children. Since working parents do not have a large quantity of time with their children, they may instead strive to have quality time with them. To some parents, quality time means pampered time during which they are reluctant to discipline their children for misbehavior. In effect, "children today are at greater risk of becoming brats" (Hellmich, 1989, d1).

■■ Summary

Rearing children is one of the most demanding tasks an individual ever undertakes, and it requires that parents keep their role in perspective. Parenthood is only one stage in the person's marriage and life. In addition, parents are only one influence in the lives of their children; the joys and problems of childrearing change as the children mature; each child is different; and the goals of childrearing may differ. Some parents want obedient children; others want children who are independent and self-reliant.

Extensive folklore has arisen to make the role of parent more palatable to adults to encourage a commitment to childrearing. Would-be parents are led to believe that childrearing is fun, that good parents will produce good children, that love is enough for successful parenting, and that their children will appreciate the sacrifices they make for them. These beliefs are not supported by facts.

There are a number of childrearing approaches to help parents with the problems of parenting. The developmental-maturational approach focuses on what the child will be able to do when and suggests that parents should not demand of children what they are developmentally unable to deliver. The behavioral approach assumes that behavior is learned and that parents can get their children to engage in the behavior they want by rewarding desirable behavior and punishing undesirable behavior. Parent effectiveness training focuses on the communication between parent and child and encourages the parents to negotiate with their children when conflicts occur. The socioteleological approach views the negative behavior of children as a result of feelings of inferiority and suggests regular family council meetings to give children a voice in what happens in the family. The reality therapy approach focuses on the necessity of letting children make their own choices and learning from them.

In addition to drug abuse, parents are also concerned about quality day care, quality education, healthy adolescent sexuality, and the potential of a fatal automobile accident or the death of their infant.

New parents will continue to enter the parenting role naively. Since most parents work outside the home, they will become increasingly concerned about the government's role in national day care. Working parents may also tend to indulge their children more.

Questions for Reflection

1. Which childrearing approach appeals to you? Why?
2. How do you feel about putting your child in day care?
3. How do you feel about "spare the rod, and spoil the child" as a method of disciplining children? (This question will become more relevant after you read the Choices section which follows.)
4. As a parent, how would you respond to your teenager abusing drugs?

References

Barber, Clifton E. Transition to the empty nest. *Aging and the Family.* Edited by Stephen J. Bahr and Evan T. Peterson. 1989. 15–32.

Belsky, Jay. The effects of infant day care reconsidered. *Early Childhood Research Quarterly,* 1988, *3,* 235–272.

Bohannon, Judy Rollins Grief responses of marital dyads following the death of a child: A longitudinal study. *Omega: The Journal of Death and Dying,* 1990, 22, 111–123.

Carpenter, C., B. Glassner, B. D. Johnson, and J. Loughlin. *Kids, drugs, and crime.* Lexington, Mass.: D. C. Heath and Company, 1988.

Cheskis-Gold, Rena. Child care: What parents want. *American Demographics,* 1988, *10,* 46–47.

Chilman, C. S. Promoting healthy adolescent sexuality. *Family Relations,* 1990, *39,* 123–131.

Clemens, A. W. and L. J. Axelson. The not so empty nest: The return of the fledgling adult. *Family Relations,* 1985, *34,* 259–264.

Conniff, Dorothy. What's best for the child? *The Progressive,* 1988, *52,* 21–24.

Cutler, B. Rock-a-bye-baby. *American Demographics,* 1990, *12,* 35–39.

Eberle, N. The full nest syndrome. *Woman's Day,* July 7, 1987, pp. 60, 62, 65.

Fabes, R. A., P. Wilson, and F. S. Christopher. A time to reexamine the role of television in family life. *Family Relations,* 1989, *38,* 337–341.

Falconer, Clark W., K. G. Wilson, and J. Falconer. A psychometric investigation of gender-tilted families: Implications for family therapy. *Family Therapy*, 1990, *39*, 8–13.

Farnsworth, Elizabeth Brooks. *Journey through grief*. Atlanta, Ga.: Susan Hunter, 1988.

Field, Tiffany, W. Masi, S. Goldstein, S. Perry, and S. Parl. Infant day care facilitates preschool social behavior. *Early Childhood Research Quarterly*, 1988, *3*, 341–359.

Ginzberg, Eli, H. S. Berliner, and M. Ostow. *Young people at risk*. London: Westview Press, 1988.

Greer, K. Today's parents: How well are they doing? *Better Homes and Gardens*, October 1986, 34–36.

Haffey, N. A. and R. F. Levant. The differential effectiveness of two models of skills training for working class parents. *Family Relations*, 1984, *33*, 209–216.

Hellmich, Nanci. Parents have less time, indulge kids. *USA Today*, July 6, 1989, p. D1.

Ho, David Y. F. Continuity and variation in Chinese patterns of socialization. *Journal of Marriage and the Family*, 1989, *51*, 149–163.

Kandel, D. B. Parenting styles, drug use, and children's adjustment in families of young adults. *Journal of Marriage and the Family*, 1990, *52*, 183–196.

Kelley, J. Teen drug use called 'alarming.' *USA Today*, August 15, 1989, p. 1.

Kelley, M. L., N. Grace, and S. N. Elliott. Acceptabilitly of positive and punitive discipline methods: Comparisons among abusive, potentially abusive, and non-abusive parents. *Child Abuse and Neglect*, 1990, *14*, 219–226.

LeMasters, E. E. and J. DeFrain. *Parents in contemporary America: A sympathetic view*, 5th ed. Belmont, Calif.: Wadsworth Publishing Co., 1989.

Lewis, R. A. The family and addictions: An introduction. *Family Relations*, 1989, *38*, 254–257.

Love, N. W., Jr., J. H. McVoy. Child abuse by the unaware. *Marriage and Family Living*, 1981, *65*, no. 11, 12–29.

Luster, K. Roades, and B. Haas. The relation between parental values and parenting behavior: A test of the Kohn hypothesis. *Journal of Marriage and the Family*, 1989, *51*, 139–147.

Mason, K. O. and K. Kuhlthau. Determinants of child care ideals among mothers of school-age children. *Journal of Marriage and the Family*, 1989, *51*, 593–603.

McGuire, M. *Parent's guide to choosing quality child care*. Compiled by National Association of Pediatric Nurse Associates and Practioners, 1989.

Meador, Louis. Personal communication. Atlantic Beach, N.C., 1990.

Noller, Patricia and R. Taylor. Parent education and family relations. *Family Relations*, 1989, *38*, 196–200.

Ordovensky, P. Six in ten favor parents picking kids' schools. *USA Today*, August 25, 1989, p. D1.

Riche, M. F. The boomerang age. *American Demographics*, 1990 12, 24–30

Rosenberg, M., C. Schooler, and C. Schoenbach. Self-esteem and adolescent problems: Modeling reciprocal effects. *American Sociological Review*, 1989, *54*, 1004–1019.

Rutter, M. Resilient children. *Psychology Today*, March 1984, 57–65.

Sanders, G. F. and D. W. Trygstad. Stepgrandparents and grandparents: The view from young adults. *Family Relations*, 1989, *38*, 71–75.

Scarr, S. What's a parent to do? *Psychology Today*, May 1984, 58–63.

Schnaiberg, A. and S. Goldenberg. *From empty nest to crowded nest: The dynamics of incompletely launched adults*, 1990.

Schroeder, A. B. and B. R. Brocota. Television and the family interaction. *Free Inquiry in Creative Sociology*, 1983, *1*, 61–64.

Shea, J. Department of Child Development and Family Relations, East Carolina University, Greenville, N.C. Personal communication, 1984. Used by permission.

Simmons, R. L. and J. F. Robertson. The impact of parenting factors, deviant peers, and coping style upon adolescent drug use. *Family Relations*, 1989, *38*, 273–281.

Statistical Abstract of the United States: 1990. 110th ed. Washington, D.C.: U.S. Bureau of the Census, 1990.

Tebes, J. K., K. Grady, and D. L. Snow. Parent-training in decision making facilitation: Skill acquisition and relationship to gender. *Family Relations,* 1989, *38,* 243–247.

Thompson, L., A. C. Acock, and K. Clark. Do parents know their children? The ability of mothers and fathers to gauge the attitudes of their young adult children. *Family Relations,* 1985, *34,* 315–320.

Waldrop, Judith. A lesson in home economics: Working wives and empty nesters mean that married couples spend differently. *American Demographics,* 1989, *11,* 26–61.

White, L. and J. N. Edwards. Emptying the nest and parental well-being: An analysis of national panel data. *American Sociological Review,* 1990, *55,* 235–242.

Williams, Allan F. Fatal motor vehicle crashes involving teenagers. *Pediatrician,* 1985, *12,* 37–40.

Wong, Morrison G. The Chinese American family. *Ethnic Families in America: Patterns and Variations.* Edited by C. H. Mindel, R. W. Habenstein, and R. Wright, Jr. New York: Elsevier, 1988a, 230–257.

Wong, Morris G. A look at intermarriage among the Chinese in the United States in 1980. Paper presented at the Conference on Racial and Ethnic Relations in the 1990s, Texas A&M University, 1988b.

York, P. and D. York. Toughlove. *Family Therapy Networker.* September-October 1982, 32–37.

CHOICES

PARENTS ARE FACED with innumerable choices in rearing their children. These include which type of punishment to use, whether to reward positive behavior, how much freedom to give how soon, and how long to allow children to continue to live at home.

Which Type of Punishment is Best?

Infants are unsocialized persons. They know only one way—their own. Parents who adopt the behavioral approach to childrearing believe that to learn appropriate behavior, developing infants and children must be rewarded for certain behaviors and punished for others. Although parents may agree that praise and privileges are ways of rewarding children for positive behavior, they may choose different forms of punishment.

Some parents (about 4 percent) have the "spare the rod, and spoil the child" philosophy and inflict physical pain on their children as punishment (Greer, 1986). Examples of such punishment include being beaten on the buttocks with a belt or leather strap, being whipped on the legs, buttocks, and back with a switch, and being slapped or knocked down. One parent said "If you don't give them a good beating now and then, they forget who's boss and they don't mind you. A good lickin' will snap a kid in line every time."

Other parents feel that corporal punishment is unnecessary or wrong and elect to put their children in "time out" (removing the child to a place of isolation) or to withhold privileges for inappropriate behavior:

When my 6-year-old says 'Nah' rather than polite 'No' or 'No ma'am,' I tell her to go to the bathroom. She knows that means she is being punished for being disrespectful. For her brother who didn't get home until 1:30 a.m., when he was supposed to be in at midnight, I took the car away from him for two weeks.

The decision to choose a corporal or noncorporal method of punishment should be based on the consequences of use. In general, the use of "time out" and withholding of privileges seem to be as effective in stopping undesirable behavior as corporal punishment. Young children who are consistently put in "time out" for inappropriate verbal behavior (saying "nah," talking back, having temper tantrums) decrease the frequency of those behaviors. Likewise, when meaningful privileges are withdrawn for inappropriate behavior (being late, not completing chores, drinking alcohol), the behaviors usually decrease.

Beatings and whippings will also temporarily decrease the negative verbal and nonverbal behaviors, but there are major side effects. First, punishing children by inflicting violence teaches them that it is okay to physically hurt someone smaller. Hence, parents may be inadvertently teaching their child to use violence in the family. Second, the person who is physically beaten learns to fear and avoid the punisher. Parents who beat their children should be aware that they are teaching their children to fear and to avoid them (the parents). Third, children who grow up in homes in which corporal punishment is used are more likely to be aggressive and disobedient (Kandel, 1990).

Increasingly, parents are becoming aware of the positive benefits of the use of noncorporal methods of punishment. Both parents who had abused their children and a control group who had not abused their children reported that the use of "time out" was more acceptable than spanking (Kelley et al., 1990).

To Reward or Not Reward Positive Behavior?

Most parents agree that some form of punishment is necessary to curb a child's inappropriate behavior, but there is disagreement over whether positive behavior (taking out the trash, cleaning up one's room, making good grades) should be rewarded by praise, extra privileges, or money. Some parents feel that a child should do the right things anyway and that to reward them is to bribe them. One parent said, "My kid is going to do what I say because I say so, not because I am going to give him something for doing it."

Other parents feel that both the child and the parent benefit when the parents reward the child for good behavior. Rewarding a child for a behavior will result in the child engaging in that behavior more often, so that the child develops a set of positive behaviors. The parents, in turn, feel good about the child.

Rather than ask whether it is good or bad to reward children for positive behavior, parents might ask, "What behavior do I want my child to engage in?" Once that behavior is identified, it is necessary to ensure that positive things happen when the behavior occurs and negative things happen when it doesn't. Children who are rewarded by praise or privileges for being polite, doing their chores, and completing their homework and who are punished by having privileges withdrawn for the opposite behaviors will soon learn to engage in the behavior their parents want them to engage in.

Which Parenting Style?

There are several styles from which parents may choose in rearing their children:

Authoritarian. Parents demand obedience from their children and severely punish disobedience. Unless tempered with love and affection, children tend to resent this style of parenting.

Permissive-Indulgent. Parents allow their children to do as they please and give them things to make them happy. There is very little conflict because the children usually get their way. Some children lose respect for parents who allowed too much freedom.

Permissive-Neglecting. Unlike permissive-indulgent parents who know where their children are and what they are doing, permissive-neglecting parents are often unaware of the child's whereabouts or behavior. The parents are preoccupied with their own lives. Children growing up under this style often feel that they are not wanted.

Permissive-Firm. Parents give children the freedom to experience their world but put firm restrictions on the children. Children learn that they can explore their world, but within parentally prescribed limits. They experience both the trust of being allowed to explore and the affection of their parent's firmness.

How Long Should Children Live With Their Parents?

Nine percent of women (ages 25–29) and 19 percent of men (ages 25–29) continue to live with their parents (Schnaiberg & Goldenberg, 1989). Their motivations are to save money, continue living in a stable environment, and avoid the psychological risk of going out on their own.

As long as offspring and parents agree with the arrangement, living with parents as an adult can be beneficial and enjoyable to both parties. But unless the rules of living together have been discussed and agreed on (most parents are concerned that their children not use drugs, not bring home late-night companions, and help with chores), parents often feel used and offspring often feel belittled. The choice to stay should be made in reference to maximizing and maintaining positive relationships with one's parents. If the young adult stays and saves money but damages the relationship with the parents in doing so, the price may be too high.

How Long Should Parents Let Adult Children Live With Them?

Parents view the dilemma of when the child should leave home from different perspectives. Most parents want to provide a home for their children but feel that it is in the best interest of the offspring to leave home and become independent—to learn to rely on their own resources—at some time.

Deciding when to nudge the reluctant offspring out of the nest isn't easy. Most parents gently encourage their offspring to get a job and an apartment. Others require that their offspring do work around the house (yard, laundry, food preparation and/or cleanup) or pay rent. Still others resort to insisting that their adult children leave. "We have our own right to live," said one parent.

Perhaps the best choice for both parents and offspring is to make their feelings known to each other. Doing so avoids the buildup of resentments that may result in a heated argument and a permanent distancing of the relationship between the respective parties.

How Should Parents Respond When Their Children Want to Return Home?

Once children leave home and get married, they may get divorced or become unemployed and want to return home. About 40% of young adults return to their parent's home to live at least once (Riche, 1990). Most parents are not prepared for the return of their children, are not pleased with the arrangement, and have problems with their offspring over "their coming and going" and "cleaning and maintenance" (Barber, 1989; Eberle, 1987; Clemens & Axelson, 1985).

The marriages of parents who have adult children living with them also suffer. Almost half of the parents in one study complained that the presence of an adult child in the home had a negative effect on their marriage (Clemens & Axelson, 1985). While most parents do not mind their adult children returning for a brief time (Greer, 1986), most parents seem to prefer to live their life independent of their children and encourage their children to do likewise.

Impact of Social Influences on Choices

How we behave as parents has more to do with the society in which we live than with our individual predispositions. "Spare the rod, and spoil the child," uninvolved fathers, and full-time mothers have been altered somewhat by the infusion of "time out for misbehavior," birthing fathers, and career women. Compared to past generations, today's parents are less likely to beat their children, fathers are more likely to be involved with their children, and women are more likely to be spending time outside the home earning money. The latter two changes have an economic base. Not only has motherhood been altered by the supposed necessity for the mother to work outside the home, but her doing so has put more pressure on the father to share in the parenting work load. Hence, forces beyond ourselves impact on our lives.

Transitions

TRADITIONALLY, THE UNITED STATES has had an adversary system of divorce in which one party was found innocent and the other guilty. Under the "fault doctrine," it was necessary to prove that one spouse had performed some specific act that had been detrimental to the other spouse. For example, the wife might say (and prove), "He beat me" (physical cruelty), or "He won't give me money for the children" (nonsupport). Likewise, the husband might accuse his wife of having an affair (adultery). Under any of these circumstances, the "innocent party" would be granted a divorce.

In 1970, as an alternative to the adversary system of divorce, California initiated the "no-fault divorce," which allows spouses to terminate their marriage if either spouse feels that there are "irreconcilable differences."

Under the no-fault system, spouses who don't want to live with each other because they are not happy, have grown apart, or don't love each other any more can get a divorce with relative ease.

By 1991, all states had adopted similar no-fault provisions. Other labels for "irreconcilable differences" include "irretrievable breakdown," "irremediable breakdown," and "no reasonable likelihood of preserving the marriage." Some states have adopted separation as a ground for divorce. Under this provision, the spouses only need to live apart for six months to one year (depending on the state) to provide evidence of "irreconcilable differences." However, in states where alimony is granted to the "innocent" spouse, adversarial legal proceedings still occur.

C H A P T E R

16

Divorce and Widowhood

CONTENTS

IS IT TRUE?

1. Ex-spouses with joint custody are usually more friendly to each other than ex-spouses when one parent has sole custody.

2. Young children tend to feel closer to fathers than to mothers after a divorce.

3. Researchers agree that the long-term effects of divorce on children are negative.

4. Blacks, Mexican Americans, and Asian Americans tend to adjust more easily to widowhood than do whites.

5. Children are usually quick to put their aging parents in a nursing home.

1 = F; 2 = F; 3 = F; 4 = T; 5 = F

:: Divorce

Divorce and death are the principal means by which marriages end. (Others are annulment and desertion.) Such endings are accompanied by many emotions—frustration, disappointment, grief, relief, hope—and sometimes by growth. In this chapter, we will explore the process of and adjustment to marital dissolution by divorce and death.

> ■ **DATA:** *Every year, there are more than 1 million divorces in the United States. The range is usually between 1,180,000 and 1,210,000* (Statistical Abstract of the United States: 1990, *Table 80*).

Preceding these divorces, spouses typically express feelings like:

> I'm tired of waiting for things to get better. I'm afraid that 20 years from now we'll be in the same stale relationship. Let's separate.
> I feel trapped and want out.
> It's not that I think bad things about you; it's just that I don't think about you at all anymore.
> I am involved in a new relationship and want a divorce.

What began at a wedding ceremony, usually with a minister, parents, and friends, ends in a courtroom with a judge, lawyers, and strangers. The reality of day-to-day living has failed to meet the hopeful expectations the partners shared during courtship.

In this section, we will look at the social and individual reasons for why spouses divorce. The social context of divorce has as much to do with divorce as the individuals who actually implement a divorce.

> Divorcees are people who have not achieved a good marriage; they are also people who would not settle for a bad one.
>
> —PAUL BOHANNAN

Causes of Divorce

Determining the causes of divorce is not easy. The reasons are embedded in the individuals, their interaction, and the society in which they live. First, let's look at the larger social context.

Societal Factors. A number of factors have combined to make divorce increasingly common in America. They include the following.

CHANGING FAMILY FUNCTIONS. Many of the protective, religious, educational, and recreational functions of the family have largely been taken over by outside agencies. Family members may now look to the police, the church or synagogue, the school, and commercial recreational facilities rather than to each other for fulfilling these needs. The result is that although meeting emotional needs remains a primary function of the family, there is less reason to keep the family together.

DECREASED ECONOMIC DEPENDENCE OF WIFE. In the past, the unemployed wife was dependent on her husband for food and shelter. No matter how unhappy her marriage was, she stayed married because she was economically dependent on her husband. Her husband literally represented her lifeline.

Finding gainful employment outside the home made it possible for the wife to afford to leave her husband if she wanted to. Now that almost 70 percent of all wives are employed (and this number is increasing), fewer and fewer wives are economically trapped in an unhappy marriage relationship. This economic independence sometimes translates into divorce.

FEWER MORAL AND RELIGIOUS SANCTIONS. The Catholic church no longer excommunicates divorced Catholics who remarry. Many priests and clergy recognize that divorce may be the best alternative in a particular marital relationship and attempt to minimize the guilt members of their congregation may feel at the failure of their marriage. Increasingly, marriage is more often viewed in secular rather than in religious terms.

> There is no society in the world where people have stayed married without enormous community pressure to do so.
> —MARGARET MEAD

DIVORCE MODELS. As the number of divorced individuals in our society increases, the probability increases that a person's friends, parents, siblings, or children will be divorced. The more divorced people a person knows, the more normal divorce will seem to that person. The less deviant the person perceives divorce to be, the greater the probability that that person will divorce if that person's own marriage becomes strained.

LESS PARENTAL CONTROL OVER MATE SELECTION. In the past, American parents have had more control over whom their son or daughter married; such factors as family background, social class, and property were given priority. The result of such parentally controlled mate selection was that the partners had more in common than love feelings. Today, however, love may be the primary consideration in the decision to marry, and feelings of love are sometimes not enough to weather 50 years together.

SOCIETAL GOAL OF HAPPINESS. The goal of happiness is viewed by society as a major reason to marry. When spouses stop having fun, they often feel there is no reason to stay married.

> I began to see an awful lot of children who were screwed up because the parents were screaming all night. I decided that it wasn't great advice to say "stay together" for the sake of the children.
> —ANN LANDERS

☐   C O N S I D E R A T I O N   ☐

The reason you stay married may not be the same reason you get married. Most people marry for love, fun, and happiness. However, marriage sometimes blunts these emotions and focuses the spouses' attentions on work and childrearing. Asian Americans and Mexican Americans have lower divorce rates than whites or blacks because they consider the family unit to be of greater value than their individual interests. To be unhappy is less likely to result in movement toward divorce for these groups (Mindel et al., 1988).

LIBERAL DIVORCE LAWS. California has one of the most liberal divorce laws in America. Marital partners who have no children and no more than $4,000 in debts, who have been married less than five years, whose community property does not exceed $12,000 in value, and who have waived alimony rights may fill out their own forms for dividing up the property. After a waiting period of six months, either the husband or wife returns to the court and asks that the judge declare the divorce legal.

All states now recognize some form of no-fault divorce. Although the legal terms are "irreconcilable differences" and "incompatibility," the reality is that spouses can get a divorce if they want to without having to prove that one of the partners is at fault (for example, adultery or drug addiction).

Individual Factors

■ **DATA:** *Women are twice as likely to petition for divorce (National Center for Health Statistics, 1990).*

Although various societal factors may make divorce a viable alternative to marital unhappiness, they are not sufficient to "cause" a divorce. One spouse must actually initiate divorce proceedings. Reasons why a spouse might seek a divorce include the following.

NEGATIVE BEHAVIOR. People marry because they anticipate greater rewards from being married than from being single. During courtship, each partner engages in a high frequency of positive verbal and nonverbal behavior (compliments, eye contact, physical affection) toward each other. The good feelings the partners share as a result of this high frequency of positive behaviors encourage them to get married to ensure that each will be able to share the same experiences tomorrow.

Just as love feelings are based on positive behavior from the partner, hostile feelings are created when the partner engages in a high frequency of negative behavior. Negative behaviors that wives typically complain about in marriage therapy sessions include "doesn't show an interest in what I say, think or feel, criticizes me, drinks too much, and doesn't help with the childcare/housework." Husbands typically complain that their wife "doesn't want sex, criticizes too much, gets upset when I want a few beers with my friends, and nags me about doing stuff."

When a spouse's negative behavior continues to the point of creating more costs than rewards in the relationship, either partner may begin to seek a more reinforcing situation. Divorce (being single again) or remarriage may appear to be a more attractive alternative than being married to the present spouse. Spouses in first marriages seem to be more tolerant and remain married longer.

■ **DATA:** *Of couples who divorced, those in first, second, and third marriages were married an average of 11, 7, and 5 years (National Center for Health Statistics, 1990).*

LACK OF CONFLICT NEGOTIATION SKILLS. Although getting a divorce is one way to handle negative behavior, negotiating the reduction of the negative behavior and replacing it with more positive behavior is sometimes a more rewarding option. One wife said her husband never spent any time with her because he was always busy with his work. So she asked him what she could do to make him want to spend more time with her. He said she could stop criticizing him and approach him for lovemaking (he was always the initiator) twice a week. The exchange worked. He began to come home earlier and not go back to the office at night, and she stopped the criticizing and initiated lovemaking. The result was a change in behavior by both partners, with a subsequent change in their feelings toward each other. "I've got a husband who likes to spend time with me," said the wife. Her husband replied, "Yes, and I've got a wife who's fun to be with."

☐   C O N S I D E R A T I O N   ☐

On our wedding day, we get three things: a wedding license, a wedding ring, and a little red wagon. As we pull our little red wagon down the marital road, inevitably stones (conflicts) flip into the wagon. If we don't get the stones out of the wagon as they collect (if we don't have the negotiating skills to get the conflicts out of our marriage), the stones pile up and the wagon gets too heavy to pull. We give up and stop pulling the wagon—we get a divorce. Within a few years, we have remarried and have gotten another little red wagon into which new stones flip. Unless we develop negotiation skills to reduce the conflicts in our relationships, we are likely to repeat the cycle.

RADICAL CHANGES.   "He's not the same man I married" is not an uncommon cry. People may undergo radical changes (philosophical or physical) after marriage. One minister married and decided seven years later that he did not like being a minister. He left the ministry, got a Ph.D. in psychology, and began to drink and have affairs. His wife, who had married him in the role of minister, now found herself married to a psychologist who spent his evenings at bars with other women. They divorced.

People who get divorced have stopped talking to each other.

Spouses may also experience severe physical changes. One wife was in an automobile accident that broke her neck and put her in a wheelchair. "The car and my neck were not the only things that were wrecked," she said of the accident. "It changed our marriage. I was no longer the worker, companion, and lover I had been. We divorced."

BOREDOM. A 26-year-old woman who had been married for four years said, "It's not that my husband is terrible. I'm just tired of the same thing all the time. I dated a lot before I was married, and I miss the excitement of new people." "Satiated" best describes her feelings. She was bored, as though she had been watching the third rerun of a TV movie. She viewed divorce as a means of freeing herself from a stale relationship.

EXTRAMARITAL RELATIONSHIP. About 50 percent of all husbands and wives have intercourse with someone other than their spouse during their marriages (Thompson, 1983). Spouses who feel mistreated by their partners or bored and trapped sometimes consider the alternative of a relationship with someone who is good to them, exciting, new, and who offers an escape from the role of spouse to the role of lover.

Extramarital involvements sometimes hurry a decaying marriage toward divorce because the partner begins to contrast the new lover with the spouse. The spouse is often associated with negatives (bills, screaming children, nagging); the lover, almost exclusively with positives (clandestine candlelight dinners, new sex, emotional closeness). The choice is stacked in favor of the lover. Although most spouses do not leave their mate for a lover, the existence of an extramarital relationship may weaken the emotional tie between the spouses so that they are less inclined to stay married.

Negative behavior, lack of negotiation skills, radical changes, boredom, and extramarital relationships are only five of the reasons people say that they want to get divorced. Others include "can't hold a job," "too much drinking," "too authoritarian," "doesn't understand me," "lousy lover," "physical abuse," and "no longer in love." Regardless of the reason, the motivation is to get away from the spouse in order to live alone or with someone new.

Movement Toward Divorce

Relationships go through certain stages when they are winding down. Figure 16.1 illustrates the progressive movement toward divorce. First, the partners in a deteriorating relationship decrease the frequency of positive behavior and increase the frequency of negative behavior toward each other. This usually results in fewer compliments, less affection, and more criticism and hostility.

Then the partners often stop spending time together. Some live apart, increasing the chance that they will divorce (Rindfuss and Stephen, 1990). Failure to spend time together makes it impossible for spouses to recreate the positive feelings necessary to motivate them to stay married.

■ **DATA:** *Thoughts about divorce are not unusual. Out of 181 spouses, 20 percent reported they had thought about separation during the previous year (Bugaighis et al., 1985–1986).*

The vow of fidelity is an absurd commitment, but it is the heart of marriage.
—FATHER ROBERT CAPON

Moving from marriage to divorce is like traveling to a foreign country; few can afford the fare, and few know how to cope en route or what to expect when we arrive.
—ELEANOR DIENSTAG

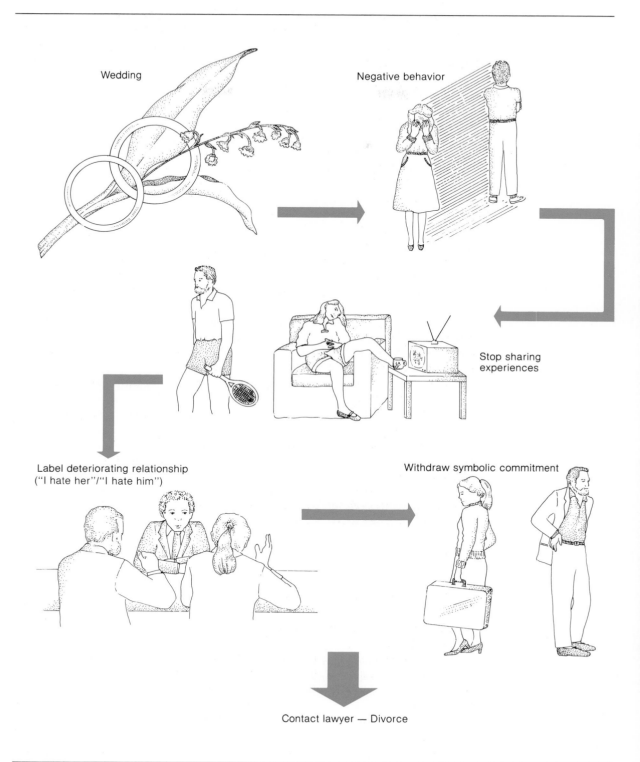

Wedding

Negative behavior

Stop sharing experiences

Label deteriorating relationship
("I hate her"/"I hate him")

Withdraw symbolic commitment

Contact lawyer — Divorce

FIGURE 16.1
Stages in a Deteriorating Relationship

As thoughts of divorce continue and feelings between the marital partners grow more distant, the deteriorating relationship may be negatively labeled. One partner, more often the wife, eventually says, "I think we should get a divorce." This labeling is significant and seems to carry the couple to the lawyer. A husband and father of two children said, "After she told me she wanted a divorce, things haven't been the same. I feel dead inside."

Then comes a public demonstration that the marriage is ending. The spouses take off their rings, go alone (or with someone new) to events they would normally attend together, and tell family, friends, children, and co-workers of the impending separation. Once the symbols of the marriage are withdrawn, one spouse often moves out. Once spouses separate, the chance that they will eventually get divorced dramatically increases.

☐   C O N S I D E R A T I O N   ☐

The progression toward divorce can be stopped at any point, but the earlier the better. The best place to stop it is in the beginning when either partner becomes upset at the behavior of the other. Talking about what is upsetting and negotiating a change in the behavior will take the source of negative feelings out of the relationship. Otherwise, the negative feelings move the spouses along toward the next stage of divorce, and the difficulty of reversing the pattern increases.

A divorce becomes final when a judge issues a judgment declaring that the marriage has ended under the laws of a particular state. If the couple has children, the divorce decree will specify custody of the children, the visitation rights of the noncustodial parent, and the amount of child support due to the custodial parent. Some spouses can decide these issues themselves and have their decisions written into the divorce agreement. Other spouses are so hostile they hire an attorney who may criticize the partner in court as punishment and an attempt to get more money. Some attorneys encourage this hostility so that they can spend more time on the case, increasing the fees they charge.

■ **DATA:** *The cost of hiring an attorney and going to court over issues of custody and division of property is around $12,000. A mediated divorce costs about $1,000 (Neumann, 1989).*

As noted in the above data reference, an alternative to litigation is mediation. Mediators assist spouses who have decided to divorce in negotiating the items of custody, visitation, division of property, and support. The negotiated agreements are then incorporated into the divorce settlement agreement. Compared to a litigated divorce, mediation is usually less expensive, less time consuming (two to three months vs. two to three years), and less apt to encourage hostility between the partners (Marlow & Sauber, 1990).

Characteristics of Divorced People

Spouses who get divorced tend to have different characteristics than those who stay married (Canabal, 1990; Pavalko and Elder, 1990; Norton & Moorman, 1987). Some of these include:

1. Marrying in teens
2. Premarital pregnancy
3. Low income
4. Having divorced parents
5. No high school education
6. Having little in common
7. Not spending time together
8. Urban residence
9. Having no children
10. Having only female children
11. Having another partner available
12. Living in the western, south central, mountain, or Pacific region
13. Interreligious marriage
14. Interracial marriage
15. Low status occupation
16. Courtship of less than one year
17. Being in a second marriage
18. Married less than five years
19. Having a seriously ill child
20. Having an alcoholic spouse
21. Not religiously devout
22. Having no preschool children
23. Thinking seriously about divorce
24. Talking about divorce with the spouse
25. Being a combat veteran

☐   C O N S I D E R A T I O N   ☐

The above list of divorce characteristics should be viewed cautiously. Although unlikely, it is possible that someone with all of the above characteristics could be happily
married, just as someone with none of these characteristics could get divorced. Each
of us is a potential candidate for divorce (even Ann Landers divorced after 36 years).

Completing the Divorce Proneness Scale in the Self-Assessment section provides
one index of the probability of getting divorced. It is only suggestive and should
be interpreted as such.

Consequences of Divorce

For most people, divorce is one of the most devastating emotional experiences
they encounter. Some reasons follow.

Loss, Disruptions, and Negative Labeling. A marriage and family counselor
who divorced after 25 years of marriage said, "I knew all about divorce, except
what it felt like." In spite of the prevalence of divorce and the suggestion that it
may be the path to greater self-actualization or fulfillment, most divorced people
report some amount of personal disorganization, anxiety, unhappiness, and
loneliness (Myers, 1989). "If I were miserable in a second marriage," said one

SELF ASSESSMENT

The Divorce Proneness Scale

This scale is designed to indicate the degree to which you are prone to get a divorce. There are no right or wrong answers. After reading each sentence carefully, circle the number that best represents your feelings.

1 Strongly agree
2 Mildly agree
3 Undecided
4 Mildly disagree
5 Strongly disagree

	SA	MA	U	MD	SD
1. My parents have a happy marriage.	1	2	3	4	5
2. My closest married friends have happy marriages.	1	2	3	4	5
3. My partner and I can negotiate our differences.	1	2	3	4	5
4. I plan to marry only once.	1	2	3	4	5
5. I am a religious person.	1	2	3	4	5
6. I will wait until my mid-twenties to marry.	1	2	3	4	5
7. I do not require a number of sexual relationships to be happy.	1	2	3	4	5
8. I think it best to marry only after I have known my partner for at least a year.	1	2	3	4	5
9. My parents approved of the person I married.	1	2	3	4	5
10. My partner and I have an adequate source of income to meet all of our expenses and some money left to play with.	1	2	3	4	5

SCORING: Add the numbers you circled. 1 (strongly agree) is the least divorce-prone response, and 5 (strongly disagree) is the most divorce-prone response. The lower your total score (10 is the lowest possible score), the less your chance of getting a divorce; the higher your score (50 is the highest possible score), the greater your chanceof getting a divorce. A score of 30 places you at the midpoint in terms of being divorce prone.

(NOTE: This Self-Assessment is intended to be thought provoking and suggestive, it is not a clinical diagnostic instrument).

spouse who was going through a divorce, "I'd stay married. I couldn't go through this again."

Feelings of depression and despair occur in response to three basic changes in the divorced person's life: termination of a major source of intimacy, disruption of the daily routine, and awareness of a new status—divorced person. Going through a divorce can also lead to feelings of failure or defeat, especially if the other partner initiated the divorce. But the partner who initiates the divorce also undergoes considerable stress and guilt in making the decision to separate. One study found that the partner who initiated the divorce experienced more trauma than the noninitiator (Buehler, 1987).

If you are married, you probably did so because you were in love and wanted to share your life with another. Like most people, you needed to experience feelings of intimacy in a world of secondary relationships. Others don't care about the intimate details of your life, nor do they have the background of a shared history to understand you. One reason divorce hurts is that you lose one of the few people who knew you and who, at least at one time, did care about you. Becoming aware that the marriage is not going to work out and thinking about divorce are the most difficult times in the divorce process.

Divorce also shatters your daily routine and emphasizes your aloneness. Eating alone, sleeping alone, and driving alone to a friend's house for companionship are role adaptations made necessary by the destruction of your marital patterns. Depression and suicide, for both whites and blacks, are much more frequent among divorced persons than married persons (Stack, 1989; Broman, 1988).

Although we tend to think of divorce as an intrinsically stressful event, one researcher suggests that the amount of stress involved in a divorce is determined by how stressful the marriage was (Wheaton, 1990). In marriages that are very stressful, a divorce may be beneficial in allowing unhappy spouses to escape from a chronically stressful situation. In very stressful marriages then, going through a divorce may actually reduce more stress than it creates.

Without forgiveness life is governed by . . . an endless cycle of resentment and retaliation.
—ROBERTO ASSAGIOLI

Financial Consequences. The media often emphasize that the wives of famous and wealthy husbands often receive large amounts of money and property in their divorce settlement. For example, in 1990, many Americans followed the media reports concerning the divorce of Ivana and Donald Trump and wondered how much of their $1.7 billion fortune Ivana would receive.

However, many studies show that divorce has detrimental economic effects on women and their children (Arendell, 1987; Day & Bahr, 1986; Weitzman, 1985). In one study of divorced women, 71 percent said that financial difficulties were their major problem (Amato & Partridge, 1987). Financial problems are most severe for women who have never worked, have no skills, have little education, and have primary physical custody of one or more children (Crossman & Edmondson, 1985).

One factor that contributes to the financial difficulties of divorced women with children is the failure of many fathers to pay child support.

■ **DATA:** *Among divorced and separated women who had been awarded child support, only 48 percent received full payment, 26 percent received a partial amount, and 26 percent received no payment (Buehler, 1989).*

Fathers may not pay child support because of intense emotional pain and isolation, revenge against the ex-wife, and/or irresponsibility. In addition, some fathers may have inadequate funds to cover overextended financial commitments (Buehler, 1989). If the father remarries, he may find it difficult to economically sustain two households.

Divorced people often become very introspective.

One researcher observed the economic consequences of divorce for women and suggested that:

> Young women must be encouraged to stay in school and invest in their own future. They must be made to realize that they may have to support their family without the help of a spouse should divorce occur (Mauldin, 1990, 145).

☐   C O N S I D E R A T I O N   ☐

One of the keys in changing the economic consequences of divorce for women is to change societal values and attitudes. Maudlin (1990) suggests that if societal attitudes encourage women to prepare for a traditional family life and discourage them from preparing to work outside the home, women will continue to suffer economic consequences following divorce.

Adjustment After Divorce

Given that divorce is, for most people, an emotionally devastating experience, what are some ways to successfully cope with this experience? The following list contains some suggestions from a clinical psychologist (Turner, 1990) who has assisted hundreds of ex-spouses through the divorce process.

1. *Consider contacting a divorce mediator rather than an attorney.* Attorneys are trained to channel divorcing spouses into an adversarial pattern of relating. This pattern keeps conflict and hostility high while minimizing the chance to relate amicably. In addition, the money spent on attorneys puts an additional financial stress on the divorcing individuals.

2. *Take some responsibility for the divorce.* Since marriage is an interaction between the spouses, one person is seldom totally to blame for a divorce. Rather, both spouses share in the demise of the relationship.

3. *Learn from the divorce.* View the divorce as an opportunity to improve one's self for future relationships. What did you do that you might consider doing differently in the next relationship?

4. *Create positive thoughts.* Divorced people are susceptible to feeling as though they are a failure and are "no good." Improving their self-esteem is important for divorced persons. This can be done by systematically thinking positive thoughts about one's self. One technique is to write down 21 positive statements about one's self ("I am honest," "I am a good cook," "I am a good parent," etc.) and transfer these to seven 3 X 5 cards each containing three statements. Take one of these cards with you each day and read the thoughts to yourself at three regularly spaced intervals (e.g., ten in the morning, four in the afternoon, ten at night). This ensures that you are thinking good things about yourself and are not allowing yourself to drift into a negative set of thoughts.

5. *Avoid alcohol and other drugs.* The stress and despair that some people feel following a divorce makes them particularly vulnerable to the use of alcohol or other drugs; women may be more vulnerable than men (Doherty et al., 1989). Drugs and alcohol should be avoided because they produce an endless negative cycle. For example, stress is relieved by alcohol; alcohol produces a hangover and negative feelings; the negative feelings are relieved by more alcohol, producing more negative feelings, etc.

6. *Relax without drugs.* Deep muscle relaxation can be achieved by systematically tensing and relaxing each of the major muscle groups in the body. Alternatively, Yoga, transcendental meditation, and intense prayer can cause a deep state of relaxation. Whatever the form, it is important to schedule a time each day to get relaxed.

7. *Engage in aerobic exercise.* Exercise not only helps to counteract stress but also to avoid it. Jogging, swimming, riding an exercise bike, or other similar exercise for thirty minutes every other day increases the oxygen to one's brain and helps facilitate clear thinking. In addition, aerobic exercise produces endorphins in the brain, which create a sense of euphoria ("runner's high").

8. *Engage in fun activities.* Divorced people tend to sit at home and brood over their "failed" relationship. This only compounds their depression. Doing what they have previously found enjoyable—movies, horseback riding, skiing, attending sporting events, etc.—provides an alternative to sitting on the couch alone.

9. *Seek others.* Divorced individuals may benefit from interaction with others. Asking friends to make you aware of people you might date, joining social clubs, or taking trips designed for singles provide opportunities for becoming involved again. Ex-spouses who do not adjust to divorce stay negatively attached to the former mate and do not develop a new intimate relationship (Tschann et al., 1989).

10. *Take time to heal.* Since self-esteem usually undergoes a battering as a result of divorce, a person is often vulnerable to making commitments before working through feelings about the divorce. The time period most people need to adjust to divorce is between 12 and 16 months (Turner, 1990). Although being available to others may help to repair one's self-esteem, getting remarried during this time should be considered cautiously.

Hatred does violence to the container in which it is held long after it hurts the victim for whom it is intended.

—ANONYMOUS

Relationship with Ex-spouse. It is assumed that ex-spouses hate each other and have only hostile interactions with each other following a divorce. Researcher Constance Ahrons, who studied the actual relationships between 98 pairs of ex-spouses, has observed four patterns (Stark, 1986).

PERFECT PALS. These ex-spouses (12 percent of the sample) continued to be involved in each other's lives. Neither spouse had remarried or was living with someone else. One such couple shared a duplex apartment, so that their children could come and go freely between the homes.

COOPERATIVE COLLEAGUES. Comprising 38 percent of the sample, these ex-spouses were able to minimize potential conflicts and to have a moderate amount of interaction. Basically, they made an effort to get along because it was in the best interest of the children.

ANGRY ASSOCIATES. Unable to contain their anger and hostility, 25 percent of the sample had a moderate amount of interaction but most of it was unpleasant. They were unable to separate their roles of spouse and parent.

FIERY FOES. Another 25 percent of the sample consisted of ex-spouses who had little interaction but always fought when they did. The divorcing couple in the film, *War of the Roses*, were fiery foes. Any interaction between them was hostile and bitter; neither was civil toward the other. Such a continued negative relationship has a negative effect on the partner's personal adjustment to the divorce (Isaacs & Leon, 1988).

The type of relationship ex-spouses have with each other is unrelated to whether they have joint custody or one partner has sole custody of their children. New partners seem to affect men and women differently. Men's psychological adjustment seems to be enhanced by having a new partner. "Women's psychological adjustment, by contrast, apparently is not so much promoted by new supportive relations, as it is negatively affected by the presence of conflictual relationships between significant family members. Women appear to be more affected by the residual hostility from the past marriage and problematic relations between partners and children in their new marriages or relationships (Coysh et al., 1989).

Relationship with Former In-laws Forty-nine separated and divorced spouses shared how their divorce had affected the relationship with their former in-laws. In general, "loss of contact and change in the quality of the relationship occurred rapidly once the separation had become known" (Amert, 1988, 684).

■ **DATA:** *Only 11 percent of the ex-spouses maintained good relationships with their former in-laws following the separation (Amert, 1988, 679).*

Sexuality After Divorce

Of the more than 2 million people getting divorced, most will have intercourse within one year of being separated from their spouse. The meanings of intercourse for the separated or divorced vary. For many, intercourse is a way to reestablish—indeed, repair—their crippled self-esteem. Divorce is often a shattering emotional experience. The loss of a lover, the disruption of a daily routine, and the awareness of a new and negative label ("divorced person") all converge on the individual. Questions like "What did I do wrong?" "Am I a failure?" and "Is there anybody out there who will love me again?" loom in the minds of the divorced. One way to feel loved, at least temporarily, is through sex. Being held by another and being told that it feels good gives people some evidence that they are desirable. Because divorced people may be particularly vulnerable, they may reach for intercourse as if for a lifeboat. "I felt that as long as someone was having sex with me, I wasn't dead and I did matter," said one recently divorced person.

Whereas some divorced people use intercourse to mend their self-esteem, others use it to test their sexual adequacy. The divorced person may have been told by the former spouse that he or she was an inept lover. One man said his wife used to make fun of him because he was occasionally impotent. Intercourse with a new partner who did not belittle him reassured him of his sexual adequacy and his impotence ceased to be a problem. A woman described how her husband would sneer at her body and say no man would ever want her because she was so fat. After the divorce, she found men who thought she was attractive and who did not consider her weight to be a problem. Other divorced men and women say that what their spouses did not like, their new partners view as turn-ons. The result is a renewed sense of sexual desirability.

Beyond these motives for intercourse, many divorced people simply enjoy the sexual freedom their divorced state offers. Freed from the guilt that spouses who have extramarital intercourse experience, the divorced can have intercourse with whomever they choose.

Before getting remarried, most divorced people seem to go through predictable stages of sexual expression. The initial impact of the separation is followed by a variable period of emotional pain. During this time, the divorced may turn to intercourse for intimacy to soothe some of the pain, although this is rarely achieved.

This stage of looking for intimacy through intercourse overlaps with the divorced person's feeling of freedom and the desire to explore a wider range of sexual partners and behaviors than marriage provided. "I was a virgin at marriage and was married for 12 years. I've never had sex with anyone but my spouse, so I'm curious to know what other people are like sexually," one divorced person said.

But the divorced person soon tires of casual sex. One man said he had been through 22 partners since his divorce a year ago. He likened his situation to that of a person in a revolving door who is in motion but isn't going anywhere. "I want to get in a relationship with someone who cares about me and vice versa." The pattern is typical. Most divorced people initially use sex to restore their ailing self-esteem and to explore sexual parameters, but they soon drift toward sex within the context of an affectionate love relationship.

▪▪ Children and Divorce

▪ **DATA:** *More than 50 percent of all divorces involve children. More than 1 million children are affected by divorce annually (National Center for Health Statistics, 1990).*

For the mother who becomes a single parent (mothers are given custody in 90 percent of all divorce cases involving children), the transition may be difficult. Due to the stress of earning an income and being solely responsible for the children, single mothers report more depression and decreased life satisfaction than married parents or single fathers (Burden, 1986). And when employed single mothers are compared to employed mothers in two-parent homes, single mothers report having much less time for themselves and very limited recreational time (Sanik & Mauldin, 1986). Of these stresses and lack of play time, one single mother said, "All of a sudden you recognize that you are on your own. You can't count on your ex-husband to pay child support, so you are stuck with paying the light bill out of your earnings."

■ **DATA:** *In a study of divorced women, 80 percent reported that "lack of money" was their primary concern (Quinn & Allen, 1989).*

Most men earn higher incomes after divorce because their incomes were higher than the women's incomes during marriage. No-fault divorce means that all income and property acquired during the marriage is divided equally. However, because the woman usually gets custody, much of her income is spent in reference to the children. In effect, in most cases, divorce means that a mother must still take care of her children—but on half the amount of money she had when she was married (Weitzman, 1985). In response to this inequity, in 1986, a New York State Court of Appeals awarded Loretta O'Brien $188,000, or 40 percent of what the court determined her husband's medical license was worth. (O'Brien and her husband had been married nine years, during which time he earned his M.D. degree.) In effect, the court viewed the ability of O'Brien's husband to earn money as property that could be divided.

Parents who fail to make their child support payments, may be required to make payments directly to the court. Alternatively, these payments may be withheld from the parent's paycheck, and back child support may be withheld from tax refunds that are due the parent. The federal child support amendment, approved in 1988, requires that the state attach the wages of parents who fall one month behind in their child support payments.

In addition to economic problems, a single parent must confront several other issues (see "Having a Child without a Spouse" on page 436). These issues include satisfying the emotional needs of children alone, satisfying adult emotional and sexual needs, and finding adequate childcare. An extended family may be helpful in coping with childcare concerns. Blacks, Mexican Americans, and Asian Americans are more likely to reach out to extended family than are whites. (Mindel et al., 1988).

Effects of Divorce on Children

The research on the effects of divorce on children has produced mixed results. In one study comparing single-parent and two-parent homes, the researchers found that the quality of the environment for children one year after the separation or divorce was very similar in both homes (Rosenthal et al., 1985–1986). In another study of 60 families five years after divorce, about one-third of the children were happy and thriving; about one-third were doing reasonably well, and about one-third were depressed (Wallerstein & Kelly, 1980). Children's grades also drop following the divorce of their parents.

The adjustment of the children of divorced parents often depends on how the parents treat each other and their children following the divorce. Children evidenced the best adjustment when parents continued a cordial relationship with each other and a stable visitation schedule was maintained (Isaacs, 1988).

The biological sex of the child may also be important in adjusting to a divorce. In general, female children seem to make a more successful adjustment than male children do. One explanation for this finding is that because women get custody in most cases, their male children suffer from the lack of regular access to their fathers who are role models for boys (Lowery & Settle, 1985).

Researchers have identified the conditions under which a divorce occurs that predict the most positive adjustment for the children (Tschann et al., 1989; Guidubaldi, 1988, 188)

1. The parents have been able to resolve their postdivorce conflict and anger.
2. Both the custodial and noncustodial parent continue a very positive relationship with their children.
3. Boys, more than girls, need a positive relationship with their father.
4. A temperament on the part of the child which allows him or her to adjust to change easily. Kalter (1989) found that the reaction of the child may have more to do with the child's temperament than with the way the parents behave. Some children are not easily frustrated and readily adapt to change; others have difficulty with even minor changes.

There are positive outcomes of divorce for children. In a review of studies on the impact of divorce, the researchers (Demo & Acock, 1988) observed that adolescents whose parents had divorced were characterized by greater maturity, feelings of efficacy, and an internal locus of control. Another study of more than 8,000 adults compared those who were living with both parents and those who were living with only one parent at age 16. No significant differences were found between the two groups. Few long-term effects were noted as being associated with family disruption of any sort. The effects that were considered important were almost all positive, indicating that the individual may have been strengthened by the experience (Nock, 1982, 38). In another study, researchers (Mechanic and Hansell, 1989) found that adolescents whose parents had divorced had a greater sense of well-being than adolescents whose parents were still together and still fighting.

☐   C O N S I D E R A T I O N   ☐

The differences in the findings of these studies may be related to the different perceptions that individuals have of an event (divorce) and not to the event itself. Divorce, by itself doesn't do anything to children. It is how the parents teach their children to regard the event and the children's relationship with the respective parents after the divorce that influences the eventual outcome.

Some research suggests that children tend to feel closer to mothers than to fathers after the divorce. Children view fathers as less available to be with them and to help them with their social and emotional problems.

■ **DATA:** *When divorced children were asked, "who do you go to when you feel down in the dumps?" 72 percent mentioned their mother but only 19 percent identified their father (Johnson et al., 1988).*

In general, research findings on the long-term effects of divorce on children are mixed and further research is needed in this area. There is less debate, however, over the short-term reactions children have to divorce. The initial reactions of children to a divorce vary and depend on such factors as their age and level of cognitive and emotional functioning. Some of the more common reactions, however, include the following:

1. A period of grief and sadness.
2. A sense of fear and insecurity. Children may wonder if their parent(s) still love them, if they will still see the parent who has left, and if the other parent may also leave.
3. Anger and resentment. Children may be angry toward the parent who leaves the unit or the parent who the child blames for the divorce.
4. Self-blame. If the couple has argued over issues concerning the children, the children may feel that they are somehow responsible for their parents' divorce. Children may also feel that their misbehavior caused a parent to leave the family unit.
5. Desire to reunite the family. Some children wish for the parents to reconcile and may even try to influence their parents to do so.

□   C O N S I D E R A T I O N   □

Some of the reactions of children to divorce described above may continue long after the initial period following the divorce. For example, children may be angry toward one or both parents for years following a divorce. In addition, some children may continue to wish that their parents were back together, even after one or both parents are remarried.

▪▪ Alternatives to Divorce

Divorce is not the only means of terminating a marriage. Others include annulment, separation (legal or informal), and desertion.

Annulment

■ **DATA:** *Ten percent of 216 Catholics reported that annulment was the way their first marriage ended (O'Flaherty & Eells, 1988).*

The concept of annulment has its origin in the Roman Catholic church, which takes the position that marriage is indissoluble, except by death. An annulment states that no valid marriage ever existed and returns both parties to their pre-marital status. Any property that has been exchanged as part of the marriage arrangement is returned to the original owner. Neither party is obligated to support the other economically.

Common reasons for annulments are fraud, bigamy, under legal age, impotence, insanity, and lack of understanding. A university professor became involved in a relationship with one of his colleagues. During courtship he promised her that they would rear a "house full of babies." But after the marriage, she discovered that he had had a vasectomy several years earlier and had no intention of having more children. The marriage was annulled on the basis of fraud—his misrepresentation of himself to her. Most annulments are for fraud.

Bigamy is another basis for annulment. In our society, a person is allowed to be married to only one spouse at a time. If another marriage is contracted at the time a person is already married, the new spouse can have the marriage annulled. All 104 wives of confessed and convicted bigamist Giovanni Vigliotto were entitled to have their marriages to him annulled.

Most states have age requirements for marriage. When individuals are younger than the minimum age and marry without parental consent, the marriage may be annulled if either set of parents does not approve of the union. However, if neither set of parents or guardians disapproves of the marriage, it may be regarded as legal; the marriage is not automatically annulled.

Intercourse is a legal right of marriage. In some states, if a spouse is impotent, refuses to have intercourse, or is unable to do so for physical or psychological reasons, the other spouse can seek and may be granted an annulment.

Insanity and a lack of understanding of the marriage agreement are also reasons for annulment. Someone who is mentally deficient and incapable of understanding the meaning of a marriage ceremony can have a marriage annulled. However, being drunk at the time of the wedding is insufficient grounds for annulment.

Although annulments are granted by civil courts, a Catholic who divorces and wants to remarry in the Church must have the first marriage annulled by the Church. Grounds for Church annulment vary widely; the result is that Catholics seeking to annul their first marriage must find a reason the Church will accept. In some cases, marriages have been annulled even though the couple has been married several years and has children. Julio Iglesias had his marriage of eight years (which included three children) annulled.

Separation

■ **DATA:** *Four percent of 216 Catholics reported that separation was the way their first marriage ended (O'Flaherty & Eells, 1988).*

An equally small proportion of unhappy relationships end in separation. Separations, or limited divorces, are sought by couples who, for religious or personal reasons, do not want a divorce or do not want one yet and who do not have grounds for an annulment. These couples contact lawyers and ask that they draw up separation papers.

Typical items in a separation agreement include: (1) the husband and wife live separately; (2) their right to sexual intercourse with each other is ended; (3) the economic responsibilities of the spouses to each other is limited to the separation agreement; and (4) custody of the children is specified in the agreement, with visitation privileges granted to the noncustodial parent. The spouses may have relationships with others, but neither party has the right to remarry. Although some couples live under this agreement until the death of one spouse, others draw up a separation agreement as a prelude to divorce. In some states, being legally separated for one year is a ground for divorce.

An informal separation is similar to a legal separation except that no lawyer is involved in the agreement. The husband and wife settle the issues of custody, visitation, alimony, and child support between themselves. Because no legal papers are drawn up, the couple is still married from the state's point of view.

Attorneys advise against an informal separation (unless it is temporary) to avoid subsequent legal problems. For example, after three years of an informal separation, a mother decided that she wanted custody of her son. Although the father would have been willing earlier to sign a separation agreement that would have given her legal custody of her son, he was now unwilling to do so. Each spouse hired a lawyer and had a bitter and expensive court fight.

☐   C O N S I D E R A T I O N   ☐

If marital partners decide that their marriage is not working out but feel that divorce is premature, they can get a legal separation. This specifies the important elements (custody, alimony, child support, visitation, and so on) of the relationship and cannot be changed arbitrarily by either partner. If the couple are unable to work out the details of the legal separation between themselves, they may consult with a mediator.

Desertion

Desertion differs from informal separation in that the deserter walks out and breaks off all contact. Although either spouse may desert, it is usually the husband who does so. A major reason for deserting is to escape the increasing financial demands of a family. Desertion usually results in nonsupport, which is a crime.

The sudden desertion by a husband sometimes has more severe negative consequences for the wife than divorce would. Unlike the divorced woman, the deserted woman is not free to remarry for several years. In addition, she receives no child support or alimony payments, and the children are deprived of a father.

Desertion is not unique to husbands. Although infrequent, wives and mothers also leave their husbands and children. Their primary reason for doing so is to escape from an intolerable marriage and feeling trapped by the role of mother. "I'm tired of having to think about my children and my husband all the time—I want a life for myself," said one woman who deserted her family. "I want to live too." But such desertion is not without its consequences. Most mothers who desert their children feel extremely guilty.

▪▪ Widowhood

A marriage relationship may also be ended by the death of one spouse.

■ **DATA:** *Approximately one-fourth of all married women will become widows by age 65, and one-half of the remaining women will become widows by age 75. During the same age span, only one man in five will lose his wife. The mean duration of widowhood for women is 14 years; for men it is just over 6 years (Pitcher & Larson, 1989, 59).*

As a society, we tend to avoid acknowledging the reality of death. We speak of people "passing away" and being placed in "memorial gardens" rather than of people dying and being buried in the ground. In our society, "we have a phobia about death" (LaNeave, 1990). To help view death as a normal part of life, courses on death and dying are being offered in some high schools (Moore, 1989), as well as in colleges and universities. The unrealistic attitudes about death that are perpetuated in our society contribute to the fact that the death of a spouse may be one of the most severe social and personal crisis events we experience. One widow described her husband's death as "the most difficult tragedy of my life, which has caused a change in my lifestyle, friends, and finances. . . . you never get over it completely. My husband has been dead 27 years, and I still think about him and the life we shared every day."

> In the long run we are all dead.
> —JOHN MAYNARD KEYNES

Although the death of a spouse may be very traumatic, in some cases it may relieve more stress than it creates. For example, caring for a spouse who is chronically ill and in great pain may be incredibly stressful. The level of stress may actually decrease after the death of the chronically ill spouse.

The level of stress experienced by a widowed person also depends on the quality of the marital relationship prior to the spouse's death. Wheaton (1990) found that a problematic marriage reduces the distress and grief felt after a spouse's death and may be less intense if the marriage was problematic.

The Bereavement Process

The bereavement process usually lasts from 12 to 18 months (Pitcher & Larson, 1989). Although every individual reacts somewhat differently, widows and widowers go through the same stages as they adjust to the death of their partner. These stages usually involve shock, denial, anger, deep grief, disorientation (sometimes), and construction of a new identity as a person without a partner.

Grief may be functional or dysfunctional. Dysfunctional grief involves retaining the pain, rather than releasing it. In contrast, functional grief is characterized by "an ability to change and an ability to manage the stresses of this period of intense physical, mental, and social difficulty" (Pitcher & Larson, 1989, 67).

☐   C O N S I D E R A T I O N   ☐

The initial impact of a spouse's death may be devastating, but most people can adjust to the loss. Time and other relationships seem to help. "It took about two years for me to get over the pain, loneliness, and self-pity I felt after she died," said one widower. "And I still get a wave of sadness at Christmas, the anniversary of her death, her birthday, and our wedding date. I'm remarried now, and that helps a lot to get over thinking about it every day." The widowed spouse might consider that the immediate and intense pain felt at the time of the spouse's death usually decreases over time.

Widowhood is usually a
very lonely experience.

Adjustment for Widows

Although both women and men go through the same stages of bereavement, each person responds differently to particular aspects of the adjustment. Many wives are married to husbands who make more money than they do, and a husband's death often means an end to the much needed regular monthly check. "Aside from missing my husband terribly," recalls one widow, "it means I'll have to move out of this house because we didn't have insurance to pay off the house and my salary won't cover the house payment each month."

Other widows experience difficulties in making decisions. "Paul and I always talked everything over, and I depended on him to make the final decision." Decisions about selling property, moving into smaller living quarters, and buying health insurance may be particularly difficult for the woman who has always depended on her husband to make such decisions.

But there are compensating factors for widows. The widow is more likely than the widower to derive emotional satisfaction from her children and grandchildren. She is also more likely to be welcome in the home of the son or daughter, where she can help with the household responsibilities.

In addition, widows have more people with whom they share a similar role than widowers do. Large churches may have Sunday school classes for widows; community centers offer special programs for them. Between interactions with other widows and with children and grandchildren, the widow is likely to continue her traditional domestic activities, which often give order and stability to her life. Although her husband is gone, what she does each day does not change that much.

The Effect of Ethnicity

Nonwhites and persons in close-knit ethnic communities are often characterized by more structured roles for widows, less of a couple orientation between husband and wife, and more developed support systems for the widowed. For these reasons, Blacks, Mexican Americans, and Asian Americans tend to have an easier adjustment to the role of widow than whites. For example, nonwhites are more likely to house and care for widows inside the kinship system, whereas whites are more likely to live alone after the death of a spouse (Pitcher & Larson, 1989).

Adjustment for Widowers

Whereas most wives expect to be a widow some day (and can have a psychological dress rehearsal), few husbands expect to be widowers. However, men who lose their spouses do not seem to face the economic hardship widows do. In a study of 27 widowers, money was not mentioned as one of the more serious concerns (Clark et al., 1986). The two most frequently cited problems were loneliness and accepting the fact that the mate had died.

■ **DATA:** *Out of 27 widowers, 63 percent reported that loneliness was the most difficult aspect of coping with the death of a spouse (Clark et al., 1986).*

Most of the men had found ways to help them cope with their loneliness. Over one-half of them saw their children at least once a week, and 85 percent reported

> I miss her as much as I ever have. It never gets easier. There are friends who would like to see me find another woman for the companionship. I wouldn't do it. It would never work.
>
> —JOHN WOODEN OF HIS WIFE, DECEASED FOR 53 YEARS.

E X H I B I T 16.1

Caring for Widowed or Elderly Parents

Not all widows are elderly, and all elderly parents are not widowed. Nevertheless, adult children are often challenged with the responsibility of taking care of elderly parents (Finley, 1989). Contrary to the myth that children in the United States abrogate responsibility for their elderly parents, children institutionalize their parents only as a last resort. Most of the time, adult children provide some type of care for their elderly parents outside of a formal institutionalized setting (Barber, 1989). "With a great deal of difficulty," answered Jeff McAllister, Executive Director of the Pitt County Council on Aging in Greenville, North Carolina. I had asked him how children of aging parents can take care of them without disrupting their own marital lives. "We have to face it," he said, "there is just no easy or simple answer. It's a very complex problem." McAllister gave two examples:

> A wife told of her widowed mother, age 86, who could not walk because of a broken hip.
> The wife had two children of her own. And with no siblings she had no brothers or sisters to help her care for her mother. She couldn't quit work to care for her mother because she needed the money. But the money she earned went to pay for the cost of having someone stay with her mother during the day when she was at work. Although there was no economic advantage to her working, she had to continue doing so to keep her own health insurance and retirement fund. Her husband was frustrated because she was always "exhausted."
> A husband whose mother had Alzheimer's disease was busy building his law practice and could not devote time to care for her. He was also an only child. So his mother came to live with him, his wife, and their young daughter. But the mother became irritable and irrational, and the wife (who did not work outside the home and was there to care for her all day) said that "she could not stand it anymore."

As these examples indicate, caring for a dependent aging parent requires a great deal of effort, sacrifice, and decision making on the part of the 5 million adults in the United States who cope with this situation daily.

And it is often the woman who ends up with the responsibility for her aging parent(s) while she is still taking care of her own children (Finley, 1989).

But men are not immune to the responsibility for aging parents. One son said he drives 2½ hours (one way) three days a week to get his father groceries, take him for a walk, and do his laundry. "I'm all he's got," said the son.

The emotional toll is heavy. Guilt, resentment, and anger are the most commonly reported feelings. The guilt comes from having promised the parents that they would be cared for when they became old and frail. Paying off the promise often entails more than the children ever expected. Or the offspring may feel guilty that they resent having to disrupt their own lives to care for their parents. Or they may feel guilty that they are angry about the frustration their parents are causing them. "I must be an awful person to begrudge taking my mother supper," said one daughter. "But I feel that my life is consumed by the demands she makes on me, and I have no time for myself."

CARING FOR A WIDOWED OR AGING PARENT—SOME SUGGESTIONS

Be Realistic. Responding to the needs of an aging parent is not easy, and there is no magic solution. Don't be unhappy if there isn't a quick answer to every problem. Accept the fact that caring for an aging parent is one of the more difficult challenges you will ever face.

Involve Siblings. More than 85 percent of all adult children have brothers or sisters. Because some offspring live closer to or have closer relationships with one or both parents, they may inadvertently wind up as almost total caretakers of their aging parents. It is a mistake not to involve your brothers and sisters in the care of parents. Tell them that your parents can no longer fend for them-

having a "close" relationship with at least one child (see Exhibit 16.1). Over 70 percent had close friends they saw each week, and many were members of a social or religious organization.

When asked what they did to help them cope with the death of their spouses, most of these men cited being with their family, reading, and believing in God. Dating someone new also helped; almost one-half of these men had done so.

selves, and ask them to help you help them. If the siblings cannot offer practical support, they may be responsible enough to send money. Try to arrange it so that they send you a specified amount every month to help pay for the costs of caring for your parents. Whatever the nature of the support, ask for it.

Communicate Openly. It is important to keep communication channels open with your parents. Tell them how you feel, try to engage them in conversation, and don't "spring" anything on them. Some children decide on their own that it is time to put their parent in a nursing home, drive them to the door, and dump them. They avoid bringing up the subject of "nursing home" for fear that their parents will react with hurt and anger. Such fears are realistic. Interviews with the elderly in need of care revealed that the elders fear being a burden, hide their troubles and feelings, and generally feel no sense of contribution to the household (Parsons et al., 1989).

Express Love. Such open discussions with your parents may be difficult and should be tempered with expressions of love. Tell your parents that you love them. Touch them. Hug them. Show them that you care about them and intend to see that their needs are taken care of. Elderly people often spend a lot of time alone and sometimes wonder if anyone cares for them.

Investigate the Meals-on-Wheels Program. For individuals with full-time jobs and children of their own, the need for support in caring for an elderly parent is particularly great. Many communities offer a Meals-on-Wheels program in which the local council on aging will send a well-balanced meal twice a day to persons who are homebound, who can't prepare food for themselves, and who have no one to do it for them.

The Meals-on-Wheels program is particularly helpful to adults whose aging parents live in another town or state. "I called up the local council on aging in the county in which my mother lives," said one daughter, "told them I had a mother who lived there and who needed food and could they help. They took food to her door twice a day, every day. It was a lifesaver for both of us."

Investigate Elderly Day Care. Another way you can get a break from constant attention to the needs of your aging parent is through a program that provides a place for you to take your parent during the day. Elderly day care, available in some communities, allows working adults to take their parents to the day care center in the morning and return after work. The parent has shelter, food, and others to interact with throughout the day and can stay with the son or daughter at night. "This is a wonderful program for us," said one daughter. "This way we didn't have to put my mother in a nursing home but had full-time coverage for her."

Investigate Chore-service Program. Similar to the Meals-on-Wheels and elderly day care programs, the chore-service program sends someone to help the elderly do chores that they cannot do by themselves. If you live in another town or state, you may be able to provide chore services for your aging parent long distance (for example, someone to mop the kitchen floor, clean the gutters, and grocery shop).

Meals-on-Wheels, elderly day care, and chore-service programs are not available in every city. You should contact your county Council on Aging or your local Social Services Department to determine the nearest location to you of self-help facilities for the elderly. Your parents' physician may also be aware of what resources for the elderly are available in your community.

Explore Organizations to Join. A number of organizations have evolved for persons who are caring for an aging parent. Children of Aging Parents (CAPS; 2761 Trenton Road; Levittown, PA 19056) has more than 12,000 members who are experiencing similar concerns. Joining such an organization helps to reduce the feeling that you are facing the problems of caring for an aging parent alone. An additional resource is the National Support Center for Families of the Aging (P.O. Box 245; Swarthmore, PA 19081). A newsletter, "Advice for Adults with Aging Parents," is available from Helpful Publications, Inc. (310 West Durham Street; Philadelphia, PA 19119).

Another problem that many widowers face is difficulty in coping with domestic tasks. Husbands who have been socialized into rigid gender role patterns of behavior may have relied on their wives to perform most domestic chores. In the event of their spouse's death, these husbands may find themselves unprepared to take care of basic domestic needs, such as cooking, shopping, and laundry.

Sexuality after Being Widowed

The 13 million widowed in the United States differ from the divorced in their sexual behavior. In general, widowed men and women have intercourse less frequently than those who are divorced. A major reason is the lack of an available partner, but others have intercourse less frequently because they feel they are "cheating" on the deceased. "It's a guilty feeling I get," expressed one widower, "that I shouldn't want to get involved with someone else and that I shouldn't enjoy it."

Social expectations also do not support sexual expression among the widowed. Some older widows are considered "too old" for sex. The lack of an available sexual partner, feelings of guilt at the idea of cheating on the deceased, and an unsupportive social context seem to conspire against the widowed. When a group of widows (ages 67–78) were asked how they coped with their sexual feelings when they had no partner, they responded:

> Only by keeping busy. Keep occupied with various activities and friends.
> Do physical exercise. Have many interests, hobbies.
> We just have to accept it and interest ourselves in other things.
> By turning to music or other arts, painting, dancing is excellent . . . using nurturant qualities, loving pets, the elderly, shut-ins. Reading, hiking. . . lots more. My mind controls my sex desires (Starr & Weiner, 1982, 165–167).

Another way that some widows may cope with their sexual needs is through masturbation. However, given the generally negative view our society has of masturbation, some widows may not consider this option.

■■ Preparation for Widowhood

Planning ahead for eventual widowhood may be difficult because it forces us to confront our own and our spouse's mortality. But as one widow said, "It's not as hard as making the arrangements later." There are several key areas to consider in preparing for the death of either spouse. Such preparation includes giving careful, early attention to wills, insurance, titles, and funeral expenses.

Wills

A will ensures that your money and property will be left to the people you want to have them. If you die intestate (without leaving a will), the state in which you lived will decide who gets what and how much. For example, suppose a married man with no children dies intestate. Although he may want his wife to have everything, she may get only half if the state law provides that his parents are entitled to half of his estate.

☐　　　　　　　C O N S I D E R A T I O N　　　　　　　☐

Before drawing up a will, consult a lawyer who is familiar with laws relating to the distribution of property and the guardianship of children in your state. If you move

continued on next page

> to another state, you might have a lawyer there check your will to make sure that it conforms to the laws in that state.

Under federal law, an estate tax (also known as an inheritance or transfer tax) return must be filed for every estate with gross assets of more than $600,000. And any tax due must be paid at the time the return is filed. Estates valued at less than $600,000 are not taxed.

Money is thicker than blood.
—JACK WRIGHT, ESTATE ATTORNEY

Although a will is necessary in preparing for the death of a spouse, two additional documents are important when either spouse becomes incapacitated. A Living Will is a document stating that should you become terminally ill, with no hope for recovery, you do not want your life prolonged by artificial means. A Living Will can be obtained from the Society for the Right to Die (250 West 57th Street, New York, NY 10107), a nonprofit organization. California, Idaho, and Wisconsin require that the document be resigned every five years; Georgia has a seven-year resigning requirement.

The second document, Power of Attorney, allows your spouse to sign papers on your behalf in the event that you become incapacitated and are unable to do so. For example, if you were brain dead and your spouse needed income, he or she could sell land that you owned if you had signed a Power of Attorney.

Insurance

Having made a will, check your life insurance policy for amount, type of payment, and ownership of policy. Assuming that the insured feels that the face value of the policy is adequate, check to see if the payments are to be made monthly or in a lump sum. One widow was only allowed to receive monthly payments of $125 instead of the lump sum she needed to pay off her house.

Titles

Valuable things such as houses, cars, and checking accounts may be subject to estate taxes if they are part of the deceased spouse's estate. If these are listed in the wife's name, they are considered her property and consequently not part of the husband's estate. Of course, if the wife dies first, the husband will face the inheritance tax problems she was to have avoided. So some balance of ownership is desirable. Retitling property to achieve a balance is only advisable, however, in a stable relationship. The transfer of ownership of large items followed by a divorce may create havoc.

Funeral Expenses

Currently, the cost of a funeral may range from $1,000 to $10,000, the average cost being around $7,000. This price includes embalming, casket, funeral service, use of the building for visitation, and cars for transportation to the cemetery.

The federal government now requires funeral homes to itemize the cost of their services and materials before an individual agrees to any arrangements. In addition, funeral homes are required to give price information over the telephone to permit customers to shop around. Embalming is often not necessary; it is usually required only if the death was caused by a specific contagious disease such as polio, diphtheria, or tuberculosis.

Alternative ways to avoid traditional funeral expenses are donating the body to medical research, cremation, and joining a memorial society. If you want to consider body donation, contact a medical school near you and ask about the procedure for donating your body for medical research and teaching. This usually involves completing an application specifying your wish that your body be donated to a certain medical school. At the time of your death, your spouse would then contact a local mortician, who would make the necessary arrangements with the medical school. Although you have donated your body to medicine, the traditional funeral service may still be held, with your body being transferred to the medical school rather than to a cemetery afterward; or your body may be removed to the medical school immediately after death, and a memorial service may be held later. In either case, the medical school usually pays the embalming fee and the cost of transporting your body up to 200 miles.

Cremation is another alternative. The cost is usually about $200. As with body donation, a memorial service may be held at a cost of around $1,000.

☐   C O N S I D E R A T I O N   ☐

Some people feel uncomfortable with both body donation and cremation but don't want to pay the high price of a traditional funeral service. By joining a memorial society or a similar organization, they buy a predetermined package of funeral services at a fixed cost before their death. Details on the nearest society can be obtained by writing to the Continental Association of Funeral and Memorial Societies (1828 L Street, N.W., Suite 1100, Washington, DC 20036).

▪▪ Trends

The number of divorces in the United States will continue to increase. Martin and Bumpass (1989) estimate that "about two-thirds of all first marriages are likely to disrupt" (p. 49). Factors which are contributing to this trend include an individualistic society, divorce models, economically independent wives, and the absence of severe negative sanctions levied against those who divorce.

Divorce mediation will also become more widespread. Rather than end their relationship in an expensive and hostile court fight, more spouses will negotiate the conditions of their settlement with the aid of a divorce mediator. Mediating the issues of custody, visitation, child support, and spouse support (if there is any), usually saves both time and money. More importantly, mediation facilitates a more cooperative co-parenting relationship between ex-spouses who have children and it sets the stage for negotiating rather than litigating subsequent issues as they come up. An increasing number of jurisdictions have mandatory child custody mediation programs, whereby parents in a custody dispute are required to attempt to resolve their dispute through mediation before their case may be heard in court. More such programs will be instituted in the coming years.

Legal changes will include more granting of joint custody, custody to the father, and the assignment of child support responsibilities to *both* parents. The legal precedent for joint child support has already been established. In *Silvia v. Silvia* (1980), the Massachusetts court ruled that the incomes of both parents should be considered in assigning the economic responsibilities of the respective parents for the support of their children.

▪▪ Summary

Societal factors contributing to divorce include the loss of family functions, more employed wives, and liberal divorce laws. Individual factors include negative behavior, lack of conflict-negotiation skills, and extramarital relationships.

Certain categories of people have a higher chance of divorce than others. These include those who were premaritally pregnant, married in their teens, and have been previously divorced.

For most, divorce represents a difficult transition. Loss of self-esteem, lack of money, and concern over children are among the potential consequences of divorce. But divorce may also represent a bridge from an unhappy relationship and personal confinement to new relationships and personal growth. For many, divorce is also the beginning of a new life. Conditions predicting a positive divorce adjustment include reducing one's stress through regular exercise and relaxation, avoiding alcohol/drugs, engaging in enjoyable activities with friends, delaying any new marital commitments for 12 to 18 months, and thinking positive thoughts about one's self.

Death terminates marriages that do not end by divorce, annulment, or desertion. Adjusting to the death of one's spouse is one of the most difficult life crises a person experiences. Although the trauma of widowhood cannot be avoided, it can be eased by attending to various concerns, such as wills, insurance, titles, and funeral arrangements. A great deal of money can often be saved by drawing up a will, having adequate life and health insurance, putting property in the wife's name, and donating one's body to a medical school.

Questions for Reflection

1. How do you feel about the high rate of divorce in the United States? Do you feel that it is a sign of a decaying society because it reflects people's lack of commitment to family life? Or is the high divorce rate a sign of family strength because it reflects that people value marriage so much that they are unwilling to remain in unhappy marriages?
2. Do you feel the people you know who have gotten divorced are glad they did so? Why do they feel this way? Do you think they are better off? Why or why not?
3. How comfortable would you be discussing funeral arrangements with your partner? Do you feel the potential money saved is worth the discomfort you might feel?

References

Amato, P. R. and S. Partridge. Women and divorce with dependent children: Material, personal, family, and social well-being. *Family Relations,* 1987, *36,* 316–320.

Amert, Anne-Marie. Relationships with former in-laws after divorce: A research note. *Journal of Marriage and the Family*, 1988, *50*, 679–686.

Arendell, T. J. Women and the economics of divorce in the contemporary United States. *Signs: Journal of Women in Culture and Society*, 1987, *13*, no. 1, 121–135.

Barber, C. E. Burden and family care of the elderly. *Aging and the Family*. Edited by Stephen J. Bahr and Evan T. Peterson. Lexington, Mass.: Lexington Books, 1989, 243–259.

Bowers, I-Chiao H. and S. J. Bahr. Remarriage among the elderly. *Aging and the Family*. Edited by Stephen J. Bahr and Evan T. Peterson. Lexington, Mass.: Lexington Books, 1989, 83–95.

Broman, C. L. Satisfaction among Blacks: The significance of marriage and parenthood. *Journal of Marriage and the Family*, 1988, *50*, 45–51.

Buehler, C. Initiator status and divorce transition. *Family Relations*, 1987, *36*, 82–86.

Bugaighis, M. A., W. R. Schumm, A. P. Jurich, and S. R. Bollman. Factors associated with thoughts of marital separation. *Journal of Divorce*, 1985–1986, *9*, 49–59.

Burden, D. S. Single parents and the work setting: The impact of multiple job and home-life responsibilities. *Family Relations*, 1986, *35*, 37–44.

Canabal, M. E. Economic approach to marital dissolution in Puerto Rico. *Journal of Marriage and the Family*, 1990, *52*, 515–530.

Clark, P. G., R. W. Siviski, and R. Weiner. Coping strategies of widowers in the first year. *Family Relations*, 1986, *35*, 425–430.

Cornell, Laurel L. Gender differences in remarriage after divorce in Japan and the United States. *Journal of Marriage and the Family*, 1989, *51*, 457–463.

Coysh, William S., J. R. Johnston, J. M. Tschann, J. S. Wallerstein, and M. Kline. Parental postdivorce adjustment in joint and sole physical custody families. *Journal of Family Issues*, 1989, *10*, 52–71.

Crossman, S. M. and J. E. Edmondson. Personal and family resources supportive of displaced homemakers' financial adjustment. *Family Relations*, 1985, *34*, 465–474.

Day, R. D. and S. J. Bahr. Income changes following divorce and remarriage. *Journal of Divorce*, 1986, *9*, no. 3, 75–88.

Demo, David H. and Alan C. Acock. The impact of divorce on children. *Journal of Marriage and the Family*, 1988, *50*, 619–648.

Doherty, William J., S. Su, and R. Needle. Marital disruption and psychological well-being. *Journal of Family Issues*, 1989, *10*, 72–85.

Dreman, Solly, Emda Orr, and Roy Aldor. Competence or dissonance? Divorcing mothers' perceptions of sense of competence and time perspective. *Journal of Marriage and the Family*, 1989, *51*, 405–416.

Farnsworth, J., M. A. Pett, and D. A. Lund. Predictors of loss management and well-being in later life widowhood and divorce. *Journal of Family Issues*, 1989, *10*, 102–121.

Finley, Nancy J. Theories of family labor as applied to gender differences in care giving for elderly parents. *Journal of Marriage and the Family*, 1989, *51*, 79–86.

Freed, D. J. and T. B. Walker. Family law in the fifty states. *Family Law Quarterly*, 1986, *19*, 331–441.

Guidubaldi, J. Differences in children's divorce adjustment across grade level and gender: A report from the NASP-Kent State Nationwide Project. *Children of Divorce: Empirical Perspectives on Adjustment*. Edited by Sharlene A. Wolchik and P. Karoly. New York: Gardner Press, Inc., 1988, 185–231.

Guidubaldi, J., H. K. Cleminshaw, J. D. Perry, B. K. Nastasi, and J. Lightel. The role of selected family-environment factors in children's post-divorce adjustment. *Family Relations*, 1986, *35*, 141–151.

Hauser-Dann, J. Divorce mediation: A growing field? *The Arbitration Journal*, 1988, *43*, 15–22.

Hobart, Charles. The family system in remarriage: An exploratory study. *Journal of Marriage and the Family*, 1988, *50*, 649–661.

Isaacs, M. B. The visitation schedule and child adjustment: A three year study. *Family Process*, 1988, *27*, 251–256.

Isaacs, M. and G. Leon. Divorce, disputation, and discussion: Communicational styles among recently separated spouses. *Journal of Family Psychology*, 1988, *3*, 298–311.

Johnson, Colleen Leahy, Linnea Klee, and Catherine Schmidt. Conceptions of Parentage and Kinship Among Children of Divorce. *American Anthropologist*, 1988, *90*, 136–144.

Kalter, Neil. *Growing up with divorce.* New York: Free Press/Macmillan, 1989.

Keshet, J. K. The remarried couple: Stresses and successes. *Relative Strangers*. Edited by William R. Beer. 1988. New Jersey: Rowman and Littlefield.

Kitson, G. C., K. B. Babri, and M. J. Roach. Who divorces and why. *Journal of Family Issues*, 1985, *6*, 255–293.

Kolata, Gina. Child Splitting. *Psychology Today*, 1988, *22*, 34–37.

LaNeave, S. Personal communication. January 28, 1990. Greenville, N.C. 27858.

Lowery, C. R. and S. A. Settle. Effects of divorce on children: Differential impact of custody and visitation patterns. *Family Relations*, 1985, *34*, 455–463.

Maccoby, E. E., C. E. Depner, and R. H. Mnookin. Coparenting in the second year after divorce. *Journal of Marriage and the Family*, 1990, *52*, 141–155.

Marlow, L. and S. R. Sauber. *The Handbook of Divorce Mediation.* New York: Plenum Publishing Corporation, 1990.

Martin. T. C. and L. L. Bumpass. Recent trends in marital disruption. *Demography*, 1989, *26*, 37–52.

Mauldin, Teresa A. Women who remain above the poverty level in divorce: Implications for family policy. *Family Relations*, 1990, *39*, 141–146.

Mechanic, David and S. Hansell. Divorce, family conflict, and adolescents' well-being. *Journal of Health and Social Behavior*, 1989, *30*, 105–116.

Mindel, C. H., R. W. Habenstein, and R. Wright, Jr. *Ethnic families in America: Patterns and variations.* New York: Elsevier, 1988.

Moore, C. M. Teaching about loss and death to junior high school students. *Family Relations*, 1989, *38*, 3–8.

Morgan, E. S. *The Puritan family.* Boston: Public Library, 1944.

Myers, M. F. *Men and divorce.* New York: Guliford Press, 1989.

National Center for Health Statistics. Advance report, final divorce statistics, 1987. Monthly vital statistics report; *38*, no. 12, suppl. 2. Hyattsville, Md.: Public Health Service, 1990.

Neumann, Diane. *Divorce mediation: How to cut the cost and stress of divorce.* New York: Holt, Henry, and Company, 1989.

Nock, S. L. Enduring effect of marital disruption and subsequent living arrangements. *Journal of Family Issues*, 1982, *3*, 25–40.

Norton, A. J. and J. E. Moorman. Current trends in marriage and divorce among American women. *Journal of Marriage and the Family*, 1987, *49*, 3–14.

O'Flaherty, Kathleen M. and Laura W. Eells. Courtship behavior of the remarried. *Journal of Marriage and the Family*, 1988, *50*, 499–506.

Pavalko, E. K. and G. H. Elder, Jr. World War II and divorce: A life-course perspective. *American Journal of Sociology*, 1990, *95*, 1213–1234.

Parsons, Ruth J., E. O. Cox, and P. J. Kimboko. Satisfaction, communication and affection in caregiving: A view from the elder's perspective. *Journal of Gerontological Social Work*, 1989, *13*, 9–20.

Pitcher, B. L. and D. C. Larson. Early widowhood. *Aging and the Family*. Edited by Stephen J. Bahr and Evan T. Peterson. Lexington, Mass.: Lexington Books, 1989, 59–81.

Quinn, Peggy and K. R. Allen. Facing challenges and making compromises: How single mothers endure. *Family Relations*, 1989, *38*, 390–396.

Rindfuss, R. R. and E. H. Stephen. Marital noncohabitation: Separation does not make the heart grow fonder. *Journal of Marriage and the Family*, 1990, *52*, 259–270.

Rosenthal, D., G. K. Leigh, and R. Elardo. Home environment of three- to six-year-old children from father-absent and two-parent families. *Journal of Divorce,* 1985–1986, *9,* 41–48.

Sanik, M. M. and T. Mauldin. Single- versus two-parent families: A comparison of mothers' time. *Family Relations,* 1986, *35,* 53–56.

Seltzer, J. A. and S. M. Bianchi. Children's contact with absent parents. *Journal of Marriage and the Family,* 1988, *50,* 663–677.

South, S. J. and G. Spitze. Divorce determinants. *American Sociological Review,* 1986, *51,* 583–590.

Stack, Steven. The impact of divorce on suicide in Norway, 1951–1980. *Journal of Marriage and the Family,* 1989, *51,* 229–238.

Stark, E. Friends through it all. *Psychology Today,* May 1986, 54–60.

Starr, B. D. and M. B. Weiner. *The Starr-Weiner report on sex and sexuality in the mature years.* New York: McGraw-Hill, 1982.

Statistical Abstract of the United States: 1990. 110th ed. Washington, D.C.: U. S. Bureau of the Census, 1990.

Thompson, A. P. Extramarital sex: A review of the research literature. *Journal of Sex Research,* 1983, *19,* 1–22.

Tschann, Jeanne M., Janet R. Johnston, Marsha Kline, and Judith S. Wallerstein. Family process and children's functioning during divorce. *Journal of Marriage and the Family,* 1989, *51,* 431–444.

Turner, Jack. When mediation fails. Presented at conference on "Mediation in Relationships" East Carolina University in Fall, 1989 and revised for this text in 1990. Used by permission of Jack Turner.

Vemer, E., M. Coleman, L. H. Ganong, and H. Cooper. Marital satisfaction in remarriage: A meta-analysis. *Journal of Marriage and the Family,* 1989, *51,* 713–725.

Wallerstein, J. S. and J. B. Kelly. *Surviving the break-up: How children actually cope with divorce.* New York: Basic Books, 1980.

Weinberg, T. Single fatherhood: How is it different? *Pediatric Nursing,* 1985, *11,* 173–176.

Weitzman, L. *The divorce revolution.* Riverside, N.J.: The Free Press, 1985.

Wheaton, Blair. Life transitions, role histories, and mental health. *American Sociological Review,* 1990, *55,* no. 2, 209–223.

White, L. K., D. B. Brinkerhoff, and A. Booth. The effect of marital disruption on child's attachment to parents. *Journal of Family Issues,* 1985, *6,* no. 1, 5–22.

CHOICES

S INCE MORE THAN one-half of all divorces involve children, a basic decision to be made in a divorce is who gets custody of the children? The options include the mother, the father, or joint custody.

There are two separate custody decisions that divorcing parents must make (or a judge must make for them). These two decisions involve the determination of legal custody and physical custody. Legal custody refers to the legal right to make decisions in reference to a minor child. Such decisions include those relating to medical care and education. Legal custody may be granted to one parent, who would have sole responsibility for making decisions in reference to the child. Alternatively, parents may have joint legal custody, whereby both parents would have legal input into the medical and educational decisions regarding the child.

Physical custody refers to where the child will live. Most custody battles are fought over physical custody, not legal custody. The following sections refer to choices involving physical custody of children.

Who Gets the Children? Custody Criteria of Parents

Nine out of 10 custody decisions after divorce result in one parent (usually the mother) receiving primary physical custody of the children with the other parent (usually the father) receiving visitation rights. This arrangement is usually decided on by the divorcing couple. "That's good," said one attorney, "because if spouses don't make their own decisions, the courts will make their choices for them."

The criteria that parents and judges use to determine who will get physical custody of the children include age of the children, sex of the children, emotional relationship of the parents with the children, time available to spend with the children, living conditions, income, and previous care (physical and emotional) of the children by the respective parents.

Who gets physical custody has implications not only for the child but also for the parents. Research demonstrates that parents who get custody of children will continue to benefit from the children being emotionally attached to them. Likewise, the emotional attachment of the children to noncustodial parents tends to decrease (White et al., 1985).

Custody to One Parent?

When the parents disagree about who should have physical custody of the children, a judge must decide. In the past, preference has been given to the mother. Awarding custody to the mother, particularly of younger children, is based on the "tender-years doctrine," which holds that young children need their mother and it is in their best interests to live with her.

This doctrine was challenged by Ken Lewis, a divorced father of two daughters, who contended that the "tender-years doctrine" was an insidious example of sex discrimination. He won custody of his children on the grounds that the word *"mother"* is a verb and that he had demonstrated better mothering skills than the biological mother. Fathers for Equal Rights of Michigan and Canada (P.O. Box 2272, Southfield, MI 48037) is an organization for fathers seeking divorce and custody reform. Dr. Lewis (Child Custody Evaluation, Inc., P.O. Box 202, Glenride, PA 19038) now specializes in interviewing all parties involved in a custody case and making recommendations to the judge. He has evaluated over 600 cases, and the judges have followed his recommendations in over 90 percent of them.

When one spouse gets primary physical custody, the relationship the child has with the noncustodial parent weakens over time (Hobart, 1988). "As time since the separation passes and as their parents remarry, children's contact with absent parents diminishes further" (Seltzer & Bianchi, 1988).

Joint Custody

An alternative to sole custody that is increasingly being considered by parents and the courts is joint custody. Over half of the states have enacted legislation authorizing joint custody. In a typical joint physical custody arrangement, the parents continue to live in close proximity to each other. The children may spend part of each week with each parent or may spend alternating weeks with each parent.

One potential disadvantage of joint custody is that it tends to put hostile ex-spouses in more frequent contact with each other, so that the marital war continues (Maccoby et al., 1990). Children do not profit from being subjected to such frequent fighting (Kolata, 1988).

But joint custody has a positive side. Ex-spouses may fight less if they have joint custody because there is no inequity in terms of the parents' involvement in the children's lives. Children will benefit from the resultant decrease in hostility between parents who have both "won" them. Unlike the sole-parent custody outcome, in which one parent (usually the mother) wins and the father is banished, children under joint custody may continue to benefit from the love and attention of both parents. Children in homes where joint custody has been awarded might also have greater financial resources available to them than children in sole-custody homes.

Joint physical custody may also be advantageous in that the stress of parenting does not fall on one parent, but rather is shared. One mother who has a joint custody arrangement with her ex-husband said, "When Jamie is with her Dad, I get a break from the parenting role, and I have a chance to do things for myself. I love my daughter, but I also love having time for myself." Another joint parenting father said, "When you live with your kids everyday, you're just not always happy to be with them. But after you haven't seen them for 3 days, it feels good to see them again."

Depending on the level of hostility between the ex-partners, their motivations for seeking sole or joint custody, and their relationship with their children, any arrangement could have positive or negative consequences for the spouses and the children. In those cases in which the spouses exhibit minimal hostility toward each other and have strong emotional attachments to their children, as well as the desire to remain an active influence in their children's lives, joint custody may be the best of all possible choices.

Relationship With Ex-Spouse

Spouses who divorce must make a choice in terms of what kind of relationship they will have with each other. This choice is crucial, in that it not only affects their lives, but also their children's lives.

Traditionally, custody "battles" have been hostile and bitter relationships between spouses, with one parent often trying to turn the children against the other parent. But everyone loses when this type relationship is allowed to develop. The parents continue to harbor negative feelings for each other, and the children are caught in the crossfire. They aren't free to develop or express love for either parent out of fear of disapproval from the other parent. Ex-spouses might consider the costs to their children of continuing the "War of the Roses" and call a truce on their behalf. Everyone will profit from the choice.

Impact of Social Influences on Choices

Although we tend to think of divorce as an individual decision, the society in which the spouses live influences whether or not divorce will occur. During the colonial period, the Puritans did not approve of spouses getting a divorce just because they were unhappy. In Massachusetts, there was an average of *one* divorce per year from 1639 to 1760 (Morgan, 1944). This is the ultimate example of social control on the private experience of marriage. Today, in contrast, you can get a divorce just because you don't like your partner (technically called "irreconcilable differences").

17

Remarriage and Stepfamilies

CONTENTS

IS IT TRUE?

1. Most studies comparing first marriages to remarriages suggest that remarriages are significantly happier than first marriages.

2. Spouses in second marriages tend to have a more equalitarian relationship than spouses in first marriages.

3. Stepfamilies have few unique characteristics; they are very similar to biological families.

4. Children are much more likely to accept a stepmother than a stepfather.

5. Spouses in stepfamilies who have a child of their own tend to be more emotionally bonded than spouses who do not have a mutual biological child.

1 = F; 2 = T; 3 = F; 4 = F; 5 = F

T he fact that a high percentage (about 80 percent) of the divorced and widowed remarry suggests that marriage is highly valued in our society. Samuel Johnson has been widely quoted as saying, "Remarriage is the triumph of hope over experience." Lewis Grizzard, the famous Atlanta journalist, said that after his third divorce he put a bumper sticker on his car, "Honk if you're married to Lewis Grizzard." In this chapter we examine the realities of remarriage and stepparenting.

:: Remarriage

Remarriages have become a visible segment of the population of the United States.

■ **DATA:** *About 20 percent (11 million) of all current marriages are remarriages. The average interval between divorce and remarriage is about 3 Years (Giles-Sims & Crosbie-Burnett, 1989). Divorced people and men are more likely to remarry and to do so sooner than widowed people and women (Bowers & Bahr, 1989, 83).*

Preparing for Remarriage

A sample of 100 men and 105 women was asked how they prepared for getting remarried. Over half of this sample prepared for remarriage by living together.

■ **DATA:** *Sixty percent of 205 persons reported that they had lived together before getting remarried as the primary way of preparing for their remarriage (Ganong & Coleman, 1989).*

When remarried spouses who had lived together were compared with remarried spouses who had not lived together, those who had cohabited reported fewer marital disagreements and problems. They also reported higher levels of affection in their relationship (Ganong & Coleman, 1989).

Some couples seek help from others in preparation for remarriage. For example, some couples go through counseling, attend support groups or remarriage/stepparent education programs, and/or consult with friends who have had experience in a remarriage situation. In addition, many couples seek advice on remarriage and stepfamily living from books and other written materials.

In preparing for remarriage, couples may also discuss important issues and concerns. Some topics that couples preparing to remarry might discuss include the following:

1. Finances
2. Discipline of children/stepchildren
3. In-laws
4. Housing
5. Careers
6. Relationship with ex-spouse

Issues Involved in a Remarriage

Whether individuals considering remarriage live together or not, they must deal with certain issues. These include the following (Roberts & Price, 1985–1986; Goetting, 1982):

Boundary Maintenance. Movement from divorce to remarriage is not a static event that happens in a brief ceremony and is over. Rather, ghosts of the first marriage in terms of the ex-spouse and, possibly, children must be dealt with. The parents must decide how to relate to the ex-spouse in order to maintain a good parenting relationship for the biological children and, at the same time, to keep an emotional distance to prevent problems from developing with the new partner. Some spouses continue to be emotionally attached to the ex-spouse and have difficulty breaking away. However, boundary ambiguity does not appear to be a major problem for remarried spouses (Pasley & Ihinger-Tallman, 1989).

Emotional Remarriage. The person begins to trust and love another person in a new relationship. Such feelings may come slowly as a result of negative experiences in the first marriage.

Psychic Remarriage. The person gives up the freedom and autonomy of being single again and develops a mental set conducive to pairing. This transition may be particularly difficult for people who sought a divorce as a means to personal growth and autonomy. These individuals may fear that getting remarried will put unwanted constraints on them.

Community Remarriage. This stage involves a change in focus from single friends to a new mate and other couples with whom the new pair will interact. The bonds of friendship established during the divorce period may be particularly valuable because they have lent support at a time of personal crisis. Care should be taken not to drop these friendships.

Parental Remarriage. Because most remarriages involve children, people must usually work out the nuances of living with someone else's children. Since mothers are usually awarded primary physical custody in 90 percent of the cases, this translates into the new stepfather adjusting to her children. If a spouse has children from a previous marriage who do not live primarily with him or her, the new spouse must adjust to these children on weekends, holidays, vacations, or other visitation times.

Getting remarried influences how often fathers who do not have primary custody see their own children. Fathers who remarry tend to see their children much less often.

■ **DATA:** *Ninety-three percent of children whose fathers had not remarried said that they saw him more than once a month. Once he remarried, the frequency dropped dramatically (Johnson et al., 1988).*

Stepparents who do things with their step-children increase the emotionald bond with them.

The first time you buy a house, you see how pretty the paint is and buy it. The second time, you look to see if the basement has termites. It's the same with men.
—LUPE VELEZ

Economic Remarriage. The second marriage may begin with economic respon-sibilities to the first marriage. Alimony and child support often threaten the har-mony and sometimes even the economic survival of second marriages. One wife said that her paycheck was endorsed and mailed to her husband's first wife to cover his alimony and child support payments. "It irritates me beyond descrip-tion to be working for a woman who lived with my husband for seven years," she added. In another case, a remarried woman who was receiving inadequate child support from her ex-spouse felt too embarrassed to ask her new husband to pay for her son's braces.

Legal Remarriage. Partners in a second marriage may have legal responsibilities in the form of alimony and child support payments to the first marriage. These responsibilities cannot be abandoned with the beginning of a new marriage. The individual must take on a new set of responsibilities while maintaining former responsibilities.

Legal documents that may be appropriate include an asset inventory (to estab-lish what each new spouse owns and brings into the marriage), a premarital agreement (to specify what assets owned by whom will go to whom if the mar-riage ends in divorce or when it ends with the death of one spouse), and a living trust, in which assets from one spouse are transferred to a third party so that the new spouse will not be tempted to ask, "Can we use that money?"

```
☐                C O N S I D E R A T I O N                ☐
```

Some spouses feel it is not romantic to draw up legal documents specifying what will happen to the assets and money in a relationship. These spouses take the position that such an action smacks of distrust. But a lawyer and social worker who have dealt with the problems in remarriages said, "facing possible outcomes does not make them happen" (Bernstein & Collins, 1985, 389).

Remarriage for the Widowed

Remarriage for the widowed is usually very different from remarriage for the divorced. The widowed are usually much older, their children are grown, and they are less likely to remarry.

A widow or widower may marry someone of similar age or someone who is radically older or younger. Marriages in which one spouse is considerably older than the other are referred to as "May-December marriages"; these marriages were discussed in Chapter 8. Here, we will discuss only "December marriages," in which both spouses are elderly.

In a study of 24 elderly couples, the need to escape loneliness or the need for companionship was the primary motivation for remarriage (Vinick, 1978). The men reported a greater need to remarry than the women. Most of the spouses met through a mutual friend or relative (75 percent) and married less than a year after their partner's death (63 percent).

The children of the couples had mixed reactions to their remarriages. Most of the children were happy that their parents were happy and felt relieved that the companionship needs of their elderly parent would now be met by someone on a more regular basis. But some children also disapproved of the marriage out of concern for their inheritance rights. "If that woman marries dad," said a woman with two children, "she'll get everything when he dies. I love him and hope he lives forever, but when he's gone, I want the farm."

The need for companionship is the primary motive for remarriage among the widowed.

Happiness in Second Marriages

How happy are second marriages when compared to first marriages?

> ■ **DATA:** *The data from 16 studies comparing first and second marriages suggest that first marriages are happier. However, "the difference appears to be miniscule and certainly not substantial" (Vemer et al., 1989, 721).*

Some aspects of remarriages may represent an improvement over first marriages. Couples who remarry point to four major differences between their second and first marriages (Keshet, 1988).

1. *Communication.* Communication in the second marriage was more open with the partners having greater skills in talking about their relationship and issues with which they were confronted.
2. *Less conflict.* The marital conflict that did occur was expected and was more easily tolerated. Unlike in their first marriages, the partners felt that it was acceptable for them to disagree.
3. *More equalitarian.* The power in the second marriage was more balanced. "The women felt more included and respected by their second husbands" (p. 30–31).
4. *Greater flexibility.* The partners in second marriages have . . .

   given up the idea that their marriage would reflect the marriage of their own parents or fulfill the impossible American dream. They start out with different names and different bank accounts. The husband can cook, the wife knows how to get the car fixed by herself . . . (p. 33).

⠿ Stepfamilies

With 50 percent of all spouses getting divorced, 80 percent of the divorced remarrying, and 55 percent of those who remarry coming to the new marriage with children from a previous marriage, stepfamilies are not unusual. In this section, we will examine how stepfamilies differ from biological families, how they are experienced from the viewpoint of women, men, and children, and the developmental tasks that must be accomplished to make a successful stepfamily. We will close this section with a look at the choices faced by those about to enter a stepfamily and suggest ways to make such decisions.

Definition and Types of Stepfamilies

A stepfamily consists of remarried spouses with at least one of the spouses having a child from a previous relationship. Stepfamilies are also referred to as reconstituted, remarried, binuclear, new extended, or blended families. The term "blended" is used because the new marriage relationship is blended with the children of at least one previous marriage.

Stepfamilies via divorce are a relatively new phenomena. The sequence of marriage-death-remarriage which was characteristic of the early 20th century has shifted to a new sequence of marriage-divorce-remarriage.

■ **DATA:** *There are 4.3 million stepfamilies in the United States. these represent 17.4 percent of all households with children under age 18 (Glick, 1989).*

Types of stepfamilies include the following:

1. Stepfamilies in which children live with their remarried parent and stepparent.
2. Stepfamilies in which the children from a previous marriage visit with their remarried parent and stepparent.
3. An unmarried couple living together in which at least one of the partners has children from a previous relationship who live with or visit them.
4. A remarried couple in which each of the spouses brings children into the new marriage from the previous marriage.
5. A couple who not only bring children from previous marriages but who, in addition, have a child of their own.

Unique Aspects of Stepfamilies

Stepfamilies are unique compared to couples who live with their biological children. Unlike the biological family, in which the children are genetically related to both parents, children in the stepfamily may be related to only one parent.

☐   C O N S I D E R A T I O N   ☐

The significance to the stepfamily of the biological tie between parent and child is the strong emotional bond that accompanies it. Although stepparents can develop love feelings for their stepchildren, they sometimes do not. The different levels of emotional bonding parents and stepparents have with their children and stepchildren create a context for negative feelings and conflict. "If you don't love my daughter, you don't love me," said a biological mother to the child's stepfather.

Stepfamilies have also experienced a crisis event. The children have been removed from one biological parent (whom they often desperately hope will reappear and reunite with the parent), and the spouse has experienced emotional disengagement and physical separation from a once-loved partner due to divorce or death. Jane, who is divorced with two children, said:

> It's been two years since I divorced Bill, and it's been hard for all of us. The children miss their father a great deal, and they still ask sometimes, "When are you and daddy getting back together?" It hurts me to know that they are separated from their father. But it would hurt even more for me to have to live with their father. Yet I miss being a family and look forward to getting remarried.

But when the remarriage comes, the problems aren't over. When stepfamilies are compared to first families, the spouses in stepfamilies tend to report problems due to the different ways the new spouses view the children—"hers," "his," and "theirs" (Hobart, 1988).

Children in a biological family have also been exposed to a relatively consistent set of beliefs, values, and behavior patterns. When children enter a stepfamily, they "inherit" a new parent who brings a new way of living into the family unit. One stepchild confided:

As long as my mother was alive, she cooked me plain ole meatloaf and potatoes for dinner. And her potatoes always were the real kind with lumps in them. My step-mother cooks all her meats in some fancy French wine sauce, and her potatoes are the instant variety. I don't like her cooking but didn't know how to tell her. And if I started to like her French cooking I might feel guilty because I would be betraying the memory of my mother.

Likewise, the new parent now lives with children who may have been reared differently from the way in which the stepparent would have reared them if he or she had been their parent all along. One stepfather explained:

It's been a difficult adjustment for me living with Molly's kids. I was reared to say "Yes sir" and "Yes ma'am" to adults and taught my own kids to do that. But Molly's kids just say "yes" or "no." It rankles me to hear them say that, but I know they mean no wrong with "yes" and "no" as long as it is said politely and that it is just something that I am going to have to live with.

Another uniqueness in stepfamilies is that the relationships between the bio-logical parent and children have existed longer than the relationships between the adults in the remarriage. Jane and her twin children have a nine-year relationship and are emotionally bonded to each other. But Jane has known her new partner only a year, and although her children like their new stepfather, they hardly know him.

☐   C O N S I D E R A T I O N   ☐

A parent's emotional bond with children (particularly if they are young and depen-dent) from a previous marriage may weaken a remarriage from the start. As one parent says, "Nothing and nobody is going to come between me and my kids." However, new spouses may view such bonding differently. One spouse said that such concern for one's own children was a sign of a caring and nurturing person. "I wouldn't want to live with anyone who didn't care about his kids." But another said, "I feel left out and that she cares more about her kids than me. I don't like the feeling of being an outsider."

The short history of the relationship between the child and stepparent is one factor that may contribute to increased conflict between these two during the child's adolescence. Hobart (1988) observed that adolescents may "become aware of their increased power and act more provocatively toward their stepparents" (p. 182).

Another unique feature of stepfamilies is that unlike children in the biological family who have one home they regard as theirs, children in stepfamilies have two homes they regard as theirs. In some cases of joint custody, children spend part of each week with one parent and part of each week with the other parent; they live with two sets of adult parents in two separate homes.

The respective adult couples may consider the time the children spend with the other couple to be a negative influence on the children. One remarried mother whose children spend a week with their father in the summer said:

It takes them a week after they come home to settle down. He buys them everything, takes them to movies and pony shows, and shows them a terrific time. They come back here, and it's rather drab. I dread their seeing their father because he interferes with the type of stable family life my new husband and I am trying to provide for them. (I won't go into the fact that my ex has a girlfriend who lives with him.)

Money, or lack of it, from the ex-spouse may be a source of conflict. In some stepfamilies, the ex-spouse is expected to send child support payments to the parent who has custody of the children. Less than one-half of these fathers send any money; those who do may be irregular in their payments. Even the amount of money awarded may be inadequate.

■ **DATA:** *The average amount of money paid by fathers annually for child support is $2,220 (Buehler, 1989).*

□   C O N S I D E R A T I O N   □

The ex-husband sending money to the biological mother creates the illusion for the stepfather that the ex-husband will take care of the expenses for the children. In reality, child support payments cover only a fraction of what is actually spent on a child, so that the new stepfather may feel burdened with more financial responsibility for his stepchildren than he bargained for. This may engender negative feelings toward the wife in the new marriage relationship.

The other side of child support is the remarried father who pays money to his ex-wife, who has custody of their children. One researcher studied 101 divorced men and observed that their remarriage was associated with an increase in voluntary support payments (Tropf, 1984).

One remarried father sent his ex-wife $500 each month in child support for their two children. But his new wife became upset that this money left their marriage every month and could not be used to buy the things they wanted. She eventually told her husband that if he were going to send his money to a wife he hated for children he never saw, she was going to leave him. The husband stopped sending the money and they moved out of the state.

New relationships in stepfamilies experience almost constant flux. Each member of a new stepfamily has many adjustments to make. Issues that must be dealt with include how the mate feels about the partner's children from a former marriage, how the children feel about the new stepparent, and how the newly married spouse feels about the spouse sending alimony and child support payments to an ex-spouse. In general, it takes at least two years for newly remarried spouses to feel comfortable together and five to seven years for the whole family to feel comfortable. Some marriages and families feel comfortable much more quickly; some never do.

Stepfamilies are also stigmatized. We are all familiar with the wicked stepmother in *Cinderella*. The fairy tale certainly gives us the impression that to be in a stepfamily with stepparents is a bad thing. Such negative stereotyping has affected stepfamilies to the degree that remarried couples often hide the fact that their children are not biologically theirs. One remarried mother said:

We moved to another state so no one would know that the children were from my former marriage. There is something better about my new husband saying "This is my son and daughter'' rather than ''This is my stepson and stepdaughter.'' The latter kind of assumes that there is something wrong with us (because we're divorced) and that something is wrong with the kids (they don't live in a ''real family'').

Finally, stepparents have no childfree period. Unlike the biological family in which the newly married couple typically have their first child about 2½ years after their wedding, the remarried couple begin their marriage with children in the house. ''We've never been alone,'' said one wife. ''We wouldn't know what it is like.''

The differences between biological families and stepfamilies are summarized in Table 17.1.

▪▪ Stages in Becoming a Stepfamily: From Outsider to Intimate

Just as there are developmental stages a person must pass through in becoming an adult, there are stages a stepfamily goes through on its way to becoming a fully

---

▪▪ TABLE 17.1 Differences Between Biological Families and Stepfamilies

BIOLOGICAL FAMILIES	STEPFAMILIES
1. Children are biologically related to both parents.	1. Children may be biologically related to only one parent.
2. Both biological parents live together with children.	2. One biological parent does not live with children as a result of divorce or death. In the case of joint physical custody, the children may live with both parents, alternating between them.
3. Beliefs and values of members tend to be similar.	3. Beliefs and values of members are more likely to be different due to different backgrounds.
4. Relationship between adults has existed longer than relationship between children and parents.	4. Relationship between children and parents has existed longer than relationship between adults.
5. Children have one home they regard as theirs.	5. Children have two homes they regard as theirs.
6. The family's economic resources come from within the family unit.	6. Some economic resources come from ex-spouse.
7. All money generated stays in the family.	7. Some money generated may leave the family in the form of alimony or child support.
8. Relationships are relatively stable.	8. Relationships are in flux: new adults adjusting to each other; children adjusting to stepparent; stepparent adjusting to stepchildren; stepchildren adjusting to each other.
9. No stigma attached to biological family.	9. Stepfamilies are stigmatized.
10. Spouses had childfree period.	10. Spouses had no childfree period.

functioning family. Papernow (1988) identified a seven stage process which may be collapsed into four:

Stage 1: *Fantasy.* Both spouses and children bring rich fantasies into the new marriage. Spouses fantasize that their new marriage will be better than the last one. If the person they are marrying has adult children, they assume that these children will not be part of the new marriage. Young children have their own fantasy—they hope that their biological parents will somehow get back together—that the stepfamily is temporary.

Stage 2: *Reality.* Instead of realizing their fantasies, new spouses find that stepchildren and ex-spouses interfere with their new life together. Stepparents feel that they are "outsiders" in an already functioning unit. "Jealousy, resentment, and inadequacy are the stepparent's everyday companions in early stepfamily life" (p. 63).

Stage 3: *Doing Something about It.* Initially the stepparent assumes a passive role and accepts the frustrations and tensions of stepfamily life. Eventually, however, the resentment reaches a level where the stepparent is driven to make changes. The stepparent makes the partner aware of the frustrations and suggests that the marital relationship should have priority some of the time. The stepparent may also make specific requests, such as reducing the number of conversations the partner has with the ex-spouse, not allowing the dog on the furniture, or requiring the stepchildren to use better table manners. This stage is successful to the degree that the partner supports the recommendations for change.

Stage 4: *Strengthening Pair Ties.* During this stage the remarried couple prioritize and solidify their relationship. At the same time, the biological parent must back away somewhat from the parent-child relationship so that the new partner can have the opportunity to establish a relationship with the stepchildren. This relationship is the product of small units of interaction and develops slowly across time. Many day-to-day activities such as watching television together, eating meals together, and driving in the car together provide opportunities for the stepparent-stepchild relationship to develop. It is important that the stepparent not attempt to replace the relationship that the stepchildren have with their biological parents.

░░ Strengths of Stepfamilies

Stepfamilies have both strengths and weaknesses. Strengths include early reality coping by children, their exposure to a variety of behavior patterns, their observation of a happy remarriage, adaptation to stepsibling relationships inside the family unit, and greater objectivity on the part of the stepparent.

Early Reality Coping

Children in stepfamilies learn about life's realities early. Whereas many biological children never have to cope with separation and divorce, stepchildren have been around the track. They have had the firsthand experience of losing someone close to them. More important, they have learned that life goes on no matter what happens and that transitions to new relationships can be for the better. One daughter said:

Looking back on my parents' divorce, I wish they had done it long ago. While I miss my dad and am sorry that I don't see him more often, I was always upset listening to my parents argue. They would yell and scream, and it would end with my mom crying. It was a lot more peaceful (and I know my mom was a lot more happy) after they got divorced. Besides, I like by stepdaddy. Although he isn't my real dad, I know he cares about me.

Exposure to a Variety of Behavior Patterns

Children in stepfamilies also experience a variety of behaviors, values, and lifestyles. They have had the advantage of living on the inside of two families. One 12-year-old said:

My real mom didn't like sports and rarely took me anywhere. My stepmother is different. She likes to take me fishing and roller skating. She recently bought me a tent and is going to take me camping this summer.

Happier Parents

Single parenting can be a demanding and exhausting experience. Remarriage can ease the stress of parenting and provide a happier context for the parent. Stepchildren often witness their parent's transition from a state of unhappiness to a state of happiness.

Adaptation to Stepsiblings

Children learning how to get along with other children in an intimate environment is another beneficial experience provided by the stepfamily. The child's world may also be expanded by new playmates and companions. This is a particular benefit for an only child whose parent marries a person with one or more children.

More Objective Stepparents

Due to the biological tie between a parent and a child, some parents seem to be incapable of discussing certain issues or topics. A stepparent often has the advantage of not being emotionally involved and can relate to the child at a different level. One 13-year-old said of the relationship with her father's new wife:

She went through her own parents' divorce and knows what it's like for me to be going through my dad's divorce. She is the only one I can really talk to about this issue. Both my dad and mom are too emotional about the subject to be able to talk about it.

:: Women in Stepfamilies

Some of the concerns women in stepfamilies have include accepting and being accepted by the new partner's children, adjusting to alimony and child support payments to an ex-wife, having the new partner accept her children and having her children accept him, and having another child in the new marriage.

Accepting Partner's Children

"She'd better think a long time before she marries a guy with kids," said one 29-year-old woman who had done so.

| ■ **DATA:** *In a study of 200 second wives, 35 percent reported children from the husband's first marriage to be the top problem in their relationship (Walker, 1984).*

This stepmother went on to explain:

It's really difficult to love someone else's children. Particularly if the kid isn't very likable. A year after we were married, my husband's 9-year-old daughter visited us for a summer. It was a nightmare. She didn't like anything I cooked, was always dragging around making us late when we had to go somewhere, kept her room a mess, and acted like a gum-chewing smart aleck. I hated her, but felt guilty because I wanted to have feelings of love and tenderness. Instead, I was jealous of the relationship she had with her father, and I wanted to get rid of her. I began counting how many days until she would be gone.

You can hide your dislike for awhile, but eventually you must tell your partner how you feel. I was lucky. My husband also thought his daughter was horrible to live with and wasn't turned off by my feelings. He told her if she couldn't act more civil, she couldn't come back. The message to every woman about to marry a guy with kids is to be aware that your man is a package deal and that the kid is in the package.

> It is very difficult to marry a man who has been married and has children.
>
> —NANCY REAGAN

Partner's Children Accepting Stepmother

| ■ **DATA:** *Of all stepparents, 18 percent are stepmothers (Glick, 1989).*

Children are much more reluctant to accept a new stepmother than a new stepfather. The role of the child's biological mother is so powerful that the stepmother's role is viewed either as marginal or nonexistent (Johnson et al., 1988). In addition, if the stepchild allows a relationship to develop with the stepmother, the biological mother may get upset. A stepchild may need to keep distance in the relationship with the stepmother to avoid conflicted loyalties (Fischman, 1988).

| ■ **DATA:** *When children in stepfamilies were asked to identify their 'families,' 100 percent included their biological mothers and only 72 percent included their stepmothers (Johnson et al., 1988).*

Adjusting to Alimony and Child Support

| ■ **DATA:** *In a study of 200 second wives, 21 percent reported financial problems to be the top problem in their relationship (Walker, 1984).*

In addition to the potential problems of not liking the partner's children, there may be problems of alimony and child support. As noted earlier, it is not unusual for a wife to become upset when her husband mails one-quarter or one-third of his income to a woman with whom he used to live. This amount of money is often equal to the current wife's earnings. Some wives in this position see themselves as working for their husband's ex-wife—a perception that is very likely to create conflict.

New Partner Accepting Her Children and Their Accepting Him

For some remarried wives, two main concerns are how her new husband will accept her children and how the children will accept him. The ages of the children are important in these adjustments. If the children are young (age 3 or younger), they will usually accept any new adult into the natural parent's life. On the other hand, if the children are in adolescence, they are struggling for independence from their natural parents and do not want any new authority figures in their lives.

Whether the new spouse will accept the children is unpredictable. Some men enjoy children and relate to them easily, as did the man who built a new house "for my new family." Other men find it difficult to enjoy children, particularly those with whom they have no biological link.

■ **DATA:** *When women with children (in a Cosmopolitan survey of 65,000) were asked how the men they dated reacted to their children, 58 percent said "with pleasure," 38 percent said "politely but not warmly," and 4 percent said "indifferent or resentful" (Bowe, 1986).*

Having Another Child

Another important issue may be whether the new husband wants to have a child with the new wife. Some men delight in the prospect of a child with their new wife. Others feel that they have had enough children and do not want any more. One husband in a second marriage said, "I've got two kids of my own, and I certainly don't want any more. But my new wife wants one, so I guess we'll have one."

CONSIDERATION

Some remarried couples feel that having their own child will help to cement their new bond. Two researchers (Ganong & Coleman, 1988) compared remarried couples who had reproduced together with couples in stepfamilies who had no mutual child. Based on measures of adjustment (Dyadic Adjustment Scale) and affect (Inventory of Family Feelings) there were no differences between the couples.

▪▪ Men in Stepfamilies

Men in stepfamilies may or may not have children from a previous relationship. Three possible stepfamily combinations include a man with children married to a woman without children, a man with children married to a woman with children, and a man without children married to a woman with children.

| ■ **DATA:** *Of all stepparents, 82 percent are stepfathers (Glick, 1989).*

Man with Children Married to a Woman without Children

Whether the man's children live with him or visit, there is a cultural expectation that the new wife care for and entertain his children. This "instant mother" phenomenon is problematic because the children may reject her or because she has had limited opportunities to develop a relationship with the children.

Another concern is whether the new wife will want children of her own.

| ■ **DATA:** *For both whites and blacks, half of women in second marriages have a child with their new partner (Wineberg, 1990).*

Man with Children Married to a Woman with Children

As more men are awarded custody of their children, an increasing number of stepfamilies will include two sets of children. Because the number of relationships to manage increases with each new person who is added to the family, such stepfamilies have most of the potential problems of stepfamilies: the adjustments of the spouses to their respective sets of stepchildren, coupled with the stepchildrens' adjustments to their new stepparent and stepsiblings. Based on longitudinal data of 50 divorces over a 40-month period, one study found that it is easier for children to relate to a new stepfather than a new stepmother (Johnson et al., 1988).

Man without Children Married to a Woman with Children

The adjustments of the never married, divorced, or widowed man without children who marries a woman with children are primarily related to her children, their acceptance of him, and his awareness that his wife is emotionally bonded to her children. Unlike childfree marital partners, who are bonded only to each other, the husband entering a relationship with a woman who has children must accept her attachment with her children from the outset. One husband said:

> By the time we decided to get married, I was already acquainted with her three children: George, who was 8, Billy, who was 6, and Susie, who was 3. I was sure they would accept me as their father, because they seemed to view me as a friend. I also assumed that every child needs and wants a father. I liked kids, especially these kids, and I expected no trouble. I was, in a word, naive (Gorman, 1983, 2).

Using a multicase study phenomenological approach, Lou Everett (1990) interviewed six stepfathers and identified two primary factors that contribute to a positive stepfather-stepchild relationship: (1) Active involvement in teaching the stepchild something mutually valued. Just spending time with the stepchild (eating meals, watching television) had no positive effect on the relationship. Teaching the stepchild (how to skate, fish, fly a kite) made the stepfather feel as though he was contributing to the development of the stepchild and endeared the stepchild to the stepfather, and (2) An intense love relationship between the stepfather and the biological mother of the stepchild. "Men who love their wives are more tolerant of their stepchildren," observed Dr. Everett.

Their daddy is still very much present in their lives, their personalities, their memories and their momentos. There is no attempt to block him out and his name is daddy. But I am concerned about what I am to be called. I want to be daddy.

—TONY GORMAN, A STEPFATHER

Here are some questions a man without children might ask a woman who has children:

1. How do you expect me to relate to your children? Am I supposed to be their friend, daddy, or what?
2. How do you feel about having another child? How many additional children are you interested in having?
3. How much money do you get in alimony and child support from your ex-husband? How long will this last?
4. What expenses of the children do you expect me to pay for? Who is going to pay for their college expenses?
5. How often are you in contact with your ex-husband? To what degree are you still emotionally involved with him?

∷ Children in Stepfamilies

| ■ **DATA:** *About 6 million children live in stepfamilies (Glick, 1989).*

Stepchildren have viewpoints and must make adjustments of their own when their parents remarry. They have experienced the transition from a family in which their biological parents lived together to either living alone with one parent (usually the mother) or alternating between the homes of both parents, to a stepfamily with a new stepparent.

Some adjustments revolve around feeling abandoned, divided loyalties, discipline, and stepsiblings.

Some stepchildren feel that they have been abandoned twice—once when their parents got divorced and again when the parents turned their attention to their new marital partners. One adolescent explained:

> It hurt me when my parents got divorced and my dad moved out. I really missed him and felt he really didn't care about my feelings. But we adjusted with just my mom, and when everything was going right again, she gets involved with this new guy and we've got baby sitters all the time. I feel like I've lost both parents in two years.

Coping with feelings of abandonment is not easy. It is best if the parents assure the children that the divorce was not their fault and that they are loved a great deal by both parents. In addition, the parents should be careful to find a balance between spending time with new partners and spending time with the children.

Divided loyalties is another issue children must deal with in stepfamilies. Sometimes they develop an attachment for a stepparent that is more positive than the relationship with the natural parent of the same sex. When these feelings develop, the children may feel they are in a bind. One adolescent boy explained:

My real dad left my mother when I was 6, and my mom remarried. My stepdad has always been good to me, and I really prefer to be with him. When my dad comes to pick me up on weekends, I have to avoid talking about my stepdad because my dad doesn't like him. I guess I love my dad, but I have a better relationship with my stepdad.

For some adolescents, the more they care for the stepparent, the more guilty they feel, so they may try to hide their attachment. The stepparent may be aware of both positive and negative feelings coming from the child.

Stepchildren may also resent their stepparents and feel that they are trying to rob them of their biological parent's love. One 14-year-old said:

My new stepdad made me feel guilty when I told him that I wanted to spend the summer with my dad. It was almost as though I was not supposed to have feelings for my real dad. I was in a bind. If I showed that I cared about my real dad, my stepdad would stop talking to me. If I didn't show the emotion I felt when my dad called to talk, I felt I was betraying myself and him.

Discipline is another issue for stepchildren. "Adjusting to living with a new set of rules from your stepparent," "accepting discipline from a stepparent," and "dealing with the expectations of your stepparent" are situations 80 percent of more than 100 adolescents in stepfamilies said they had experienced (Lutz, 1983). Their main problem was accepting rules from an "outsider":

I resented my stepdad telling me what to do. He wasn't my real dad, and I didn't want my mom to marry him anyway. It's been a problem ever since he moved in. I liked it better when my mom was a single parent. It seems as though we were all happier then.

Some unhappy adolescent stepchildren retreat into their rooms to play with their machines.

Rejecting discipline from stepparents may result in children who are more vulnerable to antisocial peer pressure. In a study comparing children who lived with both natural parents with children who lived in stepfamily environments, the latter children were more susceptible to pressure from their friends to engage in deviant behavior (Steinberg, 1987).

Siblings may also be a problem for stepchildren. They experience higher levels of stress in stepfamilies if they have stepsiblings than if they do not (Lutz, 1983). The stress seems to be a result of more arguments among the adults when both sets of children are present and the perception that parents are more fair with their own children:

> I could bounce the ball in the den and my stepdad would jump all over me. But let my stepsister bounce it and he wouldn't say a word. All I want is to be treated fairly, and that's not what's happening in this family.

Stepsiblings also compete for space, which leads to bitter territorial squabbles. The children who are already in the house may feel imposed upon and threatened. The entering children may feel out of place (Kutner, 1989, C9).

☐   C O N S I D E R A T I O N   ☐

To minimize such territorial squabbles, it is important that each child has a private space. When children fight over who gets which bedroom, some resolve the conflict by having the children change bedrooms each year (Bernstein, 1989).

In general, stepfamily life is difficult for everyone involved: remarried spouses, children, even ex-spouses, grandparents, and in-laws. While some of the problems begin to level out after 2 or 3 years, many continue for 5 to 7 years or longer (Beer, 1988). Many couples become impatient with the unanticipated problems that are slow to abate, and they divorce. The Stepfamily Success Scale provides a way to predict the degree to which you might have a relatively easy adjustment in a stepfamily.

▪▪ Developmental Tasks for Stepfamilies

A developmental task is a skill that, if mastered, allows the family to grow as a cohesive unit. Developmental tasks that are not mastered will bring the family closer to the point of disintegration. Some of the more important developmental tasks for stepfamilies are discussed in this section.

Nurture New Marriage Relationship

Because the demands of family interaction can become intense—even excessive—it is important that the new wife and husband allocate time to be alone to nurture their relationship. They must take time to communicate, to share their lives, and to have fun. One remarried couple goes out on a date each Saturday

If two people who love each other let a single instant wedge itself between them, it grows—it becomes a month, a year, a century; it becomes too late.

—JEAN GIRAUDOUX

night for dinner and a movie—without the children. "If you don't spend time alone with your partner, you won't have one," says one stepparent.

Lower Your Expectations

Because of the complexity of meshing the numerous relationships involved in a stepfamily, it is important to be realistic. Dreams of "one big happy family" often set up stepparents for disappointment, bitterness, jealousy, and guilt. "It takes from two to five years for a stepfamily to begin to emerge. Be patient" (Boley, 1989, 4). Just as biological families do not always run smoothly, neither do stepfamilies.

Accept Your Stepchildren

Rather than wishing your stepchildren were different, it is more productive "to accept your stepchild's looks, personality, habits, manners, behavior, style of dress, speech, choice of friends and feelings—all of which you had nothing to do with" (Boley, 1989, 4). All children have positive qualities; find them and make them the focus of your thinking.

In addition, it is important to relate to one's stepchildren not just as their friend but as a teacher and role model. Children will have their own friends but still have a lot to learn from adults. In some cases the stepparent can offer what the biological parent cannot:

> A stepparent, it seems, can be the ideal person for stepchildren to talk with about sex, their feelings about their parents' divorce, career choices, drugs, and other potentially highly charged subjects. The 'intimate outsider' quality is one of the most satisfying rewards of forging a stepparent role (Papernow, 1988, 279).

Some remarried spouses also become stepparents.

SELF ASSESSMENT

Stepfamily Success Scale

This scale is designed to measure the degree to which you and your partner might expect to have a successful stepfamily. There are no right or wrong answers. After reading each sentence carefully, circle the number that best represents your feelings.

1 Strongly disagree
2 Mildly disagree
3 Undecided
4 Mildly agree
5 Strongly agree

	SD	MD	U	MA	SA
1. I am a flexible person.	1	2	3	4	5
2. I am not a jealous person.	1	2	3	4	5
3. I am a patient person.	1	2	3	4	5
4. My partner is a flexible person.	1	2	3	4	5
5. My partner is not a jealous person.	1	2	3	4	5
6. My partner is a patient person.	1	2	3	4	5
7. My partner values our relationship more than the relationship with his or her children.	1	2	3	4	5
8. My partner understands that it is not easy for me to love someone else's children.	1	2	3	4	5
9. I value the relationship with my partner more than the relationship with my children.	1	2	3	4	5
10. I understand that it will be difficult for my partner to love my children as much as I do.	1	2	3	4	5

Establish Your Own Family Rituals

One of the bonding elements of nuclear families is its rituals. Stepfamilies may integrate the various family members by establishing common rituals. Such rituals may include summer vacations, visits to and from extended kin, and Christmas celebrations. "Even if one does not wholeheartedly participate, by just being part of the group one is included in its membership and its evolving history" (Whiteside, 1989, 35).

Decide about Money

Money is an issue of potential conflict in stepfamilies because it is a scarce resource and several people want to use it for their respective needs. The father wants a new computer; the mother wants a new car; the mother's children want bunk beds, a new stereo, and a satellite dish; the father's children want a larger

11. My partner and I have amicable relationships with our ex-spouses.	1	2	3	4	5
12. My children and those of my partner will live with the ex-spouse.	1	2	3	4	5
13. We will have plenty of money in our stepfamily.	1	2	3	4	5
14. I feel positively about my partner's children.	1	2	3	4	5
15. My partner feels positively about my children.	1	2	3	4	5
16. My children and those of my partner feel positively about each other.	1	2	3	4	5
17. My partner and I will begin our stepfamily in a place that neither of us has lived before.	1	2	3	4	5
18. My partner and I agree on how to discipline our children.	1	2	3	4	5
19. My children feel positively about my new partner.	1	2	3	4	5
20. My partner's children feel positively about me.	1	2	3	4	5

SCORING: Add the numbers you circled. 1 (strongly disagree) is the most negative response you can make, and 5 (strongly agree) is the most positive response you can make. The lower your total score (20 is the lowest possible score), the greater the number of potential problems and the lower the chance of success in a stepfamily with this partner. The higher your total score (100 is the highest possible score), the greater the chance of success in a stepfamily with this partner. A score of 60 places you at the midpoint between the extremes of having a difficult or an easy stepfamily experience.

(NOTE: This Self-Assessment is intended to be thought-provoking and suggestive, it is not a clinical diagnostic instrument).

room, clothes, and a phone. How do the newly married couple and their children decide how money should be spent?

Some stepfamilies put all their resources into one bank and draw out money as necessary without discriminating whose money it is or for whose child the money is being spent. Others keep their money separate; the parents have separate incomes and spend them on their respective biological children. Neither pattern is superior to the other in terms of marital satisfaction (Lown et al., 1989).

Give Authority to Your Spouse

How much authority the stepparent will exercise over the children must be discussed by the adults before they get married. Some couples divide the authority—each spouse disciplining his or her own children. But children may test the stepparent in such an arrangement when the biological parent is not around. One stepmother said, "Jim's kids are wild when he isn't here because I'm not supposed to discipline them."

□   C O N S I D E R A T I O N   □

It is often helpful for the adults to tell their respective children that they must respect the wishes of the stepparent. Stepparents can't grab authority. They must become a partner with the natural parent, who then gives authority to the new spouse. Unless children view each parent as an authority figure, they are likely to undermine the relationship between the adults.

The biological parent must support the new stepparent in front of the children. This helps prevent the children from driving a wedge between the couple and gives the children a reason to accept the new partner.

Keep Communication Channels Open

Although open lines of communication are important in any relationship, they become critical in stepfamilies. Due to the number of new relationships with varying histories and durations, the potential for problems is high. To prevent misunderstandings from festering, family members should understand that it is all right not to like something and agree on a means of telling others how they are feeling. Some families set aside regular weekly meeting times to discuss family issues or concerns.

Support Child's Relationship with Absent Parent

A continued relationship with both biological parents is critical to the emotional well-being of the child. Ex-spouses and stepparents should encourage children to have positive relationships with both parents.

■ **DATA:** *One-fourth of divorced parents in one study said that they sometimes refused to let the other parent see the children (Maccoby, et al., 1990).*

Regardless of the feelings the spouse and new partner may have about the ex-spouse, the children should be encouraged to continue a very positive relationship with the biological parent. In some cases, both stepparents and biological parents can view themselves as a coparenting team or parenting coalition. While such a coalition may be difficult, the advantages for the children are enormous (Visher & Visher, 1989).

□   C O N S I D E R A T I O N   □

Suggesting that the child call the stepparent by a name the child feels comfortable with may help to encourage a friendly rather than an authoritarian relationship. Many stepparents recognize that it would be a mistake to force their stepchildren to call them "mom" or "dad" and ask the children to call them by their first name.

Support Child's Relationship with Grandparents

It is important to support children's continued relationships with their natural grandparents. This is one of the more stable relationships in the stepchild's changing world of adult relationships. Regardless of how ex-spouses feel about their former in-laws, they should encourage their children to have positive feelings for their grandparents. One mother said, "Although I am uncomfortable around my ex-in-laws, I know my children enjoy visiting them, so I encourage their relationship."

Supporting the child's relationship with the stepgrandparents is also important. One of the advantages of being a stepchild is the potential addition of a new stepgrandparent. While grandchildren report being closer to their grandparents than stepgrandparents, the relationship between children and their stepgrandparents should be nurtured (Sanders & Trygstad, 1989).

▪▪ Trends

Due to an increased number of divorced parents getting remarried, stepfamilies will become a more visible phenomenon in American society. It is estimated that one-third of all children will become stepchildren before age 18 (Glick, 1989). The result—stepfamilies will become more normative and lose some of the stigma they now carry.

Stepfamilies will continue to reach out for help. Members of stepfamilies have already established national organizations for support. These include the Stepfamily Association of America (602 East Jappa Road, Baltimore, Maryland 21204, 301–823–7570) and Stepfamily Foundation (333 West End Avenue, Apt. 11C, New York, New York 10023, 212–877–3244). In addition, a number of self-help books on stepfamily living are available (Coleman & Ganong, 1989; Coleman & Ganong, 1988).

At the present time, family law does not provide clear and comprehensive rules about the stepparent-stepchild relationship. For example, should stepparents be legally responsible to economically support stepchildren during the remarriage? If the remarriage terminates should stepparents provide child support for stepchildren? Should stepparents have visitation rights if the remarried couple divorce? Because of the increased number of stepfamilies in our society, laws will be developed which apply to this segment of our population (Fine, 1989).

One aspect of the legal system that is becoming more fixed relates to child support. Beginning in 1994, a Federal Child Support Law will take effect which will require employers to automatically withhold child support from fathers or mothers who are under court order to pay. The amount will be determined by a fixed formula.

▪▪ Summary

About 80 percent of divorced people remarry. The issues encountered by those considering a remarriage involve establishing trust in a new relationship, boundary maintenance with the ex-spouse, meshing finances, and relating to stepchildren.

A stepfamily is a married couple in which at least one of the spouses has had a child in a previous relationship. Stepfamilies have been stigmatized as not being "real" families. The strengths of stepfamilies include early reality testing, exposure to a variety of behavior patterns, a happier parent, and greater objectivity on the part of the stepparent.

Women, men, and children sometimes experience stepfamily living differently. For women, learning to get along with the husband's children, not being resentful of his relationship with his children, and adapting to the fact that one-quarter to one-third of his income may be sent to his ex-wife as alimony or child support are skills the new wife must develop. She may also want children with her new partner or may bring her own children into the remarriage. In the latter case, she is anxious that her new husband will accept her children.

Men in stepfamilies have similar concerns. Getting along with their wife's children, paying for many of the expenses of their stepchildren, having their new partner accept their own children, and dealing with the issue of having more children are among them.

Children must cope with feeling abandoned and problems of divided loyalties, discipline, and stepsiblings.

Developmental tasks for stepfamilies include nurturing the new marriage relationship, deciding whose money will be spent on whose children, deciding who will discipline the children and how, keeping communication channels open, and supporting the child's relationship with both parents and natural grandparents, as well as stepgrandparents.

Trends include the increased visibility of stepfamilies and continued sharing of stepfamily problems and solutions by individuals involved in stepfamily living. In addition, courts will recognize that stepfamilies have issues that are not covered in traditional family law. Another trend is the establishment of mechanisms to ensure that child support money is paid.

Questions for Reflection

1. How capable do you think you are of loving someone else's children?
2. How accepting would you be of a new spouse who could not accept your children?
3. How would you feel if your stepchildren never accepted you as a member of the family? What could you do to try to change their attitude?

References

Beer, W. R., ed. *Relative strangers.* New Jersey: Rowman and Littlefield, 1988.

Bernstein, Anne C. *Yours, mine, and ours.* New York: Charles Scribner's Sons, 1989.

Bernstein, B. E. and S. K. Collins. Remarriage counseling: Lawyer and therapist's help with the second time around. *Family Relations,* 1985, *34,* 375–391.

Boley, Carol D. When you're mom no. 2. *Focus on the Family,* July 1989, 3–4.

Bowe, C. What are men like today? *Cosmopolitan,* May 1986, 263 et passim.

Bowers, I-Chiao H. and S. J. Bahr. Remarriage among the elderly. *Aging and the Family.* Edited by Stephen J. Bahr and Evan T. Peterson. Lexington, Mass.: Lexington Books, 1989, 83–95.

Buehler, C. Influential factors and equity issues in divorce settlements. *Family Relations,* 1989, *38,* 76–82.

Coleman, M. and L. H. Ganong. *Bibliotherapy with stepchildren.* Springfield, Ill.: Charles C. Thomas, 1988.

Coleman, M. and L. Ganong. Stepfamily self-help books: Brief annotations and ratings. *Family Relations,* 1989, *38,* 91–96.

Crosbie-Burnett, M. and A. Skyles. Stepchildren in schools and colleges: Recommendations for educational policy changes. *Family Relations,* 1989, *38,* 59–64.

Everett, Lou. Factors that contribute to stepfather/stepchild relationships. In press 1990.

Fine, M. A. A social science perspective on stepfamily law: Suggestions for legal reform. *Family Relations,* 1989, *38,* 53–58.

Fischman, Joshua. Stepdaughter wars. *Psychology Today,* 1988, *22,* 38–45.

Furstenberg, Frank F. The new extended family: The experience of parents and children after remarriage. *Remarriage and Stepparenting.* Edited by Kay Pasley and Marilyn Ihinger-Tallman. New York: Guilford Press, 1987, 42–61.

Ganong, L. H. and M. Coleman. Do mutual children cement bonds in stepfamilies? *Journal of Marriage and the Family,* 1988, *50,* 687–698.

Ganong, L. H. and M. Coleman. Preparing for remarriage: Anticipating the issues, seeking solutions. *Family Relations,* 1989, *38,* 28–33.

Giles-Sims, J. and M. Crosbie-Burnett. Stepfamily research: Implications for policy, clinical interventions, and further research. *Family Relations,* 1989, *38,* 19–23.

Glick, P. C. Remarried families, stepfamilies, and stepchildren: A brief demographic profile. *Family Relations,* 1989, *38,* 24–27.

Goetting, A. The six stations of remarriage: Developmental tasks of remarriage after divorce. *Family Coordinator,* 1982, *31,* 213–222.

Gorman, T. *Stepfather.* Boulder, Co.: Gentle Touch Press, 1983.

Hobart, Charles W. Perception of parent-child relationships in first married and remarried families. *Family Relations,* 1988, *37,* 175–182.

Hoffman, S. D. and G. J. Duncan. What are the economic consequences of divorce? *Demography,* 1989, *25,* 641–645.

Johnson, Colleen Leahy, Linnea Klee, and Catherine Schmidt. Conceptions of parentage and kinship among children of divorce. *American Anthropologist,* 1988, *90,* 136–144.

Keshet, J. K. The remarried couple: Stresses and successes. *Relative Strangers.* Edited by William R. Beer. New Jersey: Rowman and Littlefield, 1988.

Kutner, Lawrence. In blended families, rivalries intensify. *The New York Times,* January 5, 1989, pp. Cl et passim.

Lown, J. M., J. R. McFadden, and S. M. Crossman. Family life education for remarriage: Focus on financial management. *Family Relations,* 1989, *38,* 40–45.

Lutz, P. The stepfamily: An adolescent perspective. *Family Relations,* 1983, *32,* 367–375.

Maccoby, E. E., C. E. Depner, and R. H. Mnookin. Coparenting in the second year after divorce. *Journal of Marriage and the Family,* 1990, *52,* 141–155.

Martin, T. C. and L. L. Bumpass. Recent trends in marital disruption. *Demography,* 1989, *26,* 37–52.

Papernow, P. L. Stepparent role development: From outsider to intimate. *Relative Strangers.* Edited by William R. Beer. New Jersey: Rowman and Littlefield, 1988, 54–82.

Pasley, B. K. and M. Ihinger-Tallman. Boundary ambiguity in remarriage: Does ambiguity differentiate degree of marital adjustment and integration? *Family Relations,* 1989, *38,* 46–52.

Richmond, Gary. When families break up: The human toll. *Focus on the Family,* April 1989, 2–5.

Roberts, T. W. and S. J. Price. A systems analysis of the remarriage process: Implications for the clinician. *Journal of Divorce,* 1985–1986, *9,* 1–25.

Sanders, G. F. and D. W. Trygstad. Stepgrandparents and grandparents: The view from young adults. *Family Relations,* 1989, *38,* 71–75.

Statistical Abstract of the United States: 1990. 110th ed. Washington D.C.: U.S. Bureau of the Census, 1990.

Steinberg, Laurence. Single parents, stepparents, and the susceptibility of adolescents to antisocial peer pressure. *Child Development,* 1987, *58,* 269–275.

Tropf, W. D. An exploratory examination of the effect of remarriage on child support and personal contacts. *Journal of Divorce,* 1984, *7,* no. 3, 57–73.

Vemer, E., M. Coleman, L. H. Ganong, and H. Cooper. Marital satisfaction in remarriage: A meta-analysis. *Journal of Marriage and the Family,* 1989, *51,* 713–725.

Vinick, B. Remarriage in old age. *The Family Coordinator,* 1978, *27,* 359–363.

Visher, E. B. and J. S. Visher. Parenting coalitions after remarriage: Dynamics and therapeutic guidelines. *Family Relations,* 1989, *38,* 65–70.

Walker, G. *Second wife, second best?* New York: Doubleday, 1984.

Whiteside, M. F. Family rituals as a key to kinship connections in remarried families. *Family Relations,* 1989, *38,* 34–39.

Wineberg, J. Childbearing in remarriage. *Journal of Marriage and the Family,* 1990, *52,* 31–38.

CHOICES

NEVER MARRIED and divorced individuals with children have choices to make about entering a stepfamily. The various issues for each of these individuals to consider follow.

Should a Never Married Man Marry a Divorced Woman with Children?

The following diagrams emphasize the positive and negative consequences of a "yes" or "no" decision. They are helpful in making many kinds of decisions. First, we suggest how they may help the single man in deciding whether to marry a divorced woman with children.

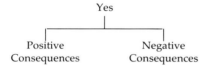

Yes

Positive Consequences   Negative Consequences

Yes

The positive consequences of marrying a divorced woman with children include continuing the love relationship with the woman, having a ready-made family, and avoiding the pain of living without the beloved. Because the man making such a decision will be emotionally involved with the woman, a major factor in his decision will be his emotional outlook. One man said:

I love her and want to be with her, whether she has kids or not. If you try to add and subtract everything about human relationships as though you are keeping a ledger, you are missing the point. My happiness depends on my being with her, and marriage means that we will continue our lives together, since we don't believe in living together.

In addition to being able to live with the loved person in a marriage relationship, another positive consequence of marrying a divorced person with children is having a ready-made family. "I've al-

ways wanted children, and I think her kids are great," said a prospective groom. "We've been camping together as a family, and it was nothing but fun. I don't see any problem down the road with these kids."

Another positive outcome is avoiding a negative one:

If I don't marry her, I'm forced to go back to bars and talk to people I'm not interested in. I love her, and deciding not to marry her would mean loneliness and pain.

Every decision has positive and negative consequences. What are the negative consequences of deciding to marry a divorced woman with children? Jealousy over the emotional bond between the woman and her children, the presence of an ex-husband who may be calling and coming by to get the kids, and the costs associated with rearing the children are potential problems. One man who married (and subsequently divorced) a woman with two children said:

It didn't work out for us. I was jealous of the time she gave to her own kids and knew that I was always second. I also didn't like her ex around, even though it was for a brief time each week. Just to see the guy who had sex with my wife for 15 years unnerved me. And the money was a real problem. Her ex never paid enough child support to cover what the kids cost, and I got tired of paying for kids who weren't really mine. Besides, they both needed braces, and that got us deeply in debt. I'd say marrying a woman with kids isn't worth it, no matter how much you love her.

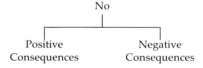

No

Positive Consequences   Negative Consequences

No

Suppose the man decides not to marry the divorced woman with children. What are the positive and negative consequences of his decision? On the positive side, he has avoided the potential problems of feeling jealous of the bond between the woman and her children, of having to deal with an ex-spouse, and of feeling financially responsible for children that are not biologically his. By making a single decision, he has avoided a lot of potential headaches (and maybe a divorce, since 60 percent of remarriages do not last).

On the other hand, there are some losses associated with deciding not to marry her. The primary one is the emotional pain he would feel as a result of terminating the relationship with her. "In these situations," said one man, "I'm a real sucker for romance. I do what I feel every time. And living without this woman is something I can't do."

After listing the positive and negative consequences of a "yes" and "no" decision, a final decision can be made by examining how the consequences look on paper. Assign weights to the different consequences if necessary. For example, on a 10-point scale (10 = tops), how important is it to have a ready-made family, to continue the love relationship, or to avoid going in debt over children who are not biologically yours? Getting the issues on paper and looking at them sometimes makes it easy to make a decision.

How the decision feels is also important. Regardless of how it looks on paper, your feelings will play an important role in determining the final decision. "If the decision doesn't feel right in your heart, it isn't right," said one person.

Should a Never Married Woman Marry a Divorced Man with Children?

It is not unusual for a single woman to become emotionally involved with a divorced man who has children. Although the ex-wife frequently has custody of their children, they may visit and he will probably pay child support. The process just described is helpful in examining the issues involved (see earlier diagrams).

Yes

The positive consequences for the single woman marrying a divorced man with children would be similar to those of the single man marrying a divorced woman with children: continuing the love relationship, benefiting from a ready-made family, and avoiding the pain of losing the partner.

The negative consequences of a "yes" decision may also include competing with the children for the husband's time. One woman said:

Since we both worked all week, I wanted the weekend to enjoy by ourselves. But he wanted his kids to visit us on the weekends. I went along with it for awhile, but finally told him I didn't like it. He said, "My kids are coming to this house every Saturday as long as they want to. If you don't like it, leave." I tried to get along with them, but I just ended up cooking and doing the laundry for them. I felt like a maid for his kids, who were interfering in our marriage.

No

The positive outcome of a decision not to marry a divorced man with children is avoiding the problems of stepchildren visiting frequently and taking money out of the marriage and giving it to the husband's ex-wife.

The negative consequence of deciding not to marry is the flood of bad feelings—loneliness, depression, and pain—that often follow a decision to walk away from an emotionally important relationship.

It is critical to keep in mind that no decision will have all positive or negative consequences. Every decision will involve trade-offs.

Should a Divorced Woman with Children and a Divorced Man with Children Marry?

Divorced people sometimes prefer each other because they know the person has an experiential understanding of the divorced state. "I won't date single people," said one divorced woman. "They have no appreciation for what it is like to be divorced and they certainly don't know anything about the parent-child bond." Marrying someone with children has its own problems. (Refer again to the earlier diagrams.)

Yes

Marrying someone who understands divorce and children is perhaps the greatest benefit of deciding to marry a divorced person with children. Because they know how intense the parent-child bond is, they are not as likely to feel jealous of this relationship. In addition, they have ex-spouses too and can empathize with the need and discomfort of interacting with an ex.

Mother and father role models for each other's children are also a benefit for adults and children. "I need a mother for my kids, and she needs a daddy for hers, so it's a good trade-off," said one father. "I wouldn't say I'm getting married for that reason, but it sure is a plus."

The negative consequences of a decision to blend two families together are problems of the wife's children accepting their stepfather, the husband's children accepting their stepmother, and the children accepting each other. These factors will influence the degree to which the new family becomes a cohesive unit. To expect that such a fusion will occur quickly and smoothly is unrealistic.

No

The decision against blending two families will result in avoiding the potentially negative consequences just described. On the other hand, such a decision will terminate an emotional relationship with someone who knows what divorce, children, and single parenting are all about.

Impact of Social Influences on Choices

Our society has not decided how it feels about stepfamilies. On the one hand, they are stigmatized as being less than a "real" family in which the adults have been married one time to each other and have their own children living with them. But with 60 percent of the divorces occurring in such "real" families with children, stepfamilies are no longer an anomaly.

The degree to which an individual who lives in a stepfamily feels stigmatized is influenced by the perceptions and attitudes of others. Since teachers are a major source of influence in the development of a child's self-concept, it is important that educators recognize the plurality of family patterns and be careful not to communicate that "biological families" are the only "real" families (Crosbie-Burnett & Skyles, 1989).

P A R T

VI

□

Special Topics

1

Budgeting, Investing, Life Insurance, and Credit

CONTENTS

O NE ASPECT OF marriage is that it is an economic partnership in which the spouses conduct the business of getting and spending money. Problems may arise when this scarce resource is not managed properly. Here, we will consider possible ways to prevent spending more than you and your partner are making and how to invest money for future needs.

:: Developing a Budget

Developing a budget is a way of planning your spending. Since money spent on X cannot be spent on Y, budgeting requires conscious value choices about which bills should be paid, what items should be bought, and what expenditures should be delayed. Couples need to develop a budget if they are always out of money long before their next paycheck, if they cannot make partial payments or pay off existing bills but keep incurring new debts, or if they cannot save money.

☐   C O N S I D E R A T I O N   ☐

The advantages of developing and following a budget include having money available when you need it, avoiding unnecessary debt, and saving money.

To develop a budget (see Table ST1.1), list and add up all your monthly take-home (after-tax) income from all sources. This figure should represent the amount of money your family will actually have to spend each month. Next, list and add up all of your fixed monthly expenses, such as rent, utilities, telephone, and car payment. Other fixed expenses include such items as life, health, and car insurance. You may not receive a bill for some of these expenses every month, so divide the yearly cost of each item by 12 so that you can budget it on a monthly basis. For example, if your annual life insurance premium is $240, you should budget $20 per month for that expense.

Set aside a minimum of 5 percent of your monthly income—and more, if possible—for savings, and include this sum in your fixed expenses. By putting a fixed amount in a savings account each month, you will not only have money available for large purchases, such as a car or a major home appliance, but you will also have an emergency fund to cover unforeseen expenses like those caused by an extended illness or a long-distance move. The size of an emergency fund should be about twice your monthly income. Although you can personally set aside some of your monthly income for savings, an alternative is to instruct the bank to transfer a certain sum each month from your checking account to your savings account, or you can join a payroll savings plan. Under the latter arrangement, a portion of your monthly salary is automatically deposited in your savings account without ever passing through your hands.

After adding together all your fixed monthly expenses, including savings, subtract this amount from your monthly take-home income. What remains can be used for such day-to-day expenses as food (groceries and restaurant meals), clothes (including laundry, dry cleaning, alterations, and new clothes), personal care (barber and hairdresser, toilet articles, cosmetics), and recreation (theater, movies, concerts, books, magazines).

▪▪ TABLE-ST1.1 **Monthly Budget for Two-Income Couple:**

BOTH SPOUSES EMPLOYED FULL TIME

Sources of Income	
Husband's take-home pay	$1,480
Wife's take-home pay	920
Interest earned on savings	17
TOTAL	$2,417
Fixed Expenses	
Rent	$ 450
Utilities	90
Telephone	70
Insurance	85
Car payments and expenses	330
Furniture payments	80
Savings	200
TOTAL	$1,295
DIFFERENCE	$1,122
(Amount available for day-to-day expenses)	
Day-to-Day and Discretionary Expenses	
Food	$ 250
Clothes	170
Personal care	90
Recreation	120
Miscellaneous	110
TOTAL	$ 740

This dual-income couple should have $382 extra at the end of each month. The reality is that many couples can't or don't live within their income and go into debt each month.

☐   C O N S I D E R A T I O N   ☐

If you come out even at the end of the month, you are living within your means. If you have money left over, you are living below your means. If you had to tap your savings or borrow money to pay your bills last month, you are living beyond your means. Knowing whether you are living within, below, or above your means depends on keeping accurate records.

And remember, you must pay taxes on what you earn. The following shows how much tax rates are for 1990.

Rate for Married Individuals—Joint Return (Two Exemptions)

15%	$0 to $ 29,750
28%	$30,950 to $ 74,850
33%	$74,850 to $177,720
An additional 28%	over $177,720

Rate for Single Individual (One Exemption)

15%	$0 to $ 18,550
28%	$18,550 to $ 44,900
33%	$44,900 to $104,330
An additional 28%	over $104,330

:: Investing

Saving should be a part of every budget. By allocating a specific amount of your monthly income to savings, having your employer do so through the payroll savings plan, or putting your change in a container on your dresser every evening, you can accumulate money for both short-term (vacation, down payment on a house) and long-term (college education for children, retirement income) goals.

CONSIDERATION

By investing, you use money to make more money. All investments must be considered in terms of their risk and potential yield. In general, the higher the rate of return on an investment, the greater the risk. Putting your money in a bank or savings and loan institution is risk-free because your deposit is insured by the federal government.

Another way to invest money and receive a fairly stable return is to buy a blue chip stock, such as American Telephone & Telegraph or Eastman Kodak. The value of these stocks is likely to increase. Also, some stocks have the potential to appreciate and pay dividends as well. Although there is greater potential return on these investment stocks than on money placed in a savings account at the

It is usually a wise decision to consult an investment counselor before investing money.

bank, there is also a risk to the investor. For example, if Nikon Camera invented a new film that offered superior quality at a lower cost, Kodak stock might plummet and take your money with it.

There is an even greater risk with speculative stocks—stocks that can radically increase or decrease in value within a short time. Suppose you could afford to lose $500 and were willing to gamble on a high return. You could buy 100 shares of stock at slightly below $5 per share. If the stock is selling for $10 one year later, your original investment would double in value: you would now have $1,000 from your initial investment of $500. But if the stock is selling for $1 per share one year later, you would only realize $100 on your $500 investment. You can lose money as fast as you can gain it. One spouse invested in a company specializing in bananas and looked forward to tripling her investment. But less than a week after she purchased the stock, a hurricane in Puerto Rico wiped out the banana crop, and the value of her stock dropped sharply.

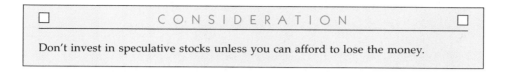

CONSIDERATION

Don't invest in speculative stocks unless you can afford to lose the money.

Fortunately, investment opportunities are not limited to banks and stocks. Table ST1.2 illustrates several investment alternatives and furnishes information on other factors that you should consider in deciding on an investment. In addition to risk and return on investment, the *liquidity*, or the ease with which your investment can be converted into cash, is an important consideration. Stocks and bonds can be sold quickly to provide cash in hand. In contrast, if you have invested in a building or land, you must find a buyer who is willing to pay the price that you are asking for your asset before you can convert it to cash.

The amount of your time that is required to make your investment grow is also important. A real estate investment can give you a considerable return on your

▪▪ TABLE ST1.2 **Some Investment Alternatives**

TYPE	RISK/YIELD	LIQUIDITY	MANAGEMENT	TAX ASPECTS
Savings account	Low/5%	Immediate	Self	Interest is taxed.
Treasury bill	Low/7%	3 months to a year	Self	Interest is taxed.
Money market	Low/6%	One week	Broker	Interest is taxed.
Annuity	Low/8%	Retirement	Company	Tax is deferred.
Real estate	Depends/0–25%	Months/years	Self or other	Good tax advantage.
Mutual fund	Moderate/3–30%	One week	Agent	Lower tax if held.
Stocks	Depends/0–100%	One week	Broker	Depends on investment.
Life insurance	Low/5%	Years	Agent	Depends on investment.
Bonds	Depends/8–10%	One week	Broker	Depends on investment.
IRA	Low/6–8%	Retirement	Broker	Deferred.
Certificate of Deposit (CD)	Low/6–8%	Variable	Self	Interest is taxed.

money, but it may also demand a lot of your time—perusing the newspaper, arranging for loans, placing ads, and showing the house, not to mention fixing leaky faucets, mowing grass, and painting rooms.

Also, consider the maturity date of your investment. For example, suppose you invest in a six-year certificate at a savings bank. Although the bank will pay you, say, 12 percent interest and guarantee your investment, you can't get your principle (the money you deposited) or the interest until the six years is up unless you are willing to pay a substantial penalty. Regular savings accounts have no maturity date. You can withdraw any amount of your money from your savings account at the bank whenever you want it, but you may earn only, say, 6 percent interest on the money while it remains in the account.

A final investment consideration is taxation. Investment decisions should be made on the basis not of how much money you can make but of how much money you can keep. Tax angles should be considered as carefully as risk and yield issues.

☐   C O N S I D E R A T I O N   ☐

Unless you are majoring in business or banking and have expertise in money management, it may be wise to ask a broker in an investment firm like Merrill Lynch, Smith Barney, E.F. Hutton to advise you. A financial advisor can tailor your investment program to accommodate your specific needs (high yield but low risk, go for broke, or whatever). Although there will be a commission if you decide to buy through the broker, there is usually no charge for the consultation. Discount brokers are available if you need no investment advice. Most banks have such brokers.

Although savings, life insurance, real estate, and stock investments are probably familiar forms of investment to you, the other types of investments listed in Table ST1.2 may need further clarification.

Annuities provide a monthly income after age 65 (or earlier if desired) in exchange for your investment of monthly premiums during your working years. For example, a 65-year-old man may receive $100 per month as long as he lives (or a lump sum) if he has paid the insurance company $238 annually since age 30.

Bonds are issued by corporations and federal, state, and local governments that need money. In exchange for your money, you get a piece of paper that entitles you to the return of the sum you lend at a specified date (up to 30 years) plus interest on that money. Although bonds are safer than stocks, you could lose all your money if the corporation you lend the money to goes bankrupt. United States Savings Bonds are safe but pay a comparatively low rate of interest.

Mutual funds offer a way of investing in a number of common stocks, corporate bonds, or government bonds at the same time. You invest your money in shares of the mutual fund, whose directors invest the fund's capital in various securities. If the securities they select increase in price, so does the value of your shares in the mutual fund.

Treasury bills (T-bills) are issued by the Federal Reserve Bank. You pay a lower price for the bill than its cash value. For example, you may pay $900 for a T-bill

Anyone who thinks there's safety in numbers hasn't looked at the stock-market pages.
—IRENE PORTER

that will be worth $1,000 on maturity. Maturity of the bill occurs at three, six, nine, or 12 months. The longer the wait, the more money paid on the investment.

Money market investments require a payment of $5,000 or more to a stockbroker who uses your money, together with the money others wish to invest, to purchase high interest securities. Your money can be withdrawn in any amount at any time. As with all investments, you pay a fee to the broker or agent for investing your money. In the past several years, increasing numbers of people have put their money in money market funds.

Individual retirement accounts (IRAs) permit you to set aside up to $2,000 each year for your personal retirement fund. The money you put in your IRA is not automatically tax-free. (You must meet certain criteria restrictions.) Each spouse can open his or her own IRA.

Certificates of deposit (CDs) are insured deposits given to the bank that earn interest at a rate from one day to several years. These high-yield, low-risk investments have become extremely popular. A minimum investment of $500 or more is usually required.

:: Life Insurance

In addition to saving and investing, it is important to be knowledgeable about life insurance. The major purpose of life insurance is to provide income for dependents when the primary wage earner dies. With dual-income couples, life insurance is often necessary to prevent having to give up their home when one wage earner dies. Otherwise, the remaining wage earner may not be able to make the necessary mortgage payments.

□   C O N S I D E R A T I O N   □

Unmarried, childfree, college students probably do not need life insurance. No one is dependent on them for economic support. However, the argument used by some insurance agents who sell campus policies is that college students should buy life insurance while they are young when the premiums are low and when insurability is guaranteed. Still, consumer advocates suggest that life insurance for unmarried, childfree college students is not necessary.

When considering income protection for dependents, there are two basic types of life insurance policies: (1) term insurance and (2) insurance plus investment. As the name implies, term insurance offers protection for a specific time period (usually one, five, 10, or 20 years). At the end of the time period, the protection stops. Although a term insurance policy offers the greatest amount of protection for the least cost, it does not build up cash value (money the insured would get upon surrendering the policy for cash).

Insurance plus investment policies are sold under various names. The first is straight life, ordinary life, or whole life, in which the individual pays a stated premium (based on age and health) as long as the individual lives. When the

When it is a question of money, everybody is of the same religion.
—VOLTAIRE

insured dies, the beneficiary is paid the face value of the policy (the amount of insurance originally purchased). During the life of the insured, the policy also builds up a cash value (which is tax-free), which permits the insured to borrow money from the insurance company at a low rate of interest. A second type of life insurance is a limited payment policy, in which the premiums are paid up after a certain number of years (usually 20) or when the insured reaches a certain age (usually 60 or 65). As with straight, ordinary life, or whole life policies, limited payment policies build up a cash value, and the face value of the policy is not paid until the insured dies. The third type of life insurance is endowment insurance, in which the premiums are paid up after a stated number of years and can be cashed in at a stated age.

Regardless of how they are sold, insurance plus investment policies divide the premium paid by the insured. Part pays for the actual life insurance, and part is invested for the insured, giving the policy a cash value. Unlike term insurance, insurance plus investment policies are not canceled at age 65.

Which type of policy, term or insurance plus investment, should you buy? An insurance agent is likely to suggest the latter and point out the advantages of cash value, continued protection beyond age 65, and level premiums. But the agent has a personal incentive for your buying an insurance plus investment policy. The commission an agent gets on this type of policy is much higher than it is on a term insurance policy.

☐   C O N S I D E R A T I O N   ☐

A strong argument can be made for buying term insurance and investing the additional money that would be needed to pay for the more expensive insurance plus investment policy.

The annual premium for $50,000 worth of renewable term insurance at age 25 is about $175. The same coverage offered in an ordinary life policy—the most common insurance plus investment policy—costs $668 annually, so the difference is $493 per year. If you put this money in the bank at a minimum interest rate of 5 percent, at the end of five years you will have $2,860.32. In contrast, the cash value of an ordinary life policy after five years is $2,350. But to get this money, you have to pay the insurance company interest to borrow it. If you don't want to pay the interest, the company will give you this amount but cancel your policy. In effect, you lose your insurance protection if you receive the cash value of your policy. With term insurance, you have the $2,860.32 in the bank earning interest, and you can withdraw it any time without affecting your insurance program.

It should be clear that for term insurance to be cheaper, you must invest the money you would otherwise be paying for an ordinary life insurance policy. If you can't discipline yourself to save, buy an insurance plus investment policy, which will ensure savings.

Finally, what about the fact that term insurance stops when you are 65, just as you are moving closer to death and needing the protection more? Again, by investing the money that you would otherwise have spent on an insurance plus investment policy, you will have as much or more money for your beneficiary than your insurance plus investment policy would earn.

Whether you buy a term policy, an insurance plus investment policy, or both, there are three options to consider: guaranteed insurability, waiver of premiums, and double or triple indemnity. All are inexpensive and generally should be included in a life insurance policy.

Guaranteed insurability means that the company will sell you more insurance in the future, regardless of your medical condition. For example, suppose you develop cancer after you buy a policy for $10,000. If the guaranteed insurability provision is in your contract, you can buy additional insurance. If not, the company can refuse you more insurance.

Waiver of premiums provides that your premiums will be paid by the company if you become disabled for six months or longer and are unable to earn an income. Such an option ensures that your policy will stay in force because the premiums will be paid. Otherwise, the company will cancel your policy.

Double or triple indemnity means that if you die as the result of an accident, the company will pay your beneficiary twice or three times the face value of your policy.

An additional item you might consider adding to your life insurance policy is a *disability income rider*. If the wage earner becomes disabled and cannot work, the financial consequences for the family are the same as though the wage earner were dead. With disability insurance, the wage earner can continue to provide for the family up to maximum of $3,500 per month or two-thirds of the individual's salary, whichever is smaller. If the wage earner is disabled by accidental injury, payments are made for life. If illness is the cause, payments may be made only to age 65. A 27-year-old spouse and parent who was paralyzed in an automobile accident said, "It was the biggest mistake of my life to think I needed only life insurance to protect my family. Disability insurance turned out to be more important."

□   CONSIDERATION   □

In deciding to buy life insurance, it may be helpful to keep four issues in mind:

1. **Compare prices.** All policies and prices are not the same. In some cases, the higher premiums are for lower coverage.
2. **Select your agent carefully.** Only one in 10 life insurance agents stay in the business. The person you buy life insurance from today may be in the real estate business tomorrow. Choose an agent who has been selling life insurance for at least 10 years.
3. **Seek group rates.** Group life insurance is the least expensive coverage. See if your employer offers a group plan.
4. **Proceed slowly.** Don't rush into buying an insurance policy. Consult several agents, read *Consumer Reports*, and talk with friends to find out what they are doing about their insurance needs.

⠿ Credit

You use credit when you take an item home today and pay for it later. The amount you pay later will depend on the arrangement you make with the seller. Suppose you want to buy a color television set that costs $600. Unless you pay cash, the seller will set up one of three types of credit accounts with you: installment, revolving charge, or open charge.

Under the installment plan, you make a down payment and sign a contract to pay the rest of the money in monthly installments. You and the seller negotiate the period of time over which the payments will be spread and the amount you will pay each month. The seller adds a finance charge to the cash price of the television set and remains the legal owner of the set until you have made your last payment. Most department stores, appliance and furniture stores, and automobile dealers offer installment credit. The cost of buying the $600 color television set can be calculated as illustrated in Table ST1.3.

Instead of buying your $600 television on the installment plan, you might want to buy it on the revolving charge plan. Most credit cards, such as MasterCard, and Visa, represent revolving charge accounts that permit you to buy on credit up to a stated amount during each month. At the end of the month, you may pay the total amount you owe, any amount over the stated "minimum payment due," or the minimum payment. If you choose to pay less than the full amount, the cost of the credit on the unpaid amount is 1.5 percent per month, or 18 percent per year. For instance, if you pay $100 per month for your television for six months, you will still owe $31.62 to be paid the next month, for a total cost (television plus finance charges) of $631.62.

You can also purchase items on an open charge (30-day) account. Under this system you agree to pay in full within 30 days. Since there is no direct service charge or interest for this type of account, the television set would cost only the purchase price. As examples, Sears and J.C. Penney offer open charge (30-day) accounts. If you do not pay the full amount in 30 days, a finance charge is placed on the remaining balance. Both the use of revolving charge and open charge accounts are wise if you pay off the bill before finance charges begin. In deciding which type of credit account to use, remember that credit usually costs money; the longer you take to pay for an item, the more the item will cost you. Exhibit ST1.1 describes the high cost of credit and one way parents of young married couples can help to reduce this burden.

▪▪ TABLE ST1.3 Calculating the Cost of Installment Credit

1. The amount to be financed:		
	Cash price	$ 600.00
	− down payment (if any)	− 50.00
	Amount to be financed	$ 550.00
2. The amount to be paid:		
	Monthly payments	$ 35.00
	× number of payments	× 18
	Total amount repaid	$ 630.00
3. The cost of the credit:	Total amount repaid	$ 630.00
	− amount financed	− 550.00
	Cost of credit	$ 80.00
4. The total cost of the color TV:		
	Total amount repaid	$ 630.00
	+ down payment (if any)	+ 50.00
	Total cost of TV	$ 680.00

E X H I B I T   ST1.1

The High Cost of Interest Over Time

"What hurts young families so often is the high rate of interest they get saddled with over a 30-year-period when they buy a house," said one father of two children. "House payments in the early years are mostly interest, so it takes forever for the kids to pay off the principal."

The first payment on a $65,000 loan at 10 percent interest for 30 years is $570.42. Only $28.75 of this amount is applied to the principal. The remainder ($541.67) is interest. Taxes and fire insurance are an additional $50 and $20, respectively, per month. To shorten the total number of years during which a family must pay the bank $570.42 every month, spouses or parents can make separate monthly payments that are applied specifically to the principal. The sooner the principal is paid off, the sooner all payments will stop.

Three Cs of Credit

Whether you can get credit will depend on the rating you receive on the "three Cs": character, capacity, and capital. *Character* refers to your honesty, sense of responsibility, soundness of judgment, and trustworthiness. *Capacity* refers to your ability to pay the bill when it is due. Such issues as the amount of money you earn and the length of time you have held a job will be considered in evaluating your capacity to pay. *Capital* refers to such assets as bank accounts, stocks, bonds, money market funds, real estate, and so on.

☐   C O N S I D E R A T I O N   ☐

It is particularly important that married individuals establish credit ratings in their own name in case they become widowed or divorced. Otherwise, their credit will depend on their spouse; if the spouse dies or divorce occurs, they will have no credit of their own.

2

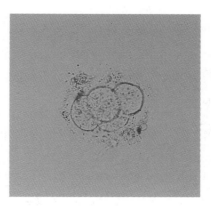

Sexual Anatomy and Physiology

CONTENTS

In the culture in which
we live, it is the custom
to be least informed
upon that subject
concerning which every
individual should
know most—namely,
the structure and
functions of his/her
own body.

—ASHLEY
   MONTAGUE

F WE THINK of the human body as a special type of machine, *anatomy* refers to that machines's part and *physiology* refers to how the parts work. In this topic, we will review the sexual anatomy and physiology of women and men and the reproductive process.

:: Female External Anatomy and Physiology

The external female genitalia are collectively known as the *vulva* (VUHL-vuh), a Latin term meaning "covering." The vulva consists of the mons veneris, the labia, the clitoris, and the vaginal and urethral openings (see Figure ST2.1). Like faces, the female genitalia differ in size, shape, and color, resulting in considerable variability in appearance.

Mons Veneris. The soft cushion of fatty tissue overlaying the pubic bone is called the *mons veneris* (mahns-vuh-NAIR-ihs), also known as the *mons pubis*. This area becomes covered with hair at puberty and has numerous nerve endings. The purpose of the mons is to protect the pubic region during sexual intercourse.

Labia. In the sexually unstimulated state, the urethral and vaginal openings are protected by the *labia majora* (LAY-bee-uh muh-JOR-uh), or "major lips"—two elongated folds of fatty tissue that extend from the mons to the *perineum*, the area of skin between the opening of the vagina and the anus. Located between the labia majora are two additional hairless folds of skin, called the *labia minora* (muh-NOR-uh), or "minor lips," that cover the urethral and vaginal openings and join at the top to form the hood of the clitoris. Some contend that the clitoral hood provides clitoral stimulation during intercourse. Both sets of labia—particularly the inner labia minora—have a rich supply of nerve endings that are sensitive to sexual stimulation.

:: FIGURE ST2.1
External female genitalia

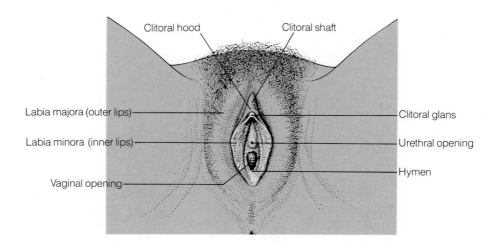

Clitoral hood   Clitoral shaft

Labia majora (outer lips)   Clitoral glans

Labia minora (inner lips)   Urethral opening

                                             Hymen

Vaginal opening

Clitoris. At the top of the labia minora is the *clitoris* (KLIHT-uh-ruhs), which also has a rich supply of nerve endings. The clitoris is a very important site of sexual excitement and, like the penis, becomes erect during sexual excitation.

Vaginal Opening. The area between the labia minora is called the *vestibule*. This includes the urethral opening and the vaginal opening, or *introitus* (ihn-TROH-ih-tuhs), neither of which is visible unless the labia minora are parted. Like the anus, the vaginal opening is surrounded by a ring of sphincter muscles. Although the vaginal opening can expand to accommodate the passage of a baby at childbirth, under conditions of tension these muscles can involuntarily contract, making it difficult to insert an object, including a tampon, into the vagina. The vaginal opening may be covered by a *hymen*, a thin membrane.

☐   C O N S I D E R A T I O N   ☐

Probably no other body part has caused as much grief to so many women as the hymen, which has been regarded throughout history as proof of virginity. A newly wed women who was thought to be without a hymen was often returned to her parents, disgraced by exile, or even tortured and killed. It has been a common practice in many societies to parade a bloody bedsheet after the wedding night as proof of the bride's virginity. The anxieties caused by the absence of a hymen persist even today; in Japan and other countries, sexually experienced women may have a plastic surgeon reconstruct a hymen before marriage. Yet the hymen is really a poor indicator of virtue. Some women are born without a hymen or with incomplete hymens. In others, the hymen is accidentally ruptured by vigorous physical activity or insertion of a tampon. In some women, the hymen may not tear but only stretch during sexual intercourse. Even most doctors cannot easily determine whether a woman is a virgin.

Urethral Opening. Just above the vaginal opening is the urethral opening where urine passes from the body. A short tube, the *urethra*, connects the bladder (where urine collects) with the urethral opening. Because of the shorter length of the female urethra and its close proximity to the anus, women are more susceptible than men to cystitis, a bladder inflammation.

:: Female Internal Anatomy and Physiology

The internal sex organs of the female include the vagina, uterus, and paired Fallopian tubes and ovaries (see Figure ST2.2).

Vagina. Leading from the vaginal opening into the women's body is the *vagina*, a thin walled elastic canal. In addition to receiving the penis during intercourse, the vagina functions as a passageway for menstrual flow and as the birth canal. The walls of the vagina are normally collapsed. Thus the vagina is actually a potential space.

■■ FIGURE ST2.2
Internal female sexual and reproductive organs.

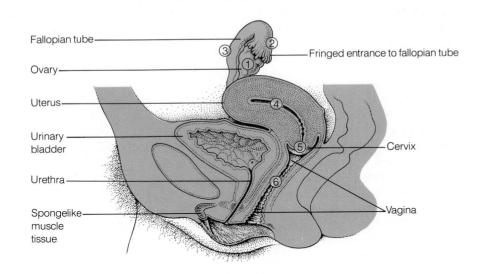

Fallopian tube
Fringed entrance to fallopian tube
Ovary
Uterus
Urinary bladder
Urethra
Cervix
Spongelike muscle tissue
Vagina

□   C O N S I D E R A T I O N   □

Some people erroneously believe that the vagina is a dirty part of the body. In fact, the vagina is a self-cleansing organ. The bacteria that are found naturally in the vagina help to destroy other potentially harmful bacteria. In addition, secretions from the vaginal walls help to maintain its normally acidic environment. The use of feminine hygiene sprays, as well as excessive douching, may cause irritation, allergic reactions, and in some cases, vaginal infection by altering the normal chemical balance of the vagina.

Some researchers believe that there is an extremely sensitive area in the front wall of the vagina 1 to 2 inches into the vaginal opening. The spot swells during stimulation, and although a woman's initial response may be a need to urinate, continued stimulation generally leads to orgasm (Perry & Whipple, 1981). Other researchers disagree about the existence of the so-called "Grafenberg spot," or "G spot," named for gynecologist Ernest Grafenberg who discovered it:

> The "G spot" does *not* exist as such, and the potential professional use of this term would be not only incorrect but also misleading. . . . The *entire* extent of the anterior wall of the vagina (rather than *one* specific spot), as well as the more deeply situated tissues, *including* the urinary bladder and urethral region, are extremely sensitive, being richly endowed with nerve endings (Hock, 1983, 166).

In one study, 48 women volunteered to allow one of several physicians to stimulate them digitally to assess the degree to which they felt erotic sensitivity in their vaginas. Of the 48 women, 45 reported erotic sensitivity located, in most cases, on the anterior wall of the vagina; of those, 66.7 percent either reached orgasm or requested the physician to stop stimulation short of orgasm. The researchers concluded that the study supported the idea of erotic sensitivity in the vagina but that it did not support the idea of a particular location (Alzate & Dippsy, 1984). A questionnaire completed by 1,292 women revealed similar results (Davidson et al., 1989).

Pubococcygeal Muscle. Also called the PC muscle, the pubococcygeal muscle is one of the pelvic floor muscles that surrounds the vagina, the urethra, and the anus. In order to find her PC muscle, a woman is instructed to voluntarily stop the flow of urine after she has begun to urinate. The muscle that stops the flow is the PC muscle. A woman can strengthen her PC muscle by performing the Kegal exercises, named after the physician who devised them. The Kegal exercises involve contracting the PC muscle several times for several sessions per day. Strengthening the PC muscle may increase the women's sexual pleasure by increasing the sensitivity of the vaginal area, and may also permit the woman to create more pleasure for her male partner. Kegal exercises are often recommended after childbirth to restore muscle tone to the PC muscle (which is stretched during the childbirth process).

Uterus. The *uterus* (YOOT-uh-ruhs), or *womb*, resembles a small, inverted pear, which measures about 3 inches long and 3 inches wide at the top in women who have not given birth. A fertilized egg becomes implanted in the wall of the uterus and continues to grow and develop there until delivery. At the lower end of the uterus is the *cervix*, an opening that leads into the vagina.

> ☐ C O N S I D E R A T I O N ☐
>
> All adult women should have a pelvic exam, including a Pap Test, each year. A Pap test is extremely important in the detection of cervical cancer. Cancer of the cervix and uterus is the third most common form of cancer in women; about 2 to 3 percent of all women develop such cancer. Some women may neglect to get a Pap test because they feel embarrassed or anxious about it or because they think they are too young to worry about getting cancer. For all women over age 20, however, having annual Pap tests may mean the difference between life and death.

Fallopian Tubes. *Fallopian* (ful-LOH-pee-uhn) *tubes* extend about 4 inches laterally from either side of the uterus to the ovaries. Fertilization normally occurs in the Fallopian tubes. The tubes transport the *ovum*, or egg, by means of *cilia* (hairlike structures) down the tube and into the uterus.

Ovaries. The *ovaries* (OH-vuhr-eez) are two almond-shaped structures, one on either side of the uterus. The ovaries produce eggs and the female hormones estrogen and progesterone. At her birth, a woman's ovaries contain about 400,000 immature ova total, each enclosed in a thin capsule forming a follicle. Some of the follicles begin to mature at puberty; only about 400 mature ova will be released in a woman's lifetime.

:: Male External Anatomy and Physiology

Although they differ in appearance, many structures of the male (see Figure ST2.3) and female genitals develop from the same embryonic tissue (the penis and the clitoris, for example).

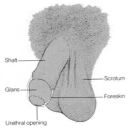

Penis. The *penis* (PEE-nihs) is the primary male sexual organ. In the unaroused state, the penis is soft and hangs between the legs. When sexually stimulated, the penis enlarges and becomes erect, enabling penetration of the vagina. The penis functions not only to deposit sperm in the female's vagina but also as a passageway from the male's bladder to eliminate urine. In cross section, the penis can be seen to consist of three parallel cylinders of tissue containing many cavities, two *corpora cavernosa* (cavernous bodies) and a *corpus spongiosum* (spongy body) through which the urethra passes. The penis has numerous blood vessels; when stimulated, the arteries dilate and blood enters faster than it can leave. The cavities of the cavernous and spongy bodies fill with blood, and pressure against the fibrous membranes causes the penis to become erect. The head of the penis is called the *glans*. At birth, the glans is covered by *foreskin*. The surgical procedure in which the foreskin is pulled forward and cut off is known as *circumcision*.

:: FIGURE ST2.3
External male organs.

□   C O N S I D E R A T I O N   □

Circumcision was performed by the Egyptians as early as 4000 B.C. and was an early religious rite for members of the Jewish and Moslem faiths. To Jewish people, circumcision symbolizes the covenant with God made by Abraham. Today, the primary reason for performing circumcision is to ensure proper hygiene. The smegma that can build up under the foreskin is a potential breeding ground for infection. But circumcision is a rather drastic procedure merely to ensure proper hygiene, which, as the Academy of Pediatrics suggests, can just as easily be accomplished by pulling back the foreskin and cleaning the glans during normal bathing. However, circumcision is indicated when the foreskin will not retract.

Scrotum. The *scrotum* (SCROH-tuhm) is the sac located below the penis, which contains the *testes*. Beneath the skin covering the scrotum is a thin layer of muscle fibers that contract when it is cold, helping to draw the testes (testicles) closer to the body to keep the temperature of the sperm constant. Sperm can only be produced at a temperature several degrees lower than normal body temperature; any prolonged variation can result in sterility.

□   C O N S I D E R A T I O N   □

It is particularly hazardous for a male to contract a case of the mumps, a viral infection that often causes swelling of the testicles. The sheath in which the testes are enclosed does not readily expand, and the resulting pressure can cause sterility.

⠿ Male Internal Anatomy and Physiology

The male internal organs, often referred to as the reproductive organs, include the testes, where the sperm is produced, a duct system to transport the sperm out of the body, and some additional structures that produce the seminal fluid in which the sperm is mixed before ejaculation (see Figure ST2.4).

Testes. The male gonads—the paired testes, or testicles—develop from the same embryonic tissue as the female gonads (the ovaries). The two oval-shaped testicles are suspended in the scrotum by the *spermatic cord* and enclosed within a fibrous sheath. The function of the testes is to produce spermatozoa and male hormones, primarily testosterone.

Duct System. Several hundred *seminiferous tubules* come together to form a tube in each testicle called the *epididymis* (ehp-uh-DIHD-uh-muhs), the first part of the duct system that transports sperm. If uncoiled, each tube would be 20 feet long. Sperm spend from two to six weeks traveling through the epididymus as they mature and are reabsorbed by the body if ejaculation does not occur. One ejaculation contains an average of 360 million sperm cells.

The sperm leave the scrotum through the second part of the duct system, the *vas deferens* (vas-DEF-uh-renz). These 14- to 16-inch paired ducts transport the sperm from the epididymis up and over the bladder to the prostate gland. Rhythmic contractions during ejaculation force the sperm into the paired ejaculatory ducts that run through the prostate gland. The entire length of this portion of the duct system is less than 1 inch. It is here that the sperm mix with seminal fluid to form *semen* before being propelled to the outside through the urethra.

Seminal Vesicles and Prostate Gland. The *seminal vesicles* resemble two small sacs, each about 2 inches in length, located behind the bladder. These vesiclesse-

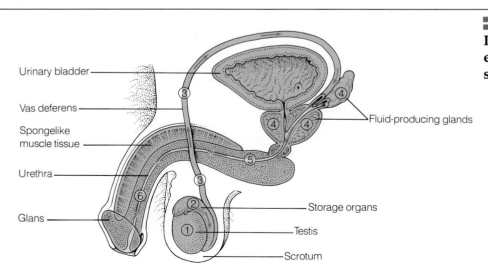

⠿ FIGURE ST2.4
Internal and external male sexual organs.

Urinary bladder

Vas deferens

Spongelike muscle tissue

Urethra

Glans

Fluid-producing glands

Storage organs

Testis

Scrotum

crete their own fluids, which empty into the ejaculatory duct to mix with sperm and fluids from the prostate gland.

Most of the seminal fluid comes from the *prostate gland,* a chestnut-sized structure located below the bladder and in front of the rectum. The fluid is alkaline and serves to protect the sperm in the more acidic environments of the male urethra and female vagina. Males over 45 should have a rectal exam annually to detect the presence of prostate cancer.

A small amount of clear, sticky fluid is also secreted into the urethra before ejaculation by two pea-sized *Cowper's,* or *bulbourethral, glands* located below the prostate gland. This protein rich fluid alkalizes the urethral passage which prolongs sperm life.

☐   C O N S I D E R A T I O N   ☐

The fluid secreted by the Cowper's glands can often be noticed on the tip of the penis during sexual arousal. It may contain stray sperm, so that withdrawal of the penis from the vagina before ejaculation is a risky method of birth control.

3

AIDS and Other Sexually Transmitted Diseases

CONTENTS

A IDS has become one of the most visible topics in our society. Of all the diseases which may be transmitted sexually, AIDS is the most life threatening. Sexually transmitted diseases (STDs) are also known as *venereal diseases*. Venus was the Roman goddess of love, and since some diseases are transmitted through various acts of love (kissing, cunnilingus, fellatio, intercourse), the term "venereal" (from Venus) has been used to describe such diseases. STDs are also referred to as *social diseases,* because they are contracted primarily through sociosexual contact. In effect, any person who has physical or sexual contact with someone who has a sexually transmitted disease may get that disease. The exposure may be through heterosexual or homosexual contacts. Table ST3.1 lists some of the myths and facts about STDs. We will review some of the more common STDs in the following sections.

:: AIDS (Acquired Immune Deficiency Syndrome)

Acquired immune deficiency syndrome (AIDS) represents the appearance in previously healthy individuals of various aggressive infections and malignancies. AIDS was first seen among homosexual and bisexual males with multiple sex partners (still the predominant victims), hemophiliacs, Haitian immigrants to the United States, and intravenous drug users.

■ **DATA:** *Five percent of all adults and 2 percent of college students in the United States have the AIDS virus (Center for Disease Control, 1989).*

:: TABLE ST3.1 **Myths and Facts About Sexually Transmitted Diseases (STDs)**

MYTH	FACT
STDs in the genitals cannot be transmitted to the mouth, and vice versa.	Transmission of STD infections from mouth to genitals and vice versa does occur.
If you have syphilis or gonorrhea, you will know it.	Some infected people show no signs of having syphilis or gonorrhea until many years later.
You can avoid having to see a physician by treating your suspected STD infection at home.	Only a physician can recommend a treatment plan for STDs.
You cannot have more than one STD at a time.	More than one half of the women who visited one STD clinic had two or more STDs.
Birth-control pills protect you from STDs.	Birth-control pills may increase a woman's chance of contracting various STDs when exposed.
Once you have been cured of an STD, you cannot get it again.	You can get an STD infection any time you come into contact with it, whether you have already had it or not.
Syphilis, gonorrhea, and AIDS can be contracted by contact with a toilet seat.	The germs of these diseases cannot live in the open air.

Although only 5 percent of AIDS cases in this country have been officially attributed to heterosexual transmission, this rate is increasing. In fact, AIDS cases attributed to heterosexual transmission are growing faster than any other category of AIDS cases. The Center for Disease Control reported that from 1988 to 1989, there was a 36 percent increase in the number of AIDS cases caused by heterosexual transmission (Hilt, 1990). The increase in the percentage of AIDS cases related to heterosexual transmission is even more evident when we look at a longer time span.

■ **DATA:** *In 1981, .5 percent of reported AIDS cases was caused by heterosexual transmission. By 1989, this percentage had risen to 5 percent, representing an increase of 900 percent (Thompson, 1990).*

Only a small percentage of AIDS victims have been infected during a blood transfusion. Fresh blood, semen, preseminal fluid, and vaginal fluid infected with HTLV-III (human T-cell lymphotrophic virus III), also referred to as AIDS virus, must enter the bloodstream for the virus to be transmitted from one person to another. The AIDS virus is not superficially transmitted. Transmission can only occur if a "critical amount of an infected body fluid gains access to an individual's bloodstream through tissue capable of absorbing it. Rectal and vaginal linings are in this group" (Campbell, 1986).

■ **DATA:** *By the end of 1992, it is estimated that 365,000 AIDS cases will have been diagnosed. Annually, there will be about 80,000 cases (Center for Disease Control, 1989). It can take as long as 3 years before the AIDS infection is evident in a blood test (Chase, 1989, 1), and 10 years from the time of initial infection until the onset of AIDS (Center for Disease Control, 1989).*

Ryan White contracted AIDS through a blood transfusion and was discriminated against by his peers, their parents, and school officials.

AIDS is not equally distributed among racial and ethnic groups.

■ **DATA:** *Of those classified as having AIDS, 60.9 percent are white, 25.5 percent are black, and 12.9 percent are hispanic. However, the risk of AIDS in blacks and hispanics is almost 3 times as great as that in whites (Selik et al., 1988).*

AIDS is also not distributed equally among women and men. About 90 percent of all diagnosed AIDS cases in the United States have been men, compared to only 10 percent women (Centers for Disease Control, 1990).

AIDS attacks the immune system of the body and makes it vulnerable to infection. The incubation period for AIDS ranges from a few months to about two years. Symptoms of AIDS include swollen glands, persistent fever, persistent dry cough, bruiselike markings on the skin, weight loss, night sweats, and persistent diarrhea. *Kaposi's sarcoma* (KS), a type of cancer, and *Pneumocystis carinii pneumonia* (PCP) have been associated with AIDS. Seventy percent of all AIDS deaths result from PCP.

AIDS patients often die because their bodies become incapable of combating other diseases and infections. Of those who contract AIDS, 80 percent are dead within three years.

A test, ELISA (enxyme-linked immunosorbent assay), can now assess the presence of antibodies in the bloodstream of a person who has been exposed to AIDS. This test does not confirm that the person has or will develop AIDS. However, the test should be taken by pregnant women who have been exposed to high-risk groups. There is a 40–60 percent chance that a pregnant woman infected with AIDS will transmit the virus to her child. Other persons who may be at risk should also be tested for AIDS. Those testing positive will be given a second test for more definitive screening.

□　　　　　　　C O N S I D E R A T I O N　　　　　　　□

To avoid getting AIDS, unprotected sexual intercourse, anal intercourse, and oral sex with persons in high-risk categories (homosexual and bisexual males; prostitutes; hemophiliacs; heterosexual partners in high-risk groups; heterosexuals exposed to high-risk partners) should be avoided. The current thinking is if you have sex with someone, you are having sex with everyone that person has had sex with in the last 10 years.

The fear of contracting AIDS is real.

■ **DATA:** *Twenty-one percent of 196 inner city adolescents in New York City said that they would commit suicide if they tested positive for AIDS (Goodman & Cohall, 1989).*

Some research suggests that the fear of AIDS has not significantly altered the sexual choices and behavior of individuals in our society. While college students report that they are fearful of contracting AIDS and have changed their behavior to reduce the chance of being infected, independent measures of their behavior change do not support their claims (Carroll, 1988). Inner city black adolescents also report that they have changed their behavior (use condoms more often or abstain from intercourse) because of fear of AIDS. However, there are no independent measures of their behavior to support the self-report data (Goodman & Cohall, 1989).

Regarding the treatment of AIDS, Azidothymidine (AZT) is useful in treating some people infected with the AIDS virus.

> Pierre Ludington, a former San Francisco schoolteacher who tested positive, remains healthy and without symptoms after two years of taking AZT (plus a drug called acyclovir) in a research project. 'I felt that if it weren't toxic to me, I'd be a fool not to take it . . . Two years later, I haven't had so much as a cold. It's important for people to know AZT isn't toxic to everyone' (Chase, 1989, 10).

Pentamidine is also helpful in treating PCP, the pneumonia associated with AIDS. When pentamidine is inhaled directly into the lungs it is dramatically effective in preventing the pneumonia. Hence, "it is important to change our conception of everyone dies from AIDS" (Thompson, 1989, 52). Physicians are now beginning to think of AIDS as diabetes. There is no cure, but it can be managed in some cases.

Another drug that has also been given FDA approval is Dideoxyinosine (ddI). In limited trials the drug seems to be as effective as AZT with fewer side effects. The drug is still considered experimental and is not to be viewed as a cure.

:: Genital Herpes

Herpes refers to more than 50 viruses related by size, shape, internal composition, and structure. One such herpes is *genital herpes*. Whereas the disease has been known for at least 2,000 years, media attention to genital herpes is relatively new. Also known as *herpes simplex virus type 2* (HSV–2), genital herpes is a viral infection that is usually transmitted during sexual contact. Symptoms occur in the form of a cluster of small, painful blisters or sores at the point of infection, most often on the penis or around the anus in men. In women, the blisters usually appear around the vagina but may also develop inside the vagina, on the cervix, and sometimes on the anus.

Another type of herpes, *labial* or *lip herpes*, originates in the mouth. Herpes simplex virus type 1 (HSV–1) is a biologically different virus with which people are more familiar as cold sores on the lips. These sores can be transferred to the genitals by the fingers or by oral-genital contact. In the past, genital and lip herpes had site specificity; HSV–1 was always found on the lips or in the mouth, and HSV–2 was always found in the genitals. But because of the increase in fellatio and cunnilingus, HSV–1 herpes may be found in the genitals and HSV–2 may be found in the lips.

| ■ **DATA:** *At least 1 in 6 U.S adults or 26 million people are infected with genital herpes (Johnson et al., 1989).*

The first symptoms of genital herpes appear a couple of days to three weeks after exposure. At first, these symptoms may include an itching or burning sensation during urination, followed by headache, fever, aches, swollen glands, and—in women—vaginal discharge. The symptoms worsen over about 10 days, during which there is a skin eruption, followed by the appearance of painful sores, which soon break open and become extremely painful during genital contact or when touched. The acute illness may last from three to six weeks. "I've got herpes,'' said one sufferer,'' and it's a very uneven discomfort. Somedays I'm okay, but other days I'm miserable.''

As with syphilis, the symptoms of genital herpes subside (the sores dry up, scab over, and disappear) and the persons feels good again. But the virus settles in the nerve cells in the spinal column and may cause repeated outbreaks of the symptoms in about one-third of those infected.

Stress, menstruation, sunburn, fatigue, and the presence of other infections seem to be related to the reappearance of the virus. Although such recurrences are usually milder and of shorter duration than the initial outbreak, the resurfacing of the virus may occur throughout the person's life. "It's not knowing when the thing is going to come back that's the bad part about herpes," said one woman.

☐   C O N S I D E R A T I O N   ☐

The herpes virus is usually contagious during the time that a person has visible sores but not when the skin is healed. However, infected people may have a mild recurrence yet be unaware that they are contagious. Aside from visible sores, itching, burning, or tingling sensations at the sore site also suggest that the person is contagious. Use a condom.

At the time of this writing, there is no cure for herpes. Because it is a virus, it does not respond to antibiotics as syphilis and gonorrhea do. A few procedures that help to relieve the symptoms and promote healing of the sores include seeing a physician to look for and treat any other genital infections near the herpes sores, keeping the sores clean and dry, taking hot sitz baths three times a day, and wearing loose-fitting cotton underwear to enhance air circulation. Proper nutrition, adequate sleep and exercise, and avoiding physical or mental stress help people to cope better with recurrences.

Acyclovir, marketed as Zovirax, is an ointment that can be applied directly on the sores, helps to relieve pain, speed healing, and reduce the amount of time that live viruses are present in the sores. A more effective tablet form of acyclovir which significantly reduces the rate of recurring episodes of genital herpes is also available. Once acyclovir is stopped, the herpetic recurrences resume. Acyclovir seems to make the symptoms of first-episode genital herpes more manageable, but it is less effective during subsequent outbreaks. Immu Vir—an alternative to acyclovir—is primarily for use by persons who have frequent outbreaks of genital herpes (once a month or more). This ointment is designed to reduce pain, healing time, and number of outbreaks. The drug has no known side effects.

☐   C O N S I D E R A T I O N   ☐

A person with genital herpes can prevent infecting someone else by avoiding genital contact until the sores have healed. It is also recommended that the man use a condom and the woman use a diaphragm for two weeks after the sores have healed-.But using the condom or diaphragm is not completely effective, because the herpes virus can pass through these synthetic membranes.

Coping with the psychological and emotional aspects of having genital herpes is often more difficult than coping with the physical aspects of the disease. Herpes victims typically go through a predictable pattern of shock, anger, bitterness, and depression. The latter may result in social withdrawal—not only from sexual encounters, but also from friends who are not sexual partners. Getting accurate information about the disease, dealing with a negative self-image, and learning how to tell someone who is sexually interested in them that they have herpes are among the challenges facing herpes sufferers.

:: Genital Warts

Also known as venereal warts, human papillomavirus, or HPV, genital warts may appear as tiny bumps or thickenings of the skin or mucous membrane. There is also an invisible variety (flat warts) which can only be detected by a Pap smear. The virus can be transmitted through sexual intercourse, oral, or rectal intercourse. In women, genital wart infection most commonly develops on the vulva, inside the vagina, on the cervix, or on or near the anus. In men, the infection appears most often on the penis but may appear on the anus or within the rectum. Sometimes there are no symptoms. If the warts are left untreated, about 70 percent of the warts may become malignant. Cervical cancer is the most dangerous outcome. Any sexual partner(s) of an infected individual should undergo prompt examination.

■ **DATA:** *About 500,000 new cases of genital warts are reported annually. Some researchers believe that 1 in 20 sexually active people have genital warts (Eisenberg, 1988; Horn, 1989).*

Treatment of genital warts involves applying local substances (podophyllin), burning or freezing the skin, or use of lasers. All methods of treatment have high failure rates (Horn, 1989). Even though these procedures may eliminate the warts, they may not necessarily eliminate the virus and the warts will recur. The best treatment is prevention—use of a condom, having sex with low-risk partners, and limiting the number of partners.

:: Chlamydia

Chlamydia (clah-MID-i-ah) has been described as the "the silent disease." It refers to one of two types of infection: (1)*Chlamydia trachomatis*, which may cause infections in the genitals, eyes, and lungs of humans, and (2) *Chlamydia psittici*, which primarily infects birds.

In this discussion, we will focus on *Chlamydia trachomatis*, or the CT variety. Public attention has been focused on CT as a result of gynecologists and urologists who, after seeing increasing numbers of sexually transmitted diseases that were not caused by gonorrhea, syphilis, or genital herpes, became aware of the devastating consequences of untreated chlamydia infections.

Several facts about chlamydia include (Sammons, 1990):

1. *Chlamydia is a bacteria.* CT was once thought to be a virus, but improved laboratory techniques have permitted medical researchers to identify CT as a bacteria. The good news about this discovery is that bacteria can be successfully treated with antibiotics; a virus cannot be.

2. *Chlamydia is transmittable.* CT is easily transmitted from person to person via sexual contact. The microorganisms are most often found in the urethra of the man, the cervix, uterus, and Fallopian tubes of the woman, or the rectums of either men or women. In addition to direct contact, CT infections can occur indirectly by contact with, as examples, a towel, handkerchief, or the side of a hot tub in which the bacteria are present.

    Genital to eye transmission of the bacteria can also occur. If a person with a genital CT infection rubs his or her own eye or the eye of a partner after touching infected genitals, the bacteria can be transferred to the eye, and vice versa. Finally, infants can get CT as they pass through the cervix of their infected mothers during delivery.

3. *Numbers infected by chlamydia.* Worldwide, it is estimated that 300 million people contract sexually transmitted chlamydial infections each year. When the eye infection, *chlamydial trachoma,* is considered, over 500 million cases are contracted yearly. At least 2 million of the 200 million people who contract *chlamydial trachoma* each year are permanently blinded by the infection; most of these people live in Asia and Africa. The rate of blindness due to chlamydial infections in the United States is much lower, due to climate and the medication readily available to control the infection.

■ **DATA:** *It is estimated that 10 to 30 percent of sexually active adolescent women in the United States have chlamydia (Leslie-Harwit & Mehus, 1989).*

4. *Chlamydia occurs as a multiple infection.* Chlamydial infections rarely occur by themselves. One-half of all persons infected with gonorrhea also have CT. In most cases, only the gonorrhea is treated, leaving the CT to flourish and be transferred to subsequent sexual partners.

5. *Chlamydia is asymptomatic.* Women and men who are infected with CT usually do not know that they have the disease. The result is that they infect new partners unknowingly, who infect others unknowingly—and unendingly. CT rarely shows obvious symptoms, which accounts for its being known as "the silent disease."

6. *Chlamydia is curable if treated early.* Although delay in treatment can be devastating, CT is curable if it is diagnosed and treated before the bacteria has had a chance to flourish. CT has often been overlooked as a cause of genital infection, because laboratory tests were not sensitive and accurate enough to reveal the presence of this bacteria until recently.

7. *Persons likely to get chlamydia.* Heterosexuals, homosexuals, and bisexuals who have intercourse or oral or anal sex with several partners are more likely to contract chlamydia than people in these groups who restrict their sexual activity to one person. Individuals who have several sexual partners are also more likely to be having sex with people who also have several sexual partners—thus compounding the risk. In general, the greater the number of sexual partners, the greater the risk of contracting CT.

8. *Diagnosing chlamydia.* Although CT often exhibits no symptoms, symptoms do occur in some cases of CT. In men, the symptoms include pus from the penis, a sore on the penis, sore testis, or a bloody stool. In women, symptoms include low back pain, pelvic pain, a boil on the vaginal lip, or a bloody discharge. Symptoms in either sex include a sore on the tongue, a sore on the finger, pain during urination, or the sensation of needing to urinate frequently. Even in the absence of such symptoms, a person who has had sex with an individual who has multiple sex partners should consult a physician. The presence of chlamydia can be determined by a laboratory test, using Chlamydiazyme, within 24 hours. The physician can then prescribe antibiotics as appropriate. (Chlamydia can be cured with tetracycline.)

░ Gonorrhea

Also known as "the clap," "the whites," "morning drop," and "the drip," gonorrhea is the second most communicable disease in the United States (the first is the common cold). *Communicable* means that, like the common cold, the disease is easily "caught" from someone who has it.

Individuals most often contract gonorrhea through having genital contact with someone who is carrying the *gonococcus* (gahn-uh-KAHK-us) *bacteria*. These bacteria live in the urethra and around the cervix of the woman and in the urinary tract of the man. During intercourse, some of the bacteria are transferred from the mucous membranes inside the urethra of one partner to the other. The bacteria may also enter the throat during oral-genital contact or the rectum during anal intercourse.

Although some infected men show no signs, 80 percent do so between three and eight days after exposure. They begin to discharge a thick, white pus from the penis and to feel pain or discomfort during urination. They may also have swollen lymph glands in the groin. Women are more likely to show no signs of the infection, but when they do, they are sometimes in the form of a discharge from the vagina along with a burning sensation. More often, a woman becomes aware of gonorrhea only after she feels extreme discomfort, which is a result of the untreated infection traveling up into her uterus and Fallopian tubes. *Pelvic inflammatory disease* (PID) is the term used to describe the inflammation in these areas caused by the gonococci or other bacteria.

☐   C O N S I D E R A T I O N   ☐

Undetected and untreated gonorrhea is dangerous. Not only does the infected person pass on this disease to the next partner, but other undesirable consequences may also result. The bacteria may affect the brain, joints, and reproductive systems. Both men and women may develop meningitis (inflammation of the tissues surrounding the brain and spinal cord), arthritis, and sterility. In men, the urethra may become blocked, necessitating frequent visits to a physician to clear the passage for urination. Infected women may have spontaneous abortions and premature or stillborn infants.

▪▪ Syphilis

Although syphilis is less prevalent than gonorrhea, the effects of syphilis are more devastating and include mental illness, blindness, heart disease—even death. The *spirochete* (SPY-roh-keet) *bacteria*—the villain germs—enter the body through mucous membranes that line various body openings. With your tongue, feel the inside of your cheek. This is a layer of mucous membrane—the substance in which spirochetes thrive. Similar membranes are in the vagina and urethra of the penis. If you kiss or have genital contact with someone harboring these bacteria, they can be absorbed into your mucous membranes and cause syphilitic infection. Your syphilis will then progress through at least three or four stages.

In stage one (primary-stage syphilis), a small sore will appear at the site of the infection between 10 and 90 days after exposure. The *chancre* (SHANK-er), as it is called, shows on the tip of the man's penis, in the labia or cervix of the woman, or in either partner's mouth or rectum. The chancre neither hurts nor itches, and if left untreated will disappear in three to five weeks. This disappearance encourages infected people to believe that they are cured—one of the tricky aspects of syphilis. In reality, the disease is still present and doing great harm, even though there are no visible signs.

During the second stage (secondary-stage syphilis), beginning from two to 12 weeks after the chancre has disappeared, other signs of syphilis appear in the form of a rash all over the body or just on the hands or feet. Welts and sores may also occur, as well as fever, headaches, sore throat, and hair loss. Syphilis has been called "the great imitator" because it mimics so many other diseases (for example, infectious mononucleosis, cancer, and psoriasis). Whatever the symptoms, they too will disappear without treatment. The person may again be tricked into believing that nothing is wrong.

For about two-thirds of those with late, untreated syphilis (latent-stage syphilis), the disease seems to have gone away and left no subsequent effects. However, the spirochetes are still in the body and can attack any organ at any time. For the other one-third, serious harm results. Tertiary syphilis—the third stage—may disable or kill. Heart disease, blindness, brain damage, loss of bowel and bladder control, difficulty in walking, and impotence may result.

Aside from avoiding contact with a person infected with syphilis, early detection and treatment is essential. Blood tests and examination of material from the infected site can help to verify the existence of syphilis. But such tests are not always accurate. Blood tests reveal the presence of antibodies, not spirochetes, and it sometimes takes three months before the body produces detectable antibodies. Sometimes there is no chancre anywhere on the person's body.

Treatment for syphilis is similar to that for gonorrhea. Penicillin or other antibiotics (for those allergic to penicillin) are effective. Infected persons treated in the early stages can be completely cured with no ill effects. If the syphilis has progressed into the later stages, any damage that has been done cannot be repaired.

☐   C O N S I D E R A T I O N   ☐

Another problem with syphilis is the effect it has on the newborn of an infected woman. If the pregnant woman does not receive treatment, her baby is likely to be born with congenital syphilis. If she is treated by the eighteenth week of pregnancy, the fetus will not be affected.

:: Getting Help

If you suspect that you have had contact with someone (see Table ST3.2) who has a sexually transmitted disease or if you have any symptoms of the STDs discussed in this Special Topic section, call the toll free national VD hotline at 800–227–8922. You will not be asked to identify yourself; you will be given information about your symptoms and told to contact STD clinics in your area that offer confidential, free treatment.

A newsletter, *The Helper,* is published quarterly to provide the latest information for herpes sufferers. The newsletter can be obtained by writing to HELP (Her-

:: TABLE 3.2 **AIDS and Other Sexually Transmitted Diseases**

GTD	SYMPTOMS	TREATMENT	COMPLICATIONS
Acquired Immunodeficiency Syndrome (AIDS)	Most people who are infected with the AIDS virus, Human Immunodeficiency Virus, show no signs or symptoms until their condition progresses to AIDS-related complex (ARC) or full-brown AIDS. Symptoms of ARC and AIDS include: - persistent cough - fever - weight loss - night sweats - skin rashes - diarrhea	There is presently no cure or vaccine to prevent the AIDS virus.	Fifty percent of individuals who develop the AIDS virus die within the first 2 years. 80 percent die within the first 3 years.
Chlamydia (a unique species of bacteria that causes the most widespread STD in the US)	Many individuals who are infected show no signs or symptoms of chlamydial infections. Symptoms include: - pain or burning upon urination - discharge form genital area - low-grade fever - lower abdominal pain - frequent need to urinate	Antibiotics.	If untreated can cause: - arthritis - sterility - permanent damage to the reproductive organs - ectopic pregnancy
Genital Herpes (an STD caused by the Herpes Simplex Virus or HSV).	Skin around genital area becomes red and sensitive. Painful blisters and bumps may appear. Other symptoms include: - swollen glands - headaches - muscle aches - fever	There is presently no cure or vaccine to prevent genital herpes. The drug, acyclovir, has been used to reduce frequency and duration of genital herpes outbreaks.	Women with genital herpes may be at an increased risk for cervical cancer.

▪▪ TABLE 3.2 **Continued**

GTD	SYMPTOMS	TREATMENT	COMPLICATIONS
Genital Warts (warts or growths that are caused by viruses called Human Papilloma Virus (HPV) and spread primarily through sexual contact).	Small to large wart or bump-like growths on the genital area. May be pink or red and appear in clusters or alone.	Treatment depends on the size and location of the warts. Podophyllin or surgical methods are commonly used in treatment.	Women with genital warts may be at an increased risk for cervical cancer.
Gonorrhea (an STD caused by a bacterial pathogen and spread through sexual contact).	Many individuals who are infected show no signs or or symptoms. Symptoms include: - discharge from the penis or vagina - burning upon urination - urge to urinate frequently - low-grade fever - fatigue	Antibiotics.	If untreated can cause: - permanent damage to the reproductive organs and/or urinary tract - pelvic inflammatory disease - possible sterility
Syphilis (caused by a bacterium that attacks the nervous and cardiovascular systems and is spread through sexual contact).	In the primary stages, a hard, painless chancre or sore will usually appear, then disappear in a few weeks. The secondary stage in characterized by a skin rash and flu-like symptoms.	Antibiotics.	If untreated can cause: - damage to the cardiovascular system - damage to the nervous system - blindness - death

SOURCE: Developed for this text by Suzanne Kellerman, R.N., Health Educator, Student Health Services, East Carolina University, Greenville, N.C. 27858. Used by permission of Suzanne Kellerman.

petics Engaged in Living Productively); 260 Sheridan Avenue; Palo Alto, CA 94306. Herpes information is also available at 415–328–7710.

Duke University in Durham, North Carolina, has opened an AIDS clinic to treat AIDS victims (919–684–2660). For special information about AIDS, call 800–342–2437; in Washington, D.C. call 646–8182.

☐   C O N S I D E R A T I O N   ☐

In addition to getting medical attention or advice for yourself and your sexual partner, sexual contact with others should be avoided until your infection is cured or is no longer contagious. You should also exercise care if you masturbate. For example, if you accidentally touch a herpes sore during masturbation, be careful not to put your finger near your mouth or eye before washing your hands.

▪▪ Prevention

The best way to avoid getting a sexually transmitted disease is to avoid sexual contact or to have contact only with partners who are not infected. This means restricting your sexual contacts to those who limit their relationships to one person. The person most likely to get a sexually transmitted disease has sexual relations with a number of partners or with a partner who has a variety of partners.

In addition to restricting sexual contacts, putting on a condom before the penis touches the partner's body will make it difficult for sexually transmitted diseases, including genital herpes, to pass from one person to another. After genital contact, it is also a good idea for the partners to urinate and to wash their genitals with soap and hot water.

Hello Hellen—I really like you. Can I have some blood and urine for a test?
—ROBIN WILLIAMS

4

Resources and Organizations

Abortion
Pro Choice
National Abortion Rights Action League
1424 K St. N. W.
Washington, DC 20005
Pro Life
National Right to Life Committee
419 Seventh St., N. W., Suite 500
Washington, DC 20045
Phone: 202–626–8800

Birth Alternatives
Nurse-Midwives
American College of Nurse-Midwives
1522 K St., N.W., Suite 1120
Washington, DC 20005
Phone: 202–347–5445

Breastfeeding
LaLeche International, Inc.
9616 Minneapolis Ave.
Franklin Park, IL 60123
Phone: 708–455–7730

Child Abuse
National Committee for Prevention of Child Abuse
332 South Michigan Ave., Suite 1600
Chicago, IL 60604–4357
Phone: 312–663–3520

National Child Abuse Hotline
Phone: 800–422–4453

Child Care
Au Pair in America
100 Greenwich Ave.
Greenwich, CT 06830

Child Custody
Joint Custody Association
10606 Wilkins Ave.
Los Angeles, CA 90024
Phone: 213–475–5352

Divorced Mothers
Mothers Without Custody
P.O. Box 56762
Houston, TX 77256–6762
Phone: 301–552–2319

Drugs
Cocaine National Treatment and Referral Information Service
Phone: 800–262–2463

Family Planning
Planned Parenthood Federation of America
2010 Massachusetts Ave., N.W.

Washington, DC 20036
Phone: 202–785–3351

Fertility
American Fertility Society
2140 11th Ave., South Suite 200
Birmingham, AL 35205
Phone: 205–933–8494

Gender Equality
National Organization for Changing Men
P.O. Box 451
Watseka, IL 60970
Phone: 815–347–2279

National Organization for Women
1000 16th St., N.W. Suite 700
Washington, DC 20036
Phone: 202–331–0066

Genetic Counseling
National Foundation for Jewish Genetic Disease
45 Sutton Place South
New York, NY 10003
Phone: 212–371–1030

Healthy Baby
Healthy Mothers-Healthy Babies Coalition
Department of Public Affairs
409 12th St., S.W.
Washington, DC 20024
Phone: 202–638–5577

Homosexual Life Style
Parents and Friends of Lesbians and Gays
P.O. Box 27605
Washington, DC 20038

Incest Prevention
Committee for Children
172 20th Ave.
Seattle, WA 98122
Phone: 206–322–5050

Interracial Parenting
Council on Interracial Books for Children
1841 Broadway Suite 608
New York, NY 10023
Phone: 212–757–5339

Marriage Enrichment
Training in Marriage Enrichment
American Guidance Service
Publisher's Building
P.O. Box 99
Circle Pines, MN 55014–1796
Phone: 612–786–4343

Marriage Therapy
American Association for Marriage and Family
Therapy
1717 K St., N.W., Suite 407
Washington, DC 20006
Phone: 202–429–1825

Mediation
Academy of Family Mediators
P.O. Box 10501
Eugene, OR 97440
Phone: 503–345–1205

Ovum Transfer
Harbor-UCLA Medical Center
1000 West Carson St.
Torrance, CA 90509
Phone: 213–533–2345

Sex Education
Sex Information and Education Council of the
United States
(SIECUS)
32 Washington Place 5th Floor
New York, NY 10003
Phone: 212–673–3850

Sexual Therapy
American Association of Sex Educators, Counselors, and Therapists (AASECT)
2000 N St., N.W., Suite 110
Washington, DC 20036

Masters and Johnson Institute
24 South Kings Highway
St. Louis, MO 63108
Phone: 314–361–2277

Loyola Sexual Dysfunction Clinic
Loyola University Hospital
2160 South First Ave.
Maywood, IL 60153
Phone: 708–531–3000

Sexual Dependency Unit
4101 Golden Valley Road
Golden Valley, MN 55422
Phone: 612–588–2771

Sexually Transmitted Diseases
AIDS Hotline
Phone: 800–342–AIDS

AZT Hotline
Phone: 800–843–9388

Centers for Disease Control
Technical Information Services
Bureau of State Services
Atlanta, GA 30333
Phone: 404–329–3311

Herpes Resource Information
260 Sheridan Ave.
Palo Alto, CA 94302
Phone: 919–361–2120

National VD Hotline
Phone: 800–227–8922
(in California: 800–982–5883)

Single Parenthood
Parents Without Partners International
8807 Colesville Rd.
Silver Springs, MD 20910
Phone: 301–588–9354

Single Mothers by Choice
1642 Gracie Square Station
New York, NY 10028
Phone: 212–988–0993

Stepfamilies
Stepfamily Association of America, Inc.
215 Centennial Mall South Suite 212
Lincoln, Nebraska, 68508

Sterilization
Association for Voluntary Sterilization, Inc.
122 East 42nd St.
New York, NY 10168
Phone: 212–351–2500

Test-tube Fertilization
Eastern Virginia Medical School
Norfolk General Hospital
Howard and Georgeanna Jones Institute for Repro-
ductive Medicine
Hofheimer Hall 6th Floor
Norfolk, VA 23507
Phone: 804–446–8948

Widowhood
Widowed Person's Service
American Association of Retired Persons
1909 K St., N.W.
Washington, DC 20049
Phone: 202–872–4700
*The addresses and phone numbers were accurate
at the time this section was printed.

References

Alzate, H. and M.L. Dippsy. Vaginal erotic sensitivity. *Journal of Sex and Marital Therapy,* 1984, *10,* 49–56.

Campbell, J.M. Sexual guidelines for persons with AIDS and at risk for AIDS. *Human Sexuality,* March 1986, 100–103.

Carroll, L. Concern with AIDS and the sexual behavior of college students. *Journal of Marriage and the Family* 1988, *50,* 405–411.

Centers for Disease Control, HIV/AIDS Surveillance Report, February 1990, 1–18.

Centers for Disease Control. AIDS and human immunodeficiency virus infection in the United States. 1988 update, MMWR 1989:38 suppl. no. s–4.

Chase, Marilyn. Many who risk AIDS now weigh carefully whether to be tested. *The Wall Street Journal,* June 13, 1989, p. 1 et passim.

Davidson, Kenneth Sr., C. A. Darling, and C. Conway-Welch. The role of the Grafenberg spot and female ejaculation in the female orgasmic response: An empirical analysis. *Journal of Sex and Marital Therapy,* 1989, *15,* 102–120.

Eisenberg, Steve. From one lover to another. *Health,* September 1988, 62–65.

Gilbert, Jersey. Money scorecard: Where to save, borrow, and invest. *Money,* January 1990, 7–12

Hilt, Philip J. AIDS advancing among heterosexuals. *The News and Observer,* Raleigh, N.C., May 1, 1990, p. 4A.

Hock, Z. The G Spot. *Journal of Sex and Marital Therapy,* 1983, *9,* 1166–167.

Horn, Janet. Genital human papillomavirus infection: New challenges from an old STD culprit. *STD Bulletin,* 1989, *9,* 3–10.

Johnson, Robert E., Andre J. Wahmias, Laurence S. Mager, Francis K. Lee, Camilla A. Brooks, and Cecelia B. Snowden. A seroepidemiologic survey of the prevalence of herpes simplex virus type 2 infection in the United States. *The New England Journal of Medicine,* 1989, *321,* 7–12.

Kelley, J. A., J. S. Rawrence, H. V. Hood, and T. L. Brasfield. Behavioral intervention to reduce AIDS risk activities. *Journal of Consulting and Clinical Psychology,* 1989, *57,* 60–67.

Kloser, P. Highlights: Fifth International AIDS Conference: Montreal, June 4–9. *Medical Aspects of Human Sexuality,* 1989, *23,* 57–64.

Lesllie-Harwit, M. and A. Mehus. Sexually transmitted disease in young people: The importance of health education. *Sexually Transmitted Diseases,* January/February, 1989, *16,* 15–20.

Perry, J.D. and B. Whipple. Pelvic muscle strength of female ejaculation: Evidence in support of a new theory of orgasm. *Journal of Sex Research,* 1981, *17,* 22–39.

Sammons, Robert. Mesa Behavioral Medicine Clinic. Grand Junction, Colorado. Personal Communication, 1990.

Selik, R. M., K. G. Castro, and M. Papaioanou. Racial/ethnic differences in the risk of AIDS in the United States. *American Journal of Public Health,* 1988, *78,* 1539–1545

Standard Federal Tax Reporter. Vol. 1. Chicago, Ill.: Commerce Clearing House, Inc., 1990.

Thompson, Dick. Longer life for AIDS patients. *Time,* June 19, 1989, p. 52.

Thompson, Dick. A losing battle with AIDS. *Time,* July 2, 1990, pp. 42–43.

PHOTO CREDITS